North Carolina Taxpayers

1679 – 1790

NORTH CAROLINA TAXPAYERS

1679 – 1790

Volume 2

Compiled by
CLARENCE E. RATCLIFF

GENEALOGICAL
PUBLISHING Co., Inc.

Dedicated to
My Son

DONALD E. RATCLIFF

$\mathcal{N}$OTE

T HIS BOOK continues the work begun in *North Carolina Tax-payers 1701–1786*. It includes most of the remaining tax lists, from the earliest known to 1790, except for a few (most of which are redundant) which were recorded shortly before or after the tax lists in this and the first volume.

Most of the names included in this book were found in the microfilmed tax lists at the North Carolina State Archives in Raleigh (Roll S.50.10), or in photocopies of some records not on microfilm at NCSA, or in tax lists published in *The North Carolinian*, later titled the *Journal of North Carolina Genealogy*, and still later titled *North Carolina Genealogy*.

Names of taxpayers are given in alphabetical order for quick reference. The name of the county of residence of each taxpayer is provided as well as the date of the tax list. This volume includes the names of about 29,000 taxpayers.

TABLE 1

County	Tax List Dates	Abbreviations
Albemarle	1679, 1694	Albe
Beaufort	1779, 1786	Beau
Bertie	1774, 1781	Bert
Bladen	1784	Blad
Brunswick	1782, 1784	Brun
Bute	1766	Bute
Camden	1782	Camd
Carteret	1779	Cart
Caswell	1784, 1786	Casw
Chowan	1785	Chow
Craven	1779	Crav
Currituck	1779	Curr
Dobbs	1780	Dobb
Duplin	1783	Dupl
Gates	1782, 1789	Gate
Granville	1771, 1785	Gran
Halifax	1783	Hali
Hertford	1779, 1784	Hert
Johnston	1784	John
Jones	1779	Jone
Martin	1779	Mart
Montgomery	1782	Mont
Nash	1782	Nash
New Bern District	1779	NewB
Northampton	1780	NorH
Onslow	1771	Onsl
Orange	1779	Oran
Pasquotank	1694, 1779, 1789	Pasq
Perquimans	1772, 1787	Perq
Pitt	1786	Pitt
Richmond	1790	Rich
Rowan	1761-1767	Rowa
Rutherford	1782	Ruth

Sampson	1784	Samp
Surry	1782	Surr
Tyrrell	1784	Tyrr
Warren	1779, 1784	Warr
Wayne	1786	Wayn
Wilkes	1782, 1784	Wilk

TABLE 2

Sources

Date	County	JNCG	NCSA
1679	Albemarle precinct - quit rents		photocopies
1694	Albemarle - survey		photocopies
1779	Beaufort		S.50.10
1786	Beaufort		S.50.10
1774	Bertie		S.50.10
1781	Bertie		S.50.10
1784	Bladen		S.50.10
1782	Brunswick		S.50.10
1784	Brunswick		S.50.10
1766	Bute		photocopies
1782	Camden	09:1138-45	S.50.10
1779	Carteret	07:771-773	S.50.10
1784	Caswell		S.50.10
1786	Caswell - census	11:1398, 2032	
1785	Chowan		S.50.10
1779	Craven		S.50.10
1779	Currituck		S.50.10
1780	Dobbs		S.50.10
1783	Duplin	19:2778, 2813	
1782	Gates		S.50.10
1789	Gates		S.50.10
1771	Granville		S.50.10
1785	Granville		S.50.10
1783	Halifax		S.50.10
1779	Hertford	13:1871-1875	S.50.10
1784	Hertford		S.50.10
1784	Johnston	15:2379-2386	S.50.10
1769	Jones	11:1405-9, 1553	
1779	Jones		S.50.10
1779	Martin	11:1461-1468	S.50.10
1782	Montgomery		S.50.10
1782	Nash	10:1249-1253	S.50.10
1779	New Bern District		S.50.10

1780	Northampton		S.50.10
1771	Onslow		S.50.10
1779	Orange	15:2349-65, 2411	S.50.10
1694	Pasquotank		photocopies
1779	Pasquotank		S.50.10
1789	Pasquotank		S.50.10
1772	Perquimans		S.50.10
1787	Perquimans		S.50.10
1786	Pitt		S.50.10
1790	Richmond		S.50.10
1761	Rowan (1761 - 1767)	17:2607, 2683, 2699-2710	
1782	Rutherford	13:1919-1923	S.50.10
1784	Sampson	14:2168-2175	S.50.10
1782	Surry		S.50.10
1784	Tyrrell		S.50.10
1779	Warren		S.50.10
1784	Warren		S.50.10
1786	Wayne	08:940-943; 1044-8	
1782	Wilkes		S.50.10
1784	Wilkes		S.50.10

AARON, Conrad	Rowa	1761	ADAMS, Isaac	Tyrr	1784
Elizabeth	Hali	1783	Isaac	Beau	1786
George	Hali	1783	James	Casw	1786
Isaac	Hali	1783	James	Hali	1783
Jacob	Rowa	1761	James	Beau	1779
Mary Ann	Hali	1783	James	Beau	1786
AARONHART, Phillip	Rowa	1761	Jane	Wilk	1782
ABBOT, Caleb	Camd	1782	John	Rowa	1761
Henry	Camd	1782	John	Casw	1784
John	Camd	1782	John	Hali	1783
Joseph	Camd	1782	John	Beau	1779
Thomas	Dobb	1780	John	Wilk	1784
Thomas	Oran	1779	John	Wilk	1782
ABERCROMBIE, Chas.	Oran	1779	Jonah	Beau	1779
Robert	Oran	1779	Jonathan	Tyrr	1784
ABERT, Geo	Surr	1782	Joshua	Beau	1779
Martin	Surr	1782	Joshua	Beau	1786
ABINGTON, Hardiman	Bert	1774	Josias	Beau	1786
Hardiman	Bert	1781	Lucy	Perq	1772
James	Bert	1774	Martin	Wilk	1782
ABNEY, Nathan	Ruth	1782	Mathias	Beau	1786
ABRAMS, Thomas B.	Hert	1784	Nancy	Beau	1779
Thomas Balis	Hert	1779	Peter	Pasq	1779
ACHISS, Thomas	Pasq	1789	Phillip	Hali	1783
ACKERMAN, Wm	Surr	1782	Rebecca	Mart	1779
ACKLAND, John	Curr	1779	Richard	Rich	1790
ACOCK, Abner	Warr	1784	Robert	Nash	1782
John	Warr	1784	Robert	Bert	1774
John Jr.	Wayn	1786	Robert	Rowa	1761
Richard	Bute	1766	Robert	Blad	1784
Richard	Bute	1766	Sam	Beau	1786
Richard	Warr	1784	Samuel	Gran	1785
Simon	Wayn	1786	Thomas	Tyrr	1784
Wm	Dobb	1780	Willibee	Pitt	1786
ACRE, David	Bert	1781	Willoughby	Crav	1779
John	Bert	1781	Wm	Nash	1782
ACREA, Isaac	Bute	1766	Wm	Rowa	1761
Wm	Warr	1784	Wm	Oran	1779
ACRES, Isaac	Warr	1784	Wm	Mart	1779
John	Warr	1784	Wm	Bert	1774
Wm	Bute	1766	Wm	Hali	1783
Wm	Warr	1784	Wm	Tyrr	1784
ADAIR, James	Ruth	1782	Wm	Crav	1779
John	Blad	1784	Wm	Wilk	1782
ADAMS, 2495	Nash	1782	Wm	Pitt	1786
Abraham	Beau	1779	ADAMSON, Aaron	Surr	1782
Abram	Beau	1786	Enos	Surr	1782
Bryan	John	1784	George	Pasq	1779
Daniel	Casw	1786	Jesse	Oran	1779
David	Crav	1779	Simon	Oran	1779
Elizabeth	Tyrr	1784	Simon	Surr	1782
Ephraim	Mart	1779	ADARE, Charles	Rowa	1770
Ezekiel	Crav	1779	Joseph	Rowa	1770
Ezekiel	Onsl	1771	ADCOCK, Bolen	Gran	1771
Ezekiel	Pitt	1786	Edmond	Casw	1786
Henry	Wilk	1782	Edmond	Bute	1766
Henry	Beau	1786	Edmond	Casw	1784
Howell	John	1784	Henry	Bute	1766

ADCOCK, Henry	Rich 1790	ALDERSON, James	Beau 1779
John	Casw 1784	John	Beau 1779
John	Gran 1771	John	Beau 1786
Joshua	Casw 1786	Simon	Beau 1779
Leonard	Gran 1771	Thomas	Beau 1786
Pierce	Casw 1784	ALDRIDGE, Drewry	Dobb 1780
ADDIMON, Thomas	Surr 1782	Elijah	Surr 1782
ADDISON, Thomas	Gran 1771	Francis	Surr 1782
ADKINS, Arthur	Bute 1766	John	Dobb 1780
David	Gran 1785	Joseph	Casw 1784
Wm	Surr 1782	Nicholas	Oran 1768
Wm	Gran 1771	Thomas	Dobb 1780
ADKINSON, Ephraim	Nash 1782	Wm	Dobb 1780
Henry	Nash 1782	Wm Sr	Oran 1768
James	Nash 1782	ALEXANDER, Abner	Tyrr 1784
Michael	Nash 1782	Allen	Stat 1773
Nathan	Nash 1782	Anthony	Hert 1779
Newitt	Nash 1782	Anthony	Tyrr 1784
Thomas	Hali 1783	Benjamin	Tyrr 1784
ADMONS, Thomas	Warr 1784	David	Rowa 1770
AERCE, John	Warr 1784	Edward	Tyrr 1784
AGENDER, Henry	Rowa 1761	Eliz	Wilk 1782
AGREE, Noah	Rich 1790	Ezekiel	Tyrr 1784
AHAIR, Wm	Onsl 1771	Gabriel	STAT 1773
AIKEN, Isham	Gran 1785	George	Rowa 1770
James	Oran 1768	George s ofGeo	Rowa 1770
James	Casw 1784	Gideon	Tyrr 1784
James Jr	Gran 1785	Henry	Hert 1779
James Sr	Gran 1785	Henry	Tyrr 1784
Joseph	Gran 1785	Isaac	Tyrr 1779
Samuel	Oran 1779	Isaac	Hert 1779
Wm	Oran 1779	Isaac Jr	Tyrr 1784
Wm Jr	Casw 1784	Isaac Sr	Tyrr 1784
AIRS, John	Bert 1774	James	Burk 1779
ALBERT, Chalkley	Perq 1772	James	Hert 1779
Mary	Oran 1779	James	Oran 1779
ALBERTSON, Albert	Albe 1679	James s of Geo	Rowa 1770
Albert	Pasq 1789	Jesse	Wilk 1784
Benj Jr	Perq 1787	Jesse	Wilk 1782
Benj Sr	Perq 1787	John	Burk 1779
Chalkley	Perq 1787	John	Hert 1779
Elias	Perq 1772	John	Rowa 1770
Elias	Pasq 1789	John	Hert 1784
Elijah	Perq 1772	John	Tyrr 1784
Elisha	Perq 1787	John Jr	Tyrr 1779
Francis	Pasq 1779	John Jr	Tyrr 1784
Francis	Perq 1772	John Sr	Tyrr 1784
John	Dupl 1779	John the Great	Hert 1779
John	Pasq 1779	Joseph	Tyrr 1784
Josiah	Perq 1787	Joseph Jr	Tyrr 1779
Mary	Perq 1787	Joseph Sr	Hert 1779
Nathaniel	Perq 1772	Joseph Sr	Tyrr 1784
Samuel	Dupl 1779	Joseph s ofGeo	Rowa 1770
Sarah	Perq 1787	Joseph s ofIsa	Tyrr 1784
Wm	Dupl 1779	Joshua	Tyrr 1779
ALBION, Robert Jr	Gran 1785	Joshua	Tyrr 1784
ALBRIGHT, Jacob	Oran 1779	Leod	Onsl 1771
Jacob Jr	Oran 1779	Martha	Tyrr 1784
John	Oran 1779	Mary	Tyrr 1784
John	Pasq 1779	Michael	Tyrr 1779
Joseph	Oran 1779	Morgan	Tyrr 1784
Lodwick	Oran 1779	Randolph	Wilk 1782
Phillip	Oran 1779	Stephen	Rowa 1770
Wm	Pasq 1789	Tibbles	Hert 1784
ALCOTT, Wm	Jone 1779	Tiblis	Hert 1779

ALEXANDER, Wm	Burk	1779	ALLEN, John	Pitt	1786
Wm	Rowa	1770	Jonathan	NBer	1779
Zilpah	Tyrr	1784	Joseph	Oran	1779
ALFORD, Benjamin	Wayn	1786	Joseph	Mont	1782
Goodrich	Bute	1766	Joseph	Surr	1782
Jacob 1138 ac.	Nash	1782	Joseph	Pitt	1786
James	Bute	1766	Mark	Mont	1782
Julius	Bute	1766	Nathaniel	Chow	1785
Lodowick	Bute	1766	Richard	Curr	1779
Lodowick Jr	Bute	1766	Richard	Wilk	1782
Thomas	Blad	1784	Richard	NorH	1780
Wm	Wayn	1786	Robert	Warr	1784
ALFRED, Jacob	Blad	1784	Robert	Gran	1785
John	Ruth	1782	Samuel	Oran	1779
Thomas	Brun	1782	Samuel	Gran	1785
ALLCOCK, Wm	Tyrr	1784	Samuel	Wilk	1782
ALLCOTT, Wm	Warr	1784	Shadrack	Pitt	1786
ALLEN, Abigail	Pasq	1789	Thomas	Pasq	1779
Abraham	Oran	1779	Thomas	Curr	1779
Adoniram	Wilk	1782	Thomas	Surr	1782
Benj	Surr	1782	Thomas Jr	Curr	1779
Benj	Pasq	1789	Thomas Sr	Curr	1779
Benjamin	Pasq	1779	Wm	Warr	1784
Benjamin	Crav	1779	Wm	NorH	1750
Callie	Chow	1785	Wm	Gran	1785
Capt	Crav	1779	Wm	Wilk	1784
Champion	Gran	1785	Wm	Mont	1782
Charles	Warr	1784	Wm	NorH	1780
Charles	Casw	1784	Wm	Surr	1782
Chas	Mont	1782	Wm	Gran	1771
Chedlin	Casw	1784	Zachariah	Oran	1779
Clifton	Casw	1786	ALLET, James	Oran	1779
Cumb.	Brun	1784	John	Oran	1779
Darius	Wilk	1782	ALLEY, Edmond	Casw	1784
Daugherty	Oran	1779	Miles	NorH	1780
David	Surr	1782	Roser	Surr	1782
Davis	Casw	1784	ALLIGOOD, Hillery	Jone	1779
Drury	Brun	1784	ALLING, Arthur	Nash	1782
Drury	Casw	1784	Thomas	Nash	1782
Drury	Brun	1782	ALLISON, Andrew	Rowa	1768
Drury	Gran	1771	Henry	Pasq	1789
Eleanor	Brun	1782	James	Gran	1785
Geo	Gate	1789	John	Oran	1779
George	Warr	1784	John	Gran	1785
George	Oran	1779	Joseph Jr	Oran	1779
Grant	Gran	1785	Joseph Sr	Oran	1779
Gresham	Wilk	1782	Robert	Gran	1785
Hezekiah	Dupl	1779	Robert	Gran	1771
Isaac	Mont	1782	Sam	Wilk	1782
Jacob	Oran	1779	Thomas	Pasq	1779
Jacob	NorH	1780	Thomas	Crav	1779
James	Oran	1779	Wm	Gran	1785
James	John	1784	Wm	Wilk	1782
James	NBer	1779	ALLISONER, John	Warr	1784
James	Curr	1779	ALLOM, Thomas	Wilk	1782
Jarvis	Curr	1779	ALLRED, Jonathan	Rich	1790
Jesse	NorH	1780	Phineas	Rich	1790
Joel	Brun	1784	Solomon	Rich	1790
Joel	Brun	1782	ALLWAYS, Obadiah	Crav	1779
John	Bert	1774	ALMOND, Canaday	Oran	1779
John	Warr	1784	David	Rich	1790
John	Oran	1779	James	Mont	1782
John	Crav	1779	John	Mont	1782
John	Surr	1782	John	Rich	1790
John	Bert	1781	Nathan	Oran	1779

ALMOND, Perrin	Crav 1779		ANDERSON, Anne	Chow 1785
ALMOTANY, Isaac	Mont 1782		Arrcuk	Oran 1779
ALPHIN, Hezekiah	Gate 1789		Bailey	Ruth 1782
Joseph	Gate 1789		Chas	Crav 1779
ALPIN, Wm	Onsl 1771		David	Oran 1779
ALSO, John	Dupl 1779		Edward	Casw 1786
ALSOBROOK, David	Hali 1783		Elmore	Onsl 1771
Drury	Hali 1783		George	Casw 1784
Elizabeth	Hali 1783		Gillett	Onsl 1771
Howell	Hali 1783		Isaac	Oran 1779
James	Hali 1783		James	Rowa 1770
Jesse	Hali 1783		James	Oran 1779
John	Hali 1783		James	Casw 1784
Thomas	Hali 1783		John	Rowa 1770
ALSTON, Francis	Brun 1784		John	Oran 1779
Geo	Gran 1771		John	Mart 1779
George	Gran 1785		John	Casw 1786
Henry	Warr 1784		John	Wayn 1786
James	Warr 1784		John	Casw 1784
John	Hali 1783		John	Tyrr 1784
Jonas	Brun 1784		John	Perq 1772
Phillip	Warr 1784		John	Perq 1787
Phillip G	Warr 1784		John Jr	Blad 1784
Phillip dec	Warr 1784		John Jr	Crav 1779
Sarah	Gran 1771		John N	Surr 1782
Thomas W	Warr 1784		John Sr	Crav 1779
Willey	Hali 1783		Jonas	Crav 1779
Wm	Warr 1784		Joseph	Crav 1779
Wm	Oran 1779		Joseph	Beau 1786
Wm	Casw 1784		Lewis	Gran 1771
Wm	Gran 1771		Peter	Nash 1782
Wm s of Philip	Bute 1766		Peter	Oran 1779
ALTMAN, Jacob	John 1784		Peter	Crav 1779
Thomas	John 1784		Peter Sr	Oran 1779
ALTON, Spencer	Mont 1782		Rebecca	Wilk 1782
ALVERSON, Archer	Casw 1786		Richard	Oran 1779
James	Tyrr 1784		Robert	Ruth 1782
James	Casw 1786		Robert	Oran 1779
John	Casw 1786		Saml	Perq 1787
ALWAYS, Henry	Crav 1779		Thomas	Crav 1779
AMAN, Dennis	Onsl 1771		Thomas	Wilk 1782
Philip	Onsl 1771		Wm	Cart 1779
AMBIGUAY, John	Wilk 1782		Wm	Oran 1779
AMBROSE, Daniel	Onsl 1771		Wm	Mart 1779
James	Tyrr 1784		Wm	Blad 1784
Jesse	Tyrr 1784		Wm	Wayn 1786
John	Wilk 1782		Wm	Bert 1781
Samson	Onsl 1771		ANDRESS, Abraham	Mart 1779
Shimea	Tyrr 1784		Andrew	Samp 1784
Wm	Onsl 1771		Daniel	Oran 1779
Zachariah	Onsl 1771		Eleazer	Casw 1784
AMES, Louis	Gran 1785		Ethelred	Mart 1779
Mary	Blad 1784		Hugh	Oran 1779
Thomas	Mart 1779		James	Rowa 1761
Wm	Gran 1785		James	Oran 1779
AMIET, Vincent	Jone 1779		John	Blad 1784
AMMITT, Benj	Onsl 1771		John	Dobb 1780
AMMONS, Howell	Samp 1784		Stephen	Blad 1784
James	Wayn 1786		Thomas	Mart 1779
Joshua	Samp 1784		Wm	Dobb 1780
Vaun	Samp 1784		Wm	Oran 1779
AMOS, Wm	Gran 1771		ANDREW, Thomas	Ruth 1782
ANDERS, Joseph	Blad 1784		ANDREWS, Adam	Jone 1779
ANDERSON, Alexander	Bute 1766		Alfred	Warr 1784
Andrew	Oran 1779		Drewry	Dobb 1780

ANDREWS, John	Bert 1781	ARCHER, Wm	Hert 1784
Wm	Bert 1781	Zachariah	Mart 1779
ANDREWSON, Jeremiah	NorH 1780	ARD, James	Blad 1784
ANGE, Francis	Mart 1779	Reuben	Blad 1784
ANGELL, Ann	Wilk 1782	Thomas	Blad 1784
Benjamin	Rowa 1768	ARGON, Robert	Dobb 1780
Chas	Surr 1782	ARGOOD, David	Onsl 1771
George	Hali 1783	ARGUE, Charles	Warr 1784
John	Ruth 1782	ARKILL, Wm	Perq 1787
John	Hali 1783	ARLINE, James	Gate 1789
Lawrence	Surr 1782	John	Gate 1789
Nicholas	Wilk 1784	ARLIS, John	Wayn 1786
Nicholas	Wilk 1782	ARMFIELD, Isaac Sr	Rowa 1761
Wm	Wilk 1782	Thomas s of Is	Rowa 1761
ANGLING, Wm	Casw 1784	Wm	Rowa 1761
Wm	Casw 1786	ARMISTEAD, Anthony	Bert 1774
ANNILL, Andrew	Casw 1784	Anthony	Bert 1781
ANNIS, Thomas	Chow 1785	Wm	Bert 1774
ANSELL, John	Curr 1779	Wm	Bert 1781
Lydia	Curr 1779	ARMOUR, David	Pasq 1779
Nathaniel	Curr 1779	Joseph	Pasq 1779
ANSLEY, John	Tyrr 1784	Joshua	Pasq 1779
Joseph	Tyrr 1784	Simon	Pasq 1779
Solomon	Tyrr 1784	Wm Jr	Pasq 1779
Wm	Oran 1779	Wm Sr	Pasq 1779
ANTHERISK, John	Rowa 1765	ARMSTEAD, Anthony	NorH 1780
Joseph	Rowa 1765	Robert	NorH 1780
ANTHONY, David	Bute 1766	ARMSTRONG, Alexander	
James	Casw 1786		Dupl 1783
John	Casw 1786	Andrew	Oran 1779
John	Casw 1784	Clement	John 1784
Jonathan	Casw 1786	Hugh	Surr 1782
Jonathan	Casw 1784	Isaac	Mont 1782
Thomas	Surr 1782	James	Ruth 1782
APEN, Joel	Surr 1782	James	Oran 1779
APLEN, Thomas	Surr 1782	John	Oran 1779
APLEY, Jacob	Blad 1784	John	Casw 1784
Joseph	Blad 1784	John	Tyrr 1784
APPERSON, Wm	Bert 1774	M	Surr 1782
APPLETON, Benjamin	Cart 1779	Margaret	Tyrr 1784
John	Surr 1782	Martin	Ruth 1782
APPLEWHITE, John	Wayn 1786	Russell	Tyrr 1784
Martha	Hali 1783	Wm	Ruth 1782
Thomas	Hali 1783	Wm	Oran 1779
APPLIN, David	Surr 1782	ARNALL, Richard	Casw 1786
ARCHDEACON, Edmund	Casw 1784	ARNETT, Andrew	Casw 1786
James	Casw 1784	James	Casw 1786
Wm	Mart 1779	Moses	Wilk 1782
ARCHEBALD, James	Beau 1779	Philemon	Wayn 1786
John	Beau 1779	ARNOLD, Aaron	Oran 1779
Nathan	Beau 1779	Ambrose	Casw 1784
Samuel	Beau 1779	Asia	Wayn 1786
ARCHER, Abel	Hert 1779	Benjamin	Wayn 1786
Abel	Hert 1784	Benjamin	Perq 1772
Armstrong	Hert 1784	David	Hali 1783
Baker	Hert 1779	Gilbert	Pasq 1779
Baker	Hert 1784	Henry	Surr 1782
Ezekiel	Hert 1784	James	Warr 1784
Jacob	Hert 1779	James	Bute 1766
Jacob	Hert 1784	John	NorH 1750
John	Bert 1774	John	Beau 1779
John	Mart 1779	John	Gate 1789
John	Hali 1783	Joseph	Wayn 1786
John	Bert 1781	Joshua	Pasq 1779
Thomas	Hert 1784	Joshua	Pasq 1789

ARNOLD, Peter	Onsl 1771	ASHETON, John	Chow 1785
Saml	Surr 1782	ASHEW, Wm	Gran 1785
Solomon	Warr 1784	ASHLEY, Charles	Oran 1779
Thomas	Surr 1782	James	Oran 1779
Wm	Bute 1766	Jeremiah	Chow 1785
Wm	Perq 1772	Joseph	Oran 1779
Wm	Gran 1771	Mede	Chow 1785
Wm	Gate 1789	Robert	Oran 1779
Wm	Perq 1787	Thomas	Bert 1774
ARP, Abraham	NorH 1780	Thomas	Bert 1781
ARRENDALL, Nathan	Dobb 1780	Wm	Bert 1774
Wm	Dobb 1780	Wm	Oran 1779
ARRINGTON, Arthur Jr		Wm	Blad 1784
	Nash 1782	Wm	Chow 1785
Arthur Sr	Nash 1782	Wm	Gran 1785
Ezekiel	Perq 1787	Wm	Surr 1782
James	Nash 1782	ASHLOCK, James	Ruth 1782
James	Samp 1784	ASHMORE, Louis	Gran 1785
Joseph	Nash 1782	Walter	Surr 1782
Richard	Perq 1772	ASKEW, Aaron	Bert 1774
Richard	Perq 1787	Aaron	Hert 1784
Thomas	Ruth 1782	Aaron	Bert 1781
Wm	Perq 1787	Charandge	Hert 1784
ARRUNDELL, Thomas	Bute 1766	Charnaday	Hert 1779
ARTHUR, Armstrong	Curr 1779	Cullen	Hert 1784
Gideon	Cart 1779	David	Bert 1781
James	Cart 1779	Godfrey	Bert 1781
James	Crav 1779	James	Hert 1779
Lanson	Beau 1786	James	Hert 1784
Seth	Cart 1779	James Jr	Hert 1779
ARTIS, Delilah	John 1784	Jesse	Bert 1781
ARTMORE, George	Rowa 1761	John	Bert 1774
ARVIN, Richard	Casw 1784	John Jr	Hert 1784
ARWIN, Richard	Casw 1786	John Scrug	Bute 1766
ASBELL, Aaron	Bert 1781	Martha	Bert 1774
James	Bert 1774	Nicholas	Hert 1779
James	Bert 1781	Nicholas	Hert 1784
John	Perq 1787	Thomas	Bert 1774
Pearce	Oran 1779	Wm	Hert 1779
Thomas	Bert 1781	Wm	Gran 1771
ASHBEE, Abel	Curr 1779	Wm Jr	Hert 1779
Elizabeth	Curr 1779	Wm s of John S	Bute 1766
Solomon	Curr 1779	Zachariah	Hert 1779
ASHBELL, James	Beau 1786	Zachariah	Hert 1784
John	Beau 1786	ASKIN, David	Bert 1774
Joseph	Beau 1786	ASKINS, James	Hert 1784
Nathan Jr	Beau 1786	ASPIL, John	Perq 1772
Nathan Sr	Beau 1786	ASWELL, Pierce	Casw 1786
Sam	Beau 1786	ATCHERSON, Etaw	Pasq 1779
ASHBURN, Anderson	Casw 1786	ATHERLY, Jonathan	Crav 1779
Anderson	Casw 1784	ATHERTON, Amos	John 1784
Benj	Bert 1781	Moses	John 1784
Benjamin	Bert 1774	Raymond	John 1784
Elisha	Bert 1781	ATKERSON, Wm	Hali 1783
Eliz	Bert 1781	ATKINS, James	Blad 1784
John	Casw 1786	James	Hali 1783
John	Casw 1784	James	Onsl 1771
Peter	Bert 1781	Joel	Blad 1784
Thomas	Bert 1774	John	Brun 1782
Wm	Bert 1774	Rodham	Warr 1784
Wm	Bert 1781	Silas	Blad 1784
ASHBURNTON, Elisha	Bert 1774	Thomas	Warr 1784
ASHBURY, John	Hali 1783	Wm	Casw 1786
ASHCROFT, John	Oran 1779	ATKINSON, Elijah	Jone 1779
Thomas	Oran 1779	Howell	Brun 1782

ATKINSON, John	Wayn 1786	
John	Casw 1784	
Roger	Casw 1784	
Samuel	Wayn 1786	
Thomas 3,500 a	Nash 1782	
Wm	Samp 1784	
ATWELL, Benjamin	Samp 1784	
ATWOOD, Thomas	Oran 1779	
AUBREY, Frederick	Bute 1766	
James	Gran 1771	
AUST, Geo	Surr 1782	
AUSTIN, Arthur	Surr 1782	
Bryant	Mont 1782	
Cornelius	Curr 1779	
Daniel	Curr 1779	
David	Wilk 1782	
Phillip	Oran 1779	
Richard	Gate 1789	
Solomon	Oran 1779	
Thomas Jr	Curr 1779	
Thomas Sr	Curr 1779	
Wm	Casw 1786	
Wm	Casw 1784	
Wm	Curr 1782	
Wm Sr	Oran 1779	
AUTRY, Cornelius	Samp 1784	
Isham	Samp 1784	
John	Samp 1784	
Theophilus	Samp 1784	
AVANT, Wm	Nash 1782	
AVENT, Mary	NorH 1780	
AVERA, Daniel	John 1784	
David	John 1784	
Samuel	John 1784	
Thomas	John 1784	
AVERITT, Ann	Bert 1781	
Arthur	Onsl 1771	
Benj	Onsl 1771	
Hanry	Bert 1781	
John	Onsl 1771	
Millie	Bert 1781	
Thomas	Bert 1781	
AVERY, Charles	Bert 1774	
Chas	Onsl 1771	
Henry	Bert 1774	
Isaac	Casw 1786	
Isaac	Casw 1784	
John	Bert 1774	
John	Crav 1779	
Nells	Bert 1774	
Robert	Perq 1787	
AVIRETT, Wm	Blad 1784	
AVIS, Abraham	Bert 1781	
David	Tyrr 1784	
Isaac	Tyrr 1784	
John Jr.	Tyrr 1784	
John Sr.	Tyrr 1784	
Sawyer	Bert 1781	
Thomas	Bert 1774	
Thomas	Tyrr 1784	
AYCOCK, Jesse	Wayn 1786	
Thomas	Wayn 1786	
AYDLOTT, Francis	Camd 1782	
AYERS, Hardwick	Rich 1790	
Henry	Surr 1782	

AYERS, Joseph	Surr 1782	
Robert	Surr 1782	
AYLER, Wm	Dobb 1780	
AYRES, Ambrose	Bert 1730	
Daniel	Surr 1782	
David	Bert 1738	
John Jr	Bert 1738	
Nathl	Surr 1782	
Thomas	Surr 1782	
AZMONT, Francis	Bert 1781	
BABB, Thomas	Bute 1766	
Wm	Bute 1766	
BABCOCK, Thomas	Pasq 1694	
BACHAM, John	Beau 1786	
BACHELOR, Samuel	Nash 1782	
Stephen Jr	Nash 1782	
Stephen Sr	Nash 1782	
Thomas	Hali 1783	
BACKERS, John	Mart 1779	
Thomas	Chow 1785	
BACKHOUSE, John	Cart 1779	
BACKLEY, James	Gran 1785	
Peter	Gran 1785	
BACKS, Joseph	Samp 1784	
BACKUS, James	Perq 1772	
Thomas	Chow 1785	
BACON, James	Hert 1779	
James	Hert 1784	
Michael	Surr 1782	
BADGETT, James	Surr 1782	
John	Gran 1785	
John	Gran 1771	
Roger	Gran 1771	
Thomas	Casw 1784	
BADHAM, Mary	Chow 1785	
BAGBY, Davis	Hali 1783	
Wm	Hali 1783	
BAGG, Thomas	Bert 1774	
BAGGE, Fagnott	Surr 1782	
BAGGETT, Abraham	NorH 1780	
Abraham	NorH 1780	
Elizabeth	Nash 1782	
Everett	Wayn 1786	
Harvey	NorH 1780	
James Jr	Rich 1790	
James Sr	Rich 1790	
John	Blad 1784	
Joseph	Blad 1784	
Shadrack	Rich 1790	
Thomas	Mart 1779	
BAGLEY, Celia	Gate 1789	
Elisha	Perq 1787	
Ephraim	Perq 1787	
Harmon	Warr 1784	
John	Wilk 1782	
John	Perq 1787	
Joshua	Perq 1787	
Nathan	Perq 1787	
Saml	Perq 1787	
Thomas	Perq 1787	
Wm	Warr 1784	
Wm	Bute 1766	

BAGLEY, Wm	Mart	1779	BAINES, Richard	Beau	1786
Wm	Wilk	1782	Richard Jr	Beau	1786
BAGNAL, James	Hert	1779	BAIRD, John	Casw	1784
BAGWELL, John	Gran	1785	BAKER, Abner	Surr	1782
Ransom	Gran	1785	Abraham	Dobb	1780
BAILES, Daniel	Surr	1782	Andrew	Wilk	1782
John & s Wm	Rowa	1768	Ann	Surr	1782
John Jr	Rowa	1768	Benjamin	Hert	1779
John Sr	Rowa	1761	Benjamin	Hert	1784
BAILEY, Abram	Onsl	1771	Benjamin Jr	Hert	1779
Benj	Wilk	1782	Benjamin Jr	Tyrr	1784
Britton	Hali	1783	Benjamin Sr	Hert	1779
Claudius	Oran	1779	Benjamin Sr	Tyrr	1784
David	Pasq	1779	Blake	Hert	1779
David	Rowa	1761	Blake	Chow	1785
David Jr	Pasq	1789	Blake	Hert	1784
David Sr	Pasq	1789	Charles	Bert	1774
Gamaliel	Surr	1782	Elijah	Dobb	1780
Henry	Wayn	1786	Elisha	Crav	1779
Henry	Pasq	1779	Henry	Rowa	1761
James	Warr	1784	Henry	Surr	1782
James	Oran	1779	Henry B	Oran	1779
James	Hert	1784	Hillery	Tyrr	1784
Jane	Pasq	1789	James	Bert	1774
Jeremiah	Gran	1785	James	Nash	1782
Jeremiah	Gran	1771	James	Dupl	1779
Jeremiah Jr	Gran	1782	James	Hert	1779
John	Oran	1779	James	Samp	1784
John	Gran	1785	James	Hali	1783
John	Hali	1783	James	Hert	1784
John	Pasq	1779	James	John	1784
John	Pasq	1789	James	Wilk	1782
John Sr	Pasq	1789	James	Gate	1789
Jonathan	Crav	1779	James	Bert	1781
Joseph	Pasq	1779	James	Bert	1781
Joseph	Onsl	1771	John	Oran	1779
Mary	Pasq	1779	John	Dobb	1780
Nancy	Pasq	1789	John	Rowa	1768
Nicholas	Onsl	1771	John	Hert	1784
Philip	Onsl	1771	John	Crav	1779
Richard	Gran	1785	John	Mont	1782
Richard	Gran	1771	John	Curr	1779
Robert	Pasq	1779	John	Wilk	1782
Robert	Mont	1782	John	Gate	1789
Robert	Pasq	1789	John	Bert	1781
Sarah	Blad	1784	John Capt	Hert	1779
Sarah	Pasq	1789	John Sr	Hert	1779
Stephen	Gran	1785	Jonathan	Bert	1781
Taylor	John	1784	Jordan	Hali	1783
Thomas	Bert	1781	Joseph	Oran	1779
Wm	Hert	1779	Judia	Dobb	1780
Wm	Gran	1785	King	Wilk	1784
Wm	Hert	1784	Laurence	Gate	1789
Wm	John	1784	Levy	Bert	1781
Wm	Rowa	1761	Morris	Wilk	1782
Wm	Rowa	1770	Moses	Surr	1782
Wm	Casw	1784	Nathan	Surr	1782
Wm	Jone	1779	Obadiah	Surr	1782
Wm	Gran	1771	Ransom	Wilk	1782
Wm Jr	Hert	1784	Richard	Wilk	1784
Wm Jr	Surr	1782	Richard	Bert	1781
Yancey	Casw	1784	Robert	Oran	1779
BAINES, George	Chow	1785	Robert	Blad	1784
George Sr	Chow	1785	Saml	Gate	1789
John	Beau	1786	Samuel	Blad	1784

BAKER, Solomon	Bert 1781		BALLARD, Benjamin	Mart 1779
Stephen	Hert 1779		Christopher	Nash 1782
Stephen	Beau 1779		David	Nash 1782
Thomas	Ruth 1782		David	Surr 1782
Thomas	Bert 1781		Debereaux	Hali 1783
Uriah	Bert 1781		Dudley	Warr 1784
Wm	Cart 1779		Elias	Mart 1779
Wm	Hert 1779		Elias	Wayn 1786
Wm	Bute 1766		Elisha	Mart 1779
Wm	Hert 1784		Elisha Jr	Mart 1779
Wm	Gate 1789		Humphrey	Bute 1766
Wm Jr	Nash 1782		Humphrey	Mont 1782
Wm Sr	Nash 1782		James	Mart 1779
Zadok	Hert 1779		Jethro	Gate 1789
Zadok	Hert 1784		Joab	Wayn 1786
BALDRIDGE, Daniel	Oran 1779		John	Nash 1782
Francis	Oran 1779		John	Bute 1766
James	Oran 1779		John	Mart 1779
John	Oran 1779		John	Mont 1782
Malcomb	Oran 1779		John	Onsl 1771
Robert	Oran 1779		Joseph	Rowa 1768
Wm	Surr 1782		Joseph	Mart 1779
BALDWIN, Charles	Blad 1784		Joseph	Onsl 1771
Edward	Casw 1786		Lucy	Warr 1784
Henry	Casw 1786		Meremon	Surr 1782
Henry	Casw 1784		Mourning	Warr 1784
Jesse	Rich 1790		Samuel	Rowa 1768
John	Oran 1779		Sarah	Warr 1784
John	Casw 1786		Silas	Mart 1779
John	Blad 1784		Thomas	Bert 1774
John Jr	Blad 1784		Thomas	Surr 1782
Joseph	Blad 1784		Walter	Hali 1783
Nathan	Blad 1784		Wm	Warr 1784
Warren	Blad 1784		Wm	Nash 1782
Wm	Blad 1784		Wm	Ruth 1782
BALE, Nancy	Bert 1774		Wm	Bute 1766
BALENDINE, Jacob	Gran 1785		Wm	Warr 1779
BALL, Alexander	NorH 1780		Wm	Mont 1782
Daniel	Warr 1784		BALLENGEE, Wm	John 1784
Daniel	Bute 1766		BALLENGER, Henry	Rowa 1765
Daniel Jret)	Warr 1784		John	John 1784
Edmund	Surr 1782		Mary	John 1784
Henry	Dobb 1780		Moses	Rowa 1765
Hogie	Curr 1779		Wm	John 1784
James	Warr 1784		BALLENTINE, Alexander	
James	Oran 1779			Blad 1784
James	Crav 1779		Edward	Mart 1779
John	Beau 1786		Henry	Curr 1779
Mary	Jone 1779		Joseph	Curr 1779
Mary	Beau 1786		BALLEY, David	Rowa 1761
Moses	Jone 1779		Wm	Rowa 1761
Nathan	Cart 1779		BALLTHROP, Augustine	
Osborn	Warr 1784			Warr 1789
Reuben	Curr 1779		John	Warr 1784
Stephen	Cart 1779		Wm	Warr 1784
Thomas	Surr 1782		BANAHER, Edward	NBer 1779
Wm	Bute 1766		BANCKE, Wm	Wilk 1782
Wm	Samp 1784		BANCO, Wm	Perq 1787
BALLANCE, Abner	Curr 1779		BANCOMBERG, James	John 1784
Benj	Beau 1786		BANDRUPED, Windant	Wilk 1784
Caleb	Curr 1779		BANGE, Thomas	Wilk 1782
John	Curr 1779		BANK, John	Beau 1779
Wm	Curr 1779		BANKS, Alexander	Hert 1779
BALLANGEE, Elisha	Tyrr 1784		Alexander Sr	Hert 1784
BALLARD, Benjamin	Rowa 1768		Benjamin	Hert 1784

BANKS, John	Crav 1779	BARDEN, Isabel	Wayn 1786
John	Wilk 1782	Jacob	Wayn 1786
Jonathan	Pasq 1779	James	Wayn 1786
Jonathan	Pasq 1789	John	Warr 1784
Joseph	Pasq 1789	Wm	Warr 1784
Liliston	Mart 1779	BARDOUR, Joseph	Perq 1772
Nathaniel	Wilk 1782	BARDOW, John	Hert 1784
Richard	Perq 1787	BARDSON, Atkin	Jone 1779
Thomas	Gran 1771	BAREFIELD, Moses	Onsl 1771
Thomas	Pasq 1789	BAREFOOT, John	Wayn 1786
Wm	Oran 1779	John	John 1784
Wm	NorH 1780	Lydia	Camd 1782
Wm	Perq 1787	Nora	John 1784
BANKSTON, Andrew	Mont 1782	Nora Jr	John 1784
Ann	Mont 1782	BARES, Daniel	Cart 1779
Daniel	Mont 1782	BARFIELD, Blake	Wayn 1786
Peter	Mont 1782	Charles	Blad 1784
Susannah	Mont 1782	David	Blad 1784
BANLIFT, Ann	Perq 1772	James	Dobb 1780
Joseph	Perq 1772	John	Dobb 1780
BANNIER, Michael	Perq 1772	John	Mart 1779
BANNISTER, Henry	Surr 1782	Mills	Dobb 1780
BANNS, Henry	Nash 1782	Richard	Blad 1784
BANTEFF, Howard	Pasq 1694	Shadrack	Blad 1784
BANTEL, John	Perq 1772	Solomon	Wayn 1786
BAPTIST, Edmund	Pasq 1779	Thomas	Dobb 1780
Eliz	Pasq 1789	Willis	Blad 1784
John	Ruth 1782	Wm	Dobb 1780
Mary Ann	Pasq 1789	BARGER, Abraham	Hert 1784
BARBER, Aaron	Perq 1787	Benj	Gran 1771
Chas	Bert 1781	G.H.	Rowa 1768
Chas	Bert 1781	BARKER, Allen	Oran 1779
Elisha	Gate 1789	Ambrose	Gran 1785
Isaac	Perq 1787	Charles	Blad 1784
Joel	Perq 1787	David	Casw 1784
John	Surr 1782	Ephraim	Wilk 1782
John	Bert 1781	George	Casw 1786
John	Beau 1786	George	Casw 1784
Joseph	Dobb 1780	George	Wilk 1782
Joseph	Beau 1779	George Jr	Casw 1786
Joshua	Hali 1783	George Jr	Casw 1784
Mitchell Jr	OnsL 1771	George Sr	Casw 1784
Richard	Onsl 1771	Israel	Casw 1786
Willis	Perq 1772	Israel	Casw 1784
Wm	Bert 1781	James	Casw 1786
BARBREE, Elizabeth	Mart 1779	John	Casw 1784
Jesse	Samp 1784	John	Beau 1786
John	Mart 1779	Joshua	Hali 1783
Peggy	Samp 1784	Joshua Jr	Hali 1783
BARBY, Christopher	Oran 1779	Samuel	Beau 1779
Gray	Oran 1779	Stephen	Hali 1783
John	Oran 1779	Thomas	Chow 1785
John Sr	Oran 1779	Thomas	Bert 1774
BARCLIFF, Ann	Perq 1787	Thomas	Bert 1774
Eliz	Perq 1787	Wm	Perq 1772
Harwood	Perq 1787	BARKLEY, Francis	Oran 1779
John	Perq 1787	Geo	NorH 1780
Joseph	Perq 1787	James	Wilk 1784
Noah	Perq 1787	James	Wilk 1782
Uriah	Perq 1787	Joseph	Wilk 1784
Wm	Perq 1787	BARKSDALE, Benjamin	Hali 1783
BARCO, Coston	Camd 1782	Wm	Hali 1783
Daniel	Cart 1779	BARLOW, Henry	Nash 1782
Judith	Camd 1782	Ralph	Blad 1784
BARDEN, Arthur	Mart 1779	Whitfield	Crav 1779

BARLOW, Wm	Blad 1784	BARNETT, Joseph	Gran 1771
BARNARD, Benoni	Beau 1786	Peter	Gran 1785
Caleb	Camd 1782	Richard	Gran 1785
Edward	Camd 1782	Sarah	Casw 1784
Jesse	Curr 1779	Sarah	Gran 1785
Rebeckah	Camd 1782	Stephen	Tyrr 1784
Robert	Curr 1779	Susie	Gran 1785
Samuel	Camd 1782	Thomas	Casw 1784
Samuel	Curr 1779	Thomas	Gran 1785
Susannah	Camd 1782	Thomas	Gran 1771
Wm	Camd 1782	Thomas Jr	Casw 1784
Wm	Curr 1779	Wm Jr	Casw 1784
BARNES, Abraham	Blad 1784	Wm Sr	Casw 1784
Anthony	Cart 1779	BARNEY, Eliz	Beau 1786
Bartholomew	Hali 1783	BARNHILL, James	Mart 1779
Benj	Gate 1789	Robert	Ruth 1782
Benjamin	Nash 1782	BARNWELL, David	Oran 1779
Britton	Blad 1784	Robert	Oran 1779
Charles	Hert 1779	Wm	Casw 1786
Charles	Hert 1784	Wm	Casw 1784
Dempsey	Nash 1782	BAROD, Jacob	Surr 1782
Demsey	Gate 1789	BARR, Wm	Gate 1789
Elias	Blad 1784	BARRELL, Thomas	NorH 1780
Elizabeth	Nash 1782	BARRETT, Edward	Hali 1783
Henry	Bert 1781	Ginn	Bert 1781
Jacob	Nash 1782	John	Hali 1783
James	Nash 1782	John	Bert 1781
James	Wayn 1786	Joseph	Surr 1782
James	Pasq 1789	Richard	Hali 1783
Jeconiah	Crav 1779	Thomas	Curr 1779
Jesse	Wayn 1786	Wm	Chow 1785
John	Nash 1782	Wm	Crav 1779
John	Blad 1784	Wm	Pitt 1786
John	Wayn 1786	BARRIMORE, Israel	Bert 1774
John	Curr 1779	Jesse	Bert 1774
John	Bert 1781	Jesse	Bert 1781
John	Rich 1790	John	Bert 1781
John Jr	Wayn 1786	John Jr	Bert 1774
Jonathan	Curr 1779	John Sr	Bert 1774
Josephia	John 1784	Thomas	Bert 1774
Merriman	Gran 1785	Thomas	Bert 1781
Merriman	Gran 1771	Wm	Bert 1781
Michael	Blad 1784	BARRINGTON, Isaac	Crav 1779
Reubin	Tyrr 1784	BARRIS, Dan	NBer 1779
Samuel	Wayn 1786	Thomas	Beau 1786
Simon	Wayn 1786	BARRON, Barnabas	Nash 1782
Stephen	Pasq 1789	Saml	Bert 1781
Thomas	Gate 1789	Samuel	Bert 1774
Thomas	Pasq 1789	Thomas	Surr 1782
Wm	Nash 1782	Wm	Casw 1784
Wm	Blad 1784	BARROT, Nathaniel	Hert 1784
Wm	Hali 1783	BARROW, Abram	Onsl 1771
Wm	Hert 1784	Daniel	Bute 1766
Wm	Tyrr 1784	Daniel	Surr 1782
Wm	Pasq 1779	David	Warr 1784
Wm	Curr 1779	Geo	Beau 1786
BARNETT, Agnes	Casw 1784	George	Beau 1779
David	Casw 1784	Jacob	Hali 1783
Hugh & s Thos	Casw 1784	James	Dobb 1780
Hugh Jr	Casw 1784	John	Albe 1679
Jesse	Gran 1785	John	Beau 1779
Jesse	Gran 1771	John	Surr 1782
John	Casw 1784	John	Beau 1786
John	Gran 1785	John Jr	Beau 1779
Joseph	Curr 1779	Samuel	Beau 1779

BARROW, Sherrod	Dobb	1780
Simon	Dobb	1780
Taylor	Dobb	1780
Wm	Hali	1783
Wm	Pasq	1779
Wm	Beau	1779
Wm	Beau	1786
Wm	Pasq	1789
BARROWS, Aaron	Perq	1787
Eli	Perq	1787
John Jr	Perq	1787
John Sr	Perq	1787
Joseph	Perq	1787
Wm	Perq	1787
BARRY, David	Cart	1779
James	Cart	1779
BARTELSON, Richard	Rowa	1761
BARTHOLOME, John	Warr	1784
BARTHOLOMEW, Charles		
	Bute	1766
Isaac	Cart	1779
BARTLETT, Blake	Camd	1782
Jesse	NorH	1780
John	Camd	1782
John	Surr	1782
Mary	Crav	1779
Samuel	Wayn	1786
Thomas	Beau	1779
Thomas	Beau	1786
BARTLEY, Robert	Oran	1779
BARTON, Benjamin	Bert	1774
Cuthbert	Casw	1786
David	Rowa	1767
David	Casw	1786
David	Wilk	1784
David	Wilk	1782
Henry	Surr	1782
James	Casw	1786
James	Casw	1784
John	Wilk	1778
John	Wilk	1784
John	Wilk	1782
Lewis	Casw	1786
Lewis	Casw	1784
Samuel	Casw	1786
Susannah	Casw	1786
Thomas	Casw	1786
Thomas]	Oran	1779
Valentine	Albe	1679
Wm	Gran	1785
BARWICK, John	Wayn	1786
Joshua s of Wm	Dobb	1780
Wm Sr	Dobb	1780
BARY, Bury	Surr	1782
BASFORD, John	Warr	1784
BASH, Daniel	Wilk	1782
BASKET, Elizabeth	Warr	1784
BASKETT, Elizabeth	Bute	1766
Elizabeth	Warr	1784
James	Bute	1766
James	Warr	1784
BASLE, John	Wilk	1782
BASLEY, Harmony	NBer	1779
BASNET, Robert	Curr	1779
BASNETT, Jacob	Tyrr	1784

BASNETT, Joseph	Tyrr	1784
Wm	Tyrr	1784
BASON, Henry	Oran	1779
Jacob	Oran	1779
John	Oran	1779
BASS, Aaron	John	1784
Abraham	Nash	1782
Alexander	Hali	1783
Alexander	Rich	1790
Andrew	Wayn	1786
Andrewe Sr	Wayn	1786
Arthur	Wayn	1786
Benj	Gran	1771
Benjamin Jr	Gran	1785
Benjamin Sr	Gran	1785
Cader	Bert	1781
Charity	Nash	1782
Daniel	NorH	1780
Demsey	NorH	1780
Edward	Wayn	1786
Edward	Gran	1785
Elisha	Wayn	1786
Ephraim	Wayn	1786
Esau	Wayn	1786
Isaac	Nash	1782
Jacob	Bute	1766
Jacob	Bert	1774
Jacob	Bert	1781
Jethro	Nash	1782
Jethro	NorH	1780
John	Wayn	1786
John	Hali	1783
John	Bert	1781
Joshua	Wayn	1786
Matthew	Surr	1782
Nathan	Gran	1785
Nathan	Gran	1771
Newit	Nash	1782
Reuben	Gran	1785
Reuben	Gran	1771
Rice	Wayn	1786
Richard	Samp	1784
Richard	Wayn	1786
Samuel	Hali	1783
Sion	Nash	1782
Stephen	Gran	1785
Theophilus	Bute	1766
Thomas	Wayn	1786
Uriah	NorH	1780
Willis	Samp	1784
Wm	Samp	1784
BASSETT, John	Hert	1779
Peter	Albe	1694
BASSNET, James	Tyrr	1784
BATCHELOR, Francis	Beau	1779
Wm	Nash	1782
BATE, Andrew	Curr	1779
Wm	Curr	1779
BATEMAN, Andrew	Tyrr	1784
Claiborne	Wayn	1786
Godfrey	Tyrr	1784
Godfrey	Tyrr	1784
Hopkins	Crav	1779
Isaac	Tyrr	1784
Isaac	Tyrr	1784

BATEMAN, Jeremiah	Tyrr 1784	BAXTER, John	Warr 1784
Jesse	John 1784	John	Curr 1779
Jesse	Tyrr 1784	Joseph	Curr 1779
Jesse	Tyrr 1784	Joshua	Curr 1779
John	Tyrr 1784	Nathaniel	Bute 1766
John	Tyrr 1784	Nathaniel	Warr 1784
John	Perq 1787	Peter	Casw 1784
John Samuel	Perq 1772	Sarah	Curr 1779
John s of Nat	Tyrr 1784	Thomas	Casw 1786
Jonathan	John 1784	BAXTEROD, Nathaniel	Warr 1784
Jonathan	Tyrr 1784	BAYBURK, James	Surr 1782
Jonathan	Perq 1787	BAYLES, John	Wayn 1786
Jonathan Sr	Tyrr 1784	BAYLEY, John	Perq 1772
Joseph	Tyrr 1784	BAYLOR, John	NBer 1779
Joseph	Perq 1787	BAYNES, John	Beau 1779
Mary	Chow 1785	Richard	Beau 1779
Nathan Sr	Tyrr 1784	BAZOR, Wm	Oran 1779
Solomon	Tyrr 1784	BEAL, John	Perq 1787
Stephen	Tyrr 1784	BEALS, Asa	Camd 1782
Thomas	Crav 1779	Bowater	Rowa 1768
Thomas	Perq 1787	James	Camd 1782
jeremiah	Tyrr 1788	Micajah	Camd 1782
BATES, Isaac	Wilk 1782	BEAM, Michael	Rowa 1761
James	Bert 1774	Peter	Rowa 1761
James	Bute 1766	BEAMAN, Francis Jr	Dobb 1780
James	Bert 1781	James	Dobb 1780
Jeffrey	Casw 1784	John	Hert 1784
John	Ruth 1782	Ozias	Hert 1784
John	Oran 1779	BEAMON, Edmond	Hert 1779
John	Casw 1786	Ozias	Hert 1779
Wm	Surr 1782	BEAN, Richard	Rowa 1768
BATHMELL, Joseph	Hert 1784	Richard	Mont 1782
BATICE, John	Mont 1782	Walter	Rowa 1768
BATON, Anguish	Mont 1782	Walter	Mont 1782
Daniel	Mont 1782	BEARD, Daniel	Blad 1784
BATTEN, George	Tyrr 1784	James	Blad 1784
John	John 1784	John	Blad 1784
BATTLE, Benjamin	Nash 1782	John Jr	Wayn 1786
James	Nash 1782	John Sr	Wayn 1786
Jesse	Nash 1782	Lewis	Rowa 1761
John	Hert 1784	Wm	Rowa 1761
John	NorH 1780	BEARDEN, Absalom	Bute 1766
Martha	Hert 1784	Benjamin	Gran 1785
Mary	Onsl 1771	Richard	Surr 1782
Sarah	Ruth 1782	Richard & s	Bute 1766
Wm	NorH 1750	BEARDON, Anthony	Warr 1784
Wm	Hert 1779	BEASLEY, Benjamin	Crav 1779
Wm	Hert 1784	Caleb	Curr 1779
Wm Jr	Nash 1782	Chas	Surr 1782
Wm Sr 1558 a	Nash 1782	Daniel	Rich 1790
BAUGH, Josiah	Oran 1779	Eleanor	Blad 1784
BAUGHERTY, Joshua	NorH 1780	Elisha	NBer 1779
BAUGHMAN, Zechariah	Casw 1784	Ezekiel	Blad 1784
BAUGHN, Wm	Hali 1783	Francis	Chow 1785
BAUGHSKY, Elisha	NorH 1780	George	Chow 1785
BAULDEN, Sam	Onsl 1771	Isaac	Rowa 1768
BAUM, John	Camd 1782	Jacob	Curr 1779
BAUME, Adam	Pasq 1779	James	Blad 1784
Peter	Pasq 1779	John	Chow 1785
Robert	Pasq 1779	John	NBer 1779
BAUTWELL, Leonard	Beau 1779	John	Wilk 1782
BAXLEY, Edmond	Blad 1784	John	Onsl 1771
Wm	Blad 1784	John B	Chow 1785
BAXTER, Cerman	Oran 1779	Major	Rowa 1768
James	Oran 1779	Major	Rowa 1770

BEASLEY, Martha	Chow 1785	BEECHAM, Edmond	Curr 1779
Richard	Casw 1786	John	Curr 1779
Richard	Casw 1784	Thomas	Curr 1779
Robert	Gran 1785	BEEK, Frederick	Gran 1785
Robert	Gran 1771	John	Gran 1785
Simon	Crav 1779	Michael	Gran 1785
Solomon	Dupl 1783	BEEMAN, Abraham	Wayn 1786
Solomon	NBer 1779	Francis	Wayn 1786
Thomas	Onsl 1771	James	Wayn 1786
Wm	Warr 1784	Ozias	Wayn 1786
Wm	Rowa 1768	BEESLEY, Abraham	Dupl 1779
Wm	Curr 1779	BEFFEL, Adam	Rowa 1761
BEASON, Benjamin	Rowa 1768	Paul	Rowa 1761
Benjamin Jr	Rowa 1761	BEGLEY, Oxford	Brun 1784
Benjamin Sr	Rowa 1761	BELATOR, Edward	Surr 1782
George	Rowa 1761	Zebulon	Surr 1782
Isaac	Rowa 1761	BELCH, James	Bert 1781
Isaac	Rowa 1768	Lewis	Bert 1781
Isaac	Rowa 1765	Mary	Hert 1779
Pearson	Rowa 1761	Mary	Hert 1784
Richard	Rowa 1768	Willis	Mart 1779
Richard	Rowa 1765	BELCHER, Woody	Dobb 1780
Wm	Rowa 1761	BELIGHAUS, Geo	Surr 1782
Wm	Rowa 1768	BELK, Wm	Dobb 1780
Wm	Rowa 1765	BELL, Abner	Cart 1779
BEATTY, George	Warr 1784	Andrew	Cart 1779
Hugh	Ruth 1782	Arthur	Rowa 1770
James	Ruth 1782	Arthur	Hali 1783
Wallace	Ruth 1782	Asel	Cart 1779
BEAVER, Jeremiah	Casw 1786	Caleb	Cart 1777
John	Casw 1786	Caleb	Cart 1779
Wm	Casw 1786	Caleb	Curr 1779
BECK, John	Blad 1784	Caleb Sr	Curr 1779
John	Samp 1784	Daniel	Surr 1782
John	Wayn 1786	David	Cart 1779
John	Surr 1782	Eden	Cart 1779
John	Beau 1786	Edward	Wilk 1782
Jonathan	Pasq 1779	Elizabeth	Nash 1782
Matthew	Hert 1784	Frances	Cart 1779
Ruth	Pasq 1789	Francis	Cart 1779
Wm	Wayn 1786	Francis	Rowa 1770
BECKER, Nicholas	Surr 1782	Frederick	Cart 1777
BECKHAM, Benjamin	Warr 1784	Geo	Gran 1771
James	Warr 1773	George	Cart 1779
James	Warr 1784	George	Dobb 1780
Jesse	Warr 1784	George	Samp 1784
John	Bute 1766	George	Hali 1783
Simon	Warr 1784	Green	Nash 1782
Stephen	Warr 1784	Hezekiah	Samp 1784
Stephen	Bute 1766	James	Warr 1784
Stephen Jr	Bute 1766	James	Nash 1782
Wm	Bute 1766	James	Cart 1779
Wm Jr	Bute 1766	James	Wayn 1786
BECKNALL, Sam	Wilk 1782	James	John 1784
BECKWITH, Amos	Nash 1782	James Jr	Cart 1779
Bolling	Nash 1782	Jesse	Warr 1784
Henry	Nash 1782	Jesse	Bute 1766
Thomas	Nash 1782	Jesse	Samp 1784
BEDGOOD, John	Nash 1782	John	Cart 1779
BEDIL, Zachariah	Gran 1785	John	Rowa 1770
BEDINGFIELD, John D.		John	Blad 1784
	John 1784	John	Brun 1784
Wm	John 1784	John	Hali 1783
BEDSCOTT, John	Crav 1779	John	Mont 1782
BEECH, Thomas Jr	Mart 1779	John	Curr 1779

BELL, John	NorH 1780		BEMBRIDGE, Elizabeth		
John	Pasq 1789			Albe 1694	
Jonathan	Bute 1766		BEMINE, Wm	Cart 1779	
Joseph	Cart 1779		BENBURY, Charles	Chow 1785	
Joseph	Bute 1766		Richard	Chow 1785	
Joseph	Camd 1782		Ruth	Chow 1785	
Joseph	Warr 1784		Thomas	Chow 1785	
Joseph	Mont 1782		BENFORD, James	NorH 1780	
Joseph Jr	Cart 1779		John	NorH 1780	
Joseph Sr	Cart 1779		BENJIN, Benj	Surr 1782	
Josephus	Cart 1779		BENNEHAN, Richard	Oran 1779	
Joshua	Gran 1785		BENNER, John	Crav 1779	
Joshua	Hali 1783		BENNETT, Crary	Mont 1782	
Josiah	Camd 1782		Elizabeth	Wayn 1786	
Lancelot	Pasq 1779		Geo	Gate 1789	
Lydia	Curr 1779		Isham	Warr 1784	
Malachi	Cart 1779		James	Warr 1784	
Mary	Warr 1784		James	Mart 1779	
Mary	Samp 1784		James	Onsl 1771	
Nathan	Cart 1779		James	Gran 1771	
Nathan	Camd 1782		Jesse	Curr 1779	
Nathaniel	Mont 1782		John	Bute 1766	
Newel	Cart 1779		John	Samp 1784	
Newel Sr	Cart 1779		John	Beau 1779	
Newel younger	Cart 1779		John	Curr 1779	
Newell	Cart 1779		Joseph	Blad 1784	
Orson	Samp 1784		Joseph	Wayn 1786	
Richard	Mont 1782		Joseph	Onsl 1771	
Robert	Samp 1784		Luke	Beau 1779	
Robert	Brun 1784		Mark	Mont 1782	
Robin	Rowa 1770		Martha	Warr 1784	
Ross	Cart 1779		Micajah	Wilk 1784	
Ross	Cart 1779		Micajah	Wilk 1782	
Ross Jr	Cart 1779		Moses	Curr 1779	
Samuel	Rowa 1770		Nathaniel	Onsl 1771	
Samuel	Camd 1782		Peter	Rich 1790	
Samuel	Samp 1784		Reuben	Warr 1784	
Samuel	Brun 1784		Richard	Bute 1766	
Samuel	Hali 1783		Richard	Warr 1784	
Samuel	Hert 1784		Richard	Rich 1790	
Samuel	Pasq 1779		Samuel	Curr 1779	
Sarah	Hali 1783		Sarah	Chow 1785	
Solomon	Cart 1777		Solomon	Mont 1782	
Solomon	Cart 1779		Thomas Jr	Mart 1779	
Thomas	Warr 1784		Thomas Sr	Mart 1779	
Thomas	Nash 1782		Wm	Mart 1779	
Thomas	Bute 1766		Wm	Chow 1785	
Thomas	Warr 1784		Wm	NorH 1780	
Wm	Nash 1782		Wm	Gran 1772	
Wm	Cart 1779		Wm	Rich 1790	
Wm	Bute 1766		BENNETTN, Richard	Warr 1784	
Wm	Rowa 1770		BENNISSELL, Sarah	NorH 1780	
Wm	Camd 1782		BENSON, Christopher	Ruth 1782	
Wm Sr	Wayn 1786		James	Blad 1784	
Zachariah	Rich 1790		John	Bute 1766	
BELLAMY, James	Beau 1779		John	Beau 1779	
BELLAS, Isaac	Casw 1784		Wm	Dobb 1780	
BELLFLOWER, James	Mart 1779		Wm	Bert 1781	
BELLONE, John	Beau 1779		BENT, Thomas	Warr 1784	
BELLOWS, Peter]	Surr 1782		Thomas		
BELOTE, John	Bert 1781		BENTHAL, Joseph	NorH 1780	
John	Bert 1781		BENTHALL, Azel	Hert 1779	
Peleg	Bert 1774		Daniel	Hert 1779	
Peter	Bert 1781		Daniel	Hert 1784	
BEMBRIDGE, Caleb	Tyrr 1784		Joseph Jr	Hert 1779	

BENTHALL, Joseph Sr	Hert	1779
BENTLEY, James	Bert	1774
James	Bert	1781
Jesse	Bert	1781
John	Onsl	1771
John	Bert	1781
Wm	Bert	1774
Wm	Crav	1779
Wm	Onsl	1771
BENTON, Bailey	Beau	1786
David	Casw	1786
Dempsey	Brun	1784
Devotion	Pasq	1789
Elkanah	Pasq	1789
Francis	Dobb	1780
Hardy	Brun	1784
Isaac	Gate	1789
James	Casw	1786
James	Casw	1784
Jeremiah	Gate	1789
Jesse	Oran	1779
Jesse	Gran	1771
Jesse	Gate	1789
Jethro	Gate	1789
Job	Brun	1784
Jonathan	Wayn	1786
Josdiah	Gate	1789
Joseph	Dobb	1780
Joshua	Dupl	1779
Josiah	Samp	1784
Margaret	Pasq	1789
Mary	Gate	1789
Michael	Brun	1784
Michael	Jone	1779
Moses	Brun	1785
Moses	Gate	1789
Peter	Gate	1789
Sam	Gate	1789
Samuel	Oran	1779
BERAYER, Abraham	Rowa	1761
George	Rowa	1761
Michael	Rowa	1761
BERGER, Michael	Hali	1783
BERGERON, Elias	Dobb	1780
John	Dobb	1780
BERGMAN, Isaac	Rich	1790
BERICK, Wm	Jone	1779
BERNARD, Joseph	Curr	1779
Julian	Curr	1779
BERNEY, Wm	Surr	1782
BEROTH, John	Surr	1782
BERRY, Daniel	Jone	1779
Hudson	Casw	1784
Hutson	Casw	1786
John	Camd	1782
John	Casw	1786
John	Casw	1784
John	Curr	1779
John	Curr	1779
John Jr	Bert	1781
John Sr	Bert	1781
Robert	Oran	1779
Samuel	Curr	1779
Solomon	Camd	1782
Thomas	Bert	1781

BERRY, Wm	Gran	1785
BERRYMAN, Edward	Gate	1789
Wm	Gate	1789
BESILL, Robert	Gran	1785
BEST, Benjamin	Dobb	1780
Cader	Bute	1766
Chas	Pasq	1789
Mary	Hert	1779
Thomas	Hert	1779
Thomas	Mart	1779
Thomas	Hert	1784
Wm	Dupl	1783
Wm	Bute	1766
Wm	Hert	1784
BETHEY, Ann	Gate	1789
James	Gate	1789
John	Gate	1789
BETSON, Joseph	Gran	1782
BETT, Abraham	Beau	1779
Jesse	Hali	1783
Jonathan	Pasq	1779
Moses	Hali	1783
Samuel	Pasq	1779
BETTUNS, Michael	Brun	1784
BEVERLY, Benj	NorH	1780
Benjamin	Hert	1779
BEVIN, Isham	Blad	1784
BIARD, Alexander	Mont	1782
BIDDLE, Charles	Cart	1779
Jacob	Onsl	1771
BIGFORD, Jeremiah	Blad	1784
BIGGS, James	Mart	1779
James s	Blad	1784
John	Nash	1782
John	Curr	1779
John Jr	Nash	1782
Joseph	Mart	1779
Kader	Mart	1779
Wm	Mart	1779
Wm	Crav	1779
BILBOA, Berryman	Warr	1784
BILLBERRY, Dennis	Beau	1779
BILLINGSLEY, Charles		
	Oran	1779
Silas	Mont	1782
BILLINGTON, Ezekiel	Wayn	1786
BINGHAM, Thomas	Surr	1782
Wm	Surr	1782
BINS, Mary	Curr	1779
BIRD, Benjamin	Dobb	1780
Chas	NorH	1780
Edward	Bert	1781
Emson	Oran	1779
Enos	Bute	1766
Enos	Bert	1781
Isaac	Blad	1784
James	Oran	1779
James Jr	Oran	1779
Jesse	Bute	1766
John	Pasq	1694
John	Bute	1766
John	Bert	1774
John	Bert	1781
Joshua	Dobb	1780
Nathan	Dobb	1780

BIRD, Nathaniel	Dobb 1780	BLACK, Thomas	Casw 1784
Nathaniel	Blad 1784	BLACKARD, Charles	Bute 1766
Needham s John	Bute 1766	Charles	Casw 1784
Peter	Hali 1783	BLACKBURN, Ambrose	Surr 1782
Phillip	NorH 1780	Augustine	Surr 1782
Richard	Dobb 1780	Benjamin	Hali 1783
Richard	Oran 1779	Edward	Surr 1782
Richard	Bert 1781	Elias	Hali 1783
Solomon	NorH 1780	James	Ruth 1782
Thomas	Bute 1766	John	Chow 1785
Thomas	Dobb 1780	John	Surr 1782
Thomas	Hali 1783	John	
Thomas	Gran 1771	Sarah	Hali 1783
Wm	Blad 1784	Thomas	Surr 1782
Wm	Hali 1783	Wm	Samp 1784
BISCO, Joseph	Curr 1779	Wm	Surr 1782
BISHOP, Avis	Wilk 1782	Younger	Surr 1782
Francis	Wilk 1784	BLACKETT, Thomas	Rowa 1767
Francis	Wilk 1782	BLACKLEDGE, Ann	Crav 1779
Isaac	Oran 1779	Ann	Pitt 1786
James	Gran 1785	Richard	Cart 1779
James	Crav 1779	Richard	NBer 1779
Jesse	Hert 1784	Richard	Beau 1786
John	Hert 1779	BLACKLEY, James	Gran 1785
John	Pasq 1694	Peter	Gran 1785
John	Hali 1783	BLACKLOCK, Mary	Pasq 1789
John	Hert 1784	BLACKMAN, Ann	Samp 1784
John	Crav 1779	Barzillian	John 1784
Joseph	Crav 1779	Esther	John 1784
Littleton	Onsl 1771	Hannah	Pasq 1779
Markus	Hert 1784	Ichabod	Samp 1784
Moses	Hali 1783	Joab	Samp 1784
Richard	Hali 1783	John	John 1784
Robert	Dupl 1779	John	Jone 1779
Roger	Wilk 1782	Josiah	Samp 1784
Thomas	Rowa 1770	Rice	Samp 1784
Wm	Hali 1783	Stephen	Samp 1784
BISMET, Wm	Gran 1784	Stephen	Brun 1784
Wm Jr	Gran 1785	Wm	Wayn 1786
BITTOCKS, John	Oran 1779	Wm	John 1784
BIZELL, David	Hert 1779	BLACKSHAW, Alexander	
David	Wayn 1786		Jone 1779
John	Wayn 1786	BLACKSHEAR, Abraham	Jone 1779
Solomon	Hert 1779	James	Jone 1779
Solomon	Hert 1784	BLACKSHIRE, Abram	Onsl 1771
Thomas	Wayn 1786	BLACKSTALK, John	Pasq 1779
Wm Jr	Wayn 1786	BLACKSTONE, Thomas	Perq 1772
BLACK, Alexander	Chow 1785	BLACKWELL, David	Surr 1782
Amy	Chow 1785	Isaiah	Ruth 1782
Francis	Chow 1785	James	Gran 1785
Frederick	Rowa 1768	Jesse	Blad 1784
Geo	Gran 1771	Joel	Ruth 1782
George	Ruth 1782	Joel	Surr 1782
George	Casw 1784	John	Gran 1785
Gilmore	Chow 1785	John	Surr 1782
Henry	Casw 1784	John	Rich 1790
Hugh	Ruth 1782	Robert	Casw 1786
Jacob	Rowa 1768	Robert	Casw 1784
Jacob	Oran 1779	Wm	Mart 1779
James	Ruth 1782	BLACKWOOD, James	Oran 1779
James	Blad 1784	John	Oran 1779
John	Ruth 1782	Wm	Oran 1779
John	Casw 1784	BLAIR, James	Rowa 1768
Patrick	Ruth 1782	James	NorH 1780
Robert	Ruth 1782	Jane	Chow 1785

BLAIR, Thomas	Oran 1779	BLOUNT, Benjamin Sr	Tyrr 1784
BLAKE, Ann	Mont 1782	Bryan	Beau 1779
Benjamin	Oran 1779	Bryan	Beau 1786
Elizabeth	Hert 1784	Charles	Perq 1772
James	Bert 1781	Edmond Jr	Tyrr 1784
John	Casw 1784	Edmond Sr	Tyrr 1784
John	Surr 1782	Edward	Chow 1785
Walter	Hert 1779	Edward	Perq 1772
BLAKLEY, Lawrence	Crav 1779	Gray	Beau 1779
BLALOCK, Jeremiah	Gran 1785	Jacob	Blad 1784
John	Rowa 1768	Jacob	Tyrr 1784
John	Surr 1782	Jacob	Crav 1779
John	Gran 1771	Jacob	Pitt 1786
Richard	Surr 1782	Jacob	Pasq 1789
Wm	Surr 1782	James	Blad 1784
Wm Jr	Surr 1782	James	Chow 1785
BLANCH, Ezekiel	Warr 1784	James	Pasq 1779
BLANCHARD, Andrew	NBer 1779	James	Beau 1779
Andrew	NBer 1779	James	Pasq 1789
Ephraim	NorH 1780	Jesse	Beau 1779
James	Wayn 1786	Jesse	Beau 1786
Micajah	Chow 1785	John	Blad 1784
Uriah	Wayn 1786	John	Chow 1785
BLANCHETT, Hudson	Warr 1784	John	Tyrr 1784
Thomas	Bute 1766	John	Beau 1786
Thomas	Warr 1784	John	Beau 1786
Thomas Jr	Warr 1784	Joseph	Chow 1785
Wm	Rowa 1768	Joseph	Perq 1772
BLAND, John	Mart 1779	Louis	Beau 1779
Stephen	Mart 1779	Louis	Beau 1786
Thomas	Mart 1779	Lovick	Tyrr 1784
Wm	Mart 1779	Mary	Pasq 1779
BLANGO, Solomon	Beau 1786	Nathan	Beau 1786
Thomas	Beau 1786	Nathaniel	Beau 1779
BLANSHARD, Abner	Gate 1789	Phillip	Blad 1784
Dempsey	Gate 1789	Reading	Beau 1779
Eliz	Gate 1789	Reading	Beau 1786
Henry	Gate 1789	Reading Jr	Beau 1779
Miles	Hert 1784	Sarah	Chow 1785
Mourning	Hert 1779	Sarah	Beau 1779
BLANTON, Charles	Hali 1783	Thomas	Blad 1784
George	Ruth 1782	Thomas	Beau 1779
Richard	Hali 1783	Wm	Samp 1784
BLANTONRD, John Sr	Mart 1779	Wm	Warr 1784
BLARNS, Patience	Beau 1779	BLUE, Dougal	Rich 1790
BLEAXTON, Thomas	Perq 1787	Dugold	Blad 1784
BLECKER, John	Surr 1782	John	Blad 1784
Moses	Surr 1782	Suffle	Rowa 1768
BLEDSOE, Bartlett	Gran 1771	BLUNT, Wm	Warr 1784
Benj	Surr 1782	BLURTON, Edward	John 1784
George	Bute 1766	BLYTHER, Wm	Blad 1784
Wm	Gran 1771	BNURGESS, Wm	Camd 1782
BLEW, Thomas	Wayn 1786	BOAM, James	Blad 1784
BLEWITT, Thomas	Rich 1790	BOBBETT, James	Warr 1784
BLOCKER, John Capt.	Blad 1784	BOBBITT, Drewry	Bute 1766
BLONGO, Sarah	Beau 1779	James	Warr 1784
Thomas	Beau 1779	John	Bute 1766
BLOOM, Jacob	Surr 1782	John	Oran 1779
BLOSS, Henry	Hali 1783	John Jr	Bute 1766
BLOTE, John	Bert 1774	John Sr	Warr 1784
BLOUINT, Benjamin Jr		Lewis	Bute 1766
	Tyrr 1784	Louis	Warr 1784
BLOUNT, Benj	Beau 1786	Miles	Bute 1766
Benjamin	Mart 1779	Miles	Warr 1784
Benjamin	Beau 1779	Sion	Gran 1785

BOBBITT, Stephen	Warr 1784		BOND, John Jr	Beau 1779
Wm	Bute 1766		Mary	Dobb 1780
Wm	Gran 1785		Michael	Chow 1785
Wm	Warr 1784		Richard	Rowa 1765
BODDIE, John	Bute 1766		Richard	Chow 1785
John	Gran 1785		Richard	Gate 1789
John	Gran 1771		Robert	Beau 1779
Martha	NorH 1780		Robert	Beau 1786
Nathan	Nash 1782		Sam	Onsl 1771
Willis	NorH 1780		Saml	Surr 1782
Wm	Nash 1782		Sarah	Beau 1779
BOGARD, Daniel	Bert 1781		Sarah	NBer 1779
BOGER, Alexander	NBer 1779		Sarah	Beau 1786
Jacob	Surr 1782		Stephen	Surr 1782
BOGGESS, Isaiah	Perq 1787		Thomas	Bert 1774
James	Casw 1786		Thomas	Bert 1781
Richard	Casw 1786		Wm	Dobb 1780
BOGGS, Andrew	Oran 1779		Wm	Perq 1772
BOGGUS, James	Casw 1784		Wm	Gate 1789
Joseph	Hali 1783		Wm	Perq 1787
Richard	Casw 1784		BONE, Archibald	Blad 1784
BOGUE, Duke	Perq 1787		John	Nash 1782
Jesse	Wayn 1786		BONECKER, Michael	Rowa 1761
Job	Perq 1787		BONEY, Henry	Gran 1785
Joseph	Perq 1787		BONGO, Jobe	Perq 1772
Wm	Perq 1787		BONN, Jacob	Rowa 1768
BOHANNON, Alexander	Surr 1782		BONNER, Abigail	Beau 1779
John	Surr 1782		Alligood	Beau 1779
Wm	NBer 1779		Ann	Beau 1786
BOLDREATH, Anguish	Blad 1784		Benj	Surr 1782
BOLEJECK, Joseph	Surr 1782		Edward	Beau 1786
BOLES, James	Surr 1782		Eliz	Beau 1786
James Sr	Oran 1779		Ephraim	Surr 1782
Jaqmes Jr	Oran 1779		Geo	Bert 1781
John	Surr 1782		Henry	Chow 1785
John Jr	Oran 1779		Henry	Surr 1782
John Sr	Oran 1779		Henry	Beau 1786
Wm	Oran 1779		James	Beau 1779
BOLEY, Alexr	Surr 1782		James	Beau 1786
BOLING, Alexander	Oran 1779		James Jr	Beau 1779
Andrew	Oran 1779		John	Beau 1786
Jane	Oran 1779		John	Beau 1786
BOLLEN, Robert	Bert 1774		Joseph	Surr 1782
BOLLING, John	Mont 1782		Joseph	Beau 1786
BOLTON, Henry	Mont 1782		Mary	Chow 1785
James	Mont 1782		Moses	Gran 1771
Jane	Hert 1779		Sam	Beau 1786
John	Hert 1784		Sarah	Beau 1786
Wm	Oran 1779		Thomas	Bute 1766
BOME, Peter	Pasq 1779		Thomas	Chow 1785
Robert	Pasq 1779		Thomas	Gran 1771
BOND, Chas	Wilk 1782		Thomas Jr	Chow 1785
Edward	Gran 1771		Wm	Beau 1786
Hannise	Hali 1783		BONNEY, Ann	Blad 1784
Henry	Chow 1785		Ephraim	Curr 1779
James	Bert 1774		Jonathan	Curr 1779
James	Mont 1782		BONNIFANT, Elizabeth	
James	Bert 1781			Hert 1779
Jesse	Wilk 1782		BOOK, Jacob	Rowa 1781
Job	Perq 1787		BOONE, Benj	NorH 1780
John	Chow 1785		Benjamin	Nash 1782
John	Nash 1782		Emanuel	Wilk 1784
John	Beau 1779		Jacob Jr	Oran 1779
John	Bert 1781		Jacob Jr	NorH 1780
John	Beau 1786		Jacob Sr	Oran 1779

BOONE, Jacob Sr	NorH	1780
James	Hert	1779
James	Hert	1784
James	Gate	1789
John	Hert	1779
John	Brun	1784
John	Hert	1784
John	NorH	1780
Jonathan	Rowa	1767
Joseph	John	1784
Martha	Bert	1781
Nathl	NorH	1780
Nicholas	Hert	1779
Nicholas	Hert	1784
Ratliff Jr	Surr	1782
Stephen	Samp	1784
Thomas	NorH	1780
Thomas	Surr	1782
Willis	Hali	1784
Wm	Samp	1784
Wm	NorH	1780
BOORE, Lawrence	Cart	1779
BOOTEY, Sarah	Crav	1779
BOOTH, Andrew	Nash	1782
Daniel	Oran	1779
Jesse	Nash	1782
John	Oran	1779
Joseph	Oran	1779
Mary	Ruth	1782
Phillip	Mart	1779
Thomas	Mart	1779
Thomas	Surr	1782
Thomas	Bert	1781
Wm	Gate	1789
BORAN, Isaac	Casw	1784
Isaac	Casw	1786
BORDEAUX, James	Brun	1784
John	Brun	1784
BORDEN, Wm	Cart	1779
BORDGER, James	NorH	1780
BORING, Francis	Dobb	1780
BORLIN, John	Gran	1771
BORMAN, Samuel	Blad	1784
BORON, John	Dobb	1780
BOROUGH, Wm	Bute	1766
BOSELEY, Wm	Curr	1779
BOSLAND, John	Wilk	1784
BOSLING, John	Wilk	1782
BOSMAN, John	Bert	1781
BOSSE, John Sr	Wilk	1782
BOSSELL, Henry	Blad	1784
Thomas	Blad	1784
BOSTER, John	Perq	1787
Joseph	Gran	1785
BOSTICK, Absalom	Surr	1782
Charles	Casw	1784
Ezra	Rich	1790
James	Rich	1790
John	Rich	1790
Nathan	Surr	1782
BOSTON, Chas	Onsl	1771
Jammes	Onsl	1771
John	Onsl	1771
BOSTWICK, Charles	Casw	1784
BOSWELL, Abram	Pasq	1789
BOSWELL, Geo	Perq	1787
George	Perq	1772
Isaac	Perq	1772
Isaac	Pasq	1789
James	Oran	1779
James	Casw	1784
James	Gran	1771
Joseph	Perq	1772
Joseph	Pasq	1789
Joshua	Perq	1787
Ransom	Gran	1771
Robert	Casw	1784
Simon	Wayn	1786
Simon	Perq	1772
Thomas	Bert	1774
Thomas		
Thomas	Perq	1787
Wm	Perq	1787
BOSWORTH, James	John	1784
BOTSFORD, James	Rowa	1768
BOTTOMS, Samuel Sr	Nash	1782
Thomas	Gran	1785
Wm	Nash	1782
BOUGE, Isaiah	Perq	1772
Jesse	Perq	1772
Joseph	Perq	1772
Robert	Perq	1772
Wm	Perq	1772
BOULTON, Aaron	Bert	1781
BOUNDS, Jesse	Rich	1790
BOUSER, Ishmael Sr	Dupl	1779
BOUSH, James	Perq	1787
BOUTTEN, Charles	Casw	1784
John	Casw	1784
BOW, Tulk	Pasq	1789
BOWDEN, Avery	Crav	1779
John	Warr	1784
Thomas	Onsl	1771
Travis	Gran	1785
Wm	Gran	1785
BOWDIN, Jonas	Brun	1782
Thomas	Gran	1771
Travis	Gran	1771
Wm	Surr	1782
BOWDON, John	Warr	1784
BOWDOWN, Travis	Gran	1771
Wm	Gran	1771
BOWEN, Abraham	Curr	1779
Alexander	Rich	1790
Benj	Bert	1781
Daniel	Samp	1784
Daniel	Dupl	1784
Edward	Albe	1679
John	Chow	1785
John	Rich	1790
Joseph	Mont	1782
Josiah	Hert	1784
Morris Jr	Curr	1779
Nathl	Bert	1781
Peggy	Rich	1790
Sarah	Blad	1784
Wm	Curr	1779
BOWER, Phillip	Gran	1785
BOWERS, Benjamin	Bute	1766
Giles & s Benj	Bute	1766

BOWERS, John	Hert 1779	BOYET, Amos	Wayn 1786
John	Surr 1782	Benjamin	Mart 1779
BOWKERS, Wm	Chow 1785	Benjamin	Wayn 1786
BOWLES, David	Pasq 1789	Delilah	Wayn 1786
John	Casw 1784	Edward	Wayn 1786
John	Hali 1783	Ethelred	Wayn 1786
Sarah	Surr 1782	Isaac	Mart 1779
Thomas	Oran 1779	Jacob	Wayn 1786
Wm	Surr 1782	James	Mart 1779
BOWLIN, John	Gran 1785	Josiah	Wayn 1786
BOWLING, Benj	Wilk 1782	Sarah	John 1784
Justice	Wilk 1782	Shadrack	Wayn 1786
BOWREN, Maximillian	Curr 1779	Solomon	Mart 1779
BOWS, Joseph	Curr 1779	Stephen	Wayn 1786
BOWSER, Luke	Dupl 1779	Thomas	John 1784
Thomas	Hert 1779	Thomas Sr	Wayn 1786
BOWSLEY, Thomas	Beau 1779	Thomass Jr	Wayn 1786
BOYCAN, Jesse	NorH 1780	Wm	Nash 1782
Job	NorH 1780	BOYETT, Shadrack	NorH 1780
John	NorH 1780	BOYKIN, Drury	Nash 1782
BOYCE, Alexander	Rich 1790	Francis	Wayn 1786
Benj	Perq 1787	Hardy	Nash 1782
Isaiah	Perq 1787	Martha	NorH 1750
John	Perq 1772	Mary	Wayn 1786
John	Perq 1787	Samuel	Rich 1790
Joseph	Perq 1787	Smedick	Samp 1784
Leah	Chow 1785	Solomon	Nash 1782
Moses	Gate 1789	Thomas	Wayn 1786
Moses	Perq 1787	Thomas	Hali 1783
Mourning	Perq 1787	Wm	Samp 1784
Wm	Blad 1784	BOYLES, Wm	Surr 1783
Wm	Gate 1789	BOZEMAN, Elizabeth	Hali 1783
BOYD, Archibald	Surr 1782	BRABBLE, Nancy	Curr 1779
Coleman	Beau 1786	BRABLE, John	Curr 1779
Job	NorH 1780	BRACHER, Benjamin	Dupl 1779
John	Gran 1785	John	Dupl 1779
John	Pasq 1779	BRACK, Ebenezer	Onsl 1771
John	Surr 1782	Geo	Onsl 1771
John	Gran 1771	George	Gran 1785
Joseph	Pasq 1779	Richard	Onsl 1771
Joseph	Surr 1782	Samuel	Gran 1785
Miriam	Chow 1785	Wm	Onsl 1771
Patrick	Gran 1779	BRACKEN, Isaac	Rowa 1779
Patrick	Warr 1784	James	Rowa 1779
Reginald	Pasq 1779	Wm	Rowa 1779
Robert	Beau 1779	BRACKET, Benjamin	Ruth 1782
Robert	Gran 1771	BRACKIN, John	Surr 1782
Samuel	Mont 1782	Samuel	Casw 1784
Solomon	Beau 1779	BRADBURY, George	Wayn 1786
Thomas	Pasq 1779	James	Wayn 1786
Thomas	Beau 1779	James	Surr 1782
Thomas	Beau 1786	Thomas	Wayn 1786
Thomas Jr	Beau 1779	BRADFORD, Bird	Gran 1785
Wm	Pasq 1779	Booker	Gran 1785
Wm	Beau 1779	David	Oran 1779
Wm	Beau 1779	David	Gran 1785
Wm	Wilk 1782	George	Oran 1779
Wm	Beau 1786	Henry	Hali 1783
Wm	Beau 1786	John	Gran 1785
Wm	Pasq 1789	John	Hali 1783
BOYER, Geo	Gran 1771	John	Gran 1771
Henry	Rowa 1767	Mary	Gran 1771
Miles	Gate 1789	Patty	Mont 1782
Sion	Gate 1789	Peter	Mont 1782
Wm	Bert 1781	Philemon	Gran 1785

BRADFORD, Philip	Gran 1771		BRAGG, Thomas	Cart 1777
Phillip	Gran 1785		Wm	Cart 1779
Richard	Gran 1785		BRAKIN, Samuel	Casw 1786
Richard	Gran 1771		BRALEY, John	Perq 1772
Thomas	NorH 1750		BRALL, Robert	Rowa 1768
Thomas	Oran 1779		BRAMBLE, Elizabeth	Blad 1784
Thomas	Gran 1771		Wm	Samp 1784
Wm	Oran 1779		BRAME, James	Gran 1785
Wm	Gran 1785		BRAMLETT, Ambrose	Surr 1782
Wm	Gran 1771		BRANAHAN, Thomas	Oran 1779
BRADLEY, Abel	Curr 1779		BRANCH, Benj	NorH 1780
Archibald	Blad 1784		Britton	Blad 1784
Benjamin	Warr 1784		Edmond	Nash 1782
Dennis	Bute 1766		Francis	NorH 1780
Edward	Surr 1782		Issacher	Perq 1787
Enoch	Oran 1779		Job	Perq 1787
Francis	Bute 1766		John	Hali 1783
James	Ruth 1782		John	NorH 1780
James	Bute 1766		John Jr	Blad 1784
James	NorH 1780		Randolph	Wayn 1786
James Jr	Casw 1784		Simon	Wayn 1786
John	Bute 1766		Wm	Blad 1784
John	Ruth 1782		Wm	Wayn 1786
John	Beau 1779		BRAND, John B	Dobb 1780
John	Wilk 1784		BRANDON, John	Rowa 1768
John	Curr 1779		BRANNON, James	John 1784
John	Wilk 1782		Thomas	John 1784
John	Surr 1782		Wm	John 1784
Joseph	Ruth 1782		BRANNUM, Benj	Wilk 1782
Joseph	Surr 1782		BRANSON, John	Surr 1782
Mooney	Wilk 1782		BRANTLEY, Benjamin	Hali 1783
Richard	Ruth 1782		Edward	Hali 1783
Samuel	Hali 1783		Jacob	Nash 1782
Sarah	Hali 1783		James	Samp 1784
Seth	Surr 1782		James	Hali 1783
Terry	Surr 1782		John	Nash 1782
Thomas	Bute 1766		John	Hali 1783
Thomas	Hali 1783		Lewis	Hali 1783
Thomas	Curr 1779		Martha	Hali 1783
Wm	John 1784		Matthew	Nash 1782
Wm	Hali 1783		Robert	Hali 1783
Wm	Curr 1779		Wm	Hali 1783
BRADLY, Wm	Beau 1779		BRANTON, Jacob	Oran 1779
BRADSHAW, John	Casw 1784		John	Blad 1784
Moses	Casw 1784		Samuel	Crav 1779
Roger	Crav 1779		BRANUM, Wm	Surr 1782
Thomas	Crav 1779		BRANWELL, Jacob	John 1784
BRADSOLE, Thomas	Blad 1784		BRASCOM, John	Surr 1782
BRADY, Benj	Beau 1786		BRASFIELD, Caleb	Gran 1785
Henry	Beau 1779		BRASSE, Richard	Wilk 1782
Henry	Beau 1786		BRASSELL, Henry	Blad 1784
Hugh	Blad 1784		Nathan	Blad 1784
James	Gate 1789		BRASSFIELD, Caleb	Gran 1771
James Sr	Gate 1789		Elias	Gran 1785
Joseph	Gate 1789		BRASSIE, Francis	Gran 1785
Wm	Ruth 1782		BRASSWELL, Arthur	Nash 1782
BRAGG, John	Warr 1784		Benj	Bert 1781
John	Crav 1779		Benjamin	Nash 1782
John	Gate 1789		Benjamin Jr	Hali 1783
Joseph	Cart 1779		Drew	Hali 1783
Moses	Gate 1789		Henry	Nash 1782
Richard	Wilk 1784		Jacob Jr	Nash 1782
Richard	Gate 1789		Jacob Sr	Nash 1782
Solomon	Cart 1779		Martha	Nash 1782
Solomon	Gate 1789		Mourning	Nash 1782

BRASSWELL, Richard Jr			BREWER, Robert	Mart	1779
	Wayn	1786	Sackville	Oran	1779
Richard Sr	Wayn	1786	Shadrack	Bute	1766
Samuel	Nash	1782	Thomas	Hali	1783
Shadrack	Wayn	1786	Wm	Surr	1782
Wm 762 a	Nash	1782	Wm Jr	Mart	1779
Wm Jr	Nash	1782	Wm Sr	Mart	1779
BRASWELL, John	Surr	1782	BREWSTER, Lot	Chow	1785
BRATCHER, Christopher			BRIAN, Thomas	Wilk	1782
	Samp	1784	BRIAR, Richard	Gran	1785
David	Onsl	1761	BRICE, George	Gran	1785
John	Samp	1784	BRICKELL, John	Hali	1783
Thomas	Onsl	1771	John	Hert	1784
BRATCHEY, Thomas	Oran	1779	Matthew Jr	Hert	1784
Thomas	Samp	1784	Matthias	Hert	1779
Wm	Oran	1779	Matthias	Hert	1784
BRATTON, Benj	Perq	1787	Thomas	Hert	1784
BRAVEBOY, David	Blad	1784	Wm	Warr	1784
John	Bert	1774	BRICKHOUSE, Benj	Curr	1779
John	Mart	1779	Caleb	Curr	1779
BRAY, David	Surr	1782	Major	Tyrr	1784
John	Tyrr	1784	Martha	Tyrr	1784
Joseph	Onsl	1771	Stephen	Beau	1779
Willis	Curr	1779	Wm	Tyrr	1784
Wm	Pasq	1694	BRICKNELL, Rachel	Wilk	1782
BRAYTON, David	Blad	1784	BRIDELOVE, Charles	Casw	1784
BRAZEL, Nathan	Rich	1790	BRIDGEFARMER, John	Rowa	1761
BRAZELTON, Jacob	Gran	1785	BRIDGER, Robert	Bert	1781
Wm	Rowa	1768	BRIDGERS, Benjamin	John	1784
BRAZOR, James	Oran	1779	Benjamin Jr	Nash	1782
John	Oran	1779	James	Dobb	1780
BREAD, Wm	Albe	1694	James	Wayn	1786
BRECETON, Nathl	NorH	1780	James	Gran	1785
BREEDLOVE, John	Gran	1785	John	Wayn	1786
BREES, Henry	Cart	1779	John	Gran	1785
Wm	Cart	1779	Joseph	Hert	1779
BREEZE, Robert	Oran	1779	Joseph	Blad	1784
Thomas	Oran	1779	Joseph	Hert	1784
BREGEN, Andrew	Surr	1782	Joseph	John	1784
BRENT, James	Curr	1779	Sampson	Blad	1784
Richard	Curr	1779	Samuel	Nash	1782
BRESTON, Wm	Gate	1789	Samuel Jr	Blad	1784
BRETT, John	Rowa	1768	Wm	Nash	1782
BRETTERSON, Nathl	Perq	1787	Wm	Dobb	1780
BREVARD, John	Rowa	1768	BRIDGES, Aaron	Ruth	1782
BREWER, Burwell	Wilk	1782	James	Gran	1771
Chas	Surr	1782	John	Ruth	1782
David	John	1784	John	Oran	1779
Geo	NorH	1780	John	NorH	1780
George	Wilk	1782	John	Gran	1771
Hubbard	Samp	1784	Moses	Ruth	1782
James	Samp	1784	Samuel	Blad	1784
Jesse	Hert	1779	Thomas	Ruth	1782
Jesse	Hali	1783	Willis	NorH	1780
Jesse	Hert	1784	Wm	Ruth	1782
John	Mart	1779	Wm	NorH	1780
John	Hali	1783	BRIDGETT, John	Beau	1786
John	John	1784	BRIDGEWATER, Wm	Casw	1786
John	NorH	1780	BRIGAN, John	Beau	1779
John	Surr	1782	BRIGGS, Chas	Perq	1787
Lewis	Hali	1783	Thomas	Surr	1782
Moses	Wayn	1786	BRIGHAM, John	Rowa	1768
Nathl	Surr	1782	BRIGHT, Aaron	Camd	1782
Peter	Oran	1779	Aaron	Curr	1779
Reece	Warr	1784	Aaron Sr	Camd	1782

BRIGHT, Amos	Bert 1781	BRINKLEY, Simon	Gate 1789
Charles	Camd 1782	Thomas	Perq 1787
Darius	Camd 1782	Wm	Hali 1783
Henry	Curr 1779	Wm Jr	Hali 1783
Hezekiah	Camd 1782	BRINN, Joseph	Chow 1785
James	Dobb 1780	Richard	Tyrr 1784
James	Camd 1782	BRINSON, Ann	Crav 1779
James	Blad 1784	Ann	Crav 1779
Jeremiah	Camd 1782	Cason	Crav 1779
Jesse	Pasq 1779	Geo	Onsl 1771
Jesse	Pasq 1789	James	Crav 1779
John	Crav 1779	Jane	Onsl 1771
John	Curr 1779	John	Tyrr 1784
Malachi	Camd 1782	John	Onsl 1771
Mary	Camd 1782	Mathew	Onsl 1771
Mary	Pasq 1789	BRISCO, Thomas	Pasq 1694
Nathan	Camd 1782	BRISSEL, Frederick	WilK 1782
Richard	Blad 1784	BRISTOE, Geo	Gran 1771
Richard	Pasq 1789	BRISTON, James	Gate 1789
Richard Jr	Pasq 1779	Wm	Perq 1787
Richard Sr	Pasq 1779	BRISTOW, David	Pasq 1779
Samuel	Burk 1777	Elias	Gran 1785
Silas	Curr 1779	George	Gran 1785
Simon	Blad 1784	James	Gran 1785
Stockwell	Crav 1779	John	Gran 1785
Willis	Camd 1782	Philemon	Gran 1785
Willis	Curr 1779	BRITAIN, John	Hert 1779
Willis	Pasq 1789	John	Hert 1784
Willis Jr	Camd 1782	BRITON, George	Jone 1779
Wm	Camd 1782	BRITSON, Jesse	NorH 1780
Wm	Crav 1779	BRITT, Abraham	Hert 1784
BRIGHTMAN, Nicholas Albe 1694		Benjamin	Blad 1784
BRIGHTWELL, Reynolds		Benjamin	Hert 1784
	Bute 1766	James	Hert 1784
BRIGMAN, Asher	Rich 1790	Joel	Hert 1784
BRILES, Adam	Rowa 1768	John	Hert 1784
Clark	Rowa 1768	Joseph	Hert 1784
Coatley	Rowa 1768	Josiah	Hert 1784
Frederick	Rowa 1768	Margaret	Dobb 1780
George	Rowa 1768	Peter	Bert 1781
Michael	Rowa 1768	Samuel	Blad 1784
BRILL, Benjamin	John 1784	Sarah	Dobb 1780
James	Hert 1784	Thomas	Hert 1784
Martin	Hert 1784	BRITTAIN, Michael	Hert 1784
BRIMER, George	Rowa 1768	BRITTLE, Charles	Nash 1782
BRINEGAR, Adam	Rowa 1768	BRITTLR, John	NorH 1750
BRINES, John	Beau 1786	BRITTON, Benjamin	Rowa 1768
BRINKLEY, Abraham	Hali 1783	Benjamin	Hert 1784
Eli	Gran 1771	Daniel	Rowa 1768
Elisha	Gate 1789	James	Rowa 1768
Ellis	Oran 1779	James	Rowa 1761
Irwin	Perq 1772	James	Rowa 1768
James	Gran 1771	James Jr	Rowa 1768
James	Perq 1787	Paul	Bert 1781
John	Gate 1789	Thomas	Chow 1785
John Davis	Perq 1772	Wm	Rowa 1768
Joseph	Gate 1789	BROACH, Jones	Casw 1786
Josiah	Gate 1789	Jones	Casw 1784
Judah	Hali 1783	BROADWAY, James	Bute 1766
Lewis	Gate 1789	John	Casw 1784
Mary	Perq 1772	BROADWELL, David	Bert 1774
Michael	Gran 1771	Wm	Bert 1774
Peter	Oran 1779	Wm	Bert 1781
Peter	Gran 1771	BROCAS, Richard	Samp 1784
Robert	Hali 1783	BROCK, Barnett	Dupl 1779
		Benjamin	NBer 1779

BROCK, Besent	Dupl 1779	BROTHERS, David	Pasq 1789
Frederick	Ruth 1782	Job	Pasq 1789
James	Dupl 1779	John	Casw 1786
Jesse	Dupl 1779	John	Casw 1784
John	Dobb 1780	John	Pasq 1779
John	Beau 1786	John	Beau 1779
Joseph	Jone 1779	John	Pasq 1789
BROCKETT, John	Camd 1782	Jonathan	Pasq 1789
Margaret	Camd 1782	Joseph	Pasq 1779
BROCKMAN, Major	Casw 1786	Joseph	Pasq 1789
BROCON, John	Warr 1784	Levi	Pasq 1789
BROGDEN, John	Bert 1779	Malachi	Pasq 1779
John	Wayn 1786	Malachi	Pasq 1789
John	Bert 1781	Miles	Pasq 1779
Thomas	Wayn 1786	Richard	Pasq 1779
BROGDON, George	Bute 1766	Richard	Pasq 1789
James	Bert 1774	Sam Sr	Beau 1786
Mary	Bert 1774	Samuel	Pasq 1779
Peterson	Bert 1774	Thomas	Pasq 1779
Wm	Bute 1766	Thomas	Pasq 1789
Wm	Bert 1781	Wm	Pasq 1779
BROMFIELD, Richard	Oran 1779	Wm	Pasq 1789
BRONSON, John	Casw 1784	BROUGHTON, Adam	Pasq 1779
Wm	Casw 1784	BROWDER, Thomas	Blad 1784
BROOK, Willoughby	Curr 1779	BROWER, Joseph	Bute 1766
BROOKER, John	NorH 1780	BROWN, Abigail	Warr 1784
BROOKINS, Abraham	Wayn 1786	Abner	Mart 1779
Bridgeman	Wayn 1786	Abraham	Casw 1784
Thomas	Wayn 1786	Abraham	Tyrr 1784
BROOKS, Arthur	Casw 1784	Abraham	Warr 1784
Benj	Gran 1771	Alexander	Mart 1779
Charles	Casw 1784	Anguish	Blad 1784
Ezekiel	Mont 1782	Archibald	Warr 1784
Geo	Gate 1789	Arthur	Samp 1784
Isaac	Curr 1779	Arthur	Bert 1781
James	Beau 1786	Benjamin	Hert 1779
John	Cart 1779	Benjamin	Dobb 1780
John	Oran 1779	Benjamin	Camd 1782
John	Samp 1784	Benjamin	Hert 1784
John	Casw 1784	Charles	Nash 1782
John	Mont 1782	Colonel	Hert 1779
John Jr	Mont 1782	Colonel	Blad 1784
John Sr	Mont 1782	Cornelius	Dobb 1780
Joseph	Onsl 1771	Daniel	Ruth 1782
Lodowick	Gate 1789	Daniel	Dobb 1780
Matthew	Surr 1782	Daniel	Camd 1782
Tabitha	Casw 1784	Daniel	Blad 1784
Thomas	Oran 1779	Daniel	John 1784
Thomas	Casw 1784	David	Mart 1779
Wm	Mont 1782	Dempsey	Jone 1779
Wm	Gate 1789	Donald	Rich 1790
BROOKSHIRE, Mannering		Edmund	Rich 1790
	Rowa 1770	Edward	Jone 1779
	Rowa 1770	Elizabeth	Hert 1779
Wm	Rowa 1770	Elizabeth	Camd 1782
BROOM, Ephraim	NorH 1780	Elizabeth	Pasq 1779
John	Bute 1766	Ephraim	Beau 1786
John	Hali 1783	Francis	Hert 1779
Major	Wayn 1786	Francis	John 1784
Mark	Blad 1784	Francis	Wilk 1782
Mason	Crav 1779	Francis	Gran 1771
Phillip	Hali 1783	Francis Jr	Hert 1779
BROSON, Wm	Casw 1784	Francis Jr	Hert 1784
BROTHERS, Andrew	Pasq 1779	Francis Sr	Hert 1784
Andrew	Pasq 1789	Frederick	Hert 1784
Covental	Pasq 1779		

BROWN, George	Blad 1784	Joseph	Tyrr 1784
Gideon	Surr 1782	Joseph	Jone 1779
Gustavius	Beau 1786	Josiah	Hert 1779
Hardy	Hert 1779	Josiah	Bute 1766
Hardy	Warr 1784	Josiah	Hert 1784
Hardy	Gate 1789	Leonard	Casw 1786
Hezekiah	Warr 1784	Leonard	Casw 1784
Howell	Jone 1779	Lewis	Hert 1779
Hugh	Blad 1784	Lewis	Hert 1779
Isaac	Beau 1786	Louis	Hert 1784
J	Hert 1779	Margaret	Blad 1784
Jacob	Rowa 1761	Mary	Blad 1784
Jacob	Beau 1786	Mary	Pasq 1779
James	Nash 1782	Mary	Pasq 1789
James	Hert 1779	Matthew	Mart 1779
James	Dobb 1780	Michael	Rowa 1761
James	Rowa 1768	Milly	Casw 1786
James	Mart 1779	Nathan	Hali 1783
James	Casw 1786	Neil	Blad 1784
James	Blad 1784	Noah	Wayn 1786
James	Casw 1784	Peter	Camd 1782
James	John 1784	Randal	Surr 1782
James	Hert 1784	Rebecca	Wilk 1784
James	Wilk 1782	Rebecca	Wilk 1782
James	Wilk 1782	Richard	Hert 1779
James	Surr 1782	Richard	Blad 1784
James	Gate 1789	Richard	Hert 1784
James	Gate 1789	Richard	Wilk 1782
James	Bert 1781	Richard	Beau 1786
James	Perq 1787	Robert	Nash 1782
Jeremiah	Nash 1782	Roderick	Hert 1784
Jeremiah	Hert 1779	Saml	Gate 1789
Jeremiah	Hert 1784	Samuel	Dobb 1780
Jeremiah	Warr 1784	Samuel	Rowa 1761
Jesse	Hert 1779	Samuel	Rowa 1765
Jesse	Hali 1783	Samuel Dr	Hert 1779
Jesse	Wayn 1786	Samuel Dr	Hert 1784
Jesse	John 1784	Sarah	Hert 1779
Jesse	Hert 1784	Sherwood	Samp 1784
Jesse	Wilk 1784	Spill	Ruth 1782
Jesse	Wilk 1782	Stephen	Hert 1779
Joel	Bert 1781	Stephen	Rowa 1761
John	Hert 1779	Stephen	Samp 1784
John	Pasq 1694	Stephen	Hert 1784
John	Ruth 1782	Sukey	Hert 1779
John	Bute 1766	Thomas	Hert 1779
John	Dobb 1780	Thomas	Dobb 1780
John	Rowa 1768	Thomas	Rowa 1765
John	Oran 1779	Thomas	Oran 1779
John	Casw 1786	Thomas	Mart 1779
John	Hali 1783	Thomas	Blad 1784
John	Blad 1784	Thomas	Hert 1784
John	Casw 1784	Thomas	Crav 1779
John	Gran 1785	Thomas	Gran 1771
John	Hert 1784	Thomas Jr	Blad 1784
John	Wilk 1784	Walter	Wilk 1782
John	Curr 1779	Willis	Camd 1782
John	Wilk 1782	Willis	Gate 1789
John	Surr 1782	Wm	Bert 1774
John	Gran 1771	Wm	Hert 1779
John	Beau 1786	Wm	Oran 1779
John (negro)	Pasq 1789	Wm	Mart 1779
John Capt	John 1784	Wm	Casw 1786
John Sr	Wilk 1784	Wm	Hali 1783
Joseph	Rowa 1765	Wm	Blad 1784

Wm	Casw 1784	BRUMSEY, Mary	Curr 1779
Wm	John 1784	BRUSH, James	Perq 1772
Wm	Hert 1784	Wm	Perq 1772
Wm	Jone 1779	BRUSSETT, John	Beau 1786
Wm	Beau 1779	BRUTON, Elizabeth	Dobb 1780
Wm	Wilk 1782	Isabel	Dobb 1780
Wm	NorH 1780	Joseph	Dobb 1780
Wm	Surr 1782	BRYAN, Arthur	Wayn 1786
Wm	Gran 1771	Arthur	John 1784
Wm	Gate 1789	Asa	John 1784
Wm	Bert 1781	Asa	Crav 1779
Wm	Beau 1786	Benj	NorH 1780
Wm	Rich 1790	Benj	Bert 1781
Wm Jr	Hert 1779	Benjamin	Dobb 1780
Wm Jr	Jone 1779	Edward	Blad 1784
Wm Sr	Wilk 1784	Eliz	Bert 1781
BROWNER, George	Rowa 1761	Geo	Bert 1781
Henry	Rowa 1761	Isaac	NBer 1779
BROWNING, Daniel	Crav 1779	James	Oran 1779
Daniel	Pitt 1786	James	Tyrr 1784
Edmond	Casw 1786	James	NorH 1780
Edmund	Casw 1784	Jean	NorH 1780
Elizabeth	Casw 1786	Jesse	Bert 1781
Geo	Pitt 1786	John	Bert 1774
George	Casw 1786	John	Rowa 1761
George	Casw 1784	John	Oran 1779
George	Crav 1779	John	Blad 1784
Jacob	Casw 1784	John	Jone 1779
James	Oran 1779	John	Crav 1779
John	Casw 1784	John	Crav 1779
John	Crav 1779	John	NorH 1780
John Jr	Mart 1779	John & s Tom	Rowa 1768
John Sr	Mart 1779	John Capt	John 1784
Joshua	Casw 1784	Joseph	Rowa 1761
Levi	Hali 1783	Joseph	Onsl 1771
Luke	Wilk 1782	Lewis	Jone 1779
Mark	Hali 1783	Louis	John 1784
Nicholas	Casw 1786	Louis	John 1784
Peregrin	Pitt 1786	Michael	Bert 1781
Perrigan	Crav 1779	Morgan	Rowa 1761
Samuel	Casw 1786	Nancy Penelope	Jone 1779
Samuel	Casw 1784	Nathan	Jone 1779
Wm	Oran 1779	Needham	John 1784
Wm	Casw 1786	Philemon	Blad 1784
BROWNLEY, John	Pasq 1789	Samuel	Rowa 1761
BRUCE, Abraham	Hert 1779	Sarah	Crav 1779
Abraham	Hert 1784	Silas	Jone 1779
Albert	Casw 1784	Stephen	Blad 1784
Alexander	Casw 1786	Thomas	Dobb 1780
Alexander	Casw 1784	Thomas	Onsl 1771
Bennett	Hert 1784	Thomas	NorH 1780
Chas	Surr 1782	Thomas	Bert 1781
Geo	Surr 1782	Thomas	Beau 1786
John	Surr 1782	Thomas s of Jn	Rowa 1768
Robert	Casw 1786	Vincent	Jone 1779
Robert	Casw 1784	Willis	Wayn 1786
Wm	Casw 1784	Wm	Rowa 1761
Wm	Hali 1783	Wm	Blad 1784
Wm	Surr 1782	Wm	Wayn 1786
BRUCKEEN, Wm	Casw 1784	Wm	John 1784
BRULER, Micajah	Hali 1783	Wm	NBer 1779
BRUMBERRY, Mathias	Oran 1779	Wm	NorH 1780
BRUMMIT, Nimrod	Gran 1785	Wm	Bert 1781
Saml	Gran 1771	Wm Jr	Dobb 1780
Thomas	Gran 1771	Wm Jr	Blad 1784

BRYANT, Barnabee	Samp 1784		BUCKLEY, Morris	Chow 1785
Bertram	Samp 1784		Richard	Casw 1784
Charles	Casw 1784		BUCKNER, John	Oran 1779
David	Samp 1784		BUCKREN, Gabriel	Jone 1779
David	Bert 1784		Gabriel	Jone 1779
David	Mont 1782		BUDS, Thomas	Pitt 1786
Elias	Mart 1779		BUFEN, John	Surr 1782
Hardy	Mart 1779		BUFFINGTON, Moses of Peter
James	Nash 1782			Rowa 1768
James	Casw 1784		Peter	Rown 1768
James	Hali 1783		BUFORD, Phillip	Warr 1784
Jane	Hali 1783		BUGBEE, Drury	Gran 1771
Jesse	Mart 1779		BUIE, John	Rich 1790
Jesse	Hali 1783		BUKLE, Job	Surr 1782
John	Nash 1782		BULA, John	Rowa 1761
John	Dupl 1783		John Jr	Rowa 1761
John	Oran 1779		Joseph	Rowa 1761
John	Mart 1779		BULEN, Rick	Jone 1779
John	Samp 1784		BULL, David	Perq 1787
John	Curr 1779		Henry	John 1784
John	Surr 1782		Jacob	Casw 1784
Kedar	Samp 1784		Jethro	John 1784
Lewis	Mart 1779		Richard	John 1784
Moses	Mart 1779		Stephen	Brun 1784
Nathaniel	Onsl 1771		Thomas	Hali 1783
Needam	Mart 1779		Wm	John 1784
Needham	Samp 1784		BULLARD, James	Blad 1784
Needham	Hali 1783		John	Samp 1784
Nicholas	Dupl 1783		John	Blad 1784
Robert	Mart 1779		Thomas	Samp 1784
Rowland	Gran 1785		Thomas	Blad 1784
Samuel	Nash 1782		BULLEN, Conrad	Rowa 1761
Sarah	Samp 1784		John	Rowa 1761
Simeon	Oran 1779		BULLISON, Samuel	Casw 1786
Thomas	John 1784		BULLO, Isaac	Rowa 1768
Wm	Nash 1782		John	Rowa 1768
Wm	Mart 1779		Joseph	Rowa 1768
Wm	Samp 1784		Moses	Rowa 1768
Wm	Hali 1783		BULLOCK, Benjamin	Samp 1784
Wm	Gran 1771		Charles	Blad 1784
Wm Jr	Casw 1784		Charles	Gran 1785
Wm Sr	Casw 1784		Ephraim	Mart 1779
BRYER, Moses	Perq 1772		Estate	Cart 1779
BRYERS, Jobe	Perq 1772		James	Samp 1784
BRYSON, John	Bert 1774		James	Gran 1785
BTITAIN, Jesse	Nash 1782		James	Gran 1771
BUCCE, Geo	Gran 1771		John	NorH 1780
BUCHAN, David	Blad 1784		John	Surr 1782
BUCHANAN, Henry	Samp 1784		John	Gran 1782
James	Ruth 1782		Micajah	Gran 1785
Matthew	Oran 1779		Micajah	Gran 1771
Wm	Oran 1779		Obadiah	Mart 1779
BUCHANNON, James	Bert 1774		Sam	Perq 1787
James	Gran 1771		Samuel	Casw 1786
James Jr	Gran 1771		Samuel	Casw 1784
Wm	Gran 1785		Samuel	Gran 1785
Wm	Rich 1790		Thomas	Perq 1772
BUCK, John	NorH 1780		Thomas	Surr 1782
Stephen	Bert 1781		Thomas	Perq 1787
Tennis	Beau 1786		Wm	Gran 1785
BUCKHAM, Philemon	Warr 1784		Wm	Gran 1771
Wm	Warr 1784		BULLOCKSON, Harley	Gran 1771
BUCKINGHAM, Joseph	Oran 1779		BUMAN, Israel	Gate 1789
BUCKLAND, Roland	Pasq 1694		BUMPAS, Edward	Casw 1784
BUCKLEY, Edward	Casw 1784		Jabez	Jone 1779

BUMPAS, John	Casw 1784	BUOY, Duncan	Blad 1784
Robert	Hali 1783	John	Blad 1784
Samuel	Casw 1784	BURBOYCON, Burrell	NorH 1780
BUNCE, Chas	Wilk 1782	BURCH, Benj	Surr 1782
Jacob	NorH 1780	James	Oran 1779
BUNCH, Cullen	Chow 1785	Jesse	Surr 1782
Embry	Bert 1781	John	Bute 1766
Fredk	Bert 1781	John	Warr 1784
Henry	Oran 1779	John	Wilk 1782
Ishmael	Chow 1785	John	Surr 1782
James	Chow 1785	Joseph	Samp 1784
Jeremiah	Oran 1779	Nicholas	Oran 1779
Jeremiah	Bert 1781	Nicholas	Gran 1771
Jesse	Perq 1772	Nicholas Jr	Gran 1771
Joshua	Perq 1787	Nicholas Sr	Gran 1785
Julius	Chow 1785	Pemberton	Oran 1779
Julius	Perq 1772	Pemberton	Casw 1784
Julius	Perq 1787	Wm	Surr 1782
Mary	Chow 1785	Wm Sr	Surr 1782
Micajah	Wilk 1782	BURCHAM, John	Surr 1782
Nazareth	Chow 1785	Joseph	Mont 1782
Nehemiah	Bert 1781	BURCHETT, James	Gran 1785
Obadiah	Chow 1785	Joseph	Gran 1785
Shadrack	Chow 1785	BURDEN, Thomas Jr	Gran 1771
Solomon	Chow 1785	BURDICK, Josiah	Chow 1785
Wm	Chow 1785	BURDINE, Nathaniel	Wilk 1782
Wm	Bert 1781	Samuel	Wilk 1782
BUNDFIELD, John	Chow 1785	BURDON, Gabriel	Hali 1783
BUNDY, Abram	Perq 1787	Peter	Blad 1784
Ann	Pasq 1779	Thomas	Gran 1785
Benj	Pasq 1789	BURFORD, Wm	Gran 1771
Caleb	Pasq 1694	BURFORT, Amey	Camd 1782
Caleb	Pasq 1779	John	Bute 1766
Caleb	Pasq 1789	Thomas	Oran 1779
David	Pasq 1789	BURGE, Alexr	Surr 1782
Demcy	Pasq 1789	Burwell	Nash 1782
Dempsey	Pasq 1779	Henry	Surr 1782
Gideon	Wayn 1786	Jeremiah	Nash 1782
John	Wayn 1786	Richard	Nash 1782
John	Pasq 1779	BURGESS, Asa	Camd 1782
John	Pasq 1789	Dempsey	Camd 1782
John	Pasq 1789	Hezekiah	Camd 1782
Jonathan	Pasq 1779	John	Camd 1782
Jonathan	Pasq 1789	John	Gate 1789
Josiah	Perq 1787	John	Pasq 1789
Moses Sr	Perq 1772	Lovett	Hali 1783
Ruth	Pasq 1779	Malachi	Blad 1784
Wm	Albe 1679	Penelope	Hali 1783
Wm	Perq 1787	Stephen	Camd 1782
BUNN, Benjamin	Nash 1782	Thomas	Camd 1782
Benjamin Sr	Nash 1782	Timothy	Casw 1786
David	Nash 1782	Wm	Cart 1779
Henry	Nash 1782	Zephaniah	Camd 1782
John	Nash 1782	BURK, Alexr	Surr 1782
Morris Sr	Curr 1779	James	Warr 1784
Redman	Nash 1782	John	Surr 1782
BUNNELL, Edward	Curr 1779	Mary	NorH 1780
BUNSON, Wm	Pasq 1694	Wm	NorH 1780
BUNTAIN, Eleanor	Wilk 1782	BURKE, Eliz	Perq 1787
BUNTEN, James	Wayn 1786	James	Surr 1782
BUNTIN, Jeremiah	Nash 1782	Joseph	Surr 1782
Wm	Nash 1782	Mary	Surr 1782
BUNTING, John deed	Dupl 1764	Saml	Surr 1782
BUNYARD, James	Wilk 1782	Thomas	Oran 1779
BUOY, Archibald	Blad 1784	BURKETT, Ann	Hert 1779

BURKETT, Ann	Hert 1784	BURRIS, John	Surr 1782
Caleb	Curr 1779	John	Camd 1782
Lemuel	Hert 1779	John	Curr 1779
Samuel	Hert 1784	Joshua	Hert 1784
Thomas	Chow 1785	Joshua	Bert 1781
Wm	Bert 1781	Robert	Curr 1779
BURKLE, James	Beau 1779	Wm	Surr 1782
BURKLOW, Isaac	Oran 1779	BURROW, Davison	Rich 1790
BURLESON, Isaac	Mont 1782	Wm	Warr 1784
BURLEY, John	Wayn 1786	BURROWS, Henry	Casw 1784
BURN, Frederick	Wayn 1786	Willie	Casw 1784
BURNAM, Mary	Bert 1781	Wm	Bute 1766
BURNBY, John	Pasq 1694	Wm Jr	Bute 1766
Wm	Pasq 1694	BURT, John	Hali 1783
BURNETT, Alexander Jr		John	Rich 1790
	Bute 1766	Joseph	Hali 1783
Alexander Sr	Bute 1766	Richard	Hali 1783
Daniel	Cart 1777	Stable	Rich 1790
David	Bute 1766	Wm	Hali 1783
Elizabeth	Bute 1766	BURTCH, John	Gran 1785
James	Mart 1779	BURTON, David	Oran 1779
John	Mart 1779	Hillery	Curr 1779
John	Chow 1784	James	Casw 1786
John	Onsl 1771	Jane	Casw 1786
Joseph	Oran 1779	John	Hert 1784
Lundry	John 1784	John	Curr 1779
Matthew	Mart 1779	John Sr	Curr 1779
Peter	Bert 1781	Robert	Casw 1786
Thomas	Surr 1782	Susannah	Oran 1779
BURNEY, Simon	Blad 1784	Thomas	Jone 1779
Wm	NBer 1779	Watson	Dupl 1783
Wm Jr	Blad 1784	BURTONSHALL, Joshua	Crav 1779
Wm Sr	Blad 1784	BUSBEE, John	Gran 1771
BURNHAM, Caleb	Perq 1772	BUSER, Wm	Gran 1771
David	Camd 1782	BUSH, Abraham	Dobb 1780
Gabriel	Camd 1782	Bibby	Dobb 1780
Isaac	Pasq 1789	Daniel	Wilk 1784
Ivey	Camd 1782	Frederick	Curr 1779
Joshua	Camd 1782	James	Samp 1784
Margaret	Camd 1782	Jeremiah	Bute 1766
Timothy	Pasq 1779	Jeremiah	Warr 1784
Timothy	Pasq 1789	John	Jone 1779
Wm	Bert 1774	John Jr	Bute 1766
BURNS, Andrew	Bert 1781	John Jr	Samp 1784
David	Wilk 1782	John Sr	Samp 1784
David	NorH 1780	Joseph	Casw 1786
Frederick	Onsl 1771	Joseph	Casw 1784
James	Gran 1771	Levi	Samp 1784
Joan	Onsl 1771	Wm	Dupl 1783
John	Rowa 1768	Wm	Samp 1784
John	Onsl 1771	BUSLEY, Ezekiel	Blad 1784
John	Bert 1781	BUSSELL, Wm	Blad 1784
Otway	Onsl 1771	BUSTIAN, Charles	Casw 1784
Owen	NorH 1780	Cuthbert	Casw 1784
Wm	Oran 1779	Samuel	Casw 1784
Wm	NorH 1780	Thomas	Casw 1784
BURNSIDE, John	Oran 1779	BUSTIN, John	Casw 1784
Robert	Oran 1779	BUTCHER, James	Oran 1779
Walter	Oran 1779	Thomas	Dobb 1780
BURRETT, Sam	Onsl 1771	Thomas	Blad 1784
BURRICK, James	Jone 1779	Valentine	Oran 1779
Thomas	Jone 1779	BUTLER, Anderson	Casw 1786
BURRIS, Benjamin	Mart 1779	Arthur	Crav 1779
Christopher	Camd 1782	Arthur	Pitt 1786
James	Bert 1781	Charles	Samp 1784

BUTLER, Chas	Crav 1779		BUTTERTON, Robert	Bert 1781
Edward	Rich 1790		Robert	Bert 1781
Elias	Mont 1782		BUTTON, Benj	Rich 1790
Grace	Gran 1785		James	Surr 1782
James	Bute 1766		Wm	Rich 1790
James	Mart 1779		BUTTREY, John	Mart 1779
James	Samp 1784		Silvanus	Mart 1779
James	Mont 1782		BUTTS, Elizabeth	Dobb 1780
James	Gran 1771		Nathan	Mart 1779
Jesse	Samp 1784		BUZZARD, John Randolph	
Jethro	Samp 1784			Gran 1771
John	Nash 1782		Wm	Perq 1772
John	Bute 1766		BYARD, Gabriel	Dupl 1779
John	Oran 1779		BYER, Mary	Gran 1785
John	Mart 1779		Wm	Gran 1785
John	Samp 1784		BYERS, John	Gran 1771
John	Crav 1779		Sarah	Ruth 1782
John	Mont 1782		Wm	Gran 1771
John	Onsl 1771		BYNHAM, Wm Jr	Hali 1783
John	Bert 1781		Wm Sr	Hali 1783
John & s John	Mart 1779		BYNUM, Gray	Surr 1782
Joseph	Blad 1784		BYRAM, Henry	Wilk 1782
Joseph	Bert 1781		Isaac	Chow 1785
Joshua	Mont 1782		Jacob	Gran 1785
Reuben	Gran 1785		James	Hert 1779
Richard	Mont 1782		James	Chow 1785
Robert	Bute 1766		James	Hali 1784
Robert	Samp 1784		Joel	Chow 1785
Robert	Bert 1781		Wm	Bute 1766
Samuel	Blad 1784		Wm	Gran 1785
Stephen	Samp 1784		BYRD, Edward	Mart 1779
Stephen	Hali 1783		Edward	Samp 1784
Thomas	Gran 1785		Isaac	Mart 1779
Thomas	Mont 1782		James	Nash 1782
Tobias	Bert 1781		John	Hert 1779
Widow	Gran 1785		John	Hert 1784
Willis	Perq 1787		Nathl	NorH 1780
Wm	Bert 1774		Robert	Hert 1784
Wm	Crav 1779		Wm	Hert 1779
Wm	Bert 1781		Wm	Hert 1784
Wm	Beau 1786		BYRNE, Matthew	Blad 1784
Wm & s Wm	Samp 1784		Peter	Blsd 1784
Zachariah	Blad 1784		Robert	Blad 1784
BUTNER, David	Rowa 1770		BYRNES, John	Beau 1779
Herman	Rowa 1770		BYRON, David	Bert 1781
Isaac	Rowa 1770		John	Bert 1781
BUTT, Abraham	Hali 1783		Barlow, Henry	Edge 1777
Caron	Hali 1783			
Jacob	Hali 1783			
James	Hali 1783			
Jesse	Hali 1783		CABAMUS, Stephen	Chow 1785
Joshua	Hali 1783		CABE, Barney	Oran 1779
Redford	Hali 1783		John	Oran 1779
Solomon	Hali 1783		CABINER, Andon	Surr 1782
BUTTER, Elisha	Dobb 1780		CADDELL, Anderson	Casw 1784
Jacob	Chow 1785		CADE, Drury	Bute 1766
Samuel	Chow 1785		Godfrey	Surr 1782
Timothy	Surr 1782		John	Blad 1784
Willis	Chow 1785		Robert	Bute 1766
Wm	Dobb 1780		Stephen	Dobb 1780
BUTTERSON, David	Bute 1766		Stephen	Blad 1784
George	Bute 1766		Waddell	Dobb 1780
Smith	Bute 1766		Wm	Crav 1767
BUTTERTON, James	Bert 1774		CADER, George	Mart 1779
James	Bert 1781		CADEWELL, Samuel	Tyrr 1784

CADLE, Benj	Surr 1782		CALLAWAY, Zebulon	Perq 1787
Mark	Surr 1782		CALLEY, John	Beau 1786
CAHLON, Dudley	Jone 1779		CALLIS, John	Curr 1779
CAHOON, Ezekiel	Tyrr 1784		CALLOE, Chas	Wilk 1782
James	Tyrr 1784		Joseph	Wilk 1782
John	Blad 1784		Richard	Wilk 1782
John	Tyrr 1784		Thomas	Wilk 1782
Joseph dec	Tyrr 1784		Wm	Wilk 1782
Micajah	Blad 1784		CALLORD, Wm & s Wm	Rowa 1761
Reuben	Tyrr 1784		CALLOWAY, Francis	Surr 1782
Wm	Blad 1784		Francis Jr	Surr 1782
Wm & s James	Tyrr 1784		Isaac	Mont 1782
CAHUNE, John	Wilk 1782		Job	Mont 1782
CAIL, Dempsey	Bert 1774		John	Mont 1782
John	Dobb 1780		Saml	Surr 1782
CAIN, Hugh Jr	Oran 1779		CALLUM, Edward	Bert 1781
Hugh Sr	Oran 1779		Willis	Bert 1781
James	Nash 1782		CALVERT, Wm	Wilk 1782
James	Blad 1784		CAMERON, Anguish	Blad 1784
James	Blad 1784		Daniel	Samp 1784
James Jr	Oran 1779		Henry Jr	Crav 1779
James Sr	Oran 1779		Henry Sr	Crav 1779
John	Brun 1784		Isaac	Samp 1784
John	Oran 1779		John	Surr 1782
John	Blad 1784		Laughlin	Blad 1784
Joseph	Blad 1784		Phillip	Samp 1784
Joseph est	Brun 1784		Rachel	Wilk 1782
Lazarus	Blad 1784		CAMFIELD, Wm	Bert 1781
Olive	Blad 1784		CAMP, Benjamin	Casw 1784
Peter	Rowa 1761		Edward	Ruth 1782
Robert	Rowa 1761		Joseph	Ruth 1782
Roger	Rowa 1770		Nathan	Ruth 1782
Samuel	Blad 1784		Thomas	Ruth 1782
Timothy	Oran 1779		Wm	Ruth 1782
Wm	Oran 1779		Zebulon	Camd 1782
Wm Jr	Blad 1784		CAMPBELL, Aaron	Wilk 1782
Wm M. Sr	Hert 1784		Allen	Rowa 1761
Wm Sr	Blad 1784		Anguish	Blad 1784
Wm est	Brun 1784		Anguish	Rich 1790
Wm s of Hugh	Oran 1779		Archibald	Casw 1784
CAIRN, Daniel	Blad 1784		Archibald	Chow 1773
CAIRNS, Alexander	Oran 1779		Catherine	Blad 1784
CAKE, Amos	NorH 1780		Daniel	Blad 1784
John	Bert 1781		Daniel	Rich 1790
Robert	Mart 1779		Dugal	Rich 1790
CALDWELL, Spencer	Dobb 1780		Elizabeth	Curr 1779
CALE, Dempsey	Bert 1781		Henry	Oran 1779
John	Bert 1781		Hugh	Blad 1784
John	Perq 1787		James	Mart 1779
Rebecca	Bert 1781		James	Bert 1774
Richard	Perq 1787		James	Beau 1779
Robert	Perq 1787		James	Crav 1779
Sarah	Bert 1781		James	NorH 1780
CALELL, Edward	NorH 1780		James	Bert 1781
CALEY, Patrick	Pasq 1694		James	Beau 1786
CALIF, James	Hert 1779		James	PItt 1786
CALL, James	Hert 1784		James	Rich 1790
CALLAHAN, Edward	Ruth 1782		John	Blad 1784
Henry	Ruth 1782		John	Casw 1784
Isaac	NBer 1779		John	Hert 1779
Wm	Ruth 1782		John	Oran 1779
CALLAWAY, Caleb	Albe 1679		John	Bert 1774
Isaac	Onsl 1771		John	Wilk 1782
Thomas	Bert 1781		John	Bert 1781
Widow	Onsl 1771		John	Rich 1790

CAMPBELL, John Capt	Hert	1779
Joseph	Crav	1779
Joshua	Camd	1782
Leven	Onsl	1771
Mary	Curr	1779
Peter	Blad	1784
Robert	Oran	1779
Robert	MecK	1772
Samuel	Oran	1779
Shadrack	Dobb	1780
Thomas	Beau	1779
Undice	NorH	1780
Willis	NorH	1780
Wm	Dobb	1780
Wm	NorH	1780
Wm	Surr	1782
Wm	Beau	1786
Wm	RicH	1790
CAMPEN, James	Beau	1786
Joseph	Beau	1786
Robert	Beau	1786
Robert	Beau	1786
CAMPERLAIN, Jacob	Surr	1782
CANADAY, Andrew	Wilk	1782
Charles	Rowa	1765
Eliz	Bert	1781
George	Tyrr	1784
Gideon	Cart	1779
Gon	Warr	1784
Jacob	Wilk	1782
John	Rowa	1765
John	Wayn	1786
John	Casw	1784
John Jr	Tyrr	1784
John Sr	Tyrr	1784
Patrick	Samp	1784
Rhoda	Samp	1784
Richard	Cart	1779
Sam	Wilk	1782
Sam	Bert	1781
Samuel	Blad	1784
Thomas	Cart	1779
Thomas	Casw	1784
Wm	Wilk	1782
CANAWAY, Thomas	Casw	1784
CANDORS, Thomas & s	Ben	
	Rowa	1761
Wm	Rowa	1761
CANE, James	Hali	1783
Jeremiah	Hali	1783
Nathaniel	Camd	1782
Thomas	Surr	1782
Thomas Jr	Surr	1782
CANNADAY, David Jr	Crav	1779
David Sr	Crav	1779
James	Bert	1781
John	Crav	1779
Joseph	Jone	1779
CANNON, Chas	Gran	1771
Daniel	Rich	1790
Edward	Crav	1779
Edward	Pitt	1786
Edward Sr	Crav	1779
Eliz	Pitt	1786
Elizabeth	Crav	1779

CANNON, Jacob	Perq	1787
James	Casw	1784
James Sr	Dobb	1780
Joel	Casw	1786
John	Dobb	1780
John	Samp	1784
John	Casw	1786
Joseph	Chow	1785
Moses	Onsl	1771
Nathl	Pitt	1786
Wm	Casw	1786
Wm	Casw	1784
CANTRELL, Jacob	Oran	1779
Joseph	Rowa	1761
Joseph	Casw	1786
Wm	Casw	1786
Wm	Casw	1784
CAPE, Thomas	Mont	1782
CAPEHART, Geo Jr	Bert	1781
Geo Sr	Bert	1781
George	Bert	1774
John	Bert	1781
Michael	Bert	1774
Michael	Bert	1781
CAPES, Matthew	John	1784
Wm	John	1784
CAPP, Elijah	Jone	1779
CAPPER, James	Pitt	1786
Thomas	Oran	1779
CAPPS, Caleb	Warr	1784
Caleb	Curr	1779
Caleb	Gran	1771
Dennis	Curr	1779
Enoch	Curr	1779
Francis	Bute	1766
Francis	Warr	1784
Henry	Warr	1784
Henry	Curr	1779
Horatio	Bute	1766
John	Bute	1766
John	Warr	1784
John	Mont	1782
John	Curr	1779
Joshua	Bute	1766
Joshua	Warr	1784
Moses	Curr	1779
Orasha	Warr	1784
Thomas	Warr	1779
Wm	Mont	1782
CARD, Joseph	Beau	1779
CARDOM, John	Surr	1782
CARDWELL, Thomas	Bute	1766
CAREY, Davison	Pasq	1789
Edward	Bute	1766
CARGILL, John	Wilk	1782
John Sr	Wilk	1782
Wm	Wilk	1782
CARKEET, Wm	Mart	1779
CARL, Elizabeth	Wilk	1782
CARLISLE, Edward	Bute	1766
Nathaniel	Hali	1783
Robert	Blad	1784
Sanders	Blad	1784
CARLSON, James	Hert	1784
CARLTON, John	NBer	1779

CARMAN, Caleb	Casw 1784		CARRAWAY, Ann	Crav 1779
Hezekiah	Casw 1784		Bedridden	Samp 1784
John	Casw 1784		Edward	NBer 1779
Samuel	Blad 1784		Elijah	Wayn 1786
CARMICHAEL, Archibald			Elizabeth	Wayn 1784
	Casw 1786		Francis	Crav 1779
Archibald	Casw 1784		James	Mart 1779
Archibald	Rich 1790		Jesse	Beau 1786
Daniel	Rich 1790		John	Wayn 1786
Duncan	Casw 1784		Joseph	Beau 1786
Hugh	Rich 1790		Phillip	Surr 1782
James	Surr 1782		Susannah	Crav 1779
Jeremiah	Casw 1784		Thomas	Wayn 1786
John	Blad 1784		Willis	Wayn 1786
John	Surr 1782		Wm	Crav 1779
CARNEL, Thomas	Mart 1779		CARRIGAN, Edward	Oran 1779
CARNELL, Benjamin	Blad 1784		Elizabeth	Oran 1779
CARNES, Edmund	Gran 1785		John	Oran 1779
Henry	Rowa 1761		Wm	Oran 1779
Joseph	Gran 1785		CARRILS, Thomas	Warr 1784
Keibard	Rowa 1761		CARRINGTON, George	Oran 1779
CARNEY, Absalom	Bert 1774		James	Oran 1779
Absalom	Bert 1781		John	Oran 1779
John	Crav 1779		John Jr	Oran 1779
Joseph	Casw 1786		CARROLL, Alexander	Samp 1784
Joseph	Casw 1784		Charles	Oran 1779
Joshua	Casw 1786		Dempsey	Samp 1784
Joshua	Casw 1784		Elizabeth	Gran 1785
Richard	Hali 1783		George	Casw 1784
Thomas	Nash 1782		Hannah	Casw 1786
CARPENTER, Burwell	Nash 1782		James	Samp 1784
George	Crav 1779		Jesse	Samp 1784
Jonathan	Hali 1783		John	Bute 1766
Jonathan	Mont 1782		John	Samp 1784
Joseph	Ruth 1782		John	Brun 1784
Mathias	Surr 1782		John	Warr 1784
Samuel	Ruth 1782		John	Wilk 1782
Samuel	Warr 1784		Luke	Gran 1771
Stephen	Chow 1785		Moses	Samp 1784
Stephen	Wilk 1784		Spencer	Gran 1785
Stephen	Wilk 1782		Stephen	Oran 1779
Thomas	Nash 1782		Thomas	Gran 1785
Wm	Hali 1783		Wm	Rowa 1768
CARPER, John	NorH 1780		Wm	Casw 1786
CARR, Barbara	Dupl 1783		Wm	Casw 1784
Hardy	NorH 1780		Wm	Gran 1785
James	Dupl 1779		Wm	John 1784
James	Rowa 1768		CARRON, George	Pasq 1779
John	Dupl 1779		CARROON, George	Camd 1782
John	Dupl 1783		Isaac	Tyrr 1784
John & s Thos	Rowa 1770		John	Tyrr 1784
Jonathan	Samp 1784		CARROTHERS, John	Ruth 1782
Joseph	Dupl 1779		Joseph	Crav 1762
Joseph	Rowa 1770		CARROWAY, Edward	NBer 1779
Matthew	Hert 1779		CARRUTHERS, Jeremiah	
Matthew	Hert 1784			Bert 1774
Nathaniel	Rowa 1768		Nathaniel	Samp 1784
Robert	Hert 1779		Samuel	Oran 1779
Robert	Hert 1784		CARSEY, Thomas	Cart 1779
Thomas	Rowa 1770		CARSON, Alexander	Oran 1779
Wm	Dupl 1779		David	Rowa 1761
Wm	Dupl 1783		James	Rowa 1761
Wm	NorH 1780		James	Oran 1779
Wm	Surr 1782		Jesse	Perq 1772
CARRAWAY, Adam	Wayn 1784		John	Ruth 1782

CARSON, Moses	Oran 1779	CARTER, Lazarus	Hert 1784
Robert	Rowa 1761	Lewis	Hert 1779
Sarah	Perq 1772	Lewis	Hert 1784
Thomas	Surr 1782	Malton	Hali 1783
Walter	Ruth 1782	Mark	Blad 1784
CARTER, Abel	Surr 1782	Mary	Nash 1782
Abraham	Bute 1766	Matthew	John 1784
Alexander	Gran 1785	Michael	Mart 1779
Ann	Gate 1789	Michael	Bert 1774
Benj	Bert 1781	Moos	Gate 1789
Benjamin	Hali 1783	Moses	Samp 1784
Charles	Nash 1782	Naomi	Wayn 1786
Charles	Hali 1783	Nathan	Surr 1782
Charles	Mont 1782	Nathaniel	Bute 1766
Chas	Gran 1771	Nathaniel	Oran 1779
Chas	Gate 1789	Phillip	Hali 1783
Dan	Bert 1774	Robert	Hali 1783
Daniel	Surr 1782	Robert	Bert 1774
David	Surr 1782	Robert Jr	Bert 1781
Edward	Dobb 1780	Robert Sr	Bert 1781
Elmore	Samp 1784	Sam	Bert 1781
Ephraim	Mont 1782	Saml	Surr 1782
Geo	Bert 1781	Samuel	Nash 1782
George	Wilk 1784	Samuel	Bert 1774
Giles	Hali 1783	Samuel	Mont 1782
Giles	Warr 1784	Simeon	Surr 1782
Henry	Samp 1784	Solomon	Nash 1782
Isaac	Hert 1784	Teneh	Rowa 1768
Isaac	Gate 1789	Thomas	Nash 1782
Isaac Jr	Hert 1779	Thomas	Gran 1785
Isaac Jr	Hert 1784	Thomas	Wilk 1782
Isaac Sr	Hert 1779	Thomas	Bert 1781
Jacob	Nash 1782	Wm	Nash 1782
Jacob	Hali 1783	Wm	Hert 1779
Jacob	Mont 1782	Wm	Oran 1779
Jacob	Surr 1782	Wm	Chow 1785
James	Nash 1782	Wm	Hali 1783
James	Hert 1779	Wm	Bert 1774
James	Hert 1784	Wm	Mont 1782
James	NorH 1780	Wm	Surr 1782
James	Gate 1789	Wm	Bert 1781
James Jr	Blad 1784	CARTRIGHT, Aliss	Pasq 1779
James Sr	Blad 1784	Benjamin	Pasq 1779
Jesse	Blad 1784	Caleb	Pasq 1779
Jesse	Gran 1785	David	Pasq 1779
Jesse	Hali 1783	Hezekiah	Pasq 1779
John	Burk 1777	Hezekiah Sr	Pasq 1779
John	Dupl 1779	James	Pasq 1779
John	Hert 1779	Jesse	Pasq 1779
John	Dobb 1780	John	Pasq 1779
John	Oran 1779	John Jr	Pasq 1779
John	Mart 1779	John Sr	Pasq 1779
John	Samp 1784	Joseph	Pasq 1779
John	Hert 1784	Matthew	Pasq 1779
John	Wilk 1782	Robert	Pasq 1779
John	NorH 1780	Sarah	Pasq 1779
John	Surr 1782	Simeon	Pasq 1779
John	Gate 1789	Thomas	Pasq 1779
John	Perq 1787	Thomas Sr	Pasq 1779
Joseph	Blad 1784	Wm	Pasq 1779
Joseph	Wayn 1786	CARTURN, Josiah	Wilk 1782
Joseph	Hali 1783	CARTWRIGHT, Ahaz	Pasq 1789
Joshua	Mont 1782	Asa	Camd 1782
Josiah	Blad 1784	Baptist	Hali 1783
Kindred	Hert 1779	Benj	Pasq 1789

CARTWRIGHT, Caleb	Camd 1782		CASHMELL, John	Blad 1784
Caleb	Pasq 1789		Thomas	Blad 1784
Caleb	Pasq 1789		CASNER, Christr	Surr 1782
Claudius	Samp 1784		CASON, John	Curr 1779
Claudius	Dupl 1784		John	Rich 1790
Clement	Camd 1782		CASSE, Thomas	Pasq 1779
Clement	Pasq 1789		CASSEE, Arthur	Pasq 1789
Darius	Pasq 1789		John	Pasq 1789
Elisha	Camd 1782		Prudence	Pasq 1789
Elizabeth	Camd 1782		Willis	Pasq 1789
H (estate)	Pasq 1789		CASSELL, Wm	Wilk 1782
Hezekiah	Pasq 1789		CASSIE, John	Pasq 1779
Isaac	Camd 1782		Prudence	Pasq 1779
Isaac	Pasq 1789		Willie	Pasq 1779
Jabez	Camd 1782		CASSO, John	Pasq 1779
Jacob	Camd 1782		Peter	Beau 1786
James	Camd 1782		Wm	Pasq 1779
James	Pasq 1789		CASTLE, Samuel	Wilk 1782
Jesse	Pasq 1789		CASTLEBERRY, Paul	Oran 1779
John	Pasq 1789		CASTLETON, John estate	
John Jr	Pasq 1789			Brun 1784
John Sr	Pasq 1789		CASWELL, Benjamin	Dobb 1780
Martha	Pasq 1789		John	Gran 1771
Mathias	Pasq 1789		Martin Col.	Dobb 1780
Matthew	Hali 1783		Richard Gov	Dobb 1778
Morgan	Camd 1782		Richard Jr Col	Dobb 1780
Moses	Camd 1782		Richard MajGen	Dobb 1780
Peter	Camd 1782		Wm Brig Gen	Dobb 1780
Robert	Camd 1782		CATAME, John	Onsl 1771
Sarah	Pasq 1789		CATCHEM, Edward	Oran 1779
Simon	Pasq 1789		Martha	Oran 1779
Thomas	Camd 1782		CATE, Barnett	Oran 1779
Thomas	Pasq 1789		Benjamin	Oran 1779
Winifred	Pasq 1789		Charles	Oran 1779
Wm	Camd 1782		John	Oran 1779
CARVER, James	Blad 1784		Joseph	Oran 1779
Job	Pasq 1779		Joshua	Casw 1784
Job	Pasq 1789		Lazarus	Oran 1779
Michael	Surr 1782		Richard	Oran 1779
Sampson	Blad 1784		Robert	Oran 1779
Thomas	Casw 1784		Robert	Casw 1784
Wm	Casw 1784		Stephen	Oran 1779
CARVIS, Wm	Casw 1784		Thomas	Oran 1779
CASE, Ezekiel	Camd 1782		Thomas	Casw 1784
Jonathan	Curr 1779		Wm	Oran 1779
Solomon Jr	Curr 1779		CATES, James	Rowa 1765
Solomon Sr	Curr 1779		Marmaduke	Rowa 1765
CASEN, Charity	Samp 1784		CATHEY, Alexander	Rowa 1761
Henry	Pasq 1694		CATHOLIC, John	Onsl 1771
Hillery	Samp 1784		CATO, Daniel	Mont 1782
John	Pasq 1694		George	Wayn 1786
CASEOVER, Jesse	Blad 1784		Moses	Perq 1772
CASEWELL, John	Tyrr 1784		CATON, John	Crav 1779
Samuel	Tyrr 1784		Moses	Crav 1779
CASEY, Elizabeth	Chow 1785		Solomon	Beau 1779
Jeremiah	Wayn 1786		Wm	Crav 1779
John	Cart 1779		CATTS, James	Ruth 1782
Micajah	Wayn 1786		CAUDELL, Lewis	Bute 1766
Wm	Warr 1784		CAUL, John	Surr 1782
CASH, David	Wilk 1782		CAUSEY, Ann	Crav 1779
James	Gran 1785		Wm	Rowa 1765
John	Casw 1784		CAUTHEN, Wm	Gran 1772
Joseph	Gran 1785		Wm	Gran 1785
Peter	Gran 1785		CAUTHORN, James	Warr 1784
Sarah	Gran 1785		John	Warr 1784

CAUTHORN, Thomas	Warr 1784	CHAMPREY, Isaac	Beau 1779
CAVANAUGH, George	Gran 1785	CHANCE, Benjamin	Wayn 1786
Thomas	Hali 1783	Elijah	Crav 1779
CAVENDER, Bryan	Crav 1779	Henry	Wayn 1786
John	Curr 1779	Margaret	Pitt 1786
Nehemiah	Onsl 1771	Nathan	Wayn 1786
CAVES, John	Curr 1779	Phillip	Wayn 1786
CAVIT, John	Bert 1781	Samuel	Waye 1786
CAWLEY, Phillip	Hali 1783	Stephen	Wayn 1786
Roger	Dobb 1780	Vincent	Dobb 1780
CAZTILLAN, Wm	Bert 1781	Vincent	Wayn 1786
CEARBY, Wm	Wilk 1782	Wm	Oran 1779
CEBURY, Edward	Beau 1779	CHANCEY, Edmund	Pasq 1779
CEETH, Cornelius	Surr 1782	Micajah	Pasq 1789
CELLER, Christian	Rowa 1761	CHANCY, Elizabeth	Pasq 1779
CELLERS, Samuel	Samp 1784	Zack	Blad 1784
CEPHANUS, Andrew	Hali 1783	CHANDLER, Bailey	Wilk 1782
CERTAIN, Lewis	Surr 1782	Chas	Curr 1779
CETRY, Hin	Surr 1782	Isel	Gran 1785
CHADWICK, David deceased		James	Gran 1785
	Cart 1779	James	Gran 1771
Gayre	Cart 1779	John	Gran 1771
Isaiah	Cart 1779	John Jr	Gran 1785
John	Gran 1785	John Sr	Gran 1785
John	Gran 1771	Joseph	Gran 1785
Martha	Nash 1782	Joseph	Gran 1771
Nathan	Gran 1785	Joshua	Gran 1785
Samuel	Cart 1779	Levin	Gran 1785
Thomas	Cart 1779	Wm	Surr 1782
CHAFFIN, Robert	Oran 1779	CHANDLOW, Joel	Wilk 1782
CHAINEY, James	Wilk 1782	Robert	Wilk 1782
CHALK, Wm	Perq 1787	Timothy	Wilk 1782
CHAMBERLIN, Henry	Camd 1782	CHANEY, Philip	Onsl 1771
Jeremiah	Camd 1782	Saml	Surr 1782
John	Camd 1782	CHANNELL, John	Hali 1783
Robert	Pasq 1779	CHAPEL, Christopher	Mont 1782
Willis	Camd 1782	Moses	Bert 1774
CHAMBERS, Edward Jr	Mont 1782	Thomas	Curr 1779
Edward Sr	Mont 1782	CHAPLIN, Caleb	Curr 1779
Francis	Onsl 1771	Gro	Bert 1781
Henry	Wilk 1784	James	Curr 1779
James	Casw 1784	CHAPMAN, Benjamin	Oran 1779
John	Casw 1784	Chas	NorH 1780
Josiah	Casw 1784	George	Gran 1785
Martha	John 1784	Henry	Hali 1783
Moses	Rich 1790	James	Casw 1786
Rachel	Rich 1790	Jesse	Pitt 1786
Samuel	Oran 1779	John	Nash 1782
Wm	Casw 1784	John	Crav 1779
Wm Sr	Gran 1771	John	Wilk 1782
CHAMBLEE, Isaac	Hert 1779	Joseph	Tyrr 1784
CHAMNESS, Joseph	Rowa 1768	Richard	Tyrr 1784
CHAMPION, Charles	Gran 1785	Samuel	Crav 1779
Chas	Gran 1771	Thomas	Tyrr 1784
Hart	Hali 1783	Weeks	Crav 1779
John	Gran 1785	Wm	Ruth 1782
John	Hali 1783	Wm	Casw 1786
John	Gran 1771	Wm	Wilk 1782
John Jr	Gran 1785	Wm Jr	Nash 1782
John Jr	Gran 1771	CHAPPEL, Job	Perq 1772
Joseph	Bert 1781	John	Hali 1783
Samuel	Mont 1782	John	Perq 1772
Wm	Blad 1784	Josiah	Chow 1785
Wm	Hali 1783	Malachi	Perq 1772
Wm	Gran 1771	Mark	Perq 1772

CHAPPEL, Moses	Bert 1781	CHERRY, James	Hert 1779
Robert	Perq 1772	James	Hert 1784
Thomas	NorH 1750	James	Bert 1774
CHAPPELL, Isaac	Perq 1787	Jesse	Mart 1779
James	Perq 1787	Joab	Mart 1779
John Jr	Perq 1787	Job	Mart 1779
John Sr	Perq 1787	John	Mart 1779
Joseph	Perq 1787	John	Bert 1774
Malachi	Perq 1787	John	Bert 1781
Mark	Perq 1787	John	Beau 1786
Robert	Perq 1787	John Jr	Beau 1786
CHAPPEl, Micajah	Chow 1785	Jonathan	Mart 1779
CHARLES, Henry	Beau 1779	Josiah	Curr 1779
John	Gran 1771	Luke	Curr 1779
Michael	Oran 1779	Mary	Mart 1779
Oliver	Surr 1782	Robert	Bert 1781
Saml	Perq 1787	Samuel	Mart 1779
Samuel	Perq 1772	Solomon	Bert 1774
Sarah	Surr 1782	Solomon Jr	Bert 1774
CHARLESCRAFT, David	Dobb 1780	Wm	Bert 1774
John	Dobb 1780	Wm	Bert 1781
Levi	Dobb 1780	CHESHIRE, Henry	Chow 1785
CHARLTON, Geo	Pitt 1786	CHESKEN, Wm	Blad 1784
Jasper	Bert 1781	CHESNUTT, Alexander	Samp 1784
John	Chow 1785	Charles	Samp 1784
Joseph	Crav 1779	Jacob	Samp 1784
Joseph	Pitt 1786	John	Samp 1784
Thomas	Chow 1785	Joshua	Dupl 1779
CHARY, John	Hali 1783	Joshua Jr	Samp 1784
CHASON, Joseph	Blad 1784	CHESON, Richard	Blad 1784
Richard	Onsl 1771	CHESSIER, James	Surr 1782
CHATEN, Benj	NorH 1780	CHESSON, John	Tyrr 1784
CHATWIN, Joseph	Onsl 1771	Joshua	Tyrr 1784
CHAUNCEY, Ann	Beau 1779	Samuel	Tyrr 1784
Samuel	Beau 1779	Wm	Tyrr 1784
CHAVERS, Gibea	Gran 1771	CHESTER, Henry	Tyrr 1784
Henry	Hert 1784	Henry	Beau 1779
John	Blad 1784	John	Beau 1779
Joseph	Hali 1783	John	Beau 1786
Phillip	Blad 1784	Thomas	Mont 1782
Wm	Blad 1784	CHILDERS, David	Surr 1782
Wm Sr	Gran 1771	John	Ruth 1782
CHAVES, James	Brun 1784	Michael	Wilk 1782
James	Gran 1785	CHILDRESS, Abraham	Warr 1784
Wm	Gran 1785	Abraham	Surr 1782
Wm	Gate 1789	Abram	Casw 1784
CHEATAM, James	Warr 1784	James	Wilk 1782
CHEBIS, Nehemiah	Rich 1790	John	Warr 1784
CHEEK, John	Rowa 1767	John	Surr 1782
John	Warr 1784	Joseph	Surr 1782
John	Mont 1782	Richard	Surr 1782
Jonathan	Bute 1766	Robert	Warr 1784
Randolph	Mont 1782	CHILDS, Hezekiah	Gran 1771
Richard	Surr 1782	John	NorH 1780
Robert	Bute 1766	Nathan	Gran 1771
Robert	Oran 1779	CHILES, Nathan Jr	Gran 1785
Sam	Bert 1781	Thomas	Mont 1782
Wm	Warr 1784	CHILLEY, Brittain	Mart 1779
Wm & s Jonath	Bute 1766	CHIMMEY, Thomas	Onsl 1771
CHENEY, Abiel	Cart 1777	CHIPPENHALL, Samuel	Oran 1779
CHERRY, Aaron	Bert 1781	Wm	Oran 1779
Cader	Bert 1774	CHITHAM, Sarah	Curr 1779
Chas	Beau 1786	CHITTY, Benj	Surr 1782
Ezekiel	Bert 1781	Edward	NorH 1750
Faithful	Mart 1779	CHITWOOD, Alice	Ruth 1782

CHITWOOD, James	Ruth	1782		CLARK, Benjamin	Blad	1784
Richard	Ruth	1782		Benjamin	Gran	1785
CHRIST, Randolph	Surr	1782		Benjamin	Hert	1784
CHRISTIAN, Christopher				Bowling	Surr	1782
	Mont	1782		Charles	Blad	1784
Drury	Warr	1784		Christr	Bert	1781
Jesse	Mont	1782		Colen	Bert	1774
Nicholas	Mont	1782		Cornelius	Pasq	1789
CHRISTIE, Jesse	Hali	1783		Daniel	John	1784
John	Hali	1783		Daniel	Rich	1790
CHRISTMAN, Belshazzar				David	Samp	1784
	Surr	1782		David	Blad	1784
Daniel	Surr	1782		David	Surr	1782
Jacob	Ruth	1782		Edward	Rowa	1761
John	Ruth	1782		Edward	Rowa	1768
CHRISTMAS, Gideon	Gran	1785		Edward	Crav	1779
John	Oran	1779		Edward	Pitt	1786
John	Casw	1786		Eldridge	Warr	1784
Richard	Oran	1779		Geo	Beau	1786
Thomas	Bute	1766		George	Rowa	1768
Thomas	Warr	1784		George	Blad	1784
CHRISTOPHER, Ephraim				George	Curr	1779
	Oran	1779		Goshen	Pasq	1789
Thomas	Gran	1785		Gregory	Samp	1784
Wm	Gran	1785		Henry	Ruth	1782
CHUMNEY, Wm	Gran	1771		Henry	Blad	1784
CHUN, Silvester	Rich	1790		Henry	Warr	1784
CHURCH, John	Rowa	1761		Henry	Rich	1790
John	Surr	1782		Isaac	Pitt	1786
John Jr	Wilk	1782		Isaac	Pasq	1789
John Sr	Wilk	1782		James	Oran	1779
Thomas	Surr	1782		James	Casw	1784
Thomas	Perq	1787		James	Bert	1781
CHURCHILL, James	Hali	1783		Janet	Bert	1781
Simon	Hali	1783		John	Hert	1779
CHURCHWELL, Henry	Bert	1781		John	Dobb	1780
James	Bert	1774		John	Rowa	1761
James	Bert	1781		John	Rowa	1768
CICKES, John	Bute	1766		John	Oran	1779
CILLEY, Catherine	Beau	1779		John	Blad	1784
Charles	Beau	1779		John	Hert	1784
Curtis	Beau	1779		John	Beau	1779
John	Beau	1779		John	Crav	1779
Michael	Wilk	1784		John	NorH	1780
CIMBERLAND, Martin	Oran	1779		John	Beau	1786
CISBLER, Seth	NorH	1780		John	Perq	1787
CITRAL, Jonathan	Crav	1779		John Jr	Hert	1779
CIVIL, Wm Sr	NBer	1779		John Jr	Hert	1784
CLAGHORN, Shubel	Mart	1779		Jonathan	Surr	1782
CLAIF, Ralph	Beau	1786		Joseph	Rowa	1761
CLANDY, James	Blad	1784		Joseph	Pasq	1779
CLANTON, Joel	Gran	1771		Joseph	NBer	1779
Richard	Gran	1771		Leonard	Gran	1785
Thomas	Surr	1782		Martha	Pasq	1789
Wm	Warr	1784		Mary	Pasq	1694
CLAPP, John	Oran	1779		Mary	Pasq	1779
Margaret	Oran	1779		Micajah	Pasq	1779
CLAPTON, Richard	Bute	1766		Micajah	Surr	1782
CLARK, Aaron	Hali	1783		Nathaniel	Warr	1784
Abraham	Ruth	1782		Nicholas	Rich	1790
Amelia	Bert	1781		Nunn	Onsl	1771
Ann	Beau	1779		Osburn	Pitt	1786
Benj	Crav	1779		Patrick	Oran	1779
Benj	Pasq	1789		Robert	Nash	1782
Benjamin	Samp	1784		Ruth	Pasq	1789

Samuel	Rowa	1768
Samuel Jr	Rowa	1768
Stephen	Pasq	1779
Stewart	Rowa	1761
Thomas	Bert	1774
Thomas	Bute	1766
Thomas	Rowa	1761
Thomas	Rowa	1768
Thomas	Oran	1779
Thomas	Brun	1784
Thomas	NorH	1780
Thomas	Surr	1782
Wm	Hert	1779
Wm	Oran	1779
Wm	Blad	1784
Wm	Hert	1784
Wm	Warr	1784
Wm	Crav	1779
Wm	Crav	1779
Wm	Onsl	1771
Wm	Surr	1782
Wm	Gran	1771
Wm	Beau	1786
Wm Jr	Hert	1784
Wm Jr	Warr	1784
Wm s of James	Oran	1779
CLARKSON, Thomas	Chow	1785
CLARY, John	Beau	1779
Wm	Pasq	1789
CLASBY, Elijah	Surr	1782
CLASSINGTON, Nicholas	NorH	1780
CLAWZELL, John Lewis	Gate	1789
CLAXTON, James	Gran	1785
James	Gran	1771
CLAY, Edward	Casw	1784
John	Rowa	1768
Samuel	Gran	1785
Wearcobie	Samp	1784
CLAYBORNE, Leonard	Ruth	1782
CLAYTON, Benoni	Blad	1784
Daniel	Casw	1784
Daniel	Gran	1771
Elizabeth	Surr	1782
Francis	Surr	1782
John	Bute	1766
John	Hali	1783
John	Surr	1782
John	Perq	1787
John Jr	Casw	1784
John Sr	Casw	1784
Mary	Surr	1782
Richard	Perq	1772
Richard	Gran	1771
Stephen	Surr	1782
Stephen Sr	Surr	1782
Thomas	Bute	1766
Thomas	Casw	1784
Wm	Surr	1782
Wm	Perq	1787
CLEARE, Saml	Rich	1790
CLEARY, Charles	Perq	1787
John	Perq	1787
CLEAVES, John	Hali	1783
CLEAVES, Robert	Hali	1783
CLEGHORN, Wm	Ruth	1782
CLEMENT, Charlton	Bert	1781
Geo	Bert	1781
John	Chow	1785
John	Gran	1785
Keziah	Gran	1771
Neely	Ruth	1782
Obadiah	Gran	1785
Samuel	Gran	1785
Simon	Gran	1785
Stephen	Gran	1785
Thomas	Gran	1785
Zephaniah	Gran	1785
CLEMENTS, Henry	Oran	1779
Peyton	Gran	1771
Richard	Oran	1779
Zephaniah	Gran	1771
CLEMMONS, George	Mart	1779
Henry	Casw	1786
Robert	Perq	1772
Wm	Warr	1784
Wm	Perq	1787
Wm George	Perq	1772
CLEMONS, Henry	Surr	1782
John	Rich	1790
CLENDENIN, Charles	Oran	1779
CLENNEY, Samuel	Oran	1779
Wm	Oran	1779
CLENTON, Benj	Surr	1782
CLERK, Henry	Curr	1779
Major	Curr	1779
CLEVELAND, Absalom	Wilk	1782
Benj	Wilk	1782
James	Nash	1782
Jeremiah	Wilk	1782
John	Wilk	1782
Larkin	WiLK	1782
Robert	Wilk	1782
CLEWIS, George	Brun	1784
CLIFFORD, James	Beau	1779
James	Beau	1786
CLIFT, John	Casw	1784
CLIFTON, Benj	NorH	1780
Benjamin	Hert	1779
Charles	Tyrr	1784
Covington	Gran	1771
Ezekiel	Onsl	1771
John	Tyrr	1784
John	Onsl	1771
Lydia	NorH	1780
Peter	Bert	1774
Peter	Bert	1781
Robert	Tyrr	1784
CLINCH, Joseph J	Nash	1782
Milly	Nash	1782
CLINE, Christr	Surr	1782
CLINGMAN, Alexander	Rowa	1761
CLINTON, Matthew	Oran	1779
CLISBY, John	Casw	1784
CLITHERALL, Dr	NBer	1779
CLOUD, Daniel Quaker	Oran	1779
Isaac	Surr	1782
Joseph	Surr	1782

CLOUD, Joseph Quaker		COCKBURN, Andrew	Mart 1779
	Oran 1779	Francis	Mart 1779
Wm	Surr 1782	George	Mart 1779
CLOWER, George	Oran 1779	George Sr	Mart 1779
CLYBURN, John	Blad 1784	John	Mart 1779
John Jr	Blad 1784	Wm	Hali 1783
Joshua	Blad 1784	COCKERHAM, Thomas	Rich 1790
Robert	Blad 1784	COCKERMAN, Thomas	Mont 1782
Wm	Blad 1784	COCKLEY, James	Oran 1779
COALE, Wm	Hert 1779	COCKRELL, Jacob	Nash 1782
COALTER, Martin	Rowa 1761	John	Nash 1782
COART, John	Dobb 1780	Thomas	John 1784
COATES, George	Camd 1782	Wm	Casw 1784
James	Camd 1782	COCKSTON, John	Curr 1779
Malachi	Camd 1782	COE, Isaiah	Surr 1782
Robert	Oran 1779	John	Surr 1782
COBB, Abel	Surr 1782	Timothy	Surr 1782
Absalom	NorH 1780	COEN, Benj	Pasq 1789
Benjamin	Wayn 1786	Caleb	Pasq 1789
David	Wayn 1786	John	Pasq 1789
Hannah	Bert 1781	COFF, Stephen	Pasq 1694
Henry	Casw 1786	COFFEE, Ambrose	Wilk 1784
Henry	Casw 1784	Chesley	Wilk 1782
Henry	Bert 1781	Jacob	Curr 1779
James	Mart 1779	James	Wilk 1784
James	Wayn 1786	Joel	Wilk 1782
James	Bert 1781	Joshua	Casw 1784
Jesse	Dobb 1780	Nathan	Wilk 1782
John	Casw 1786	Richard	Beau 1779
John	Casw 1784	Thomas	Wilk 1784
John	NorH 1780	Thomas	Wilk 1782
John	Gran 1771	Wm	Beau 1779
John	Bert 1781	COFFER, Averille	Hali 1783
John Petty	Nash 1782	COFFEY, Abner	Beau 1786
Lewis	Bert 1781	Becham	Beau 1786
Nathan	Wayn 1786	Benj	Wilk 1782
Nathl	Bert 1781	Isaac	Wilk 1782
Noah	Casw 1786	James	Wilk 1782
Noah	Casw 1784	James	Surr 1782
Patience	Wayn 1786	James Sr	Wilk 1782
Wm	Bert 1781	Jane	Wilk 1782
COBEY, Nathl	NorH 1780	Jesse	Wilk 1782
COBLE, Adam	Oran 1779	COFFIELD, Benjamin	Chow 1785
Anthony	Oran 1779	David	Hali 1783
David	Oran 1779	David	Bert 1781
George	Oran 1779	Edward	Chow 1785
Henry	Oran 1779	Gresham	Bert 1781
John	Oran 1779	John	Chow 1785
COCHRAN, Daniel	Surr 1782	COFFIN, Cliff	Surr 1782
David	Casw 1784	COFTEN, Francis Sr	Onsl 1771
Humphrey	Surr 1782	John	Onsl 1771
James	Casw 1784	COGDELL, Charles	Wayn 1786
John	Casw 1784	David	Wayn 1786
John Jr	Casw 1786	Francis	Wayn 1786
John Sr	Casw 1786	COGDILL, Richard	Beau 1786
Moses	Surr 1782	COGGAN, John	Warn 1784
Reuben	Casw 1786	John & s Wm	Bute 1766
Reuben	Casw 1784	Thomas	Samp 1784
Thomas	Bert 1781	Wm	Warr 1784
Wm	Casw 1786	COGGIN, John	Warr 1784
Wm	Casw 1784	Wm	Warr 1784
Wm	Jone 1779	COGWELL, Israim	Warr 1785
Wm	Wilk 1782	Isrome	Bute 1766
COCKALEER, Michael	Gran 1771	James	Warr 1784
Tabott	Gran 1771	COHORN, Cornelius	Rowa 1765

COHORN, Thomas	Rowa 1765		COLEMAN, John	Ruth 1782
COKE, Phillip	Blad 1784		John	Blad 1784
Robert	Bert 1774		John	Hali 1783
Wm	Surr 1782		John	Warr 1784
COKER, Benj	NorH 1780		John	Rich 1790
Hardy	Crav 1779		Miles	Wayn 1786
Joseph	Surr 1782		Moses	Blad 1784
Millie	Mont 1782		Peter	Warr 1784
Robert	Surr 1782		Peter	Surr 1782
Whitley	NorH 1780		Richard	Ruth 1782
COLBERY, John	Bert 1781		Richard	Casw 1784
COLBREATH, Anguish	Samp 1784		Richard	Warr 1784
Daniel	Samp 1784		Richard Jr	Bute 1766
Neil	Samp 1784		Richard Sr	Ruth 1782
Torkle	Samp 1784		Robert	Gran 1785
COLCLOUGH, John	Bute 1766		Robert	Hali 1783
John	Warr 1784		Spill	Casw 1786
Mary	Warr 1784		Spill	Casw 1784
Wm & s Wm	Bute 1766		Theophilus	Nash 1782
COLE, David	Ruth 1782		Thomas	Crav 1779
Francis	Rich 1790		Thomas	Pitt 1786
Geo	Rich 1790		Wm	Warr 1784
James	Wayn 1786		Young	Surr 1782
James Esq	Rich 1790		COLER, Elizabeth	Wilk 1782
Jeremiah	Bert 1781		Isaac	Rowa 1761
Job	Wilk 1784		COLES, Wm Temple	Rowa 1767
Job	Bert 1781		COLESON, Chesley	Wilk 1782
John	Bute 1766		Chester	Nash 1782
John	Rowa 1768		Elizabeth	Hert 1784
John	Gran 1785		Gabriel	Perq 1772
John	Perq 1772		Henry	Rowa 1768
John	Wilk 1782		John	Hert 1784
John	Rich 1790		Wm	Perq 1772
John Sr	Rich 1790		COLEY, Charles	Bute 1766
Joseph	Perq 1787		Charles	Hali 1783
Josiah	Casw 1784		Edward	Bute 1766
Peter	Rich 1790		James	Hali 1783
Rhoda	Gran 1785		Jeffrey	Hali 1783
Richard	Perq 1772		Jesse	Hali 1783
Robert	Ruth 1782		Levy	Hali 1783
Robert	Perq 1772		Moses	Hali 1783
Samuel	Oran 1779		Robert	Hali 1783
Stephen	Rich 1790		COLF, Charles	Pasq 1694
Thomas	Casw 1786		COLLETT, Abraham	Rowa 1761
Thomas	Casw 1784		COLLEY, Charles	Beau 1779
Thomas	Warr 1784		George	Mont 1782
Warrington	Gran 1785		Laban	Beau 1779
Wm	Ruth 1782		Samuel	Perq 1772
Wm	Rowa 1768		COLLIER, Also	NorH 1780
Wm	Samp 1784		David	Surr 1782
Wm	Gran 1785		Drury	Mont 1782
Wm	Hert 1784		Jesse	NorH 1780
Wm	Bert 1774		John	Wilk 1782
Wm	Warr 1784		Joshua	NorH 1780
COLECLOUGH, John	Warr 1784		Thomas	Wilk 1782
Mary	Warr 1784		COLLIFER, Isaac	Tyrr 1784
COLEMAN, Charity Mrs			James	Tyrr 1784
	Warr 1784		John	Tyrr 1784
Charles	Oran 1779		COLLING, Sam	Wilk 1782
Chas	Wilk 1784		COLLINGAME, Elisha	Rich 1790
Chas	Curr 1779		COLLINGHAM, Wm	Rich 1790
David	Perq 1772		COLLINS, Andrew	John 1784
James	Casw 1786		Anthony	Surr 1782
James	Crav 1779		Army	Beau 1779
John	Pasq 1694		Brice	Oran 1779

COLLINS, Caleb	Tyrr 1784		COLLSOM, Thomas	NorH 1780
Chas	Rich 1790		COLSON, James	Hert 1779
Christopher	Perq 1772		John (younger)	Hert 1779
Christopher	Perq 1787		John Jr	Hert 1779
Deal	John 1784		John Sr	Hert 1779
Edward	Bert 1774		COLSTON, Wm	Perq 1787
Elisha	Rich 1790		COLTEN, John	Surr 1782
Elizabeth	Gran 1785		COLTRAINE, John	Mart 1779
Enoch	Oran 1779		Wm	Rowa 1761
Ephraim	Mart 1779		Wm	Rowa 1770
Geo	Rich 1790		COLTSON, James	NorH 1780
George	John 1784		Joseph	NorH 1780
George	Camd 1782		COLVIN, Francis	Blad 1784
Henry	Beau 1786		COMAS, Nathaniel	Casw 1784
Isaiah	Bert 1774		COMBS, Bryan	Blad 1784
James	Dobb 1780		Canon	Blad 1784
James	Gran 1771		Francis	Surr 1782
Jeremiah	Surr 1782		Geo	Wilk 1782
Jeremiah	Perq 1786		George	Wilk 1784
Jesse	Nash 1782		Gilbert	Blad 1784
Jesse	Bert 1774		John	Wilk 1784
John	Gran 1785		John	Wilk 1782
John	Ruth 1782		John	Surr 1782
John	Oran 1779		Nathaniel	Blad 1784
John	Mart 1779		Robert	NorH 1780
John	Camd 1782		Thomas	Casw 1784
John	Casw 1784		Wm	Oran 1779
John	Perq 1772		Wm	Wilk 1784
John	Wilk 1784		Wm	Wilk 1782
John	Onsl 1771		COMFORT, Charles	Beau 1779
John	Bert 1781		COMMANDER, John	Pasq 1779
John	Perq 1787		John	Pasq 1789
Joseph	Chow 1785		Joseph	Pasq 1694
Joseph	Cart 1779		Joseph	Pasq 1779
Joseph	Bert 1774		Joseph Jr	Pasq 1789
Joseph	Bert 1781		Tukes	Pasq 1779
Josiah	Bert 1781		COMMISEK, Duke	NorH 1780
Luke	Bert 1781		COMPON, Robert	Beau 1779
Malachi	Camd 1782		Thomas	Beau 1779
Margaret	Mart 1779		COMPTON, Aquilla	Oran 1779
Matthew	Pasq 1694		Aquilla	Casw 1786
Michael	Bute 1766		Mary	Bert 1781
Obadiah	Surr 1782		Stephen	Wilk 1784
Ralph	Pasq 1779		CONANT, Hardy	Surr 1782
Richard	Camd 1782		CONAWAY, Edward	Surr 1782
Roger	Surr 1782		Wm Rev War	Hali 1782
Solomon	Nash 1782		CONDICE, Dennis	Beau 1779
Thomas	Camd 1782		George	Beau 1779
Thomas	Bert 1774		John	Beau 1779
Thomas	Surr 1782		Wm	Beau 1779
Thomas	Bert 1781		CONDREY, Dennis	Beau 1786
Thomas	Bert 1781		John	Beau 1786
Timothy	Mart 1779		Wm	Beau 1786
Timothy	Beau 1786		CONDRY, Clayburn	Ruth 1782
Watson	Surr 1782		James	Rowa 1768
Wm	Chow 1785		John	Rowa 1768
Wm	Pasq 1694		Thomas	Rowa 1768
Wm	Ruth 1782		CONE, Joseph	Beau 1786
Wm	Bute 1766		Joshua	Nash 1782
Wm	Oran 1779		Neal Jr	Mart 1779
Wm	Mart 1779		Neal Sr	Mart 1779
Wm	Surr 1782		Stephen	Beau 1786
Wm	Gate 1789		Thomas	Bert 1781
COLLISUM, Pritchard	Blad 1784		Wm	Mart 1779
COLLONIL, Benjamin	Oran 1779		CONER, Rader	Pasq 1779

CONGLECON, James	Beau 1786	COOK, Ephraim	Oran 1779
Thomas	Beau 1786	Frederick	Warr 1784
Wm	Beau 1786	Henry	Rowa 1765
CONLEY, Patrick	Pasq 1694	Henry	Oran 1779
CONN, James	Ruth 1782	Henry	Samp 1784
CONNALLY, George	Casw 1784	Jacob	Bute 1766
John Jr	Blad 1784	James	Ruth 1782
Thomas	Oran 1779	James	Oran 1779
CONNELL, Davis	Nash 1782	James	Samp 1784
John	Surr 1782	James	NorH 1780
CONNER, Burwell	Hert 1779	Jiles	NorH 1780
Darby	Oran 1779	John	Cart 1779
Dempsey	Pasq 1779	John	Bute 1766
Dempsey	Pasq 1789	John	Rowa 1761
Edward	Brun 1784	John	Oran 1779
James	Hali 1783	John	Samp 1784
James	Beau 1779	John	Blad 1784
James	Beau 1786	John	Hali 1783
John	Brun 1784	John	Pasq 1779
John	Surr 1782	John	NBer 1779
Lewis	Surr 1782	John	Wilk 1782
Mark	Jone 1779	John	NorH 1780
Merrick	Beau 1786	John	Surr 1782
Moses	Onsl 1771	John	Bert 1781
Susannah	Brun 1784	John	Pasq 1789
Wm	Ruth 1782	John Jr	Hali 1783
Wm	Hert 1779	John Sr	Hali 1783
Wm	Hert 1784	Joseph	Oran 1779
CONNERLY, Wm	Jone 1779	Joseph	Warr 1784
CONRAD, Christian	Surr 1782	Joshua	Surr 1782
CONSTANT, Wm	Rowa 1768	Josiah	Pasq 1789
CONWAY, James	Rowa 1770	Lazarus	Samp 1784
Wm	Onsl 1771	Lemuel	Camd 1782
CONYERS, James	Beau 1779	Mark	Hali 1783
John	Brun 1784	Martha	Wayn 1786
Susannah	Brun 1784	Mary	Surr 1782
COOB, James	Bert 1774	McDonaldson	Gran 1771
COOK, Abel	Surr 1782	Mercurius	Samp 1784
Abraham	Rowa 1765	Pat	Curr 1779
Abraham	Beau 1779	Pettit	Tyrr 1784
Abraham	Wilk 1782	Rentin	Bert 1774
Abraham	Gran 1771	Reuben	Bert 1781
Arthur	Wayn 1786	Richard	Gran 1785
Benj	Bert 1781	Richard	Warr 1784
Benjamin	Hert 1779	Sam	Bert 1781
Benjamin	Bute 1766	Samuel	Crav 1779
Benjamin	Waye 1786	Shem	Gran 1785
Benjamin	Hali 1783	Stephen	Beau 1779
Benjamin	Hert 1784	Thomas	Bute 1766
Berryman	Gran 1771	Thomas	Wayn 1786
Charles	Bute 1766	Thomas	Warr 1784
Charles	Beau 1779	Thomas	Beau 1779
Chas	Beau 1786	Thomas	Crav 1779
Cornelius	Rowa 1765	Thomas	Surr 1782
Cornelius	Samp 1784	Thomas & sons	Bute 1766
Daniel	Hert 1779	Thomas Jr	Crav 1779
Daniel	Blad 1784	Wm	Blad 1784
Daniel	Hert 1784	Wm	Gran 1785
Dempsey	Bert 1774	Wm	Hali 1783
Dempsey	Bert 1781	Wm	Bert 1774
Donald	Gran 1785	Wm	Bert 1774
Drury	Gran 1785	Wm	Surr 1782
Edward	Perq 1772	Wm	Gran 1771
Edward	Perq 1787	Wm	Bert 1781
Ephraim	Ruth 1782	Wm Jr	Surr 1782

Wm Sr	Bert 1781	COOPER, Wm	Mart 1779
COOKINGS, Joseph	Beau 1779	Wm	Samp 1784
COOLEY, Abraham	Surr 1782	Wm	Gran 1785
Edward	Bute 1766	Wm	Warr 1784
Gabriel	Wayn 1786	Wm	NorH 1780
John	Bute 1766	Wm	Gran 1771
John	Surr 1782	Wm	Bert 1781
Patrick	Pasq 1694	Wm & son Wm	Bute 1766
Robert	Pasq 1694	COOR, Thomas Jr	Wayn 1786
Samuel	Chow 1785	Thomas Sr	Wayn 1786
Wm	Samp 1784	COORS, David	Mont 1782
COON, Michael	Rowa 1761	COPE, Williamson	Gran 1785
Valentine	Rowa 1761	COPELAND, Aaron	Perq 1787
COONS, Wm	Hert 1784	Charles Jr	John 1784
COOPER, Alexander	Ruth 1782	Charles Sr	John 1784
Benjamin	Bute 1766	David	Oran 1779
Benjamin	Blad 1784	Eli	Hert 1779
Benjamin	Pasq 1779	Eli	Hert 1784
Cader	Bert 1781	Elisha	Hert 1779
Cannon	Bute 1766	Henry	Gate 1789
Cannon	Gran 1785	Hollowell	Hert 1779
Cannon	Gran 1771	Hollowell	Hert 1784
Coor	Samp 1784	Hugh	Oran 1779
Corneliis	Gran 1771	Isaiah	Chow 1785
Cornelius	Gran 1785	James	Hert 1779
David	Cart 1779	James	Hert 1784
David	Mart 1779	James Jr	Hert 1779
Edward	Nash 1782	James Jr	Hert 1784
Edward	Mart 1779	Jesse	Chow 1785
Fleet	Samp 1784	John	Hert 1779
Henry	Casw 1786	John	Blad 1784
Henry	Casw 1784	John	Hert 1784
Howell	Warr 1784	John	Surr 1782
James	Nash 1782	John Jr	Hert 1784
James	Blad 1784	Joseph	Chow 1785
James	Beau 1779	Joshua	Chow 1785
Jesse	Bert 1774	Samuel	Hali 1783
Jesse	Mart 1779	Silas	Gate 1789
John	Ruth 1782	Thomas	Hert 1779
John	Samp 1784	Thomas	Chow 1785
John	Casw 1784	Thomas	Hert 1784
John	Warr 1784	Wm	NorH 1780
John	Mont 1782	Zachariah	Gate 1789
John	Curr 1779	COPER, Thomas	Bert 1774
John	Onsl 1771	COPES, Jacob	Crav 1779
John	Surr 1782	COPHAM, Alger	Jone 1779
John Jr	Onsl 1771	COPLE, Wm	NorH 1780
Joseph	Mart 1779	COPLEY, John	Oran 1779
Joseph	Tyrr 1784	COPLIN, Isaac	Surr 1782
Joseph	Pasq 1779	COPPADGE, James	Bute 1766
Joseph	Gran 1771	COPPAGE, Wm	Perq 1787
Josiah	Curr 1779	COPPER, Micajah	Pasq 1789
Marcom	Nash 1782	COPPERSMITH, Benjamin	
Martha	Crav 1779		Pasq 1779
Orasha	Casw 1786	John	Pasq 1779
Reuben	Nash 1782	John	Pasq 1789
Russell	Warr 1784	CORBETT, Abel	Blad 1784
Samuel	Curr 1779	James	Brun 1782
Seth	Camd 1782	Joshua	John 1784
Thomas	Pasq 1694	Wm	John 1784
Thomas	Beau 1779	CORBIN, Benjamin	Hali 1783
Thomas	Curr 1779	Charnal	Hali 1783
Willis	Tyrr 1784	David	Gran 1771
Wm	Nash 1782	James	Brun 1784
Wm	Ruth 1782	James	Pitt 1786

CORBIN, Wm	NorH	1780	COTTON, James	Hert	1784
CORBITT, Samuel	Wayn	1786	Joab	Hali	1783
Wm	Wayn	1786	John	Dobb	1780
CORDELL, Abraham	Blad	1784	John	NorH	1780
Isham	Gran	1771	Josiah	NorH	1780
James	Gran	1771	Lydia	NorH	1780
John Sr	Gran	1771	Robert	Hali	1783
CORDEN, James	Gran	1785	Samuel	Wayn	1786
CORDER, Joel	Casw	1786	Theophilus	Hali	1783
John	Casw	1786	Thomas	Hert	1779
John	Gran	1771	Thomas	Hert	1784
Lewis	Casw	1786	Thomas	Wilk	1782
Patience	Gran	1771	Wm	Hert	1779
CORDEROY, Thomas	Beau	1779	Wm	Hall	1783
CORDES, Joel	Casw	1784	COTTRELL, Thomas	Wilk	1782
John	Casw	1784	COTTUM, Thomas	Wilk	1782
Joseph	Casw	1784	COUCH, Dedrick	Wayn	1786
Lewis	Casw	1784	John	Wilk	1782
CORDIN, Thomas	Beau	1786	Thomas	Oran	1779
CORDING, Benjamin	Beau	1779	Wm	Oran	1779
CORDWELL, Thomas	Surr	1782	COULTER, Alexander	Ruth	1782
COREY, Benjamin	Mart	1779	COUNCIL, Charles	Mart	1779
Eleazer	Cart	1779	Charles	Blad	1784
John	Gran	1771	David	Blad	1784
John Sr	Mart	1779	James	Mart	1779
CORKER, David	NorH	1780	James	Blad	1784
CORLEAN, John	Hali	1783	John	Blad	1784
CORLEW, John	NorH	1750	Michael	Nash	1782
John	Hali	1783	Nathan	Hali	1783
Wm	Hali	1783	Robert	Blad	1784
CORLEY, Catlet	Bute	1766	COUNCILL, Jesse	Surr	1782
John & son	Bute	1766	COUNCILMAN, Jacob	Oran	1779
CORNELIUS, Benj	Surr	1782	COUNTS, George	Rowa	1761
Roling	Surr	1782	COURT, John	Tyrr	1784
West	Surr	1782	COURTNER, Daniel	Oran	1779
Wm	Ruth	1782	Peter	Oran	1779
Wm	Wilk	1782	COURTNEY, John	Pasq	1779
CORPREW, John	Tyrr	1784	Wm	Oran	1779
Jonathan	Tyrr	1784	COURTRIGHT, John	Pasq	1779
Joshua	Tyrr	1784	COVEN, John	Hali	1783
Matthew	Tyrr	1784	COVINGTON, Benj	Rich	1790
Thomas	Tyrr	1784	Henry	Rich	1790
CORPUS, Thomas	Beau	1786	John	Rich	1790
CORRIE, Simeon Jr	Pasq	1779	John Jr	Rich	1790
CORRINDER, John	Wayn	1786	Levin	Crav	1779
CORRNICE, John	Casw	1784	Wallis	Rich	1790
CORRY, Thomas Sr	Pasq	1779	COWAN, Robert	Casw	1784
CORUN, Wm	Casw	1784	COWARD, Ann widow ofWm		
COSAND, Aaron	Perq	1787		Dobb	1780
Gabriel	Pasq	1789	Edward	Dobb	1780
COSTEN, Christian	Gate	1789	Edward Sr	Dobb	1780
Isaac	Gate	1789	Elisha s of Wm	Dobb	1780
James	Gate	1789	Frederick ofWm	Dobb	1780
COTHER, Wm	Oran	1779	James	Dobb	1780
COTTAL, Timothy	Camd	1782	James son ofWm	Dobb	1780
COTTER, Lewis	Rowa	1767	Joel	Rich	1790
Timothy	Pasq	1789	John	Dobb	1780
COTTON, Arthur	Hert	1779	John	Bert	1781
Arthur	Hert	1784	John B	Surr	1782
Cullen	Hert	1779	Needham	Dobb	1780
Cullen	Hert	1784	Wm	Hert	1779
Ephraim	Wayn	1786	COWEL, John	Curr	1779
Goscin	Hert	1784	Solomon	Curr	1779
Henry	Hali	1783	COWELL, Butler	Beau	1786
James	Hert	1779	Thomas	Tyrr	1784

COWELL, Wm	Tyrr 1784	COX, Thomas	Bute 1766
COWEN, Edward	Wilk 1782	Thomas	Rowa 1768
John	Wilk 1782	Thomas	Chow 1785
Thomas	Wilk 1782	Thomas	Curr 1779
COWLEY, Susannah	Pasq 1779	Wm	Oran 1779
COX, Aaron	Crav 1779	Wm	Gran 1785
Aaron	Onsl 1771	Wm	Beau 1786
Aaron	Pitt 1786	Wm Jr	Gran 1785
Abraham	Crav 1779	Zachariah	Rowa 1761
Abram	Beau 1786	Zachariah	Rowa 1768
Andrew	Dobb 1780	COYER, Sam	NorH 1780
Benj	Bert 1781	COYLE, Benjamin Jr	NBer 1779
Benjamin	Bert 1774	Elizabeth	Casw 1784
Cary	John 1784	John Jr	Rowa 1761
Chas	Onsl 1771	Patrick	Rowa 1761
Corey	Hali 1783	COZART, Ann	Gran 1785
Eleanor	Gran 1771	Anthony	Oran 1779
Elijah	Brun 1784	David	Gran 1785
Elijah	Brun 1782	Jacob	Gran 1785
Elisha	Chow 1785	John	Casw 1784
Gilbert	Blad 1784	Peter	Casw 1784
Herman	Dobb 1780	COZZARD, Anthony	Gran 1771
Howard	Gran 1785	Jacob	Gran 1771
Isaac	Oran 1779	John	Gran 1771
Jacob	Pasq 1789	CRAB, Benjamin	Curr 1779
James	Nash 1782	CRABB, Thomas	Bute 1766
James	Surr 1782	Wm	Hali 1783
Jeremiah	Pitt 1786	CRABTREE, Thomas	Oran 1779
John	Nash 1782	Wm Jr	Oran 1779
John	Dupl 1783	Wm Sr	Oran 1779
John	Dobb 1780	CRADDOCK, Eleazer	Tyrr 1784
John	Rowa 1768	Jodeph	Tyrr 1784
John	Blad 1784	Thomas	John 1784
John	Brun 1784	CRAFFORD, David	Surr 1782
John	Hali 1783	CRAFT, Chas	Onsl 1771
John	Brun 1782	John	Blad 1784
John	Pasq 1789	John	Gran 1771
Joseph	Surr 1782	Thomas	Gran 1771
Joseph Jr	Dupl 1783	CRAGG, John	Gran 1771
Joseph Sr	Dupl 1783	CRAIG, David	Oran 1779
Joshua	Surr 1782	James	Oran 1779
Josiah	Wayn 1786	John	Oran 1779
Levi	Crav 1779	John	Gran 1785
Lewis	Curr 1779	Richard	Pasq 1694
Marmaduke	Jone 1779	Samuel	Oran 1779
Marmaduke	Curr 1779	Wm	Oran 1779
Mary	Wayn 1786	CRAIN, John	Pasq 1779
Matthew	Surr 1782	CRANDALL, James	Beau 1786
Micajah	Wayn 1786	CRANE, Ambrose	Wilk 1782
Milley	Surr 1782	Elizabeth	Ruth 1782
Moses	Dobb 1780	Jacob	Surr 1782
Moses	Onsl 1771	James	Wilk 1782
Moses Sr	Dobb 1780	John	Ruth 1782
Nathan	Wilk 1782	John	Surr 1782
Peter	Warr 1784	Philemon	Wilk 1782
Phillip	Surr 1782	Thomas	Mont 1782
Phoeby	Wayn 1786	Wm	Ruth 1782
Presley	Hali 1783	Wm	Wilk 1784
Richard	Surr 1782	Wm	Wilk 1782
Robert	Bert 1774	CRANFORD, John	Onsl 1771
Robert	Pasq 1694	CRANK, Levi	Tyrr 1784
Seth	Pasq 1779	CRANSFORD, John	Onsl 1771
Simon	Blad 1784	CRANTZ, Christopher	Oran 1779
Solomon	Rowa 1768	CRASTARPHEN, James	Hali 1783
Thomas	Cart 1779	Perkins	Hali 1783

CRASTARPHEN, Robert	Hali	1783
Wm	Hali	1783
CRASWICK, Wm	Warr	1784
CRAVEN, John	Hali	1783
CRAWFORD, Benjamin	John	1784
Chas	Beau	1786
Don	Beau	1779
Henry	NorH	1750
Hugh	Oran	1779
Isaac	Ruth	1782
James	Gate	1789
John	Ruth	1782
Joseph	Pasq	1789
Lazarus	Wayn	1786
Mary	NorH	1780
Moses	Oran	1779
Richard	Wayn	1786
Robert	Wayn	1786
Samuel	Wilk	1782
Thomas	Hali	1783
Thomas	Rich	1790
Thomas	Rich	1790
Wm	Wayn	1786
Wm	Gate	1789
Wm	Beau	1786
CRAWFSON, John	Rich	1790
CRAWLEY, Daniel	Gran	1785
Daniel	Hali	1783
CRAWSON, Thomas	Beau	1786
CRAY, Wm	Onsl	1771
CRAYS, Margaret	Ruth	1782
CREAGER, Geo	Surr	1782
Henry	Surr	1782
CREAGHOM, Wm	NorH	1780
CRECKMAN, Joshua	Pasq	1779
CREECH, Ezekiel	Dobb	1780
Henry	Pasq	1694
James	Camd	1782
John	Dobb	1780
CREECY, Eliezer	Perq	1787
Frederick	Chow	1785
Levi	Perq	1787
Mary	Chow	1785
Nathan	Chow	1785
Samuel	Chow	1785
Thomas	Perq	1787
CREED, Bennett	Surr	1784
Matthew	Surr	1782
CREEKMAR, George	Nash	1782
CREEKMORE, Sam Jr	Curr	1779
Samuel	Curr	1779
CREEL, Charles	Dobb	1780
John	Dobb	1780
John Jr	Dobb	1780
Thomas	Dobb	1780
CREIGHTON, James	Beau	1779
CRENS, Stanley	Surr	1782
CRENSHAW, Abraham	Gran	1785
Chas	Wilk	1782
CRESAN, Joshua	Surr	1782
CRESBEY, Mary	Beau	1779
CRESON, Abraham	Rowa	1761
Abraham	Surr	1782
CRETCH, George	Bert	1781
CRETCHET, Jane	Albe	1694

CREW, Caleb	Gran	1785
Eliza his dau	Albe	1694
Elizabeth	Albe	1694
Gideon	Gran	1785
John	Albe	1694
CREWS, Gideon	Gran	1771
CRIMSHAW, Gideon	Gran	1771
CRIN, Macon	Surr	1782
Thomas	John	1784
CRISENBERRY, Mary	Casw	1784
Nicholas	Casw	1784
CRISHAM, James	Hert	1784
CRISP, Benjamin	Mart	1779
John	Casw	1784
Joseph	Crav	1779
Wm	Mart	1779
CRISWELL, John	Oran	1779
CRITCHARD, Thomas	Gran	1771
CRITCHER, Esther	Gran	1785
James	Gran	1785
Thomas	Gran	1785
CRITCHET, Bashink	John	1784
CRITCHFIELD, Amos	Surr	1782
Joshua	Surr	1782
Nathl	Surr	1782
Richard	NBer	1779
Wm	Surr	1782
CRITCHLOW, Bowman	Hert	1779
Carmichael	Hert	1779
Wm	Hert	1779
CRITTENDEN, Henry	NorH	1780
Robert	NorH	1780
CROCKER, Jacob	Bute	1766
John	Pasq	1779
John	Pasq	1789
CROCKETT, Saml	Surr	1782
CROFLIN, Jonas	Bute	1766
CROFT, John	Gran	1785
Thomas	Gran	1785
CROFTEN, Samuel	Gran	1785
CROFTON, Ambrose	Beau	1779
Thomas	Beau	1779
CROMDER, Stephen	Surr	1782
CROOKHAM, John	Pasq	1789
CROOKS, Clement	Tyrr	1784
Wm	Tyrr	1784
CROOM, Charles	Wayn	1786
Daniel	Wayn	1786
Hardy	Dobb	1780
Jesse Sr	Wayn	1786
John	Dobb	1780
Joshua	Dobb	1780
Major	Dobb	1780
Major Jr	Dobb	1780
CROPLEY, Ann	Albe	1694
Ann Jr	Albe	1694
Elizabeth	Albe	1694
John	Albe	1694
Mary	Albe	1694
Vines	Albe	1694
CROSS, Abel	Gate	1789
Benj	Wilk	1782
Benj Jr	Wilk	1782
Cyprian	Gate	1789
Davalts	Rowa	1761

CROSS, David	Gate 1789	CULPEPPER, Elizabeth	
Edward	Wilk 1782		Nash 1782
Elisha	Gate 1789	Henry	Mart 1779
Hardy	Gate 1789	Henry	Curr 1779
Henry	Mart 1779	James	Nash 1782
John	Hert 1779	Peter	Curr 1779
John	Mart 1779	Wm	Mont 1782
John	Hert 1784	CULPEPPPER, Erasmus	Nash 1782
Sarah	Gate 1789	CUMBO, Jacob	Brun 1784
Thomas	Mart 1779	John	Brun 1784
CROUCH, James	Rich 1790	Thomas	Brun 1784
John	Rich 1790	CUMMINGS, Benjamin	Crav 1779
CROW, Isaac	Wayn 1786	Charity	Perq 1772
John	Wayn 1786	David	Crav 1779
Sarah	Wayn 1786	James	Crav 1779
CROWDER, Matthew	Gran 1785	John	Crav 1779
CROWELL, Edward Sr	Hali 1783	Thomas	Onsl 1771
Edward Jr	Hali 1783	CUMMINS, Elizabeth	Tyrr 1784
James	Hali 1783	Francis	Tyrr 1784
Samuel	Hali 1783	George	Onsl 1771
CROWEll, Benjamin	Hali 1783	John	Ruth 1782
CROWLEY, David	Hali 1783	Jonathan	Casw 1786
CROWSON, John	Bute 1766	Joseph	Surr 1782
CROXON, Benjamin	Hali 1783	Saml	Surr 1782
CRUCH, Joshua	John 1784	CUMP, Aaron	Surr 1782
CRUIZE, Hardy	Casw 1784	CUNNINGHAM, Bruth	Hert 1784
CRUM, John	Surr 1782	James	Hert 1779
Joseph	NorH 1780	Jesse	Warr 1784
CRUMERLY, Wm	Blad 1784	John	Chow 1785
CRUMMETT, Absalom	Casw 1784	Nathaniel	Casw 1784
CRUMP, James	Mont 1782	Samuel	Hali 1783
John	Mont 1782	Wm	Bute 1766
Robert	Surr 1782	Wm	Warr 1784
CRUMPLER, Jacob	Samp 1784	Wm	Surr 1782
John	Samp 1784	CUNSEY, Thomas	Gran 1785
Matthew	Samp 1784	CURITAN, John	NorH 1780
West	Nash 1782	CURL, Thomas	Mart 1779
CRUMPTER, James	Casw 1784	Willis	Nash 1782
CRUMPTON, Aquilla	Casw 1784	Wilson	Nash 1782
Thomas	Casw 1784	CURLE, James	Gate 1789
CRUNMORE, James	Beau 1786	CURLIN, Courtney	Curr 1779
CRURY, Wm	Perq 1787	CURLING, Jacob	Camd 1782
CRUTCHFIELD, Mary	Jone 1779	CURRIER, James	Casw 1786
Richard & s Wm	Bute 1766	James	Casw 1784
Samuel	Warr 1784	Richard	Casw 1786
CUFF, John	Gate 1789	Richard	Casw 1784
CULBERHOUSE, Wm	Surr 1782	CURRIN, Elizabeth	Gran 1785
CULBERSON, David	Surr 1782	Hugh	Gran 1785
CULBERTSON, David	Casw 1784	James	Gran 1785
James	Casw 1786	James	Gran 1771
James	Casw 1784	CURRY, Alexander	Blad 1784
Wm	Casw 1786	Anguish	Rich 1790
Wm	Casw 1784	Archibald	Blad 1784
CULLEN, Jacob	Chow 1785	Daniel	Brun 1782
James	Beau 1779	Daniel	Rich 1790
John	Beau 1779	David	Bert 1781
Moses	Beau 1779	Duncan	Rich 1790
Nathan	Bert 1774	Edward	Rich 1790
Nathanl	Bert 1781	Elizabeth	Blad 1784
Nehemiah	Crav 1779	Jacob	Bert 1781
CULLEY, Francis	Crav 1779	James	Oran 1779
Thomas	Cart 1779	James	Casw 1784
CULLIFER, Nathl	Beau 1786	James	Bert 1781
CULLUM, Wm	Hali 1783	James & s John	Casw 1786
CULPEPPER, Daniel	Mont 1782	John	Blad 1784

CURRY, John	Casw 1784		DANCY, Jacob	NorH 1780
John	Surr 1782		James	NorH 1780
John Sr	Casw 1786		DANDLESTONES, Jacob	Ruth 1782
John s of Jams	Casw 1786		Wm	Ruth 1782
Malcomb	Blad 1784		DANFORD, Abraham	Brun 1784
Malcomb	Surr 1782		DANIEL, Abraham	Hert 1784
Mary	Casw 1786		Ambrose	Hali 1783
Samuel	Blad 1784		Ann	Gran 1771
Wm	Wilk 1784		Barton	Mont 1782
Wm	Surr 1782		Charley	Gran 1771
CURTIS, Ann	Beau 1779		Chisley	Gran 1785
David	Wilk 1784		David	Curr 1779
Henry	Casw 1786		Edmund	Hali 1783
James	Rowa 1768		James	Gran 1785
John	Beau 1779		James	Surr 1782
John	Beau 1786		James	Gran 1771
Joshua	Rowa 1761		John	Rich 1790
Joshua	Rowa 1768		John Wm	Gran 1785
Joshua	Wilk 1784		John Wm	Gran 1771
Moses	Mont 1782		Joseph	Gran 1785
Russell	Mont 1782		Joseph	Hali 1783
Samuel	Rowa 1761		Joseph	Hert 1784
Samuel & s Joe	Rowa 1768		Laughten	Onsl 1771
Thomas	Rowa 1768		Louis	Hali 1783
Thomas	NBer 1779		Mary	Hali 1783
CUSEY, Ann	Pitt 1786		Paul	Mont 1782
CUSTARD, James	Gran 1785		Peter	Hali 1783
CUSTER, John	Mont 1782		Reuben	Gran 1785
CUTHBERT, Benj	Wilk 1782		Thomas	Hali 1783
CUTHRELL, Moses	Crav 1779		Wm	Hali 1783
Thomas	Crav 1779		Wm	Hert 1784
CUTHRITE, Joshua	Crav 1779		Wm	Mont 1782
CUTLER, Aaron	Beau 1786		DANIELS, Archibald	Blad 1784
John	Beau 1786		Arthur	Beau 1786
Moses	Beau 1786		Belteshazar	Curr 1779
Robert	Beau 1786		Capt	Mart 1779
CUTONHOUSE, Thomas	Gran 1785		Daniel	Wayn 1786
Wellman	Gran 1785		David	Nash 1782
CVHANDLER, Wm	Surr 1782		Delilah	Dobb 1780
CYLERSON, Joseph	Pasq 1779		Edward	Beau 1786
			Ephraim	Wayn 1786
			Frederick	Nash 1782
			Geo	Beau 1786
DABLEY, Jacob	Oran 1779		George	Blad 1784
DABNEY, Cornelius	Casw 1786		Henry	Bert 1781
DACKARY, Thomas	Rich 1790		Isaac	Samp 1784
DADE, John Jr	NorH 1780		Isaac	Wayn 1786
DAFFER, Joseph	NorH 1780		Jacob	Cart 1779
DAFFIN, John	Hali 1783		Jacob	Samp 1784
DAFFORD, Jeremiah	Blad 1784		James	Nash 1782
DAGGET, Jeremiah	Hali 1783		James	Wayn 1786
DAILEY, Enoch	Camd 1782		James	Beau 1786
Jesse	Pasq 1789		James Jr	Wayn 1786
Wm	Oran 1779		John	Jone 1779
DALCHICH, James	Pasq 1789		John	Dobb 1780
DALE, Henry	Oran 1779		John	Oran 1779
Isaac	Oran 1779		John	Wayn 1786
Thomas	Dobb 1780		John	Beau 1786
Wm	Hali 1783		Joseph	Nash 1782
DAMERELL, Tegnel	Hali 1783		Joseph	Wayn 1786
DAMERON, Onesiphorus			Joseph	Curr 1779
	Perq 1787		Joseph Jr	Hert 1779
DAMMON, Onesiphorus	Pasq 1779		Joseph Sr	Hert 1779
DANBY, Elisha	Beau 1779		Matthew	Casw 1784
DANCE, Ethelred	Nash 1782		Nathan	Wayn 1786

DANIELS, Patterson	Oran 1779		DAUGE, James	Camd 1782
Robert	Mart 1779		James	Curr 1779
Robert	Brun 1784		John	Camd 1782
Robert Jr	Mart 1779		Mark	Camd 1782
Roger	Oran 1779		Mitchell	Curr 1779
Samuel	Curr 1779		Peter	Camd 1782
Sarah	Hert 1779		Tully	Curr 1779
Sarah	Dobb 1780		Unro	Curr 1779
Simon	Mart 1779		Willoughby	Curr 1779
Stephen	Brun 1784		DAUGHAN, James	NorH 1780
Widow	Blad 1784		John	NorH 1780
Wm	Hert 1779		DAUGHERTY, Agnes	Ruth 1782
Wm	Mart 1779		Anthony Jr	Oran 1779
Wm	Samp 1784		Anthony Sr	Oran 1779
Wm	Blad 1784		Benjamin	Samp 1784
Wm	Surr 1782		Bryan	NorH 1771
Wm Jr	Curr 1779		Edward	Gate 1789
Wm Sr	Curr 1779		Elisha	NorH 1780
DANK, John	Surr 1782		Everett	Hert 1779
DANOLD, Amy	Warr 1784		Isaac	Rowa 1761
DANUM, Hugh	Surr 1782		James	Ruth 1782
DARBY, George	Casw 1784		Jeremiah	Hert 1784
John	Albe 1694		Jethro	Hert 1779
Joseph	Bert 1781		Jethro	Hert 1784
Wm	Albe 1694		Phoebe & sons	Rowa 1761
DARDEN, Ann	Bute 1766		Simon	NorH 1780
Ann	Warr 1784		Wm	Hert 1779
David	Hert 1779		Wm	Rowa 1761
David	Hert 1784		Wm	Hert 1784
Elisha	Hert 1779		Wm	Gate 1789
Elisha	Hert 1784		DAUGHETY, John	Dobb 1780
James	Bute 1766		Solomon	Dobb 1780
James	Warr 1784		DAUGHKINS, Richard	Rowa 1761
Jesse	Samp 1784		DAUGHTERY, Jesse	NorH 1780
Jethro	Hert 1779		DAUGHTON, Mandrew	NorH 1780
Jethro	Hert 1784		DAUGHTRY, Arthur	Wayn 1786
John	Hert 1779		Jacob	Wayn 1786
John	Gate 1789		Joshua	Samp 1784
John Wm	Hert 1784		Lawrence	Wayn 1786
John the Elder	Hert 1779		DAVENPORT, Ann	Tyrr 1784
Joseph	Hert 1779		Augustine	Rowa 1768
Martha	Hert 1784		Daniel	Tyrr 1784
Reddick	Hert 1784		David	Tyrr 1784
Willie	Hert 1784		Dorrell	Nash 1782
Wm	Hert 1779		Elizabeth	Tyrr 1784
Wm	Samp 1784		Ephraim	Tyrr 1784
DARDIN, Ann	Warr 1784		Francis	Gran 1771
James	Warr 1784		Frederick	Tyrr 1784
DAREN, Anthony	Surr 1782		Gabriel	Casw 1784
DARLET, Anthony	Bert 1781		Hezekiah	Tyrr 1784
DARNAL, Charles	Bute 1766		Isaac	Tyrr 1784
Waugh & s Mose	Bute 1766		Jacob Jr	Tyrr 1784
DARNELL, Isaac	Wilk 1782		Jacob Sr	Tyrr 1784
Joseph	Surr 1782		James Sr	Tyrr 1784
Rachell	Wilk 1782		James s of Wm	Tyrr 1784
DARNIL, Peter	Bert 1774		John	Cart 1750
DARNOLD, Joseph	Warr 1784		John	Nash 1782
DARWIN, John	Surr 1782		John	Tyrr 1784
DAUCH, John	Dobb 1780		Joseph Jr	Tyrr 1784
Waller	Dobb 1780		Joseph Sr	Tyrr 1784
DAUGE, Angelus	Curr 1779		Joshua	Tyrr 1784
Benjamin	Curr 1779		Moses	Tyrr 1784
Caleb	Camd 1782		Rachel	Tyrr 1784
Elias	Curr 1779		Wm	Surr 1782
Hezekiah	Curr 1779		DAVEY, James	Blad 1784

DAVEY, James	Casw 1784	DAVIS, Hardiway	Warr 1784
John	Oran 1779	Henry	Casw 1786
Robert	Casw 1784	Henry	Samp 1784
Wm	Casw 1784	Henry	Casw 1784
DAVIDSON, Alexander	Ruth 1782	Henry	NorH 1780
Amos	Bert 1781	Henry Jr	Casw 1784
David	Surr 1782	Henry Sr	Casw 1786
George	Mont 1782	Henry Sr	Casw 1784
Henry	Hali 1783	Hester	Gran 1785
John	Bert 1781	Hezekiah	Blad 1784
Thomas	NorH 1780	Hezekiah	Casw 1784
Wm	Gate 1789	Hugh	Wayn 1786
DAVIS, Abraham	Pasq 1779	Humphrey	Gran 1771
Absalom	Gran 1785	Ichabod	Dobb 1780
Absalom	Gran 1771	Isaac	Cart 1779
Andrew	Oran 1779	Isham	Hali 1783
Anthony	Pasq 1779	Isom	Wilk 1784
Anthony	Pasq 1789	Jacob	John 1784
Archibald	Hali 1783	James	Pasq 1694
Archibald	Pasq 1779	James	Dobb 1780
Arthur	Hali 1783	James	Rowa 1768
Arthur	John 1784	James	Oran 1779
Arthur	Pasq 1779	James	Samp 1784
Arthur	Pasq 1789	James	Wayn 1786
Augustine	Gran 1785	James	Gran 1785
Augustine	Gran 1771	James	Hali 1783
Baxter	Blad 1784	James	NBer 1779
Baxter	Gran 1771	James	Wilk 1782
Benj	Beau 1786	James	Surr 1782
Benj	Pasq 1789	James	Gate 1789
Benjamin	Jone 1779	James Jr	Dobb 1780
Benjamin	Cart 1779	Jane	Bute 1766
Benjamin	Oran 1779	Jesse	Hali 1783
Benjamin	Hali 1783	Jesse	Pasq 1779
Boswell	Casw 1784	Jesse	Bert 1781
Caleb	Pasq 1779	Jesse	Pasq 1789
Caleb	Perq 1787	John	Warr 1784
Chas	Surr 1782	John	Nash 1782
Cornelius	Casw 1786	John	Albe 1679
Daniel	Hert 1784	John	Pasq 1694
David	Dobb 1780	John	Bute 1766
David	Pasq 1779	John	Oran 1779
Dedrick	Pasq 1779	John	Mart 1779
Dedrick	Pasq 1789	John	Samp 1784
Delphin	Hali 1783	John	Blad 1784
Devotion	Pasq 1779	John	Wayn 1786
Devotion	Pasq 1789	John	Casw 1784
Devotion Jr	Pasq 1789	John	John 1784
Devotion Sr	Pasq 1789	John	Pasq 1779
Dinah	Perq 1772	John	Warr 1784
Diocletion	Nash 1782	John	NorH 1780
Edward	NorH 1780	John	Surr 1782
Elias	Curr 1779	John	Gran 1771
Elisha	Tyrr 1784	John	Gate 1789
Eliz	Pasq 1789	John	Perq 1787
Evan	Wilk 1782	John	Pasq 1789
Francis	Camd 1782	John Capt	Hali 1783
Frederick	Pasq 1779	John Jr	Casw 1784
Frederick	Gran 1771	John Jr	Tyrr 1784
Frederick	Pasq 1789	John Sr	Tyrr 1784
Gabriel	Mont 1782	John Sr	Pasq 1779
Geo	Bert 1781	Jonathan	Warr 1784
George	Curr 1779	Jonathan	Casw 1786
George A	Casw 1786	Jonathan	Casw 1784
Goodoram	Hali 1783	Jonathan	Rich 1790

Joseph	Cart 1779	Solomon	Cart 1779
Joseph	Dobb 1780	Solomon	Grsn 1785
Joseph	Blad 1784	Solomon	Gran 1771
Joseph	Pasq 1779	Stephen	Bute 1766
Joseph	Brun 1782	Tabitha	Nash 1782
Joseph	Pasq 1789	Thomas	Warr 1784
Joshua	Dobb 1780	Thomas	Dupl 1779
Joshua	Wayn 1786	Thomas	Dobb 1780
Joshua	Pasq 1779	Thomas	Wayn 1786
Josiah	Cart 1779	Thomas	Brun 1784
Josiah	Curr 1779	Thomas	Hali 1783
Josias	NorH 1780	Thomas	Hert 1784
Lawson	Pitt 1786	Thomas	Tyrr 1784
Letitia	Surr 1782	Thomas	Pasq 1779
Levi	Pasq 1789	Thomas	Wilk 1784
Lewis	Bute 1766	Thomas	Brun 1782
Lewis	Gran 1771	Thomas	Onsl 1771
Littleton	Crav 1779	Thomas	Gran 1771
Margaret	Casw 1784	Thomas	Pasq 1789
Marmaduke	Perq 1772	Thomas Capt	Pasq 1789
Martha	Dobb 1780	Thomas Jr	Pasq 1789
Mary	Dobb 1780	Tufloh	Pitt 1786
Mary Ann	Pasq 1789	Turner	Blad 1784
Matilda	Tyrr 1784	Wicker	Cart 1779
Matthew	Warr 1784	Windall	Dobb 1780
Matthew	Bute 1766	Wm	Warr 1784
Matthew	Surr 1782	Wm	Jone 1779
Milcah	Tyrr 1784	Wm	Rowa 1761
Morgan	Surr 1782	Wm	Rowa 1765
Moses	Gate 1789	Wm	Oran 1779
Nancy	Hali 1783	Wm	Blad 1784
Nathan	Cart 1779	Wm	Brun 1784
Nathan	Pasq 1789	Wm	Hali 1783
Nathaniel	Mont 1782	Wm	John 1784
Nicholas	Oran 1779	Wm	Pasq 1779
Nicholas	Casw 1786	Wm	Wilk 1782
Nicholas	Casw 1784	Wm	NorH 1780
Peter	Warr 1784	Wm	Surr 1782
Peter & sons	Bute 1766	Wm	Beau 1786
Ransom	Warr 1784	Wm	Pasq 1789
Reuben	Pasq 1789	Wm & s Wm Jr	Bute 1766
Reuben Jr	Pasq 1789	Zephaniah	Tyrr 1784
Reuben Sr	Pasq 1779	DAVISSON, John	Mart 1779
Richard	Wayn 1786	Moreland	Mart 1779
Richard	Tyrr 1784	DAW, John	Crav 1779
Robert	Oran 1779	DAWES, Ann	Hert 1784
Robert	Casw 1784	Benjamin	Hert 1779
Robert	Tyrr 1784	James	Hert 1779
Robert	Pasq 1779	James	Hert 1784
Robert	Pasq 1789	John	Pasq 1694
Roger	Brun 1784	DAWKINS, Geo	Rich 1790
Saml	Surr 1782	John	Rich 1790
Sampson	Samp 1784	Saml	Rich 1790
Samson	Surr 1782	DAWLEY, Jonathan	Curr 1779
Samuel	Warr 1784	DAWSON, Dempsey	Nash 1782
Samuel	Pasq 1694	Edward	Rowa 1765
Samuel	Hali 1783	Henry	NorH 1780
Samuel	Hert 1784	Joel	Dobb 1780
Samuel	Pasq 1779	John	Hali 1783
Samuel	Warr 1784	Lemuel	Beau 1786
Samuel	NBer 1779	Levi	Crav 1779
Sandford	Pasq 1789	Patience	Wayn 1786
Sanford	Pasq 1779	Richard	Bert 1781
Shadrack	Pasq 1779	Solomon	Hali 1783
Shadrack	Pasq 1789	Solomon	NorH 1780

DAWSON, Thomas	Dobb 1780	DEFREES, John	Wilk 1782
Wm	Wayn 1786	DEHULAK, MIcajah	Gran 1784
DAY, Edward	NorH 1780	DELANEY, Benjamin	Dup] 1783
Francis	Casw 1784	Wm	Rowa 1761
John	Casw 1784	DELBERY, Isham	NorH 1780
Robert	Bute 1766	DELOACH, Nathl	NorH 1780
Wm & Mary	Brun 1782	Thomas	NorH 1780
Wm Jr	Brun 1782	Wm	NorH 1780
DAYNAS, Jeremiah	Rich 1790	DELON, Charles	Pasq 1779
DEAL, Edward	Dobb 1780	Chas	Pasq 1789
Milbery	NorH 1780	Mark	PasQ 1779
Richard	NorH 1780	Mark	Pasq 1789
Wm	Dobb 1780	DEMOPSON, Abraham	Wilk 1782
Wm	Wayn 1786	DEMOS, Louis	Wilk 1784
Wm	Perq 1787	DEMOSS, Lewis	Wilk 1782
DEAN, Abraham	Hali 1783	DEMPSEY, Geo	NorH 1780
Anthony	Beau 1786	Geo	Bert 1781
Daniel	Hert 1784	Joshua	Bert 1781
Henry	Nash 1782	Melvin	Bert 1781
Isaac	Hali 1783	Thorogood	Hali 1783
James	Nash 1782	DEMRY, Samuel	NorH 1780
John	Bert 1781	DENBY, Benj	Pasq 1789
Moses Jr	Beau 1786	James	Bute 1766
Moses Sr	Beau 1786	John	Bute 1766
Richard	Samp 1784	Nathan	Pasq 1789
Sam	Bert 1781	Sam	Beau 1786
Solomon	Bert 1781	Samuel	Bute 1766
Thomas	Rowa 1768	DENMAN, Moses	Wilk 1782
Wm	Bute 1766	DENMARK, Wm	Crav 1779
DEANES, Daniel	Hert 1779	DENNEY, Aaron	Wilk 1782
DEANS, Daniel	Wayn 1786	Benjamin	Gran 1785
Dempsey	Wayn 1786	Edmund	Wilk 1782
James	Wayn 1786	James	Oran 1779
Jeremiah	Nash 1782	James	Gran 1771
Richard	Nash 1782	John	Oran 1779
DEARMAN, Thomas	Rich 1790	Robert	Gran 1771
DEARSON, Solomon	Rich 1790	Zachariah	Casw 1784
DEATHERIDGE, Geo	Surr 1782	DENNING, Robert	Wayn 1786
John	Surr 1782	Wm	Wayn 1786
Kellis	Surr 1782	DENNIS, Andrew	Mont 1782
Wm	Surr 1782	Daniel	Dobb 1780
DEBENPORT, Wm	Pitt 1786	Edward	Rowa 1768
DEBERRY, Absalom	NorH 1780	Ignatius	Casw 1784
Benj	NorH 1780	John	Casw 1786
Henry	Mont 1782	John	Casw 1784
John	NorH 1780	John	Wilk 1784
Peter	NorH 1780	Samuel	Rowa 1768
Solomon	NorH 1780	Thomas	Rowa 1768
DEBORD, Geo	Surr 1782	Thomas	Mont 1782
George	Bute 1766	Wm	Wilk 1784
DEBOW, Benjamin	Casw 1784	DENNISON, Geo	Beau 1786
Frederick	Casw 1784	DENNY, Azariah	Surr 1782
John Rev	Oran 1779	David	Dobb 1780
Mrs	Oran 1779	George	Wilk 1784
DECAMP, John	Blad 1784	James	Wilk 1779
DEENING, David	Oran 1779	John	Wilk 1784
DEENS, Thomas	Nash 1782	John	Beau 1786
DEERE, George	Albe 1694	Wm	Surr 1782
John	Albe 1694	DENSON, Benjamin	Nash 1782
DEES, Gabriel	Rich 1270	James	NorH 1780
James	Rich 1790	Jethro	Nash 1782
DEESE, Hardy	Samp 1784	John	Wayn 1786
Sampson	Samp 1784	John	Rich 1790
Wm	Blad 1784	Joseph	Nash 1782
DEFNELL, John	Hali 1783	Mary	Nash 1782

DENSON, Thomas	Wayn 1786	DICKEY, James	Oran 1779
Wm	Bute 1766	James & s John	Rowa 1768
DENT, Joshua	Perq 1772	James Jr	Rowa 1768
DENTON, Arthur	Surr 1782	John	Oran 1779
B.	Gran 1785	John	Casw 1786
Elizabeth	Hali 1783	Zachariah	Oran 1779
James	Hert 1779	DICKINSON, Daniel	Wayn 1786
James Jr	Hert 1784	David	Hert 1779
James Sr	Hert 1784	David	Wayn 1786
Saml	Gran 1771	Griffin	Warr 1784
DENVER, Chas	Bert 1781	Henry	Wayn 1786
DESAM, Frederick	Surr 1782	Isaac	Wayn 1786
DESERN, Francis	Oran 1779	James	Hert 1779
James	Oran 1779	Joel	Wayn 1786
DESMOND, Benj	Rich 1790	Joseph	Hert 1779
Jeremiah	Dobb 1780	Lewis	NBer 1779
John	Dobb 1780	Martin	Warr 1784
DEVAUGHAN, Thomas	Gran 1785	Samuel	Chow 1785
DEVENY, Aaron	Ruth 1782	Shadrack	Wayn 1786
DEVINE, Michael	Oran 1779	Wm	Nash 1782
DEW, John	Nash 1782	DICKS, John	Gate 1789
DEWBERRY, Giles	Bute 1766	Nathan	Rowa 1765
Jenkins	NorH 1780	Zachariah	Rowa 1765
DEWER, Sarah	Curr 1779	DICKSON, Aaron	NBer 1779
DEWEY, David	Rowa 1765	George	Cart 1779
DEWITT, Joseph	Brun 1784	Henry	Cart 1779
DIAS, Wm	Beau 1786	James	Cart 1779
DICKENS, Benjamin	Hali 1783	James	Dupl 1783
David	Casw 1786	John	Wilk 1782
Ephraim	Hali 1783	John	Rich 1790
Henry	Warr 1784	Joseph	Dupl 1783
Henry	Bute 1766	Louis	Chow 1785
James	Casw 1786	Murphrey	Dobb 1780
James	Casw 1784	Richard	Rich 1790
Joseph	Hali 1783	Robert	Dupl 1783
Joseph	Hert 1784	Solomon	Cart 1779
Robert	Casw 1784	Thomas	Bute 1766
Robert	Gran 1771	Wm	Bute 1766
Wm	Hali 1783	DIFFEY, Wm	Rowa 1761
DICKERSON, David	NorH 1780	DILL, Annela	Casw 1786
Esau	Hert 1779	Edward	Cart 1779
Esau	NorH 1780	Elizabeth	Ruth 1782
Francis Jr	Gran 1771	John	Oran 1779
Francis Sr	Gran 1771	John	Casw 1786
Griffin	Bute 1766	John Jr	Casw 1786
Griffith	Surr 1782	John Sr	Casw 1786
Isaac	NorH 1780	Richard	Casw 1786
James	Cart 1779	DILLAHUNTY, Daniel	Dobb 1780
John	Cart 1779	John	Dobb 1780
John	Hert 1779	Samuel	Dobb 1780
John	Hert 1784	DILLARD, Wm	Hali 1783
John	NorH 1780	Zachariah	Hali 1783
John	Gran 1771	DILLON, Daniel	Rowa 1765
John Jr	Gran 1785	Ichabod	Perq 1772
John Sr	Gran 1785	James	Tyrr 1784
Martha	NorH 1780	James	Surr 1782
Martin	Bute 1766	John	Gran 1785
Martin	Warr 1779	John	Tyrr 1784
Nathaniel	Casw 1786	DILSON, Edward Jr	NorH 1780
Wm	Bute 1766	Edward Sr	NorH 1780
Wm	Gran 1785	John	NorH 1780
Wm	Gran 1771	DIMSEY, John	Blad 1784
DICKEY, Anthony	Ruth 1782	DINBEE, John	Pasq 1779
David	Ruth 1782	DINKINS, Dion	Warr 1784
David	Casw 1786	James	Wayn 1786

DINKINS, John	Warr	1784
DINUM, Maston	Wilk	1782
DINWIDDIE, Henry	Oran	1779
John	Casw	1784
Sarah	Blad	1784
DIRRAH, John	Blad	1784
DIRSOR, Wm	Warr	1784
DISHANNON, Augustine		
	Chow	1785
DISON, Francis	Curr	1779
Thomas	Jone	1779
DIX, Peter	Rowa	1760
Peter & s Jame	Rowa	1768
Wm	Casw	1786
Zachariah	Oran	1779
DIXON, Adam	Oran	1779
Benj	Beau	1786
Benjamin	Beau	1779
Charles	Casw	1784
Christopher	Casw	1786
Elisha	Hali	1783
Eliz	Beau	1786
Henry	Casw	1784
Henry, Est	Casw	1784
Hosea	Nash	1782
Jacob	Casw	1784
James	Oran	1779
James	Beau	1779
James	Beau	1786
Jesse	Hali	1783
John	Oran	1779
John	Casw	1784
John	Perq	1787
Josiah	Hali	1783
Josias	Casw	1784
Martha	Casw	1786
Michael Jr	Casw	1784
Pilman	Casw	1784
Thomas	Oran	1779
Thomas	Beau	1779
Thomas	Wilk	1782
Thomas	Beau	1786
Thomas Jr	Beau	1779
Tillman	Casw	1786
Wm	Oran	1779
Wm	Beau	1779
Wynne	Casw	1786
DIXSON, Wm	Crav	1779
DOAK, James	Surr	1782
John s James	Rowa	1761
Robert of John	Rowa	1761
DOAN, Esther	Blad	1784
Jeremiah	Blad	1784
John	Blad	1784
DOBBINS, Campbell	Casw	1784
Catherine	Casw	1784
Hugh	Casw	1784
John	Casw	1784
Rachel	Casw	1784
Robert	Oran	1779
DOBBS, John	Wilk	1782
Laddy	Wilk	1782
Richard	Crav	1779
DOBIE, Farmsell	Pasq	1694
James	Pasq	1694

DOBIE, John	Pasq	1694
DOBSON, John	Rowa	1772
Wm	Surr	1782
DOCK, Isaac	NorH	1780
DODD, Aaron	Wayn	1786
David	Samp	1784
Richard	Gran	1771
DODRILL, John	Bert	1781
DODSON, Charles	Gran	1785
Chas	Gran	1771
Hightower	Nash	1782
Reuben	Surr	1782
Wm	Gran	1785
Wm	Gran	1771
DOEREO, John	Albe	1679
DOLBY, Abraham	Curr	1779
Gerard	Hert	1779
Israel	Hert	1784
DOLDAY, Henry	Gate	1789
Joseph	Gate	1789
DOLES, Benjamin	Hali	1783
Jesse	Hali	1783
John	Hali	1783
Sarah	Hali	1783
DOLLAR, Ambrose	Casw	1784
Elisha	Oran	1779
John	Gran	1785
Lewis	Gran	1785
Wm	Samp	1784
DOLLARHIDE, Aquilla	Casw	1784
Cornell	Casw	1784
Ezekiel	Casw	1784
Francis	Casw	1784
DOLLESON, Francis	Surr	1782
DOLLING, Mary	Chow	1785
DONALD, Thomas	Rowa	1760
DONALDS, Robert	Chow	1785
DONALDSON, Andrew	Perq	1787
Hannah	Casw	1784
Robert	Casw	1784
DONELSON, Thomas	Ruth	1782
Thomas Sr	Ruth	1782
DONLDSON, Wm	NorH	1780
DONNAN, David	Wayn	1786
DONNELLY, John	Blad	1784
DONOHO, Thomas	Casw	1784
Wm	Casw	1786
Wm	Casw	1784
DORCEY, John	Curr	1779
DORCH, Elizabeth	Nash	1782
Isaac	Nash	1782
Lewis	Nash	1782
DORCHESTER, James	Rowa	1760
DORMAN, John	Nash	1782
DORRES, Wm	Casw	1786
DORSETT, Nancy	Oran	1779
Phillip	Oran	1779
Wm	Oran	1779
DORTON, David	Ruth	1782
DOSHER, Richard	Brun	1784
Tully	Blad	1784
DOTHAN, Hawkins	Wilk	1782
DOTSON, Joshua	Surr	1782
DOUD, John	Blad	1784
DOUGAN, Thomas	Rowa	1768

DOUGH, George	Curr 1779		DRAKE, Albridgton	Nash 1782
John	Curr 1779		Cornelius	Camd 1782
Richard	Curr 1779		Edmund	Nash 1782
Samson	Curr 1779		James	Nash 1782
DOUGHTY, Edward	Curr 1779		Jonathan	Mart 1779
DOUGLAS, Abel	Curr 1779		Matthew	Nash 1782
Abraham	Surr 1782		Nathaniel	Nash 1782
Alexander	Wilk 1782		Tristram	Hali 1783
Alexr	Gran 1771		Wm 800 acres	Nash 1782
Andrew	Wilk 1782		DRAPER, Hannah	Perq 1772
Benjamin	Casw 1784		John	John 1784
Daniel	Mont 1782		Joseph	Perq 1772
Daniel	Rich 1790		Joseph	Perq 1787
David	Oran 1779		Silas	Perq 1787
Hannah	Pasq 1789		Thomas	Perq 1787
James	Curr 1779		Wm	Rowa 1768
John	Dupl 1783		DREDDING, John	Dobb 1780
John	Oran 1779		DRENAN, Robert	Surr 1782
John	Casw 1784		DRESSLER, Joseph	Pasq 1789
John	Surr 1782		DREW, John	Brun 1784
John	Rich 1790		Joshua	Hali 1783
Joseph	Gran 1785		Newitt	Samp 1784
Radham	Wayn 1786		Solomon	Hali 1783
Sarah	Mont 1782		Thomas	Hali 1783
Stephen	Chow 1785		Wm	Samp 1784
Thomas	Casw 1784		DREWRY, Amey	Gran 1785
Thomas	NorH 1780		Charles	Warr 1784
Wm	Oran 1779		Ellis	Gran 1771
DOUTEY, Benajah	Onsl 1771		DRINKLE, Timothy	Gran 1771
DOVE, John	Rich 1790		DRISCOLL, Joseph	Gran 1785
Thomas	Surr 1782		Timothy	Gran 1785
DOVER, Job	NorH 1780		DRIVER, Bird	Gran 1785
DOW, Seth	Blad 1784		Dempsey	Nash 1782
Wm	Beau 1779		Giles & s Shaw	Bute 1766
DOWDAY, John	Cart 1779		John	Nash 1782
DOWDY, Billy	Beau 1779		John	Hert 1779
James Sr	Beau 1779		Joseph	Pasq 1779
DOWELL, James	Casw 1784		Samuel	Hert 1784
John	Casw 1784		Wm	Hert 1779
DOWLEY, Wm	Blad 1784		Wm	Hert 1784
DOWN, David	Hali 1783		DROLLINGER, Henry	Oran 1779
DOWNEY, Daniel	Blad 1784		DRONEBERRY, Lodwick	Oran 1779
James	Gran 1785		DRY, Mrs Mary Jane	Brun 1784
James Jr	Gran 1785		Wm estate	Brun 1784
John	Gran 1785		DUACKS, James	Hali 1783
DOWNING, Elisha	Dobb 1780		Magdalen	Samp 1784
Elisha	Wayn 1786		DUBBERLY, Jack	Crav 1779
George	Dobb 1780		John	Crav 1779
George	Wayn 1786		Wm	Crav 1779
James	Mart 1779		DUBOIS, John	Blad 1784
Joseph	Dobb 1780		Stephen	Blad 1784
Richard	Wayn 1786		DUDLEY, Aaron	Mart 1779
Wm	Hert 1779		Abraham	Cart 1779
Wm	Hert 1784		Chas	Surr 1782
DOWNS, Richard	Mont 1782		Christopher	Casw 1786
Thomas	Mont 1782		Daniel	Samp 1784
Wm	Hali 1783		Guilford	Hali 1783
DOYLE, Daniel	Surr 1782		John	Curr 1779
Edward	Casw 1784		Levi	Samp 1784
James	Blad 1784		Nal	Curr 1779
James	Surr 1782		Sarah	Mont 1782
DOZIER, Daniel	Tyrr 1784		Stephen	Cart 1779
John	Nash 1782		Susannah	Cart 1779
Wm, deceased	Nash 1782		Thomas	Warr 1784
DOZWELL, John	Gran 1771		Thomas	Cart 1779

DUDLEY, Thomas	Curr 1779	DUNCAN, John	Rowa 1770
Wm	Curr 1779	John	Oran 1779
Wm	Onsl 1771	John	Camd 1782
DUFF, Dennis	Ruth 1782	John	Wilk 1782
DUFFY, Hugh	Pasq 1789	John Jr	Gran 1785
DUGGAN, Aaron	Mart 1779	John Sr	Gran 1785
John	Gran 1785	John Wm	Gran 1785
Wm	Mart 1779	Laurence	Wilk 1782
Wm	Bert 1781	Mary	Casw 1784
DUGGS, Benjamin	Wilk 1782	Thomas	Surr 1782
DUKE, Andrew	Curr 1779	Wm	Gran 1785
Arthur	Dobb 1780	Wm	Hali 1783
Benjamin	Warr 1784	Wm	Surr 1782
Britain	Warr 1784	Wm Drury	Brun 1782
Burwewll	Warr 1784	DUNFORD, Wm	Gate 1789
Elizabeth	NorH 1771	DUNKIN, Elias	Brun 1782
Green	Warr 1784	Wm Drury	Brun 1782
Harold	Warr 1784	DUNKINS, Wm	Oran 1768
Hezekiah	Tyrr 1784	DUNLAP, James	Rowa 1761
Jacob	Nash 1782	James	Surr 1782
James	Crav 1779	John	Surr 1782
John	Warr 1784	DUNLOP, James	Oran 1779
John	Bute 1766	DUNMAN, Joseph	Oran 1779
John	Dobb 1780	DUNN, Benjamin	Wayn 1786
John	Oran 1779	Francis	Crav 1779
John	Crav 1779	George	Hert 1779
John	NorH 1780	Jacob	Samp 1784
John	Gate 1789	James	Onsl 1771
Joseph & s Maj	Bute 1766	John	Crav 1779
Mary	Warr 1784	John	NorH 1780
Matthew	Warr 1784	John Jr	Crav 1779
Peter	Crav 1779	Joseph	Ruth 1782
Robert	Tyrr 1784	Patrick	Oran 1779
Samuel	Warr 1784	Richard	Samp 1784
Samuel & s Bri	Bute 1766	Richard	Mont 1782
Simon	Warr 1784	Thomas	Oran 1779
Sterling	Warr 1784	Thomas	Wayn 1786
Wm	Warr 1784	Thomas	Crav 1779
Wm	Oran 1779	Walter	Dobb 1780
Wm & s Green	Bute 1766	Wm	Ruth 1782
DULANEY, Thomas	Onsl 1771	Wm	Crav 1779
Thomas Jr	Onsl 1771	Wm	Mont 1782
DUMAN, Thomas	Curr 1779	DUNNAGIN, Thomas	Surr 1782
DUNAHO, Ann	Wilk 1782	DUNNAWAY, Abraham	Casw 1784
DUNBAR, James	Tyrr 1784	DUNNEGAN, Charles	Oran 1779
James	Beau 1779	Wm	Oran 1779
James	Beau 1786	DUNNIGAN, James	Surr 1782
Susannah	Beau 1779	John Jr	Surr 1782
DUNCAN, Abraham	Casw 1784	Joseph	Surr 1782
Andrew	Rich 1790	Thomas Sr	Surr 1782
Benj	Wilk 1782	DUNNING, Jeremiah	Bert 1781
David	Rowa 1761	Jesse	Bert 1781
David	Camd 1782	John	Bert 1781
David	Brun 1782	Sam	Bert 1781
Dennis	Brun 1784	Shadrack	Bert 1781
Elias	Brun 1782	DUNSCOMB, James	Chow 1785
Elijah	Casw 1784	DUNSTON, Edmund	Bert 1781
George	Gran 1785	DUNTON, Martin	Tyrr 1784
George	Hali 1783	DUPORT, Anna	Mart 1779
Harrison	Gran 1785	DUPREE, James	Blad 1784
Henry	Wilk 1782	Jesse	NorH 1780
James	Beau 1779	Lewis	Brun 1784
James	Surr 1782	DURANT, George	Albe 1679
Jesse	Casw 1784	DURDELL, Blackman	Gran 1785
John	Gran 1779	DURDEN, Elisha	Hert 1779

DURDEN, Wm	Hert 1779	
DURDINS, Cornelius	Wayn 1786	
Jacob	Wayn 1786	
John Jr	Wayn 1786	
John Sr	Wayn 1786	
Richard	Wayn 1786	
Wm	Wayn 1786	
DURGAN, Jeremiah	Bert 1781	
DURHAM, Achilles	Oran 1779	
Edward	Warr 1784	
Edward	Bute 1766	
Elizabeth	John 1784	
Humphrey	Surr 1782	
Isaac	Casw 1786	
James	Warr 1784	
James	Perq 1772	
James	Surr 1782	
John	Warr 1784	
John	Bute 1766	
John	Oran 1779	
Mary	Casw 1786	
Matthew	Oran 1779	
Matthew & s Sa	Bute 1766	
Sam	Bute 1766	
Thomas	Oran 1779	
Thomas	Mont 1782	
Wm	Oran 1779	
Wm	John 1784	
Wm	Warr 1784	
Wm & son Wm	Bute 1766	
Wm Jr	Warr 1784	
DURNAL, Wm	Ruth 1782	
DURNING, James	Oran 1779	
DUROW, Sarah	Perq 1787	
DURRELL, John	Onsl 1771	
DURST, Hezekiah	Casw 1784	
DUTLEY, Hugh	Pasq 1779	
DUTY, Absalom	NBer 1779	
Matthew	Bute 1766	
Richard	Gran 1785	
Richard	Gran 1771	
Wm	Bute 1766	
Wm	Casw 1784	
Wm	Warr 1784	
DUVAUGHAN, Samuel	Nash 1782	
DWYER, Dennis	Bert 1781	
Jonathan	Bert 1781	
Patrick	Bert 1781	
Sam	Bert 1781	
DYAR, James	Curr 1779	
James	Gran 1771	
DYE, Averitt	Blad 1784	
Martin	Warr 1784	
Stephen	Blad 1784	
DYER, Elisha	Wilk 1782	
Elizabeth	Wilk 1782	
Haman	Wilk 1782	
James	Gran 1785	
Joel	Wilk 1782	
John	Wilk 1782	
John	Surr 1782	
Manoah	Wilk 1782	
Mary	Wilk 1782	
Saml	Surr 1782	
Samuel	Casw 1784	

DYSON, Jane	Blad 1784	
Solomon dec	Blad 1784	
EADY, Samuel	Curr 1779	
Sarah	Curr 1779	
EAGAN, Robert	Chow 1785	
EAGERTON, James	Wayn 1786	
James	Warr 1784	
Timothy	Warr 1784	
EAGLE, Joseph	Brun 1784	
EAGLESON, James	Blad 1784	
EAK, Wm	Casw 1784	
EAKES, Zechariah	Gran 1772	
EARL, Daniel	Chow 1785	
Jesse	Gran 1785	
John	Ruth 1782	
John	aasq 1789	
John Jr	Gran 1785	
John Sr	Gran 1785	
Thomas	Gran 1785	
Wm	Bute 1766	
Wm	Tyrr 1784	
EARLE, Gamaliel	Gran 1771	
John	Gran 1771	
EARLEY, Wm	Mont 1782	
Wm Jr	Mont 1782	
EARLS, Wm	Mont 1782	
EARLY, General	Hert 1784	
George	Hert 1779	
James	Bert 1774	
John	Hert 1779	
Patrick	Surr 1782	
Sarah	Hert 1779	
EARTHMAN, Isaac	Oran 1779	
EASLEY, Benj	Bert 1781	
James	Hali 1783	
James	Bert 1781	
John	Surr 1782	
Millington	Gran 1771	
Wm	Gran 1785	
EASLICK, Isaac	Cart 1779	
EASON, Abner	Bert 1781	
Abraham	Gate 1789	
Alexr	Gate 1789	
Benjamin	Samp 1784	
Frederick	Gate 1789	
George	Gate 1789	
Gregory	Perq 1772	
Isaac	Gate 1789	
Jacob	Chow 1785	
Jacob	Gate 1789	
James	Surr 1782	
Jesse	Gate 1789	
John	Samp 1784	
Joseph	Samp 1784	
Joseph	Surr 1782	
Levi	Gate 1789	
Major	Gran 1785	
Mary	Surr 1782	
Peter	Bert 1781	
Reuben	Mart 1779	
Robert	Chow 1785	
Samuel	Ruth 1782	

EASON, Samuel Jr	Ruth 1782		EDMUNDS, James	Gran 1785
Seth	Gate 1789		John	NorH 1780
EAST, Joseph	Surr 1782		Wm	Hali 1783
Thomas	Surr 1782		EDMUNDSTONES, John	Ruth 1782
Wm	Surr 1782		EDNEY, Newton	Camd 1782
EASTER, John	Gran 1785		EDWARDS, Absalom	Wayn 1786
John	Surr 1782		Ambrose	Bute 1766
EASTERLING, Henry	Dobb 1780		Ambrose	Mont 1782
Wm	Dobb 1780		Andrew	Surr 1782
EASTMAN, Benj	Pasq 1789		Ann	Bert 1781
EASTON, John	Cart 1779		Anshott	Hali 1783
Richard	Casw 1784		Benjamin	Dobb 1780
EASTRIDGE, Abraham	Gran 1771		Benjamin	John 1784
EASTWOOD, Israel	Gran 1785		Britton	Beau 1786
Israel	Tyrr 1784		Brown	Hali 1783
Israel	Surr 1782		Cader	Surr 1782
Israel	Gran 1771		Charity	NorH 1780
John	Mart 1779		Charles	Cart 1779
EATER, Christian	Surr 1782		Charles	Gran 1785
EATHERGAIN, George	Mart 1779		Chas	Gran 1771
EATMAN, John	Nash 1782		Cullen	Dobb 1780
EATON, Charles	Gran 1785		Cullen	Hali 1783
John	Hali 1783		David	Rowa 1768
Leonard	Wilk 1782		David	Oran 1779
Rebecca	NorH 1780		David	Wayn 1786
Thomas	Bute 1766		David	Beau 1779
Thomas	Warr 1784		David	Beau 1786
EAVES, Mary	Wilk 1782		Edward	Oran 1779
EBORN, Elisha	Beau 1779		Edward	Surr 1782
ECCLES, John	Oran 1779		Enoch	Bute 1766
Wm	Oran 1779		Gideon	Surr 1782
ECCOLS, Frederick	Dobb 1780		Grace	Onsl 1771
ECHLIN, John	Beau 1786		Hugh	Oran 1779
ECHOLS, Geo	Beau 1786		Isaac	NorH 1780
Tredwick	Beau 1786		Isaac	Beau 1786
Wm	Beau 1786		Jacob	John 1784
ECKLIN, Christopher	Beau 1779		James	Gran 1785
Joshua	Beau 1779		James	Beau 1779
ECKRIDGE, Malachi	Beau 1779		James	Beau 1786
ECTOR, Samuel	Oran 1779		James	Perq 1787
EDDINGTON, Wm	Casw 1784		Jarrett	Hali 1783
EDDINS, Abraham	Wilk 1782		Jean	Onsl 1771
Wm	Wilk 1782		Jesse	Hali 1783
EDDLEMON, Peter	Surr 1782		John	Bute 1766
EDEMAN, Saml	Surr 1782		John	Oran 1779
Wm	Surr 1782		John	Wayn 1786
EDENS, Elias	Onsl 1771		John	Gran 1785
EDENTON, Hardy	Bert 1781		John	Hali 1783
EDGARTON, James	Warr 1784		John	Hali 1783
EDGE, Jeremiah	Oran 1779		John	Mont 1782
John	Blad 1784		John	Onsl 1771
Nehemiah	Oran 1779		John	NorH 1780
Richard	Albe 1679		John Jr	Oran 1779
Thomas	Blad 1784		Joseph	Hali 1783
Wm	Samp 1784		Joseph	John 1784
Wm	Blad 1784		Joseph	Wilk 1782
EDGERTON, Joseph	Wayn 1786		Joshua	Rowa 1768
Thomas	Wayn 1786		Josiah	Onsl 1771
EDGINGTON, Wm	Crav 1779		Madock	Bute 1766
EDMONDSON, Elizabeth			Mary	Dobb 1780
	Hali 1783		Matthew	Bute 1766
John	Dobb 1780		Matthew	NorH 1780
Wm	Mart 1779		Micajah	John 1784
EDMUNDS, Ambrose	Hali 1783		Nathan	Bert 1781
Bryant	Hali 1783		Nathaniel	Mont 1782

EDWARDS, PamFret	Gran 1785		ELLEGE, Jacob	Wilk 1782
Philemon	Mont 1782		ELLER, Jacob	Rowa 1760
Richards	Oran 1779		Michael	Rowa 1760
Robert	Blad 1784		ELLIFF, John	Chow 1785
Sam	NorH 1780		ELLIGOOD, Francis	Beau 1786
Samuel	Blad 1784		Jacob	Beau 1786
Solomon	Nash 1782		John	Beau 1786
Stephen	John 1784		ELLIN, Howell	Nash 1782
Sylvanus	Oran 1779		ELLINGTON, Daniel	Gran 1785
Thomas	Nash 1782		James	Warr 1784
Thomas	Samp 1784		John	Warr 1784
Thomas	Brun 1784		Wm	Warr 1784
Thomas	Gran 1785		ELLIOTT, Abel	Perq 1772
Thomas	Hali 1783		Abel	Perq 1787
Thomas	Bert 1774		Abram	Perq 1787
Thomas	Brun 1782		Benjamin	Perq 1772
Thomas	Onsl 1771		Caleb	Perq 1787
Thomas	Bert 1781		Caleb	Pasq 1789
Thomas & s Tom	Dobb 1780		Cornelius	Pasq 1789
Titus	Bert 1781		Demsy	Perq 1787
Triscilla	Warr 1779		Elizabeth	Pasq 1779
Walker	Beau 1786		Ephraim	Perq 1772
Walter	Beau 1779		Ephraim	Perq 1787
Wm	Bute 1766		Exum	Perq 1787
Wm	Dobb 1780		Geo	NorH 1780
Wm	Oran 1779		George	Casw 1784
Wm	Samp 1784		George	Gran 1785
Wm	John 1784		Isaac	Perq 1772
Wm	Onsl 1771		Isaac	Perq 1787
Wm	Bert 1781		Jacob & s Jaco	Rowa 1768
Young	Oran 1779		James	Casw 1784
EELBUK, Elizabeth	Hali 1783		James	Perq 1787
Henry	Hali 1783		John	Rowa 1768
Joseph	Hali 1783		John	Perq 1772
Montfort	Hali 1783		John	Beau 1779
EGGERTON, Henry	Cart 1779		John	Onsl 1771
James & bros	Bute 1766		John	Perq 1787
John	Bute 1766		Joseph	Perq 1772
John Jr	Bute 1766		Joseph	Perq 1787
Scrup & bros	Bute 1766		Joseph Jr	Perq 1787
Wilmot & bros	Bute 1766		Joseph Sr	Perq 1787
EILBACK, Joseph	Chow 1785		Josiah	Perq 1787
ELDER, Ephraim	Surr 1782		Mary	Perq 1787
Peter	Surr 1782		Miles	Perq 1787
Saml	Surr 1782		Mordica	Perq 1787
ELEY, Eli	Hert 1779		Moses	Pasq 1779
Eli	Hert 1784		Nathan	Pasq 1779
Elsey	Bute 1766		Nathan	Pasq 1789
Samuel	Bute 1766		Peter	Bert 1781
ELIAS, Thomas	Oran 1779		Peter	Beau 1786
ELKES, Ann	Albe 1694		Ruth	Wilk 1782
Margaret	Albe 1694		Saml	Perq 1787
Richard	Albe 1694		Seth	Perq 1787
Richard Jr	Albe 1694		Shirley	Perq 1772
ELKINS, James	Samp 1784		Solomon	Perq 1772
John	Samp 1784		Solomon	Perq 1787
Nathaniel	Rich 1790		Thomas	Perq 1772
Richard	Rich 1790		Thomas	Surr 1782
Samuel Jr	Samp 1784		Thomas	Perq 1787
Samuel Sr	Samp 1784		Thomas	Perq 1787
ELLECE, Benj	Wilk 1782		Winslow	Perq 1787
Francis	Wilk 1782		Wm	Hali 1783
Joseph	WilK 1782		Wm	Casw 1784
ELLEDGE, Isaac	Wilk 1784		Wm	Wilk 1782
ELLEGE, Abraham	Wilk 1782		Wm	Surr 1782

ELLIOTT, Wm	Beau 1786	ELLIS, Wm	Gate 1789
Zackariah	Casw 1784	Wright	Gate 1789
ELLIS, Aaron	Gate 1789	ELLISON, Alanso	Beau 1779
Absalom	Wayn 1786	Alderson	Beau 1786
Benjamin	Rowa 1761	Francis	Beau 1786
Benjamin	Warr 1784	Jesse	Mart 1779
Christopher	Surr 1782	ELLLISON, Thomas	Beau 1779
Daniel	Gate 1789	ELLOMS, John	Bute 1766
Edward	Warr 1784	ELLROOD, Christopher	
Edward & s Ed	Bute 1766		Rowa 1761
Elisha	Gate 1789	Robert	Rowa 1761
Ellis	Hali 1783	ELLSBERRY, Isaac	Surr 1782
Ephraim	Bute 1766	ELMORE, Abijah	Surr 1782
Ephraim	Warr 1784	Charles	Casw 1786
Evan	Blad 1784	Charles	Casw 1784
Freeman	Cart 1779	Christopher	Casw 1786
Jacob	Dobb 1780	George	Casw 1786
Jacob	Wayn 1786	John	Oran 1779
James	Ruth 1782	Joseph	Bert 1781
James	Rowa 1761	Peter	Casw 1786
James	Blad 1784	Peter	Casw 1784
James	Gate 1789	Reuben	Wayn 1786
Jesse	Bute 1766	Thomas	Wilk 1782
Jesse	Hert 1784	Travis	Wayn 1786
Jesse	Warr 1784	Travis	Casw 1784
John	Bute 1766	Wm	Blad 1784
John	Dobb 1780	ELMS, Edward	Hali 1783
John	Rowa 1761	John	Ruth 1782
John	Blad 1784	ELROD, Rachel	Surr 1782
John	Wayn 1786	Robert	Surr 1782
John	Warr 1784	Susannah	Surr 1782
John	Onsl 1771	ELSBERRY, John	Surr 1782
John	Gate 1789	ELWELL, Benjamin	Blad 1784
John & sons	Bute 1766	ELY, Mahan	Beau 1786
John Jr	Bute 1766	EMANUEL, Ephraim	Samp 1784
Joseph	Dobb 1780	EMBRY, Robert	Casw 1786
Joshua & sons	Bute 1766	Robert	Casw 1784
Joshua Jr	Bute 1766	Wm	Casw 1786
Josiah	Wayn 1786	EMERSON, James	Pasq 1789
Lewis	Surr 1782	John	Bute 1766
Mary	Warr 1784	John	Warr 1784
Miles	Gate 1789	EMERY, Balaam	NorH 1780
Nathan	Brun 1784	Edward	Hali 1783
Nimrod	Gran 1785	Ephraim	Gran 1785
Nimrod	Gran 1771	John	NorH 1780
Oswell	Hert 1784	John	Surr 1782
Richard	Bute 1766	EMESON, James	Mart 1779
Richard	Warr 1784	EMET, Moses	Crav 1779
Richard	NBer 1779	EMPSON, John	Camd 1782
Robert	Blad 1784	EMUL, Aaron	Crav 1779
Robert	Hali 1783	ENDICOTT, Moses	Surr 1782
Robert	NorH 1780	ENDLESS, Thomas	Chow 1785
Robert	Beau 1786	ENGLAND, Daniel	Surr 1782
Robert	Beau 1786	John	Surr 1782
Shadrack	Gate 1789	John Sr	Surr 1782
Thomas	Chow 1785	Joseph	Surr 1782
Thomas	Gate 1789	ENGLES, Charles	Rowa 1768
Walter	Casw 1784	ENGLISH, Cornelius	Mont 1782
Wm	Bute 1766	John	Wayn 1786
Wm	Rowa 1761	John	Mont 1782
Wm	Mart 1779	Joseph	Mont 1782
Wm	Blad 1784	ENNALS, Joseph	Curr 1779
Wm	Warr 1784	ENNIS, John	Ruth 1782
Wm	Mont 1782	ENOCH, Benjamin	Casw 1784
Wm	Surr 1782	Benjamin	Casw 1786

ENOS, Saml	Gate 1789		ETHERIDGE, Solomon	Curr 1779	
ENTRY, Dan	Surr 1782		Tarte	Curr 1779	
ENYART, Abraham	Surr 1782		Thomas	Camd 1782	
Christr	Surr 1782		Thomas	John 1784	
John	Rowa 1761		Thorogood	Curr 1779	
Peter	Surr 1782		Timothy	Curr 1779	
Silas	Rowa 1761		Willis	Camd 1782	
ENZOR, Ambrose	Samp 1784		Willis	Pasq 1779	
Summers	Samp 1784		Willis	Curr 1779	
EPPERSON, Wm	Surr 1782		Willis Jr	Camd 1782	
EPSON, Thompson	Wilk 1782		Wm	Hali 1783	
ERICKSON, Anderson	Onsl 1771		Wm	Curr 1779	
ERWIN, Edward	Dobb 1780		ETHRIDGE, John	Brun 1782	
Francis	Dobb 1780		Malachi	Beau 1786	
John	Dobb 1780		EUBANK, Elijah	Jone 1779	
John	Perq 1772		Thomas	Jone 1779	
Richard	Dobb 1780		EUDLOT, David	Curr 1779	
Wm	Dobb 1780		EURE, Chas	Gate 1789	
Wm	Perq 1772		Daniel	Gate 1789	
ESKRIDGE, Richard	Casw 1784		James	Gate 1789	
ESLEY, Daniel	Surr 1782		John	Gate 1789	
ESON, Demcy	Edge 1777		Millie	Gate 1789	
EST, Morley	Blad 1784		Stephen	Gate 1789	
ESTES, Ephraim	Oran 1779		Uriah	Gate 1789	
John	Oran 1779		EUSTICE, Judith	Blad 1784	
John	Warr 1784		Richard	Casw 1784	
Richard	Casw 1786		EVANS, Bartholomew	Pasq 1789	
Thomas	Oran 1779		Benjamin	Hert 1779	
Wm	Oran 1779		Benjamin	Mart 1784	
Wm	Gran 1785		Benjamin	Curr 1779	
ESTRIDGE, Ephraim	Bute 1766		Charles	Nash 1782	
John	Bute 1766		Charles	Bert 1774	
Thomas	Bute 1766		Cornelius	Hert 1779	
ETHAN, Artinatus	Chow 1785		Cornelius	Mart 1784	
Maude	Chow 1785		Daniel	Casw 1786	
ETHERIDGE, Aaron	Hali 1783		Daniel	Casw 1784	
Aaron Jr	Hali 1783		David	Nash 1782	
Abel	Curr 1779		David	Wayn 1786	
Abram	Camd 1782		David	NBer 1779	
Adam	Curr 1779		David	Surr 1782	
Amos Jr	Curr 1779		Edward	Surr 1782	
Amos Sr	Curr 1779		Elizabeth	Blad 1784	
Caleb	Curr 1779		Ezekiel	Curr 1779	
Caleb Sr	Hall 1783		Francis	Hert 1779	
Caleb Jr	Hali 1783		Francis	Mart 1784	
David	Camd 1782		Grace	Pasq 1789	
Dempsey	Camd 1782		Henry	Hali 1783	
Ephraim	Tyrr 1784		Isom	Wayn 1786	
George	Hali 1783		James	Dupl 1783	
Grandy	Camd 1782		James	Mart 1779	
James	Curr 1779		James	Warr 1784	
James Sr	Curr 1779		James	Onsl 1771	
Jesse	Curr 1779		Joel	Wayn 1786	
John	Brun 1784		John	Nash 1782	
John Jr	Curr 1779		John	Cart 1779	
John Sr	Curr 1779		John	Chow 1785	
Joshua	Camd 1782		John	Onsl 1771	
Josiah	Curr 1779		John	NorH 1780	
Marmaduke	Brun 1782		John	Pasq 1789	
Mathew	Curr 1779		John Jr	Wayn 1786	
Peter	Nash 1782		Joseph	Curr 1779	
Richard	Curr 1779		Nathan	Oran 1779	
Samson	Curr 1779		Phillip	Surr 1782	
Samuel	Brun 1782		Powell	Warr 1784	
Samuel	Curr 1779		Robert	Hert 1779	

EVANS, Robert	Mart 1784	EXUM, Arthur	NorH 1780
Robert	Pasq 1789	Benjamin	Bute 1766
Robert Jr	Perq 1787	Benjamin	Dobb 1780
Robert Sr	Perq 1787	Elijah	Samp 1784
Saml	Surr 1782	John	Nash 1782
Sarah	Curr 1779	Joseph	Nash 1782
Thomas	Hert 1779	EZARD, Thomas	Warr 1784
Thomas	Casw 1786	EZEL, Gillium	Rich 1790
Thomas	Casw 1784	John	Rich 1790
Thomas	Mart 1784	Wm	Rich 1790
Thomas	John 1784	EZELL, Benjamin	Hert 1779
Thomas	Crav 1779	Benjamin	Hert 1784
Thomas	Surr 1782	John	Hert 1779
Thomas Jr	Casw 1784	John	Warr 1784
Thomas Sr	Casw 1784		
Wm	Hert 1779		
Wm	Camd 1782		
Wm	NBer 1779	FADDLES, Andrew	Oran 1779
Wm	Surr 1782	FAGAN, Geo	Gran 1771
Wm	Bert 1781	Mary	Tyrr 1784
Wm Sr	Mart 1784	Shadrack	Tyrr 1784
Zackariah	Casw 1786	Wm	Tyrr 1784
EVELAND, David	Oran 1779	FAGEN, Wm	Bert 1774
Peter	Oran 1779	FAIR, Barns	Surr 1782
EVEN, John	Pasq 1779	FAIRCHILD, Abijah	Wilk 1782
EVENT, Lawrence	Rich 1790	Ebenezer	Wilk 1782
EVERARD, Merida	Hali 1783	FAIRCLOTH, Benjamin	Samp 1784
EVERETT, Alexander	Hali 1783	Hardy	Samp 1784
Ethel	Hert 1784	Jesse	Camd 1782
Ethelred	Hert 1779	John	Samp 1784
James	Beau 1786	Robert	Samp 1784
James dec	Mart 1779	Samuel	Samp 1784
Jerusiah	Tyrr 1784	Thomas	Dobb 1780
Jesse	Hali 1783	Thomas	Surr 1782
John	Mart 1779	Wm	Dobb 1780
John	Beau 1786	Wm	Samp 1784
Joseph	Wayn 1786	Wm Sr	Dobb 1780
Joseph	Tyrr 1784	FAIRFAX, John	NorH 1780
Nathaniel	Mart 1779	FAIRLESS, Robert	Hert 1779
Nathaniel	Tyrr 1784	Wm	Hert 1784
Samuel	Mart 1779	Zadok	Hert 1784
Thomas	Tyrr 1784	FAISON, Francis	Samp 1784
Turner	Mart 1779	James Jr	Samp 1784
Wm	Mart 1779	James Sr	Samp 1784
Wm	Samp 1784	Kilbee	Samp 1784
EVERGIN, Edward	Pasq 1779	FAITHFUL, Wm	Blad 1784
EVERIGEN, Edward	Pasq 1789	FALLOW, Wm	Chow 1785
EVERS, James	Blad 1784	FALLS, Gillie	Rowa 1761
EVERTON, John	Curr 1779	FANN, Ann	Warr 1784
Thomas	Curr 1779	Jesse	Warr 1784
Wm	Pasq 1779	John	Warr 1784
EVES, Benjamin	Bute 1766	Wm	Warr 1784
Graves	Ruth 1782	FANNELL, Ephraim	Blad 1784
Sarah	Cart 1779	FANNEY, Wm	Hert 1784
Wm	Ruth 1766	FANNING, Hezekiah	Casw 1786
EVESON, Burwell	Gran 1785	Hezekiah	Casw 1784
EVITT, John	Beau 1786	John	Dobb 1780
Thomas	Beau 1786	FANNY, Wm	Hert 1779
EWAN, John	Rich 1790	FANSQUER, James	Casw 1784
EWBANK, Don	Jone 1779	FARAUGE, Wm	Pasq 1789
EWBANKS, George	Hali 1783	FARLEY, Alexander	Rich 1790
James	Hali 1783	Archibald	Rich 1790
Joseph	Hali 1783	David	Oran 1779
EWEN, John	Camd 1782	James	Casw 1784
EXON, Sam	NorH 1780	John	Casw 1784

FARLEY, John	Rich	1790	FEARNS, Martin	Cart	1779
FARLOW, George	Rowa	1768	FELL, Edward	Hert	1779
Michael & sons	Rowa	1768	FELLINGHIM, Robert	Crav	1779
Wm	Rowa	1768	FELLINGIM, Benjamin	Crav	1779
FARMER, Benj	Surr	1782	Jarvis	Crav	1779
Cassandra	Casw	1784	John	Crav	1779
Isaiah	Gran	1785	Margaret	Crav	1779
Job	Oran	1779	Samuel	Crav	1779
John	Gran	1785	FELLOW, John	Wayn	1786
John	Surr	1782	Robert	Wayn	1786
Joseph	Gran	1771	Wm	Wayn	1786
Joseph	Bert	1781	FELTON, Ameriah	Surr	1782
Josiah	Gran	1785	Anna	Chow	1785
Nicholas	John	1784	Elisha	Hert	1784
Samuel	Rowa	1761	Job	Rowa	1761
Samuel	Ruth	1782	Job	Surr	1782
Samuel	Brun	1784	Noah	Gate	1789
Thomas	Oran	1779	Sarah	Gate	1789
Thomas	Casw	1784	Shadrack	Chow	1785
Thomas	Bert	1781	Thomas	Gate	1789
Wm	Bert	1781	Wm	Chow	1785
FARNELL, Thomas	Onsl	1771	FELTS, Aaron	Wilk	1782
FARRAR, Wm	Gran	1771	Allen	Warr	1784
FARRELL, Charles	Casw	1784	Francis	Warr	1784
Enoch	Casw	1784	Frederick	Bute	1766
John	Wayn	1786	Isham	Hali	1783
Wm	Wayn	1786	Isham	Warr	1784
Wm	Crav	1779	John	Ruth	1782
FARROW, Christopher	Curr	1779	John	Warr	1784
Fraish	Gate	1789	Jordan	Warr	1784
Francis	Curr	1779	Nathan	Warr	1784
Hezekiah	Curr	1779	Nathaniel	Bute	1766
Isaac	Curr	1779	Nathaniel	Warr	1784
Jacob	Curr	1779	Randolph	Warr	1784
Jacob Jr	Curr	1779	Rowland	Warr	1784
Tench	Chow	1785	Wm	Warr	1784
Thomas	Curr	1779	Wm	Warr	1784
Vinah	Curr	1779	FENDALL, John	Albe	1694
FASON, James	Blad	1784	Robert	Albe	1694
FAT, Richard	Jone	1779	FENDER, Christian	Surr	1782
FATHERNE, Ann	Beau	1786	FENN, Chas	Surr	1782
FAUCETT, David	Oran	1779	FENNELL, John	Pasq	1789
George	Oran	1779	Sam	NorH	1780
James	Oran	1779	FENNER, Robert	Hali	1783
Ralph	Oran	1779	FENNETT, John	Pasq	1779
Richard	Oran	1779	Mary	Onsl	1771
Robert	Oran	1779	FENTERS, Malachi	Cart	1779
Thomas	Oran	1779	FENTON, Sarah	Curr	1779
Wm	Oran	1779	FENTRESS, Wm	Pasq	1789
FAULK, John	John	1784	FERGUSON, Adam	Crav	1779
Thomas	John	1784	James	Wilk	1784
Wm	Surr	1782	James	Blad	1784
FAULKNER, Abraham	Casw	1784	James	Wilk	1782
Emanuel	Warr	1784	Jeremiah	Wilk	1784
Emmanuel	Bute	1766	John	Wilk	1784
John	Warr	1784	John	Oran	1779
Moses	Warr	1784	John	Wilk	1782
Wm	Warr	1779	John	Rich	1790
FAUTHER, Jacob	Rowa	1768	John Jr	Blad	1784
John	Rowa	1768	John Sr	Blad	1784
FAWN, Ann	Hert	1779	Joseph	Wilk	1784
Ann	Hert	1784	Joseph	Wilk	1782
FAY, John	Jone	1779	Malcomb	Blad	1784
FAYE, Catherine	Bert	1774	Malcomb	Mont	1782
FEALER, Andrew	Surr	1782	Nehemiah	Wilk	1782

FERGUSON, Neil	Blad 1784	FIELDS, Brittle	Dobb 1780
Rebecca	Surr 1782	George	John 1784
Robert	Casw 1786	John	Rowa 1761
Roger	Wilk 1784	John	Rowa 1768
Slocum	Crav 1779	Joseph	Rown 1768
Thomas	Wilk 1784	Lan	Surr 1782
Thomas	Wilk 1782	Moses	Dobb 1780
Wm	Ruth 1782	Richard	Surr 1782
Wm	Oran 1779	Robert	Rowa 1761
Wm	Wilk 1784	Robert	Rowa 1768
Wm	Wilk 1782	Thomas	Wilk 1782
FERREBEE, George	Curr 1779	Wm	Rowa 1768
James	Curr 1779	FIFE, David	Crav 1779
Jesse	Curr 1779	FIGG, James	Gate 1789
John	Curr 1779	Joseph	Gate 1789
Joseph	Camd 1782	FIGURES, Richard	Hert 1779
Joseph	Curr 1779	Thomas	Hert 1784
Leah	Beau 1786	Wm	Hert 1779
Peter	Curr 1779	Wm	Hert 1784
Wm	Camd 1782	FILGO, Anthony	Bert 1774
Wm	Curr 1779	Wm	Bert 1781
FERREBOW, Jacob	Gran 1785	FINCH, Edward	Gran 1785
FERREE, Ephraim	Oran 1779	Edward	Wilk 1782
FERRELL, Benjamin	Camd 1782	John	Gran 1785
Catherine	Camd 1782	John	Gran 1771
Cornelius	John 1784	John Sr	Gran 1785
Henry	Casw 1784	Thomas	Pasq 1694
Jacob	John 1784	Williamson	Gran 1785
Jacob	Crav 1779	Wm	Nash 1782
James	Camd 1782	Wm	Gran 1771
John	Dobb 1780	FINCHER, Jonathan	Rowa 1768
John	Casw 1784	FINDLAY, James	Wilk 1784
John & s Bryan	Bute 1766	FINDLEY, Hugh	Oran 1779
Joseph	Camd 1782	FINLEY, Duncan	Rich 1790
Joseph	Hali 1783	James	Wilk 1782
Nicholas Jr	John 1784	James	Surr 1782
Nicholas Sr	John 1784	FINN, Peter	Surr 1782
Samuel	Camd 1782	FINNEY, John	Rowa 1768
Sarah	Camd 1782	John	Onsl 1771
Wm	Bute 1766	John	Gate 1789
Wm	Dobb 1780	Joseph	Oran 1779
Wm	Mart 1779	Thomas	Hert 1784
Wm	Hali 1783	Thomas	Gate 1789
Wm	Gran 1771	Wm	NorH 1780
FERRINGTON, Samuel	Rowa 1768	FIPS, John	Wilk 1782
FERRIS, Abigail	Onsl 1771	FIRDS, Sam	Onsl 1771
Drury	NorH 1780	FISH, George	Perq 1772
Ishmael	Blad 1784	Thomas	Crav 1779
John	Casw 1784	Thomas	Pitt 1786
John	Blad 1784	FISHEL, Adam	Surr 1782
Joseph	Casw 1784	FISHER, Bailey	Samp 1784
Peter	Casw 1784	Casper	Surr 1782
Roger	Pasq 1694	Elijah	Samp 1784
Samuel	Blad 1784	George	Crav 1779
Wm	Casw 1784	George	Onsl 1771
Wm	Gran 1785	Gideon	Casw 1784
FERRISS, Wm	Bert 1774	James	Albe 1694
FEUTT, Joseph	Chow 1785	John	Ruth 1782
FEW, James	Oran 1779	Malcolm	Surr 1782
James Jr	Oran 1779	Nicholas	Ruth 1782
FIDLER, James	Rowa 1768	Sarah	Surr 1782
FIELD, Davis	Surr 1782	Southey	Samp 1784
Stephen	Surr 1782	Thomas	Hert 1779
FIELDER, James	Surr 1782	Wm	Cart 1779
John	Surr 1782	FISKIS, Adam	Surr 1782

FISKIS, Fredk	Surr 1782	FLEWELLEN, Taylor	Hali 1783
FITCH, Thomas	Oran 1779	Wm	Hali 1783
Wm	Oran 1779	Wm Jr	Hali 1783
FITCHETT, Christian	Blad 1784	Wm Sr	Hali 1783
FITTS, Andrew	Gran 1771	FLINN, Ann	Brun 1782
Henry	Warr 1784	Geo	Surr 1782
FITZGERALD, Charles	Casw 1786	Jacob	Surr 1782
John	Hali 1783	John	Casw 1784
Wm	Casw 1786	John	Surr 1782
FITZPATRICK, John	Surr 1782	John	Bert 1781
Saml	Surr 1782	Saml	Surr 1782
Thomas	Tyrr 1784	Thomas	Surr 1782
Thomas	Surr 1782	FLINTHUM, James	Oran 1779
FITZRANDOLPH, Benjamin		FLOCK, Jacob	Jone 1779
	Blad 1784	FLOOD, Absalom	Hert 1779
FIVEASH, Dempsey	Blad 1784	Phillip	Bert 1781
John	Blad 1784	Wm	Tyrr 1784
John	Perq 1787	Wm	Bert 1779
FLACK, John	Ruth 1782	FLORENCE, Obediah	Casw 1786
Wm	Ruth 1782	Obediah	Casw 1784
FLAGER, Christr	Surr 1782	FLORYCER, Wm	Gran 1785
FLAGLER, Wm	Brun 1784	FLOWER, John	Curr 1779
FLANCHER, Richard	Beau 1786	FLOWERS, Benjamin	Nash 1782
FLECK, Baptist	Rowa 1768	David	Brun 1784
FLEETWOOD, Dan	Bert 1774	David	Brun 1782
Edmund	Bert 1781	Edward	Blad 1784
James	Bert 1774	Henry	Nash 1782
James	Bert 1781	Ignatius	Blad 1784
Jeremiah	Bert 1781	Jacob	Nash 1782
Sarah	Bert 1774	Jacob	Wayn 1786
Wm	Bert 1774	John	Nash 1782
Wm	Bert 1781	John	Samp 1784
FLEMING, George	Ruth 1782	John	Wayn 1786
James	Mart 1779	John Jr	Blad 1784
John	Ruth 1782	Jonathan	Blad 1784
John	Warr 1784	Ransford	NorH 1780
John-Sr	Gran 1785	Simon	Wayn 1786
Peter	Ruth 1782	Wm	Blad 1784
Thomas	Gran 1785	Wm	Waye 1786
Wm	Gran 1785	FLOYD, Austin	Dobb 1780
FLEMMING, Bailey	Gran 1771	Benjamin	Nash 1782
Henry	Gran 1771	Chas	Gran 1771
John	Warr 1784	Griffin	Beau 1786
John	Gran 1771	James	Casw 1784
Peter	Gran 1771	James	Bert 1781
FLEMMON, John	Surr 1782	Jesse	NorH 1780
FLESSION, Joseph	Brun 1782	John	Bert 1774
FLETCHER, Francis	Pasq 1779	John	NorH 1780
Francis	Pasq 1789	John	Bert 1781
James	Mont 1782	John	Beau 1786
James Jr	Casw 1784	Joseph	Bert 1781
James Sr	Casw 1784	Margaret	Hert 1784
Joseph	Gran 1771	Morris	Gran 1785
Margaret	Curr 1779	Norris	NorH 1780
Margaret	Perq 1787	Peter	Beau 1779
Ralph	Wayn 1786	Peter	Beau 1786
Richard	Mont 1782	Richard	Bute 1766
Sally	Wayn 1786	Simeon	Beau 1779
Wm	Wilk 1782	Simon	Beau 1786
Wm	Surr 1782	Simon	Beau 1786
FLEURY, Henry	Chow 1785	Solomon	Hert 1784
FLEWELLEN, James	Hali 1783	Thomas	Surr 1782
Richard Jr	Hali 1783	Valentine	Hert 1779
Richard Sr	Hali 1783	Wm	Gran 1785
Sarah	Beau 1779	Wm	Gran 1771

FLUKER, David	Bute 1766		FORBISH, Robert	Surr 1782
David	Warr 1784		FORBUSH, David	Wilk 1782
George	Warr 1784		John	Camd 1782
John	Warr 1784		FORD, Absalom	Gran 1785
FLURRY, Lucy	Curr 1779		Calvin	Casw 1784
Thomas	Curr 1779		Isaac	Surr 1782
FLYNN, Daniel	Blad 1784		John	Rowa 1770
John	Blad 1784		John	Camd 1782
Wm	NorH 1780		John	Blad 1784
FOANNON, John	Perq 1787		John	Hali 1783
FOANS, John Sr	Mart 1779		Joseph	Blad 1784
FOGARTY, Edmond	Blad 1784		Merriman	Gran 1771
FOGG, Joseph	Warr 1784		Simeon	Casw 1786
FOGLE, Saml	Surr 1782		Simeon	Casw 1784
FOGLEMAN, George	Oran 1779		Thomas	Camd 1782
Malachi	Oran 1779		Wm	Chow 1785
Michael	Oran 1779		Wm	Hali 1783
Peter	Oran 1779		Wm	Gran 1771
FOLEY, Mason	Casw 1784		FORDHAM, Benjamin	Jone 1779
FOLGER, Latham	Surr 1782		FORE, Archelaus	Surr 1782
FOLK, John	Bert 1774		Daniel	Nash 1782
Jolk	Bert 1781		Richard	Nash 1782
Simon	Hert 1784		FORECLOTH, Mary	Mont 1782
FOLKNER, James	Dobb 1780		FOREHAND, Anthony	Camd 1782
Wm	Dobb 1780		Benj	Perq 1787
FOLKS, Jacob	Blad 1784		Boswell	Camd 1782
James	Blad 1784		Cornelius	Perq 1772
John	Blad 1784		Cornelius	Perq 1787
Richard	Blad 1784		David	Pasq 1779
Solomon	Wayn 1786		David	Pasq 1789
Wm	Blad 1784		Eliz	Pasq 1789
Wm	Wayn 1786		Irwin	Perq 1772
FOLLIS, Wm	Surr 1782		James	Wayn 1786
FOMPOL, Robert	Pasq 1694		James	Pasq 1779
Wm	Pasq 1694		James Sr	Wayn 1786
FONES, John Jr	Mart 1779		Jarvis	Chow 1785
FONNEVILLE, John	NBer 1779		Lemuel	Pasq 1779
Mary	NBer 1779		Lemuel	Pasq 1789
FONNVILLE, Richard	NBer 1779		Wm	Wayn 1786
Wm	NBer 1779		FOREMAN, Benjamin	Hali 1783
FONVIELLE, Jeremiah	Onsl 1771		George	Nash 1782
FOOST, John	Bert 1774		Gideon	Gran 1785
FOOT, Henry	Bute 1766		Samuel	Hali 1783
FOOTE, George Jr	Casw 1786		Wm	Cart 1779
George Jr	Casw 1784		FOREN, Ruth	Crav 1779
George Sr	Casw 1786		FORKNER, John	Surr 1782
George Sr	Casw 1784		Wm	Surr 1783
Newton	Casw 1786		FORKS, Odom	NorH 1780
FORBES, Aaron	Camd 1782		FORLAW, John	Tyrr 1784
Adam	Camd 1782		FORNER, Thomas	Crav 1779
Bailey	Camd 1782		FORNETH, Lucas	Hali 1783
Caleb	Camd 1782		FORREST, Benjamin	Oran 1779
Eliab	Camd 1782		Henry	Dobb 1780
Henry	Camd 1782		Henry	Gate 1789
Isaac Jr	Camd 1782		Hezekiah	Oran 1779
Isaac Sr	Camd 1782		Isaac	Oran 1779
Jacob	Camd 1782		James	Oran 1779
James	Camd 1782		John	Oran 1779
Joshua	Camd 1782		Lovisa	Oran 1779
Luke	Camd 1782		Martin	Warr 1784
Moses	Camd 1782		Shadrack	Oran 1779
Peter	Pasq 1789		Stephen	Oran 1779
Thomas	Camd 1782		FORSETT, Francis	Hert 1779
Wm	Camd 1782		FORSTER, Anne	Camd 1782
FORBISH, Geo	Surr 1782		Christopher	Bute 1766

FORSTER, Francis	Camd 1782	FOWLER, Richard	Gran 1785
James	Rowa 1769	Richard	Gran 1771
John	Bute 1766	Samuel	Bute 1766
Mary	Bute 1766	Samuel Jr	Bute 1766
Thomas	Casw 1786	Thomas	Gran 1771
FORSYTHE, James	Gran 1785	Wm	Casw 1784
John	Gran 1785	Wm	Surr 1782
Robert	Oran 1779	Wm	Gran 1771
FORT, Arm.	Hali 1783	FOX, Allen	Wilk 1784
Benjamin	Wayn 1786	James	Hali 1783
John	Samp 1784	James	Wilk 1782
John	Hali 1783	John	Wilk 1782
Micajah	Hali 1783	Joseph	Pasq 1779
Peter	Samp 1784	Joseph	Mont 1782
Sherwood	Samp 1784	Joseph	Pasq 1789
Sherwood	Hali 1783	Moses	Onsl 1771
Wm	Wayn 1786	Titus	Wilk 1782
FORTNER, Robert	Wayn 1786	Wm	Pasq 1789
FOSCUE, Richard	Crav 1779	FOY, John	Crav 1779
FOSSHE, Charles	Casw 1784	FOZER, James	Onsl 1771
FOSTER, Francis	Perq 1772	FRADDLE, George	Oran 1779
Francis	Perq 1787	George Jr	Oran 1779
George	Wilk 1782	FRANCHY, Jacob	Blad 1784
Haley	Surr 1782	FRANCIS, Andrew	NorH 1780
Hugh	Rowa 1768	Matthew	Wilk 1782
James	Rowa 1768	Phillip	Surr 1782
James	Surr 1782	FRANK, Barnett	Wilk 1782
James	Gran 1771	Thomas	Brun 1784
Jeremiah	Curr 1779	FRANKLIN, Edmund	Surr 1782
John	Albe 1694	Edward	Casw 1784
John	Casw 1786	James	Surr 1782
John	Casw 1784	Jesse	Wilk 1782
John	Tyrr 1784	John	Bute 1766
John	Crav 1779	John	Surr 1782
John	Surr 1782	Malachi	Surr 1782
John	Pasq 1789	Richard	Beau 1779
Kimmy	Onsl 1771	Thomas	Crav 1779
Margaret	NorH 1780	Wm	NorH 1780
Mary	Perq 1787	FRANKS, Wm	Rowa 1761
Richard	Oran 1779	FRAPER, Wm	Gate 1789
Richard	Gran 1771	FRASER, Wm	Surr 1782
Silas	Tyrr 1784	FRAZELL, John	Chow 1785
Thomas	Blad 1784	FRAZER, George	Samp 1784
Thomas	Casw 1784	George	Dupl 1784
Wm	Blad 1784	Micajah	Cart 1779
Wm	Perq 1772	Wm	Ruth 1782
Wm	Onsl 1771	FRAZIER, Aaron	Rowa 1761
FOUCH, Jonathan	Ruth 1782	Aaron	Rowa 1768
FOUST, John	Oran 1779	Daniel	Crav 1779
Phillip	Oran 1779	Daniel	Gran 1771
FOUTS, Daniel	Rowa 1768	Daniel	Perq 1787
John	Rowa 1768	Duncan	NBer 1779
FOWLER, Alexander	Warr 1784	Ephraim	Gran 1785
Daniel	Samp 1784	James	Rowa 1768
Daniel	Casw 1784	Jeremiah	Gran 1785
Edward	Blad 1784	Jeremiah	Tyrr 1784
Elias	Surr 1782	Jeremiah	Gran 1771
Francis	Gran 1771	John	Rowa 1761
Geo	Beau 1786	John	Rowa 1768
Henry	Gran 1785	Rev James	Oran 1779
James	Gran 1785	Sarah	Gran 1785
John	Blad 1784	Thomas	Crav 1779
Joseph	Samp 1784	Wm	Gran 1785
Joseph	Wilk 1782	Wm	Mont 1782
Molley	Surr 1782	Wm	Surr 1782

FRAZIER, Wm	Gran 1771	FRENCH, Samuel	Casw 1784
FREDERICK, Wm	Dupl 1783	Samuel Sr	Ruth 1782
FREE, Archibald	Bert 1774	Thomas	Ruth 1782
FREECER, Winifred	Hali 1783	FRESHWATER, Thaddeus	
FREELAND, James	Oran 1779		Pasq 1779
FREEMAN, Aaron	Surr 1782	Thaddeus	Pasq 1789
Abraham	Brun 1784	Wm	Cart 1779
Abraham	Brun 1782	Wm A	Camd 1782
Amos	Surr 1782	FRIDDLE, Casper	Blad 1784
Benjamin	Blad 1784	FRINK, Samuel	Brun 1784
Bridges	Bute 1766	FRITZ, John	Surr 1782
Chas	Bert 1781	FRIZE, George	Cart 1779
Daniel	Oran 1779	FRIZZELL, Jason & s Wm	
Edward	Bute 1766		Rowa 1768
Elisha	Dobb 1780	FRIZZLE, Jonathan	Pasq 1779
Elisha	Bert 1774	Jonathan	Pasq 1789
Elisha	Bert 1781	FROHOCK, John	Rowa 1761
Elizabeth	Bute 1766	FRUIT, James	Oran 1779
Gabriel	Rowa 1768	FRUTHET, Silvester	Wilk 1782
Ging	Bert 1781	FRY, Catherine	Bert 1781
Hartmel	Mont 1782	Christian	Rowa 1761
Henry	Nash 1782	Henry	Surr 1782
Henry	Gran 1785	James	Mont 1782
Jacob	Surr 1782	Joseph & s Rob	Rowa 1768
James	Wilk 1784	Joseph Jr	Mont 1782
James	Wilk 1782	Joseph Sr	Mont 1782
James	Surr 1782	Michael	Surr 1782
James	Gate 1789	Peter	Rowa 1761
James	Beau 1786	Thomas	Rowa 1768
James Capt	Bert 1781	Thomas	Mont 1782
Joel	NorH 1780	Valentine	Surr 1782
John	Bute 1766	FRYER, Isaac	Gate 1789
John	Dobb 1780	Jacob	Samp 1784
John	Oran 1779	James	Samp 1784
John	Bert 1774	Jean	Samp 1784
John	Bert 1781	Jean	Dupl 1784
Joseph	Bert 1774	Jonathan	Samp 1784
Joshua	Surr 1782	Mary	Hert 1779
Joshua	Bert 1781	Thomas	Gate 1789
King	Bert 1774	Wm	Hert 1784
Moses	Bert 1774	Wm	Gate 1789
Moses	Bert 1781	FRYLEY, Frederick	Rowa 1761
Moses	Bert 1781	FRYMAN, John Conrad	Gran 1771
Reuben	Dobb 1780	FUERS, James	Bert 1781
Richard	Gate 1789	FUGATE, Randolph	Wilk 1782
Roger	Blad 1784	FULCHER, Henry	Casw 1784
Saml	Surr 1782	Jacob	Crav 1779
Samuel	Bute 1766	James	Casw 1784
Samuel	Oran 1779	Maximillian	Beau 1779
Sarah	Gate 1789	Thomas	Cart 1779
Solomon	Bert 1774	Wm	Casw 1784
Solomon	Bert 1781	FULFORD, George	Surr 1782
Stephen	Blad 1784	James	Cart 1779
Tabitha	Bert 1781	John	Cart 1779
Thomas	Gran 1785	Josiah	Curr 1779
Wm	Bute 1766	Stephen	Cart 1779
Wm	Mart 1779	Wm	Cart 1779
Wm	Blad 1784	FULGHAM, John	Wayn 1786
Wm	Tyrr 1784	Michael	Wayn 1786
Wm	Surr 1782	Rayford	Wayn 1786
Wm	Gate 1789	FULK, Andrew	Surr 1782
FRENCH, Benjamin	Casw 1786	John A	Surr 1782
Moses	Ruth 1782	FULKS, Wm	NorH 1780
Samuel	Ruth 1782	FULLER, Alexander	Onsl 1771
Samuel	Casw 1786	David	Cart 1779

FULLER, David	Gran 1785	GABRIEL, Nathaniel	Crav 1779
Edward	Cart 1779	GADDIS, Isaac	Oran 1779
Elijah	Casw 1786	John	Oran 1779
Elijah	Casw 1784	Thomas	Casw 1786
Ezekiel	Gran 1771	GADDY, Thomas	Mart 1779
George	Casw 1784	GAGE, Aaron	Ruth 1782
Henry	Casw 1786	Daniel	Ruth 1782
Henry	Casw 1784	David	Ruth 1782
Henry	Gran 1771	James	Ruth 1782
Henry Jr	Casw 1784	Mary	Ruth 1782
Henry Sr	Gran 1785	GAINER, Ann	Hali 1783
Henry Sr	Casw 1784	Arthur	Mart 1779
Hezekiah	Gran 1785	James	Mart 1779
Israel	Gran 1771	John	Beau 1786
James	Gran 1785	Joseph	Beau 1786
James	Casw 1784	Sam	Beau 1786
James	Gran 1771	Sarah	Mart 1779
John	Cart 1779	Wm	Nash 1782
John Jr	Casw 1784	Wm	Hali 1783
John Sr	Casw 1784	Wm	Mont 1782
Joseph	Gran 1785	GAINES, Edward	Casw 1784
Mordica	Wilk 1782	Moses	Hali 1783
Nathan	Cart 1779	GAINS, Eliz	Bert 1781
Peter Jr	Casw 1784	GALBREATH, John	Oran 1779
Peter Sr	Casw 1784	Wm	Oran 1779
Saml	Gran 1771	GALE, Cornelius	Camd 1782
Samuel Sr	Gran 1785	GALLEMOOD, John	Gran 1771
Solomon	Gran 1771	GALLENTON, Wm	Mart 1779
Wm Jr	Casw 1784	GALLION, Jacob	Wilk 1784
Wm Sr	Casw 1784	Jacob	Surr 1782
FULLERTON, Wm	Beau 1786	Thomas	Surr 1782
FULLILSON, JOHN	Gran 1771	GALLLOWAY, John	Beau 1786
FULLER, Edward	Cart 1779	GALLOP, Abel	Camd 1782
FULLWIDER, Jacob	Rowa 1761	Isaac	Camd 1782
FULTON, James	Oran 1779	John	Camd 1782
Jesse	Oran 1779	Jonah	Curr 1779
Joshua	Perq 1772	Joshua	Camd 1782
Robert	Oran 1779	Judith	Camd 1782
FULWOOD, Andrew	Onsl 1771	Luke	Camd 1782
FUQUA, Wm	Hali 1783	Mark	Camd 1782
FURY, James	Oran 1779	GALLOWAY, Anne	Blad 1784
John	Oran 1779	John	Dobb 1780
FUSSELL, Aaron	Warr 1784	John	Brun 1784
Fornash	Warr 1784	Wm	Beau 1779
Moses	Oran 1779	GAMBILL, Mary	Wilk 1784
Wm	Warr 1784	GAMBLE, Henry	Wilk 1782
FUTERAL, Frederick	Hert 1784	John	Wilk 1782
FUTRELL, Arthur	NorH 1780	Martin	Wilk 1782
Benj	NorH 1780	Mary	Wilk 1782
David	NorH 1780	Thomas	Wilk 1782
Ephraim	NorH 1780	GAMBLING, James	Camd 1782
John	NorH 1780	Joshua	Camd 1782
Moore	NorH 1780	GAMMETT, John	Curr 1779
Thomas	NorH 1780	GAMMON, Merritt	Mart 1779
Wm	NorH 1780	GAMWELL, James	CUrr 1779
FUTS, Thomas	Wilk 1784	John	Curr 1779
FYAN, Elizabeth	Albe 1694	Wm	Curr 1779
Hannah	Albe 1694	GANDY, Brinkley	Nash 1782
Mercy	Albe 1694	Britain	Nash 1782
Wm	Albe 1694	Edward	Nash 1782
		Isham	Nash 1782
		GANET, Jesse	Bert 1781
		GANEY, Bartholomew	Samp 1784
GABRIEL, Ann	Cart 1779	Jacob	Samp 1784
Emanuel	Cart 1779	Wm	Samp 1784

GANNON, Joshua	Hali 1783	GARNES, Wm		Casw 1784
GANSON, Wm	Pasq 1694	GARRARD, Anthony		Oran 1779
GANT, Edward	Oran 1779	Milley		Oran 1779
Isom	Bute 1766	GARRELL, Wm		Pitt 1786
James	Bute 1766	GARRESUS, Matthew		Hali 1783
John	Oran 1779	GARRETT, Averard		Oran 1779
Wm	Bute 1766	Benj		Beau 1786
GARDINER, Alexander	Bert 1781	Charles		Camd 1782
Daniel	Surr 1782	Daniel		Tyrr 1784
Edward	Crav 1779	Deborah		Chow 1785
Edward Sr	Crav 1779	Edward		Chow 1785
Elias	Rich 1790	Frederick		Chow 1785
Isaac	Crav 1779	Fredk		Perq 1787
James	Blad 1784	Henry		Oran 1779
James	Bert 1781	Isaac		Camd 1782
Jesse	Crav 1779	James		Rowa 1770
John Jr	Bert 1781	James		Camd 1782
Martin	Bert 1781	James		Chow 1785
Wm	Ruth 1782	James		Tyrr 1784
GARDNER, Demcy	Pasq 1789	Jesse		Gran 1785
Edward	Camd 1782	John		Mart 1779
Edward	Pitt 1786	John		Camd 1782
George	Hali 1783	John		Chow 1785
Isaac	Mart 1779	John		Tyrr 1784
Isaac	Pitt 1786	John		Beau 1779
James	Bert 1774	John		Surr 1782
James	Oran 1779	John		Beau 1786
Jesse	Pitt 1786	John Jr		Tyrr 1784
John	Bert 1774	Joseph		Warr 1784
Josiah	Hali 1783	Major		Camd 1782
Martin	Bert 1774	Matthew		Warr 1784
Prior	Hali 1783	Richard		Chow 1785
Samuel Jr	Mart 1779	Samson		Camd 1782
Samuel Sr	Mart 1779	Shadrack		Beau 1786
Sterling	Hali 1783	Thomas		Warr 1784
Thomas	Mart 1779	Thomas Jr		Tyrr 1784
Thomas	Hali 1783	Thomas Sr		Tyrr 1784
Thomas Sr	Mart 1779	Welcome		Surr 1782
Valentine	Hali 1783	Wm		Camd 1782
Wm	Mart 1779	Wm		Warr 1784
GARETT, Thomas	Chow 1785	GARRIS, John s of Amos		
GARGANUS, James	Onsl 1771			Dobb 1780
Jesse	Onsl 1771	Joshua		Wayn 1786
John	Onsl 1771	GARRISON, Benj		Wilk 1782
Nicholas	Onsl 1771	Ephraim		Dupl 1783
Samuel	Mart 1779	Garrett		Oran 1779
Zachariah	Onsl 1771	George		Oran 1779
GARLAND, James	Samp 1784	Henry		Oran 1779
John	Dobb 1780	Isaac		Wilk 1782
John Jr	Wayn 1786	Isaac		Surr 1782
Jonathan	Hali 1783	Isaiah		Oran 1779
Patrick	Hali 1783	Jacob		Oran 1779
GARNER, Conway	Gran 1771	James		Wilk 1784
John	Cart 1779	Jane		Dupl 1783
John	Gran 1785	Judah		Oran 1779
John	Surr 1782	Richard		Oran 1779
Lewis	Oran 1779	GARRON, James		Rowa 1768
Parrish	Oran 1779	GARROT, Blount		Surr 1782
Ralph	Pasq 1694	GARROTT, Matthew & son		
Samuel	Cart 1779			Bute 1766
Wm	Cart 1779	Thomas		Bute 1766
Wm	Gran 1785	GARZIA, John		Beau 1786
Wyatt	Surr 1782	GASKILL, Adam		Cart 1779
GARNES, John	NorH 1780	Benjamin		Cart 1779
Tobias	Beau 1779	James		Cart 1779

GASKILL, John	Cart 1779	GAUSE, Charles	Brun 1784
Joseph	Cart 1779	John, estate	Brun 1784
Thomas	Cart 1779	Matthew	Surr 1782
Wm	Cart 1779	Susannah	Brun 1784
Zerubabel	Cart 1779	Wm	Brun 1784
GASKINS, Ann	Crav 1779	GAVEN, James	Beau 1786
David	Bert 1781	GAVIN, Charles	Samp 1784
Herman	Crav 1779	Jarred	Samp 1784
John	Hali 1783	Lewis	Samp 1784
Thomas	Pasq 1779	Samuel	Samp 1784
Thomas	Crav 1779	GAY, Ann	NorH 1780
Thomas	Pasq 1789	Henry	NorH 1780
Wm	Crav 1779	James	Hert 1779
GASTON, Alexander	NBer 1779	James Jr	Hert 1779
Clary	Wilk 1782	James Jr	Hert 1784
David	Bert 1774	James Sr	Hert 1784
GATELY, Isham	Casw 1784	Jesse	NorH 1780
Joseph	Casw 1784	John	NorH 1780
Thomas	Casw 1784	Jonathan	NorH 1780
Wm	Casw 1784	Joshua	Hert 1779
GATER, Samuel	Mart 1779	Lemuel	Dupl 1779
GATES, Edward	Blad 1784	GAYLOR, James	Samp 1784
Jane	Blad 1784	GAYLORD, Benj	Beau 1786
John	Blad 1784	Winfield	Beau 1786
Lovick	Gran 1785	GEDDY, John	Hali 1783
Peter	Blad 1784	GEDINE, John	Wayn 1786
Saml	Gran 1771	GEE, Drury	NorH 1780
GATEWOOD, Dudley	Casw 1786	Howell	Hali 1783
Dudley	Casw 1784	John	Oran 1779
GATLIN, David	Crav 1779	GEER, David	Oran 1779
Edward	Hert 1779	GENEWAY, Joseph	Surr 1782
Edward	Crav 1779	GENN, Wm	Gate 1789
Eliz	Pitt 1786	GENTRY, Allen	Casw 1784
Hardy	Crav 1779	Allen	Surr 1782
James	Hert 1779	Artha	Surr 1782
James	Crav 1779	Hezekiah	Surr 1782
John	Crav 1779	Joseph	Surr 1782
Joshua	Crav 1779	Nathl	Surr 1782
Lazarus	Crav 1779	Nicholas	Surr 1782
Levi	Crav 1779	Richard	Surr 1782
Levi	Pitt 1786	Robert	Surr 1782
Shadrack	Crav 1779	Runnel	Surr 1782
Stephen	Pitt 1786	Saml	Surr 1782
Thomas	Crav 1779	Shadrack	Casw 1784
GATLING, Ann	Hert 1779	Shelton	Surr 1782
Arthur	Hert 1784	GEORGE, Allen	Oran 1779
Benj	NorH 1780	David	Dobb 1780
David	Hert 1779	David	Wayn 1786
David	Hert 1784	David	Pasq 1779
Geo	Gate 1789	David	Pasq 1789
Hardy	Hert 1779	Jesse	Surr 1782
Hardy	Hert 1784	Peter	Surr 1782
James	Hert 1784	Reuben	Surr 1782
John	Gate 1789	Thomas	Rich 1790
Lazarus	Dobb 1780	Wm	Crav 1779
Rachel	Hert 1779	GERBY, Howell	NorH 1780
Rachel	Hert 1784	GERKIN, Jeremiah	Mart 1779
Thomas	Dobb 1780	GERRALL, Jesse	Bert 1774
Wm	Hert 1779	GERRARD, Forbes	Beau 1786
Wm	Hert 1784	Geo	Beau 1786
Wm Sr	Gate 1789	GESKIN, Benjamin	Beau 1779
GATMAN, Wm	Crav 1779	Charles	Beau 1779
GAUNN, Charles	Brun 1784	GESS, George	Oran 1779
GAURE, Suzanne	Brun 1784	GHANER, George	Blad 1784
GAUS, Frederick	Rowa 1761	GHIBSON, John	Surr 1782

GIATT, Joseph	Surr 1782		GILBERT, John	Perq 1772	
GIBBLE, Dedrick	Cart 1779		John	Mont 1782	
GIBBONS, George	Cart 1779		John	Surr 1782	
Hen	Onsl 1771		John Jr	Hert 1779	
Jonathan	Onsl 1771		John Jr	Hert 1784	
Joshua	Curr 1779		John Sr	Hert 1779	
Robert	Cart 1779		John Sr	Hert 1784	
Stephen	Curr 1779		Joseph	Jone 1779	
Wm	Oran 1779		Joseph	Perq 1787	
GIBBS, George	Blad 1784		Josiah	Pasq 1789	
Nathaniel	Cart 1779		Matthew	Hali 1783	
Nicholas	Oran 1779		Moses	Brun 1784	
Samuel	Blad 1784		Nicholas Jr	Tyrr 1784	
Shadrack	Casw 1786		Nicholas Sr	Tyrr 1784	
Thomas	Samp 1784		Wm	Ruth 1782	
GIBSON, Chas	NorH 1780		Wm	Hali 1783	
Churchill	Hali 1783		Wm	Tyrr 1784	
David	Cuur 1779		Wm	Jone 1779	
Garrett	Surr 1782		GILCHRIST, Job	Jone 1779	
Geo	Onsl 1771		John	Blad 1784	
Ginnins	Oran 1779		Thomas	Hali 1783	
Henry Jr	Curr 1779		GILES, John	Tyrr 1784	
James	Rowa 1767		Richard	Rowa 1768	
James	Casw 1786		Thomas	Mont 1782	
James	Casw 1784		Wm	Chow 1785	
James	Mont 1782		GILGOW, Tobin	Crav 1779	
James	Rich 1790		GILKEY, Robert	Ruth 1782	
Joel	Casw 1786		GILL, David	Warr 1784	
John	Casw 1786		James	Oran 1779	
John	Casw 1784		James	Hali 1783	
John	Tyrr 1784		Joseph	Gran 1785	
John	Perq 1772		Joseph	Gran 1771	
John	Surr 1782		Richard	Bert 1774	
Joseph	Surr 1782		Richard	Bert 1781	
Julius	Wilk 1784		Robert	Casw 1784	
Martha	Camd 1782		Thomas	Hali 1783	
Nelson	Rich 1790		Thomas	Surr 1782	
Peter	Curr 1779		Wm	Gran 1785	
Robert	Curr 1779		Wm	Surr 1782	
Thomas	Rich 1790		Young	Surr 1782	
Valentine	Surr 1782		GILLAM, Chas	Gran 1771	
Wm	Oran 1779		Ephraim	Bute 1766	
Wm	Mont 1782		Harriett	Gran 1785	
Wm	Onsl 1771		Harris	Gran 1771	
Wm	Surr 1782		John	Gran 1785	
GIDDENS, Jacob	Onsl 1771		Moses	Bert 1781	
James	Surr 1782		Wm	Gran 1785	
GIDDINGS, Jacob Jr	Onsl 1771		Wm	Gran 1771	
Wm	Surr 1782		Wm Sr	Gran 1771	
GIDDINS, Francis	Surr 1782		GILLESPIE, Archibald		
Margaret	Surr 1782			Onsl 1771	
Roger	Surr 1782		GILLEY, Francvis	Wilk 1782	
GIFFORD, John	Gran 1785		Peter	Wilk 1782	
GILBERT, Benjamin	Camd 1782		GILLIAM, Burwell	NorH 1780	
Chas	Wilk 1782		Hinchia	Perq 1787	
David	Jone 1779		GILLIKIN, Alexander	Cart 1779	
Guy	Jone 1779		Benjamin	Cart 1779	
James	Hali 1783		Charles	Cart 1779	
James	Tyrr 1784		Joseph	Cart 1779	
Jeremiah	Pasq 1779		Thomas	Cart 1779	
Jeremiah	Pasq 1789		GILLION, Wm	Casw 1784	
Jesse	Mont 1782		GILLIS, Daniel	Rich 1790	
Joel	Wayn 1786		John	Blad 1784	
John	Camd 1782		John	Rich 1790	
John	Samp 1784		Neil	Blad 1784	

GILLISON, David	Casw 1784	GLOVER, Joab	Gran 1785
GILLISPIE, James	Dupl 1783	John	Gran 1785
James	Casw 1784	John	Hali 1783
Robert	Gran 1785	John	Warr 1779
Wm	Casw 1784	John	Wilk 1782
GILMORE, Charles	Bute 1766	John	Surr 1782
GILPIN, Henry	Gran 1785	Joseph	Gran 1785
GILREATH, Alex	Wilk 1782	Joseph	Gran 1771
John	Wilk 1782	Nathaniel	Hali 1783
Wm	Bute 1766	Reuben	Surr 1782
Wm	Wilk 1782	Thomas	Warr 1779
Wm Sr	Wilk 1782	Thomas	NorH 1780
GILTON, Abraham	Casw 1786	Thomas	Surr 1782
John	Casw 1786	Wm	Albe 1694
GINN, Henry	Dobb 1780	Wm	Gran 1785
Jacob	Wayn 1786	GLOWER, Thomas	Perq 1772
Jesse	Wayn 1786	GLUTON, Joseph	Dobb 1780
GINNET, Thomas	Wayn 1786	GOBER, George	Gran 1785
GINNIS, John	Oran 1779	GODDARD, George	Mart 1779
GIPSON, David	Wilk 1782	John	Surr 1782
Elizabeth	Pasq 1779	Shadrack	Mart 1779
Wm	Curr 1779	GODFREY, Constable	Onsl 1771
GIRKEN, John	Tyrr 1784	Francis	Albe 1694
GIST, Moses	Rowa 1767	Jacob	Camd 1782
Wm	Rowa 1767	James	Gran 1785
GIVEN, John	Surr 1782	Jesse	Camd 1782
GLADHOUSE, Elijah	Wilk 1784	Joan	Albe 1694
GLADIS, Richard	Rich 1790	John	Albe 1694
GLADWIN, John	Bert 1774	John	Camd 1782
GLASGO, Caleb	Pasq 1789	Joseph	Camd 1782
GLASGOW, Ann	Pasq 1779	Joseph	Perq 1787
Caleb	Pasq 1779	Joshua	Camd 1782
James	Dobb 1780	Matthew	Bert 1781
James	Curr 1779	Thomas	Onsl 1771
Richard	Gran 1785	Tulla	Perq 1787
Solomon	Pasq 1779	Wm	Albe 1679
Thomas	Curr 1779	Wm	Albe 1694
Wm	Curr 1779	Wm	Blad 1784
GLASS, Josiah	Casw 1784	Wm	Gran 1771
Wm	Gran 1785	GODLEY, Elias	Beau 1786
GLASSON, Joseph	Oran 1779	John	Beau 1786
GLAZE, Benj	Gran 1771	Nathan	Beau 1786
Josiah	Casw 1784	Nathan Sr	Beau 1786
Reuben	Gran 1785	Thomas	Beau 1786
Samuel	Casw 1784	GODWIN, Alexdander	John 1784
Thomas	Gran 1785	Anne	Blad 1784
GLENN, Beverly	Casw 1784	Barnaby	Hert 1779
Hugh	Onsl 1771	Barnaby	Hert 1784
Patience	Surr 1782	Edmund	John 1784
Wm	Casw 1784	Ezekiel	Tyrr 1784
Worham	Oran 1779	Jacob Jr	Samp 1784
GLISSON, Daniel	Hert 1784	James	Samp 1784
Daniel	Bert 1774	James	Brun 1784
Daniel	Bert 1781	James	Hert 1784
Henry	Hert 1779	John	Tyrr 1784
Isaac	Mart 1779	Jonathan	Samp 1784
James	Bert 1774	Joseph	Samp 1784
Joseph	Wayn 1786	Joseph	Tyrr 1784
GLODOM, Ann	Wilk 1782	Josiah	Hert 1779
GLOHON, James W Sr	Hert 1784	Kearney	Hert 1779
James WJR	Hert 1784	Kerney	Hert 1784
GLOVER, Benj	Wilk 1782	Nathan	Samp 1784
Henry	Bute 1766	Pierce	Blad 1784
Henry	Warr 1784	Richard	Samp 1784
James	Wilk 1782	Samuel	John 1784

GODWIN, Selby   Tyrr 1784
    Stephen   John 1784
    Thomas   John 1784
    Willis   Hert 1779
    Willis   Hert 1784
    Wm   Hert 1779
    Wm   Samp 1784
GOFF, Lewis   Dupl 1779
    Thomas   Samp 1784
    Thomas   Casw 1784
GOFORTH, Andrew   Ruth 1782
GOING, Alexander   Ruth 1782
    Judrick   Casw 1784
    Wm   Ruth 1782
GOINS, James   Surr 1782
    Thomas   Surr 1782
GOLAR, Stephen   Blad 1784
GOLD, Daniel   Curr 1779
    David   Casw 1784
    Joseph   Casw 1784
    Wm   Beau 1786
GOLDEN, Archibald   Hali 1783
GOLDSBEY, Drury   Surr 1782
GOLDSON, Joseph   Casw 1784
GOLIGHTLY, John   Bute 1766
    John Jr   Bute 1766
    Wm   Bute 1766
GOOCH, Amos   Gran 1785
    Billy   Casw 1784
    Gideon   Gran 1785
    James   Casw 1786
    James   Casw 1784
    John   Gran 1785
    Joseph   Gran 1785
    Roland   Gran 1785
    Wm   Casw 1784
    Wm Jr   Casw 1786
    Wm Jr   Casw 1784
    Wm Sr   Casw 1786
    Wm Sr   Casw 1784
GOOD, Edward   Hali 1783
    Isham   Bute 1766
    John   Hali 1783
    John   Surr 1782
    Joseph Jr   Rich 1790
    Joseph Sr   Rich 1790
    Peter   Wilk 1784
    Peter   Wilk 1784
    Richard   Surr 1782
    Thomas Jr   Surr 1782
    Thomas Sr   Surr 1782
    Wm   Hali 1783
    Wm   NBer 1779
GOODBREAD, John   Ruth 1782
    Joseph   Ruth 1782
    Phillip   Ruth 1782
GOODEN, James   Bert 1774
    Willis   Samp 1784
GOODIN, Aaron   Jone 1779
    George   John 1784
    Wm   John 1784
GOODING, Daniel   Dobb 1780
    Francis   NBer 1779
    John   NBer 1779
    Lewis   Rich 1790

GOODINGMORE, Morrow Beau 1786
GOODLOE, Robert   Gran 1785
GOODMAN, Benj   Gran 1771
    Henry   Dobb 1780
    Henry   Samp 1784
    Isaac   Gate 1789
    Jacob   Curr 1779
    James   Dobb 1780
    John   Gate 1789
    Lewis   Dobb 1780
    Luke   Samp 1784
    Mary   Dobb 1780
    Overton   Ruth 1782
    Solomon   Samp 1784
    Timothy   Dobb 1780
    Wm   Wayn 1786
    Wm   Brun 1784
    Wm   Wilk 1782
    Wm   Gate 1789
GOODNER, John   Oran 1779
GOODNIGHT, George   Rowa 1761
GOODRICH, Matthew   Warr 1784
    Matthew   Warr 1779
GOODRICK, George   Wayn 1786
GOODSON, Jesse   NorH 1780
    Mander   NorH 1780
    Uzzel   Nash 1782
GOODWIN, Alexander Mont 1782
    Exum   Chow 1785
    George   Mont 1782
    Isaac   Perq 1772
    Jacob   Samp 1784
    Jacob   Perq 1787
    James   Nash 1782
    Jesse   Hali 1783
    John   Bute 1766
    John   Perq 1772
    John   Perq 1787
    Joseph   Chow 1785
    Josiah   Hali 1783
    Louis   Perq 1787
    Lucy   Bute 1766
    Mark   Bute 1766
    Peter   Bute 1766
    Richard   Perq 1772
    Richard   Perq 1787
    Samuel   Gran 1785
    Theophilu & s   Bute 1766
    Theophilus Jr   Bute 1766
    Thomas   Cart 1779
    Thomas   Bute 1766
    Thomas   Chow 1785
    Thomas   Gran 1785
    Wm   Perq 1772
    Wm   Onsl 1771
GOOGMAN, Henry   Gate 1789
GORDON, Abraham   Pasq 1789
    Alex   Rich 1790
    Benj   Gate 1789
    Benj Jr   NorH 1780
    Chas   Wilk 1782
    David   Dobb 1780
    David   Wilk 1782
    Francis   NBer 1779
    George   Wilk 1778

GORDON, George	Wilk 1782	GOWER, Wm	John 1784
George	NorH 1780	GRACE, Geo	Surr 1782
Isaac	Pasq 1789	James	Wayn 1786
Jacob	Gate 1789	John	Surr 1782
James	Pasq 1779	Wm	Dobb 1780
John	Nash 1782	GRADY, John	Dobb 1780
John	Oran 1779	GRAGG, Wm	Gran 1771
John	Hali 1783	GRAHAM, Alexander	Blad 1784
John	Tyrr 1784	Archibald	Rich 1790
John	Gran 1779	Arthur	Blad 1784
John	Gate 1789	Dugal	Rich 1790
John	Bert 1781	Ebenezer	Gate 1789
Joseph	Pasq 1779	Edward	Casw 1786
Joseph	Pasq 1789	Edward	Casw 1784
Mary	Wilk 1782	Edward	Wilk 1784
Moses	Jone 1779	Edward	Wilk 1782
Nathaniel Sr	Wilk 1782	Edward	Rich 1790
Nathl	Perq 1787	Geo	Rich 1790
Peter	Curr 1779	James	Surr 1782
Thomas	Wilk 1782	John	Oran 1779
Thomas	Surr 1782	John	Casw 1786
Thomas	Rich 1790	John	Casw 1784
Wm	Oran 1779	John	Rich 1790
Wm	Gate 1789	Peter	Casw 1786
Wm	Pasq 1789	Wm	Casw 1786
GORE, Wm	Brun 1782	Wm	Casw 1784
GORMAN, Wm	Jone 1779	Wm	Rich 1790
GOSE, Anthony	Bert 1781	Wm Jr	Casw 1784
GOSLIN, John	Surr 1782	GRAINGE, John Jr	Brun 1784
GOSS, Joseph	Gran 1785	John Sr	Brun 1784
Shearmore	Gran 1785	GRAINGER, John	Dobb 1780
Thomas	Casw 1784	Samuel	Crav 1779
Thomas	Gran 1771	GRANBERRY, Wm	NorH 1780
Zacheriah	Gran 1771	GRANBURY, Josiah	Gate 1789
GOSSAGE, Daniel	Casw 1786	Wm	Crav 1779
GOSSETT, James	Rowa 1768	GRANDY, Absalom	Camd 1782
Thomas	Rowa 1768	Ammon	Camd 1782
Wm	Rowa 1768	Anne Jr	Camd 1782
GOSTEN, Elizabeth	Surr 1782	Anne Sr	Camd 1782
John	Perq 1772	Caleb	Camd 1782
GOSTOPHER, Wm	Casw 1784	Charles	Camd 1782
GOSWICK, Joseph	Bute 1766	David	Camd 1782
GOTT, Richard	Oran 1779	Malachi	Camd 1782
Robert	Oran 1779	Noah	Camd 1782
GOTTON, Jesse	Bert 1781	Solomon	Camd 1782
GOUCH, Amos	Gran 1785	Thomas	Camd 1782
Gideon	Gran 1785	Thomas Jr	Camd 1782
John	Gran 1785	GRANGER, John	Brun 1782
Joseph	Gran 1785	GRANT, Abraham	NorH 1780
Roland	Gran 1785	Alexander	Ruth 1782
GOUGE, John	Bute 1766	Alexander	Onsl 1771
GOUGH, Joseph	Wilk 1782	Daniel	Gran 1771
Wm	Bert 1774	James	Nash 1782
GOWEN, Edward	Gran 1785	James	Casw 1786
Edward	Gran 1771	James	Casw 1784
John	Gran 1785	John	Dobb 1780
John	Mont 1782	John	Casw 1786
John	Gran 1771	John	Wayn 1786
Joseph	Gran 1771	John	Casw 1784
Moses	Gran 1771	John	NBer 1779
Thomas	Mont 1782	John	Surr 1782
Thomas	Gran 1771	Mathew	Onsl 1771
Walter	Albe 1679	Michael	Wayn 1786
Wm	Gran 1785	Richard	NorH 1780
GOWER, John	John 1784	Sarah	Onsl 1771

GRANT, Walter	Curr 1779	GRAY, John	Oran 1779
Wm	Ruth 1782	John	Camd 1782
Wm	Wayn 1786	John	Pasq 1779
Wm	Casw 1784	John	Wilk 1782
Wm	Onsl 1771	John	Onsl 1771
GRANTHAM, Edward	Blad 1784	John	Pasq 1789
Jacob	Wayn 1786	Joseph	Camd 1782
James	Hert 1779	Joshua Jr	Camd 1782
James	Wayn 1786	Joshua Sr	Camd 1782
James	Blad 1784	Lodowick	Dobb 1780
James	Hert 1784	Lovick	Tyrr 1784
Jesse	Wayn 1786	Mary	Pasq 1779
Joel	Wayn 1786	Nancy	Ruth 1782
Phereby	Wayn 1786	Nathanl	Pasq 1789
Richard	Blad 1784	Robert	Oran 1779
Wm	Hert 1779	Robert	Pasq 1779
Wm	Hert 1784	Robert	Curr 1779
GRASHANY, Peter	Chow 1785	Robert	Pasq 1789
GRASNTHAM, Mary	Wayn 1786	Samuel	Wilk 1782
GRAVES, Ann	NBer 1779	Stephen	Bert 1781
Barzilla	Casw 1786	Thomas	Bute 1766
Barzilla	Casw 1784	Thomas	Hali 1783
Benj	NorH 1780	Thomas	Pasq 1779
Boston	Oran 1779	Thomas	Curr 1779
Henry	Gran 1771	Timothy	Camd 1782
Henry Jr	Gran 1785	Wm	Rowa 1768
Henry Sr	Gran 1785	Wm	Oran 1779
Jacob	Oran 1779	Wm	Pasq 1779
John	Oran 1779	Wm	Warr 1784
John	Casw 1784	Wm	Bert 1774
John	Gran 1785	Wm	Warr 1784
John Jr	Oran 1779	Wm	Curr 1779
John Jr	Casw 1786	Wm	Wilk 1782
John Jr	Casw 1784	Wm	Onsl 1771
John Sr	Casw 1786	Wm	Bert 1781
Robert	Oran 1779	Wm H	Surr 1782
Tabitha	Albe 1694	Zachariah	Surr 1782
Thomas	Casw 1786	GRAYBLE, Stephens	Bert 1781
Thomas	Casw 1784	GREAT, Benj	Beau 1786
Thomas	Brun 1782	GREAVES, Rhoda	Pasq 1789
Wm	Oran 1779	GREAVEY, Benjamin	Brun 1784
Wm	GRan 1785	GREEN, Abraham	Bute 1766
Wm	Gran 1771	Abraham	Warr 1784
GRAY, Abraham	Blad 1784	Abraham	Gate 1789
Anthony	Pasq 1779	Abraham & son	Bute 1766
Edward	Camd 1782	Ann	Crav 1779
Edward	NBer 1779	Benjamin	Hali 1783
Edward	Curr 1779	Caleb	Blad 1784
Elizabeth	Dupl 1783	Daniel	Oran 1779
Elizabeth	Camd 1782	Daniel	Hali 1783
George	Chow 1785	Elijah	Oran 1779
George	Onsl 1771	Geo	Surr 1782
Godfrey	Tyrr 1784	Hannah	Hali 1783
Griffith	Curr 1779	Hartley	Gran 1785
Henry	Tyrr 1784	Henry	Gran 1785
Israel	Onsl 1771	Henry	Hali 1783
James	Ruth 1782	Isaac	Gate 1789
James	Bute 1766	James	Rowa 1761
James	Warr 1784	James	Rowa 1768
James	Mont 1782	James	Blad 1784
James	Wilk 1782	James	Jone 1779
James	Onsl 1771	James	Beau 1786
James	Beau 1786	James & s Jams	Rowa 1761
John	Albe 1694	James & s John	Rowa 1768
John	Dobb 1780	James West	Hali 1783

GREEN, Job	Gran 1785	GREER, James	Rich 1790
John	Oran 1779	John	Perq 1772
John	Blad 1784	John	Wilk 1782
John	Brun 1784	Joseph	Perq 1772
John	Chow 1785	Joshua	Wilk 1784
John	Hali 1783	Samuel	Casw 1786
John	NBer 1779	GREESON, Nicholas	Oran 1779
John	Warr 1784	GREGORY, Abner	Camd 1782
John	Onsl 1771	Absalom	Ruth 1782
John	Surr 1782	Arthur	Camd 1782
John Jr	Oran 1779	Arthur	NorH 1780
John Sr	Oran 1779	Asahel	Camd 1782
Joseph	Hert 1779	Benjamin	Chow 1785
Joseph	Bute 1766	Chas	NorH 1780
Joseph	Rowa 1761	Cornelius	Curr 1779
Joseph	Rowa 1768	David	Camd 1782
Joseph	Wayn 1786	Eleanor	Chow 1785
Joseph	Hert 1784	Ethelred	John 1784
Joseph	NBer 1779	Griffith Jr	Curr 1779
Joseph deceasd	Warr 1784	Griffith Sr	Curr 1779
Josiah	Warr 1784	Hardy	Onsl 1771
Leonard	Mont 1782	Hosea	Pasq 1789
Littlebury	Hali 1783	Isaac	Camd 1782
Lucy	Casw 1784	James	Camd 1782
Mahala	Hert 1784	James	Casw 1784
Malachi	Hert 1784	James	Gate 1789
Malachi	Bert 1781	Jesse	Curr 1779
Mathew	Onsl 1771	John	Camd 1782
Mathias	Gate 1789	John	John 1784
Nathan	Hali 1783	John	Onsl 1771
Obed	Warr 1784	Joseph	Ruth 1782
Peter	Bute 1766	Joseph	Camd 1782
Peter	Surr 1782	Judith	Camd 1782
Phillip	Surr 1782	Luke	Chow 1785
Randolph	Hert 1784	Matthew	Jone 1779
Reuben	Samp 1784	Nathan	Camd 1782
Richard	Mont 1782	Nathan Sr	Camd 1782
Richard	Gate 1789	Noah	Camd 1782
Robert	Hali 1783	Price	Hert 1784
Saml	Gate 1789	Richard	Camd 1782
Samuel & s Geo	Bute 1766	Ruth	Camd 1782
Sarah	Hali 1783	Sampson	Camd 1782
Simon	Blad 1784	Samson	Camd 1782
Solomon	Hert 1784	Thomas	Hert 1779
Thomas	Warr 1784	Thomas	Samp 1784
Thomas	Crav 1779	Willis	Camd 1782
Thomas	Wilk 1782	Wm	Camd 1782
Wm	Bute 1766	Wm	Chow 1785
Wm	Blad 1784	Wm	Perq 1787
Wm	Gran 1785	GRESHAM, Oliver	Hali 1783
Wm	Warr 1784	GRICE, Alexander	Nash 1782
Wm	Jone 1779	James	Nash 1782
Wm	NBer 1779	James	John 1784
Wm	Onsl 1771	John	Brun 1784
Zachariah	Surr 1782	Louis	John 1784
GREENHAW, Jonathan	Casw 1784	Moses	Blad 1784
Jonathan	Casw 1786	Robert	Blad 1784
GREENLEE, James	Wilk 1782	Samuel	Casw 1784
GREENSTREET, Peter	Wilk 1782	Theophilus	Nash 1782
GREENWAY, Sarah	Beau 1779	Wm	Blad 1784
GREER, Ann	Casw 1786	Wm	John 1784
Bartley	Gran 1785	GRIDER, John	Wilk 1782
Daniel	Wilk 1782	GRIER, Ann	Wilk 1782
Geo	Rich 1790	Aquilla	Wilk 1782
James	Dupl 1779	Benj	Wilk 1782

GRIER, Jesse	Wilk 1782	GRIFFIN, Wm	Perq 1772
John	Wilk 1782	Wm	Bert 1781
Joshua	Perq 1772	Wm	Perq 1787
Joshua	Wilk 1782	GRIFFINGEN, Wm	Onsl 1771
GRIEVES, Lydia	Pasq 1789	GRIFFIS, Edward	Beau 1786
GRIFFE, Benj	Surr 1782	GRIFFITH, Andrew	Oran 1779
GRIFFIN, Amos	Perq 1772	Catson	Oran 1779
Amos	Beau 1779	John	Hert 1779
Amos	Perq 1787	John	Hert 1784
Andrew	Casw 1784	Thomas	Oran 1779
Andrew Jr	Blad 1784	Wm	Hert 1779
Andrew Sr	Blad 1784	Wm	Oran 1779
Arthur	NorH 1780	Wm	Curr 1779
Benjamin	Mart 1779	GRIGGS, George Jr	Curr 1779
David	Mart 1779	George Sr	Curr 1779
Delilah	Nash 1782	John	Beau 1786
Dempsey	Wayn 1786	Moses	Surr 1782
Drury	Dobb 1780	Rhoda	Warr 1784
Edward	Mart 1779	Wm	Beau 1786
Edward	Bert 1781	GRILL, Benjamin	Beau 1779
Eliab	Perq 1787	GRIMES, Barney	Oran 1779
Elizabeth	Wilk 1782	Charles	Oran 1779
Epenetes	Mart 1779	Duncan	Blad 1784
Evan	Dobb 1780	George	Wilk 1784
Hardy	Nash 1782	John	Blad 1784
Henry	Gate 1789	Robert	Jone 1779
Isabel	Hali 1783	Sam	Bert 1781
Jacob	Dobb 1780	Samuel	Bert 1774
James	Nash 1782	Thomas	Mart 1779
James	Wayn 1786	GRIMSLEY, George	Dobb 1780
James	Hali 1783	John	Dobb 1780
James	Pasq 1779	Sherrod	Dobb 1780
James	Perq 1772	GRIMSTEAD, Holly	Curr 1779
James	NorH 1780	GRINAWAY, Thomas	Gran 1771
James	Perq 1787	GRINSTEAD, Wm	Hali 1783
James	Pasq 1789	GRISHAM, Archibald	Oran 1779
Jesse	Dobb 1780	Benjamin	Gran 1785
Jesse	Perq 1787	David	Oran 1779
Job	NorH 1780	Edward	Oran 1779
John	Mart 1779	Edward	Gran 1785
John	Camd 1782	George	Oran 1779
John	Tyrr 1784	Harris	Oran 1779
John	NorH 1780	Henry	Gran 1785
Joseph	Pasq 1779	James	Gran 1785
Joseph	Pasq 1789	John	Oran 1779
Joseph Jr	Nash 1782	Richard	Gran 1785
Joseph Sr	Nash 1782	Robert	Oran 1779
Joshua	Pasq 1789	Stephen	Gran 1785
Josiah	Perq 1787	Whater	Gran 1785
Lodowick	Camd 1782	GRISSET, Wm	Brun 1782
Martin	Mart 1779	GRISSETT, George	Brun 1782
Phoebe	Mart 1779	Reuben	Brun 1782
Pierce	Nash 1782	GRISSOM, James	Rowa 1768
Robert	Albe 1694	GRIST, Benj	Beau 1786
Robert	Wayn 1786	John	Beau 1786
Robert	NorH 1780	John & s Wm	Rowa 1768
Roland	NorH 1780	Reading	Beau 1786
Sam	Onsl 1771	Richard	Beau 1786
Samuel	Dobb 1780	Wm	Beau 1786
Simon	Dobb 1780	GRISVETT, Delilah	Brun 1784
Thomas	Perq 1772	Wm Jr	Brun 1784
Willis	Chow 1785	GRIZZARD, Thomas	Dobb 1780
Wm	Dobb 1780	GRIZZETT, Reuben	Brun 1784
Wm	Mart 1779	Wm	Brun 1784
Wm	Camd 1782	GROCE, Devol	Surr 1782

GROCE, Simon	Surr 1782	GURLEY, George	John 1784
GROFS, Godfrey	Surr 1782	Jacob	John 1784
Wm	Surr 1782	Joel	Wayn 1786
GROFTEN, Wm	Perq 1772	Joel	Surr 1782
GROSS, Francis	Nash 1782	John	John 1784
Joshua	Nash 1782	Joseph	John 1784
GROVE, David	Beau 1779	Lazarus	John 1784
GROVER, James	Bert 1781	Lewis	Wayn 1786
GROVES, Allen	Bute 1766	Mary	John 1784
Daniel	Beau 1786	Nicholas	Hali 1783
Henry	Gran 1785	Robert	Wayn 1786
John	Gran 1785	Sarah	John 1784
Thomas	Hali 1783	GUSTATON, Wm	Bert 1779
Wm	Gran 1785	GUTHRIE, Charles	Cart 1779
Wm	Beau 1786	Daniel	Cart 1779
GRUBB, Henry	Rowa 1761	Frederick	Cart 1779
GRUBBS, Richard	NBer 1779	Henry	Hali 1783
GRUBE, John	Crav 1779	Jesse	Hali 1783
GTREEN, John	Bute 1766	John	Cart 1779
GUARD, Joshua	Tyrr 1784	John	Casw 1784
GUARTNEY, Hannah	Pitt 1786	John	Hali 1783
GUBBAGE, Wm	Hali 1783	Levi	Cart 1779
GUDAH, Martin	Beau 1779	Reuben	Hali 1783
GUESS, Geo	Gran 1771	Samuel	Cart 1779
Pleasant	Gran 1771	Wm	Gran 1785
GUEST, Benjamin	Wilk 1784	Wm	Hali 1783
Benjamin	Wilk 1782	GUTTING, Garrett	Casw 1784
Elias	Gran 1785	GUY, Benjamin	Gran 1785
Godfrey	Surr 1782	John	Mart 1779
John	Gran 1785	John	Beau 1786
John	Wilk 1784	Wm	Mart 1779
Joseph	Crav 1779	Wm	Beau 1786
Moses	Wilk 1784	Wm	Pasq 1789
Moses	Wilk 1782	GUYAN, Joseph	Mart 1779
Richard	Beau 1786	GUYER, John	Perq 1787
Wm	Wilk 1784	Joseph	Perq 1787
Wm	Wilk 1782	Joshua	Perq 1787
Wm Jr	Wilk 1782	GUYTON, Samuel	Blad 1784
GUFFEY, John	Ruth 1782	GWINN, Daniel	Casw 1786
GUILFORD, Isaac	Camd 1782	Daniel	Casw 1784
John	Pasq 1694	Daniel	Gate 1789
GUIN, Almon	Surr 1782	Edward	Oran 1779
Saml	Pasq 1789	John	Casw 1784
GULLET, Daniel	Wilk 1782	Mordecai	Oran 1779
Geo	Rich 1790	Moses	Oran 1779
GULLEY, John Jr	John 1784	Saml	Surr 1782
John Sr	John 1784	Thomas	Oran 1779
GUNN, Geo	Rich 1790	Thomas	Wayn 1786
John	Hali 1783	Wm	Oran 1779
Joseph	Oran 1779	Wm	Casw 1784
Mary	Casw 1784	Wm	Warr 1784
Thomas	Casw 1784	Wm	Gate 1789
Wm	Oran 1779	GYER, Sarah	Wilk 1782
Wm	Warr 1784	GYMON, Isaiah	Surr 1782
GUNTER, John	Jone 1779		
Lazarus	Hali 1783		
Richard	Jone 1779		
GUNTHER, John	Gran 1771	HABS, John	Perq 1772
GUPTON, James	Bute 1766	HACKETT, John	Hert 1784
Stephen & s Ja	Bute 1766	HACKNEW, John	Warr 1784
GURGANUS, Joshua	Beau 1779	HACKNEY, Rachel	Nash 1782
GURGOIN, John	Albe 1679	Wm	Nash 1782
GURLEY, Ann	John 1784	HADDOCK, Andrew	Casw 1784
Edward	John 1784	Drury	Blad 1784
Frederick	Chow 1785	HADLEY, Ambrose	Hali 1783

HADLEY, Benjamin	Hali 1783	HALL, David	Cart 1777
Joseph	Hali 1783	David	Oran 1779
Wm	Hali 1783	David	Camd 1782
Wm	Rich 1790	David	Casw 1784
HADNOT, Stephen	Cart 1779	Edmund	Camd 1782
Stephen	Onsl 1771	Edward	Perq 1787
Whitcher	Onsl 1771	Edward Jr	Perq 1787
Wm	Onsl 1771	Enoch	Blad 1784
HADSACK, Peter	Wayn 1786	Geo	Beau 1786
HAFNER, Jacob	Surr 1782	George	Beau 1779
HAGAN, Danby	Beau 1779	Henry	Perq 1772
HAGEN, Balthager	Surr 1782	Ignatius	Hali 1783
Darby	Beau 1786	Isaac	Blad 1784
HAGERTY, Patrick	Gate 1789	Isaac	Wayn 1786
HAGGARD, David	Casw 1784	Isaiah	Perq 1787
Edmund	Casw 1786	Jacob	Perq 1772
Edmund	Casw 1784	James	Oran 1779
Saml	Surr 1782	James	Wayn 1786
Wm	Casw 1786	James	Jone 1779
Wm	Casw 1784	James	Perq 1787
HAGLER, John	Mont 1782	Jarman	Beau 1786
HAGOOD, Bird	Oran 1779	Joel	Rich 1790
George	Oran 1779	John	Bute 1766
Jesse	Oran 1779	John	Rowa 1768
HAGUE, Henry	Gran 1785	John	Oran 1779
James	Casw 1784	John	Samp 1784
John	Oran 1779	John	Casw 1784
HAIGHOVER, Geo	Gate 1789	John	Chow 1785
HAILES, Samuel	Blad 1784	John	Gran 1785
HAILEY, James	Hert 1779	John	Perq 1772
Joel	Hert 1779	John	Mont 1782
Nehemiah	Rowa 1761	John	Wilk 1782
Wm	Bute 1766	John	Surr 1782
HAINES, Stephen	Crav 1779	John	Gate 1789
HAIOR, James	Wilk 1782	John	Perq 1787
HAIR, John	Samp 1784	John	Rich 1790
John	NorH 1780	John Sr	Wilk 1782
Wm	Samp 1784	Joll	Beau 1786
HAIRFOOT, Malachi	Pitt 1786	Jonathan	Cart 1779
HAIST, John	Surr 1782	Joseph	Dobb 1780
HALBERT, John	Surr 1782	Joseph	Rowa 1768
HALE, James	Hert 1779	Joseph	Gran 1785
Jesse	Bert 1781	Joseph	Rich 1790
Joel	Hert 1779	Joseph Jr	Rich 1790
John	Dobb 1780	Lazarus	Samp 1784
John	Hali 1783	Lemuel	Pasq 1789
Jonas	NorH 1780	Levi	Oran 1779
Jonas	Bert 1781	Lewis Jr	Blad 1784
Reuben	Hert 1779	Lewis Sr	Blad 1784
HALEY, Holiday	NorH 1780	Mills	Wilk 1782
John	Rich 1790	Moses	NorH 1780
Randall	Rich 1790	Nathan	Blad 1784
Silas	Rich 1790	Nathaniel	Curr 1779
Wm	Rich 1790	Phillip	Casw 1784
HALIBEE, Wm	Wayn 1786	Poole	Dobb 1780
HALIBURTON, John	Casw 1784	Priscilla	Samp 1784
HALILEE, Sarah	Camd 1782	Randall	Surr 1782
HALL, Absalom	Camd 1782	Rebecca	NorH 1780
Armager	Samp 1784	Richard	Bute 1766
Benjamin	Oran 1779	Richard	Rowa 1768
Benjamin	Samp 1784	Robert	Hali 1783
Burwell	Dobb 1780	Robert Jr	Oran 1779
Caleb	Wayn 1786	Robert Jr	Pasq 1779
Charlton	Perq 1787	Robert Sr	Oran 1779
Clement	Chow 1785	Robert Sr	Pasq 1779

Simon	Cart 1779	HAMBRICK, Samuel	Ruth 1782
Spencer	Curr 1779	HAMELL, Adam	Chow 1785
Techell	Gran 1785	HAMER, James	Beau 1786
Thomas	Hert 1779	HAMILTON, Alexander	Chow 1785
Thomas	Oran 1779	Archibald	Oran 1779
Thomas	Hert 1784	Barnaby	Wayn 1786
Thomas	Warr 1784	Francis	Nash 1782
Thomas	NBer 1779	Guy	Wayn 1786
Thomas Jr	Crav 1779	John	Dobb 1780
Thomas L	Hali 1783	John	Chow 1785
Thomas Sr	Crav 1779	Joseph	Oran 1779
Wm	Nash 1782	Sarah	Dobb 1780
Wm	Dupl 1783	Thomas	Nash 1782
Wm	Rowa 1768	Wm	Oran 1779
Wm	Samp 1784	HAMLET, Richard	Warr 1784
Wm	Blad 1784	HAMLIN, Jonathan	Hali 1783
Wm	Casw 1784	HAMM, Erastus	Wayn 1786
Wm	Hali 1783	Henry	Wayn 1786
Wm	Crav 1779	Joseph	Surr 1782
Wm	Onsl 1771	Richard	Bute 1766
Wm	Beau 1786	Richard	Wayn 1786
Wm	Rich 1790	Thomas	Surr 1782
HALLEY, Thomas	Perq 1772	Wm	Dobb 1780
Wm	Ruth 1782	Wm Jr	Wayn 1786
Wm	Bute 1766	Wm Sr	Wayn 1786
HALLIBURTEN, Charles		Zackariah	Wayn 1786
	Casw 1784	HAMMER, John	Perq 1772
HALLIBURTON, David	Casw 1784	HAMMET, Robert	Surr 1782
Wm	Casw 1784	HAMMIL, Adam	Hali 1783
HALLOM, Jeremiah	Bert 1774	HAMMITER, Stewart	Tyrr 1784
John	Bert 1774	HAMMOCK, Charles	Gran 1785
HALLOWAY, David	Hali 1783	Chas	Gran 1771
HALLSING, David	Wilk 1782	David	Gran 1785
HALLSON, Anthony	Mont 1782	John	Gran 1771
HALLSTEAD, Drew	Pasq 1779	Wm	Gran 1785
Edward	Pasq 1779	HAMMON, Charles	Cart 1779
John	Pasq 1779	James	Chow 1785
HALSEY, Daniel	Chow 1785	Joseph	Wilk 1782
Edmond	Perq 1787	Wm	Wilk 1782
Fredk	Perq 1787	HAMMOND, Benjamin	Onsl 1771
James	Chow 1785	Edward	Onsl 1771
Malachi	Chow 1785	Henry	Bert 1781
Malachi	Chow 1785	Jesse	Hali 1783
Richard	Gran 1785	Job	Gran 1785
Wm	Chow 1785	John	Camd 1782
HALSTEAD, Edward	Pasq 1789	John	Warr 1784
Jarvis	Pasq 1789	John	Beau 1779
John	Curr 1779	John	Beau 1786
John	Pasq 1789	Lucy	Beau 1786
Samuel	Curr 1779	Martin	Onsl 1771
HALTSELOW, Henry	Surr 1782	Mel	Beau 1786
HAMBE, John	Wilk 1779	Phillip	Beau 1786
HAMBLET, Richard	Hali 1783	Samuel Jr	Gran 1785
HAMBLETON, David	Cart 1779	Samuel Sr	Gran 1785
John	Beau 1779	Shadrack	Hali 1783
John	Crav 1779	Wm	Hali 1783
HAMBLETT, James	Casw 1784	Wm	Rowa 1770
John	Mont 1782	Wm	Onsl 1771
Peter	Mont 1782	HAMMONS, Ambrose	Wilk 1782
HAMBLIN, Charles	Hali 1783	Ambrose	Surr 1782
HAMBRICK, Benj	Wilk 1782	Benjamin	Wilk 1782
Enoch	Ruth 1782	John	Samp 1784
Jeremiah	Ruth 1782	John	Blad 1784
Patrick	Wilk 1782	John	Wilk 1782
Saml	Gran 1771	John	Surr 1782

HAMPHILL, Wm	Warr 1784	HANKINS, John	Pasq 1694
HAMPTON, Andrew	Ruth 1782	Wm	Surr 1782
Collin	Surr 1782	HANKS, Elijah	Gran 1771
Ephraim	Gran 1771	Epaphroditus	Dobb 1780
Ezekiel	Gran 1771	John	Wayn 1786
Jacob	Wilk 1782	Mary	Dobb 1780
James	Wilk 1782	Mott	Dobb 1780
James	Surr 1782	Thomas	Nash 1782
Joel	Wilk 1782	Wm	Gran 1771
John	Surr 1782	HANLEY, James	Surr 1782
John	Gran 1771	John	Onsl 1771
Jonathan	Ruth 1782	HANNA, John	Surr 1782
Preston	Surr 1782	John Doak	Surr 1782
Richard	Surr 1782	HANNAH, Hillery	Curr 1779
Saml	Surr 1782	James	Wayn 1786
Thomas	Crav 1779	Sarah	Onsl 1771
Thomas	Wilk 1782	Wm	Oran 1779
HANCHY, Adam	Dupl 1783	HANNAN, Martin	Mont 1782
Moses	Dupl 1783	HANNON, Rebecca	Bert 1774
HANCOCK, Benjamin	Cart 1779	HANSELL, Joseph	Mart 1779
Benoni	Gran 1750	Wm	Bute 1766
David	Hert 1779	HANSFORD, Henry	Hali 1783
David	Hert 1784	Jenkins	Hert 1784
Henry	Cart 1779	HANSON, Andrew	Casw 1784
James Jr	Crav 1779	Benedict	Surr 1782
James Sr	Crav 1779	Vincent	Casw 1784
John	Surr 1782	HARALSON, Jonathan	Casw 1784
Nathaniel	Onsl 1771	HARBERT, Charles	Curr 1779
Nehemiah	Hert 1779	Jonathan	Beau 1779
Nehemiah	Hert 1784	HARBIN, John	Casw 1784
Robert	NorH 1780	John	Casw 1786
Roger	Crav 1779	Thomas	Wilk 1782
Samuel	Gran 1785	Wm	Casw 1784
Samuel & s Sim	Bute 1766	Wm	Casw 1786
Simon	Bute 1766	Wm	Wilk 1782
Simon	Gran 1785	HARBOUR, Adonijah	Surr 1782
Stephen	Albe 1679	HARDCASTLE, Elijah	John 1784
Wm	Bute 1766	James	John 1784
Wm	Tyrr 1784	HARDEN, Charles	Rowa 1768
Wm	Crav 1779	David	Ruth 1782
Wm	Onsl 1771	Henry	Surr 1782
HAND, Henry	Surr 1782	John	NorH 1780
John	Surr 1782	Mark	Surr 1782
John	Surr 1782	Nicholas	Oran 1779
HANDLEY, Edmund	Bert 1781	Presley	Casw 1786
James	Bute 1766	Saul	Wayn 1786
James	Wayn 1786	HARDESTY, Benjamin	Cart 1779
John	Wayn 1786	Joseph	Cart 1779
Joseph	Pasq 1779	Thomas	Cart 1779
Wm	Rich 1790	HARDGRAVES, Francis	Wilk 1782
HANEY, Benj	Onsl 1771	HARDIE, John	Pitt 1786
Bridger	Casw 1786	HARDIMAN, Uriah	Wilk 1782
Bridger	Casw 1784	HARDIN, Ann	Perq 1787
Charles	Casw 1786	Benjamin	Ruth 1782
Charles	Casw 1784	David	Samp 1784
John	Ruth 1782	James	Hali 1783
Reuben	Casw 1786	Jonathan	Ruth 1782
Thomas	Nash 1782	Richard	Bert 1781
Wm	Casw 1786	Solomon	Samp 1784
Wm	Casw 1784	Stephen	Beau 1786
HANKE, Ardell	Gran 1785	Thomas	Wilk 1784
Wm	Gran 1785	Thomas	Bert 1781
HANKIN, John	Pasq 1789	Wm	Hali 1783
HANKINS, Dennis	Brun 1784	Wm	Wilk 1782
James	Gran 1785	Wm	Perq 1787

HARDING, David	Hali 1783	HARE, Willis	Hert 1779
Israel	Beau 1786	Willis	Hert 1784
John	Casw 1784	Wm	Crav 1779
Presley	Casw 1784	HARFORD, John	Chow 1785
Wm	Casw 1784	HARGANS, Jeremiah	Hert 1779
HARDISON, Benjamin	Mart 1779	HARGATE, John	Blad 1784
Benjamin	Chow 1785	HARGET, Frederick	Jone 1779
Chas	Onsl 1771	HARGIS, Abraham Jr	Casw 1784
David	Mart 1779	Abraham Sr	Casw 1784
James	Mart 1779	Abram	Ruth 1782
John	Mart 1779	Richard	Casw 1784
John Jr	Mart 1779	Shadrack	Casw 1784
Joseph	Mart 1779	Thomas	Casw 1784
Joshua	Mart 1779	Wm	Oran 1779
Richard Sr	Mart 1779	Wm	Casw 1784
Thomas	Mart 1779	Wm	Wilk 1782
Wm	Mart 1779	HARGROVE, Arthur	Samp 1784
Wrenby	Onsl 1771	Bray	Samp 1784
HARDMAN, Adam	Rowa 1761	Britton	Blad 1784
Harman	Rowa 1761	Burrell	Blad 1784
HARDWICK, Aaron	Bute 1766	Howell	Surr 1782
Allen	Blad 1784	John	Hali 1783
James	Bute 1766	John	Oran 1779
Lindsell	Blad 1784	John	Gran 1771
Thomas	Blad 1784	Moses	Samp 1784
HARDY, Benjamin	Dobb 1780	Richard	Oran 1779
Edward	Bert 1774	Richard	Gran 1771
Edward	Bert 1781	Samuel	Brun 1784
Francis	Chow 1785	Sarah	Hali 1783
Henry	Bert 1781	Wm	John 1784
Humphrey	Bert 1774	HARGROVES, Benjamin	Gran 1785
Jesse	Bert 1774	John	Gran 1785
Jesse	Bert 1781	Leary Wm	Gran 1785
John	Bert 1774	Richard	Gran 1785
John	Crav 1779	HARKER, Ebenezer	Cart 1779
John	Bert 1781	James	Cart 1779
Joseph	Bert 1781	Susannah	Brun 1784
Laud	Bert 1781	Zechariah	Cart 1779
Lemuel	Dobb 1780	HARKINS, Aaron	Pasq 1779
Michael	Bert 1781	John	Rowa 1761
Robert	Chow 1785	Thomas	Rowa 1761
Robert	Bert 1774	HARMAN, Thomas	Perq 1772
Thomas	Dobb 1780	HARMON, Eliz	Perq 1787
Thomas	Hali 1783	George & son	Rowa 1768
Wm	Bert 1774	James	Perq 1787
Wm	Bert 1781	Jeremiah	Perq 1787
HARE, Benjamin	Hert 1784	John	Wilk 1782
Henry	Gate 1789	Mathias	Rowa 1768
Henry	Perq 1787	Nicholas	Bert 1781
James	Tyrr 1784	Phillip	Rowa 1768
John	Hert 1779	Thomas	Rowa 1768
John	Hert 1784	Thomas	Perq 1787
John	Gate 1789	Webb	Tyrr 1784
John	Beau 1786	HARNAGE, George	Hert 1779
John L	Hert 1784	George	Hert 1784
Joseph	Hert 1779	HARP, Henry	Gran 1785
Joseph	Hert 1784	John	Gran 1785
Joseph	Gate 1789	Sampson	Gran 1785
Luke	Hert 1779	Simon	Gran 1785
Mary	Beau 1786	Thomas	Gran 1785
Moses Jr	Gate 1789	Thomas Sr	Gran 1785
Moses Sr	Gate 1789	HARPER, Abner	Nash 1782
Thomas	Samp 1784	Abraham	Crav 1779
Thomas	Bert 1774	Alexander	Dobb 1780
Thomas	Bert 1781	Ambrose	Hali 1783

HARPER, Francis	Dobb 1780	HARRELL, Enoch	Surr 1782
Francis Sr	DObb 1780	Esther	Mart 1779
George	Blad 1784	Etheldred	John 1784
Henry	Hali 1783	Geo	NorH 1780
Isaac	Hali 1783	Gideon	Bert 1774
Jacob	Hali 1783	Hardy	Bert 1781
Jesse	Gran 1785	Henry	Gate 1789
Jesse	Gran 1771	Henry	Bert 1781
John	Oran 1779	Isaac	Gate 1789
John	Warr 1784	Isaac	Bert 1781
John	Surr 1782	Isaac Jr	Bert 1774
Matthew	Ruth 1782	Isaiah	Bert 1774
Reuben	Hali 1783	Isaiah	Gate 1789
Samuel	Ruth 1782	Isham	Wilk 1782
Samuel	Warr 1784	Jacob	Bert 1781
Sarah	Cart 1779	James	Mont 1782
Shadrack	Brun 1782	James Jr	Bert 1781
Susannah	Brun 1784	James Sr	Bert 1781
Thomas Sr	Crav 1779	Jesse	Blad 1784
Vincent	Hali 1783	Jesse	Hert 1779
Wm	Dobb 1780	Jesse	Hert 1784
Wm	Oran 1779	Jesse	Gate 1789
Wm	Samp 1784	Jesse Jr	Bert 1781
Wm	Jone 1779	Joel	Bert 1781
HARPERT, Samuel	Warr 1784	John	Wayn 1786
HARPET, John	Jone 1779	John	Hert 1779
HARRALSON, Elijah	Casw 1784	John	Hert 1784
Gideon	Casw 1784	John	Bert 1774
Herndon	Casw 1784	John	Curr 1779
Jane	Casw 1784	John	Surr 1782
HARREL, Jesse	Bert 1781	John	Surr 1782
John	Mart 1779	John	Bert 1781
Wm	NorH 1780	Jonathan	Surr 1782
HARRELL, Aaron	Gate 1789	Joseph	Dobb 1780
Aaron Jr	Gate 1789	Joshua	Bert 1781
Abner	Perq 1787	Josiah Jr	Bert 1781
Abraham	Bert 1774	Josiah Sr	Bert 1781
Absalom	Bert 1781	Kader	Dupl 1783
Adam	Mart 1779	Lemuel	Perq 1787
Adam	Chow 1785	Lott	Mart 1779
Adam	Bert 1774	Matthew	Mont 1782
Adam Jr	Bert 1774	Millie	Gate 1789
Adam Sr	Bert 1774	Nathan	Hert 1779
Amos	Bert 1781	Nathaniel	Hert 1784
Ann	Gate 1789	Noah	Gate 1789
Ann (widow)	Bert 1781	Nora	Bert 1781
Arthur	Bert 1781	Paul	Casw 1784
Asa	Gate 1789	Peter	Gate 1789
Balis	Bert 1781	Reuben	Bert 1781
Benj	Bert 1781	Saml	Gate 1789
Benjamin	Hert 1779	Samuel	Wayn 1786
Benjamin	Bert 1774	Samuel	Hert 1779
Christopher	Bert 1781	Samuel	Hert 1784
David	Bert 1781	Samuel	Perq 1772
Demcy	Perq 1787	Samuel	Bert 1774
Dempsey	Gate 1789	Shadrack	Bert 1774
Dempsey	Bert 1781	Shadrack	Bert 1781
Edward	Wayn 1786	Silas	Perq 1787
Edward	Bert 1774	Solomon	Bert 1774
Elijah	Hert 1779	Solomon	Bert 1781
Elijah	Hert 1784	Thomas	Mart 1779
Elisha	Blad 1784	Thomas	Bert 1774
Elisha	Chow 1785	Thomas	Gate 1789
Elisha	Gate 1789	Thomas	Bert 1781
Elizabeth	Dobb 1780	Thomas (Quaker	Bert 1781

Willis	Wayn 1786	HARRIS, George	Pasq 1694
Wm	Hert 1779	George	Pasq 1779
Wm	Bert 1774	George	Rowa 1768
Wm	Bert 1781	George	Mart 1779
Wm	Bert 1781	George	Gran 1785
HARREN, Henry	Surr 1782	Gibson	Gran 1785
HARRICK, Mary	Samp 1784	Gideon	NorH 1780
Mary	NewH 1782	Gillam	Gran 1771
HARRIMAN, David	Surr 1782	Gilliam	Gran 1785
HARRINGTON, David	Casw 1786	Goldman	Casw 1784
Drury	Hali 1783	Henry	Hali 1783
Henry	Rich 1790	Hezekiah	Pasq 1779
John	Beau 1779	Hezekiah	Pasq 1789
John	NBer 1779	Isham	Gran 1785
Nathaniel	Rich 1790	Isham	Gran 1771
Thomas	Bute 1766	Jacob	Beau 1779
HARRIOCK, Thomas	Wilk 1782	James	Oran 1779
HARRIS, Abraham	Chow 1785	James	Bute 1766
Amos	Warr 1784	James	Gran 1785
Amos	Bert 1781	James	Warr 1784
Archer	Oran 1779	James	Warr 1779
Archibald	Warr 1784	James	Mont 1782
Arthur	Mont 1782	James	Surr 1782
Bidford	Warr 1784	James Sr	Warr 1784
Bidford	Warr 1784	Jane	Bute 1766
Brantley	Mont 1782	Jane & s Drewr	Bute 1766
Brin	Cart 1779	Jeremiah	Oran 1779
Britain	Bute 1766	Jesse	Cart 1779
Burrill son of	Bute 1766	Jesse	Mont 1782
Charles	Gran 1785	Joel	Warr 1784
Charles	Warr 1784	Joel son of Jo	Bute 1766
Charles & son	Bute 1766	Johjn	NBer 1779
Christopher	Gran 1785	John	Oran 1779
Christr	Gran 1771	John	Dobb 1780
Clayborn	Warr 1784	John	Casw 1784
Clayborn	Gran 1771	John	Gran 1785
Clayborne	Warr 1784	John	Pasq 1779
Claybourn	Gran 1785	John	Warr 1784
Dabney	Surr 1782	John	Bert 1774
Darwin	Gran 1785	John	Crav 1779
David	Gran 1785	John	Mont 1782
David	Gran 1771	John	Surr 1782
David	Pasq 1789	John	Gran 1771
David Sr	Gran 1785	John	Bert 1781
Drewry	Bute 1766	John	Beau 1786
Edmond	Bute 1766	John & son Rd	Bute 1766
Edmund	Warr 1784	John Jr	Pasq 1789
Edward	Bute 1766	Jordan	Bute 1766
Edward	Oran 1779	Jordan	Warr 1784
Edward	Gran 1785	Jordan	Warr 1784
Edward	Warr 1784	Joseph	Dobb 1780
Edward	Wilk 1782	Joseph	Pasq 1779
Edward	NorH 1780	Joseph	Warr 1784
Edward	Gran 1771	Joseph	Pitt 1786
Eli	Hali 1783	Joseph	Pasq 1789
Elias	Hali 1783	Joseph & son J	Bute 1766
Elijah	Beau 1779	Major	Blad 1784
Elisha	Gran 1771	Mary	Surr 1782
Elisha	Gate 1789	Matthes	Hali 1783
Elizabeth Mrs	Warr 1784	Matthew	Bute 1766
Etheldred	Mont 1782	Matthew	Warr 1784
Ethelred	Bute 1766	Matthew	Gran 1771
Frederick	Warr 1784	May	Mont 1782
Frederick s of	Bute 1766	Mial	Bute 1766
George	Cart 1779	Miol	Warr 1784

Moses	Bute	1766	HARRISON, Benjamin	Wayn	1786
Moses	Warr	1784	Benjamin	Casw	1784
Mrs Elizxabeth	Warr	1784	Benjamin	Hert	1784
Nathan	Warr	1784	Benjamin	Tyrr	1784
Nathaniel	Warr	1784	Daniel	Jone	1779
Nathl	NorH	1780	Edmund	Tyrr	1784
Nathl	Surr	1782	Edward	Albe	1694
Nehemiah	Cart	1779	Edward	Blad	1784
Nehemiah	Cart	1779	Edward	Tyrr	1784
Nelson	Warr	1784	Elisha	Hali	1783
Newett	NorH	1780	Elisha	Warr	1784
Newit	Bute	1766	Hannah	Albe	1694
Norfleet	Hali	1783	Isaiah	Curr	1779
Parnall	Mont	1782	James	Warr	1779
Peter	Rowa	1768	James	Samp	1784
Richard	Bute	1766	James	Hert	1784
Richard	Mart	1779	James	Tyrr	1784
Richard	Gran	1785	Jethro	Nash	1782
Richard	Gran	1771	John	Nash	1782
Richard Jr	Gran	1785	John	Dobb	1780
Richmond	Oran	1779	John	Blad	1784
Robert	Hali	1783	John	Gran	1785
Robert	Warr	1784	John	Tyrr	1784
Robert	Surr	1782	John	Jone	1779
Robert	Gran	1771	John	Beau	1779
Robert & son B	Bute	1766	John	Curr	1779
Robert Esq	Gran	1785	John Jr	Blad	1784
Robert Jr	Gran	1785	John T.	Jone	1779
Robert Jr	Warr	1784	John W	Camd	1782
Robert Jr	Gran	1771	Jonathan	Tyrr	1784
Roe	Hali	1783	Joseph	Pitt	1786
Roland	Mont	1782	Joseph	Pasq	1789
Samuel	Casw	1784	Joshua	Curr	1779
Samuel	Gran	1785	Josiah	Tyrr	1784
Sherwood	Gran	1785	Mathias	Pasq	1789
Sherwood	Gran	1771	Millie	Gran	1785
Simon	Warr	1784	Ninnian	Casw	1784
Simon	NorH	1780	Richard Jr	Blad	1784
Stalling	Warr	1784	Robert	Surr	1782
Stephen	Wilk	1782	Samuel	Casw	1784
Sterling	Bute	1766	Stephen	Beau	1786
Thomas	Bute	1766	Thomas	Ruth	1782
Thomas	Crav	1779	Thomas	Casw	1784
Thomas	NorH	1780	Thomas	Perq	1772
Thomas	Gran	1771	Thomas	Bert	1774
Turner	Bute	1766	Thomas	Pasq	1789
Tyra	Chow	1784	Thomas Jr	Casw	1784
Tyree Jr	Casw	1786	Thomas Jr	Tyrr	1784
Tyree Sr	Casw	1786	Thomas Sr	Tyrr	1784
Uresiam	Gran	1785	Thomas s of Jo	Tyrr	1784
Wes	Mont	1782	Wm	Blad	1784
Wes Sr	Mont	1782	Wm	Tyrr	1784
West & sons	Bute	1766	Wm	Warr	1784
Wm	Nash	1782	Wm	Onsl	1771
Wm	Oran	1779	Wm	NorH	1780
Wm	Ruth	1782	Wm	Surr	1782
Wm	Gran	1785	HARROD, John	Samp	1784
Wm	Hali	1783	HARRY, Evan & s Evan		
Wm	Curr	1779		Rowa	1768
Wm	Gate	1789	HART, Arthur Jr	NorH	1780
HARRISDON, Robert	Gran	1771	Col. Thomas	Oran	1779
HARRISON, Abner	Camd	1782	David	Casw	1786
Abraham	Pasq	1779	David	Wayn	1786
Andrew	Casw	1784	Hartwell	Nash	1782
Benj	Gran	1771	Henry	NorH	1780

HART, Henry Phillip	Gran	1771
James	Oran	1779
John	Oran	1779
John	Gran	1785
John	Jone	1779
John	NorH	1780
John	Surr	1782
John	Surr	1782
John	Gran	1771
Joseph	Oran	1779
Joseph	Gran	1785
Joseph	Surr	1782
Joseph	Gran	1771
Micajah	Dobb	1780
Miles	Surr	1782
Moses	Dobb	1780
Peter	Oran	1779
Pleasant	Gran	1771
Samuel	Oran	1779
Stephen	Oran	1779
Thomas	Nash	1782
Thomas	NorH	1780
Thomas Jr	Oran	1779
Warren	NorH	1780
Wm	Gran	1785
Wm	Gran	1771
HARTLEY, Francis	Rowa	1768
John	Oran	1779
Wm	Crav	1779
HARTMAN, John	Surr	1782
HARTON, Howell	Warr	1784
John	Warr	1784
Samuel	Bute	1766
Thomas	Bute	1766
Thomas	Warr	1784
HARTSFIELD, David	Dobb	1780
Jacob	Bute	1766
John	Dobb	1780
John Jr	Dobb	1780
Paul	Dobb	1780
Paul Jr	Dobb	1780
HARVEY, Andrew	Casw	1784
Ann	Crav	1779
Ann	Pitt	1786
Ann	Perq	1787
Benj	Perq	1787
Caleb	Oran	1779
Ellison	Gran	1771
Isaac	Oran	1779
James	Beau	1779
John	Oran	1779
John	Blad	1784
John	Perq	1772
John	Beau	1779
John	Beau	1786
John Jr	Surr	1782
John Sr	Surr	1782
Joseph	Perq	1787
Mary	Perq	1787
Mathias	Dobb	1780
Michael	Rowa	1768
Miles	Perq	1787
Robert	Blad	1784
Robert	Perq	1787
Saml	Surr	1782

HARVEY, Thomas	Hali	1783
Thomas	Perq	1772
Thomas	Beau	1779
Thomas	Beau	1786
Thomas	Perq	1787
Thomas Jr	Perq	1787
Travis	Blad	1784
Wm	Rowa	1768
Wm	Oran	1779
Wm	Hali	1783
Wm	Wilk	1782
HARWOOD, Union	Onsl	1771
HASEL, Wm	Surr	1782
HASELL, Joseph Sr	Tyrr	1784
HASELWOOD, George	Bute	1766
Randolph	Bute	1766
Thomas	Bute	1766
HASKELL, Joseph	Perq	1787
HASKET, Joseph	Perq	1787
HASKETT, Abraham	Rowa	1768
Anthony Sr	Albe	1694
Giles	Perq	1787
Jesse	Perq	1787
John	Perq	1787
Joshua	Perq	1787
Silas	Perq	1787
Thomas	Perq	1787
HASKINS, Caleb	Bert	1774
Solomon	OnsL	1771
HASLEWEOOD, Warwick	Warr	1784
HASLEWOOD, George	Warr	1784
Randolph	Warr	1784
HASLIP, Labourn	Gran	1785
Thomas	Ruth	1782
HASSELL, Abraham	Tyrr	1784
Ann	Tyrr	1784
Caldwell	Tyrr	1784
Edward Jr	Tyrr	1784
Edward Sr	Tyrr	1784
Jesse	Tyrr	1784
John	Tyrr	1784
John	Tyrr	1784
Levi	Tyrr	1784
Solomon	Tyrr	1784
Susannah	Tyrr	1784
Wm	Tyrr	1784
Zebulon	Tyrr	1784
HASTE, Sarah	Bert	1781
HASTEN, Thomas	NBer	1779
HASTIE, Martha	Bert	1774
HASTINGS, Devotion	Camd	1782
James	Oran	1779
John	Warr	1784
Joseph	Oran	1779
Joshua	Wayn	1779
Wm	Pasq	1779
HASTINGS', Henry	Oran	1779
HASTY, James	Wayn	1786
John	Wayn	1786
Matthew	Hert	1779
HATCH, Anthony	Jone	1779
Don	Jone	1779
Durant	Jone	1779
Edman estate	Cart	1779
Edmund	Jone	1779

HATCH, John	Onsl 1771	HAWKINS, Joshua	Ruth 1782
Lucy	Jone 1779	Joshua	Oran 1779
Narsipa	Jone 1779	Major	Beau 1779
Sam	Onsl 1771	Major	Beau 1786
Samuel	Jone 1779	Matthew	Gran 1785
HATCHEL, Henry	Cart 1779	Obediah	Onsl 1771
Richard	Cart 1779	Philemon	Bute 1766
Wm	Oran 1779	Philemon	Gran 1785
HATCHER, Benjamin	Casw 1784	Philemon	Warr 1784
James	Curr 1779	Phillip Jr	Gran 1771
John	Gran 1785	Samuel	Oran 1779
Ralph	Albe 1679	Solomon	Hali 1783
Robert	Samp 1784	Stephen	Onsl 1771
Timothy	Blad 1784	Thomas	Oran 1779
Timothy	Samp 1784	Thomas	Hali 1783
HATFIELD, Benjamin	Hert 1784	Thomas	Tyrr 1784
Jesse	Tyrr 1784	Thomas	Bert 1774
John	Hert 1779	Thomas Sr	Bert 1781
Mary	Casw 1786	Willoughby	Dobb 1780
Mildred	Tyrr 1784	Wm	Brun 1782
Richard	Perq 1787	Wm	Surr 1782
Richard Jr	Perq 1787	HAWLEY, Benj	NorH 1780
HATFORD, Joseph	Bert 1774	Dicey	Wayn 1786
HATH, Thomas	Hali 1783	Joseph	Gran 1785
HATHAWAY, Allen	Chow 1785	Joseph	Gran 1771
Woolsey	Chow 1785	Millie	Wayn 1786
HATHCOCK, Benjamin	Mont 1782	Thomas	Pasq 1779
Holiday	Samp 1784	HAWORTH, Micajah	Rowa 1768
Isham	Hali 1783	Rachel	Rowa 1768
Wm	Warr 1784	Stephen	Rowa 1768
HATMAKER, Malachi	Oran 1779	HAWTHORNE, John	Blad 1784
HATTAWAY, Wm	Hali 1783	Nathaniel	Blad 1784
HATTEN, Peter	Nash 1782	Thomas	Dupl 1783
HAUSER, Geo	Surr 1782	Wm	Dupl 1783
Geo Jr	Surr 1782	HAY, Alexr	Beau 1786
Jacob	Surr 1782	Charles Jr	Samp 1784
John	Surr 1782	Charles Sr	Samp 1784
Martin	Surr 1782	George	Dobb 1780
Nicholas	Surr 1782	George	Wilk 1784
Peter	Surr 1782	James	Wilk 1784
HAVARD, James	Samp 1784	Jesse	Wilk 1784
Joseph	Camd 1782	John	Samp 1784
Thomas	Camd 1782	Peter	Samp 1784
HAVNER, Wm	Pasq 1694	Reuben	Dobb 1780
HAW, John	Onsl 1771	Theophilus	Hali 1783
HAWK, James	Surr 1782	Thomas	Bute 1766
John	Crav 1779	HAYCROFT, John	Onsl 1771
HAWKINS, Alexander	Surr 1782	HAYES, Benjamin	Gran 1785
Benj	Beau 1786	Ezekiel	Bert 1774
Benj Jr	Surr 1782	Ezekiel	Bert 1781
Benj Sr	Surr 1782	Hardy	Bert 1774
Benjamin	Warr 1784	Hardy	Bert 1781
Eaton	Ruth 1782	Henry Jr	Gran 1785
Edward	Bert 1774	Henry Sr	Gran 1785
Frederick	Ruth 1782	Jacob	Brun 1784
Hannah	Crav 1779	Jacob	Gate 1789
Isham	Warr 1784	James	Casw 1784
James	Gran 1785	James	Gate 1789
John	Oran 1779	Jesse	John 1784
John	Gran 1785	John	Rowa 1768
John	Wilk 1782	John	Gran 1785
John Jr	Bute 1766	John	Gate 1789
John Major	Warr 1784	John estate	Wayn 1786
Joseph	Hali 1783	Joseph	Gran 1785
Joseph	Warr 1784	Joseph	Gran 1771

HAYES, Joshua	Blad 1784		HEARN, Mason	Dobb 1780
Joshua	Gran 1771		Michael	Mart 1779
Joshua Sr	Gran 1785		HEARNDON, Benjamin	Oran 1779
Peter	Bert 1774		David	Casw 1784
Sam	NorH 1780		George	Oran 1779
Samuel	Bute 1766		Pomphrey	Oran 1779
Samuel	Ruth 1782		HEARNE, Elisha	Onsl 1771
Sarah	Gran 1785		Thomas	Onsl 1771
Southey	Blad 1784		HEARTGROVE, Francis	Wilk 1778
Thomas	NorH 1780		HEATH, Abraham	Hali 1783
Thomas	NorH 1780		Adam	Hali 1783
Wm	Hali 1783		Ann Margaret	Curr 1779
Wm	Hert 1784		Elizabeth	Hali 1783
Wm	Gate 1789		Jacob	Tyrr 1784
Wright	Gate 1789		James	Dupl 1783
HAYLE, Aris	Hali 1783		James	Curr 1779
Jonathan	Hali 1783		Jesse	Hali 1783
Wm	Hali 1783		Jesse	Gate 1789
HAYMAN, Henry	Tyrr 1784		John	Hali 1783
John	Curr 1779		Mark	Dobb 1780
Thomas	Curr 1779		Moses	Hali 1783
HAYNES, Anthony	Warr 1784		Richard	Hali 1783
Beth	Surr 1782		Richard	Surr 1782
Beth Sr	Surr 1782		Richard Jr	NBer 1779
Christopher	HalI 1783		Robert	Pasq 1779
Daniel	Surr 1782		Sarah	Hali 1783
Elizabeth	Curr 1779		Sarah	Curr 1779
Henry	Curr 1779		Thomas	Dupl 1783
Herbert	Warr 1784		Thomas	Curr 1779
Jacob	Brun 1782		Thomas	Surr 1782
John	Surr 1782		Wm	Cart 1779
Mark	Surr 1782		Wm	Hali 1783
Richard	Ruth 1782		HECK, Audrey	Rich 1790
Richard	Surr 1782		HEDGEPETH, Benjamin	Nash 1782
Samuel	Blad 1784		Daniel	Wayn 1786
Thomas	Blad 1784		Dempsey	Hert 1784
Wm	Samp 1784		Ezekiel	Wayn 1786
HAYNIA, John	Bute 1766		James	Hert 1779
HAYNIE, Benjamin	Hali 1783		James	Bert 1774
Jesse	Hali 1783		James	Bert 1781
Louis	Hali 1783		John	Wayn 1786
HAYS, Joseph	Nash 1782		Peter	Blad 1784
Thomas	Ruth 1782		HEDRICK, Isham	Warr 1784
Wm	Hert 1779		HEEDY, Thomas	Cart 1779
HAYWOOD, Egbert	Hali 1783		HEFLIN, Charles	Gran 1785
HAZEWELL, Sampson & son			Fielding	Gran 1785
	Bute 1766		James Jr	Gran 1785
Thomas	Bute 1766		James Sr	Gran 1785
HAZLETT, Moses	Surr 1782		John	Gran 1771
HAZLEWOOD, George	Warr 1784		John Sr	Gran 1771
Randolph	Warr 1784		Wm	Gran 1783
Richard	Surr 1782		HEIDEN, Elisha	Wilk 1782
Warwick	Warr 1784		Gilbert	Wilk 1782
HEAD, Elizabeth	Surr 1782		HEIGHT, Abner	Surr 1782
Isaac	Gran 1771		HELLAR, Henry	Rowa 1761
James	Gran 1771		HELSBECK, Frederick	Surr 1782
John	Gran 1771		Jacob	Surr 1782
Richard	Gran 1785		HELTON, John	Surr 1782
Richard	Gran 1771		Winthrop	Hali 1783
Wm	Surr 1782		HELTZEL, MichaeL	Rowa 1768
Wm	Gran 1771		Sainbright & s	Rowa 1768
HEADLEY, Simon	Surr 1782		HEMBLY, John	Dobb 1780
Thomas	Surr 1782		HEMBRE, James	Surr 1782
HEADON, Douglas	Rowa 1768		HEMMONS, James	Onsl 1771
Wm & son	Rowa 1768		HEMP, Joseph	Blad 1784

HEMPHILL, Hugh	Casw 1784		HENRY, Samuel	Tyrr 1779
HENDBY, John	Pasq 1779		Stephen	Crav 1779
HENDEN, Josiah	Blad 1784		Thomas	Rich 1790
Wm	Blad 1784		HENSLEY, David	Casw 1786
HENDERSON, Alexander			John	Casw 1786
	Blad 1784		John	Casw 1784
Duncan	Blad 1784		Macksfield	Casw 1786
Elias	Gran 1785		Maxwell	Casw 1784
James	Gran 1771		Wm	Casw 1786
Jasper	Beau 1779		Wm	Casw 1784
John	Dobb 1780		HENTS, Godfrey	Oran 1779
John	Mont 1782		HERACK, John	Hali 1783
John	Wilk 1782		HERALD, Amos	Bert 1774
John	Surr 1782		Benjamin	Bert 1774
Joseph	Mont 1782		Cader	Bert 1774
Michael	Surr 1782		David	Bert 1774
Nathaniel	Bute 1766		Henry	Bert 1774
Richard	Gran 1785		James	Bert 1774
Richard	Gran 1771		Jesse	Bert 1774
Saml	Gran 1771		Jesse Jr	Bert 1774
Samuel	Casw 1784		John	Bert 1774
Sarah	Hali 1783		Reuben	Bert 1774
Shadrack	Oran 1779		Solomon	Bert 1774
Thomas	Rowa 1768		Willis	Bert 1774
Trimilan	Blad 1784		HERBERT, John	Surr 1782
Watson	Pasq 1779		HERED, John George	Gran 1785
HENDLEY, Daniel	Oran 1779		HERING, John	Wayn 1786
Elmore	Oran 1779		HERN, James	Mont 1782
Joseph	Pasq 1779		Joshua	Mont 1782
HENDRICK, Benj	Gran 1771		Stephen	Mont 1782
Francis	Pasq 1694		Thomas	Mont 1782
John	Crav 1779		HERNDON, Benj	Wilk 1782
Wm	Nash 1782		Comp	Gran 1771
HENDRICKS, David	Crav 2779		HERNE, John	Surr 1782
Elizabeth	Bert 1781		HERRENDINE, James	Samp 1784
Nathan	Crav 1779		Wm	Samp 1784
Peter	Oran 1779		HERRIN, John	Crav 1779
Wm	Wilk 1782		Wm	Blad 1784
HENDRICKSON, Isaac	Bert 1781		HERRING, Abraham	Samp 1784
Job	Perq 1787		Armwell	Dobb 1780
Job Jr	Perq 1787		Benjamin	Dobb 1780
John	Cart 1779		Bridgett	Wayn 1786
Nathan	Perq 1787		Edward	Dobb 1780
Solomon	Perq 1787		Edward	Oran 1779
HENDRIE, Gilmore	Hali 1783		Frederick	Wayn 1786
Michael	Hali 1783		Jacob	Wayn 1786
Nicholas	Hali 1783		James	Dobb 1780
HENDRIX, Benjamin	Wilk 1782		Joel	Wayn 1786
HENDRY, Robert	Bert 1781		John	Dobb 1780
HENDY, Thomas	Perq 1787		Jonathan	Camd 1782
HENESY, Clements	Gran 1771		Joseph	Samp 1784
HENEY, Wm	Wilk 1782		Joshua	Dobb 1780
HENLEY, Joseph	Pasq 1789		Matchet	Dobb 1780
HENLY, Darby	Casw 1784		Michael	Wayn 1786
Edmund	Casw 1784		Owen	Oran 1779
James	Bute 1766		Richard	Samp 1784
Jesse	Rowa 1768		Samuel	Dobb 1780
Jesse	Casw 1784		Samuel	Wayn 1786
John	Rowa 1761		Samuel of S.C.	Wayn 1786
Wm	Gran 1785		Simon	Dobb 1780
HENRY, Alexander	Blad 1784		Simon	Wayn 1786
Isom	Rich 1790		Solomon	Wayn 1786
James	Blad 1784		Stephen	Dobb 1780
John	Warr 1784		Uzzel	Samp 1784
Robert	Blad 1784		Wm	Wayn 1786

HERRINGTON, Chas	Beau 1779		HICKMAN, Edwin	Surr 1782
Chas	Beau 1779		Jacob	Pitt 1786
Jacob	Beau 1779		Richard	Crav 1779
John & son Joe	Bute 1766		Samuel	Brun 1784
Joseph	Bute 1766		Wm	Brun 1784
Matthew	Camd 1782		Wm	Brun 1782
Silas	Brun 1784		Wm	Surr 1782
Thomas	Dobb 1780		HICKS, Avery	Mont 1782
HERRINTON, Phillip	Cart 1779		Billy	Casw 1784
HERRITAGE, John	Dobb 1780		Charles	Bute 1766
HESKETH, John Jr	Gran 1785		Charles	Warr 1784
John Sr	Gran 1785		Charles	Wilk 1782
HESKETT, Chas	Rich 1790		Daniel	Casw 1784
HESTER, Benjamin	Gran 1785		Daniel	Mont 1782
Charles	Brun 1782		David	Gran 1785
David	Gran 1771		Drury	Blad 1784
Henry	Gran 1785		Henry	John 1784
James	Gran 1785		James	Bute 1766
James	Gran 1771		Jesse	Blad 1784
Jasper	Blad 1784		Job	Chow 1784
John	Blad 1784		John	Casw 1784
John	Gran 1771		John	Warr 1784
Joseph	Blad 1784		John & sons	Bute 1766
Robert	Casw 1784		John J.	Warr 1784
Robert	Gran 1785		John Jr	Bute 1766
Robert	Gran 1771		Leonard	Gran 1785
Stephen	Blad 1784		Mary	Gran 1771
Thomas	Blad 1784		Robert	Gran 1785
Wm	Blad 1784		Robert	Gran 1771
Wm	Gran 1785		Saml Jr	Gran 1771
Wm	Gran 1771		Saml Sr	HGrn 1771
Zechariah	Gran 1771		Samuel	Gran 1785
HESTON, Wm	Bert 1781		Solomon	Cart 1779
HETHCOCK, James	NorH 1780		Stephen	Gran 1785
Meshack	NorH 1780		Stephen	Gran 1771
HEUEN, Evan	Rowa 1768		Thomas	Samp 1784
HEW, Sarah	Perq 1772		Thomas	Gran 1785
HEWELL, Wm	Cart 1779		Wm	Gran 1785
HEWITT, David	Brun 1784		Wm	Rowa 1761
Ebenezer	Brun 1784		Wm	Chow 1784
Jacob	Brun 1784		Wm	Gran 1771
James	Rowa 1768		Zebedee	Casw 1784
John	Gran 1771		HICKSON, Timothy	Pasq 1779
John Jr	Onsl 1771		HIGGINS, Holton	Rowa 1768
Joseph	Brun 1784		Robert	Wilk 1782
Phillip	Oran 1779		Wm	Rowa 1768
Phillip	Brun 1784		Wm	Gran 1785
Thomas	Gran 1785		Wm	Wilk 1782
Thomas	Onsl 1771		HIGGS, Abraham	Bert 1774
Wm	Gran 1785		Abram	Bert 1781
HIATT, Geo	Surr 1782		Isaac	Bert 1774
George	Rowa 1768		John	Bert 1774
Jesse	Gate 1789		Leonard	Gran 1785
John	Rowa 1768		Wm	Bute 1766
John	Surr 1782		Wm	Bert 1781
Joseph	Rowa 1768		Zechariah	Gran 1785
Thomas	Gate 1789		HIGH, Abigail	Bute 1766
Wm	Rowa 1768		Gerner	Mont 1782
Wm	Surr 1782		Milly Miss	Warr 1784
HIBBS, Jonathan	Cart 1779		Samuel	Bute 1766
HICKER, John	Bute 1766		HIGHATT, Sam	Pitt 1786
HICKERSON, David	Wilk 1782		HIGHFIELD, Hezekiah	Gran 1785
HICKMAN, Benjamin	Crav 1779		HIGHGATE, George	Blad 1784
Corbin	Gran 1785		HIGHSMITH, Thomas	Surr 1782
Edward	Surr 1782		Wm	Mart 1779

HIGHTOWER, Augustine		
	Oran 1779	
Charnell	Casw 1784	
Eppie	Casw 1784	
Gregory	Bute 1766	
Henry	Oran 1779	
John	Oran 1779	
Turner	Casw 1784	
Wm	Oran 1779	
HILBORN, Hamblin	Samp 1784	
HILBOURNE, Vaughn	Wayn 1786	
HILDRETH, Reuben	Mont 1782	
Sarah	Mont 1782	
Wm	Mont 1782	
HILES, Joshua	Hert 1784	
HILL, Ann	Oran 1779	
Asa	Tyrr 1784	
Barsheba	Bert 1781	
Bathsheba & so	Hert 1779	
Benjamin	Hert 1779	
Benjamin	Bute 1766	
Briggs	Dobb 1780	
Busheby	Hert 1784	
C B	Surr 1782	
Charles	Warr 1784	
Col. Whitmell	Mart 1779	
Daniel	Surr 1782	
David	Curr 1779	
Elizabeth	Hali 1783	
Ephraim	Ruth 1782	
Ezekiel	Blad 1784	
Francis	Samp 1784	
Green	Bute 1766	
Hamrick	Gate 1789	
Hardy	Bert 1774	
Henry	Bute 1766	
Henry	Mart 1779	
Henry	NorH 1780	
Henry	Surr 1782	
Henry	Gate 1789	
Henry	Bert 1781	
Herman	Beau 1779	
Human	Beau 1786	
Isaac	Cart 1779	
Isaac	Hert 1779	
Isaac	Surr 1782	
Isham	Hali 1783	
Jacob	Pasq 1779	
James	Ruth 1782	
James	Blad 1784	
James	Surr 1782	
Jane	Samp 1784	
Jeremiah	Wayn 1786	
Jesse	Tyrr 1784	
Joel	Brun 1784	
John	Cart 1779	
John	Blad 1784	
John	Gran 1785	
John	Tyrr 1784	
John	Beau 1779	
John	Crav 1779	
John	Mont 1782	
John	Curr 1779	
John	Surr 1782	
John	Gate 1789	
HILL, Joseph	Gran 1771	
Kedar	Gate 1789	
Levi	Dobb 1780	
Lewis	Nash 1782	
Marjorie	Hali 1783	
Mary	Hert 1779	
Micajah	Blad 1784	
Michael	Hert 1779	
Michael	Hert 1784	
Milbrough	Curr 1779	
Moses	Blad 1784	
Moses	Gate 1789	
Mrs Bathsheba	Hert 1779	
Nathl	Surr 1782	
Nicholas	Bute 1766	
Peter	Casw 1786	
Rhoda	Wayn 1786	
Richard	Dobb 1780	
Richard	Hali 1783	
Richard	Rich 1790	
Robert	Dobb 1780	
Robert	Pasq 1779	
Samuel	Hali 1783	
Samuel	Jone 1779	
Sion	Nash 1782	
Solomon	Hali 1783	
Stephen	Crav 1779	
Susannah	Wayn 1786	
Thomas	Bute 1766	
Thomas	Rowa 1768	
Thomas	Mart 1779	
Thomas	Hali 1783	
Thomas	John 1784	
Thomas	Bert 1781	
Wise	Cart 1779	
Wm	Hert 1779	
Wm	Bute 1766	
Wm	Blad 1784	
Wm	Hali 1783	
Wm	Hert 1784	
Wm	Wilk 1782	
Wm	Onsl 1771	
Wm	Surr 1782	
Wm Jr	Surr 1782	
Wm Sr	Surr 1782	
HILLARD, Benj	Onsl 1771	
Elias	NorH 1780	
Francis Sr	Wayn 1786	
John	NorH 1780	
Major	Wayn 1786	
Margaret	NorH 1780	
HILLIARD, Isaac	Nash 1782	
John	Blad 1784	
Joseph	Gran 1785	
Margaret	Hali 1783	
Thomas	Gran 1785	
HILLIMAN, John	Hert 1784	
Kinchen	Hert 1784	
HILLINS, Wm	Pitt 1786	
HILLS, Abel	Ruth 1782	
HILLSMAN, Bennett & son		
	Bute 1766	
Hind	Bute 1766	
HILTON, Abraham	Oran 1779	
James	Rowa 1768	

HILTON, John	Oran 1779	HINTON, Wm	Bert 1781
Joseph	Warr 1784	Zadock	Gate 1789
Peter	Oran 1779	HIPSWORTH, John	Casw 1784
HINCHEY, John	Oran 1779	HIRCUM, Wm	Gran 1771
HINDE, Samuel	Wilk 1782	HITCHCOCK, Isaac	Oran 1779
HINDLEY, James	Dobb 1780	HITCHEN, Joseph	Blad 1784
Joseph	Dobb 1780	HITT, Peter	Casw 1784
Wm	Gran 1771	HIVCKS, James	Warr 1784
HINDS, Joseph	Rowa 1761	HIVELY, Joseph	Chow 1785
Joseph	Rowa 1768	HIVER, John Sr	John 1784
Joseph	Rand 1779	HIX, David	Casw 1786
Joshua	Wayn 1786	James	Ruth 1782
Peter	Wayn 1786	Jesse	Dobb 1780
HINES, Absalom	Rich 1790	John	Casw 1786
Cader	Wayn 1786	Thomas	Ruth 1782
Charles	Wayn 1786	Thomas	Dobb 1780
Charles Jr	Wayn 1786	Wm	Dobb 1780
Elizabeth	Brun 1784	HJARRIS, Josiah	Pasq 1789
Hardy	Wayn 1786	HOBB, James	Jone 1779
Isaac	Dobb 1780	HOBBINS, Adam	Curr 1779
John	Bute 1766	HOBBS, Abram	Hert 1784
Joseph	Rich 1790	Drew	Hert 1779
Moses	Gate 1789	Edmund	Gate 1789
Reuben	Wayn 1786	George	Samp 1784
Thomas	Warr 1784	Hardy	Hert 1784
HINNANT, James	John 1784	Henry	Hert 1779
Wm Jr	John 1784	Henry	Hert 1784
Wm Sr	John 1784	Henry	Gate 1789
HINSLEY, Martha	Chow 1785	Isaac	Hert 1779
HINSMON, John C	Surr 1782	Isaac	Blad 1784
HINSON, Aaron	Dobb 1780	Jacob	Gate 1789
Allen	Ruth 1782	James	Bute 1766
Isaac	Ruth 1782	James	Onsl 1771
James	Wayn 1786	John	Samp 1784
James	Wilk 1782	Joseph	Hert 1784
Jeremiah	Dobb 1780	Joseph Jr	Hert 1779
Jesse	Dobb 1780	Joseph Sr	Hert 1779
Joseph	Dobb 1780	Millicent	Gate 1789
Paul	Wilk 1782	Patience	Gate 1789
Richard	Casw 1786	Reuben	Gate 1789
Wm	Mart 1779	Robert	Bert 1781
HINTON, Allen	Ruth 1782	Simon	Samp 1784
Amos	Hert 1779	Simon	Onsl 1771
Amos	Hert 1784	Thomas	Chow 1785
Christopher	Casw 1784	Wm	Hert 1779
Christopher	Hali 1783	Wm	Bute 1766
Christopher	Bert 1774	Wm	Oran 1779
Isaac	Ruth 1782	Wm	Samp 1784
James	NorH 1780	Wm	Hert 1784
John	John 1784	HOBBY, Reuben	John 1784
John	Bert 1781	HOBDAH, Robert	Bert 1774
John Jr	Bert 1774	HOBDAY, Sarah	Hali 1783
John Sr	Bert 1774	HOBGOOD, Elijah	Hali 1783
John Sr	Bert 1781	Francis	Hali 1783
Kedar	Gate 1789	Hezekiah	Gran 1771
Micajah	Bert 1774	John	Hali 1783
Micajah	Bert 1781	Samuel	Hali 1783
Noah	Chow 1785	Wm	Hali 1783
Noah	Bert 1774	HOBGOODEN, Hezekiah	Gran 1785
Noah	Bert 1781	HOBISON, Edward	Wilk 1782
Reuben	Bert 1781	HOCCO, John	Pasq 1779
Seabrook	Gate 1789	HOCKADAY, James	Hali 1783
Thomas	Casw 1784	Wm	Hali 1783
Thomas	Gate 1789	HOCKINGS, Abraham	Rowa 1770
Wm	Gate 1789	Benjamin	Rowa 1770

HOCOFF, Richard	Hert 1779		HOLCOMB, Lawrence	Surr 1782
HODDER, Wm	Bert 1774		Philemon	Surr 1782
HODGE, Isaac	Casw 1784		Thomas	Surr 1782
John	Casw 1784		Wm	Bute 1766
Joseph	Blad 1784		Wm	Casw 1784
Matthew	Bert 1781		HOLDECRAFT, James	Hali 1783
Robert	Blad 1784		HOLDEN, Thomas	Oran 1779
HODGES, Abner	Surr 1782		HOLDER, Chas	Surr 1782
Bartholomew	Surr 1782		Elisha	Bert 1781
Chrisr	Perq 1787		Geo	Surr 1782
Edmond	Surr 1782		George	Samp 1784
Francis	Dobb 1780		George	Surr 1782
George	Oran 1779		James	Bert 1781
Henry	Hali 1783		John	Oran 1779
James	Samp 1784		John	Samp 1784
John	Dobb 1780		John	Wilk 1782
John	Oran 1779		John	Surr 1782
John	Surr 1782		John	Bert 1781
Joseph	Samp 1784		Joseph	Surr 1782
Joseph	Gran 1771		Lewis	Surr 1782
Joshua	Dobb 1780		Mary Ann	Wilk 1782
Matthew	Bert 1774		Thomas	Bert 1781
Richard	Dobb 1780		HOLDERNESS, Wm	Casw 1784
Thomas	Beau 1779		HOLDERT, John	Surr 1782
Thomas	NorH 1780		HOLDING, Amos	Brun 1784
Willis	Hali 1783		Benjamin	Brun 1784
Wm	Oran 1779		James	Brun 1784
Wm	Beau 1779		Job	Brun 1784
HODGIN, George	Rowa 1768		John	Albe 1679
John	Rowa 1768		Joshua	Brun 1784
HODGSON, Charles	Bert 1774		HOLEBROOK, John	Surr 1782
Chas	Bert 1781		HOLEFIELD, Wm	Surr 1782
HOFFLER, John	Gate 1789		HOLEMAN, Thomas	Wilk 1782
Thomas	Gate 1789		HOLIFIELD, Valentine	
HOGAN, Cordial	NorH 1780			Surr 1782
Edward	Ruth 1782		HOLINGS, Francis	Beau 1786
Henry	Surr 1782		HOLINS, James	Curr 1779
James	Oran 1779		HOLLAND, Archer	Gate 1789
John	Oran 1779		Dempsey	Bert 1774
John	Gran 1771		Demsey	Samp 1784
Lemuel	Hali 1783		Fred	Bert 1781
Shadrack	Mont 1782		Henry	Samp 1784
Thomas	Wilk 1782		Henry	Wayn 1786
HOGG, Andrew	Casw 1784		Hugh	Surr 1782
Gideon	Casw 1786		Jacob	Gate 1789
Gideon	Casw 1784		James	Ruth 1782
James	Oran 1779		James	Wayn 1786
James	Hali 1783		James	Beau 1779
Patrick	Bert 1774		James	Surr 1782
Thomas	Hali 1783		Jewel	Bert 1774
HOGGARD, John	Bert 1781		Joel	Bert 1781
Patrick	Bert 1781		John	Rowa 1767
HOGGETT, Joseph	Rowa 1768		John Jr	Wayn 1786
Phillip	Rowa 1768		John Sr	Wayn 1786
Wm	Rowa 1768		Joseph	Bert 1774
HOGGETt, John	Rowa 1768		Joseph	Gate 1789
HOGGINS, Wm	Rowa 1768		Leonard	Wilk 1784
HOGWOOD, Bird	Wilk 1782		Matthew	Wayn 1786
John	NorH 1780		Phillip	Beau 1786
Partin	Wilk 1782		Richard	Nash 1782
HOLBROOK, Wm	Rowa 1768		Richard	Beau 1786
Wm	Wilk 1782		Spear	Tyrr 1784
HOLBROOKS, John	Wilk 1782		Wm	Perq 1772
Randolph	Wilk 1782		Worth	Beau 1786
HOLCOMB, Geo	Surr 1782		HOLLEY, Edward	Samp 1784

HOLLEY, James	Bert 1774	HOLLOMAN, Wm	Warr 1784
James Jr	Bert 1781	Wm	Surr 1782
James Sr	Bert 1774	HOLLOWAY, Absalom	Hert 1784
James Sr	Bert 1781	Hannah	Perq 1787
John	Samp 1784	Leah	Perq 1772
Nathaniel	Bert 1774	Levy	Mart 1779
Nathl	Bert 1781	Luke	Chow 1785
Osborne	Samp 1784	Marmaduke	Perq 1772
HOLLIDAY, Hardy	Mart 1779	Martha	Oran 1779
Henry	Oran 1779	Obadiah	Casw 1786
John	Mart 1779	Obadiah	Casw 1784
Joseph	Dobb 1780	Stephen	Wilk 1782
Robert	Oran 1779	Thomas	Wayn 1786
Samuel	Dobb 1780	Thomas	Perq 1787
Thomas	Mart 1779	Wm	Curr 1779
Wm	Mart 1779	HOLLOWELL, Abner	Chow 1785
HOLLIMAN, Aaron	Hert 1784	Absalom	NorH 1780
Christopher	Wayn 1786	Cader	Bert 1781
Christopher	Hert 1784	Eliz	Bert 1781
Coleinus	Hert 1784	Elizabeth	Bert 1774
Edmund	Hert 1784	Henry	Perq 1787
Ezekiel	Wayn 1786	Joel	Perq 1787
Jane	Wayn 1786	Joseph	Wayn 1786
Jedidiah	Wayn 1786	Reuben	Bert 1781
John	Hert 1784	Saml	Pasq 1789
Matthew	Hert 1784	Samuel	Pasq 1779
Nathan	Warr 1784	Silas	Wayn 1786
Samuel Jr	Hert 1784	Thomas	Perq 1787
Samuel Sr	Hert 1784	Wm	Perq 1787
HOLLINGS, Elias	Chow 1785	HOLLYMAN, Reuben	Mont 1782
Nicholas	Chow 1785	HOLMAN, Daniel	Wilk 1782
HOLLINGSWORTH, Chas	Onsl 1771	Joseph	Wilk 1782
Henry	Samp 1784	HOLMES, :Lewis	Samp 1784
Henry Jr	Samp 1784	Alexander	Bert 1774
Isaac	Blad 1784	Charles	Wayn 1786
James	Samp 1784	Gabriel	Samp 1784
John	Samp 1784	George	Bert 1774
Samuel	Samp 1784	Hardy	Samp 1784
Stephen	Samp 1784	Henry	Tyrr 1784
Zebulon	Samp 1784	Hillary	Hert 1779
HOLLIS, Harmon	Tyrr 1784	James	Dobb 1780
Isaac	Crav 1779	James	Oran 1779
James	Tyrr 1784	Jesse	Dobb 1780
James	Crav 1779	John	Dobb 1780
John	Rowa 1770	John	Oran 1779
Kermit	Tyrr 1784	John	Wayn 1786
Wm	Crav 1779	Joseph	Oran 1779
HOLLOMAN, Aaron	Hert 1779	Joseph	Crav 1779
Arthur	NorH 1780	Joseph	Wilk 1782
Christopher	Hert 1779	Moses	Blad 1784
Cornelius	Hert 1779	Owen	Samp 1784
Edmund	Hert 1779	Robert	Oran 1779
Edward	Bute 1766	Robert	Chow 1785
Edward	Warr 1784	Saml	Gran 1771
Herman	Bute 1766	Samuel	Oran 1779
John	Hert 1779	Shadrack	Bert 1781
John	Bute 1766	Simon	Dobb 1780
Malachi	Hert 1779	Thomas	Rowa 1761
Martha	Hert 1779	Thomas	Bert 1781
Richard	Casw 1784	Timothy	Dobb 1780
Samuel	Hert 1779	Wm	Chow 1785
Silas	Hert 1779	HOLSMAN, Bennett	Bute 1766
Silas	Wayn 1786	HOLSON, Wm	Tyrr 1784
Solomon	Hert 1779	HOLSTED, Jesse	Curr 1779
Thomas	Wilk 1782	HOLSTON, Jacob	Tyrr 1784

HOLSTON, Nicholson	Gran	1771	HOOKS, Wm		Nash	1782
HOLSWORTH, John	Hert	1779	Wm		Mart	1779
Wadkins	Hert	1779	Wm		Wayn	1786
HOLT, Charles	Gran	1785	HOOPER, Frillin		Rowa	1761
Christopher	Oran	1779	James		Wilk	1782
Edmund	Surr	1782	Obadiah		Casw	1784
Francis	Surr	1782	Rachel		Curr	1779
Frank Sr	Surr	1782	HOOTEN, Caleb		Pitt	1786
George	Oran	1779	John		Bert	1781
George Jr	Oran	1779	Wm Jr		Bert	1781
Hillery	Wilk	1782	Wm Sr		Bert	1781
Jacob	Oran	1779	HOOTS, Jacob		Surr	1782
James	Oran	1779	HOOVER, Andrew & son			
James	Hali	1783			Rowa	1768
James	John	1784	Henry		Crav	1779
John	Oran	1779	James or Jonas		Rowa	1768
John	Gran	1771	HOPKINS, Aaron		Bert	1781
John Jr	Oran	1779	Alexander		Bert	1781
Joseph	Hali	1783	Andrew		Jone	1779
Joseph	Wilk	1782	Andrew		Dobb	1780
Michael	Oran	1779	Elizabeth		Tyrr	1784
Michael Jr	Oran	1779	James		Dobb	1780
Nicholas	Oran	1779	James		Oran	1779
Shadrack	Oran	1779	James		Casw	1786
Thomas	Hali	1783	James		Casw	1784
Wm	Ruth	1782	James		Gran	1771
HOLTON, David	Beau	1779	Jesse		Gran	1785
David	Beau	1786	Job		Jone	1779
George	Crav	1779	John		Oran	1779
Jeremiah	Bert	1781	John		Hali	1783
Vinson	Wilk	1782	John		Tyrr	1784
Wm	Mont	1782	John		Gran	1771
Wm Sr	Mont	1782	John		Bert	1781
HOLZER, Henry	Surr	1782	John		Perq	1787
HONEY, Abner	Samp	1784	John Jr		Bert	1774
HONEYCUTT, Ambrose	Oran	1779	Joseph		Wilk	1784
Bowlin	Rich	1790	Joseph		Wilk	1782
Drury	Oran	1779	Joseph		Bert	1781
HOOD, Absalom	Hert	1784	Parker		Hali	1783
Charles	John	1784	Philip		Rowa	1770
Nathaniel	Wayn	1786	Phillip		Tyrr	1784
Thomas	NorH	1780	Richard		Bute	1766
Wm	Wayn	1786	Richard		Mont	1782
Wm (Mulatto)	Casw	1786	Solomon		Oran	1779
HOOFMAN, Geo	Surr	1782	Thomas		Tyrr	1784
Lewis	Surr	1782	HOPPER, Charles		Rowa	1761
HOOK, Daniel	Rich	1790	Geo		Surr	1782
Edward	Wilk	1782	Geo Jr		Surr	1782
John	Brun	1784	Harman		Casw	1786
HOOKER, Hamrick	Dobb	1780	James		Casw	1786
Jacob	Jone	1779	James		Casw	1784
James	Hert	1779	James		Gran	1771
John	Gran	1785	John		Casw	1786
John	Tyrr	1784	John		Casw	1784
John·Jr	Gran	1785	Matthew		Surr	1782
Samuel	Hert	1779	Susannah		Casw	1786
Wm	Dobb	1780	Thomas		Rowa	1761
Wm	Bert	1774	Thomas		Wilk	1782
Wm Sr	Bert	1774	Thomas & son		Rowa	1761
HOOKS, Charles	Mart	1779	HOPSON, Martin		Oran	1779
Hardy	Wayn	1786	Richard		Oran	1779
Joseph	Mart	1779	HOPTON, Charles		Wayn	1786
Mary	Mart	1779	HORLEY, Henry		Casw	1784
Robert	Wayn	1786	HORN, Edith		Nash	1782
Thomas	Dupl	1779	Enoch		John	1784

HORN, Geo	Beau 1786		HORTON, Samuel	Bute 1766
George	Beau 1779		Sarah	Oran 1779
Hannah	Nash 1782		Thomas	Hert 1779
Henry	Nash 1782		Thomas	Bute 1766
Henry	Hali 1783		Thomas	Hert 1784
James	John 1784		Thomas	Warr 1784
James	NorH 1780		Townsend	Casw 1784
Jesse	Surr 1782		Williford	Hert 1784
Joel	John 1784		Wm	Hert 1779
John	Surr 1782		Wm	Oran 1779
Joseph	Bert 1781		Wm	Hert 1784
Michael	Nash 1782		Wm	NorH 1780
Moses	NorH 1780		Wm Jr	Hert 1784
Nathan	Nash 1782		HOSEA, Abraham	Pasq 1789
Rhoda	Nash 1782		Seth	Pasq 1789
Richard	Hali 1783		Thomas	Perq 1787
Richard	John 1784		HOSINCY, Danl	Surr 1782
Thomas	Nash 1782		HOSKINS, John	Tyrr 1784
Thomas	NorH 1780		Thomas	Tyrr 1784
Thomas	Surr 1782		HOSMER, Sylvester	Pasq 1789
Thomas	Beau 1786		HOST, Thomas	Jone 1779
Wm	Nash 1782		HOTTEN, Alexander	Wilk 1782
Wm	John 1784		Brazeller	Beau 1786
Wm	Bert 1774		James	Beau 1779
Wm	Bert 1781		James	Beau 1786
HORNADY, Christopher			Joseph	Bert 1781
	Oran 1779		HOUGH, Hezekiah	NorH 1780
John	Oran 1779		HOUGHEY, John	Rowa 1768
HORNBEY, Wm	Mont 1782		HOUGHT, James	Rich 1790
HORNBLOW, John	Chow 1785		HOUGHTON, Charles	Chow 1785
HORNE, Henry	Waye 1786		Jeremiah	Chow 1785
James	Oran 1779		John	Perq 1772
Jeremiah	Wayn 1786		Jonathan	Chow 1785
John	Oran 1779		Richard	Chow 1785
John	Mart 1779		Richard	Perq 1772
Joshua	Oran 1779		HOUSE, Balus	Bert 1781
Nathan	Blad 1784		Dudley	Hali 1783
Thomas	Oran 1779		Dudley	Warr 1784
Thomas	Wayn 1786		Everett	Dobb 1780
Wm	Oran 1779		James	Warr 1784
HORNER, George	Oran 1779		James	Onsl 1771
Samuel	Gran 1785		James	Bert 1781
HORNLEY, John	Chow 1785		Mary	Bert 1781
HORNSBEY, Wm	Gran 1771		Sam	Bert 1781
HORNSBURGER, Wm	Gran 1785		Thomas	Oran 1779
HORNYARD, Drury	John 1784		Thomas	Bert 1774
HORTON, Abraham	Surr 1782		Wm	Warr 1784
Abraham Jr	Surr 1782		Wm	Bert 1774
Charles	Oran 1779		Wm	Bert 1781
Daniel	Surr 1782		HOUSEMAN, Joseph	Oran 1779
Francis(Quaker	Crav 1779		HOUSTON, Christopher	
Henry	Oran 1779			Casw 1786
Howell	Warr 1784		Christopher	Casw 1784
Hugh	Hert 1784		George	Casw 1784
Hugh Jr	Hert 1779		James	Casw 1784
Hugh Jr	Hert 1784		Peter	Samp 1784
Hugh Sr	Hert 1779		Wm	Casw 1784
Jacob	Bert 1774		HOWARD, Bartholomew	Crav 1777
James	Oran 1779		Benjamin	Tyrr 1784
James Jr	Oran 1779		Benjamin	Wilk 1782
Jeremiah	Oran 1779		Edward	Hert 1779
John	Surr 1782		Edward	Gran 1785
John	Perq 1787		Edward	Onsl 1771
Matthew	Hert 1784		Elijah	Bert 1781
Rawlings	Casw 1786		Elisha	Hert 1779

HOWARD, Elisha	Hert 1784	HOWELL, Absalom	Chow 1785
Elisha	Bert 1774	Admiral	Wayn 1786
Francis	Casw 1784	Archelaus	Wayn 1786
Francis	Gran 1771	Arthur	Wayn 1786
George	Cart 1779	Benj	NorH 1780
George	Brun 1782	Benjamin	Oran 1779
Grover	Gran 1785	Benjamin	Wayn 1786
Groves	Gran 1771	Daniel	Dobb 1780
Henry	Rowa 1761	Daniel	Wayn 1786
Hezekiah	Blad 1784	David	Surr 1782
Hiram	Casw 1784	Edmund	NorH 1780
Hiram	Rich 1790	Elias	Beau 1786
James	Samp 1784	Ethelred	Wayn 1786
James	Hali 1783	Francis	Casw 1784
James	Bert 1774	Henry Jr	NorH 1780
James	Onsl 1771	Hyroneus	Tyrr 1784
James Jr	Hert 1779	James	Mart 1779
James Sr	Hert 1779	James	Surr 1782
Jane	Surr 1782	Jethro	Mart 1779
John	Bute 1766	John	Oran 1779
John	Rowa 1761	John	Wayn 1786
John	Gran 1785	John	Gran 1785
John	Wilk 1782	John	Hali 1783
John	Gran 1771	Joseph	Casw 1784
John	Rich 1790	Joshua	Wayn 1786
John (Quaker)	Crav 1779	Major	Wayn 1786
Joseph	Oran 1779	Matthew	Hali 1783
Joseph	Hert 1784	Mills	Wayn 1786
Joseph	Crav 1779	Ozburn	Wayn 1786
Joseph	Onsl 1771	Phillipson	Warr 1784
Joseph	NorH 1780	Rachel	Wayn 1786
Luke	Hert 1779	Richard	Tyrr 1784
Luke	Hert 1784	Silvanus	Curr 1779
Mary	Wilk 1782	Thomas	Samp 1784
Moses	Hert 1779	Thomas	Wayn 1786
Moses	Hert 1784	Thomas	Hali 1783
Nathan	Rowa 1768	Thomas	Surr 1782
Nathan	Mont 1782	Thomas	Gran 1771
Old	Rowa 1761	Watson	Gate 1789
Parmenus	Blad 1784	Wm	Bute 1766
Phillip	Surr 1782	Wm	Wayn 1786
Robert	Surr 1782	Wm	Tyrr 1784
Samuel	Dobb 1780	Wm	Gran 1771
Sarah	Surr 1782	HOWETT, Abram	Perq 1787
Solomon	Bert 1774	Francis	Hert 1784
Solomon	Gran 1771	Rowan	Pasq 1789
Thomas	Oran 1779	HOWEll, Daniel	Pasq 1694
Thomas	Samp 1784	HOWLAND, Samuel	Cart 1779
Thomas	Blad 1784	Zepha	Cart 1779
Thomas	Tyrr 1784	HOYLE, Benjamin	Hert 1784
Thomas	Pasq 1789	HUBBARD, Benjamin	Casw 1784
Wm	Albe 1679	Bird	Bert 1781
Wm	Tyrr 1784	Joseph	Casw 1784
Wm	Warr 1784	Wm	Cart 1779
Wm	Gran 1771	HUBBERT, Benjamin	Casw 1786
Wm Jr	Cart 1779	Omar	Wilk 1782
HOWCOTT, Nathaniel	Chow 1785	HUCKABY, James	Bute 1766
HOWE, Arthur	Bert 1774	John	Bute 1766
Geo	Surr 1782	Saml	Gran 1771
Henry	Bert 1774	Samuel	Gran 1785
Mary	Bert 1781	Thomas	Gran 1771
Thomas	Bute 1766	HUCKING, John	Surr 1782
Thomas estate	Brun 1784	HUDDLEBURY, John	Onsl 1771
Thos Clifford	Brun 1782	HUDDLESTON, David	Ruth 1782
HOWELL, Abraham	Wayn 1786	David Jr	Ruth 1782

HUDDLESTON, James	Ruth 1782	HUFFMAN, Kit	Onsl 1771
John	Ruth 1782	HUGGINS, Charles	Dupl 1783
Wm	Ruth 1782	Jacob	Onsl 1771
Wm	Gran 1771	James	Oran 1779
HUDGIN, Ambrose	Casw 1784	Michael	Onsl 1771
Joshua	Dupl 1779	HUGH, John	Brun 1784
Wm	Casw 1784	HUGHES, Billy	Casw 1784
HUDGINS, Humphrey	Gate 1789	Charles	Casw 1786
HUDNALL, Huffman	Blad 1784	Charles	Casw 1784
HUDSON, Abiah	Perq 1787	Charles	Chow 1785
Chamberlain	Bute 1766	David	Casw 1784
Charles	Mart 1779	Edward	Rowa 1761
Cornelius	Perq 1772	Elijah	Camd 1782
Cuthbert	Gran 1771	Geo Jr	Bert 1781
Edward	Bute 1766	Geo Sr	Bert 1781
Elijah	Tyrr 1784	James	Casw 1786
Henry	Bute 1766	James	Casw 1784
Henry	Warr 1784	James	Surr 1782
Isaac	Bute 1766	James	Bert 1781
James	Hert 1779	John	Oran 1779
James	Warr 1784	John	Camd 1782
James	Beau 1779	John	Casw 1786
James Sr	Beau 1786	John	Casw 1784
Jesse	Beau 1786	John	John 1784
Job	Samp 1784	John	Surr 1782
John	Bute 1766	John Sr	Camd 1782
John	Dobb 1780	Joseph	Chow 1785
John	Mart 1779	Leander	Surr 1782
John	Gran 1785	Richard	Casw 1784
John	Beau 1786	Roland	Casw 1786
John	Perq 1787	Roland	Casw 1784
John Jr	Dobb 1780	Rolling	Oran 1779
John s of Cham	Bute 1766	Solomon	Bert 1781
Joseph	Warr 1784	Thomas	Dobb 1780
Joseph	Beau 1786	Thomas	Surr 1782
Joseph	Perq 1787	Thomas	Bert 1781
Joseph Sr	Mart 1779	Timothy	Oran 1779
Joshua	Casw 1784	Willis	Gate 1789
Lewis	Samp 1784	Wm	Rowa 1770
Shadrack	Casw 1784	Wm	Camd 1782
Thomas	Dobb 1780	Wm	Casw 1786
Wm	Bute 1766	Wm	Bert 1781
HUDSPETH, Airs	Gran 1771	HUGHESON, Shadrack C	
Ariers	Surr 1782		Hert 1784
Carter	Surr 1782	HUGHESTON, George	Casw 1786
Carter	Gran 1771	HUGHEY, George	Ruth 1782
Carter Jr	Gran 1785	James	Ruth 1782
Carter Sr	Gran 1785	James	Oran 1779
Catherine	Surr 1782	HUGHLET, Wm	Surr 1782
David	Surr 1782	HULEN, Thomas	Jone 1779
Giles	Gran 1771	HULET, Henry	Dobb 1780
Israel	Gran 1771	HULING, Arthur	Hali 1783
Jiles	Surr 1782	HULL, Elias	Beau 1786
Mary	Surr 1788	Wm	Onsl 1771
HUDSTAFF, Ralph	Gran 1771	HULM, John	Warr 1784
HUEN, Ann	Tyrr 1784	HULMAN, John	Hali 1783
HUFF, Daniel	Surr 1782	Robert	Hali 1783
Richard	Cart 1779	HUMDEN, John	Onsl 1771
HUFFMAN, Andrew	Oran 1779	HUMPHREY, Benj	Surr 1782
Barney	Surr 1782	Benjamin	Blad 1784
Christian	Oran 1779	Chambers	Blad 1784
Daniel	Oran 1779	David	Chow 1785
Jacob	Gran 1785	Elijah	Hali 1783
John	Oran 1779	Jacob	Onsl 1771
Josias Sr	Beau 1786	James	Rowa 1768

HUMPHREY, John	Blad 1784		HUNT, Thomas	Pasq 1694
John	Wayn 1786		Thomas	Rowa 1768
John	Curr 1779		Thomas	Wilk 1784
John	Onsl 1771		Thomas & son	Bute 1766
John	Surr 1782		Wm	Rowa 1768
Joseph	Wilk 1782		Wm	Blad 1784
Justice	Onsl 1771		Wm	Gran 1785
Mary	Oran 1779		Wm	Gran 1771
Richard	Chow 1785		Wm Jr	Gran 1785
Saml	Surr 1782		Wm Sr	Gran 1785
Thomas	Onsl 1771		HUNTER, Alexander	Oran 1779
Wm	Hert 1779		Brassell	Blad 1784
Wm	Blad 1784		Cader	Bert 1781
Wm	Hert 1784		Daniel	Gran 1785
Wm	Onsl 1771		Elisha	Perq 1772
HUMPHREYS, Wm	Ruth 1782		Ezekiel	Cart 1779
HUMPHRIES, Adam	Camd 1782		Ezekiel	Onsl 1771
Benj	Surr 1782		Hardy	Bert 1774
Daniel	Camd 1782		Hardy	Bert 1781
David	Surr 1782		Henry	Hali 1783
Elijah	Surr 1782		Isaac	Dupl 1783
George	Casw 1784		Isaac	Warr 1784
Jonathan	Camd 1782		Isaac	Gate 1789
Joseph	Camd 1782		Isaac Capt	Gate 1789
Joseph	Brun 1784		James	Oran 1779
Thomas	Camd 1782		James	Pasq 1694
Wm	Camd 1782		James	Rich 1790
Wm	Perq 1772		Jesse	Warr 1784
Wm	Bert 1774		Job	Bert 1774
Wm	Wilk 1782		John	Oran 1779
Wm	Perq 1787		John	Gate 1789
Wm Jr	Wilk 1782		John Jr	Oran 1779
HUNNICUTT, Meredith	Samp 1784		John Sr	Oran 1779
Wm	Samp 1784		Joseph	Bert 1781
HUNNINGS, Zachariah	Tyrr 1784		Libias	Cart 1779
HUNT, Charles	Curr 1779		Nicholas	Dupl 1783
Christr	Gran 1771		Robert	Oran 1779
David	Nash 1782		Samuel	Oran 1779
Eleazer	Rowa 1768		Theophilus	Gate 1789
Elizabeth	Oran 1779		Thomas	Nash 1782
Ezra	Rowa 1768		Thomas	Mart 1779
George	Gran 1785		Thomas	Gate 1789
Hardy	Bute 1766		Thomas	Gate 1789
Henry	Bute 1766		Timothy	Bert 1774
Henry (Cypres)	Bute 1766		Timothy	Bert 1781
Howell	Wilk 1782		Wm	Gate 1789
James	Bute 1766		Wm	Rich 1790
James	Gran 1785		Wm Jr	Rich 1790
James	Gran 1771		HUNTSINGER, Mathias	Rowa 1768
James Jr	Gran 1785		HURDLE, Abraham	Gate 1789
Jesse	Nash 1782		Benjamin	Chow 1785
John	Bute 1766		Hardin Sr	Chow 1785
John	Nash 1782		Hardy Sr	Chow 1785
John	Pasq 1694		Harmon	Chow 1785
John	Gran 1785		Henry	CHOW 1785
John	Wilk 1784		Isaiah	Chow 1785
John	Gran 1771		Joseph	Gate 1789
John Sr	Nash 1782		Joseph	Perq 1787
Mary	Mont 1782		Martin	Chow 1785
Momican	Gran 1771		Martin	Perq 1787
Mourning	Gran 1771		Thomas	Gate 1789
Samuel	Gran 1785		HURLER, Zachariah	Gran 1785
Samuel big	Ruth 1782		HURLEY, Edmond	Rowa 1768
Samuel little	Ruth 1782		Edmund	Mont 1782
Thomas	Nash 1782		Joseph	Mont 1782

HURLEY, Moses	Rich 1790		HYMAN, Michael	Crav 1779
HURST, Dinah	Hall 1783		Peter	Crav 1779
James	Bert 1774		Rachel	Crav 1779
John	Casw 1784		Wm	Mart 1779
Phillip	Wayn 1786		HYMES, Thomas	Hali 1783
Thomas	Mart 1779		HYNE, Jacob	Surr 1782
Wm	Wayn 1786		Joel	Surr 1782
Wm	Casw 1784		HYNES, Christopher	Mart 1779
HURT, Elisha	Hali 1783		Isham	Nash 1782
Joel	Hali 1783		Lewis	Nash 1782
John	Surr 1782		Wm	Mart 1779
Wm	Hali 1783			
HUSBAND, Edmund	Wilk 1784			
John	Rich 1790			
Wm	Rich 1790		IBES, Joseph	Perq 1787
HUSK, Edward	Oran 1779		IFLER, John	Jone 1779
HUSMAN, Daniel	Rowa 1770		ILEZ, John	Hali 1783
HUSSEY, Edward	Onsl 1771		IMMANUEL, Isaac Sr	Surr 1782
Mary	Blad 1784		INGMAN, James	Wilk 1782
Peter & s John	Rowa 1768		INGRAM, Andrew	Rowa 1768
Simon	Onsl 1771		Benj	Rich 1790
Stephen	Rowa 1768		Benjamin	Casw 1784
HUSTICE, John	Samp 1784		Charles	Dobb 1780
HUTCHENS, Don	Jone 1779		Charlotte	Casw 1784
Francis	Gran 1771		Edwin	Rich 1790
James	Rich 1790		Fereby	Samp 1784
John	Curr 1779		Isaac	Dobb 1780
Miles	Crav 1779		Jacob	Dobb 1780
Nathaniel	Curr 1779		James	Casw 1786
Richard	Curr 1779		James	Casw 1784
Robert	Crav 1779		James Jr	Dobb 1780
Thomas	Curr 1779		James Sr	Dobb 1780
Thomas Sr	Curr 1779		John	Rowa 1768
HUTCHESON, Daniel & s Wm			John	Casw 1786
	Surr 1782		John	Casw 1784
Wm	Surr 1782		Joshua	Bute 1766
HUTCHINS, Elijah	PItt 1786		Wm	Rowa 1768
Exod	Pitt 1786		INMAN, John	NorH 1780
James	Oran 1779		IPOCK, Jacob	Rowa 1761
Moses	Oran 1779		IRBY, Edmund	Hali 1783
HUTCHINSON, Joshua	Gran 1785		Elizabeth	Hali 1783
HUTCHISON, James	Oran 1779		Henry	Hali 1783
HUTER, Joseph	Gran 1785		IRELAND, Grafton	Hert 1779
Robert	Gran 1785		Grafton	Hert 1784
HUTSON, Forest	Wilk 1784		IRVIN, John	Bert 1774
James	Wayn 1786		John	Bert 1781
John	Oran 1785		Samuel	Hert 1784
HUTTON, Lewis	Rowa 1768		IRWIN, Henry	Beau 1786
HUX, Wm	Hali 1783		Samuel	Hert 1779
HUZIL, Wm	Gran 1771		ISAAC, Buck	Beau 1786
HYDE, Benjamin	Ruth 1782		Elijah	Wilk 1784
Caswell	NorH 1780		Elijah	Wilk 1782
David	NorH 1780		Elijah & son	Rowa 1768
Geo	Surr 1782		Elisha	Rowa 1768
Henry	NorH 1780		Elisha	Wilk 1782
Stephen	Surr 1782		Rachel	Wilk 1782
HYDER, Benjamin	Ruth 1782		Sam	Wilk 1782
Jacob	Ruth 1782		Samuel	Rowa 1768
HYMAN, Eleazer	Mart 1779		Samuel	Wilk 1784
Elizabeth	Mart 1779		Thomas	Rowa 1768
Hugh	Bert 1781		ISBELL, Benj	Surr 1782
John	Mart 1779		Christopher	Surr 1782
John	Bert 1774		Francis	Wilk 1782
John	Bert 1781		Godfrey	Wilk 1788
Lemuel	Bert 1781		James	Wilk 1782

ISBELL, Jason	Surr 1782		JACKSON, George	Casw 1786
Loveston	Wilk 1782		Henry	Warr 1784
Pelion	Wilk 1782		Isaac	Hali 1783
Thomas	Wilk 1782		Isaac Quaker	Oran 1779
Thomas	Surr 1782		Jacob	Dobb 1780
Zechariah esta	Rown 1768		Jacob	Surr 1782
ISDO, Wm	Jone 1779		James	Dobb 1780
ISEDELL, James	Chow 1785		James	Oran 1779
ISENZY, Henry	Rowa 1768		James	Mart 1779
ISLEY, Conrad	Oran 1779		James	Blad 1784
Malachi	Oran 1779		James	Surr 1782
Phillip	Oran 1779		Jesse	Pasq 1789
ISRAEL, Michael	Wilk 1784		Joab	Pasq 1789
Michael	Wilk 1782		John	Casw 1786
Samuel	Wilk 1784		John	Blad 1784
ISTER, Richard	Jone 1779		John	Casw 1784
IVES, Abigail	Curr 1779		John	Jone 1779
John	Crav 1779		John	Surr 1782
Thomas	Curr 1779		John	Surr 1782
Timothy	Hali 1783		John & sons	Rowa 1768
Timothy	Bert 1774		John (Little)	Samp 1784
Timothy	Curr 1779		John Jr	Samp 1784
Wm	Crav 1779		John Jr	Crav 1779
IVEY, Charles	Bute 1766		John Sr	Samp 1784
Curtis	Samp 1784		Joseph	Crav 1779
Curtis	Samp 1784		Joseph	Pitt 1786
George	Tyrr 1784		Joseph Sr	Crav 1779
Henry	Oran 1779		Joshua	Pasq 1779
James	Camd 1782		Lemuel	Pasq 1789
John	Oran 1779		Lewis	Samp 1784
John	Wayn 1786		Mary	Perq 1772
Robert	Wayn 1786		Mordicai	Pasq 1789
Robert	Hali 1783		Moses	Perq 1772
Thomas	Samp 1784		Moses	Perq 1787
IZARD, Hansel	Bute 1766		Moses Sr	Perq 1787
IZZELL, George	Samp 1784		Nathan	Samp 1784
			Nathan & son	Rowa 1768
			Peter	Bute 1766
			Peter	Warr 1784
JACKS, Churchill	Wilk 1782		Peter	Mont 1782
Edward	Rowa 1768		Priscilla	Pasq 1779
James	Wilk 1782		Rachel	Perq 1787
John	Rowa 1768		Robert	Rowa 1768
Wm	Wilk 1782		Rosannah	Pasq 1779
JACKSDON, Moses	Pasq 1779		Sam	Perq 1787
JACKSON, Archibald	Samp 1784		Saml	Surr 1782
Asa	Pasq 1779		Samuel	Mart 1779
Bailey	Pasq 1789		Samuel	Gran 1785
Benjamin	Hali 1783		Samuel	Pasq 1789
Benjamin	Warr 1784		Samuel	NorH 1780
Courtney	Pasq 1779		Sarah	Tyrr 1784
Curtis	Surr 1782		Seth	Samp 1784
Daniel	Pasq 1789		Shadrack	Casw 1786
David	Pasq 1789		Shadrack	Casw 1784
Dempsey	Pasq 1789		Simeon	Rowa 1768
Drury	Warr 1784		Smid	Edge 1777
Edward	Nash 1782		Thomas	Blad 1784
Edward	Rowa 1768		Thomas	Gran 1785
Eleanor	Beau 1786		Thomas	Hali 1783
Eleazer	Beau 1786		Wm	Pasq 1694
Eliz	Pasq 1789		Wm	Bute 1766
Francis	Cart 1779		Wm	Rowa 1768
George	Nash 1782		Wm	Oran 1779
George	Mart 1779		Wm	Mart 1779
George	Samp 1784		Wm	Samp 1784

Wm	Chow 1785	JANNETT, Abraham	Perq 1772
Wm	Mont 1782	JARMAIN, Hall	Dobb 1780
Wm	Perq 1787	John	Dobb 1780
Wm	Perq 1787	Joseph	Dobb 1780
Wm Jr	Oran 1779	Rachel	Dobb 1780
Zachariah	Pasq 1779	Robert	Dobb 1780
Zachariah	Pasq 1789	JARMAN, John	Onsl 1771
JACOB, Wm	Gran 1771	Littleton	Cart 1779
JACOBS, Abraham	Samp 1784	Mary	Onsl 1771
Benjamin	Casw 1784	Thomas	Onsl 1771
Fizer	Rowa 1770	JARRATT, Wm	Warr 1784
Henry	Chow 1785	JARRELL, Frederick	Crav 1779
Henry	Mont 1782	Fredk	Pitt 1786
Jonathan	Bert 1774	Henry Jr	Pitt 1786
Phillip	Rowa 1770	Henry Sr	Crav 1779
Richard	Casw 1786	Henry Sr	Pitt 1786
Sarah	Cart 1779	James	Crav 1779
Thomas	Samp 1784	Wm	Crav 1779
Wm	Gran 1785	Wm	Wilk 1782
JACOBSON, Hagar	Perq 1772	JARVIS, Foster	Curr 1779
JACOCKS, Eliz	Perq 1787	Jabez	Surr 1782
JAINE, Nathl	Surr 1782	James	Curr 1779
JAMES, Absalom	Mart 1779	John	Curr 1779
Benj	Bert 1781	Malissia	Curr 1779
Benjamin	Oran 1779	Maximillian	Curr 1779
Benjamin	Bert 1774	Rezia	Surr 1782
Charles	Warr 1784	Samuel	Curr 1779
Charles	Crav 1779	Solomon	Curr 1779
David	Samp 1784	Thomas	Curr 1779
Edward	Rowa 1770	Wm	Hali 1783
George	Warr 1784	Wm	Curr 1779
James	Dupl 1783	JASMON, Benj	Beau 1786
James	Rich 1790	JASONSHIELD, Roger	Albe 1679
Jesse	NorH 1780	JASPER, James	Beau 1786
John	Mart 1779	Jonathan	Beau 1786
John	Casw 1784	JAY, James	Casw 1784
John	Surr 1782	James Jr	Hert 1784
John Jr	Rich 1790	James Sr	Hert 1784
Joseph	Crav 1779	JAYCOCKS, Jonathan	Beau 1779
Joshua	Casw 1784	Jonathan	Bert 1781
Lemuel	Pasq 1789	JEAN, Phillip	Casw 1784
Morater	Onsl 1771	Thomas	Curr 1779
Noah	Camd 1782	JEFFERS, Patience	Mart 1779
Phillip	Rich 1790	JEFFERSON, Levi	Beau 1779
Samuel	Pasq 1779	Levy	Beau 1786
Solomon	Oran 1779	Obediah	Beau 1786
Thomas Sr	Rich 1790	JEFFREY, James	Mont 1782
Winnie	Crav 1779	Joseph	Warr 1784
Wm	Rowa 1768	Wm	Gran 1785
Wm	Rowa 1770	JEFFREYS, Debra	Casw 1784
Wm	Beau 1779	John	Bute 1766
Wm	Bert 1774	Joseph	Bute 1766
Wm	Surr 1782	Paul	Casw 1784
Wm	Beau 1786	Thomas	Bute 1766
Wm Sr	Pasq 1779	Thomas	Casw 1784
JAMESON, James	Rowa 1770	Wm	Bute 1766
Wm	Oran 1779	JEFFRIES, James	Ruth 1782
Wm Jr	Oran 1779	JELKS, Ethelred	Nash 1782
JAMISON, Bard	Chow 1785	John	Nash 1782
Elizabeth	Onsl 1771	Milakin	Nash 1782
James	Nash 1782	JEMISON, George	Curr 1779
JANE, Loter	Surr 1783	JENETT, Joseph	NorH 1780
JANETTE, James	Chow 1785	JENKINS, Abraham	Bert 1774
JANNET, Easter	Curr 1779	Abram	Bert 1781
Joseph	Curr 1779	Benjamin	Hert 1784

JENKINS, Cader	Bert 1781	JENNINGS, Demcy	Pasq 1789
Charles	Hert 1779	Dempsey	Pasq 1779
Charles	Hert 1784	Elizabeth	Pasq 1779
Demsy	Hert 1784	Hannah	Pasq 1789
Ephraim	NorH 1780	Isaac	Pasq 1779
Fisher	Onsl 1771	Isaac	Pasq 1789
Francis	Rowa 1768	James	Pasq 1779
Gary	Warr 1784	James	Wilk 1782
Henry	Hert 1779	Jarvis	Pasq 1789
Henry	Hert 1784	Jesse	Pasq 1779
Hugh	Rowa 1770	Jesse	Pasq 1789
Israel	Bert 1774	John	Pasq 1694
James	Rowa 1770	John	Mont 1782
James	Gran 1785	John	Wilk 1782
James	Bert 1774	John	Pasq 1789
James	Wilk 1782	Joseph	Pasq 1779
James Jr	Bert 1781	Joseph	Pasq 1789
James Sr	Bert 1781	Lemuel	Pasq 1789
John	Rowa 1768	Rebecca	Pasq 1779
John	Rowa 1770	Saml	Pasq 1789
John	Oran 1779	Samuel	Pasq 1779
John	Samp 1784	Thomas	Pasq 1789
John	Warr 1784	Wm	Pasq 1694
John	Bert 1774	Zachariah	Pasq 1789
John	Bert 1781	JENTRY, Elkins	Onsl 1771
John	Rich 1790	JEREL, John	Surr 1782
John Jr	Bert 1774	JERNIGAN, Arthur	Wayn 1786
Jonathan	Wilk 1782	Benj	Bert 1781
Jonathan	Onsl 1771	David	Bert 1781
Lennie	Bert 1774	David Jr	Wayn 1786
Levin	Onsl 1771	David Sr	Wayn 1786
Lewis	Nash 1782	Frederick	Wayn 1786
Lewis	Hert 1779	Geo	Bert 1781
Lewis	Blad 1784	George Jr	Wayn 1786
Lewis	Bert 1781	George Sr	Wayn 1786
Mansfield	Gran 1785	Jacob	Bert 1781
Nathl	Bert 1781	Jesse	Samp 1784
Padlock	Bert 1781	Jesse	Bert 1781
Reuben	Bute 1766	Jesse Jr	Blad 1784
Robert	Oran 1779	Joseph estate	Wayn 1786
Robert	Bert 1781	Josiah	Wayn 1786
Roderick	Rowa 1770	Mills	Wayn 1786
Roger	Nash 1782	Needham	Hert 1779
Thomas	Rowa 1768	Patience	Wayn 1786
Thomas	Rowa 1770	Stephen	Wayn 1786
Thomas	Gran 1785	Thomas	Blad 1784
Thomas	Warr 1784	Wm	Rich 1790
Webb	Hert 1784	JERVIS, Jabez	Surr 1782
Winborn	Hert 1784	John	Surr 1782
Winborne	Hert 1779	JESSOP, Mary	Perq 1787
Wm	Hert 1779	Thomas	Perq 1787
Wm	Hali 1783	JESSUMS, Benjamin	Hert 1784
Wm	Hert 1784	JESSUP, Isaac	Blad 1784
Wm	Onsl 1771	Joseph	Surr 1782
Wm	Bert 1781	Thomas	Rowa 1770
JENKINSON, John	Oran 1779	Thomas Jr	Rowa 1770
JENNER, Joseph	Tyrr 1784	Timothy	Cart 1779
JENNETT, Jabez	Curr 1779	Wm	Surr 1782
Jesse	Curr 1779	JESTER, Jacob	Rowa 1761
Job	Curr 1779	JETER, Edward	NorH 1780
JENNINGS, Anthony	Pasq 1779	John	NorH 1780
Arthur	Pasq 1779	JETT, Stephen	Gran 1771
Arthur	Pasq 1789	JILLS, Paron	Rowa 1770
Benj	Pasq 1789	Wm	Rowa 1770
Benjamin	Pasq 1779	JINNETT, Joseph	Wayn 1786

JOHANNES, Joseph	Gate 1789	JOHNSON, Phillip	Warr 1784
JOHN, David	Rowa 1768	Randall Jr	Tyrr 1784
JOHNS, Arthur	Surr 1782	Randall Sr	Tyrr 1784
Daniel	Pasq 1694	Robert	Bute 1766
John	Oran 1779	Robert	Rich 1790
Obediah	Surr 1782	Samuel	Blad 1784
Richard	Beau 1779	Simon	Blad 1784
Robert	Brun 1782	Thomas	Dobb 1780
Thomas	Oran 1779	Thomas	Blad 1784
Thomas	Beau 1779	Thomas	Wilk 1784
JOHNSON, Abraham	Hali 1783	Thomas	Wilk 1782
Alexander	Rowa 1768	Thomas	Surr 1782
Alexander	Casw 1786	Thomas	Rich 1790
Amos	Cart 1779	Tillah	Blad 1784
Anguish	Blad 1784	Travis	John 1784
Ashley	Surr 1782	Winney	Rich 1790
Benj	Wilk 1782	Wm	Ruth 1782
Benjamin	Warr 1784	Wm	Bute 1766
Benjamin	Wilk 1784	Wm	Blad 1784
Charles	Blad 1784	Wm	Hali 1783
Charles	Chow 1785	Wm	John 1784
Charles	John 1784	Wm	Warr 1784
Chas	Wilk 1782	Wm	Wilk 1784
Chas	Surr 1782	Wm	Wilk 1782
Duke	Warr 1784	Wm	Surr 1782
Elizabeth	Hali 1783	Wm	Surr 1782
Ethelred	John 1784	Wm	Rich 1790
Francis	Bute 1766	JOHNSTON, Absalom	Beau 1779
Geo	Surr 1783	Alexander	Blad 1784
George	Wilk 1784	Alexander	Casw 1784
Henry	Dobb 1780	Alexander & sn	Rowa 1768
Henry	Sury 1782	Barnaby	NorH 1780
Hezekiah	Blad 1784	Benj	Onsl 1771
Isaac	Surr 1782	Benj	Onsl 1771
Jacob	Dobb 1780	Benj	Gran 1771
Jacob	Hert 1784	Benjamin	Casw 1784
Jacob	Surr 1783	Benjamin	Gran 1785
James	Rowa 1768	Burwell	Bert 1774
James	Blad 1784	Charles	Oran 1779
James	Warr 1784	Charles	Crav 1779
James	Mont 1782	Collinson	Jone 1779
James s of Mar	Dobb 1780	Daniel	Blad 1784
Jeffrey	Wilk 1782	Daniel	Casw 1784
Jeffrey	Surr 1782	Daniel	NorH 1780
Jesse Jr	Samp 1784	Darden	NorH 1780
Joab	John 1784	David	Onsl 1771
John	Bute 1766	David	NorH 1780
John	Rowa 1768	David & son	Rowa 1768
John	Blad 1784	Drury	Oran 1779
John	Hali 1783	Elijah	Dobb 1780
John	Mont 1782	Ephraim	Samp 1784
John	Surr 1782	Francis	Bute 1766
John	Surr 1782	Francis	Rowa 1761
John	Perq 1787	Francis	Casw 1784
John	Rich 1790	Gabriel Gov	Crav 1756
Jonathan	Tyrr 1784	Gen	NorH 1780
Julius	Bute 1766	Geo	NorH 1780
Lewis	Blad 1784	George	Oran 1779
Lucy	Oran 1779	George	Casw 1784
Mary	Dobb 1780	Gideon	Rowa 1768
Mary	John 1784	Gideon	Gran 1785
Matthew	John 1784	Henry	Mart 1779
Moses	Surr 1782	Henry	Wayn 1786
Nehemiah	Blad 1784	Henry	Crav 1779
Philemon	John 1784	Hezekiah	Crav 1779

JOHNSTON, Isaac	Rowa 1768	Richard	Gran 1771
Isham	Gran 1785	Robert	Mart 1779
Jacob	Samp 1784	Robert	Blad 1784
Jacob	Crav 1779	Robert & sons	Rowa 1768
James	Camd 1782	Sam	Wilk 1782
James	Casw 1786	Samuel	Blad 1784
James	Casw 1784	Samuel	Casw 1784
James	Gran 1785	Samuel	Chow 1785
Jarrett	Onsl 1771	Samuel	Gran 1785
Jesse	Mart 1779	Sarah	Bute 1766
Jesse	Samp 1784	Soasby	Samp 1784
Jesse	Gran 1785	Solomon Jr	Samp 1784
Joel	Samp 1784	Solomon Sr	Samp 1784
John	Albe 1679	Thomas	Dupl 1783
John	Oran 1779	Thomas	Rowa 1768
John	Mart 1779	Thomas	Oran 1779
John	Samp 1784	Thomas	Mart 1779
John	Blad 1784	Thomas	Onsl 1771
John	Casw 1784	Thomas	Gran 1771
John	Jone 1779	Tillah	Blad 1784
John	Bert 1774	Wm	Rowa 1768
John	Wilk 1782	Wm	Oran 1779
John	Onsl 1771	Wm	Samp 1784
John	Gran 1771	Wm	Casw 1784
John	Bert 1781	Wm	Gran 1785
John	Bert 1781	Wm	John 1784
John	Pasq 1789	Wm	Wilk 1782
John & sons	Rowa 1768	Wm	Bert 1781
John H	Bert 1781	Wm James	Wayn 1786
John Jr	Casw 1784	Wm Jr	Oran 1779
John s of Alex	Rowa 1768	Wm Jr	Gran 1771
Jonathan	Gran 1785	JOINER, Charles	Hert 1784
Joseph	Samp 1784	Henry	Hali 1783
Joseph	Casw 1784	James	NorH 1780
Joseph	Chow 1785	Jiles	NorH 1780
Joseph	Gran 1785	John	Hali 1783
Joseph	Onsl 1771	John	Surr 1782
Joseph	NorH 1780	Joiner	Dobb 1780
Joseph	Gran 1771	Joseph	Hert 1779
Joshua	Mart 1779	JOINS, Eaekiel	Wilk 1782
Joshua	Casw 1784	JOLLEY, Solomon	Beau 1786
Joshua	Chow 1785	JOLLY, James	Nash 1782
Joshua	Beau 1779	Wm	Ruth 1782
Joshua	Onsl 1771	JONAS, Arthur	Wayn 1786
Joshua	NorH 1780	David	Casw 1784
Joshua	Beau 1786	Elking	Blad 1784
Judith	Gran 1785	Francis	Chow 1785
Julius	Bute 1766	Gen Allen	NorH 1780
Lancelot	Casw 1786	Hardy	Wayn 1786
Lancelot	Casw 1784	Hezekiah	Chow 1785
Langhorn	John 1784	Isaiah	Chow 1785
Lazarus	Blad 1784	James	Wayn 1786
Lazham	Gran 1785	James	Casw 1784
Levy	Bert 1781	John	Bert 1781
Linda	Bert 1781	Jonathan	Blad 1784
Mary	Dobb 1780	Nicholas	Casw 1784
Matthew	Oran 1779	Richard	Casw 1784
Matthew	Gran 1771	Robert	Blad 1784
Moses Jr	John 1784	Samuel	Chow 1785
Moses Sr	John 1784	Simon	Rowa 1768
Noah	Gran 1785	Solomon	Blad 1784
Peregrine	Samp 1784	Thomas	Chow 1785
Peter	Casw 1784	Thomas Jr	Casw 1784
Richard	Casw 1786	Thomas Sr	Casw 174
Richard	Casw 1784	Willis	Wayn 1786

JONAS, Wm	Wayn 1788	JONES, Edward	Rowa 1768
Wm	Brun 1784	Edward	Warr 1784
Wm	Casw 1784	Elisha	Surr 1782
JONATHAN, John	Albe 1679	Eliz	Beau 1786
JONCY, Littlebury	Wilk 1782	Elizabeth	Chow 1785
JONES, Abraham	Gran 1785	Emanuel	Onsl 1771
Abraham	Crav 1779	Evan	Tyrr 1784
Abraham	Gran 1771	Evan	Crav 1779
Abram	Hert 1779	Evan Jr	Curr 1779
Aden	Cart 1779	Evan Sr	Curr 1779
Albritton	Hali 1783	Fowler	Gran 1785
Ambrose	Cart 1779	Francis	Nash 1782
Ambrose	Gran 1785	Francis	Casw 1784
Ambrose	Gran 1771	Francis	Perq 1772
Amey	Hert 1779	Francis	Perq 1787
Ann	Dobb 1780	Francis Capt	Hali 1783
Ann	Casw 1786	Frederick	Bute 1766
Aquilla	Oran 1779	Frederick	Dobb 1780
Avin	Dobb 1780	Frederick	Nash 1782
Bactron	Gran 1785	Frederick	Hali 1783
Barbara	Nash 1782	Frederick	Dobb 1780
Barnaby	Wayn 1786	Frederick s of	Bute 1766
Bartlett	Tyrr 1784	Friley	Tyrr 1784
Benj	Surr 1782	George	Warr 1784
Benj	Gran 1771	George	Perq 1772
Benjamin	Mart 1779	Gideon	Curr 1779
Benjamin	Samp 1784	Griffin	Dobb 1780
Benjamin	Mart 1779	Hananiah	Perq 1772
Benjamin	Warr 1784	Harwood	NorH 1780
Berry	Ruth 1788	Henry	Hali 1783
Bess	Perq 1772	Henry	Pasq 1694
Bilhah	Tyrr 1784	Henry	Samp 1784
Binkler	Gran 1785	Henry	Bute 1766
Britton	Blad 1784	Henry	Pasq 1779
Britton	Hali 183	Henry	Warr 1784
Burrell	Bute 1766	Henry	Jone 1779
Cadwalider	Surr 1782	Henry	Wilk 1782
Charles	Pasq 1694	Henry	Pasq 1789
Charles	Samp 1784	Hezekiah	Gate 1789
Charles	Crav 1779	Higgins	Mart 1779
Charles	Mont 1782	Humphrey	Hert 1779
Chas	Gate 1789	Isaac	Blad 1784
Cooper	Nash 1782	Isaac	Warr 1784
Corbit	Tyrr 1784	Isaac	Mont 1782
Crowalier	Surr 1782	Isaac	Surr 1782
Davey	Perq 1772	Isaac	Pasq 1789
David	Hert 1779	Jacob	Crav 1779
David	Dobb 1780	James	Hert 1779
David	Hali 1783	James	Bute 1766
David	Samp 1786	James	Dobb 1780
David	Hert 1784	James	Rowa 1768
David	Tyrr 1784	James	Casw 1786
David	Beau 1779	James	Tyrr 1784
David	Curr 1779	James	Warr 1784
David	Onsl 1771	James	Jone 1779
David	Surr 1782	James	Beau 1779
David	Surr 1784	James	Wilk 1784
David	Beau 1786	James	Bert 1774
David Jr	Gate 1789	James	Crav 1779
David Sr	Gate 1789	James	Surr 1782
Demcy	Onsl 1771	James	Gran 1771
Dempsey	Gate 1789	James	Gate 1789
Drury	Casw 1784	James	Bert 1781
Edward	Pasq 1694	James	Bert 1781
Edward	Gran 1785	James	Pasq 1789

James sof John			Mary	Nash 1782
	Gran 1771		Mary	Rowa 1761
Jarvis	Pasq 1779		Mary	Jone 1779
Jarvis	Pasq 1789		Mary	NorH 1780
Jesse	Cart 1779		Merriam	Pasq 1779
Jesse	Gate 1789		Michael	Gran 1785
Jesse	Bert 1781		Moses	Gate 1789
Job	Surr 1782		Musgrave	Blad 1784
John	Hali 1783		Nathan	Samp 1784
John	Pasq 1694		Nathaniel	Onsl 1771
John	Ruth 1782		Nathl	NorH 1780
John	Bute 1766		Newsome	Nash 1782
John	Dobb 1780		Owen	Onsl 1771
John	Nash 1782		Peter	Dobb 1780
John	Samp 1784		Peter	Wilk 1782
John	Casw 1784		Peter	Gran 1771
John	Gran 1785		Phillip	Hali 1783
John	Mart 1779		Phillip	Wilk 1784
John	Casw 1786		Phillip & son	Bute 1766
John	Tyrr 1784		Polly	Warr 1784
John	Pasq 1779		Randall	Curr 1779
John	Warr 1784		Richard	Bute 1766
John	Beau 1779		Richard	Dobb 1780
John	NBer 1779		Richard	Samp 1784
John	Bert 1774		Richard	Casw 1784
John	Mont 1782		Richard	Gran 1785
John	Curr 1779		Richard	Warr 1784
John	NorH 1780		Richard	NorH 1780
John	Surr 1782		Richard	Gran 1771
John	Gran 1771		Robert	Ruth 1782
John	Gate 1789		Robert	Bute 1766
John	Beau 1786		Robert	Tyrr 1784
John	Rich 1790		Robert	Warr 1784
John (short)	Dobb 1780		Roger	Bute 1766
John Jr	Hali 1783		Roger	Crav 1779
John Jr	Rich 1790		Roger	Beau 1786
John Sr	Mart 1779		Russell	Wilk 1782
Jonathan	Oran 1779		Saml	Surr 1782
Jonathan	Camd 1782		Samuel	Gran 1785
Jonathan	Beau 1786		Samuel	Tyrr 1784
Joseph	Hert 1779		Samuel & sons	Bute 1766
Joseph	Mart 1779		Sarah	Hert 1779
Joseph	Rowa 1768		Sarah	Hali 1783
Joseph	Casw 1786		Sarah	Camd 1782
Joseph	Tyrr 1784		Sarah	Hert 1784
Joseph	Surr 1782		Sarah	Curr 1779
Joseph	Perq 1787		Simon	Rowa 1768
Joshua	Casw 1784		Simon Edward	Jone 1779
Joshua	Hali 1783		Solomon	Mart 1779
Joshua	Casw 1786		Solomon	Bert 1781
Josiah	Bute 1782		Stephen	Casw 1784
Josiah	Beau 1779		Sugars	Warr 1784
Josiah	Gate 1789		Sylvanus	Dobb 1780
Josias Sr	Beau 1786		Tamar	Camd 1782
Lancelot	Samp 1784		Thomas	Bute 1766
Levi	Rowa 1761		Thomas	Dobb 1780
Lewis	Oran 1779		Thomas	Casw 1786
Lewis	NorH 1780		Thomas	Blad 1784
Lewis	Gate 1789		Thomas	Gran 1785
Lovick	Crav 1779		Thomas	Rowa 1768
Lucy	Hali 1783		Thomas	Beau 1779
Lurana	Rich 1790		Thomas	Curr 1779
Margaret	Dobb 1780		Thomas	Surr 1782
Martha	Warr 1784		Thomas	Gran 1771
Mary	Ruth 1782		Thomas	Beau 1786

Thomas	Perq	1787
Thomas & son	Bute	1766
Thomas (river)	Bute	1766
Thomas Jr	Bute	1766
Thomas Sr	Wilk	1782
Vinson	Wilk	1782
Walter	Beau	1779
Walter	Crav	1779
Walter	Beau	1786
Walter	Pitt	1786
Willey	Hali	1783
Willie	Bert	1781
Willis	Bert	1774
Winkler	Gran	1771
Wm	Bute	1766
Wm	Dobb	1780
Wm	Chow	1785
Wm	Hali	1783
Wm	Oran	1779
Wm	Casw	1786
Wm	Hert	1784
Wm	Hali	1782
Wm	Perq	1772
Wm	Beau	1779
Wm	Onsl	1771
Wm	NorH	1780
Wm	Gran	1771
Wm	Bert	1781
Wm	Beau	1786
Wm	Pitt	1786
Wm	Perq	1787
Wm (short)	Dobb	1780
Wm Jr	Gran	1785
Wm Sr	Gran	1785
Zariah	Cart	1779
Zeriah	Cart	1779
JONEY, James	HalI	1783
JORDAN, Alexander	Wilk	1782
Arthur	Gran	1771
Benjamin	Chow	1785
Caleb	Chow	1785
Charles	Chow	1785
Charles	Mont	1782
Edward	Hali	1783
Francis	Mont	1782
Gare	Bert	1781
Henry	NorH	1780
Hezekiah	Bert	1774
Isaiah	Chow	1785
Jacob	Chow	1785
James	NorH	1780
Jeremiah	Gate	1789
John	Mart	1779
John	Gran	1785
John	Tyrr	1784
John	Bert	1774
John	Mont	1782
John	Wilk	1782
Jonathan	Chow	1785
Joseph	Hali	1783
Joseph	Bert	1781
Joseph	Perq	1787
Joseph Jr	Bert	1774
Joseph Sr	Chow	1785
Joseph Sr	Bert	1774

JORDAN, Joshua	Pasq	1789
Josiah	Pasq	1779
Josiah	Perq	1787
Keston	Wilk	1782
Maximillian	Warr	1784
Munn	NorH	1780
Nathan	Chow	1785
Nicholas	Chow	1785
Pleasant	Hert	1779
Pleasant	Hert	1784
Robert	Oran	1779
Sarah	Samp	1784
Thomas	Oran	1779
Thomas	Wayn	1786
Thomas	Pasq	1779
Thomas	Crav	1779
Thomas	Wilk	1782
Thomas	Pasq	1789
Wm	Mart	1779
Wm	Samp	1784
Wm	Chow	1785
Wm	Hali	1783
Wm	Crav	1779
Wm	Mont	1782
Wm	Bert	1781
Wm	Pasq	1789
Wm Jr	Bert	1781
Wm Sr	Bert	1774
Zechariah	Pasq	1779
JOSEPH, John	Rowa	1761
Peter	Rowa	1770
JOSEY, John	Rowa	1768
John	NorH	1780
Willis	NorH	1780
JOY, Henry	Hali	1783
JOYCE, Alexander	Rowa	1770
Alexr	Surr	1782
Caleb	Mart	1779
Elijah	Rowa	1770
Isaac	Surr	1782
John	Mart	1779
Martin	Mart	1779
Thomas	Rowa	1770
JOYNER, Blount	Hali	1783
Bridgeman	Hali	1783
Eli	Hali	1783
Henry	Hali	1783
Jacob	Nash	1782
Joel	Samp	1784
Joel	Hali	1783
John	Nash	1782
Jonathan	Hali	1783
Nathan	Nash	1782
Nathan	Hali	1783
Solomon	Nash	1782
Theophilus	Hali	1783
Wm	Samp	1784
Wm Jr	Nash	1782
Wm Sr	Nash	1782
JRNKINS, Elisha	Curr	1779
Henry	Onsl	1771
Jesse	Warr	1784
John	Warr	1784
JUBERY, Jiles	Bute	1766
JUDD, Nathaniel	Wilk	1782

JUDD, Roland	Wilk 1778	KEE, Matthew	NorH 1780
Roland Jr	Wilk 1782	KEEL, Chas	Pasq 1789
Rowland	Wilk 1782	James	Beau 1786
JUDDELL, Absalom	Casw 1784	Nathan	Beau 1786
JUDGE, Bryan	Oran 1779	Nathaniel	Beau 1779
Israel	Hali 1783	Samuel	Warr 1784
James	Hali 1783	KEELE, Charles	Pasq 1779
JUDKINS, Thomas	Warr 1784	Jacob	Hert 1779
JUDSON, Arthur	Gran 1785	Jacob	Hert 1784
JULER, Samuel	Gran 1785	James	Hert 1784
JUMP, Wm	Dobb 1780	John	Oran 1779
JURDEN, Edward	Pitt 1786	Joseph	Mart 1779
Wm	Pitt 1786	Lewis	Hert 1779
JURNIGAN, David	Bert 1774	Liddy	Hert 1784
George	Bert 1774	Mary	Hert 1779
Jacob Jr	Bert 1774	KEELER, Charles	Brun 1784
Jacob Sr	Bert 1774	Jacob	Gran 1771
Jesse	Bert 1774	KEELING, Benj	Surr 1782
Wm	Bert 1774	KEEN, George	Bert 1774
JUSON, Gabriel	Rowa 1768	Monez	Hali 1783
James	Rowa 1768	Nicholas	Oran 1779
Joseph	Rowa 1768	Sam	Gate 1789
JUSTICE, John	Hali 1783	Sion	Samp 1784
John	Oran 1779	KEER, Alexr	Surr 1782
John	Samp 1784	John	Surr 1782
Reuben	Gran 1785	KEES, John	Wilk 1782
Thomas	Ruth 1782	KEETER, John	Camd 1782
Wm	NorH 1780	KEETLEY, John Sr	Wayn 1786
JUTON, Abram	Rowa 1770	KEETON, Lawrence	Albe 1694
		Wm	Surr 1782
		KEETOR, Solomon	Camd 1782
		KELER, Mathias	Surr 1782
KAGLE, David & son	Rowa 1768	KELLAM, Theophilis	Curr 1779
John	Rowa 1768	KELLOW, Wm	NorH 1780
KAILE, Amos	Bert 1774	KELLY, Archibald	Blad 1784
John	Bert 1774	Charles	Oran 1779
Sarah	Bert 1774	Chas	Surr 1782
KALE, Richard	Gran 1771	Chas	Beau 1786
KANEY, Abraham	Rowa 1768	Christopher	Gran 1785
KAPP, Joseph	Rowa 1768	Curtis	Beau 1786
KARNEY, Abraham	Jone 1779	Daniel	Ruth 1782
KARR, David	Rowa 1768	Daniel	Oran 1779
James	Rowa 1768	David	Surr 1782
John	Rowa 1768	Delphia	Hert 1784
KATTEREL, Jonathan	Pitt 1786	Duncan	Blad 1784
KAYES, Thomas	Rowa 1768	Edward	Casw 1784
KEA, Robert	Samp 1784	Edward	Gate 1789
Thomas	Samp 1784	Elizabeth	Hali 1783
KEADLE, John	Surr 1782	Francis	Gran 1771
KEARS, Matthew	Beau 1779	James	Bute 1766
KEATON, Caleb	Pasq 1779	James	Oran 1779
Daniel	Pasq 1779	James	Camd 1784
Henry	Pasq 1779	James	Gran 1785
Henry	Pasq 1789	James	Hali 1783
John	Pasq 1779	James	Gran 1771
John	Pasq 1789	John	Oran 1779
Joseph Jr	Pasq 1779	John	Blad 1784
Joseph Jr	Pasq 1789	John	Wilk 1782
Joseph Sr	Pasq 1779	John	Surr 1782
Joseph Sr	Pasq 1789	John	Gran 1771
Lewis	Pasq 1779	Joseph	Samp 1784
Patrick	Pasq 1789	Kelly	Rowa 1770
Stephen	Pasq 1789	Laban	Beau 1786
Wm	Pasq 1789	Matthew	Blad 1784
Zechariah	Pasq 1779	Nelson	Wilk 1782

KELLY, Patrick	Camd 1782		KENYON, John	Perq 1787
Richard	Ruth 1782		Joseph	Pasq 1789
Robert	Oran 1779		Joshua	Perq 1779
Robert	Surr 1782		Roger	Perq 1772
Samuel	Casw 1786		KERBY, Absalom	John 1784
Samuel	Casw 1784		Archibald	John 1784
Samuel	Mont 1782		Edmund	Wilk 1782
Thomas	Gran 1785		Francis	Wilk 1782
Thomas	Hali 1783		Henry	Wilk 1782
Wm	Ruth 1782		Henry	Surr 1782
Wm	Casw 1786		Jesse	John 1784
Wm	Casw 1784		Jesse	NorH 1780
Wm	Gran 1771		Joel	Surr 1782
Wm	Gate 1789		Saml	Surr 1782
Wm	Bert 1781		Wm	Gate 1789
KELON, Charlton	Wilk 1782		KERLOCK, Henry	Ruth 1782
Osburn	Wilk 1782		KERN, Gilbert	Surr 1782
KEMP, Hannah	Crav 1779		Masa	Surr 1782
Isaac	Crav 1779		KERNEY, Edward	Warr 1784
Isaac	Pitt 1786		John	Warr 1784
Joshua	Crav 1779		John	Crav 1779
Thomas	Crav 1779		Phillip	Warr 1784
KENCH, Nathl	Beau 1786		Shemiele	Bute 1766
KENDALL, Thomas	Rowa 1770		KERNS, John	Rowa 1768
KENDRICK, John Jr	Crav 1779		KERR, Alexander	Casw 1786
John Sr	Crav 1779		Alexander	Casw 1784
Jones	Oran 1779		James	Oran 1779
Thomas	Gran 1785		John	Casw 1786
KENNEDY, Daniel	Rowa 1768		John	Casw 1784
Edmund	Ruth 1782		KERSEY, John	Casw 1784
Ephraim	Mart 1779		Peter	Blad 1784
George	NBer 1779		Wm	Bert 1781
Henry	Dobb 1780		KERSHAW, John	Rich 1798
Isaac	Mart 1779		KESTER, Wm	Bert 1774
James	Oran 1779		KETNER, Francis	Surr 1782
James	Camd 1782		KETTERSIDES, James	Ruth 1782
James	Casw 1784		KETTLE, Peter	Rowa 1768
James	Onsl 1771		KEY, Jonathan	Onsl 1771
John	Dobb 1780		Luck	Warr 1784
John	Rowa 1768		Thomas	Gran 1771
John	Oran 1779		KEYS, Joseph	Oran 1779
John	Mart 1779		Thomas	Rowa 1768
John	Wayn 1786		KIBBLE, James	Onsl 1771
John	NBer 1779		KIDWELL, Thomas	Rowa 1768
John	Beau 1779		KIER, Randolph	Surr 1782
John	Brun 1782		KIFF, Ephraim	Mart 1779
John	Beau 1786		Wm	Onsl 1771
John	Pitt 1786		KIGER, Adam	Surr 1782
Joseph	Rowa 1768		KIGHTE, Elisha	Curr 1779
Robert	Camd 1782		KILBEY, Adam	Wilk 1782
Walter	Dobb 1780		Elizabeth	Wilk 1782
Wm	Oran 1779		Michael	Wilk 1782
KENNEDY;, Stephen	Wayn 1786		Wm	Wilk 1782
KENNELL, Britain	Bute 1766		KILBURN, Amos	Wilk 1782
Moses & son	Bute 1766		Amos	Surr 1782
KENT, Henry	Mart 1779		KILGORE, Lydda	Casw 1786
Jesse	Nash 1782		Thomas Jr	Casw 1784
John Jr	Nash 1782		KILLETT, John	Wayn 1786
Joseph	Bert 1774		KILLEY, Jiles	Surr 1782
Thomas Wm	Mart 1799		KILLIAN, Andrew	Rowa 1768
KENTERY, Pottana	Pitt 1786		John	Rowa 1768
KENYON, Benj	Perq 1787		Michael	Oran 1779
Duke	Perq 1787		KILLINGSWORTH, Mark Jr	
Joab	Perq 1787			Hali 1783
Jobe	Perq 1772		Wm	Hali 1783

KILPATRICK, Alexander		KING, Charles	Oran	1779
	Oran 1779	Charles	Samp	1784
Easter	Dobb 1780	Charles	Bert	1774
Wm	Dobb 1780	Chas	Wilk	1782
KIMBALL, Bartholomew		Chas Sr	Bert	1781
	Gran 1785	Cuthbert	Warr	1784
Benjamin	Bute 1766	David	Warr	1784
Benjamin	Warr 1784	Duncan	Blad	1784
Benjamin Jr	Warr 1784	Edward	Oran	1779
Charles	Bute 1766	Edward	Casw	1786
David	Warr 1784	Edward	Hali	1783
Drury	Gran 1785	Edward	Wilk	1782
Drury	Gran 1771	Eliz	Bert	1781
Joseph	Gran 1771	Francis	Gran	1771
Stella	Warr 1784	George	Rowa	1770
Winney	Warr 1784	George	Gran	1785
Winnie	Warr 1784	Henry	Surr	1782
Wm	Warr 1784	Henry	Gate	1789
KIMBERLAND, Martin	Oran 1779	Henry	Bert	1781
KIMBOROUGH, John	Mont 1782	Higason	Mart	1779
KIMBROUGH, Bradley	Rowa 1770	James	Bute	1766
Bradley & son	Rowa 1768	James	Rowa	1770
Eleanor	Casw 1786	Jeremiah	Crav	1779
Eleanor	Casw 1784	Jesse	Hert	1779
Frederick	Oran 1779	Jesse	Hert	1784
Henry	Oran 1779	Joel	Crav	1779
John	Rowa 1770	John	Albe	1694
John	Oran 1779	John	Ruth	1782
John	Casw 1786	John	Rowa	1770
John	Casw 1784	John	Wayn	1786
Leonard	Oran 1779	John	Hali	1783
Marmaduke	Rowa 1770	John	Tyrr	1784
Powell	Oran 1779	John	Onsl	1771
Robert	Casw 1786	John	NorH	1780
Robert	Casw 1784	John	Surr	1782
Thomas	Rowa 1768	John Jr	Oran	1779
Thomas	Casw 1786	John Sr	Oran	1779
Thomas	Casw 1784	Johnson	Rowa	1770
Wm	Casw 1786	Johnson Jr	Rowa	1770
Wm	Casw 1784	Johnston Jr	Rowa	1768
KINAST, Christopher	Rowa 1768	Johnston Sr	Rowa	1768
KINCAID, James	Rowa 1768	Joseph	Jone	1779
KINCHIN, John	Oran 1779	Julian	Nash	1782
John	Hali 1783	Julian	Bute	1766
KINDALL, Arm.	Hali 1783	Julius	Oran	1779
Dennis	Hali 1783	Julius	Gran	1771
Wm	Mont 1782	Margaret	Jone	1779
KING, Aaron	Wilk 1782	Martha	Bert	1781
Andrew	Surr 1782	Michael	Samp	1784
Anthony	Warr 1784	Michael	Bert	1774
Ark	Warr 1779	Michael	Bert	1781
Armour	Oran 1779	Michael Jr	Bert	1781
Arrington	Crav 1779	Michael Sr	Bert	1781
Baker	Wilk 1784	Miles	Gran	1785
Baxter	Oran 1779	Miles	Rich	1790
Benajer	Surr 1782	NathanieL	Casw	1784
Benijah	Rowa 1770	Nathaniel	Oran	1779
Britain	Crav 1779	Nathaniel	Casw	1786
Britain	Pitt 1786	Nathl	Beau	1786
Burrill	Hali 1783	Parks	Surr	1782
Cader	Bert 1774	Peter	Rowa	1768
Cader	Bert 1781	Peter	Surr	1782
Catherine	Bert 1781	Richard	Rowa	1770
Charles	Hert 1779	Robert	Rowa	1770
Charles	Dobb 1780	Robert	Mart	1779

Robert	Casw 1786		KITCHEN, Joseph	Edge 1777
Robert	Casw 1784		Joshua	Perq 1787
Robert	Wilk 1782		KITE, Henry	Crav 1779
Saml	Surr 1782		John	Camd 1782
Samuel	Ruth 1782		Willie	Camd 1782
Samuel	Rowa 1770		Zechariah	Camd 1782
Solomon	Gate 1789		KITRELL, Moses	Gate 1789
Stephen	Samp 1784		KITSMILLER, John	Oran 1779
Thomas	Nash 1782		KITT, Ephraim	Bert 1774
Thomas	Chow 1785		KITTLE, Ben	Surr 1782
Thomas	Rowa 1770		Peter	Rowa 1761
Thomas	Oran 1779		KITTLEBREW, Hinkley	Jone 1779
Thomas	Chow 1785		KITTRELL, Charles	Bert 1774
Thomas	Curr 1779		Dempsey	Bert 1781
Thomas	Surr 1782		Geo	Bert 1781
Thomas	Gran 1771		George	Bert 1774
Thomas & son	Rowa 1768		Isaac	Gran 1785
Thomas Sr	Surr 1782		James Jr	Gran 1785
Wm	Oran 1779		James Sr	Gran 1785
Wm	Samp 1784		John	Gran 1785
Wm	Bert 1774		John	Bert 1774
Wm	Onsl 1771		John	Bert 1781
Wm	Surr 1782		Jonathan	Gran 1771
Wm	Gate 1789		Joshua	Gran 1785
Wm	Bert 1781		Priscilla	Bert 1781
Wood	Warr 1784		Saml	Gran 1771
KINLAW, Thomas	Blad 1784		Samuel	Gran 1785
KINLEY, John	Beau 1779		KNAUE, Teeter	Rowa 1770
KINMAN, James	Rowa 1770		KNEWES, Phillip	Beau 1786
KINNEN, Anthony Jr	Beau 1786		KNIGHT, Abel	Rowa 1768
KINNEON, Daniel	Curr 1779		Abel & sons	Rowa 1770
John	Curr 1779		Ann	Hert 1784
KINNEY, Joseph	Jone 1779		Dempsey	Hert 1779
KINSEY, Absalom	Samp 1784		Dempsey	Hert 1784
Edward	Dobb 1780		Elisha	Nash 1782
Henry	Hert 1779		Emanuel	Pasq 1779
John	Dobb 1780		Ephraim	Hali 1783
John Jr	Wilk 1782		George	Nash 1782
Samuel	Dobb 1780		James	Gate 1789
Solomon	Tyrr 1784		John	Nash 1782
KINSLE, Frederick	Surr 1782		John	Rowa 1768
KINSON, John	Gran 1785		John	Rowa 1770
KIRBY, Duncan	Blad 1784		John	Oran 1779
Wm	Nash 1782		John	Gran 1785
KIRCHNER, Christopher			John	Hali 1783
	Rowa 1768		Jonathan	Rowa 1770
KIRK, George	Bute 1766		Jonathan	Gran 1771
George	Mont 1782		Nehemiah	Hert 1779
Isaac	Oran 1779		Nehemiah	Hert 1784
Isaac	Hali 1783		Richard	Mart 1779
Lewis	Oran 1779		Robert	Hali 1783
Stephen	Oran 1779		Solomon	Rowa 1770
Thomas	Pasq 1694		Thomas	Rowa 1770
KIRKLAND, Joseph	Oran 1779		Thomas	Pasq 1789
Thomas	Oran 1779		Thomas & sons	Rowa 1768
KIRKLEY, George	Hali 1783		Wm	Hert 1779
KIRKMAN, Elijah	Surr 1782		Wm	Gran 1785
KIRKPATRICK, James	Rowa 1770		Wm	NorH 1780
John	Rowa 1770		Wm	Surr 1782
Mary	Surr 1782		Wm	Gran 1771
Moses	Surr 1782		KNOLES, Thomas	Perq 1772
Wm	Rowa 1770		Wm	Perq 1772
Wm	Blad 1784		KNOLL, David	Gran 1785
KITCHEN, James	Casw 1786		James	Gran 1785
James	HalI 1783		John	Gran 1785

KNOP, Wm	Jone 1779	LACEY, John	Oran 1779
KNOTT, James	Gran 1771	Joseph	Perq 1787
James	Bert 1781	Nathan	Perq 1787
James Sr	Bert 1781	LACKEY, John	Casw 1786
John	Gran 1771	John	Casw 1784
Joseph Jr	Bert 1774	LACY, Wm	Mont 1782
Joseph Sr	Bert 1774	LADD, Amos	Surr 1782
Sarah	Bert 1781	Constant	Surr 1782
Wm	Bert 1781	Noble	Rowa 1770
Wm Sr	Bert 1774	Noble Jr	Surr 1782
KNOTTS, John	Dobb 1780	Noble Sr	Surr 1782
KNOWLAND, Charles	Gran 1785	LAFIELD, Thomas	Bert 1781
Daniel	Gran 1785	LAFOY, James	Surr 1782
KNOWLES, Abner	Perq 1787	John	Surr 1782
George	Blad 1784	LAIN, Benj	Perq 1787
James	Blad 1784	Demsey	Perq 1787
Lawrence	Bute 1766	John	Perq 1787
Wm	Warr 1784	Lettison	Perq 1787
Wm	Perq 1787	Miles	Perq 1787
Wm & bro	Bute 1766	Moses	Perq 1787
KNOWLIN, Daniel	Gran 1771	Wm	Perq 1787
Edward	Gran 1771	LAKE, Jacob	Oran 1779
Peter	Gran 1771	Manasseh	Rowa 1761
KNOX, Absalom	Rowa 1770	LAKEW, Peter	Brun 1784
Ambrose	Pasq 1779	LAMB, Arthur	Blad 1784
Ambrose	Pasq 1789	Campbell	Blad 1784
Andrew	Pasq 1779	Cornelius	Wayn 1786
Andrew	Perq 1772	Eliz	Perq 1787
James	Hert 1784	Elizabeth & so	Rowa 1761
James	Beau 1786	Elizabeth wido	Rowa 1768
Jane & sons	Rowa 1770	Hardy	Wayn 1786
John	Rowa 1770	Isaac	Wayn 1786
John	Crav 1779	Jacob	Rowa 1761
John	NorH 1780	Jacob	Rowa 1768
John	Beau 1786	Jacob	Wayn 1786
Joseph	Rowa 1770	Jacob Sr	Wayn 1786
Robert	Bert 1774	James	Rowa 1768
Samuel	Rowa 1770	Jesse	Hert 1779
Thomas	NorH 1780	John	Blad 1784
Wm	Rowa 1770	John	Bert 1774
KOFFLER, Adam	Rowa 1768	Joseph	Rowa 1768
KOONAS, Christian	Jone 1779	Joseph son of	Rowa 1768
KOONCE, Jacob	Jone 1779	Joshua	Rowa 1768
KOONES, Nicholas	Oran 1779	Joshua	Wayn 1786
KOPP, Jacob	Surr 1782	Luke	Camd 1782
KORNES, John	Jone 1779	Manus	Rowa 1768
KOWLE, Maj	Beau 1786	Mercy	Blad 1784
KRAMER, Adam	Rowa 1768	Phineas	Perq 1787
KRAPE, Wm	Mont 1782	Recon	Perq 1787
KREGER, Nicholas	Surr 1782	Reuben	Wayn 1786
KREIGER, Nicholas	Rowa 1768	Robert	Rowa 1768
KRENIZER, Andrew	Surr 1782	Thomas	Rowa 1761
KRETER, Jacob	Rowa 1768	Thomas & son J	Rowa 1768
KROFER, Jacob	Surr 1782	Wm	Mart 1779
KROUSE, Gottleib	Surr 1782	Wm	Blad 1784
John	Surr 1782	Wm	Wayn 1786
Wm	Surr 1782	Zachariah	Perq 1787
KUKER, John	Warr 1784	LAMBERT, Courtney	Blad 1784
KUTLEY, John	Dobb 1780	John	Mart 1779
KYLE, John	Onsl 1771	John	Camd 1782
		Joseph	Pasq 1779
		Richard	Blad 1784
		Sylvanus	Pasq 1779
LACEFIELD, Joseph	Rowa 1770	LAMBIRD, Wm	Pitt 1786
Wm & son	Rowa 1770	LAMBKIN, Charles	Warr 1784

LAMMON, John	Casw 1784	LANE, John	Pasq 1789
LAMON, Archibald	Nash 1782	Levi Capt.	Hali 1783
Duncan	Nash 1782	Newit	Nash 1782
LANCASTER, Aaron	Bute 1766	Samuel	Chow 1785
Aaron	Warr 1779	Thomas	Dobb 1780
Absalom	Nash 1782	Thomas	Bert 1774
Henry	Pasq 1789	Wm	Dobb 1780
James	Warr 1779	Wm	Wayn 1786
Joel	Bute 1766	Wm	Hali 1783
Joel	Warr 1784	Wm	Perq 1772
John	Cart 1779	Wm	Pasq 1789
John	Warr 1784	LANER, Adams	Mart 1779
John	Surr 1782	LANFORD, Jonathan	Wilk 1779
John & son	Bute 1766	LANG, John	Hert 1779
John Jr	Warr 1784	LANGE, Nathan	Beau 1779
John Jr	Surr 1782	LANGFORD, Henry	Surr 1784
Laurence	Warr 1784	James	John 1784
Laurence Jr	Warr 1784	Robert	Surr 1782
Lawrence & son	Bute 1766	LANGLEY, Geo	Beau 1786
Lawrence Jr	Bute 1766	James	John 1784
Lawrence Jr	Warr 1784	John	Nash 1782
Lawrence Sr	Warr 1784	John	Edge 1777
Levy	Wayn 1786	Ozwell	Wayn 1786
Mary	Bert 1774	Thomas	Casw 1786
Mary	Bert 1781	Thomas	Casw 1784
Moses	Bute 1766	LANGSTON, David	Hert 1784
Moses	Warr 1784	Dempsey	Gate 1789
Richard	Cart 1779	Francis	Dobb 1780
Samuel	Bute 1766	Isaac	Gate 1789
Sanders	Wayn 1786	James	Gran 1771
Wm	Nash 1782	Jeconiah	Bute 1766
Wm	Wayn 1786	John	Dobb 1780
Wm Jr?	Wayn 1786	John	Hert 1784
Wright	Wayn 1786	John & son Jec	Bute 1766
LANCE, Mary	NBER 1779	Joseph	Gran 1771
LAND, Bird	Tyrr 1784	Luke	Hert 1779
Michael	Curr 1779	Luke	Hert 1784
Thomas	Wilk 1782	Macy	Wayn 1786
LANDERS, Anna	Wilk 1782	Martha	Hert 1779
Duke	Gran 1771	Martha	Hert 1784
Jacob	Gran 1771	Mary	Wayn 1786
John	Gran 1785	Solomon	Gran 1771
John	Gran 1771	Thomas	Gate 1789
Joseph	Gran 1771	Uriah	Wayn 1786
Luke	Gran 1785	Wm	Hert 1779
Stephen	Wilk 1782	Wm	Hert 1784
LANDING, James	Gate 1789	LANGWORTHY, John G	Crav 1779
John	Gate 1789	LANIER, Adam	Mart 1779
Richard	Beau 1779	Benjamin	Dupl 1779
LANDMON, James	Casw 1786	Benjamin	Bert 1774
LANDON, Amos	Surr 1782	Francis	Gran 1771
Richard	BeaU 1786	Henry	Pasq 1694
LANDRIFF, John	Wilk 1782	James	Dupl 1779
LANE, Abraham	Dupl 1779	Jesse	Mont 1782
Alexander	Dupl 1779	John	Warr 1784
David	Hali 1783	John	Pasq 1694
Isaac	Chow 1785	John	Mart 1779
Isom Jr	Wayn 1786	John	Beau 1786
Isom Sr	Wayn 1786	Lewis	Dupl 1779
James	Cart 1779	Martha	Beau 1786
James	Chow 1785	Martha (widow)	Beau 1786
James	Bert 1774	Robert	Pasq 1694
James	Bert 1781	Robert	Surr 1782
John	Pasq 1779	Robert	Beau 1786
John	Perq 1772	Thomas	Pasq 1694

LANIER, Wm	Pasq 1694		LASWELL, Benjamin	Ruth 1782
Wm	Mart 1779		LATHAM, Chas	Beau 1786
Wm	Beau 1786		Noll	Beau 1786
LANKFORD, George	Warr 1784		Phineas	Beau 1786
John	Warr 1784		LATTA, Benjamin	Ruth 1782
John	Surr 1782		James	Ruth 1782
John Jr	Surr 1782		James	Oran 1779
Judith	Warr 1784		John	Oran 1779
Thomas	Surr 1782		Thomas	Oran 1779
Sam	Surr 1782		LATTERMORE, Sam	Perq 1787
LANNUM, Tabitha	Casw 1786		LATTIMORE, Daniel	Ruth 1782
LANSDALE, Benjamin	Blad 1784		John	Ruth 1782
LANSDELL, John	Blad 1784		LAUD, John	Hali 1783
LANSDOWN, Wm	Wilk 1782		LAUGHINGHOUSE, Andrew	
LANSLEY, Thomas	Oran 1779			Beau 1786
Thomas Sr	Oran 1779		John	Camd 1782
LANTRIP, John	Surr 1782		John	Beau 1786
LAREY, Darby	Bert 1774		Richard	Beau 1786
Jari	Onsl 1771		Robert	Beau 1786
John	Bert 1774		Thomas Sr	Beau 1786
LARKINS, James	Blad 1784		LAUGHLIN, James	Wayn 1786
LARRY, Carolus	Pasq 1694		John	Wayn 1786
LARWELL, Obediah	Hert 1784		Mary	Oran 1779
LASBY, John	Blad 1784		Richard	Oran 1779
LASEWELL, Wm	Ruth 1782		Wm	Oran 1779
LASH, Geo	Surr 1782		Wm	Wayn 1786
Jacob	Rowa 1770		LAUGHTER, Henry	Bute 1766
LASHLEY, Barnabee	Oran 1779		James	Bute 1766
Thomas	Oran 1779		John	Bute 1766
LASSELL, Othneil	Pasq 1789		LAUGHTON, James Jr	Bert 1774
Othniel	Pasq 1789		LAVENDER, Samuel	Jone 1779
LASSITER, Aaron	Gate 1789		Wm	Jone 1779
Abishai	Gate 1789		LAW, Thomas	Hali 1783
Absalom	Gate 1789		LAWHEN, James	Wayn 1786
Amos	Gate 1789		John	Wayn 1786
Arthur	Nash 1782		Wm	Wayn 1786
Fredk	Bert 1781		LAWLEY, Wm	Crav 1779
Geo	Gate 1789		LAWRENCE, Abner	Bert 1781
George	Samp 1784		Abraham	Gran 1785
Hansalom	Nash 1782		Ann	Bert 1774
Jacob	Dobb 1780		Ann	Bert 1781
Jacob	Bert 1774		Arum	Hert 1784
James	Bert 1774		Asa	Bert 1781
James	Gate 1789		Clayburn	Surr 1782
Jason	Hert 1784		David	Rowa 1768
John	Nash 1782		Fredk	Bert 1781
John	Bert 1774		George	Gran 1785
John	Bert 1781		James	Surr 1782
Jonathan	Gate 1789		John	Cart 1779
Joseph	Rich 1790		John	Pasq 1779
Josiah	Gate 1789		John	Bute 1766
Lemuel	Nash 1782		John	Gran 1785
Michael	Gate 1789		John	Hali 1783
Moses	Gate 1789		John	NorH 1780
Nathan	Dobb 1780		John	Bert 1781
Reuben	Gate 1789		John Jr	Bert 1774
Thomas	Bert 1774		John Sr	Bert 1774
Timothy	Gate 1789		Joseph	Bert 1774
Tobias	Nash 1782		Joseph	NorH 1780
Wm	Bute 1766		Laban	Cart 1779
Wm	Hert 1779		Michael	Gate 1789
Wm	Gran 1785		Obediah	Tyrr 1784
Wm	Hert 1784		Peter	Rowa 1768
Zadok	Hert 1779		Reuben	Bert 1781
Zadok	Hert 1784		Richard	NorH 1780

LAWRENCE, Richard	Surr 1782		LEA, John s of Wm	Casw 1784
Robert	Bert 1774		Maier	Casw 1784
Robert	NorH 1780		Owen	Casw 1784
Robert	Bert 1781		Richard	Oran 1779
Thomas	Wilk 1782		Richard	Casw 1784
Thomas	Bert 1781		Thomas	Casw 1784
Williamson	Bert 1781		Wm	Casw 1786
Wm	Albe 1678		Wm	Casw 1784
Wm	Hert 1784		Wm	Bert 1781
Wm	NBer 1779		Wm Capt	Casw 1784
LAWS, Andrew	Dupl 1783		Zachariah	Casw 1784
David	Wilk 1782		LEACE, Jonas	Pasq 1789
George	Oran 1779		LEACH, Eliz	Beau 1786
George Jr	Oran 1779		Stephen	Rowa 1761
Thomas	Mont 1782		Thomas	Gran 1771
Wm	Oran 1779		LEADHAM, Elizabeth	Hert 1779
Wm	Wilk 1782		LEAKE, Bryant	Casw 1786
LAWSON, Francis	Blad 1784		Wm	Casw 1786
James Jr	Dobb 1780		LEALE, George Jr	Rowa 1767
James Sr	Dobb 1780		George Sr	Rowa 1767
John	Dobb 1780		LEAMON, Henry	Oran 1779
John	Casw 1784		Isaac	Oran 1779
John	Mont 1782		Peter	Oran 1779
John	Surr 1782		LEARY, Cornelius	Tyrr 1784
Jonas	Surr 1782		John	Chow 1785
Morrman	Surr 1782		LEASCH, Adam	Rowa 1770
Samuel	Crav 1779		George	Rowa 1770
LAWTHER, Wm	Casw 1784		LEATH, Charles	Beau 1779
LAWTON, Peleg	Perq 1787		Compton	Beau 1779
LAWYER, John	Blad 1784		LEATHER, James	Gran 1771
LAY, Chas	Surr 1782		LEATHERS, Moses	Oran 1779
Jesse	Wilk 1784		Wm	Oran 1779
Jesse	Wilk 1782		Wm	Surr 1782
John	Casw 1786		LEATHWORTH, Joseph	Pitt 1786
John	Brun 1784		LEBETON, Luke	Beau 1786
John	Casw 1784		LECK, Jeremiah	Pasq 1779
John	Brun 1782		Joel	Pasq 1779
Thomas	Wilk 1784		Josiah	Hali 1783
Thomas	Wilk 1782		Wm	Hali 1783
Wm	Oran 1779		LEDBETTER, Chas	Mont 1782
LAYCOCK, Thomas	Oran 1779		Daniel	Casw 1784
Wm Jr	Oran 1779		Drury	Mont 1782
LAYNE, John	NorH 1780		George	Ruth 1782
LAYTON, Francis	Perq 1787		Henry	Casw 1784
Henry	Blad 1784		James	Bute 1766
James	Casw 1784		Joel	Casw 1784
James	Bert 1781		Zedekiah	Mont 1782
John	Blad 1784		LEDFORD, John	Rowa 1768
John	Casw 1784		John & son Joh	Rowa 1768
John	Gran 1771		Wm	Rowa 1768
Joseph	Perq 1787		LEE, Abram	Bert 1781
LEA, Ambrose	Casw 1784		Adam Sr	Curr 1779
Barnett	Casw 1784		Arthur	Curr 1779
Carter	Casw 1784		Benj	Beau 1786
Edmund	Casw 1784		Charles	Nash 1782
Elliott	Casw 1784		Christopher	Mart 1779
GabrieL	Casw 1784		Dory	Jone 1779
George	Casw 1784		Drury	NorH 1780
Isaac	Bert 1781		Francis	Hert 1779
James	Casw 1786		Frederick	Hali 1783
James	Casw 1784		Garrison	Ruth 1782
James	Bert 1781		Henry	Hert 1779
John	Oran 1779		Henry	Mart 1779
John	Casw 1784		Henry	Gate 1789
John Jr	Casw 1784		Henry	Bert 1781

LEE, Isaac	Samp 1784		LEGGETT, Samuel	Mart 1779
Isaiah	Curr 1779		Thomas	Bert 1781
Jacob	Jone 1779		LEGGITT, Louis	Beau 1786
James	Hert 1779		LEGHORN, Joseph	Wilk 1782
James	Mont 1782		LEKEN, Hance	Rowa 1761
Jean	Curr 1779		LEMLEY, George	Rowa 1761
Jesse Jr	Blad 1784		LEMMON, Geo	Gran 1771
John	Hert 1779		LEMMONS, Arthur	Curr 1779
John	Blad 1784		Henry	Curr 1779
John	Chow 1785		LENNEN, Dennis	Blad 1784
John	Hali 1783		Duncan	Blad 1784
John	Beau 1779		John	Blad 1784
John	Curr 1779		LENNON, Thomas	Perq 1772
John	Onsl 1771		LENNOX, Robert	Bert 1779
John	Bert 1781		LENOIR, Robert	Bert 1781
John Henry	Hert 1784		Wm	Wilk 1782
Joseph	Ruth 1782		LEONARD, Benj	Pasq 1789
Joseph	Mart 1779		Benjamin	Oran 1779
Joshua	Blad 1784		Benjamin	Pasq 1779
Josiah	Curr 1779		Davis	Blad 1784
Levi	Gate 1789		James	Pasq 1779
Linton	Curr 1779		James	Pasq 1789
Lucy	Blad 1784		John	Bute 1766
Mary	Tyrr 1784		John	Rowa 1768
Mary	Bert 1774		Joseph	Rowa 1768
Mason	Mart 1779		Samuel	Brun 1784
Morasha	Curr 1779		LESLIE, Mary	Hali 1783
Nathaniel	Curr 1779		LESTER, Abel	Cart 1779
Noah	Samp 1784		Archibald	Surr 1782
Peter Jr	Samp 1784		Bannister	Onsl 1771
Peter Sr	Samp 1784		Wm	Onsl 1771
Robert	Ruth 1782		LETCHWORTH, Elizabeth	
Sampson	Samp 1784			Crav 1779
Samuel	Curr 1779		Joseph	Crav 1779
Shadrack	Blad 1784		LETT, Samuel	Hert 1784
Stephen	Onsl 1771		Thomas	Hert 1784
Steven	Mart 1779		Wm	Oran 1779
Thomas	Jone 1779		LEUTEN, Absalom	Chow 1785
Thomas	Curr 1779		Sarah	Chow 1785
Timothy	Beau 1786		LEVEL, Edward	Gran 1785
Westbrook	Samp 1784		LEVERETT, Richard	Mont 1782
Wm	Oran 1779		LEVERTON, John	Beau 1779
Wm	Samp 1784		LEVIN, Frederick	Wayn 1786
Wm	Curr 1779		Wm	Bert 1774
Wm Jr	Samp 1784		LEVINE, John	Rich 1790
Wm Sr	Samp 1784		LEVING, Riddick	Wayn 1786
LEECH, Edward	Curr 1779		LEVISTON, Wm Jr	Rowa 1770
Joseph	NBer 1779		Wm Sr	Rowa 1770
Wm	Wilk 1782		LEVY, Alexander	Hert 1779
LEEK, Isaac	Pasq 1789		LEWEIS, Nathaniel Col.	
Thomas	Pasq 1789			Oran 1779
LEEPER, James	Rowa 1770		LEWELLIN, John	Ruth 1782
LEFFERS, Samuel	Cart 1779		John	Mart 1779
LEGETT, Louis	Bert 1781		Wm	Rowa 1768
LEGGETT, Benjamin	Mart 1779		Wm	Mart 1779
Daniel	Tyrr 1784		LEWIS, Abel	Ruth 1782
David	Mart 1779		Arch	Beau 1786
Debra	Bert 1774		Benjamin	Wilk 1784
Ezekiah	Mart 1779		Berry	Gran 1785
James	Bert 1781		Charles	Ruth 1782
James Jr	Mart 1779		David	Wilk 1782
James Sr	Mart 1779		David	Gate 1789
John	Mart 1779		Eden	Hert 1779
John	Bert 1781		Eden	Hert 1784
Luke	Tyrr 1784		Edmund	Casw 1784

LEWIS, Elisha	NorH 1780	Thomas Sr	Cart 1779
Elizabeth	Crav 1779	Valentine	Gran 1785
Elkanah	Surr 1782	Wm	Cart 1779
Enoch	Oran 1779	Wm	Hert 1779
Fielding	Casw 1784	Wm	Dobb 1780
George	Wilk 1784	Wm	Rowa 1770
George	Wilk 1782	Wm	Samp 1784
Gideon	Wilk 1782	Wm	Cart 1779
Griffin	NorH 1780	Wm	Wayn 1786
Henry	NorH 1780	Wm	Gran 1785
Howell	Gran 1771	Wm	Wilk 1784
Howell Jr	Gran 1785	Wm	Crav 1779
Howell Sr	Gran 1785	Wm	Wilk 1782
Isaac	Hert 1779	Wm	Onsl 1771
Isaac	Hert 1784	Wm	Surr 1782
Jacob	Dobb 1780	Wm	Gate 1789
James	Dobb 1780	Wm Sr	Wilk 1784
James	Blad 1784	Wm Sr	Wilk 1782
James	Gran 1785	Wm Terrell	Wilk 1782
James	Wilk 1782	Zachariah	Hali 1783
James	NorH 1780	LEWISTON, Geo	Gran 1771
Jeremiah	Gran 1771	John	Wilk 1782
Jesse	Tyrr 1784	LEYN, Wm	Surr 1782
Jesse	NBer 1779	LEZETIN, Dutton	Wilk 1782
John	Ruth 1782	LIGGETT, James	Beau 1786
John	Rowa 1761	LIGHTFOOT, John	Mont 1782
John	Rowa 1770	LILES, Burgess	Ruth 1782
John	Oran 1779	Charles	Bute 1766
John	Mart 1779	David	Ruth 1782
John	Casw 1784	LILLY, Benjamin	Mont 1782
John	Hali 1783	Edward	Mont 1782
John	Beau 1779	Isaac	Perq 1772
John	Onsl 1771	Jeremiah	Perq 1772
John	Beau 1786	Job	Perq 1787
Jonathan	Beau 1786	John	Mont 1782
Joseph	Surr 1782	Joseph Jr	Mart 1779
Josiah Jr	Blad 1784	Joseph Sr	Mart 1779
Josiah Sr	Blad 1784	Joshua	Perq 1772
Littlebury	Wilk 1784	Reuben	Mart 1779
Luke	Hert 1779	Reuben	Perq 1787
Luke	Hert 1784	Timothy	Mart 1779
Luten	Gate 1789	Wm	Perq 1772
Margaret Jr	Hali 1783	Wm Jr	Perq 1787
Margaret Sr	Hali 1783	Wm Sr	Perq 1787
Martha	NorH 1780	Zachariah	Mart 1779
Mary	Cart 1779	LILLYBRIDGE, Joseph	Onsl 1771
Miles	Gate 1789	LIND, Thomas	Beau 1786
Nathaniel	Crav 1779	LINDER, Lewis	Dobb 1780
Nicholas	Hali 1783	LINDLEY, Simon	Oran 1779
Phillip	Gran 1785	Wm	Oran 1779
Phillip	Gran 1771	LINDSAY, Dinah	Camd 1782
Phillip	Gate 1789	Elisha	Gran 1785
Richard	Rowa 1761	John	Hali 1783
Richard	Hali 1783	John	NBer 1779
Robert	Oran 1779	Mathew	Oran 1779
Robert	Casw 1784	Walter	Rowa 1770
Robert	Gran 1785	Wm	NBer 1779
Robert	Gran 1771	LINDSEY, Benjamin	Curr 1779
Solomon	Blad 1784	David	Curr 1779
Stephen	Dobb 1780	James	Surr 1782
Thomas	Nash 1782	Jeremiah	Wilk 1782
Thomas	Cart 1779	John	Curr 1779
Thomas	Oran 1779	Thomas	Curr 1779
Thomas	Cart 1779	LINES, Mary	Crav 1779
Thomas Jr	Cart 1779	LINGLE, Lawrence	Rowa 1761

LINLEY, Jonathan	Oran 1779	LITTLETON, Edmund	Jone 1779
Thomas	Oran 1779	Jarman	Cart 1779
LINNVILLE, Aaron	Rowa 1768	John	Jone 1779
David	Rowa 1768	Thomas	Cart 1779
Humphrey	Rowa 1768	LITTON, Isaac	Camd 1782
John	Rowa 1761	LIVELY, Gillim	Ruth 1782
Richard	Rowa 1768	Wm	Ruth 1782
Wm	Rowa 1761	LIVERMAN, Herman	Hert 1784
Wm	Rowa 1768	John	Oran 1779
Wm & son Humph	Rowa 1768	John	Tyrr 1784
LINSEY, Diana	Nash 1782	John Jr	Tyrr 1784
Joseph	Gran 1771	John s of Wm	Tyrr 1784
Leonard	Gran 1771	Luke	Hert 1779
Sarah	Beau 1779	Thomas	Tyrr 1784
Wm	Nash 1782	Wm	Hert 1779
LINTON, David	Beau 1779	Wm	Tyrr 1784
Hezekiah	Camd 1782	LIVERSAGE, Mary	Chow 1785
Lazarus	Perq 1787	Sarah	Beau 1786
Lemuel	Curr 1779	LIVINGSTON, John	Wayn 1786
Tabitha widow	Dobb 1780	LLOYD, Amos	Onsl 1771
LINVILL, Moses	Surr 1782	David	Blad 1784
LINVILLE, Thomas	Wilk 1782	Ebenezer	Gran 1785
LION, John	Surr 1782	Edward	Gran 1785
Wm	Wilk 1782	Edward	Gran 1771
LIPPS, Elizabeth	Curr 1779	Frederick	Oran 1779
LIPSCOMB, Andrew	Rich 1790	Isaac	Gran 1785
Willis	Bert 1781	Isaac	Gran 1771
LISTER, Benjamin	Brun 1782	Israel	Gran 1785
Daniel	Pasq 1789	John	Rowa 1768
Elisha	Pasq 1779	John	Oran 1779
Elisha	Pasq 1789	Joseph	Onsl 1771
Jacob	Pasq 1789	Mary	Blad 1784
Lylie	Casw 1784	Nicholas	Gran 1785
LITCHFIELD, Abraham	Curr 1779	Richard	Blad 1784
Jacob	Curr 1779	Stephen	Oran 1779
Peter	Curr 1779	Thomas	Gran 1785
LITTESON, Isaac	Perq 1787	Thomas	Onsl 1771
Joseph	Perq 1787	Thomas	Surr 1782
Thomas	Perq 1787	Thomas Jr	Oran 1779
LITTLE, Abraham	Rowa 1761	Thomas Sr	Oran 1779
Abraham	Jone 1779	Wm	Hert 1779
Alexander	Blad 1784	Wm	Gran 1785
Archibald	Blad 1784	Wm	Onsl 1771
Catherine	Blad 1784	LOCK, Benjamin	Blad 1784
Chas	Wilk 1782	David Jr	Blad 1784
Daniel	Rowa 1761	David Sr	Blad 1784
Duncan	Blad 1784	Elizabeth	Blad 1784
Frank	Wilk 1782	Francis	Rowa 1768
George	Hert 1779	Gibson	Rowa 1768
George	Hert 1784	James	Rowa 1770
Henry	Rowa 1768	James	Hali 1783
Jacob	Beau 1786	John	Brun 1784
James	Mart 1779	John	Gran 1785
John	Blad 1784	John	Bert 1781
Josiah	Beau 1786	John Jr	Hali 1783
Micajah	Mart 1779	John Sr	Hali 1783
Moses	Mart 1779	Jonathan	Hali 1783
Thomas	Rowa 1768	Joseph	Blad 1784
Thomas	Samp 1784	Josiah	Hali 1783
Thomas	Blad 1784	Leonard	Blad 1784
Thomas	Beau 1786	Mathew & son	Rowa 1768
Wm	Curr 1779	Thomas	Blad 1784
LITTLEDALE, Mary	Chow 1785	LOCKABEY, Thomas	Surr 1782
LITTLEJOHN, Thomas	Rowa 1761	LOCKALIER, Jacob	Blad 1784
Wm	Chow 1785	John	Blad 1784

LOCKALIER, Joseph	Blad 1784	LONG, Geo	Surr 1782
Robert	Blad 1784	George	Rowa 1770
Wm	Blad 1784	George	Oran 1779
LOCKALIN, Daniel	Blad 1784	George	Gran 1785
LOCKE, Eliz	Gran 1771	Giles	Hali 1783
Wm	Gran 1771	Giles	Tyrr 1784
LOCKER, Elijah	Blad 1784	Henry	Nash 1782
Henry	Pitt 1786	Henry	Hali 1783
Hue	Cart 1779	Henry	Beau 1786
LOCKERMAN, Jacob	Samp 1784	Isaac	Tyrr 1784
Jacob Jr	Samp 1784	James	Albe 1679
James	Samp 1784	James	Oran 1779
LOCKHART, Eliz	Bert 1781	James	Casw 1784
Elizabeth	Bert 1774	James	Tyrr 1784
Geo	Bert 1781	James	Gate 1789
George	Bert 1774	James	Rich 1790
Sam	NorH 1780	James Capt	Tyrr 1784
Thomas	Oran 1779	James Jr	Tyrr 1784
LOCKINGBURG, Jacob	Rowa 1761	James Sr	Tyrr 1784
LOCUS, Francis	Nash 1782	John	Warr 1784
James	Nash 1782	John	Hali 1783
LODONTOUN, Thomas	Rowa 1768	John	Hert 1784
LOEBICK, Robert	Hali 1783	John	NorH 1780
LOFNUCHER, Shadrack	NorH 1780	John	Gate 1789
LOFTEN, Thomas	NBer 1779	John	Rich 1790
Wm Col	Mont 1782	John Jr	Tyrr 1784
LOFTIN, Elkanah	Dobb 1780	John Sr	Tyrr 1784
Ezekiel	Dobb 1780	John son of Wm	Tyrr 1784
Francis	Dobb 1780	Jonathan	Bert 1774
Frederick	Dobb 1780	Joshua	Perq 1787
Jeremiah	Dobb 1780	Lemuel	Perq 1787
Leonard	Albe 1694	Littleton	Hali 1783
Leonard	Dobb 1780	Nathan	Beau 1786
Samuel	Dobb 1780	Nathl	Perq 1787
LOFTLY, Daniel	Wayn 1786	Nehemiah	Hert 1784
LOFTON, Joseph	Crav 1779	Nehemiah	NorH 1780
LOGAN, Francis	Ruth 1782	Reuben	Perq 1787
John	Ruth 1782	Richard	Hali 1783
John	Surr 1782	Robert	Casw 1784
Nathan	Casw 1784	Samuel	Wilk 1782
Patrick	Surr 1782	Sarah	Bert 1781
Private	Rowa 1770	Stephen	Tyrr 1784
Wm	Ruth 1782	Thomas	Albe 1679
Wm	Oran 1779	Thomas	Oran 1778
LOLLIRON, Charles	Beau 1779	Thomas	Perq 1772
LONDON, Edward	Albe 1694	Thomas	Surr 1782
Wm	Surr 1782	Thomas	Perq 1787
LONG, Alexander	Hali 1783	Wm	Ruth 1782
Ambrose	Casw 1784	Wm	Oran 1779
Andrew	Tyrr 1784	Wm	Hert 1784
Anthony	Perq 1772	Wm	Perq 1787
Aquilla	Mart 1779	Zachariah	Gran 1785
Arthur	Hali 1783	LONGHREE, Charles	Chow 1785
Barre Sr	NorH 1780	LONGINO, John	Surr 1782
Basham	NorH 1780	Thomas	Surr 1782
Benj	Rich 1790	LONGINS, Wm	Gran 1785
Benjamin Jr	Casw 1784	LONGIST, Caleb	Cart 1779
Benjamin Sr	Casw 1784	LOOKEBY, John	Rowa 1761
Christian	Oran 1779	LOOMIS, Jonathan	Beau 1786
Conrad	Oran 1779	LOP, Jacob	Rowa 1761
Darby	Bert 1781	LOPWATTER, Joseph	Rowa 1761
Davis	Hali 1783	LORD, Lord	Casw 1784
Frederick	Rowa 1770	Peter	Blad 1784
Frederick	Surr 1782	Wm	Brun 1784
Gabriel	Warr 1784	LOTT, Mark	Rowa 1770

LOUIS, Arthur	Nash 1782	LOWE, George	Pasq 1779
LOVE, Alexander	Blad 1784	Hannah	Pasq 1789
Daniel	Blad 1784	Isaac	Rowa 1770
David	Rich 1790	Isaac	Wilk 1782
Doc	Hali 1783	John	Pasq 1789
James	Casw 1784	Mary	Wilk 1782
James	Wilk 1782	Mary	Pasq 1789
Jane	Casw 1786	Samuel	Rowa 1768
John	Rowa 1768	Stephen	Bute 1766
John	NorH 1780	Thomas	Rowa 1768
John	Surr 1782	Thomas	Wilk 1782
Jonathan	Casw 1784	Thomas	Pasq 1789
Murdock	Samp 1784	Wm	Hali 1783
Rachel	Casw 1784	Wm	NorH 1780
Samuel	Oran 1779	LOWELL, Ann	Bert 1781
Samuel Jr	Casw 1784	Chas	Bert 1781
Samuel Sr	Casw 1784	Dempsey	Hert 1784
Thomas	Oran 1779	Francis	Gran 1771
Thomas	Camd 1782	James	Perq 1787
Thomas	Pasq 1789	Obadiah	Hert 1784
Wm	Oran 1779	Richard	Hert 1784
Wm	Camd 1782	Sarah	Bert 1781
Wm	NorH 1780	Stephen	Bert 1781
Wm	Surr 1782	Thomas	Bert 1781
Wm	Rich 1790	Wm	Rowa 1761
LOVELACE, John	Wilk 1782	LOWL, Edward	Perq 1772
LOVELATTY, Samuel	Rowa 1761	LOWRY, Andrew	Surr 1782
LOVELL, Edward	Surr 1782	Benj	Pasq 1789
Francis	Bert 1781	Benjamin	Pasq 1779
John	Wilk 1782	Cornelius	Dobb 1780
Wm	Hali 1783	Jacob	Surr 1782
Wm	Wilk 1782	James	Oran 1779
Wm	Surr 1782	James	Blad 1784
LOVEN, Thomas	Surr 1782	James	Surr 1782
Wm	NorH 1780	John	Albe 1679
LOVETT, Arthur	Casw 1784	John	Dobb 1780
David	Dobb 1780	John	Surr 1782
Edward	Dobb 1780	John	Pasq 1789
John	Dobb 1780	Mary	Pasq 1789
John	Cart 1779	Noah	Pasq 1779
John	Pasq 1779	Noah	Pasq 1789
John Sr	Cart 1779	Patrick	Ruth 1782
Morris	Dobb 1780	Peter	Pasq 1789
Richard	Crav 1779	Robert	Pasq 1779
LOVICK, Ann	Crav 1779	Robert	Pasq 1789
Thomas	Crav 1779	LOY, George	Oran 1779
LOVING, Arthur	Casw 1786	Henry	Oran 1779
Gabriel	Wilk 1782	John	Oran 1779
Gabriel	Wilk 1782	LOYD, Margaret	Hert 1784
Wm	Wilk 1784	LOwe, Frederick	Rowa 1768
Wm	Wilk 1782	LRVERETT, Robert	Mont 1782
LOW, Aaron	Surr 1782	LUCAS, Charles	Blad 1784
Daniel	Surr 1782	Francis	Blad 1784
John	NorH 1780	George	Rowa 1768
John	NorH 1780	George	Blad 1784
John	Surr 1782	George & son	Rowa 1768
Mary	NorH 1780	Henry	Beau 1779
Thomas	NorH 1780	Jesse	Beau 1786
Wm	NorH 1780	John	Samp 1784
LOWE, Aaron	Pasq 1779	Lewis	Samp 1784
Aaron	Pasq 1789	Martha	NorH 1780
Anna	Pasq 1779	Samuel	Beau 1779
Barnaby	Pasq 1789	Wm	Blad 1784
Caleb	Wilk 1782	LUCTON, Constant	Pasq 1779
Christian	Rowa 1768	LUCY, Burwell	NorH 1780

LUCY, Isham	Warr 1784		LYNN, Wm	Rowa 1761
Isham	Bute 1766		LYON, Henry	Gran 1785
Isham	Warr 1784		Jacob	Wilk 1784
Isom	Bute 1766		James	Oran 1779
LUDELL, Benoni	Pasq 1694		John	Rowa 1768
LUDLAM, Jeremiah	Brun 1784		John	Rich 1790
LUDWICK, Peter	Rowa 1770		Mary	Blad 1784
LUDWIG, Peter	Surr 1782		Mathew	Oran 1779
LUFFMAN, Lazarus	Pasq 1789		Peter	Casw 1784
LUKE, James	Casw 1784		Robert	Casw 1786
Jeremiah	Pasq 1779		Robert	Casw 1784
Wm Jr	Casw 1784		Thomas	Chow 1785
Wm Sr	Casw 1784		Thomas	Wilk 1784
LUKENSON, Daniel	Wilk 1782		Wm	Casw 1786
LUMBERSHON, John	Pasq 1694		LYONS, Wm	Pitt 1786
LUNESFORD, James	Oran 1779			
LUNN, James	Ruth 1782			
LUNS, Nicholas	Curr 1779			
LUNSFORD, Benj	Gran 1771		MABLEY, Robert	Hali 1783
Elisha	Wilk 1784		MABRAY, Benjamin	Rowa 1768
James	Gran 1771		Francis & son	Bute 1766
John	Wilk 1784		George & son	Rowa 1768
John	Gran 1771		Isaac	Rowa 1768
John	Perq 1787		James	Rowa 1768
Joseph	Warr 1784		Jesse	Bute 1766
Wm	Gran 1771		Joseph	Rowa 1768
LUPTON, Christopher	Cart 1779		MABREY, John	Gran 1785
LURAY, Daniel	Brun 1784		Wm	Pasq 1694
LURRY, Evan	Camd 1782		MABRY, Burwell	NorH 1780
Mary	Curr 1779		Dilk	Warr 1784
Simon	Pasq 1789		Francis	NorH 1780
Wm	Bert 1781		James	NorH 1780
LURY, Thomas	Camd 1782		Joshua	Warr 1784
LUSK, Sarah	Ruth 1782		Matthew	Warr 1784
LUSSMAN, Wm	Pasq 1789		Moseland	Warr 1784
LUTE, Joss	NorH 1780		Nathl	NorH 1780
LUTEN, Henderson	Chow 1785		Randall	NorH 1780
Henry	NorH 1780		Repps	Warr 1784
Thomas	Hert 1779		Wm	NorH 1780
LUTHER, Ingrum	Pasq 1789		MACE, John	Cart 1779
LUTTON, Frasncis	Perq 1787		MACIELLE, John	Bute 1766
Fredk	Perq 1787		MACK, Wm	Mont 1782
LYCAN, Goodin	Wilk 1782		MACKADNIE, John	Rowa 1761
Hance	Wilk 1782		MACKELROY, John Jr	Crav 1779
LYDEN, Wm	Perq 1772		Wm	Beau 1786
LYLE, James	Mont 1782		MACKEY, Alexander	Ruth 1782
Wm	Gran 1785		Ann	Beau 1786
LYLES, Jeremiah	Bert 1774		Caleb	Pasq 1779
John	Warr 1784		Joseph	Perq 1787
LYMAN, James	Blad 1784		Thomas	Tyrr 1784
LYMBECK, Abraham	Surr 1782		Wm	Tyrr 1784
Benj	Surr 1782		MACKLEMORE, James	Gran 1771
Joseph	Surr 1782		MACON, Elizabeth	NBer 1779
Lodowick	Surr 1782		MADDIN, John	Oran 1779
LYNCH, Cornelius	Wayn 1786		Stephen	Oran 1779
Cornelius	John 1784		MADES, James	Cart 1779
Holly	John 1784		MADISON, Abraham	Casw 1784
James	John 1784		Peyton	Oran 1779
John	Surr 1782		Peyton	Gran 1771
Joshua	Wayn 1786		Reuben	Pasq 1779
Phillip	Mont 1782		MADREN, John	Pasq 1779
Thomas	Oran 1779		John	Pasq 1789
LYNN, Aaron	Pasq 1779		Joseph	Pasq 1779
Francis	Perq 1772		Mathias	Pasq 1789
John	Oran 1779		Reuben	Pasq 1779

MADREN, Reuben	Pasq 1789	MALLETT, Thomas	Warr 1784
Thomas	Pasq 1789	MALLORY, Francis	Hali 1783
Wm	Pasq 1779	John	Casw 1786
MADRY, Alexander	Pasq 1789	John Jr	Casw 1784
John	Bute 1766	Wm	Gran 1785
Richard	Bute 1766	MALONE, Daniel	Casw 1784
Thomas	Pasq 1779	Daniel	Gran 1771
Wm	Pasq 1789	David	Bute 1766
MAGEE, Benj	Gran 1771	Edward	Warr 1779
Chas	Gran 1771	Elizabeth	Warr 1784
John	Gran 1771	Frederick	Warr 1784
Nathan	Gran 1771	George	Gran 1785
MAGET, Wm	Curr 1779	Isham	Gran 1771
MAGETT, John	Hert 1779	John	Bute 1766
Nicholas	Hert 1779	Nathaniel	Casw 1784
Samuel	Hert 1779	Robert	Ruth 1782
MAGGETT, John	Hert 1784	Robert	Gran 1785
Nick	Hert 1784	Simon	Bute 1766
MAGNESS, Benjamin	Ruth 1782	Simon	Gran 1785
Peregrin	Ruth 1782	Simon	Warr 1784
MAGNUS, John	Hali 1783	Simon	Gran 1771
MAHAFFY, James	Oran 1779	Wm	Casw 1784
Thomas	Oran 1779	MALONEY, John	Casw 1784
MAHAN, Wm	Casw 1786	John	Beau 1786
MAHOLLAND, John	NorH 1780	Wm	Casw 1784
MAHON, Wm	Wayn 1786	MANCEY, James	Hert 1784
MAHONEY, John	Hali 1783	MANCY, Edward	Onsl 1771
John	Curr 1779	MANDEN, Henry	Jone 1779
Wm Jr	Hali 1783	MANDLEY, Abel	Hert 1784
Wm Sr	Hali 1783	Gilbert	Hert 1784
MAHOON, Ezekiel	Mart 1779	James	Wayn 1786
Hezekiah	Bert 1774	Littleton	Hert 1784
MAIL, Reuben	Hert 1784	Major M.	Hert 1784
MAIN, Arnold	Gran 1785	Mons	Hert 1784
John	Gran 1785	MANER, Henry	Onsl 1771
Wm	Crav 1779	Jacob	Onsl 1771
MAINARD, Gipson	Wilk 1782	Jethro	Onsl 1771
Jacob	Wilk 1782	John	Onsl 1771
Wm	Bute 1766	MANGHAM, Howell	Gran 1785
Wm	Wilk 1782	Joseph	Gran 1785
MAINER, Benjamin	Samp 1784	MANGRUM, Jacob	Rich 1790
John	Mart 1779	MANGUM, Arthur	Oran 1779
John	Beau 1786	Christopher	Hert 1779
Josiah	Samp 1784	Joseph	Bute 1766
Stephen	Samp 1784	Joseph	Gran 1771
Wm	Bert 1781	Solomon	Oran 1779
MAINES, John	Blad 1784	Wm	Bute 1766
Samuel	Camd 1782	Wm	Oran 1779
MAINS, Absalom	Bert 1781	MANIE, Richard	Gran 1785
Robert	Oran 1779	MANIER, John	Gran 1785
Samuel	Oran 1779	MANKIN, Richard	Crav 1779
Wm	Oran 1779	MANLEY, Absalom	Surr 1782
MAITLAND, Joseph	Bute 1766	Bassell	Blad 1784
Wm	Bute 1766	Littlejohn	Hert 1779
MAJORS, John	Surr 1782	MANN, Benjamin	Tyrr 1784
John Sr	Surr 1782	Elizabeth	Cart 1779
Robert	Surr 1782	Elizabeth	Casw 1784
MALCOMB, Alexander	Oran 1779	John	Casw 1784
MALDEN, Micajah	NorH 1780	John	Beau 1779
MALKINS, Wm	Pasq 1789	John	Curr 1779
MALLARD, Don	Jone 1779	Joseph	Pasq 1779
George	Dupl 1783	Richard	NorH 1780
John	Dupl 1783	Thomas	Nash 1782
John	Jone 1779	Thomas	Tyrr 1784
Joseph	Dupl 1783	Thomas	NorH 1780

MANN, Thomas	Pasq	1789
Thomas Sr	Tyrr	1784
MANNING, Benj	Bert	1781
Benjamin	Bert	1774
Francis	Gran	1771
John	Nash	1782
John	Mart	1779
Jordan	Surr	1782
Joshua	Hali	1783
Marcum	Mart	1779
Mathias	Nash	1782
Moses	Dobb	1780
Richard	Nash	1782
Sala	Nash	1782
Sam	Pitt	1786
Samuel	Gran	1785
Willoughby	Nash	1782
Wm	Nash	1782
MANOR, George	Pasq	1779
MANSFIELD, Thomas	Hert	1779
Thomas	Hert	1784
Wm	Blád	1784
Zebulon	Chow	1785
MANSWELL, Philemon	Surr	1782
MANTIN, Tucker	Jone	1779
MANUEL, Levi	Samp	1784
Lucretia	Samp	1784
MAPP, Littleton	Gran	1771
MAPRAY, Joseph	Wilk	1782
MARBURY, Thomas	Bute	1766
MARCH, Bernard	Gate	1789
Rudolph	Rowa	1761
Thomas	Bute	1766
Wm	Gate	1789
MARCHANT, Cader	Curr	1779
John	Curr	1779
MARCOM, John	Oran	1779
Samuel	Oran	1779
Thomas	Oran	1779
Wm	Oran	1779
MARDENEN, Richard	Pasq	1694
MARDIKE, John	Oran	1779
MARDRA, Darling	Warr	1784
Wm	Warr	1784
MARDRY, Richard	Bute	1766
MARGOT, Lettice	Beau	1786
MARIE, John	Chow	1785
MARIS, George	Oran	1779
MARKHAM, Anthony	Pasq	1779
Anthony	Pasq	1789
Charles	Pasq	1779
Chas	Pasq	1789
Joshua	Pasq	1779
Joshua	Pasq	1789
Lowry	Pasq	1789
Matthew	Surr	1782
Richard	Pasq	1779
Robert	Surr	1782
Thomas	Pasq	1779
Thomas	Pasq	1789
MARKLAND, Charles	Dobb	1780
MARKLE, Christr	Surr	1782
MARKS, Fennil	Gran	1771
MARLEY, Adam Jr	Oran	1779
Adam Sr	Oran	1779

MARLOW, John	Hali	1783
MARMADUKE, Elijah	Curr	1779
MAROON, John	Ruth	1782
Peter	Ruth	1782
MARQUIS, Ellis	Bute	1766
MARRELL, John	Onsl	1771
MARRINER, Maxim	Tyrr	1784
Tabitha	Tyrr	1784
MARROW, Bartholomew	Surr	1782
Kozer	Onsl	1771
MARSEY, James	Wilk	1782
MARSH, George	Hert	1784
James	Blad	1784
James	Bert	1774
James	Bert	1781
Rebecca	Hert	1779
MARSHALL, Charles	Warr	1784
Charles	Crav	1779
David	Hali	1783
David	NBer	1779
Fredk Wm	Surr	1782
George	Dobb	1780
Isaac	NorH	1780
Jacob	Oran	1779
Jamers Jr	Warr	1784
Jean	NorH	1780
John	Cart	1779
John	Brun	1784
John	Hali	1783
Jonas	Wilk	1782
Joseph	Onsl	1771
Richard	Warr	1784
Samuel	Warr	1784
Stedia	Warr	1784
Stephen	Warr	1784
Tabitha	Warr	1784
Tabitha	Warr	1784
Thomas	Bute	1766
Thomas	Hali	1783
Thomas	Gate	1789
Wm	Hali	1783
Wm	Surr	1782
MARSHAWN, James	Wilk	1782
MARSHBURN, Edward	Onsl	1771
Jethro	Hert	1784
Matthew	Hert	1784
MARTIN, Aaron	Wayn	1786
Abraham	Oran	1779
Abraham	Surr	1782
Alex	Rich	1790
Andrew	Bute	1766
Andrew	Blad	1784
Andrew	Surr	1782
Anthorite	Casw	1786
Benj	Wilk	1782
Benj	Surr	1782
Daniel	Rich	1790
Francis	Mart	1779
Francis	Wayn	1786
Gabriel	Gate	1789
George	Bute	1766
George	Casw	1786
George	Casw	1784
Gibson& son Wm	Bute	1766
Henry	Oran	1779

MARTIN, Henry	Wilk 1784	MASON, Benjamin	Crav 1779
Higglety	Dobb 1780	David	Gran 1785
Isaac	Wilk 1782	Elijah	Casw 1786
James	Casw 1786	Elijah	Surr 1782
James	Hali 1783	Elizabeth	Hali 1783
James	Surr 1782	Gideon	Warr 1784
Jesse	Gate 1789	Henry	Nash 1782
Jiles	Wilk 1782	Henry	Oran 1779
Job	Surr 1782	Henry	Pasq 1779
John	Bute 1766	Hunt	Warr 1784
John	Wilk 1784	Jacob	Oran 1779
John	Bert 1774	John	Warr 1784
John	Crav 1779	John	Pasq 1694
John	Crav 1779	John	Ruth 1782
John	Mont 1782	John	Crav 1779
John	Wilk 1782	John	Curr 1779
John	Surr 1782	Joseph	Onsl 1771
John	Bert 1781	Joshua	Cart 1779
John	Rich 1790	Mark Jr	Nash 1782
Joseph	Bute 1766	Mark Sr	Nash 1782
Joseph	Casw 1786	Mathew	Dobb 1780
Joseph	Wayn 1786	Matthew	Samp 1784
Lydia	Bert 1781	Nathaniel	Warr 1784
Mary	Surr 1782	Ralph	Nash 1782
Michael	Bert 1781	Samuel	Warr 1784
Moses	Surr 1782	Thomas	Oran 1779
Neil	Rich 1790	Thomas	Casw 1784
Obediah	Oran 1779	Thomas	Hali 1783
Patrick	Hali 1783	Turner	Hali 1783
Paul	Wayn 1786	MASSEY, Abijah	Oran 1779
Peter	Onsl 1771	Abraham	Oran 1779
Richard	Casw 1784	Adkins	Tyrr 1784
Robert	Casw 1786	Elizabeth	John 1784
Salathiel	Surr 1782	Ezekiel	NorH 1780
Sarah	Wilk 1784	John	Gran 1785
Sarah	Wilk 1782	MASSIE, John & sons	Wm
Thomas	Mart 1779		Bute 1766
Thomas	Bert 1774	John Jr	Bute 1766
Thomas	Bert 1781	P. Raymond	Nash 1782
Thomas Wm	Beau 1779	MASSINGALE, Abraham	NorH 1780
Valentine	Surr 1782	George	Nash 1782
Wm	Bute 1766	James Jr	Nash 1782
Wm	Dobb 1780	Mark	Nash 1782
Wm	Wayn 1786	Matthew	Nash 1782
Wm	Chow 1785	Walter	Nash 1782
Wm	Hali 1783	MAST, Abraham	Bert 1774
Wm	Perq 1779	MASTER, Joseph	Crav 1779
Wm	Beau 1779	MASTERS, Enoch	Crav 1779
Wm	Surr 1782	Thomas	Crav 1779
Wm	Beau 1786	Wm	Surr 1782
Wm (Guilford)	Surr 1782	MATHENEY, Francis	Mont 1782
Zachariah	Surr 1782	MATHENY, Robert	Wilk 1782
Zachariah	Pasq 1789	Thomas	Wilk 1782
MASH, Dudley	Rich 1790	Wm	Mont 1782
George	Hert 1779	MATHER, Thomas	Crav 1779
Pleasant	Rich 1790	MATHERS, Humphrey	Jone 1779
Wm	Rich 1790	MATHIAS, Isaiah	Perq 1772
MASHBERN, Benj	Onsl 1771	JOhn	Camd 1782
Daniel	Onsl 1771	Joseph	Perq 1772
MASHBURN, Daniel	Hert 1779	Joseph	Perq 1787
James	Oran 1779	Thomas	Chow 1785
Jethro	Hert 1779	Wm	Gate 1789
Matthew	Hert 1779	MATHIS, Alexander Jr	
MASHMONT, Wm	Onsl 1771		Dobb 1780
MASINGALE, Joseph	Blad 1784	Alexander Sr	Dobb 1780

MATHIS, Anthony	Dobb 1780		MAULTSBY, James	Blad 1784
David	Hali 1783		John	Blad 1784
Edmund	Hert 1779		Samuel	Brun 1784
Isaac	Hali 1783		MAXEDON, John	Oran 1779
James	Hali 1783		MAXFIELD, Francis	Dobb 1780
James	Surr 1782		MAXIM, Edward	Beau 1779
James & son J	Rowa 1761		George	Beau 1779
James Jr	Rowa 1761		MAXWELL, James	Beau 1786
Jeremiah	Hali 1783		MAY, Daniel	Oran 1779
John	Samp 1784		John	Warr 1784
Luke	Mart 1779		John	Jone 1779
Mary	Samp 1784		John Jr	Oran 1779
Mary	Hali 1783		John Sr	Oran 1779
Oliver	Rowa 1768		Joseph	Curr 1779
Richard	Hali 1783		Samuel	Oran 1779
Samuel	Hali 1783		Thomas	Oran 1779
Sarah	Hali 1783		Wm	Mart 1779
Stephen	Hali 1783		MAYBERRY, Francis	Mont 1782
Susannah	Hali 1783		MAYBURY, Duke	Hali 1783
Thomas	Hali 1783		MAYFIELD, Abraham	Warr 1784
Wm	Dobb 1780		Abraham	Bute 1766
MATTHEW, James	Surr 1782		Abraham & son	Bute 1766
MATTHEWS, Anthony	Gate 1789		Isaac	Gran 1771
Benjamin	Nash 1782		John	Warr 1784
Bond	Gate 1789		Robert	Bute 1766
Chas	Rich 1790		Stephen	Bute 1766
Daniel	Blad 1784		Thomas	Warr 1784
Daniel	Mont 1782		Thomas	Wilk 1782
Farmer	Hert 1779		Valentine	Gran 1785
George	Tyrr 1784		MAYFIRLD, Abraham	Gran 1785
Giles	Hert 1779		MAYHOE, Duke	Camd 1782
Giles	Hert 1784		Thomas	Camd 1782
James	Oran 1779		MAYLE, Thomas	Crav 1779
James	Gate 1789		MAYNOR, Sarah	Hert 1779
Joel	Nash 1782		Wm	Hert 1779
John	Gran 1785		MAYO, Chas	Surr 1782
John	Hali 1783		Edward	Pasq 1694
John	Onsl 1771		John	Surr 1782
John	Gran 1771		Jonas	Mart 1779
John	Rich 1790		Joseph	Perq 1772
John Jr	Wilk 1782		Nathan	Mart 1779
Mathias	Curr 1779		Solomon	Beau 1779
Moses	Hali 1783		Williamson	Surr 1782
Reuben	Surr 1782		MAYS, Solomon	NorH 1780
Richard	Hert 1779		Solomon	Beau 1786
Richard	Hert 1784		MCCRANEY, Hugh Jr	Blad 1784
Robert	Hert 1779		Hugh Sr	Blad 1784
Step	Bute 1766		MCCRAY, Alexander	Blad 1784
Wm	Gran 1771		Daniel	Blad 1784
Wm	Gate 1789		Phillip	Blad 1784
MATTOCK, Nicholas	Casw 1784		MCCREERY, Hugh	Rowa 1761
MATTON, Samuel	Hali 1783		MCCUBBINS, Wm	Casw 1784
MATTOX, Robertson	Wayn 1786		MCCUBER, Benjamin	Gran 1785
MAUD, Gershom	Jone 1779		Nathan	Gran 1785
MAUDLIN, John	Perq 1772		MCCULLER, John Sr	John 1784
Joseph	Perq 1772		MEABURN, Matthew	Ruth 1782
Joseph	Perq 1787		MEACHAM, Banks	NorH 1780
Thomas	Perq 1772		Henry	NorH 1780
Thomas	Perq 1787		Henry	NorH 1780
Wm	Perq 1772		John	Rich 1790
Wm	Perq 1787		MEADE, James	Ruth 1782
MAUDLING, Dempsey	Hert 1784		Wm	Ruth 1782
MAULDEN, John	Gran 1771		MEADOR, James	Warr 1784
MAULFORD, Ephraim	Blad 1784		MEADOWS, Daniel	Bute 1766
MAULTSBY, Ann	Blad 1784		Daniel	Casw 1784

MEADOWS, Hannah	Warr 1784	MELLON, Henry	Gran 1771
Isaac	Cart 1779	Richard	Bert 1781
Isham	Warr 1784	Rosamond	Gran 1785
Isham	Bute 1766	MELTON, Benjamin	Casw 1784
Jacob	Cart 1779	Daniel	Casw 1786
James	Rowa 1761	David	Surr 1782
James	Gran 1785	Elizabeth	NorH 1780
James	Warr 1784	Jethro	Gate 1789
James	Gran 1771	John	Nash 1782
Jesse	Gran 1785	Josiah	Nash 1782
Joel	Cart 1779	Josiah	Hert 1779
John	Wilk 1782	Neil	Casw 1784
Mary	Cart 1779	Robert	Onsl 1771
Thomas	Cart 1779	Zechariah	Nash 1782
Wm	Casw 1784	MELVIN, Daniel	Blad 1784
MEADS, James	Cart 1779	John	Blad 1784
Thomas	Cart 1779	Solomon	Onsl 1771
MEALER, James	Warr 1784	Thomas	Crav 1779
MEARNS, Wm S.	Nash 1782	MENDENHALL, Mordecai	
MEARS, Mark	Dobb 1780		Rowa 1768
Thomas	Rowa 1761	Mordecai & son	Rowa 1768
Wm	Dobb 1780	Moses	Rowa 1768
MEARYON, John	Surr 1782	Richard	Rowa 1768
MEBANE, Alexander Jr		Stephen	Rowa 1768
	Oran 1779	Stephen & son	Rowa 1768
Alexander Sr	Oran 1779	Thomas	Rowa 1768
James	Oran 1779	MENDON, Joseph	Wilk 1782
John	Oran 1779	MERADIM, Jacob	Wilk 1782
Wm	Oran 1779	MERCER, Bryan	Curr 1779
MECAN, Solomon	Wilk 1782	Christopher	Dobb 1780
MECKLE, George	Gran 1785	Coye	Camd 1782
John	Gran 1785	James	Camd 1782
MEDEREST, Rice	Wilk 1782	Jeremiah Jr	Curr 1779
MEDFORD, James	Mart 1779	Jeremiah Sr	Curr 1779
MEDGET, Samuel Jr	Curr 1779	John	Camd 1782
Samuel Sr	Curr 1779	John	Curr 1779
MEDICI, Capt	Hali 1783	Joshua	Camd 1782
MEDLAR, Bryan	John 1784	Peter	Camd 1782
Nicholas	John 1784	Shadrack	Dobb 1780
MEDLIN, Benjamin	Dobb 1780	Silas	Hali 1783
Bryan	Dobb 1780	Stephen	Camd 1782
Bryan Jr	Dobb 1780	Thomas	Dobb 1780
Joseph	Bute 1766	Thomas	Curr 1779
Nicholas	Dobb 1780	Wm	Camd 1782
Ryal	Bute 1766	MERCHANT, Christopher	
Timothy	Bute 1766		Camd 1782
Wm	Bute 1766	MERDES, James	Casw 1784
Wm	Wilk 1782	MEREDITH, David	Bert 1781
Wm Sr	Dobb 1780	Henry	Oran 1779
MEDLING, John	NOrH 1780	James	Surr 1782
MEEDS, Thomas	Pasq 1789	James B	Surr 1782
Timothy	Pasq 1789	John	Surr 1782
MEEKER, James	Brun 1784	Lewis	Hert 1779
MEEKINS, Isaac	Tyrr 1784	Lewis	Hert 1784
Isaac Sr	Tyrr 1784	Meredith	Chow 1785
John	Tyrr 1784	Nathaniel	Blad 1784
MEERS, Moses	Surr 1782	Thomas	Oran 1779
MEESE, John	Beau 1786	Wm	Bert 1774
MEETS, John	Pasq 1779	Wm	Surr 1782
Thomas	Pasq 1779	MERINEY, James	Surr 1782
MEGAHORN, John	Pitt 1786	MERONEY, Henry	Gate 1789
MEIZE, Joshua	Wilk 1784	MERRILL, Absalom	Hali 1783
MEKES, Matthew	Surr 1782	Arthur	Cart 1779
MELLION, Wm	Beau 1786	George	Hali 1783
MELLON, Evan	Curr 1779	Jacob	Hali 1783

MERRILL, John	Bert 1774	
John	Wilk 1782	
Sarah	Hali 1783	
Thomas Jr	Hali 1783	
Thomas Sr	Hali 1783	
Timothy	Bert 1781	
Wm	Rowa 1761	
Wm	Rowa 1768	
MERRIMAN, Benjamin	Bute 1766	
Charles & son	Bute 1766	
Chas	Mont 1782	
Chas	Gran 1771	
MERRIT, Benj	Wilk 1782	
Jonathan	NBer 1779	
MERRITT, Absalom	Samp 1784	
Ann	Casw 1784	
Arthur	Hali 1783	
Benjamin	Edge 1777	
Benjamin	Casw 1784	
Daniel	Samp 1784	
Edward	Surr 1782	
Ephraim	Hali 1783	
Frederick	Samp 1784	
Frederick	Hali 1783	
George	Wilk 1782	
James	Warr 1784	
James	Surr 1782	
James & son Ja	Bute 1766	
James Jr	Warr 1784	
James son of J	Bute 1766	
John	Oran 1779	
John	Hali 1783	
John	Wilk 1784	
John	Surr 1782	
Joseph	Warr 1784	
Maderick	Hali 1783	
Michael	Samp 1784	
Nathaniel	Samp 1784	
Phillip	Samp 1784	
Reuben	Bute 1766	
Robert Sr	Samp 1784	
Sarah	Nash 1782	
Shadrack	Hali 1783	
Silvanus	Warr 1784	
Stephen	Gran 1785	
Stephen	Gran 1771	
Thomas	Warr 1784	
Thomas	Bute 1766	
Thomas	Hali 1783	
Thomas Jr	Warr 1784	
Wm	Hali 1783	
MERRY, Jonathan	Casw 1784	
MERRYMAN, Charles	Gran 1785	
John Jr	NorH 1780	
Wm	Gran 1785	
MERRYMOON, Francis	NorH 1780	
John	NorH 1780	
MERRYWEATHER, John	Albe 1694	
MESER, Christian	Surr 1782	
MESHAW, Matthew	Tyrr 1784	
MESSER, Henry	Blad 1784	
Smith	Oran 1779	
Solomon	Blad 1784	
Stephen	Oran 1779	
MESSISTON, John	Beau 1786	
METCALF, Francis	Rowa 1768	
METHOLME, Charles	Bute 1766	
METT, Wm	Jone 1779	
METTS, Frederick	Jone 1779	
George Sr	Jone 1779	
MEW, John	Crav 1779	
MEWBOON, Elizabeth	Bert 1774	
MEYERS, Thomas	Surr 1782	
MEZICK, Joshua	Cart 1779	
Margaret	Cart 1779	
MICHAEL, Barnett	Rowa 1761	
Burrell	Mart 1779	
Frederick	Rowa 1761	
George	Wayn 1786	
Isaac	Mart 1779	
Randolph	Wilk 1784	
Thomas	Mart 1779	
Wm	Wilk 1782	
MICHAL, Tamar	Perq 1772	
MICHESON, Edward	Wilk 1782	
Wm	Wilk 1782	
MIDDLEBROOK, Ann	Casw 1786	
Isaac	Casw 1786	
John	Casw 1786	
John	Casw 1784	
MIDDLETON, James	Dupl 1783	
John	Chow 1785	
Thomas	Tyrr 1784	
Thomas	Onsl 1771	
MIDGET, Christopher	Curr 1779	
Joseph	Curr 1779	
Samuel	Curr 1779	
Thomas	Curr 1779	
MIDGETT, John	Tyrr 1784	
MIGGENSON, Thomas	Mont 1782	
MILAM, Adam	Warr 1784	
James	Warr 1784	
John	Warr 1784	
MILBURN, Elias	Wilk 1784	
James	Bert 1781	
Samuel	Bert 1774	
Thomas	Wilk 1784	
MILDER, Catherine	Casw 1784	
MILES, Abraham	Casw 1786	
Abram	Casw 1784	
Alexander	Casw 1784	
Benjamin	Samp 1784	
David	Samp 1784	
Jacob	Casw 1784	
Jacob Jr	Casw 1784	
James	Wayn 1786	
John	Casw 1786	
John	Casw 1784	
Stephen	Chow 1785	
Thomas	Casw 1786	
Thomas	Casw 1784	
Thomas	Hali 1783	
Wm	Rich 1790	
MILGOWS, Andrew	Curr 1779	
MILION, Thomas	Bert 1774	
MILKER, Amey	Hert 1784	
MILLER, Amy	Hert 1779	
Andrew	Hali 1783	
Andrew	Surr 1782	
Andrew	Pasq 1789	

MILLER, Barney	Rowa 1761	Wm	NBer 1779
Bushrod	Dobb 1780	Wm Sr	Dobb 1780
Caleb	Curr 1779	MILLEY, Wm	Blad 1784
Campbell	Cart 1779	MILLIGAN, Benjamin	Brun 1784
Christian	Surr 1782	Samuel	Brun 1784
Clinton	Chow 1785	MILLIKEN, Andrew	Ruth 1782
Daniel	Dobb 1780	James	Ruth 1782
Daniel	Beau 1779	James	Oran 1779
Daniel	Beau 1786	James	NorH 1780
David	Ruth 1782	John	Ruth 1782
Elizabeth	Dobb 1780	Robert	Oran 1779
Elizabeth	Wilk 1784	Samuel	Rowa 1770
Evan	Curr 1779	Wm	Rowa 1770
Frederick	Surr 1782	Wm & son Sam	Rowa 1761
George	Dobb 1780	MILLION, Wm	Beau 1779
George	Oran 1779	MILLNER, Patoles	Bute 1766
Harmon	Surr 1782	MILLS, Anthony	Dobb 1780
Henry Jr	Gran 1771	Anthony	Crav 1779
Isaac	Gate 1789	Benjamin	Brun 1784
Jacob	Surr 1782	Daniel	Hali 1783
James	Ruth 1782	George	Rowa 1768
James	Casw 1786	George Thomas	Edge 1777
James	Tyrr 1784	Henry	Rowa 1768
James	Bert 1774	James	Dupl 1783
James	Bert 1781	James	Brun 1784
James Sr	Ruth 1782	James	NorH 1780
Jesse	Oran 1779	John	Rowa 1768
Job	Perq 1787	John	NorH 1780
John	Warr 1784	Jonathan Jr	Bert 1774
John	Hert 1779	Mordica	Wilk 1782
John	Ruth 1782	Moses	Tyrr 1784
John	Rowa 1761	Rebecca	Rowa 1768
John	Oran 1779	Reuben	Rowa 1768
John	Surr 1782	Richard	Rowa 1768
John Anderson	Crav 1779	Robert	Gran 1785
Jonathan	Bert 1781	Robert Jr	Gran 1771
Joseph	Surr 1782	Samuel	Warr 1779
Joseph	Gran 1771	Simon	Wilk 1784
Joshua	Dobb 1780	Simon	Wilk 1782
Leonard	Rowa 1761	Thomas	Wilk 1784
Leonard	Wilk 1782	Willobee	NorH 1780
Little	Ruth 1782	Wm	Brun 1784
Malachi	Chow 1785	Wm	Gran 1785
Mary	Chow 1785	Wm	Gran 1771
Mary	Crav 1779	Wm Jr	Onsl 1771
Mary	Bert 1781	Wm Sr	Onsl 1771
Mason	Chow 1785	MILLSAPS, Robert	Rowa 1768
Moses	Curr 1779	Thomas	Rowa 1768
Nathl	Beau 1786	MILNER, James	Gran 1785
Rachel	Gate 1789	Wm	Gran 1785
Ralph	Blad 1784	MILSAPS, Matthew	Rich 1790
Randall	Surr 1782	MILTON, Edward	Onsl 1771
Randolph	Samp 1784	James	Onsl 1771
Robert	Dupl 1783	John	NorH 1780
Robert	Chow 1785	Joseph	Onsl 1771
Samuel	Nash 1782	Wm	OnsL 1771
Stephen	Bert 1781	MIMES, Wm	Onsl 1771
Thomas	Warr 1784	MIMS, David	Blad 1784
Thomas	Dupl 1783	James	Blad 1784
Thomas	Curr 1779	Thomas	Blad 1784
Thomas Jr	Warr 1784	Thomas	Rich 1790
Tobias	Jone 1779	MINDERWOOD, Wm	Surr 1782
Wendell	Rowa 1761	MING, Thomas	Chow 1785
Willis	Curr 1779	MINIAR, Nathaniel	Chow 1785
Witty	Dupl 1779	MINOR, John	Gran 1785

MINOR, Wm	Gran 1785	MITCHELL, Joseph	Camd 1782
MINSHEW, Isaac	Dobb 1780	Joshua	Wilk 1782
Jacob	Dobb 1780	Josiah	Gran 1785
John	Wayn 1786	Josiah	Gran 1771
Mary	Gate 1789	Major	Gran 1785
Nathan	Dobb 1780	Matthew	Bert 1774
Richard	Casw 1784	Matthew	Bert 1781
MINTON, James	Bert 1774	Mial	Nash 1782
James	Bert 1781	Nancy	Cart 1779
James Sr	Bert 1781	Nancy	Cart 1779
Jesse	Nash 1782	Nicholas	Wilk 1782
Joseph Jr	Nash 1782	Reuben	Wayn 1786
Joseph Sr	Nash 1782	Richard	NBer 1779
Merida	Wilk 1782	Richard	Chow 1785
Shadrack	Nash 1782	Richard	NBer 1779
MINTOR, Joseph	Gran 1771	Richard	Gate 1789
MINYARD, Israel	Gate 1789	Wm	Dobb 1780
John	Hert 1779	Wm	Casw 1786
John	Hert 1784	Wm	Bute 1766
Joseph	Hert 1779	Wm	Casw 1784
Wm	Bute 1766	Wm	Hert 1784
MIRES, Nathan Jr	Bert 1774	Wm	Bert 1774
Thomas	Warr 1786	Wm	Wilk 1782
Thomas	Bert 1774	Wm	Wilk 1782
MISE, Joshua	Wilk 1782	Wm	NorH 1780
MITCHELL, Abram	Gran 1771	Wm	Bert 1781
Adam	Surr 1782	MITCHEM, George	Casw 1784
Amos	Curr 1779	John	Chow 1785
Andrew	Oran 1779	MITCHENER, John	NorH 1780
Archibald	Gran 1785	MIXAM, Hannah	Chow 1785
Cader	Bert 1781	MIXCAN, Elijah	Beau 1779
Daniel	NorH 1780	MIXON, Elijah	Beau 1786
David	Ruth 1782	Zachariah	Beau 1786
David	Gran 1785	MIZE, Howell	Gran 1771
David	Gran 1771	Jeremiah	Gran 1771
David	Gran 1771	John	Gran 1771
David Jr	Casw 1784	MIZELL, Aaron	Bert 1774
David Sr	Casw 1784	Aaron	Bert 1781
Elijah	Gran 1785	Edward	Mart 1779
Ephraim	Bert 1781	Henry	Bert 1781
Francis	Camd 1782	James	Mart 1779
George	Casw 1786	James Sr	Mart 1779
Isham	Gran 1785	John	Mart 1779
Jacob	Gran 1785	John	Bert 1781
James	Warr 1784	Luke Jr	Mart 1779
James	Ruth 1782	Luke Sr	Mart 1779
James	Bert 1774	Mark	Mart 1779
James	Wilk 1782	Wm	Mart 1779
James	Gran 1771	Wm	Bert 1781
James Sr	Gran 1771	MIZES, Isaac	Surr 1782
Jeremiah	Bert 1774	MOBLEY, Biggars	Samp 1784
Jeremiah	Bert 1781	MOCK, John	Blad 1784
Jesse	NorH 1780	Paul	Rowa 1761
John	Oran 1779	MODLIN, Edmund	Wayn 1786
John	Casw 1784	John	Perq 1787
John	Gran 1785	MODRIC, John	Bert 1774
John	Hali 1783	MOLBRON, Lemuel	Cart 1779
John	Beau 1779	MOLER, Louis	Surr 1782
John	Bert 1774	MOLIN, Bryan	John 1784
John	Crav 1779	MOLINRUIK, Joshua	Bert 1774
John	NorH 1780	MOLLISTON, Job	Cart 1779
John	Gran 1771	John	Crav 1779
John	Bert 1781	MOLSON, Robert	Rich 1790
John Jr	Oran 1779	MOLTON, John	Wayn 1786
John Sr	Oran 1779	Joseph	Casw 1784

MONASTO, Jeremiah	Mont 1782		MOORE, Abraham	Casw 1784
MONCRIEF, Caleb	Hali 1783		Alexander	Casw 1784
MONCRIES, Maxey	Hali 1783		Alexander	Gran 1785
MONEY, John	Blad 1784		Alexr	Surr 1782
MONGILLE, Nathl	NorH 1780		Amaziah	Dobb 1780
MONK, Jacob	Bert 1781		Andrew	Surr 1782
John	Dobb 1780		Arthur	Casw 1784
Menan	Dobb 1780		Arthur	NorH 1780
Nottingham	Bert 1781		Azariah	Dobb 1780
MONROE, Absalom	NorH 1780		Benjamin	Gran 1785
Arthur	Ruth 1782		Benjamin	Curr 1779
Frederick	NorH 1780		Britain	Dobb 1780
George	Ruth 1782		Charles	Casw 1784
Hector	Blad 1784		Charles	Gran 1785
James	Oran 1779		Charles	Hali 1783
John	Blad 1784		Chas	Gran 1771
John	Rich 1790		Chas Jr	Perq 1787
Lewis	Blad 1784		Chas Sr	Perq 1787
Louis	Blad 1784		Cidenalgo	Mont 1782
Malcomb	Blad 1784		Dan	NBer 1779
Thomas	Chow 1785		David	Oran 1779
Wm	Ruth 1782		David	Onsl 1771
Wm	Chow 1785		Dempsey	Casw 1784
Wm	NorH 1780		Edward	Warr 1784
MONTAGUE, Henry	Gran 1785		Edward	Cart 1779
MONTFORT, Henry	Oran 1779		Edward	Hert 1779
Henry	Hali 1783		Edward	Hert 1784
Richard	Hali 1783		Edward	Surr 1782
Wm	Bert 1774		Edward	Gran 1771
MONTGOMERY, Ansley	Bert 1781		Edward Esq	Nash 1782
Benjamin	Oran 1779		Elizabeth	Curr 1779
James	Casw 1784		Epaphroditus	Hert 1779
James	Bert 1774		Epaphroditus	Bert 1781
John	Hert 1779		Ephraim	Dobb 1780
John	Hert 1784		Ezekiel	Mart 1779
Michael	Casw 1784		Francis	Curr 1779
Robert	Hert 1779		George	Mart 1779
Robert	Hert 1784		Henry	Hert 1779
Sarah	Chow 1785		Henry	Hert 1784
Wm	Rowa 1768		Higdon	Warr 1784
Wm	Oran 1779		Hodges	Mart 1779
MONTJOY, Allen	Bute 1766		James	Nash 1782
MOODY, Benj	NorH 1780		James	Hert 1779
Gillian	NorH 1780		James	Oran 1779
Jabez	Bute 1766		James	Mart 1779
Joel	Oran 1779		James	Samp 1784
John	Bute 1766		James	Samp 1784
John	Oran 1779		James	Blad 1784
Joseph	NorH 1780		James	Hali 1783
Surrell	NorH 1780		James	Hert 1784
MOON, John	Oran 1779		James	Bert 1774
John	Mart 1779		James	Crav 1779
Richard	Rowa 1768		James	Surr 1782
MOONEY, Jacob	Casw 1784		James	Gran 1771
John	Blad 1784		James	Bert 1781
John	Brun 1784		James	Pitt 1786
John	Brun 1782		James Jr	Blad 1784
Robert	Casw 1784		James Sr	Blad 1784
Thomas	Blad 1784		Jesse	Pasq 1779
Thomas	Brun 1782		Jesse	Casw 1784
Wm	Brun 1784		Jesse	Pasq 1789
MOONEYHAM, Thomas	Nash 1782		John	Ruth 1782
MOOR, Samuel	Perq 1772		John	Rowa 1770
MOORE, Aaron	Hert 1779		John	Oran 1779
Aaron	Hert 1784		John	Samp 1784

Name	Place	Year	Name	Place	Year
John	Pasq	1779	Stephen	Casw	1784
John	Blad	1784	Stephen	NBer	1779
John	Wayn	1786	Thomas	Oran	1779
John	Casw	1784	Thomas	Blad	1784
John	Gran	1785	Thomas	Perq	1787
John	Hali	1783	Willis	Hert	1779
John	Hert	1784	Willis	Casw	1784
John	Beau	1779	Willis	Hert	1784
John	Bert	1774	Willis	Gate	1789
John	Crav	1779	Wm	Hert	1779
John	Wilk	1782	Wm	Dobb	1780
John	Surr	1782	Wm	Oran	1779
John	Gran	1771	Wm	Mart	1779
John	Bert	1781	Wm	Blad	1784
John	Beau	1786	Wm	Casw	1784
John Jr	Hert	1779	Wm	Gran	1785
John Jr	Hert	1784	Wm	Beau	1779
John Sr	Hert	1779	Wm	Crav	1779
Joseph	Rowa	1770	Wm	Surr	1782
Joseph	Oran	1779	Wm	Beau	1786
Joseph	Blad	1784	Wm	Perq	1787
Joseph	Casw	1784	Wm Jr	Dobb	1780
Joseph Jr	Mart	1779	Wm Jr	Surr	1782
Joseph Sr	Mart	1779	Wm Sr	Surr	1782
Joshua	Perq	1787	MOOREHEAD, James	Blad	1784
Lewis	Samp	1784	MORAN, Basel	Hali	1783
Louis	John	1784	Samuel	Hali	1783
Luke	Hert	1779	Wm	Hali	1783
Luke	Hert	1784	MORBEN, Ambrose	Pasq	1694
Major	Gran	1785	MOREEN, Wm	Cart	1779
Mark	Warr	1784	MOREHEAD, James	Rich	1790
Mary	Blad	1784	Joseph	Rich	1790
Mary	Beau	1779	MORELAND, Barrett Jr		
Mary	Bert	1774		Hali	1783
Matthew	Surr	1782	Barrett Sr	Hali	1783
Maurice	Mart	1779	Edward	Hali	1783
Michael	Mont	1782	Francis	Oran	1779
Moses	Casw	1784	Thomas	Oran	1779
Moses	Bert	1774	MOREMAN, Thomas	Rich	1790
Moses	Bert	1781	Wm	Rich	1790
Nathan	Cart	1779	Zechariah	Rich	1790
Prudence	Bert	1781	MORGAN, Abram	Gate	1789
Rachel	Ruth	1782	Andrew	Crav	1779
Rachel	Hert	1784	Ann	Bert	1781
Reuben	Hali	1783	Asa	Camd	1782
Richard	Beau	1786	Asa	Pasq	1789
Richardson	Curr	1779	Benj	Pasq	1789
Robert	Oran	1779	Benjamin	Gran	1785
Robert	Casw	1784	Benjamin	Pasq	1779
Robert	Casw	1784	Benjamin	Perq	1772
Robert Jr?	Casw	1784	Benjamin	Wilk	1782
Rod	Surr	1782	Caleb	Hali	1783
Sam	Bert	1781	Charles	Rowa	1768
Saml	Beau	1786	Charles	Pasq	1779
Saml	Perq	1787	Charles	Bert	1774
Samuel	Dobb	1780	Chas	Pasq	1779
Samuel	Mart	1779	Claude	Camd	1782
Samuel	Casw	1786	Davis	Dobb	1780
Samuel	Casw	1784	Edith	Hert	1784
Samuel	Bert	1774	Edward	Samp	1784
Samuel Sr	Crav	1779	George	Cart	1779
Schinkling	Blad	1784	George	Dobb	1780
Seth	Casw	1784	Hardy	Nash	1782
Shadrack	Hert	1779	Hardy	Oran	1779
Shadrack	Hert	1784	Hardy	Hert	1784

MORGAN, Humphrey	NorH 1780		MORRIS, Chislieu	Hali 1783
Isaac	Wilk 1782		Cornelius	Perq 1772
Jacob	Hert 1779		Doneston	Hali 1783
Jacob	Hert 1784		Edward	Mart 1779
James	Nash 1782		Edward	Mont 1782
James	Albe 1679		Edward	Onsl 1771
James	Hert 1784		Elisha	Beau 1786
James	Pasq 1789		Geo	Wilk 1782
John	NasH 1782		George Jr	Hali 1783
John	Cart 1779		George Jr	Wilk 1782
John	Pasq 1694		George Sr	Hali 1783
John	Oran 1779		Griffin	Hali 1783
John	Samp 1784		Hadley	Hali 1783
John	Gran 1785		Henry	Oran 1779
John	Crav 1779		Henry Sr	Oran 1779
John	NorH 1780		Hezekiah	Hali 1783
John	Surr 1782		Isaac	Wayn 1786
John	Gran 1771		Jacob	Mart 1779
John	Gate 1789		James	Ruth 1782
John	Perq 1787		James	Bert 1781
John Jr	NorH 1780		Jeremiah	Perq 1772
Joseph	Warr 1784		Jesse	Hali 1783
Joseph	Pasq 1779		John	Mart 1779
Joseph	Wilk 1782		John	Casw 1784
Joseph	Onsl 1771		John	Gran 1785
Joshua	Wilk 1782		John	Jone 1779
Lemuel	Pasq 1779		John	Mont 1782
Mark	Camd 1782		John	Wilk 1782
Massey	Mont 1782		John	Gran 1771
Mathias	Gate 1789		John	Pasq 1789
Ozmund	Surr 1782		Jonathan	Pasq 1779
Peter Jr	Hali 1783		Joseph	Pasq 1779
Peter Sr	Hali 1783		Joseph	Bert 1774
Phillip	Camd 1782		Joseph	Perq 1787
Sam	Wilk 1782		Joseph	Pasq 1789
Samuel	Casw 1786		Joseph Sr	Pasq 1779
Samuel	Casw 1784		Linner	Camd 1782
Sarah	Oran 1779		Mary	Warr 1784
Seth	Pasq 1779		Mary	Pasq 1779
Seth	Pasq 1789		Millicent	Pasq 1789
Timothy	NorH 1780		Mitchell	Nash 1782
Wilis	Hert 1784		Mordica	Pasq 1779
Willis	Hert 1779		Mordica	Pasq 1789
Wm	Rowa 1768		Moses	Cart 1779
Wm	Casw 1786		Nathan	Pasq 1789
Wm	Brun 1784		Nathaniel	Pasq 1779
Wm	Casw 1784		Philemon	Hali 1783
Wm	Onsl 1771		Rebecca	Pasq 1779
MORING, Burwell	Wayn 1786		Richard	Oran 1779
Wm	Wayn 1786		Richard	Surr 1782
MORMON, Andrew	Rich 1790		Ruth	Pasq 1779
Archelaus	Rich 1790		Samuel	Warr 1784
Benj	Rich 1790		Savannah	Pasq 1779
John	Rich 1790		Thaner	Pasq 1779
MORPUS, Bashford	Nash 1782		Thomas	Nash 1782
John	Nash 1782		Thomas	Blad 1784
MORRELL, Britton	Hert 1784		Thomas	Pasq 1779
Wm	Gran 1771		Thomas	NBer 1779
MORRIS, Aaron	Pasq 1789		Thomas	Bert 1774
Aaron Jr	Pasq 1779		Thomas	Onsl 1771
Aaron Jr	Pasq 1789		Thomas	Pasq 1789
Aaron Sr	Pasq 1779		Travis	Surr 1782
Abraham	Bert 1774		Valentine	Rich 1790
Benjamin	Wayn 1786		Wm	Oran 1779
Benjamin	Pasq 1779		Wm	Hali 1783

Wm	Jone 1779	MOSELEY, Thomas	Dobb 1780
Wm	Wilk 1784	West	Surr 1782
Wm	Bert 1774	MOSELY, Joseph	Surr 1782
Wm	Surr 1782	MOSER, Peter	Surr 1782
Wm	Pasq 1789	MOSES, Nathan	Bert 1774
Zachariah	Wayn 1786	Stephen	Surr 1782
Zachariah Sr	Wayn 1786	MOSIER, John	Rowa 1768
MORRISET, John	Camd 1782	MOSLEY, Daniel	Surr 1782
Joseph	Camd 1782	Saml Sr	Surr 1782
Peter	Camd 1782	MOSS, Aaron Jr	Pasq 1789
MORRISON, Anguish	Rich 1790	Abram	Gran 1771
Joel	Ruth 1782	Benjamin	Warr 1784
John	Casw 1784	Christopher	Hali 1783
John	Mont 1782	David	Warr 1784
John	Rich 1790	Howell	Gran 1771
Nathaniel	Oran 1779	John	Wilk 1784
Norman	Rich 1790	Joseph	Wilk 1782
Robert	Oran 1779	Richard	Warr 1784
MORROUGH, John	Brun 1782	Wilkins	Warr 1784
MORROW, David	Surr 1782	Wm	Casw 1786
Harmond	Surr 1782	Wm	Casw 1784
John	Brun 1782	Wm	Mont 1782
Robert	Casw 1784	MOSSON, Richard	Hert 1784
Wm	Casw 1784	MOTHERALL, Joseph	Casw 1784
Wm Jr	Casw 1784	Samuel	Casw 1784
MORSE, Benjamin	Bert 1774	MOTHERSHEAD, Christopher	
Howell	Gran 1785		Bute 1766
James	Cart 1779	MOTHRELL, Samuel	Casw 1786
Jesse	Gran 1785	MOTT, Jethro	Samp 1784
Joseph	Cart 1779	Joseph	Cart 1779
Joseph Jr	Cart 1779	MOTTLOW, John	Bute 1766
Joshua	Cart 1779	MOUNTYRE, John	Curr 1779
Moses	Cart 1779	MOUS, Wm	Pitt 1786
Nehemiah	Curr 1779	MOY, Geo	Pitt 1786
Nicholas	Gran 1771	MOYE, Thomas	Hali 1783
Reuben	Gran 1785	MOZAR, Frederick	Oran 1779
Reuben	Gran 1771	Jacob	Oran 1779
Samuel	Gran 1785	MOZINGO, Booth	Dobb 1780
MORTON, Fredk	NorH 1780	Pierce	Dobb 1780
Isom	Rich 1790	MRRRITT, Jacob	Samp 1784
James	Rich 1790	MUCKELROY, Adam	Beau 1779
Joel	Oran 1779	Adam	Beau 1786
Joseph	Onsl 1771	MUDY, Isaiah	Bute 1766
Meshack	Casw 1784	MUGART, Alex	Bert 1781
Meshack	Casw 1786	MUIR, Wm	Hali 1783
Patrick	Surr 1782	MUIRHEAD, John	Bute 1766
Peter	Onsl 1771	MULHOLLAND, Thomas	Oran 1779
Richard	Onsl 1771	MULLEN, Henry	Wilk 1782
Wm	Dobb 1780	James	Hert 1779
Wm	Rich 1790	James	Hert 1784
MOSBY, Saml Jr	Surr 1782	John	Hert 1779
MOSELEY, Emperor	Pasq 1789	Joseph	Perq 1787
Gimmeser	Pasq 1779	Patrick	Hert 1779
James	Warr 1784	Patrick	Hert 1784
James & son Ja	Bute 1766	Scott	Hert 1779
Jesse	Warr 1784	Wm	Hert 1779
Joel	Gran 1771	Wm	Hert 1784
John	Warr 1784	Zadock	Perq 1787
John	Bute 1766	MULLENS, Mike	WilK 1782
John	Gran 1785	Sarah	Wilk 1784
John	Warr 1784	MULLER, Thomas	Gran 1785
John	Surr 1782	Thomas	Gran 1771
John Jr	Warr 1784	MULLINS, Abraham	Bert 1774
Matthew	Dobb 1780	Wm	Surr 1782
Michael	Gran 1771	MUMFORD, Zack	Onsl 1771

MUNDEN, Elisha	Perq 1787		MURPHY, Neil	Blad 1784
Hugh	Onsl 1771		Simon	Bute 1766
Jeremiah	Pasq 1779		Thomas	Casw 1786
John	Perq 1772		Thomas	Crav 1779
Levi	Perq 1787		Timothy	Dupl 1783
Simon	Pasq 1789		Wm	Warr 1784
Wm	Perq 1772		Wm	Hert 1779
Wm	Perq 1787		Wm	Samp 1784
Wm	Pasq 1789		Wm	Crav 1779
MUNDINE, Kittrell	Cart 1779		Wm	Pitt 1786
MUNDY, Arthur	Hert 1784		MURRAY, Adam	Onsl 1771
Peter	Pasq 1779		Alexander	Tyrr 1784
MUNGER, Henry	Mont 1782		Barnabus	Oran 1779
MUNK, Silas	Surr 1782		Barney	Oran 1779
MUNSHEW, David	Oran 1779		Dominick	Chow 1785
Richard	Oran 1779		Hugh	Oran 1779
MUNTS, Matthew	Blad 1784		James	Ruth 1782
MURBOUGH, Josiah	Perq 1787		James	Oran 1779
MURCHISON, John	Mont 1782		James	Casw 1786
MURD, Robert	Gran 1771		Jesse	Onsl 1771
MURDEN, Isaac	Camd 1782		John	Oran 1779
Jeremiah	Pasq 1789		John	Surr 1782
MURDOCK, Andrew	Oran 1779		Jonathan	Casw 1786
David	Dupl 1779		Jonathan	Onsl 1771
Elizabeth	Oran 1779		Louis	Tyrr 1784
James	Oran 1779		Mark	Hali 1783
James Jr	Oran 1779		Mathew	Onsl 1771
John	Oran 1779		Morgan	Bute 1766
John	Rich 1790		Thomas	Ruth 1782
MURKISON, Finley	Blad 1784		Tobias	Jone 1779
MURN, Drew	Tyrr 1784		Wm	Oran 1779
MURPHERY, Charles	Samp 1784		Wm	Bert 1781
John	Samp 1784		MURRELL, Barnaby	NorH 1780
Miles	Samp 1784		Benj	NorH 1780
Richard	Samp 1784		George	NorH 1780
MURPHREE, Hardy	Hert 1779		John	Onsl 1771
Hardy	Hert 1784		Mark	NorH 1780
Hugo	NorH 1780		Mary	NorH 1780
James	Surr 1782		Robert	NorH 1780
Wm	Hert 1779		Zackariah	NorH 1780
Wm Sr	Hert 1784		MURROW, James	Dupl 1783
MURPHREY, Jethro	Dobb 1780		John	Bert 1774
John	Dobb 1780		MUSCLEWHITE, Jesse	Blad 1784
Michael	Dobb 1780		Mary	Blad 1784
Wm	Dobb 1780		Milbey	Blad 1784
MURPHY, Alexander	Casw 1784		Thomas	Blad 1784
Archibald	Blad 1784		MUSGROVE, Caleb	Wayn 1786
Archibald	Casw 1784		Joel	Wayn 1786
Arthur	Bute 1766		Moses	Wayn 1786
Daniel	Wilk 1782		Thomas	Wayn 1786
David	Dupl 1783		MUSICK, Abraham	Ruth 1782
Edward	Blad 1784		George	Ruth 1782
Edward	Crav 1779		Jane	Casw 1786
Gabriel	Casw 1786		Lewis	Ruth 1782
Gabriel	Casw 1784		Thomas	Ruth 1782
Hugh	Blad 1784		MUSLAND, Wm	Warr 1784
James	Rowa 1768		MUZZLE, Joseph	Surr 1782
James	Blad 1784		MYAS, Thomas	Hert 1779
John	Casw 1786		MYERS, Benj	Bert 1781
John	Blad 1784		Joseph	Surr 1782
John	Casw 1784		Nathl	Bert 1781
John	Rich 1790		Noah	Jone 1779
Joseph	Warr 1784		Peter	Surr 1782
Keziah	Surr 1782		Phillip	Oran 1779
Martha	Pasq 1779		MYHAND, James	Hali 1783

MYHAND, Silas	Samp 1784		McCALLEY, John Sr	Mont 1782
MYRICK, James	Warr 1784		McCALLIP, John	Oran 1779
James	Bute 1766		Wm	Ruth 1782
Matthew	Warr 1784		McCALLOM, Duncan	Rich 1790
Matthew Jr	Warr 1784		McCALLUM, Daniel	Blad 1784
Moses	Warr 1784		Duncan	Blad 1784
Moses	Bute 1766		Edward	Blad 1784
Wm	Warr 1784		John	Casw 1786
Mahoon, Samson	Mart 1779		John	Blad 1784
Mattox, Alexander	Pasq 1779		John	Oran 1779
McADAMS, Hugh	Oran 1779		McCANDLESS, James	Oran 1779
James	Oran 1779		McCANNON, Donald	Rich 1790
John	Ruth 1782		McCARLEY, Andrew	NorH 1780
John	Oran 1779		McCARROLL, Francis	Oran 1779
Joseph	Perq 1787		Isbell	Surr 1782
Samuel	Oran 1779		John	Blad 1784
McALLISTER, Alexander			Thomas	Surr 1782
	Brun 1784		McCARTER, Alexander	Blad 1784
Anguish	Rich 1790		McCARTNEY, James	Gran 1771
George	Casw 1784		McCARTY, Neil	Blad 1784
John	Casw 1784		McCARVER, James	Casw 1784
John	Rich 1790		McCARVEY, Neil	Blad 1784
Mary	Blad 1784		McCASKETT, John	Mont 1782
Mrs James	Oran 1779		McCASKEY, John	Mart 1779
McALPINE, Malcomb	Blad 1784		McCATO, Wm	Beau 1779
Neil	Blad 1784		McCAUL, Daniel	Rich 1790
McANNLEY, Chas	Surr 1782		Daniel Jr	Rich 1790
Jesse	Surr 1782		Dennis	Rich 1790
John	Surr 1782		John	Rich 1790
McARMAIG, Gilbert	Blad 1784		Paul	Rich 1790
McARTHUR, Alexander	Blad 1784		Robert	Oran 1779
Daniel	Blad 1784		McCAULEY, Matthew	Oran 1779
Donald	Blad 1784		Wm	Oran 1779
John Jr	Blad 1784		McCAULLEY, Benj	Rich 1790
Peter	Blad 1784		McCAWLEY, John	Mont 1782
McBEE, David	Wilk 1782		McCAY, Daniel	Rowa 1768
McBOYD, Thomas	Gran 1771		McCILLEY, Samuel	Edge 1777
McBRIDE, Andrew	Oran 1779		McCLAIN, Alexander	Pasq 1779
Archibald	Blad 1784		McCLAM, Solomon	Samp 1784
Elisha	Camd 1782		Wm	Wayn 1786
James	Oran 1779		Wn	Samp 1784
James	Wilk 1782		McCLANE, Wm	Wilk 1782
John	Oran 1779		McCLAREN, John	Blad 1784
John	Blad 1784		McCLARNEY, Henry	Casw 1786
John	Surr 1782		Paul	Casw 1784
Manasseh	Surr 1782		Paul	Casw 1786
Wm	Surr 1782		Wm	Casw 1786
McBRIDGE, Duncan	Rich 1790		McCLEASE, John	Tyrr 1784
McBRIDGERS, Anguish	Blad 1784		McCLELLAN, John	Brun 1782
McBRIER, Samuel	Ruth 1782		McCLELLAND, Andrew	Blad 1784
McBROOM, Andrew	Oran 1779		John	Blad 1784
Andrewe Jr	Oran 1779		John	Bert 1774
McCABE, John	Pasq 1779		John	Beau 1786
John Rev.	Oran 1779		Malcomb	Blad 1784
Wm	Beau 1786		Rebecca	Oran 1779
McCAFFE, Malcomb	Mont 1782		Thomas	Blad 1784
McCAIN, Archibald	Rich 1790		Wm	Oran 1779
Daniel	Rich 1790		McCLELLEN, Wm	Hali 1783
Murdock	Blad 1784		McCLENDEN, Ezekiel	Mont 1782
McCALEPH, Alexander	Blad 1784		Israel	Mont 1782
McCALL, Alexander	Blad 1784		Jesse	Mont 1782
Francis	Brun 1784		McCLENDOL, Elizabeth	
Frank	Brun 1782			Samp 1784
McCALLER, Peter	Blad 1784		Shadrack	Samp 1784
McCALLEY, Anguish	Mont 1782		McCLENNY, James	Perq 1787

McCLINDEN, Isel	Mont 1782	McCRANEY, John	Blad 1784
Jacob	Ruth 1782	McCRAW, Benj	Surr 1782
Joel	Mont 1782	John	Rich 1790
Mark	Mont 1782	Wm	Surr 1782
Thomas	Mont 1782	McCRAY, Alex	Rich 1790
McCLOUD, Daniel	Mont 1782	Christian	Rich 1790
Daniel	Gran 1771	Christopher	Rich 1790
Duncan	Mont 1782	Colin	Mont 1782
Malcomb	Mont 1782	Dennis	Rich 1790
McCLURE, Henry	Oran 1779	John	Mont 1782
John	Ruth 1782	Mary	Mont 1782
Richard	Ruth 1782	Murdock	Rich 1790
McCLUSKEY, Edmund	Casw 1784	Nancy	Mont 1782
Edward	Oran 1779	Rankin	Mont 1782
Edward	Casw 1786	McCULLEN, Bryan	Wayn 1786
Edward	Casw 1784	John	Wayn 1786
McCOLEMAN, John	Rich 1790	John Sr	Samp 1784
McCOLLAR, Neil	Rich 1790	McCULLER, John Jr	John 1784
McCOLLEY, Malcomb	Rich 1790	Wm Jr	John 1784
McCOLLUM, Malcomb	Casw 1784	Wm Sr	John 1784
McCOLTER, Hezekiah	Crav 1779	McCULLEY, John	Casw 1784
McCOMAS, Laughlin	Rich 1790	John	Casw 1786
McCONE, Ephraim	Hert 1779	McCULLOCH, Alexander	
Wm Jr	Hert 1779		Hali 1783
Wm Sr	Hert 1779	Benjamin	Hali 1783
McCONN, Wm Jr	Hert 1784	James	Oran 1779
McCONNEL, John	Surr 1782	John	Dupl 1783
McCOOL, Benjamin	Oran 1779	John	Oran 1779
McCORMICK, Daniel	Rich 1790	Patrick	Oran 1779
Hugh	Rich 1790	Robert	Gate 1789
McCORNING, Archibald		McCULLOCK, Swain	Mont 1782
	Blad 1784	McCURY, Wm	Wilk 1782
Duncan	Blad 1784	McDADE, Edward	Oran 1779
John	Blad 1784	McDANIEL, Alexander	Ruth 1782
McCOULSKEY, James	Blad 1784	Alexander Jr	Ruth 1782
Neil	Blad 1788	Andrew	Beau 1786
McCOY, Archibald	Rich 1790	Caleb	Pasq 1779
Christopher	Rich 1790	Caleb	Pasq 1789
Daniel	Camd 1782	Drucilla	Beau 1786
Daniel	Rich 1790	Eli	Oran 1779
James	Camd 1782	Elias	Casw 1784
John	Camd 1782	James	Ruth 1782
John	Curr 1779	James	Pasq 1779
John	Wilk 1782	John	Rowa 1768
John	Rich 1790	John	Samp 1784
John Jr	Camd 1782	John	Brun 1784
Joshua	Camd 1782	John	Pasq 1779
Josiah	Camd 1782	John	Pasq 1789
Kezia	Camd 1782	John	Rich 1790
Neal	Casw 1786	Joshua	Curr 1779
Neil	Casw 1784	Josiah	Pasq 1779
Wm	NBer 1779	Peter	Pasq 1779
Wm	Camd 1782	Rachel	Pasq 1779
Wm	Wilk 1782	Sarah	Pasq 1779
Wm	Rich 1790	Silvanus	Camd 1782
Wm Jr	Camd 1782	Wm	Wayn 1786
McCRACKEN, Alexander		Wm	Casw 1784
	Oran 1779	Wm	Tyrr 1784
James	Ruth 1782	Wm	Surr 1782
Jeremiah	Oran 1779	Wm	Beau 1786
John	Oran 1779	Zack	Rich 1790
Samuel	Oran 1779	McDANIELS, Joseph	Gran 1771
Thomas	Oran 1779	McDONALD, Alex	Rich 1790
McCRANE, Jacob	Surr 1782	Alexander	Blad 1784
John	Onsl 1771	Alexander	Mont 1782

McDONALD, Anguish	Blad 1784	McFARLING, Walter	Bert 1774
Anguish	Rich 1790	Wm	Oran 1779
Catherine	Bert 1774	McFARSHION, Wm	Dobb 1780
Daniel	Blad 1784	McFATTER, Daniel	Blad 1784
Daniel	Mont 1782	Malcomb	Blad 1784
Daniel	Rich 1790	Mary	Blad 1784
David	Blad 1784	Wm	Blad 1784
David	Onsl 1771	McFEE, Wm	Surr 1782
Dennis	Rich 1790	McFULTON, Daniel	Blad 1784
Donald	Blad 1784	McGAUCHEY, Alexander	
George	Blad 1784		Ruth 1782
James	Blad 1784	John	Ruth 1782
James	Gran 1785	McGEE, Daniel	Dobb 1780
James	Rich 1790	Jacob	Dupl 1779
John	Blad 1784	James	Samp 1784
John	Mont 1782	John	Dupl 1779
John	Pasq 1789	John	Samp 1784
Joseph	Gran 1785	John Jr	Samp 1784
Malcomb	Rich 1790	Mary	Blad 1784
Randall	Beau 1786	Michael	Oran 1779
Thomas	Gran 1785	Monford	Casw 1784
Wm	Blad 1784	Phillip	Samp 1784
Wm	Chow 1785	Robert	Dupl 1779
Wm	Rich 1790	Robert	Samp 1784
McDONOCK, Henry	Beau 1786	Shadrack	Dupl 1783
John	Beau 1786	Solomon	Samp 1784
McDONOUGH, Andrew	Beau 1779	Thomas	Samp 1784
Andrew Jr	Beau 1779	Willis	Samp 1784
Henry	Beau 1779	Wm	Dupl 1783
John	Beau 1779	Wm	Hali 1783
McDOUGALD, Archibald		Wm	Wilk 1782
	Blad 1784	McGEEHEE, David	Bute 1766
Hugh	Blad 1784	Joseph	Gran 1785
McDOWELL, Benjamin	Casw 1784	McGEORGE, Duncan	Rich 1790
James	NorH 1780	Malcomb	Rich 1780
Stephen	Bert 1774	Peter	Rich 1790
Thomas	Tyrr 1784	McGILL, Allen	Rich 1790
Wm	Camd 1782	Anguish	Rich 1790
Wm	Rich 1790	Archibald	Blad 1784
McDUFFEE, Anguish	Rich 1790	Neil	Blad 1784
John	Rich 1790	McGINNIS, John	Blad 1784
McDUFFY, Daniel	Blad 1784	McGINNISS, Malcomb	Rich 1790
McEACHAM, Daniel	Blad 1784	McGIRETT, Archibald	Blad 1784
Duncan	Blad 1784	McGLANAHAN, Edmund	Bert 1774
Robert	Blad 1784	John	Bert 1774
McELROY, John	Ruth 1782	John	Bert 1781
McEUTNEY, John	Rowa 1768	Mary	Perq 1787
McFADDEN, Alexander	Ruth 1782	Wm	Bert 1781
Samuel	Ruth 1782	McGLAUGHAN, Jeremiah	
McFAIL, Daniel	Samp 1784		Crav 1779
McFALL, John	Blad 1784	McGLOHON, James	Hert 1779
Mary	Blad 1784	McGONEGAL, Patrick	Casw 1784
McFARLAN, Daniel	Casw 1784	Patrick	Casw 1786
James	Casw 1784	McGOWAN, John	Rowa 1761
John	Casw 1784	McGOWEN, James	Rowa 1768
Margaret	Casw 1784	Wm	Tyrr 1784
McFARLANE, Walter	Hert 1779	McGRATH, Wm	Chow 1785
Walter	Hert 1784	McGRAW, James	Hert 1784
McFARLIN, Dougal	Rich 1790	McGREGOR, Arthur	NorH 1780
Duncan	Rich 1790	John	NorH 1780
John	Rich 1790	Wm	Mont 1782
Neil	Rich 1790	McGRIGGER, Anthony	Hali 1783
McFARLING, John	Oran 1779	McGUIRE, John	Chow 1785
Peter	Oran 1779	Phillip	Chow 1785
Thomas	Oran 1779	Phillip Jr	Chow 1785

McGUIRE, Samuel	Chow 1785		McKEEL, John	Beau 1779
Wm	Rich 1790		John	Beau 1786
McHENRY, George	Mart 1779		John	Pasq 1789
Gustin	Mart 1779		Joseph	Beau 1779
James	Surr 1782		McKEEN, Agnes	Casw 1784
Samuel	Tyrr 1784		McKEITHEN, Daniel	Blad 1784
McHOIN, James	Surr 1782		Dougal	Blad 1784
McHOIST, Benjamin	Warr 1784		Gilbert	Blad 1784
McINNIS, Duncan	Rich 1790		McKENITH, Kenneth	Blad 1784
John	Rich 1790		McKENZIE, Gilbert	Blad 1784
McINNISS, Finloh	Rich 1790		McKESSICK, Archibald	
McINTIRE, Daniel	Rich 1790			Blad 1784
McINTOSH, Alexander	Casw 1786		McKEWN, John	Blad 1784
Alexander	Casw 1784		McKEY, Joel	Surr 1782
Charles	Casw 1786		John	Surr 1782
Charles	Casw 1784		McKILLISON, Amos	Mont 1782
John	Casw 1786		McKILWEAN, John	Dobb 1780
John	Casw 1784		Stringer	Oran 1780
Lovine	Rich 1790		McKINLE, Daniel	Blad 1784
Murdock	Blad 1784		McKINLEY, Daniel	Blad 1784
Thomas	Casw 1784		Robert	Blad 1784
Wm	Casw 1786		McKINNEY, Daniel	Mont 1782
Wm	Casw 1784		Isaac	Crav 1779
McINTYRE, Alexander	Ruth 1782		John	Ruth 1782
Andrew	Dupl 1783		John	Dobb 1780
Ann	Ruth 1782		John	Blad 1784
James	Ruth 1782		John	Onsl 1771
John	Ruth 1782		Joseph	Tyrr 1784
John	Blad 1784		Richard	Wayn 1786
John	Rich 1790		Thomas	Tyrr 1784
Robert	Oran 1779		Wm Jr	Wayn 1786
Wm	Ruth 1782		Wm Sr	Wayn 1786
McINVALE, John & s James			McKINNIS, Daniel	Blad 1784
	Bute 1766		Donald	Blad 1784
McIVER, John	Blad 1784		John	Blad 1784
Margaret	Rich 1790		Murdock	Blad 1784
McKACHER, Geo	Rich 1790		McKINNON, Daniel	Rich 1790
James	Rich 1790		John	Rich 1790
McKANE, John	Cart 1779		Neil	Blad 1784
John	Dupl 1779		McKINSEY, Katy	Rich 1790
McKASKILL, Allen	Rich 1790		Kenith	Rich 1790
Daniel	Rich 1790		Wm	Hali 1783
Finlah	Rich 1790		McKIPHEN, John	Rich 1790
John	Rich 1790		McKISSICK, Thomas	Casw 1784
Kenneth	Rich 1790		McKNIGHT, Andrew	Casw 1784
McKAY, Alexander	Rich 1790		David & s Davi	Rowa 1768
Anguish	Blad 1784		George	Rowa 1761
Daniel	Blad 1784		James	Casw 1784
Daniel	Rich 1790		McLAIN, Archibald	Blad 1784
Duncan	Rich 1790		Chas	Rich 1790
Flora	Blad 1784		Daniel	Blad 1784
Henry	Brun 1782		David	Dobb 1780
Iver	Blad 1784		Hector	Blad 1784
John	Blad 1784		Hugh	Blad 1784
McKEACHEN, John	Blad 1784		John	Rich 1790
Peter	Blad 1784		John Jr	Blad 1784
McKEE, George	Blad 1784		McLAMORE, James	Gran 1785
John	Oran 1779		John	Gran 178
McKEEL, Benj	Beau 1786		McLANE, Archibald	Rich 1790
Edmund	Beau 1779		Thomas	Casw 1786
Edmund	Beau 1786		McLAREN, Duncan	Rich 1790
Eliz	Beau 1786		McLAUGHLIN, Daniel	Rich 1790
James	Beau 1779		Dougald	Blad 1784
James	Beau 1786		John	Rowa 1770
John	Pasq 1779		John	Blad 1784

McLAURAN, Duncan	Rich	1790
McLEAD, Alexandra	Rich	1790
McLEMORE, Adkin	Bute	1766
Archibald	Samp	1784
Atkins	Warr	1784
Drew	Samp	1784
Drewry	Samp	1784
Ephraim	Surr	1782
Sterling	Surr	1782
West	Samp	1784
Wm	Samp	1784
Young	Warr	1784
Young	Bute	1766
McLEOD, Alex	Rich	1790
Alexander	Blad	1784
Ann	Rich	1790
Murdock	Blad	1784
Norman	Blad	1784
McLESTER, Joseph	Mont	1782
McLIN, Charles	Crav	1779
Thomas	Crav	1779
McLINDEN, Malcomb	Blad	1784
McLOUD, Murdock	Blad	1784
Neil	Samp	1784
McMAHAN, Bryan	Beau	1779
McMAHON, Daniel	Oran	1779
McMAIN, Robert	Pasq	1789
McMANEMY, John	Casw	1786
McMANIME, Robert	Pasq	1779
McMICHAEL, John	Surr	1782
McMILLEN, Alex	Rich	1790
Anguish	Rich	1790
Archibald	Blad	1784
Archibald	Rich	1790
Daniel	Blad	1784
Dugald	Blad	1784
John	Blad	1784
John	Rich	1790
Malcomb	Blad	1784
Neil	Blad	1784
Nevin	Blad	1784
Richard	Perq	1787
Robert	Blad	1784
Wm	Blad	1784
McMINAMY, Alexander	Casw	1784
Daniel	Casw	1784
John	Casw	1784
Wm	Casw	1784
McMIRTH, Elizabeth	Cart	1779
McMOSIAN, Robert	Pasq	1789
McMULLEN, Henry	Casw	1786
Henry	Casw	1784
James	Hali	1783
John	Casw	1786
John	Casw	1784
Matthew	Bute	1766
Mr	Oran	1779
Samuel	Oran	1779
Wm	Hali	1783
McMUNN, James	Oran	1779
McMURRAY, John	Casw	1784
Samuel	Ruth	1782
Samuel	Casw	1784
Thomas	Ruth	1782
Wm	Ruth	1782

McNABB, James	Blad	1784
McNAIR, Daniel	Rich	1790
Daniel Jr	Blad	1784
Edward	Rich	1790
Gilbert	Rich	1790
John	Rich	1790
Malcomb	Rich	1790
Neil	Blad	1784
Neil	Rich	1790
Roger	Rich	1790
McNEAL, Alec	Blad	1784
Anne	Casw	1784
Daniel	Blad	1784
George	Wilk	1782
Hector	Blad	1784
James	Blad	1784
John	Oran	1779
John	Blad	1784
John	Casw	1784
Keaton	Rich	1790
Malcomb	Blad	1784
Mary	Blad	1784
Neil Jr	Blad	1784
Neil Sr	Blad	1784
Tirgville Jr	Blad	1784
Tirgville Sr	Blad	1784
Wm	Blad	1784
McNEER, Edward	Rich	1790
John	Blad	1784
McNEIL, Archibald	Rich	1790
F.	Hali	1783
John	Rich	1790
McNEMAR, Francis	Ruth	1782
McNEWCHY, Wm	Blad	1784
McNICHOLS, Coleman	Blad	1784
Sarah	Blad	1784
McNISS, Isaiah	Dobb	1780
McPEALE, Geo	Perq	1787
McPHALL, Mary	Blad	1784
McPHERSON, Daniel	Camd	1782
Daniel	Blad	1784
Daniel	Rich	1790
Edward	Rich	1790
Elizabeh	Camd	1782
James	Camd	1782
Jesse	Pasq	1789
John	Blad	1784
Joseph Jr	Camd	1782
Joseph Sr	Camd	1782
Joshua	Camd	1782
Stephen	Camd	1782
Wm	Oran	1779
Wm	Rich	1790
McQUEEN, Malcomb	Rich	1790
Samuel	Wilk	1782
McQUILLEN, Alexander		
	Jone	1779
Nathaniel	Jone	1779
Phillip	Jone	1779
McRAE, Alexander	Rich	1790
Daniel	Rich	1790
Duncan	Rich	1790
Farguard	Rich	1790
Fasdward	Rich	1790
John	Rich	1790

McRAE, Malcomb	Rich 1790		NATION, Christopher	Rowa 1761
Nelly	Rich 1790		Christopher &	Rowa 1768
McREE, Samuel	Blad 1784		John	Rowa 1768
Wm	Blad 1784		John	Surr 1782
Wm Jr	Blad 1784		John & sons	Rowa 1761
McREYNOLDS, Jesse	Casw 1784		Joseph	Rowa 1761
Joseph	Casw 1786		Joseph	Rowa 1768
Robert	Casw 1784		Thomas	Rowa 1768
Roland	Casw 1786		NAWL, Wm	Wilk 1782
Roland	Casw 1784		NAZERY, Wm	Wilk 1782
Samuel	Casw 1784		NBUNDY, Caleb	Perq 1787
McRICE, Robert	Blad 1784		NEAL, Abner	Crav 1779
McRORY, John	Oran 1779		Andrew	Rowa 1761
McSKILL, Malcomb	Rich 1790		Daniel	Onsl 1771
McSWAIN, David	Oran 1779		James	Oran 1779
John	Blad 1784		Jeremiah	Bute 1766
Roger	Blad 1784		Jeremiah	Warr 1784
Thomas	Oran 1779		Joseph	Gran 1785
McVAY, Daniel	Oran 1779		Mary	Blad 1784
David	Ruth 1782		Rebecca	BeaU 1786
John	Ruth 1782		Richard	Crav 1779
John	Oran 1779		Thomas	Hali 1783
Patrick	Oran 1779		Thomas	Surr 1782
McVEY, Patrick	Wilk 1784		Thomas Jr	Brun 1784
McVICAR, Margaret	Blad 1784		Thomas Jr	Brun 1782
Wm	Blad 1784		Thomas Sr	Brun 1784
McVINCHEY, John	Oran 1779		Thomas Sr	Brun 1782
McWHORTER, Aaron	Ruth 1782		Wm	Tyrr 1784
McWORLEY, Joseph	Hali 1783		Wm Jr	Warr 1784
			NEALE, Christopher	Jone 1779
			NEARN, Benjamin	Rowa 1768
			NEBER, John	John 1784
NAIL, Jeremiah	Hert 1784		NEEDHAM, Gideon	Camd 1782
Robert	Oran 1779		Gideon Jr	Camd 1782
NAILING, Wm	Gran 1785		John	Pasq 1779
NAIRN, Aquilla	Nash 1782		John	Pasq 1789
Jesse	Hali 1783		Joseph	Camd 1782
John	Nash 1782		Thomas	Camd 1782
Wm	Nash 1782		NEELY, Andrew	Samp 1784
NANCE, Daniel	Samp 1784		James	Rowa 1761
John	Beau 1779		James &son Jam	Rowa 1768
Richard	Gran 1771		John	Oran 1779
Sherwood	Casw 1786		Richard	Rowa 1761
Sherwood	Casw 1784		Samuel	Casw 1784
Thomas	Casw 1784		Thomas	Casw 1784
Wm	Bert 1774		NEIL, Patrick	Blad 1784
Wynne	Samp 1784		NEILL, Samuel	Ruth 1782
NARSON, Isaiah	Mont 1782		NEITHERCOTT, Sarah	Cart 1779
NASCOM, Frede	Chow 1785		NELMS, George	Samp 1784
John	Chow 1785		Jeremiah	Hali 1783
NASH, Abram	Jone 1779		John	Nash 1782
Caleb	Camd 1782		NELSON, Abraham	Oran 1779
Dempsey	Pasq 1789		Abraham	NorH 1780
Edward	Casw 1784		Alexander	Rowa 1768
John	Pasq 1694		Ananias	Cart 1779
John	Gran 1785		Eleazor	Crav 1779
Joseph	Nash 1782		Eli	Crav 1779
Sally	Camd 1782		George	Cart 1779
Thomas	Casw 1784		George	Rowa 1768
Wm	Nash 1782		George	Oran 1779
Wm	Jone 1779		George	Crav 1779
NASSER, Jesse	Hert 1784		Hardy	Crav 1779
NASWORTH, Agnes	NorH 1780		Isabelle	Oran 1779
NASWORTHY, John	Hali 1783		James	Cart 1779
John	NorH 1780		John	Crav 1779

NELSON, John	Surr 1782		NEWBY, Thomas	Gran 1771
Joseph	Rowa 1768		Thomas	Perq 1787
Joseph	Surr 1782		Thomas(Quaker	Pasq 1779
Lemuel	Oran 1779		Wm	Perq 1772
Mary	Cart 1779		Wm	Perq 1787
Moses	NorH 1780		Wm Simon	Perq 1772
Nathan	Dobb 1780		Zachariah	Perq 1787
Nathan	Beau 1786		NEWCAN, Edward	Onsl 1771
Samuel	Rowa 1761		NEWELL, Absalom	Beau 1786
Samuel	Oran 1779		James	Curr 1779
Thomas	Crav 1779		James	Beau 1786
Thomas	NorH 1780		John	Wayn 1786
Wm	Cart 1779		John	Warr 1784
Wm	Rowa 1768		NEWLIN, James	Oran 1779
Wm	Crav 1779		John	Oran 1779
Wm	Surr 1782		John Sr	Oran 1779
NESON, Osten	Gate 1789		NEWMAN, Hardy	Blad 1784
NETTLES, Shadrack	Ruth 1782		Henry	Rich 1790
NEU, Phillip	Jone 1779		James	Beau 1786
Wm	Jone 1779		John	Beau 1779
NEVIL, George	Ruth 1782		Richard	Beau 1786
Jesse	Ruth 1782		Sarah	Samp 1784
Jesse	Oran 1779		Thomas	Warr 1784
Wm	Ruth 1782		NEWSOM, Booth	NorH 1780
Wm Capt	Camd 1782		James	NorH 1780
NEVILL, Benjamin	Hali 1783		John	NorH 1780
Thomas	Hali 1783		Moses	NorH 1780
Wm	Hali 1783		NEWSOME, Charles	Hert 1784
NEVILLs, John	Gran 1771		David	Wayn 1786
NEW, David	Hert 1784		Gilliam	Hali 1783
NEWBERRY, Jesse	Blad 1784		Hosea	Hert 1784
John	Blad 1784		Isaac	Nash 1782
John Jr	Blad 1784		Joel	Wayn 1786
Jonathan	Rich 1790		Joel	Hert 1784
Thomas	Wilk 1782		Wm	Wayn 1786
Wm	Rich 1790		NEWSON, Wm	Wilk 1782
Wm Jr	Rich 1790		NEWTON, Benjamin	Casw 1784
NEWBOLD, John	Onsl 1771		Elijah	Onsl 1771
Sam	Perq 1787		Elizabeth	Wilk 1782
Thomas	Onsl 1771		George	Oran 1779
Wm	Perq 1787		John	Casw 1784
NEWBY, Benjamin	Pasq 1779		John	Onsl 1771
Eliz	Perq 1787		John	Gran 1771
Exum	Perq 1787		Reuben	Casw 1784
Francis	Perq 1787		Wm	Hert 1779
Gabriel	Perq 1772		Wm	Hert 1784
Gabriel	Perq 1787		NICE, Elizabeth	Albe 1693
Gideon	Perq 1772		NICHOLAS, George	Gran 1785
Jacob	Pasq 1779		Jacob	Wilk 1784
Jacob	Pasq 1789		James	Onsl 1771
James	Pasq 1779		John	Hert 1779
Jesse	Perq 1787		Nathaniel	Nash 1782
Jonathan	Perq 1787		Nathaniel	Hert 1779
Joseph	Perq 1772		Nicholas	Curr 1779
Joseph	Perq 1787		Phillip	Curr 1779
Joseph Jr	Perq 1787		Willis	Hert 1779
Joseph Sr	Perq 1787		Willis	Casw 1784
Mark	Perq 1772		Wm	Hert 1779
Mordica	Pasq 1779		NICHOLS, Anthony	Pasq 1779
Robert	Perq 1772		Anthony	Pasq 1789
Robert	Perq 1787		Burkett	Surr 1782
Robert Sr	Perq 1787		David	Pasq 1779
Samuel	Perq 1772		David	Mont 1782
Sarah	Pasq 1779		Edmund	Mont 1782
Thomas	Perq 1772		George	Cart 1779

NICHOLS, Humphrey	Bert	1781	NICHOLSON, Robert	Perq	1787
Isaiah	Bert	1774	Samuel	Hali	1783
Jabez	Pasq	1789	Sarah	Perq	1787
Jacob	Nash	1782	Susannah	Blad	1784
Jacob	Wilk	1782	Thomas	Mart	1779
James	Tyrr	1784	Thomas	Pasq	1789
James	Mont	1782	Urban	Bute	1766
James	Pasq	1789	Urban	Warr	1784
Jeremiah	Nash	1782	NICKENS, Carter	Hert	1779
John	Oran	1779	James	Hert	1779
John	Hert	1784	James	Hert	1784
John	Bert	1774	Richard	Hert	1784
John	Mont	1782	NICKSON, Robert	Onsl	1771
John	Bert	1781	NIESTLESON, Henry	Bute	1766
Jonathan	Oran	1779	NINSON, Drury	Hert	1784
Jonathan	Gate	1789	Elisha	Hert	1784
Joseph	Pasq	1789	Hardy	Hert	1784
Josiah	Bert	1781	James	Hert	1784
Keziah	Pasq	1779	James Jr	Hert	1784
Luke	Hali	1783	Peter	Hert	1784
Nathaniel	Hert	1784	NIPPER, Wm	Gran	1785
Richard	Hert	1784	NIXON, Albertson	Perq	1787
Robert	Perq	1772	Austin	Perq	1772
Samuel	Pasq	1779	Delight	Perq	1772
Thomas	Camd	1782	Delight	Perq	1787
Thomas	Pasq	1779	Francis	Perq	1772
Thomas	Pasq	1789	Francis	Perq	1787
Willis	Hert	1784	Francis	Rich	1790
Willis	Pasq	1779	Hannah	Perq	1772
Willis	Pasq	1789	Hannah	Perq	1787
Willobee	Pasq	1789	Henry	Wayn	1786
Wm	Oran	1779	James	Pasq	1789
Wm	Hert	1784	Jeremiah	Perq	1772
Wm	Mont	1782	John	Wayn	1786
Wm	Pasq	1789	John	Perq	1772
Wm Jr	Pasq	1779	John	Perq	1787
Wm Sr	Pasq	1779	Joseph	Perq	1787
Wm Sr	Mont	1782	Mary	Perq	1772
Zaber	Pasq	1779	Phineas	Perq	1787
NICHOLSON, Absalom	Hali	1783	Sarah	Perq	1772
Alexander	Warr	1784	Thomas	Perq	1772
Archibald	Warr	1784	Zachariah	Perq	1772
Benj	Rich	1790	Zachariah	Perq	1787
Benjamin	Oran	1779	NMORTH, James	Surr	1782
Charles	Mart	1779	NOBLE, George	Dobb	1780
Christopher	Pasq	1779	Isaac	Beau	1786
Christopher Jr	Pasq	1789	John	Beau	1786
Christopher Sr	Pasq	1789	Joseph	Blad	1784
Edward	Nash	1782	Philemon	Dobb	1780
Henry	Bute	1766	Ralph	Gran	1785
Isaiah	Curr	1779	Samson	Mont	1782
James	Warr	1784	Samuel	Cart	1779
James	Pasq	1789	Thomas	Mont	1782
James & sonJam	Bute	1766	Wm	Mont	1782
James Jr	Warr	1784	NOBLIN, Richard	Hali	1783
John	Bute	1766	NOE, John	Oran	1779
John	Mart	1779	Joseph	Oran	1779
John	Warr	1784	Lutisia	Cart	1779
Josiah	Nash	1782	Peter	Oran	1779
Josiah	Curr	1779	NOEL, Edward	Casw	1786
Malachi	Nash	1782	James	Casw	1786
Nathaniel	Bute	1766	NOELIN, Wm	Gran	1771
Nicholas	Perq	1772	NOLES, Richard	Dobb	1780
Nicholas	Perq	1787	NOLL, Charles	Pasq	1694
Peter	Rich	1790	NOLLEY, Josiah	Samp	1784

NOLLS, Mosess	Wilk 1784		NORTH, Wm	NBer 1779
NOONE, Thomas	Bert 1781		Wm	Bert 1781
NORFLEET, Abraham	Chow 1785		NORTHCOTT, Anthony	Hert 1784
Cordial	NorH 1780		John	Hert 1779
Elisha	Chow 1785		John	Hert 1784
Elisha	Perq 1772		John Jr	Hert 1784
Elisha	Gate 1789		Wm	Hert 1779
Eliz	Gate 1771		Wm	Hert 1784
James	Perq 1772		NORTHERN, John	Curr 1779
James	Gate 1789		Wm	Curr 1779
Joseph	Gate 1789		NORTHON, Solomon	Crav 1779
Reuben	Bert 1774		NORTON, Asahel	Curr 1779
Reuben	Bert 1781		Edward	Rowa 1768
Sarah	Chow 1785		James	NorH 1780
NORMAN, Eli	Surr 1782		Jesse	Bert 1774
Frederick	Perq 1772		John	Curr 1779
Geo	Gran 1771		Joseph	Crav 1779
George	Gran 1785		Susannah	Camd 1782
Henry	Tyrr 1784		Thomas	Rowa 1768
Henry	Surr 1782		Wm	Pasq 1779
Isaac	Tyrr 1784		NORVEL, James	Bert 1774
Isaac	Wilk 1782		James	Gran 1771
James	Tyrr 1784		NORVILLE, Benjamin	Hert 1779
James	Wilk 1782		Benjamin	Hert 1784
Joel	Tyrr 1784		Benjamin Jr	Hert 1779
John	Tyrr 1784		Dempsey	Hert 1784
John	Warr 1784		James	Hert 1779
Joseph	Oran 1779		James	Hert 1784
Joseph	Tyrr 1784		NORWOOD, Benjamin	Gran 1785
Mary widow ofS	Tyrr 1784		Carolyn	NorH 1780
Mary widowofEl	Tyrr 1784		Geo	NorH 1780
Nehemiah	Tyrr 1784		Gilliam	Gran 1785
Thomas	Ruth 1782		John	Bute 1766
Thomas	Bute 1766		John	Hali 1783
Thomas	Gran 1785		John	Crav 1779
Thomas	Warr 1784		Jordan	Gran 1785
Thomas	Surr 1782		Nathl	NorH 1780
Thomas	Perq 1787		Nathl	Gran 1771
Thomas Jr	Ruth 1782		Richard	Hali 1783
Wm	Surr 1782		NOTHERN, Edmund	Wilk 1782
NORRILL, James	Gran 1785		NOWELL, Demsey	Hert 1779
NORRIS, Abram	Bert 1781		Edward	Casw 1786
James	Nash 1782		James	Bert 1781
Joseph	Bute 1766		Septimus	Mart 1779
Richard	Wilk 1784		Wm	Hert 1779
Thomas	Oran 1779		NOWLAND, Edward	Gran 1785
Thomas	Brun 1784		NOWLING, Lewis	Surr 1782
Thomas	Bert 1781		NUCOMB, Timothy	Oran 1779
Wm	Onsl 1771		NULL, Jacob	Surr 1782
Wm Jr	Bert 1781		Michael	Surr 1782
NORSWORTHY, James	Warr 1784		NUNAN, Wm	Oran 1779
Moyal	Warr 1784		NUNN, Elijah	Casw 1784
Wm	Warr 1784		Francis	Dobb 1780
Wm Moyal	Warr 1784		Joshua	Dobb 1780
NORTH, Edmund	Beau 1779		Richard	Surr 1782
John	Wilk 1782		Wm	Surr 1782
Joseph	Bert 1774		Wm Jr	Oran 1779
Joseph	Bert 1781		NUNRE, Jemimah	Jone 1779
Malachi	Pasq 1789		NUSBEY, Thomas	Gran 1785
Tamar	Pasq 1789		NUSOM, Hosea	Hert 1779
Thomas	Crav 1779			
Thomas	Brun 1782			
Thomas	Gate 1789			
Thomas	Pasq 1789		O'BRYANT, Dennis	Gran 1785
Vernon	Beau 1779		Patrick	Gran 1785

O'DANIEL, Henry	Oran 1779	ODOM, Wm	Gate 1789
Jacob	Hali 1783	ODOWDEY, Caleb	Curr 1779
John	Oran 1779	Joseph	Curr 1779
Joseph	Camd 1782	Wm	Curr 1779
O'DEAN, Thomas	Oran 1779	OENMEDLEN, Wm	Bute 1766
O'MALLEY, Matthew	Chow 1785	OGG, George	Hali 1783
O'NEALE, Arthur	Rowa 1761	OGILVIE, Harris	Gran 1785
Edmond	Rowa 1761	OGLAND, Phillip	Beau 1786
Edward	Casw 1786	OGLESBEE, Benjamin	Cart 1779
Henry	Chow 1785	Elizabeth	Cart 1779
Peter	Chow 1785	John	Cart 1779
Richard	Tyrr 1784	Joseph	Cart 1779
Sarah	Chow 1785	Thomas	Cart 1779
Wm	Cart 1779	OGLEVIE, Kimberly	Gran 1785
Wm	Oran 1779	Wm	Gran 1771
O'NEILL, Arthur	Nash 1782	OLDFIELD, Richard	Onsl 1771
O'QUINN, Alexander	Samp 1784	OLDHAM, George	Casw 1786
David	Blad 1784	George	Casw 1784
Farlow	Blad 1784	James	Casw 1786
Farlow Jr	Blad 1784	James	Casw 1784
John	Samp 1784	Jesse	Casw 1786
John	Blad 1784	Jesse	Casw 1784
Patrick	Samp 1784	John	Casw 1786
OAKES, Wm	Surr 1782	John	Casw 1784
OAKLEY, Elizabeth	Curr 1779	Moses	Casw 1786
Francis	Gran 1771	Moses	Casw 1784
John	Casw 1784	Richard Jr	Casw 1786
John	Gran 1771	Richard Jr	Casw 1784
Joseph	Gran 1771	Richard Sr	Casw 1784
Joseph Jr	Gran 1785	OLDS, Arthur	Dobb 1780
Joseph Sr	Gran 1785	OLIPHANT, Jesse	Blad 1784
Richard	Gran 1785	Wm	Blad 1784
Thomas	Gran 1785	OLIVER, Alexander	Tyrr 1784
Thomas Jr	Gran 1771	Andrew	Tyrr 1784
Walter	Oran 1779	Andrew	Bert 1774
Walter	Casw 1784	Douglas	Casw 1784
Wm	Gran 1785	Francis	Gran 1785
Wm	Gran 1771	Henry	Wayn 1786
OATES, Artisha	Samp 1784	James	Onsl 1771
Jesse	Samp 1784	John	Gran 1785
Samuel	Samp 1784	John	John 1784
OBANION, Wm	Bute 1766	John	Tyrr 1784
OBAR, Daniel	Surr 1782	John	Bert 1774
OBER, Robert	Surr 1782	John	Gran 1771
ODEN, Richard	Beau 1786	John	Bert 1781
ODOM, Aaron	Blad 1784	John	Rich 1790
Abraham	Samp 1784	John Jr	Hert 1779
Dempsey	Gate 1789	John Sr	Hert 1779
Jacob	Hert 1779	JohnJr	Hert 1784
Jacob	Wayn 1786	Joseph	Tyrr 1784
Jacob	Hert 1784	Peter	Gran 1785
Jacob	NorH 1780	Peter	Gran 1771
James	NorH 1780	Samuel	Crav 1779
Jethro	Wayn 1786	Sollom	Pitt 1786
John	Samp 1784	Solomon	Crav 1779
John	Blad 1784	Wm	Dobb 1780
John	Gate 1789	OLLIS, John	Warr 1784
Kedar	Gate 1789	OLLIVER, Andrew	Bert 1781
Miles	Gate 1789	OMARY, Jacob	Beau 1786
Richard	Beau 1779	OMERAY, Richard	Warr 1784
Richard	Rich 1790	OMERY, Richard	Warr 1784
Theophilus	Bute 1766	ONLEY, John	Perq 1772
Uriah	Gate 1789	ONLY, Penelope	Gate 1789
Wm	Samp 1784	OPENPINE, Henry	Rich 1790
Wm	Blad 1784	OPETS, Harrell	Surr 1782

ORANGE, Wm	Hali 1783	OUTLAW, Joseph	Perq 1787
ORENDILL, Benjamin	Bute 1766	Josiah	Bert 1774
ORENDINE, Charles	Blad 1784	Josiah	Bert 1781
ORMAND, Wm	Dobb 1780	Levi	Gate 1789
ORME, Richard	Bert 1781	Lewis	Bert 1781
ORR, Alexander	Ruth 1782	Rachel	Hert 1784
James	Casw 1784	Ralph	Bert 1774
James	Casw 1786	Ralph	Bert 1781
ORRELL, Amy	Beau 1786	Thomas	Hert 1784
John	Beau 1779	Thomas	Bert 1774
Lewis	Beau 1779	Thomas	NorH 1780
Sarah	Beau 1786	Thomas	Bert 1781
Stephen	Beau 1786	Thomas Jr	Hert 1779
Wm	Beau 1786	Wm	Hert 1779
OSBORNE, Abraham	Rowa 1768	Wm	Hert 1784
Benjamin	Oran 1779	Wm	Bert 1774
Caleb	Rowa 1761	Wm Capt	Hert 1784
Daniel	Rowa 1768	Wm Sr	Bert 1781
Ephraim	Rowa 1761	OVEDYFORD, Green	Blad 1784
James	Oran 1779	OVERMAN, Aaron	Wayn 1786
John	Bute 1766	Ann	Pasq 1779
John	Rowa 1761	Benj	Pasq 1789
John	Rowa 1768	Benjamin	Pasq 1779
Jonathan	Rowa 1761	Charity	Pasq 1789
Joseph	Rowa 1761	Charles	Pasq 1779
Joseph	Rowa 1768	Charles	Perq 1772
Matthew	Rowa 1761	Chas	Perq 1787
Matthew	Rowa 1768	Chas	Pasq 1789
Phillip	Tyrr 1784	Enoch	Pasq 1789
Samuel	Ruth 1782	Ephraim	Pasq 1789
Samuel	Bute 1766	Ephraim Jr	Pasq 1779
Samuel	Rowa 1761	Ephraim Sr	Pasq 1779
Samuel	Rowa 1768	Isaac	Pasq 1779
Wm	Rowa 1761	Isaac	Pasq 1789
Wm	Hali 1788	Jacob	Perq 1772
OSMAN, Francis	Bert 1774	James	Pasq 1779
OSTEN, Claiborn	Gate 1789	James	Pasq 1789
OSTON, Wm	Hali 1783	James	Pasq 1789
OTTERY, Absalom	Ruth 1782	John	Wayn 1786
Simon	Rowa 1768	John	Pasq 1779
OTWELL, Wm	Casw 1786	John	Perq 1772
OUTERBRIDGE, Stephen		John	Perq 1787
	Mart 1779	John	Pasq 1789
Stephen	Bert 1781	Joseph	Pasq 1779
Wm	Mart 1779	Joshua	Pasq 1779
OUTLAND, Cornelius	Wayn 1786	Morgan	Perq 1787
Joseph	Perq 1772	Nathan	Pasq 1779
Josiah	NorH 1780	Nathan	Pasq 1789
Thomas	Wayn 1786	Onias	Pasq 1789
OUTLAW, Aaron	Bert 1781	Othniel	Pasq 1789
Benj	Onsl 1771	Ozias	Pasq 1789
David	Bert 1774	Rachel	Perq 1787
David	Bert 1781	Reuben	Pasq 1779
Delilah	Brun 1784	Robert	Pasq 1789
Edmund	Bert 1774	Saml	Pasq 1789
Edward	Bert 1781	Samuel	Pasq 1779
Geo	Gate 1789	Sarah	Pasq 1779
Geo	Bert 1781	Sarah	Pasq 1789
Jacob	Gate 1789	Sarah Jr	Pasq 1789
Jacob	Bert 1781	Sarah Sr	Pasq 1789
James	Hert 1779	Taylor	Pasq 1779
James	Gate 1789	Thomas	Wayn 1786
James	Bert 1781	Thomas	Pasq 1779
John	Bert 1781	Thomas	Perq 1772
John Jr	Bert 1774	Thomas	Pasq 1789

OVERMAN, Wm	Pasq 1779		OWENS, Brannock	Beau 1786
Wm	Pasq 1789		Henry	Rowa 1768
Zephraim	Pasq 1779		John	Oran 1779
OVERSTREET, Henry	Hali 1783		John	Samp 1784
Phereby	Blad 1784		John	Blad 1784
OVERTON, Benjamin	CamD 1782		Stephen	Beau 1779
Christopher	Hert 1779		Stephen	Beau 1786
Daniel	Perq 1772		Thomas	Tyrr 1784
David	Camd 1782		Thomas	Onsl 1771
Demsey	Camd 1782		Wm	Samp 1784
Edward	Tyrr 1784		Zachariah Jr	Tyrr 1784
Eli	Camd 1782		Zachariah Sr	Tyrr 1784
Elijah	Perq 1787		OWNLEY, John	Ruth 1782
Francis	Camd 1782		OXFORD, Edward	Casw 1784
Gershom	Camd 1782		OXLEY, George	Dobb 1780
James	Hert 1779		John	Bert 1774
James	Camd 1782		John	Bert 1781
James	Hert 1784		OZIAR, Wm	Mont 1782
James	Pasq 1789		O°BRIEN, Patrick	Gran 1771
James Jr	Hert 1784		O°BRYAN, Dennis	Rich 1790
John	Camd 1782		Lawrence	Rich 1790
Joseph	Camd 1782		Pilletson	Rich 1790
Joshua	Camd 1782		O°NEAL, Christopher	Curr 1779
Josiah	Camd 1782		John	Curr 1779
Lazarus	Camd 1782		John	Onsl 1771
Nathaniel	Hert 1779		Sarah	Curr 1779
Nathaniel	Hert 1784		Thomas	Curr 1779
Peter	Camd 1782		Thomas	Onsl 1771
Richard	Camd 1782		Wm	Curr 1779
Robert	Camd 1782		aichael	Curr 1779
Sam	Perq 1787			
Willis	Curr 1779			
OWEN, Bailey	Warr 1784			
Barnett	Wilk 1782		PACE, Burwell	Surr 1782
Daniel	Nash 1782		John	Mont 1782
David	Wilk 1782		Keziah	Surr 1782
Elizabeth	Surr 1782		Sam	Bert 1781
Francis	Gran 1771		Sarah	Surr 1782
Geo	Wilk 1782		Thomas	Hali 1783
George	Wilk 1784		Wm	Nash 1782
Hezekiah	Surr 1782		Wm	Bute 1766
James	Gran 1785		Wm	NorH 1780
James	Gran 1771		PACKER, Joseph	Samp 1784
John	Bute 1766		Joseph	Gran 1771
John	Blad 1784		PACQUENET, James	Cart 1779
John	Gran 1785		John	Cart 1779
John	Wilk 1782		PACQUINETT, James	Cart 1779
John	Gran 1771		Mrs (JACOB?)	Cart 1779
John Jr	Gran 1785		PADGETT, Benj	Surr 1782
John Sr	Gran 1785		Elizabeth	Surr 1782
Richardson	Gran 1771		Ephraim	Surr 1782
Stephen	Beau 1786		John	Mart 1779
Thomas	Blad 1784		John	Blad 1784
Thomas	Gran 1785		John	Chow 1785
Thomas	Wilk 1782		John	Surr 1782
Thomas	NorH 1780		Thomas	Surr 1782
Thomas	Gran 1771		PADRICE, Joseph	Warr 1784
Tuder	Rich 1790		PADRICK, John	Curr 1779
Wm	Gran 1785		Joseph	Cart 1779
Wm	Wilk 1782		Peter	Curr 1779
Wm	Gran 1771		PAGE, Jacob	Wayn 1786
Wm Jr	Wilk 1782		Jesse	John 1784
Wm s of James	Gran 1785		John	Wayn 1786
OWENS, Adam	Tyrr 1784		Nathan	Bert 1781
Amaziah	Beau 1779		Nathaniel	Casw 1786

PAGE, Nathaniel	Casw 1784	PARDUE, Patram	Warr 1784
Nathaniel	Bert 1774	PARHAM, Avery	Gran 1785
Sam	NorH 1780	Avery	NorH 1780
Samuel	Wayn 1786	Avery	Gran 1771
Samuel	Bert 1774	Avery Jr	Gran 1785
Solomon	Brun 1784	Cannon	Gran 1785
Thomas	Albe 1694	Ephraim	Gran 1785
Thomas	Samp 1784	Henry	Gran 1771
Thomas	Bert 1774	Isham	Gran 1771
Thomas	Bert 1781	John	Gran 1785
Thomas Jr	Bert 1774	John	Gran 1771
Wm	Casw 1786	John Sr	Gran 1771
PAGGETT, John	Tyrr 1784	Louis	Gran 1785
PAGIER, Henry	Surr 1782	Thomas	Gran 1785
PAGOT, Jacob	Onsl 1771	Thomas Jr	Gran 1785
PAIGE, Amos	Hali 1783	Thomas Sr	Gran 1785
Bythel	Hali 1783	Wm	Gran 1785
PAINE, Benjamin	Albe 1694	Wm	Gran 1771
James	Warr 1784	PARIS, George	Ruth 1782
James Jr	Bute 1766	Meschall	Rowa 1768
Joseph	Albe 1694	Moses & sons	Rowa 1768
Michael	Hert 1779	PARK, Daniel	Perq 1787
Thomas	Curr 1779	Elizabeth Mrs	Warr 1784
Thomas Sr	Curr 1779	Joseph	Gran 1771
PAKS, John	Rowa 1768	Robert	Gran 1771
PALIN, Eliz	Pasq 1789	Wm	Nash 1782
Henry	Pasq 1694	PARKER, Aaron	Nash 1782
Thomas	Pasq 1789	Aaron	Chow 1785
PALL, Richard	Perq 1772	Aaron	Hali 1783
PALLISERS, John	Surr 1782	Amos	Oran 1779
PALMER, Ann	Pasq 1789	Amos	Gate 1789
Demcy	Pasq 1789	Ann	Gate 1789
James	Beau 1786	Arthur	Samp 1784
John	Bute 1766	Arthur	Wayn 1786
Joseph	Beau 1786	Azarican	Curr 1779
Joseph	Pasq 1789	Benj	Gate 1789
Joseph Jr	Casw 1784	Benj	Bert 1781
Joseph Sr	Casw 1784	Benjamin	Bert 1774
Malachi	Pasq 1779	Burwell	John 1784
Margaret	Beau 1786	Charles	Hali 1783
Martin	Oran 1779	Chas	Surr 1782
Robert	Pasq 1779	Danny	Gate 1789
Thomas	Ruth 1782	David	Surr 1782
Thomas	Casw 1784	Elisha	Casw 1784
Thomas	Pasq 1779	Elisha	Gate 1789
Thomas	Pasq 1789	Eliz	Gate 1789
Thomas Jr	Casw 1784	Elizabeth	Nash 1782
Thomas Sr	Casw 1784	Ephraim	Hert 1784
Willis	Pasq 1779	Ezekiel	Blad 1784
Willis	Pasq 1789	Francis	Nash 1782
Wm	Bute 1766	Francis	Samp 1784
Wm	Gran 1785	Francis	Onsl 1771
Wm	Beau 1779	Francis	NorH 1780
Wm	Pasq 1789	Francis	Gate 1789
PALMERLY, Ephraim	Wilk 1782	Gabriel	Nash 1782
Jiles	Wilk 1782	Gabriel	John 1784
PANELL, John	Oran 1779	Gen	Beau 1786
PANFORD, John	Surr 1782	Howell	Mont 1782
PANKEY, John	Rich 1790	Hubbard	John 1784
PARAGON, Henry	Surr 1782	Isaac	Hert 1779
John	Surr 1782	Isaac	Dobb 1780
PARDUE, Beverly	Warr 1784	Isaac	Wayn 1786
Joseph Jr	Warr 1784	Isaac	Casw 1784
Morris	Warr 1784	Isaac	Chow 1785
Partram	Warr 1784	Isaac	Hert 1784

PARKER, Isaac	Gate 1789	Solomon	Onsl 1771
Isaac Sr	Gate 1789	Stephen	Rich 1790
Jacob	Mart 1779	Thomas	Curr 1779
Jacob	NorH 1780	Thomas	Gate 1789
James	Dobb 1780	Thomas Jr	Curr 1779
James	Camd 1782	Willis	Gate 1789
James	Hali 1783	Wm	Hert 1779
James	Curr 1779	Wm	Ruth 1782
James	Gate 1789	Wm	Samp 1784
James	Gate 1789	Wm	Blad 1784
Jesse	Gran 1771	Wm	Hali 1783
Job	Chow 1785	Wm	Gate 1789
John	Nash 1782	Wm Sr	Hert 1784
John	Hert 1779	Zachariah	Gate 1789
John	Dobb 1780	PARKINSON, Joel	Gran 1785
John	Rowa 1761	John	Crav 1779
John	Rowa 1768	PARKS, Benonia	Perq 1787
John	Mart 1779	Chas	Wilk 1782
John	Samp 1784	George	Wilk 1782
John	Blad 1784	Henry	Wilk 1782
John	Hert 1784	Humphrey	Perq 1787
John	Wilk 1782	James	NorH 1780
John	Onsl 1771	John	Wilk 1778
John	Surr 1782	John	Oran 1779
John	Gate 1789	John	Chow 1785
John	Perq 1787	John	Wilk 1782
Jonathan	Samp 1784	John Jr	Wilk 1782
Jonathan	Gran 1785	Joseph	Perq 1787
Joseph	Blad 1784	Nathan	Perq 1787
Joseph	NorH 1780	Reuben	Wilk 1782
Joseph	Bert 1781	Robert	Casw 1786
Josiah	Gate 1789	Robert	NorH 1780
Kedar	Gate 1789	Sam	Wilk 1782
Linius	Dobb 1780	Samuel	Oran 1779
Mary	Gate 1789	Solomon	Casw 1786
Matthew	John 1784	Thomas	Wilk 1782
Micajah	Wayn 1786	PARNAGAM, Needham	Hert 1784
Miles	Gate 1789	PARNALL, Jeremiah	John 1784
Mills	Gate 1789	PARNEL, Edward	Rowa 1761
Moses	Dobb 1780	John	Blad 1784
Moses	Oran 1779	PARNELL, Reuben	Surr 1782
Nathan	Chow 1785	Thomas	Surr 1782
Nathaniel	NorH 1780	PARR, Daniel	Curr 1779
Nicholas	Samp 1784	James	Bert 1781
Nicholas	Mont 1782	Jesse	Curr 1779
Penelope	Nash 1782	Noah	Curr 1779
Peter	Hert 1779	Noah	Pasq 1789
Peter	Chow 1785	Wm Jr	Casw 1784
Peter	Hert 1784	Wm Sr	Casw 1786
Peter	Gate 1789	PARREMORE, Benjamin	Dobb 1780
Peter Sr	Hert 1779	PARRISH, Ansil	Oran 1779
Richard	Chow 1785	Bailey	Gran 1785
Richard	Mont 1782	Bris	Gran 1771
Robert	Gate 1789	Charles	Gran 1785
Robert Jr	Gate 1789	Charles	John 1784
Sam	NorH 1780	Chas	Gran 1771
Saml	Surr 1782	Claybourne	Gran 1785
Samuel	Wayn 1786	David	Gran 1785
Samuel	Gran 1785	David	Gran 1771
Samuel	Hert 1784	Edward	Bute 1766
Samuel Jr	Hert 1779	Edward	Chow 1785
Samuel Sr	Hert 1779	Elijah	Gran 1785
Seth	Chow 1785	Elijah	Gran 1771
Silas	Hert 1779	Henry	Oran 1779
Silas	Hert 1784	Henry Jr	Oran 1779

PARRISH, Jesse	Bute 1766		PASCHALL, Wm	Casw 1784
Jesse	Gran 1785		Wm	Warr 1784
John	Chow 1785		PASLEY, Robert	Oran 1779
John	Gran 1785		PASMORE, Humphrey	Oran 1779
Joseph	Chow 1785		John	Nash 1782
Joseph	Gran 1771		Mary	Nash 1782
Justice	Gran 1785		Robert	Hali 1783
Justice	Gran 1771		PASS, Nathaniel	Casw 1784
Samuel	Cart 1779		Wm	Hali 1783
Sherwood	Gran 1785		PASTEUR, Charles	Hali 1783
Sherwood	Gran 1771		James	Hali 1783
Wm	Gran 1771		PATCHETT, Phillip	Surr 1782
Wm Jr	Gran 1788		PATE, Catherine	Dobb 1780
Wm Sr	Gran 1785		Charles Jr	Blad 1784
PARRISHER, Joseph	Pasq 1779		Daniel	Wayn 1786
PARROCK, James	Ruth 1782		Isaac	Dobb 1780
PARROT, Anthony	Mont 1782		Isom	Wayn 1786
Augustine	Hali 1783		John	Dobb 1780
James	Cart 1779		Joseph	Dobb 1780
John	Dobb 1780		Mary	Wilk 1784
Joseph	Nash 1782		Mary	Wilk 1782
Needham	Nash 1782		Saml	Rich 1790
PARROTT, John	Onsl 1771		Shadrack	Wayn 1786
PARSHALL, Israel	Hert 1779		Thorogood	Rich 1790
PARSON, Nicholas	Albe 1694		PATEL, John	Beau 1779
PARSONS, Jeremiah	Crav 1779		PATNER, John	Pasq 1779
John Jr	Crav 1779		PATON, Chas	Gran 1771
John Sr	Crav 1779		PATRICK, Isaac	Tyrr 1784
Joseph	Hali 1783		Joel	Pitt 1786
Levi	Tyrr 1784		John	Tyrr 1784
Richard	Surr 1782		John	Surr 1782
Samuel	Tyrr 1784		John	Pitt 1786
Solomon	Wayn 1786		Louis	Warr 1784
Thomas Jr	Crav 1779		Mary	Brun 1784
Thomas Sr	Crav 1779		Micajah	Pitt 1786
PARTAIN, Henry	Hert 1779		Paul	Bute 1766
Hubbard	Hert 1779		Paul	Surr 1782
PARTEE, Charles	Gran 1785		Saml	Surr 1782
PARTEN, John	Hali 1783		Solomon	Wilk 1782
Wm	Hali 1783		Wm	Surr 1782
PARTIN, Benjamin	Hali 1783		PATTELS, Henry	Gran 1785
Henry	Hert 1784		PATTEN, Anna	Beau 1786
Hubbard	Hert 1784		Sarah	Beau 1786
PARTON, Benjamin	Oran 1779		PATTERPOOL, John	Gran 1771
James	Oran 1779		Seth	Gran 1771
Wm	Oran 1779		PATTERSON, Alex	Rich 1790
PARTRICK, Edward	Crav 1779		Andrew	Oran 1779
Joel	Dobb 1780		Andrew	Gran 1785
John	Dobb 1780		Daniel	Blad 1784
Margaret	Crav 1779		David	Bute 1766
Menon	Dobb 1780		Duncan	Blad 1784
Minoah	Dobb 1780		Elizabeth	Chow 1785
Welmoth	Warr 1784		George	Bute 1766
PARVIS, John	NorH 1780		George	Warr 1784
PASCHALL, Dennis	Gran 1785		George	Warr 1784
Elisha	Gran 1785		Greenberry	Surr 1782
Elisha	Gran 1771		James	Ruth 1782
Isaiah	Gran 1771		James	Oran 1779
James	Gran 1785		James	Gran 1771
James	Warr 1784		James	Rich 1790
John	Warr 1784		John	Oran 1779
John	Gran 1771		John	Blad 1784
Phineas	Bute 1766		John	Warr 1784
Samuel	Warr 1784		Joseph	NorH 1780
Thomas	Warr 1784		Joseph	Beau 1786

PATTERSON, Lewis	Bute 1766		PEACOCK, Levy	Tyrr 1784
Lucas	Warr 1784		Patience	Wayn 1786
Mark	Oran 1779		Peter	Wayn 1786
Matthew	Ruth 1782		Samuel	Wayn 1786
Nathaniel	Oran 1779		Simon	Wayn 1786
Nathl	Gran 1771		Uriah	Tyrr 1784
Smith	Bute 1766		PEAKE, John Comer	Gran 1785
Wm	Oran 1779		PEAL, John	Blad 1784
Wm	NorH 1780		PEALE, Alexander	Mont 1782
Wm	Beau 1786		Dempsey	Hert 1784
PATTON, Abraham	Rowa 1768		Edward	Hert 1779
Alexander	Oran 1779		Edward	Hert 1784
Andrew	Oran 1779		Edward	Hert 1784
Henry	Pasq 1779		Edward	NorH 1780
John	Oran 1779		Jesse	Wayn 1786
John	Beau 1779		John	Hert 1779
Joseph	Pasq 1779		John	NorH 1780
Robert	Oran 1779		Moses	Hert 1784
Samuel	Oran 1779		Passco	Wayn 1786
Thomas	Oran 1779		Reuben	Wayn 1786
Thomas	Pasq 1779		Robert	Hert 1779
PAUL, Andrew	Rowa 1761		Robert	Hert 1784
Jacob	Dobb 1780		Sam	NorH 1780
James	Oran 1779		Samuel	NorH 1780
Robert	Casw 1786		Thomas	Hert 1779
Robert	Casw 1784		Thomas	Hert 1784
Samuel	Casw 1786		Wm	Hert 1779
Samuel	Casw 1784		Wm	Hert 1784
Wm	Beau 1786		PEALER, Anthony	Oran 1779
PAYNE, Edward	Beau 1779		Benjamin	Oran 1779
Greenwood	Casw 1786		PEARCE, Benjamin	Hali 1783
Greenwood	Casw 1784		Daniel	Hert 1779
James	Oran 1779		Edmund	Crav 1779
John	Ruth 1782		Edward	Crav 1779
John	Rowa 1768		Geo	Beau 1786
John	Oran 1779		George & sons	Bute 1766
John	Casw 1786		George (Jr)	Bute 1766
John	Tyrr 1784		Hezekiah	Beau 1786
John Capt	Casw 1784		Isaac	Hert 1779
Josiah	Oran 1779		Jeremiah	Bert 1781
Josiah	Casw 1786		John	Albe 1679
Michael	Chow 1785		John	Bute 1766
Nehemiah	Oran 1779		John	Surr 1782
Robert	Casw 1784		Lazarus	Beau 1786
Thomas	Oran 1779		Richard	Hert 1779
Wm	Casw 1784		Snowden	Dupl 1783
PAYTHETON, George	Albe 1679		Theophilus	Wayn 1786
PAYTON, Wm	Beau 1779		Wm	Bert 1774
Wm Jr	Beau 1779		PEARMAN, Wm	Hali 1783
PEACE, John	Gran 1785		PEARN, George	Gran 1785
John	Gran 1771		PEARSALL, James	Dupl 1783
John Jr	Gran 178		Jeremiah	Dupl 1783
John Sr	Gran 1785		PEARSE, Thomas	NBer 1779
Joseph	Gran 1771		PEARSON, Ann	NBer 1779
Joseph Jr	Gran 1785		Christopher	Wayn 1786
Joseph Jr	Gran 1771		Eleazer	Perq 1787
Joseph Sr	Gran 1785		Henry	Ruth 1782
Nicholas	Gran 1785		Ichabod	Wayn 1786
Samuel	Gran 1785		John	Bert 1774
PEACOCK, Abraham	Wayn 1786		Jonathan	Perq 1787
Archelaus	Wayn 1786		Mark	Wayn 1786
David	Samp 1784		Nathyan	Pasq 1789
Isaac	Tyrr 1784		Wm	Chow 1785
Jesse	Tyrr 1784		Wm	Perq 1787
John	Wayn 1786		PEAT, Henry	Bute 1766

PEAVEY, Benjamin	Brun 1784		PENDERGRASS, Robert	Oran 1779
Caleb	Brun 1784		Spencer	Bute 1766
Caleb	Brun 1782		Wm	Bute 1766
Charles	Brun 1784		Wm	Oran 1779
Charles	Brun 1782		PENDLESON, Henry	Pasq 1694
Joseph	Oran 1779		Thomas	Pasq 1694
PECK, Frederick	Gran 1771		PENDLETON, Abimelech	
John	Gran 1771			Mart 1779
Leonard	Gran 1771		Caleb	Pasq 1779
PEDRICK, Lurannah	Camd 1782		Caleb	Pasq 1789
PEEBLES, Amelia	Warr 1784		Frederick	Pasq 1789
Henry	NorH 1780		George	Pasq 1779
Nathan	Bute 1766		Henry	Pasq 1779
Nathaniel	Bute 1766		Jesse	Pasq 1789
Robert	NorH 1780		John	Pasq 1779
PEED, Henry	Nash 1782		John	Pasq 1789
PEELE, Isaiah	Bert 1774		John Jr	Pasq 1789
James	Bert 1774		Joseph	Pasq 1779
James	Bert 1781		Joseph (minor)	Pasq 1789
Jethro	Bert 1774		Joseph Jr	Pasq 1779
Jethro	Bert 1781		Joseph Jr	Pasq 1789
John	Bert 1774		Joseph Sr	Pasq 1779
John	Bert 1781		Joshua	Pasq 1789
Joseph	Gate 1789		Lemuel	Pasq 1789
Joshua	Bert 1774		Robert	Pasq 1779
Josiah	Bert 1781		Robert	Pasq 1789
Wm	Bert 1781		Samuel	Pasq 1779
PEELER, Anthony	Gran 1771		Thomas	Pasq 1779
Benj	Gran 1771		Thomas	Pasq 1789
Christian	Gran 1771		Thomas Sr	Pasq 1779
Michael	Gran 1771		Thomas Sr	Pasq 1789
PEGRAM, DanieL	Warr 1784		Timothy	Pasq 1789
Daniel	Bute 1766		Zachariah	Pasq 1789
Daniel	Warr 1784		PENITON, Benajah	Wilk 1782
Daniel & sons	Bute 1766		Micajah	Wilk 1782
Edward	Warr 1784		Wm	Wilk 1782
Edward	Warr 1784		PENIX, John	Casw 1784
George	Bute 1766		PENN, John	Gran 1785
George	Warr 1784		PENNEY, Thomas	Blad 1784
Gideon	Warr 1784		PENNINGTON, Abimeleck	
PELL, John	Curr 1779			Beau 1786
Joseph	Camd 1782		Ephraim	Rowa 1761
Wm	Ruth 1782		John	Beau 1779
PELTS, Henry	Pitt 1786		Levi	Rowa 1768
John	Pitt 1786		Sarah	Pasq 1779
PEM, Isaac	Surr 1782		Stephen	Onsl 1771
PEMBERTON, John	Blad 1784		PENNY, James	Onsl 1771
John	Rich 1790		PENRICE, Thomas	Perq 1787
John	Rich 1790		PENROY, John	Surr 1782
Maremont	Blad 1784		PENSLEY, John	Bert 1781
Richard	Hali 1783		PENSON, Aaron	Gran 1785
PEMET, John	Gran 1785		PERCAN, Chas	Surr 1782
PENDEGRASS, James	Wilk 1782		PERDUE, Dennis	Dobb 1780
PENDER, Dennis	Crav 1779		PERISHO, Devotion	Tyrr 1784
Joseph	Oran 1779		James	Wayn 1786
Solomon	Bert 1781		James	Tyrr 1784
Wm	Bert 1781		Joseph	Perq 1787
PENDERGRASS, David	Casw 1786		Rufus	Tyrr 1784
John	Bute 1766		Samuel	Rowa 1761
John	Casw 1786		PERKINS, Abraham	Casw 1786
John	Warr 1784		Abram	Casw 1784
John	Gran 1771		Amey	Camd 1782
Luke	Oran 1779		Asa	Camd 1782
Luke	Casw 1786		Elijah	Bert 1774
Richard	Casw 1784		Elisha	Bert 1781

PERKINS, George	Crav 1779	PERRY, James	Bert 1774
Henry Jr	Hali 1783	James	Surr 1782
Henry Sr	Hali 1783	Jeremiah	Bute 1766
Jacob	Rich 1790	Jeremiah	Hali 1783
James	Casw 1786	Jesse	Perq 1772
James	Casw 1784	Jesse	Perq 1787
Jeremiah	Wayn 1786	John	Bute 1766
Jeremiah	NorH 1780	John	Dobb 1780
Jesse	Casw 1786	John	Mart 1779
John	Casw 1786	John	Blad 1784
Jonathan	Crav 1779	John	Hali 1783
Joshua	Chow 1785	John	Jone 1779
Joshua	Curr 1779	John	Curr 1779
Mack	Camd 1782	John	Onsl 1771
Peter	Surr 1782	Joseph	Perq 1787
Phoebe	Curr 1779	Joshua	Bute 1766
Robert	Chow 1785	Joshua	Warr 1784
Thomas	Oran 1779	Josiah	Pasq 1779
Thomas	Camd 1782	Josiah	Pasq 1789
Thomas	Wilk 1782	Micajah	Mart 1779
Wm	Camd 1782	Miles	Perq 1787
Wm	Hali 1783	Mordica	Gate 1789
Wm	Beau 1779	Mourning	Hert 1779
Wm	Curr 1779	Nathan	Perq 1787
Wm	Beau 1786	Nathaniel & so	Bute 1766
PERNALL, John	Blad 1784	Nicholas	Hert 1779
PERNELL, Wm	Gran 1771	Peter	Gran 1785
PERRY, Abner	Hert 1784	Phillip	Perq 1772
Abraham	Bert 1774	Phillip	Perq 1787
Absalom	Bert 1781	Reuben	Perq 1787
Amos	Chow 1785	Robert	Jone 1779
Benj	Perq 1787	Samuel	Rowa 1768
Benjamin	Perq 1772	Samuel	Chow 1785
Burrill	Bute 1766	Seth	Perq 1787
Christmas	Gate 1789	Shadrack	Hert 1779
Dempsey	John 1784	Simon	Bute 1766
Docker	Bert 1781	Thomas	Bert 1774
Dr	Hert 1784	Thomas	Bert 1781
Drury	Bute 1766	Wm	Hert 1779
Druscilla	Perq 1787	Wm	Rowa 1768
Ebenezer	Surr 1782	Wm	Camd 1782
Elisha	Hert 1779	Wm	Surr 1782
Elisha	Hert 1784	Wm & sons Wm	Bute 1766
Ephraim	Bute 1766	PERSER, David	Beau 1786
Ezekiel	Hert 1779	James	Beau 1786
Ezekiel	Hert 1784	James Sr	Beau 1786
Francis	Bute 1766	Robert	Beau 1786
Francis	Chow 1785	PERSINGER, JOhn	Rowa 1761
Herbert	Hali 1783	PERSON, Ann	Warr 1784
Isaac	Bert 1774	Benjamin	Bute 1766
Isaac	Bert 1781	George	Rowa 1768
Isaiah	Bert 1774	James	Wilk 1782
Isaiah	Bert 1781	Jesse	Warr 1784
Isham	Bute 1766	John	Bute 1766
Isom	Bute 1766	John	Mont 1782
Israel	Perq 1787	Joseph	Bute 1766
Jacob	Hert 1779	Margaret	Bert 1781
Jacob	Hert 1784	Peter	Wayn 1786
Jacob	Perq 1787	Peter	Wilk 1782
Jacob Sr	Perq 1787	Richard	Gran 1771
James	Hert 1779	Salsbery	Onsl 1771
James	Bute 1766	Samuel	Warr 1784
James	Dobb 1780	Samuel	Mont 1782
James	Hali 1783	Thomas	Rowa 1768
James	Hert 1784	Thomas	Gran 1771

PERSON, Thurgood	Gran 1785	PHELPS, Henry	Bert 1781
Wm	Bute 1766	Isham	Warr 1784
Wm	Warr 1784	James	Casw 1786
Wm Jr	Bute 1766	James	Gate 1789
PERVIANCE, Elizabeth		James Capt	Tyrr 1784
	Chow 1785	James Sr	Tyrr 1784
PERY, Phillip	Blad 1784	James son of J	Tyrr 1784
PETERS, Anne	Samp 1784	Joanna widow J	Tyrr 1784
Charles	Crav 1779	John	Warr 1784
Etheldred	Pitt 1786	John Jr	Tyrr 1784
Joseph	Crav 1779	John Sr	Tyrr 1784
Joseph	Pitt 1786	John deceased	Tyrr 1784
Mark	Rich 1790	Jonathan	Tyrr 1784
PETERSON, Aaron	Samp 1784	Joseph Jr	Tyrr 1784
Godfrey	Surr 1782	Joseph Sr	Tyrr 1784
James	Casw 1784	Joseph son of	Tyrr 1784
John	Samp 1784	Joshua	Tyrr 1784
John	Casw 1784	Josiah Sr	Tyrr 1784
John	NorH 1780	Kedar	Gate 1789
Joseph	Casw 1784	Micajah	Chow 1785
Kinchen	NorH 1780	Micajah	Gate 1789
Moses	Samp 1784	Nathaniel	Bute 1766
Nels	Surr 1782	Sarah	Perq 1787
Wm	Samp 1784	Seth	Tyrr 1784
Wm	NorH 1780	Thomas	Casw 1786
PETREE, Jacob	Surr 1782	Wm	Dobb 1780
PETTEY, Absalom	Bute 1766	Wm	Tyrr 1784
James	Bute 1766	Wm	Beau 1779
James & sons	Bute 1766	PHILGO, David	Nash 1782
PETTICE, Dinah	Wayn 1786	PHILGRAVE, James	Onsl 1771
PETTIFORD, Drury	Gran 1785	PHILLIP, Jethro	Nash 1782
Elias	Gran 1785	Wm	Surr 1782
George	Gran 1785	PHILLIPPE, Robert	Gran 1785
Laurence	Gran 1771	PHILLIPS, Ann	Curr 1779
Lawrence	Gran 1785	Benjamin	Camd 1782
Phillip	Gran 1785	Benjamin	Warr 1784
Wm	Gran 1785	Benjamin	Mont 1782
PETTIGREW, Chas	Perq 1787	Daniel	Camd 1782
John	Oran 1779	David	Oran 1779
Wm	Oran 1779	David	Gran 1785
PETTIJOHN, Abraham	Chow 1785	Elijah	Bute 1766
John	Chow 1785	Elizabeth	Camd 1782
PETTIPOOL, John Jr	Gran 1785	Ephraim	Nash 1782
John Sr	Gran 1785	Geo	Surr 1782
Seth	Gran 1785	Isham	Hali 1783
Stephen	Gran 1785	Jacob	Crav 1779
PETTIT, Benjamin	Surr 1782	James	Bute 1766
Thomas Jr	Surr 1782	James	Dobb 1780
Thomas Sr	Surr 1782	James	Blad 1784
PETTY, George	Gran 1785	James	Crav 1779
Wm	Surr 1782	James	Curr 1779
PETTYJOHN, Jacob	Surr 1782	James	Rich 1790
PEYN, George	Wilk 1782	James Jr	Pitt 1786
PHAFF, Isaac	Surr 1782	Jean	Curr 1779
Peter	Surr 1782	Jesse	Oran 1779
PHARAOH, Joshua	Blad 1784	John	Dupl 1783
PHELPS, Amos	Tyrr 1784	John	Hali 1783
Aquilla	Rowa 1761	John	Crav 1779
Asa	Tyrr 1784	John	Onsl 1771
Cuthbert	Tyrr 1784	John	Surr 1782
Edmund	Tyrr 1784	John Jr	Surr 1782
Edward	Tyrr 1784	Jonathan	Pitt 1786
Edward	Beau 1786	Joseph	Nash 1782
Enoch	Tyrr 1784	Levi	Mont 1782
Godfrey	Tyrr 1784	Major	Gate 1789

PHILLIPS, Mannado	Cart 1779		PIERCE, Moses	Casw 1786
Mark	Dobb 1780		Nathaniel	Beau 1779
Mark	Surr 1782		Phillip	Mart 1779
Mason	Dobb 1780		Phillip	John 1784
Mitchell	Camd 1782		Richard	Hert 1784
Priscilla	Hali 1783		Ruth	Albe 1694
Richard	Surr 1782		Sarah	Dobb 1780
Solomon	Rich 1790		Shadrack	John 1784
Thomas	Crav 1779		Solomon	Gran 1785
Thomas	Gran 1771		Solomon	Beau 1779
Thomas	Pitt 1786		Thomas	Albe 1694
Thomas	Rich 1790		Thomas	Tyrr 1784
Thomas Sr	Crav 1778		Thomas	Perq 1787
Thomas Sr	Pitt 1786		Wm	Hali 1783
Wm	Nash 1782		Wm	Surr 1782
Wm	Oran 1779		Wm	Gate 1789
Wm	NorH 1780		PIERCEY, Charles	Mart 1779
PHILPOTT, Charles	Mart 1779		PIERSON, George	Hali 1783
John	Pasq 1694		Jacob	Casw 1784
Thomas	Casw 1784		Nathan	Pasq 1779
Wm	Gran 1785		PIGGOTT, Benjamin	Oran 1779
PHIPPS, Jacob	Crav 1779		Culpepper	Cart 1779
John	Wilk 1782		Jeremiah Quake	Oran 1779
Wm	Crav 1779		John	Cart 1779
PHISOCK, Peter	Crav 1779		John	Cart 1779
PICKEL, Michael	Dobb 1780		Oliver	Cart 1779
PICKELL, John	Warr 1784		Samuel	Oran 1779
Wm	Rich 1790		Wm	Cart 1779
PICKENS, Moses	Jone 1779		PIKE, Benjamin	Pasq 1779
PICKETT, Edward	Oran 1779		John	Wayn 1786
Gideon	Blad 1784		John	Pasq 1779
James	Rich 1790		John	Pasq 1789
Wm	Oran 1779		Lewis	Casw 1784
PICKHART, John	Oran 1779		Lewis	Casw 1786
PICKRELL, Benjamin	Bute 1766		Nathan	Wayn 1786
Richard	Bute 1766		Samuel	Oran 1779
Wm	Bute 1766		Samuel	Wayn 1786
PICKRIEN, Aaron	Jone 1779		Samuel	Bert 1774
PICKRON, John	Jone 1779		Wm	Hali 1783
PIENNER, Rachel	Hert 1784		PILAND, Ann	Gate 1789
PIERCE, Abner	Gate 1789		David	Gate 1789
Abner	Perq 1787		Edward	Gate 1789
Abraham	Gate 1789		Geo	Gate 1789
Arthur	Mont 1782		James	Gate 1789
Christopher	Gate 1789		John	Gate 1789
Daniel	Hert 1784		Stephen	Gate 1789
David	Perq 1787		Thomas	Gate 1789
Elisha	Surr 1782		Thomas Sr	Gate 1789
Ephraim	NBer 1779		PILCHER, Edward	Bute 1766
Isaac	Hert 1784		Robert	Mont 1782
Isaac	Gate 1789		PILKINSON, Richard	John 1784
Jacob	NorH 1780		Richard Jr	John 1784
Jacob	Surr 1782		PILLEY, John	Beau 1779
Jacob	Gate 1789		John	Beau 1786
Jesse	Mart 1779		Thomas	Beau 1786
John	Albe 1694		PINCOM, Irma	Beau 1786
John	Hert 1784		PINDER, Hardy	Wayn 1786
John	NBer 1779		Solomon	Bert 1774
John	Perq 1787		Thomas	John 1784
Joseph	Hali 1783		PINE, James	John 1784
Joseph	Beau 1779		PINER, James	Cart 1779
Joseph	Perq 1787		Joab	Cart 1779
Joshua	Nash 1782		Peter	Cart 1779
Mary	Beau 1779		Thomas	Cart 1779
Miles	Tyrr 1784		Thomas	Onsl 1771

PINKERTON, David	Oran	1779
David Jr	Oran	1779
Edward	Wilk	1782
John	Oran	1779
Robert	Oran	1779
Wm	Oran	1779
PINKHAM, Zephaniah	Cart	1779
PINKIT, Zachariah	Mart	1779
PINKLEY, Frederick	Surr	1782
John	Surr	1782
Peter	Surr	1782
PINNELL, John	Bute	1766
Joshua	Bute	1766
Richard & s Ri	Bute	1766
Richard son of	Bute	1766
Thomas	Bute	1766
PINNER, Wright	Brun	1784
PINNEX, John	Casw	1786
PINNON, Thomas	Wilk	1782
PINSON, Aaron	Wilk	1782
Aaron	Gran	1771
Aaron Jr	Wilk	1782
John	Wilk	1782
Joseph	Wilk	1782
Richard	Surr	1782
Wm	Rowa	1768
PIPER, Alexander	Oran	1779
John	Oran	1779
John Jr	Surr	1782
Samuel	Oran	1779
Silvanus	Surr	1782
PIPES, John Jr	Surr	1782
Matthew	Surr	1782
Silvanus	Surr	1782
PIPKIN, Arthur	Wayn	1786
Asher	Samp	1784
Elisha	Wayn	1786
Isaac	Gate	1789
Jesse	Dobb	1780
Jesse	Wayn	1786
Joseph	Wayn	1786
Luke	Wayn	1786
Phillip	Wayn	1786
Stephen	Wayn	1786
Willis	Wayn	1786
PIPPIN, Benjamin	Mart	1779
Benjamin Jr	Mart	1779
John	Mart	1779
Joseph	Mart	1779
PIQUIT, Joseph	Beau	1786
PITCHARD, Thomas	NBer	1779
PITCHFORD, George	Casw	1784
PITCOCK, Stephen	RiCH	1790
Stephen	RiCH	1790
PITT, Hardy	Hali	1783
John	NBer	1779
Lewis	Hali	1783
Mark	Hali	1783
PITTARD, Samuel	Gran	1785
PITTMAN, Ambrose	Hali	1783
Arthur	Hali	1783
Elijah	Hali	1783
Gideon Jr	Casw	1784
Gideon Sr	Casw	1784
Hardy	Blad	1784

PITTMAN, Isham	Blad	1784
Jesse	Blad	1784
Joel	Nash	1782
Joel	Blad	1784
John	Wayn	1786
John	Hali	1783
John	Crav	1779
John	NorH	1780
Joseph	Casw	1784
Joseph	Hali	1783
Lot	Hali	1783
Mary	Crav	1779
Nathan	Blad	1784
Noel	Blad	1784
Samuel	Hali	1783
Thomas	Hali	1783
Thomas	Crav	1779
Thomas Jr	Blad	1784
Thomas Sr	Blad	1784
PITTS, Andrew	Rowa	1761
Martha	Surr	1782
Mary	Onsl	1771
Rachel	Crav	1779
Saml	Surr	1782
Thomas	Onsl	1771
PLEASANT, Blueford	Casw	1786
John	Casw	1786
PLEDGER, Thomas	Gran	1785
PLIES, Reuben	Gran	1771
PLUMMER, Aaron	Blad	1784
Jeremiah	Blad	1784
Jeremiah Jr	Blad	1784
John	Blad	1784
Moses	Curr	1779
Richard	Blad	1784
Wm	Blad	1784
Zack	Blad	1784
PLUNKETT, Christopher		
	Ruth	1782
PLUTY, Joseph	Gate	1789
POE, John	Wilk	1782
Jonathan	Casw	1786
Stephen	Wilk	1782
POGUE, John	Casw	1784
Joseph	Casw	1784
POINDEXTER, David	Surr	1782
Thomas	Surr	1782
POINTER, Daniel	Hali	1783
John	Pasq	1779
Samuel	Gran	1785
Samuel	Pasq	1779
POKESHICK, Thomas	Rowa	1768
POLAND, John	Nash	1782
John Jr	Nash	1782
Wm	Nash	1782
POLLARD, Jacob	Beau	1786
John	Crav	1779
John	Pitt	1786
Thomas	Crav	1779
Thomas	Mont	1782
POLLOCK, Cullen	Hert	1779
Cullen	NorH	1780
Cullen	Bert	1781
Jacob	Bert	1774
Wm	Bert	1774

POLSON, Caleb	Gate 1789		POPE, Samuel Sr	Dobb 1780
Edward	Gate 1789		Solomon	Wayn 1786
James	Gate 1789		Thomas	Samp 1784
John	Casw 1786		West	Samp 1784
Sarah	Gate 1789		Winkfield	Wayn 1786
POMFRET, John	Gran 1785		Wm	Blad 1784
POND, Patty	Mont 1782		POPLEWELL, George	Curr 1779
Richard	Oran 1779		POPLIN, John	Mont 1782
Walter	Casw 1784		POPPERWELL, George	Tyrr 1784
PONDER, Morgan	Casw 1786		PORCH, Thomas	NorH 1780
Morgan	Casw 1784		PORCUPINE, John	Blad 1788
Thomas	Casw 1786		PORIGE, John	Pasq 1694
POOL, Jonathan	Pasq 1779		PORTER, Abraham	Hert 1784
Joseph	Pasq 1779		Abram	Hert 1779
Patrick	Pasq 1779		Absalom	Samp 1784
Patrick Sr	Pasq 1779		Alexander	Casw 1786
Robert	Pasq 1779		Alexander	Casw 1784
Solomon	Pasq 1779		Christopher	Oran 1779
Wm	Pasq 1779		Christopher	Casw 1786
POOLE, Aaron	Dobb 1780		Edmond	Gran 1785
Ann	Pasq 1789		Edward	Albe 1679
Jacob	Rowa 1761		Isaac	Blad 1784
James	Pasq 1789		James	Hert 1779
John	Tyrr 1784		John	Samp 1784
John	Pasq 1789		John	Crav 1779
John Jr	John 1784		Joseph	Wilk 1782
Joseph	Dobb 1780		Robert	Ruth 1782
Joshua	Pasq 1789		Samuel	Samp 1784
Patrick Jr	Pasq 1789		Samuel	Blad 1784
Patrick Sr	Pasq 1789		Samuel	Hali 1783
Petty	Casw 1784		Spence	Hert 1784
Robert	Pasq 1789		Spencer	Hert 1779
Samuel	Dobb 1780		Wm	Hert 1779
Solomon	Pasq 1789		Wm	Ruth 1782
Thomas	Gran 1785		Wm	Hert 1784
POOR, Alexander	Wilk 1782		Wm	Crav 1779
John	Surr 1782		PORTICE, John	Nash 1782
Thomas	Casw 1786		Lucy	Nash 1782
POPE, Abner	Gran 1785		PORTLOCK, Caleb	Camd 1782
Amos	Hali 1783		POSTLOCK, Thomas	Perq 1787
Arthur	John 1784		POSTON, Jeremiah	Casw 1784
Charles	Bute 1766		Jeremiah	Casw 1786
Charles	Wayn 1786		Jonathan	Rowa 1761
Elijah	Hali 1783		POTED, John	Gran 1771
Hardyman	Nash 1782		POTEET, John	Oran 1779
Henry	Blad 1784		John	Casw 1784
Jacob	Dobb 1780		Wm	Oran 1779
Jeremiah	Samp 1784		POTTER, Ann	Brun 1782
Jesse	Samp 1784		Daniel	Warr 1779
Jesse	Hali 1783		Daniel & sonWm	Ruth 1782
Joel	Casw 1784		Ephraim	Casw 1784
John	Bute 1766		James	Cart 1779
John	Dobb 1780		James	Dobb 1780
John	Warr 1784		John	Ruth 1782
John Jr	Gran 1785		John	Dobb 1780
John Sr	Gran 1785		Joshua	Cart 1779
Lazarus	Nash 1782		Miles	Brun 1784
Pool	Dobb 1780		Wm	Ruth 1782
Richard	Pasq 1694		Wm	Dobb 1780
Richard	John 1784		Wm	Gran 1771
Robert	Samp 1784		POTTS, Am	Hali 1783
Samuel	Dobb 1780		George	Ruth 1782
Samuel	Blad 1784		Mary	Ruth 1782
Samuel	Rowa 1768		POUND, Wm	Oran 1779
Samuel	Hali 1783		POUTT, Joseph	Perq 1772

POWEL, Cader	Warr 1784	POWELL, Paul	Beau 1779
POWELL, Aaron	Hert 1784	Petelman	Hali 1783
Abner	Warr 1784	Peter	Wayn 1786
Abraham	Rowa 1768	Rachel	NorH 1780
Abraham	Blad 1784	Richard	Mont 1782
Ann	Gate 1789	Richard	Rich 1790
Barbara	Camd 1782	Richard	Rich 1790
Barnaby	NorH 1780	Sampson	Nash 1782
Benj	Rich 1790	Sarah	Nash 1782
Benj	Rich 1790	Solomon	NorH 1780
Benjamin	Hali 1783	Starling	Wayn 1786
Cader	Bert 1781	Stephen	John 1784
Cally	Nash 1782	Thomas	Samp 1784
Charles	Blad 1784	Willis	Hall 1783
Charles	Hert 1784	Willoughby	Nash 1782
Chas	Bert 1781	Wm	Bute 1766
Daniel	Dobb 1780	Wm	Mart 1779
Dempsey	Hert 1784	Wm	Wayn 1786
Demsey	Hert 1779	Wm	Hali 1783
Douglas	Samp 1784	Wm	Warr 1784
Elie	Wayn 1786	Wm	Bert 1774
Elijah	Nash 1782	Wm	NorH 1780
Elijah	Blad 1784	Wm	Gate 1789
Elijah	Wayn 1786	Zachariah	Hall 1783
Elizabeth	NorH 1780	POWER, Charles	Bert 1774
Enoch	Bute 1766	John	Warr 1784
Etheridge	Curr 1779	POWERHAM, Rebeccah	Hali 1783
Fanny	Dobb 1780	POWERS, Absalom	Hali 1783
George	Hert 1779	Caleb	Curr 1779
George	Dupl 1783	Caleb Jr	Curr 1779
George	Hert 1785	Caleb Sr	Curr 1779
Hardy	NorH 1780	Chas	Bert 1781
Henry	Rowa 1768	George	Curr 1779
Henry	Rowa 1761	George Jr	Curr 1779
Henry	Mont 1782	Isaac	Tyrr 1784
Honorias	Warr 1784	James	Beau 1779
Jacob	Bute 1766	Jesse	Hali 1783
James	Hert 1779	John	Blad 1784
James	Casw 1786	John	Chow 1785
James	Hali 1783	John	Hali 1783
James	Hert 1784	John	Tyrr 1784
James	Gate 1789	Jonathan	Curr 1779
Jesse	Nash 1782	Joseph	Blad 1784
John	Nash 1782	Josephiah	Tyrr 1784
John	Rowa 1768	Joshua	Tyrr 1784
John	Dobb 1780	Robert Jr	Hali 1783
John	Casw 1786	Robert Sr	Hali 1783
John	Blad 1784	Samuel	Tyrr 1784
John	Casw 1784	Seth	Tyrr 1784
John	Mont 1782	Wm	Hali 1783
John	Gate 1789	Wm	Curr 1779
John Jr	Oran 1779	Wm	Curr 1779
Joseph	Nash 1782	POWNELL, Wm	Bute 1766
Lemuel	Pasq 1779	POYERLY, Jacob	Rowa 1761
Lewis	Hert 1779	POYNER, Humphrey	Curr 1779
Louis	Blad 1784	Humphrey	Curr 1779
Lydia	Nash 1782	Joel	Curr 1779
Matthew	NorH 1780	John	Camd 1782
Moses	Hali 1783	John	Blad 1784
Nathan	Mont 1782	Jonathan	Curr 1779
Nathaniel	Nash 1782	Peter	Curr 1779
Nathaniel	Rich 1790	Peter	Curr 1779
Nathaniel	Rich 1790	Thomas	Curr 1779
Nehemiah	Casw 1784	Wm Sr	Curr 1779
Nichols	Wayn 1786	POYNTER, John	Pasq 1789

PRATER, Edward	Surr	178	PRICE, Saml	Pasq	1789
John	Surr	1782	Samuel	Pasq	1779
PRATHER, Wm	Surr	1782	Shadrack	Mart	1779
PRATT, Jonathan	Wilk	1782	Thomas	Pasq	1694
Mrs	Oran	1779	Thomas	Dobb	1780
Richard	Perq	1787	Thomas	Mart	1779
Wm	Casw	1784	Thomas	Chow	1785
Wm	Pasq	1779	Wm	Dobb	1780
Zebulon	Perq	1787	Wm	Mart	1779
PREME, Benj	Onsl	1771	Wm	Warr	1784
PRENESS, Mary	Warr	1784	Wm Sr	Dobb	1780
PRESCOTT, Aaron	Cart	1779	PRICHARD, Benj	Pasq	1789
Benj	Beau	1786	Carey	Mont	1782
John	Blad	1784	PRIDDY, Geo	Gran	1771
John	Beau	1779	George	Gran	1785
John	NBer	1779	Robert	Gran	1785
John	Beau	1786	Thomas	Gran	1785
Major	Onsl	1771	PRIDE, Wesley	Casw	1784
Moses	Onsl	1771	PRIDGEON, David	Nash	1782
Thomas	Cart	1779	Jesse	Nash	1782
Wm	Beau	1779	John Jr	Samp	1784
PRESNELL, James	Surr	1782	John Sr	Samp	1784
PRESSLEY, James & Lucy			Matthew	Samp	1784
	Rowa	1768	Matthew	Blad	1784
Wm	Rowa	1768	Peter	Blad	1784
PRESTON, Isaac	Wilk	1782	Thomas assessr	Dobb	1780
PRETOR, Ben	Surr	1782	PRIMROSE, Wm	Gran	1785
PRETZEL, Godfrey	Surr	1782	PRINCE, Andrew	NorH	1780
PREWIT, Chas	Surr	1782	Gilbert & son	Bute	1766
PREWITT, Joseph	Wilk	1782	Gilbert son of	Bute	1766
PRICE, Absalom	Dobb	1780	James	Brun	1784
Ann	Wilk	1782	James & son Jo	Bute	1766
Dempsey	Pasq	1779	John	Bute	1766
Demsey	Camd	1782	Nathan	Perq	1787
Dixon	John	1784	PRINGLE, Abraham	Crav	1779
Edward	John	1784	PRITCHARD, Arthur	Pasq	1779
Elijah	Mart	1779	Benj	Pasq	1789
Ephraim	Warr	1784	Benjamin	Pasq	1779
Etheldred	John	1784	Christian	Bert	1781
Francis	Ruth	1782	David	Pasq	1694
Frederick	Ruth	1782	David	Camd	1782
James	Crav	1779	David	Pasq	1779
James Jr	Chow	1785	David	Pasq	1789
James Jr	John	1784	David Jr	Camd	1782
James Sr	Chow	1785	Elisha	Pasq	1779
James Sr	John	1784	Elisha Jr	Pasq	1789
Jeremiah	John	1784	Elisha Sr	Pasq	1789
John	Ruth	1782	Eliz	Beau	1786
John	Dobb	1780	Enoch	Camd	1782
John	Oran	1779	Herbert	Bert	1774
John	Mart	1779	Herbert	Bert	1781
John	Casw	1784	Hugh	Camd	1782
John	Chow	1785	James	Camd	1782
John	John	1784	James	Pasq	1779
John	Pasq	1779	James	Bert	1781
John	Jone	1779	Jeremiah	Jone	1779
John	Pasq	1789	John	Pasq	1779
Jonathan	Pasq	1789	John	Pasq	1789
Joseph	Mart	1779	John Jr	Pasq	1779
Joseph	Surr	1782	John Sr	Pasq	1779
Lucretia	Crav	1779	Joseph	Camd	1782
Reis	John	1784	Joseph	Pasq	1789
Rice	Wayn	1786	Joshua	Pasq	1789
Richard	John	1784	Mary	Pasq	1789
Saml	Pasq	1789	Pethia	Pasq	1789

PRITCHARD, Richard	Pasq	1789
Samuel	Pasq	1779
Samuel	Pasq	1789
Sarah	Pasq	1779
Thomas	Pasq	1694
Thomas	Pasq	1779
Thomas	Pasq	1789
Wm	Bert	1774
PRITCHETT, Abraham	Beau	1786
Abram Jr	Beau	1786
Benj	Beau	1786
Benjamin	Bute	1766
Christopher	Hali	1783
Jacob	Beau	1786
John	Hali	1783
Phillip	Beau	1786
Wm	Hali	1783
Wm	Surr	1782
PRITCHFIELD, John	Surr	1782
PRITLOW, Keziah	Perq	1787
PROBY, Wm	Pasq	1779
PROCTOR, Micajah	Ruth	1782
Richard Jr	Bute	1766
Thomas	John	1784
PROPHETT, John	Wilk	1782
Wm	Wilk	1782
PROSSER, John	Jone	1779
PROWELL, Wm	Casw	1784
PRUDEN, James	Gate	1789
PRUITT, Levi	Surr	1782
Wm	Rowa	1761
PRYOR, Ann	Casw	1784
Ann	Gran	1771
Haden	Gran	1771
Hardin	Casw	1784
Henry	Casw	1784
John	Casw	1784
Matthew	Casw	1784
Robert	Gran	1771
Wm	Hali	1783
PUCKETT, Benjamin	Warr	1784
Isham	Surr	1782
James	Gran	1771
Thomas	Surr	1782
PUEL, John	Gran	1771
PUFF, Andrew	Blad	1784
PUGH, Amos	Surr	1782
Ann	Hali	1783
Daniel	Oran	1779
David	Hali	1783
Francis	Bert	1774
Francis	Bert	1781
George	Curr	1779
Hugh Jr	Crav	1779
Hugh Jr	Pitt	1786
Hugh Sr	Crav	1779
Hugh Sr	Pitt	1786
John	Oran	1779
Lewis	Hali	1783
Peter	Pasq	1789
Poll	Bert	1774
Shadrack	Samp	1784
Thomas	Curr	1779
Thomas	Bert	1781
Thomas Jr	Bert	1774

PUGH, Thomas Jr	Bert	1781
Thomas Sr	Bert	1774
Thomas W	Bert	1781
Whitmell	Bert	1774
Wm	Wilk	1784
Wm	Bert	1774
Wm	Curr	1779
Wm	Bert	1781
Wm 1165 a.	Nash	1782
PULLEN, Barnett	Gran	1785
David	Hali	1783
Isham	Hali	1783
John	Beau	1779
John	Gran	1771
Thomas	Hert	1779
Thomas	Ruth	1782
Thomas	Hert	1784
Wm	Hali	1783
PULLEY, Benjamin	Hali	1783
David	Hali	1783
James	Hali	1783
Wm	Mart	1779
Wm	Hali	1783
Wm	NorH	1780
PULLING, John	Beau	1779
Thomas	Beau	1779
PULLINS, James	Casw	1784
PUMPHREY, Henry	Wilk	1782
PUQUIT, Joseph	Beau	1786
PURDIE, James	Blad	1784
PURDY, Iva	Chow	1785
PURLEE, Isaac	Wilk	1782
PURNALL, John	Hali	1783
PURSELL, Edward	Nash	1782
Jeremiah	Nash	1782
PURSLEY, Alice	Camd	1782
PURVIANCE, Elizabeth		
	Chow	1785
PURVICE, James	Bert	1774
PURVIS, Moses	Bert	1781
PURVISE, John	Wayn	1786
Lewis	Mart	1779
Wm	Pasq	1779
Wm	Mart	1779
PURYEAR, John	Gran	1785
Robert	Gran	1785
Wm	Gran	1785
Wm	Gran	1771
PUSEN, Timothy	Mont	1782
PUTMAN, Benjamin	Bute	1766
Benjamin	Gran	1785
John	Beau	1779
Thomas & son B	Bute	1766
PUTTNELL, John	Beau	1786
PYLAND, Robert	Nash	1782
PYLES, Conrod	Oran	1779
PYOTT, Wm	NBer	1779
PYRANT, John	Casw	1786
QUALLS, Peter	Hali	1783
QUEEN, John	Rowa	1768
QUILLEN, Daniel	Dobb	1780
Teague	Surr	1782

QUILLING, Edward	Pitt	1786
QUINBY, Jesse	Hert	1779
Jesse	Hert	1784
Jonas	Wayn	1786
QUINN, Benjamin	Casw	1786
Benjamin	Casw	1784
Henry	Casw	1784
Mary	Casw	1786
Peter	Ruth	1782
Wm	Casw	1786
Wm Jr	Casw	1784
Wm Sr	Casw	1784
Wm Sr	Casw	1786
QUINNEY, Hollister	Crav	1779
Wm	Crav	1779
QUINNILY, Patk	Pitt	1786
QUINSY, Ann	Pitt	1786
QUOTURMUS, Patrick	Pitt	1786
QYARLES, Alexander	Tyrr	1784
RABON, Silrany	Surr	1782
RABUN, Matthew	Hali	1783
RABY, Adam	Bert	1774
Cader	Bert	1774
James	Tyrr	1784
Luke	Bert	1781
RACHELL, Sterling	Rich	1790
Sterling	Rich	1790
RACKLEY, John	Samp	1784
John Mills	Bute	1766
Joseph	Bute	1766
Persons & son	Bute	1766
RADFORD, John	Warr	1784
Wm	Wayn	1786
Wm	Surr	1782
RAE, Thomas	Perq	1787
RAGLAND, Amey	Gran	1785
Benj	Gran	1771
Evan	Gran	1771
Stephen	Gran	1785
Stephen	Hali	1783
Stephen	NorH	1780
Wm	Gran	1771
RAGLIN, Wm	Wilk	1784
Wm	Wilk	1782
RAGON, Armond	Beau	1786
Jesse	Casw	1784
John	Casw	1784
Joseph	Chow	1785
Nathan	Casw	1784
Owen	Casw	1784
Timothy	Casw	1786
RAGSDALE, John	Casw	1784
Thomas	Casw	1784
Wm	Casw	1784
RAIBORN, George	Warr	1784
RAIFORD, James	Mont	1782
Joseph	Beau	1786
Matthew	Mont	1782
Phillip	John	1784
Robert	Blad	1784
Wm	Wayn	1786
RAIL, Sam	Surr	1782

RAILEY, George	Rowa	1768
RAINER, John	Mart	1779
Solomon	Mart	1779
Thomas	Mart	1779
RAINES, Ambrose	John	1784
Fred	Hali	1783
Henry	John	1784
John	Gran	1785
John	Gran	1771
Samuel	Bert	1774
RAINEY, Buckham	Warr	1784
David	Oran	1779
Elizabeth	Casw	1784
John	Oran	1779
John	Casw	1784
Wm	Oran	1779
Wm	Casw	1784
RAINS, George	Rowa	1761
John	Nash	1782
RAINWATER, Arm	Hali	1783
James	Bute	1766
James	Surr	1782
John	Bute	1766
John	Surr	1782
Mary	Surr	1782
Moses	John	1784
Wm	Warr	1784
RALE, Leah	Curr	1779
RALEIGH, James	Casw	1784
RALLS, Abraham	Bert	1774
Phillip	Bert	1774
RALLYS, Wm	John	1784
RALPH, John	Pasq	1694
Louis	Casw	1784
Thomas	Pasq	1694
Wm	Pasq	1694
RAMBLE, Frederick	Chow	1785
RAMEY, Joseph	Surr	1782
Thomas	Surr	1782
Wm	Surr	1782
RAMPER, Isom	Perq	1772
RAMSEY, Anderson	NorH	1788
Daniel	Casw	1784
David	Rowa	1770
Gilbert	Blad	1784
Gordon	Brun	1784
Henry	NorH	1780
James	Dobb	1780
John	Rowa	1770
John	Bert	1781
Neil	Blad	1784
Robert	Rowa	1770
Wm	Onsl	1771
RAN, John	Bute	1766
RANCKE, John	Rowa	1770
Michael	Rowa	1770
RANDALL, Colby	Mont	1782
Edmond	Mont	1782
Giles	Hali	1783
John	Mont	1782
John Capt	Mont	1782
Joseph	Brun	1784
Josias	Mont	1782
Peter	Mont	1782
Richard	Mont	1782

RANDLEMAN, Christopher		RATCLIFF, Benjamin (T.L)		
	Rowa 1770		John 1784	
John	Rowa 1770	Benjamin (T.L)	John 1784	
John	Surr 1782	Benjamin (T.L.	John 1784	
Stephen	Rowa 1761	Benjamin (deed	John 1754	
RANDOLPH, Andrew	Surr 1782	Benjamin (deed	John 1754	
Benj	Mont 1782	Charles (deed)	Onsl 1739	
Giles	NorH 1771	Charles (deed)	Onsl 1739	
James Jr	Casw 1784	Elam (deed)	Leno 1800	
James Sr	Casw 1784	Elam (deed)	Leno 1800	
John	Mont 1782	Elisha (T.L.)	Anso 1763	
Wm	Casw 1784	Elisha (T.L.)	Anso 1763	
RANK, Michael	Surr 1782	Elisha (pet)	Anso 1769	
RANKHORN, Joseph	Tyrr 1784	Elisha (pet)	Anso 1769	
RANKIN, James	Casw 1784	James (deed)	Samp 1774	
Robert	Ruth 1782	James (deed)	Dupl 1772	
Robert	Rowa 1768	James (deed)	Dupl 1779	
Wm	Casw 1784	James (deed)	Samp 1774	
RANNELS, Jesse	Hert 1784	James (deed)	Dupl 1772	
RANNER, George	Rowa 1770	James (deed)	Dupl 1779	
John	Rowa 1770	Jesse (will)	Rand 1779	
RANSOM, Amey	Warr 1784	Jesse (will)	Rand 1779	
Benjamin	Casw 1786	John Jr (deed)	John 1754	
James	Bute 1766	John Jr (deed)	Dobb 1775	
James	Warr 1784	John Jr (deed)	Dobb 1777	
James Jr	Warr 1784	John Jr (deed)	Chat 1772	
John	Gran 1771	John Jr (deed)	John 1754	
Joseph	Surr 1782	John Jr (deed)	Dobb 1775	
Joseph	Gate 1789	John Jr (deed)	Dobb 1777	
Simon	Blad 1784	John Jr (deed)	Chat 1772	
Wm	Warr 1784	John Jr (will)	Chat 1796	
RAPER, Benjamin	Pasq 1779	John Jr (will)	Chat 1796	
Cornelius	Pasq 1779	John Sr	Dobb 1767	
Cornelius	Pasq 1789	John Sr	Dobb 1767	
Enoch	Perq 1772	John Sr (deed)	Crav 1739	
Enoch	Perq 1787	John Sr (deed)	Crav 1745	
Henry	Perq 1772	John Sr (deed)	John 1750	
Henry Jr	Perq 1787	John Sr (deed)	Dobb 1760	
Henry Sr	Perq 1787	John Sr (deed)	John 1754	
Isom	Perq 1772	John Sr (deed)	Crav 1739	
John	Perq 1787	John Sr (deed)	Crav 1745	
John	Pasq 1789	John Sr (deed)	John 1750	
Luke	Perq 1787	John Sr (deed)	Dobb 1760	
Robertson	Perq 1787	John Sr (deed)	John 1754	
Wm	Rowa 1770	John Sr estate	Dobb 1772	
RARDIN, Capt	Wilk 1784	John Sr estate	Dobb 1772	
Nancy	Hert 1784	Joseph (deed)	Dobb 1787	
RASBERRY, Abram	Onsl 1771	Joseph (deed)	Dobb 1761	
Francis	Dobb 1780	Joseph (deed)	Dobb 1787	
James	Hert 1784	Joseph (deed)	Dobb 1761	
John	Dobb 1780	Joseph of John	Dobb 1780	
RASCO, James	Wayn 1786	Moses (T.L.)	Dobb 1769	
RASCOW, Daniel Jr	Tyrr 1784	Moses (T.L.)	Dobb 1769	
Daniel Sr	Tyrr 1784	Moses (deed)	John 1775	
RASOR, Eliz	Bert 1781	Moses (deed)	Dobb 1775	
RASP, Melchior	Rowa 1770	Moses (deed)	Dobb 1775	
RATCLIFF, Aaron (deed)		Moses (deed)	Dobb 1771	
	Leno 1811	Moses (deed)	Dobb 1762	
Aaron (deed)	Leno 1812	Moses (deed)	Kins 1763	
Aaron (deed)	Leno 1813	Moses (deed)	John 1775	
Aaron (deed)	Leno 1814	Moses (deed)	Dobb 1775	
Aaron (deed)	Leno 1811	Moses (deed)	Dobb 1775	
Aaron (deed)	Leno 1812	Moses (deed)	Dobb 1771	
Aaron (deed)	Leno 1813	Moses (deed)	Dobb 1762	
Aaron (deed)	Leno 1814	Moses (deed)	Kins 1763	

Richard (deed)		
	Dupl	1768
Richard (deed)	Samp	1768
Richard (deed)	Dupl	1768
Richard (deed)	Samp	1768
Riding (will)	Rand	1787
Riding (will)	Rand	1787
Sam Jr (T.L.)	Anso	1763
Sam Jr (T.L.)	Anso	1763
Sam Jr (deed)	Dupl	1760
Sam Jr (deed)	Samp	1760
Sam Jr (deed)	Dupl	1760
Sam Jr (deed)	Samp	1760
Samuel & Mary	Anso	1767
Samuel & Mary	Anso	1767
Samuel (L.O.)	Bert	1730
Samuel (L.O.)	Bert	1730
Samuel (deed	Dupl	1755
Samuel (deed	Dupl	1755
Samuel (deed)	Samp	1755
Samuel (deed)	Dupl	1764
Samuel (deed)	Samp	1764
Samuel (deed)	Dupl	1751
Samuel (deed)	Anso	1761
Samuel (deed)	Anso	1761
Samuel (deed)	Samp	1755
Samuel (deed)	Dupl	1764
Samuel (deed)	Samp	1764
Samuel (deed)	Dupl	1751
Samuel (deed)	Anso	1761
Samuel (deed)	Anso	1761
Samuel (pet)	Ansa	1763
Samuel (pet)	Ansa	1763
Samuel Jr pet	Anso	1769
Samuel Jr pet	Anso	1769
Samuel census	Anso	1784
Samuel census	Anso	1784
Thomas (T.L.)	Dobb	1769
Thomas (T.L.)	Dobb	1769
Thomas (will)	Chat	1787
Thomas (will)	Chat	1787
Wm (T.L.)	Dobb	1780
Wm (T.L.)	Dobb	1769
Wm (T.L.)	Dobb	1769
Wm (deed)	Dobb	1775
Wm (deed)	Dobb	1773
Wm (deed)	Leno	1791
Wm (deed)	Dobb	1775
Wm (deed)	Dobb	1773
Wm (deed)	Leno	1791
RATHEW, Thomas	Surr	1782
RATLIFF, Cornelius	Perq	1787
Damaris will	Pasq	1734
Damaris estate	Perq	1734
Damaris estate	Perq	1734
Elijah (deed)	Anso	1811
Elijah (deed)	Anso	1811
James (will)	Anso	1777
James (will)	Anso	1777
Jesse (deed)	Anso	1811
Jesse (deed)	Anso	1811
Jesse (deed)	Anso	1811
Jesse (deed)	Anso	1811
John (will)	Anso	1777
John (will)	Anso	1777

RATLIFF, Joseph	Perq	1787
Joseph	Perq	1784
Joseph	Perq	1784
Richard	Surr	1782
Richard (deed)	Anso	1811
Richard (deed)	Anso	1783
Richard (deed)	Anso	1811
Richard (deed)	Anso	1783
Richard estate	Perq	1724
Richard estate	Perq	1724
Richard will	Perq	1724
Robt Clothier	Anso	1777
Robt Clothier	Anso	1777
Thomas	Perq	1787
Thomas (deed)	Anso	1783
Thomas (deed)	Anso	1783
Thomas (will)	Anso	1777
Thomas (will)	Anso	1777
Wm	Surr	1782
Wm (deed)	Anso	1811
Wm (deed)	Anso	1771
Wm (deed)	Anso	1811
Wm (deed)	Anso	1771
Wm (will)	Anso	1777
Wm (will)	Anso	1777
Zachariah (wi)	Anso	1777
Zachariah (wi)	Anso	1777
Zachariah pet	Anso	1783
Zachariah pet	Anso	1783
RATZE, Francisco	Wilk	1782
RAVENS, John	Gran	1771
RAWLES, Absalom	Hert	1779
Francis	Mart	1779
Jesse	Mart	1779
John	Nash	1782
Joshua	Mart	1779
Phillip	Hali	1783
Wm	Mart	1779
RAWLEY, James	Casw	1784
RAWLINGS, Mark	John	1784
Roadham	Hali	1783
Samuel	Hali	1783
Wm	John	1784
RAWLINS, John	Nash	1782
Nathaniel	Nash	1782
RAWLS, Jesse	Hert	1784
Levi	Hert	1784
Levy	Bert	1781
Rebecca	Bert	1781
RAWSON, Wm	Bute	1766
RAXON, John	Pasq	1694
RAY, Anguish	Blad	1784
David	Oran	1779
Gabriel	Bute	1766
Geo	Surr	1782
Hugh	Oran	1779
James	NorH	1780
James	Bert	1781
Jean	Blad	1784
John	Oran	1779
John	Beau	1779
John	Bert	1774
John	Bert	1781
John	Beau	1786
Jonathan	Bute	1766

RAY, Joseph	Oran 1779	REDDICK, Solomon	Perq 1787
Reuben	NorH 1780	Thomas	Mart 1779
Robert	Cart 1779	Wm Jr	Dobb 1780
Robert	Casw 1784	Wm Sr	Dobb 1780
Robert	Oran 1779	REDDIN, John	Oran 1779
Robert	Onsl 1771	Joseph	Mart 1779
Samuel	Bert 1774	Thomas	Oran 1779
Stephen	Bert 1774	REDDING, Ann	Pasq 1779
Thomas	Casw 1784	Benjamin	Pasq 1779
Thomas	Wilk 1782	Clarkie	Pasq 1779
Usley	Surr 1782	Joseph	Pasq 1779
Wm	Oran 1779	Joseph	Pasq 1789
RAYBURN, John	Oran 1779	Joseph Jr	Pasq 1779
Thomas	Oran 1779	Joshua	Pasq 1779
RAYBURY, Daniel	Brun 1784	Millerson	Pasq 1779
RAYFIELD, Babel	Hali 1783	Rhuhum	Blad 1784
RAYMOND, Wm	Pasq 1694	Robert	Pasq 1779
RAYNER, Amos	Hert 1784	Thomas	Pasq 1779
Amos	Bert 1781	Thomas	Pasq 1789
David	Samp 1784	REDMAN, Barbary	Casw 1786
James	Bert 1781	John	Oran 1779
John	Bert 1781	REDOAKES, John	Rowa 1768
Richard	Bert 1774	John & son Joh	Rowa 1768
Richard	Bert 1781	Joseph	Rowa 1768
Saml	Bert 1781	REDWINE, Jacob	Oran 1779
Wm	Bert 1781	Lodowick	Gran 1771
REA, James	Rowa 1779	REECE, Travers	Bute 1766
Samuel Jr	Chow 1785	Valentine	Rowa 1768
Samuel Sr	Chow 1785	Will	Rowa 1768
Thomas	Chow 1785	REED, Alexander Jr	Rowa 1770
READ, Robert	Cart 1779	Alexander Sr	Rowa 1770
READING, John	Wilk 1782	Andrew	Oran 1779
READY, John	Chow 1785	Benj	Gate 1789
REAGAN, Charles & sons		Benj	Perq 1787
	Bute 1766	Charles	Crav 1779
Edward	Rowa 1761	Christian	Bert 1774
James	Bute 1766	Christian	Bert 1781
Jesse	Bute 1766	Dempsey	Warr 1784
John	Bute 1766	Eldad	Rowa 1770
John	Rowa 1770	Field	Gran 1785
Joseph	Bute 1766	Frederick	Nash 1782
Peter	Bute 1766	George	Rowa 1761
Powell	Bute 1766	George	Rowa 1770
Thomas	Blad 1784	George	Casw 1784
Wm	Rowa 1768	George	Rowa 1770
REAP, Peter	Rowa 1770	Griffin	Hali 1783
REARDEN, Ann	Wilk 1782	Hambleton	Hert 1784
Henry	Gran 1785	Henry	Rowa 1770
John	Wilk 1784	Hugh	Rowa 1770
Michael	Beau 1779	Isaac	Crav 1779
REAVES, Ameriah	Oran 1779	Isaac	Gate 1789
Edward	Blad 1784	Jacob	Bert 1774
Geo	Wilk 1782	James	Rowa 1770
George	Oran 1779	James	Perq 1787
John	Oran 1779	Jesse	Hali 1783
REDDICK, David	Mart 1779	John	Rowa 1770
Jacob	Perq 1787	John	Casw 1786
James	Mart 1779	John	Gran 1785
John	Dobb 1780	John	Hali 1783
John	Mart 1779	John	Bert 1774
Josiah	Perq 1787	John	Wilk 1782
Mary	Chow 1785	John	Gran 1771
Robert	Perq 1787	Joseph	Rowa 1761
Ruth	Perq 1787	Joseph	Rowa 1770
Seth	Perq 1787	Joseph	Perq 1772

REED, Joseph	Wilk 1782		REEVES, Samuel	Gran 1785
Joseph	Surr 1782		Samuel	Mont 1782
Joseph	Surr 1782		Solomon	Brun 1782
Medad	Rowa 1770		Wm	Rowa 1770
Moses	Hali 1783		Wm	Rowa 1768
Nathan	Rowa 1761		Wm	Wayn 1786
Nathaniel	Casw 1786		Wm	Gran 1785
Nathaniel	Casw 1784		Wm	Mont 1782
Nathaniel & so	Rowa 1770		Wm	NorH 1780
Nathl	Surr 1782		Wm	Gran 1771
Robert	Cart 1779		Wm & son Georg	Rowa 1770
Robert	Gran 1785		REGAN, Ann	Blad 1784
Robert	Wilk 1784		Charles	Warr 1784
Robert	Bert 1774		John	Blad 1784
Robert	Gran 1771		Ralph	Blad 1784
Samuel	Rowa 1770		Richard	Blad 1784
Thomas	Bute 1766		REGISTER, Benjamin	Samp 1784
Thomas	Oran 1779		John	Samp 1784
Thomas	Pasq 1779		John Sr	Samp 1784
Thomas	Warr 1784		Joseph	Samp 1784
Thomas	Perq 1772		Shadrack	Samp 1784
Thomas	Fran 1771		Silas Jr	Samp 1784
Tommy	Bert 1774		Thomas Jr	Samp 1784
Wm	Bute 1766		Thomas Sr	Samp 1784
Wm	Hali 1783		Wm	Samp 1784
Wm	Pasq 1779		REID, Andrew	Rowa 1768
Wm	Perq 1772		George	Rowa 1761
Wm	Curr 1779		John	Rowa 1768
Wm	Perq 1787		Joseph	Rowa 1761
Zerubabel	Gran 1771		Nathan	Rowa 1761
REEKS, Thomas	Gran 1785		Samuel	Ruth 1782
REEL, George	Rowa 1770		REIGHLEY, Mary	Hert 1779
James	Crav 1779		Sarah	Hert 1779
REES, Thomas	Cart 1779		REILLY, Andrew	Bute 1766
REESE, Abraham	Surr 1782		Morris & son A	Bute 1766
John	Casw 1784		REIZ, Matthew	Rowa 1770
Luke	John 1784		RELFE, Dorcas	Pasq 1779
Tobin	Mont 1782		Enoch	Psaq 1779
Valentine	Surr 1782		John	Pasq 1694
REESNER, Josiah	NorH 1780		John	Pasq 1779
REEVES, Allen	Gran 1785		Rebecca	Camd 1782
Benjamin	Rowa 1770		Robert	Pasq 1779
Burgess	Gran 1785		Thomas	Pasq 1694
David	Surr 1782		Thomas	Pasq 1779
Frederick	Gran 1785		Wm	Pasq 1694
George	Gran 1785		Wm	Pasq 1779
Isaac	Wilk 1782		RELSE, Dorcas	Pasq 1789
James	Rowa 1770		Eliz	Pasq 1789
James	Wilk 1782		Enoch	Pasq 1789
James	Surr 1782		Joseph	Pasq 1789
Jeremiah	Rowa 1770		Nathan	Pasq 1789
Jesse	Surr 1782		RENCHER, Abraham	Rowa 1770
John	Ruth 1782		RENSHAW, Thomas	Rowa 1768
John	Wayn 1786		RENTFRO, Jacob	Wayn 1786
John	NorH 1780		James	Wayn 1786
John Jr	Gran 1785		Wm	Wayn 1786
John Sr	Gran 1785		RESCESS, Robert	Beau 1786
Jonathan	Gran 1771		Thomas	Beau 1786
Josias	Mont 1782		RESSER, Isham	Hali 1783
Malachi	Gran 1785		RESTES, Thomas	Beau 1786
Malachi	Gran 1771		RESTESS, Esther	Beau 1786
Mark	Brun 1784		John	Beau 1786
Mark	Brun 1782		Polly	Beau 1786
Matthew	Blad 1784		Richard	Beau 1786
Samuel	Rowa 1770		Thomas	Beau 1786

REUDETT, Alexr	Beau 1786	RHODES, Robert	Bert 1781
Louis	Beau 1786	Stephen	Tyrr 1784
REUTER, Christian	Rowa 1770	Thomas	Oran 1779
REVELL, Edmund	Blad 1784	Thomas	Bert 1781
Edmund	Wayn 1786	Wm	Oran 1779
Elijah	Nash 1782	Wm	Samp 1784
Matthew	Hert 1779	Wm Jr	Wayn 1786
Micajah	Nash 1782	RHONE, Thomas	Casw 1786
Nathaniel	Samp 1784	RIBELS, Mary	Hert 1784
Simphey	NorH 1780	RICE, Asa	Casw 1786
Solomon	Brun 1784	Benjamin	Ruth 1782
REVIER, Richard	Warr 1784	Daniel	Oran 1779
REVIS, George	Ruth 1782	David	Gate 1789
REX, Thomas	Bute 1766	Edward	Wilk 1782
REYNOLDS, Abraham	Blad 1784	Eliz	Gate 1789
Abraham	Brun 1782	Ephraim	Crav 1779
Amy	Wilk 1782	Evan	Crav 1779
Chas	Wilk 1782	Haines	Gran 1785
Christopher	Dobb 1780	Hardy	Gate 1789
Dudley	Casw 1784	Hezekiah	Casw 1786
Elisha	Wilk 1782	Hezekiah	Casw 1784
Ezekiel	Surr 1782	Isaac	Ruth 1782
Francis	Wilk 1782	James	Casw 1786
Hamilton	Casw 1784	James	Wilk 1782
Humphrey	Blad 1784	James	Gate 1789
James	Rowa 1768	Jefferson	Casw 1786
James	Wilk 1784	Jephthah	Casw 1786
James	Wilk 1782	Jeptha	Casw 1784
Jeremiah	Rowa 1761	John	Nash 1782
Jeremiah	Rowa 1768	John	Casw 1786
Jesse	Hert 1784	John	Casw 1784
Mark	Blad 1784	John	Gran 1785
Mark	Jone 1779	John	Gate 1789
Mathew	Wilk 1782	John Jr	Casw 1784
Richard Jr	Blad 1784	John Sr	Casw 1784
Richard Sr	Blad 1784	Micajah	Gate 1789
Thomas	Rowa 1768	Moses	Ruth 1782
Wm	Rowa 1761	Nathan	Casw 1786
Wm	Blad 1784	Nathan	Casw 1784
Wm	Brun 1784	Nathaniel	Casw 1786
Wm	Wilk 1782	Nathaniel	Casw 1784
Wm & son Henry	Rowa 1770	Samuel	Wilk 1782
RHEEM, Jacob	Dobb 1780	Simon	Pasq 1694
RHEW, John	Oran 1779	Thomas	Oran 1779
RHODES, Abraham	Hert 1784	Thomas	Casw 1786
Aquilla	Oran 1779	Thomas	Casw 1784
Arthur	Tyrr 1784	Thomas	Wilk 1782
Benjamin	Oran 1779	Wm	Samp 1784
Elisha	Bert 1781	Wm	Casw 1786
Henry	Bert 1774	Wm	Casw 1784
Henry	Onsl 1771	Wm	Mont 1782
Henry	Bert 1781	Wm	Bert 1781
Henry Jr	Bert 1781	Wm H	Casw 1784
Henry Sr	Bert 1781	Wm H	Casw 1786
Isaac	Bert 1781	Zachariah	Dobb 1780
Jacob	Wayn 1786	Zeri	Casw 1784
James	Wayn 1786	Zerubabel	Gran 1785
James	Bert 1781	RICH, Isaac	Onsl 1771
John	Oran 1779	John	Rowa 1770
John Jr	Oran 1779	John	Rowa 1768
John Jr	Bert 1781	John	Samp 1784
John Sr	Bert 1781	John	Pasq 1779
Leven	Tyrr 1784	John	Onsl 1771
Penelope	Bert 1781	John	NorH 1780
Richard	Oran 1779	Lot	Samp 1784

RICH, Mary	Samp 1784	RICHARDSON, Thomas	Casw 1784
Obadiah	Pasq 1789	Thomas	Pasq 1779
Thomas	Oran 1779	Thomas	Pasq 1789
RICHARD, Respes	Beau 1786	Tobias	Pasq 1779
RICHARDS, George	Bute 1766	Wm	Nash 1782
James	Brun 1784	Wm	Bute 1766
James	Pasq 1789	Wm	Hali 1783
John	Cart 1779	Wm	John 1784
John	Bute 1766	Wm	Pasq 1789
John	Oran 1779	RICHESON, Daniel	Wilk 1782
John	Jone 1779	RICHEY, John	Rowa 1770
John	NBer 1779	Samuel	Rowa 1768
John	NorH 1780	Wm	Rowa 1768
Maurice	Blad 1784	Wm	Rowa 1770
Ralph	Beau 1786	Wm & son John	Rowa 1770
Richard	Hali 1783	RICHMOND, James	Casw 1786
Thomas	Beau 1786	John	Casw 1786
Walter	Rowa 1770	John Sr	Casw 1786
Wm	Bute 1766	Matthew	Casw 1786
Wm	Oran 1779	Wm	Casw 1786
Wm	Perq 1772	RICHTER, Johannes	Rowa 1770
Wm	Perq 1787	RICK, Jacob	NorH 1780
RICHARDSON, Adiston	Casw 1784	Thomas	Gran 1771
Alex	Wilk 1782	Wm	NorH 1780
Ann	Pasq 1779	RICKER, Jacob	Rowa 1761
Appelew	John 1784	Jacob Jr	Rowa 1770
Benj	Onsl 1771	RICKETTS, Reason	Oran 1779
Benj	Pasq 1789	Samuel	Oran 1779
Benjamin	Hali 1783	RICKHOUSE, Absalom	Beau 1786
Benjamin	Pasq 1779	RICKMAN, Mark	Hali 1783
Daniel	Pasq 1789	RICKS, Abraham	Nash 1782
Edward	Bute 1766	Ann	Nash 1782
Evan	Pasq 1779	Isaac	Nash 1782
James	Nash 1782	Isaac	Hali 1783
James	Casw 1786	Jacob	Nash 1782
James	Blad 1784	Joel	Nash 1782
James	Casw 1784	John	Nash 1782
James	Wilk 1784	John	Hali 1783
Jeremiah	Tyrr 1784	Thomas	Nash 1782
John	Camd 1782	Wm	Nash 1782
John	Blad 1784	RICe, Thomas	Casw 1786
John	Pasq 1789	RIDDELL, Isaiah	Bert 1774
John Jr	Pasq 1779	Peter	Bert 1774
John Sr	Pasq 1779	RIDDENCE, Wm Jr	Rowa 1770
Joseph	Camd 1782	Wm Sr	Rowa 1770
Joseph	Pasq 1779	RIDDENS, David	Surr 1782
Joseph	Pasq 1789	John	Surr 1782
Lal	Casw 1786	Millie	Surr 1782
Lawrence	Casw 1786	Wm	Surr 1782
Lawrence	Casw 1784	RIDDICK, Abraham	Gate 1789
Lebus	Pasq 1789	Alexander	Bert 1781
Mathias	Surr 1782	Benjamin	Rowa 1768
Moses	Casw 1784	Christopher	Gate 1789
Richard	Pasq 1789	David	Perq 1772
Robert	Blad 1784	Jacob	Perq 1772
Robert	Wilk 1784	Job	Gate 1789
Samuel	Rowa 1768	John	Rowa 1768
Samuel	Blad 1784	John	Rowa 1770
Samuel	Pasq 1779	John	Perq 1772
Stephen	Camd 1782	John	Gate 1789
Stephen	Pasq 1779	Joseph	Rowa 1768
Stephen	Pasq 1789	Joseph	Rowa 1770
Thomas	Nash 1782	Joseph	Perq 1772
Thomas	Casw 1786	Joseph	Gate 1789
Thomas	Blad 1784	Josiah	Bert 1781

RIDDICK, Micajah	Gate 1789	RILEY, Jacob	Oran 1779
Mills	Gate 1789	James	Rowa 1768
Nathan	Perq 1772	James	Rowa 1770
Peter	Bert 1781	James	Oran 1779
Reuben	Gate 1789	John	Oran 1779
Silas	Perq 1772	Phillip	Beau 1786
Willis	Gate 1789	Wm	Brun 1784
RIDDICKS, Seth	Gate 1789	RIMER, James	Casw 1784
RIDDLE, Bazel	Surr 1782	RING, James	Hali 1783
John	Mont 1782	John	Hali 1783
Stephen	Rowa 1761	Thomas	Gran 1771
Stephen	Rowa 1770	RINZE, Frederick	John 1784
RIDER, Henry	Rowa 1770	RIPLEY, Ann	Pasq 1789
Michael	Rowa 1770	Spencer	Pasq 1779
Stuffie	Rowa 1770	Wm	Cart 1779
RIDGE, Godfrey	Rowa 1768	RIPPEY, Edward	Oran 1779
Winny	Surr 1782	Mathew	Oran 1779
Wm	Rowa 1768	RISDON, Wm	Rowa 1770
RIDGEN, Frederick	Wayn 1786	RISING, James	Blad 1784
RIDLEY, Arthur	Hert 1779	RISTON, Millie	NorH 1780
Bromfield	Gran 1771	RISTOP, Thomas	Beau 1779
Broomfield	Gran 1785	Thomas Jr	Beau 1779
Elizabeth	Hert 1784	RITTER, James	Surr 1782
Martha	Hert 1779	Moses	Samp 1784
RIFFIN, James	Mart 1779	Wm	Gate 1789
RIFTUSS, John	Beau 1779	RIVELL, Matthew	Hert 1784
Richard	Beau 1779	RIVER, Don	Jone 1779
RIGAN, Jesse	Warr 1784	RIVERS, Joshua	Warr 1784
John	Warr 1784	RIVETTE, George	Hert 1779
RIGBY, Spencer	Perq 1772	RIX, James	Rowa 1768
RIGGAN, Charles	Warr 1784	ROACH, Charles	Crav 1779
Francis	Warr 1784	David	Crav 1779
Jacob	Warr 1784	James	Oran 1779
Jesse	Warr 1784	John	Samp 1784
John	Warr 1784	John	Hali 1783
RIGGELS, Mark	Rich 1790	John	Surr 1782
Mark	Rich 1790	Sasnitt	Wayn 1786
RIGGINS, Nehemiah	Pasq 1779	Thomas	Hali 1783
RIGGS, Abram	Camd 1782	ROADES, David	Camd 1782
Bethuel	Wilk 1782	Hezekiah	Rowa 1770
Edward	Rowa 1770	Jacob	Dobb 1780
George	Oran 1779	Jacob	Rowa 1770
Giles	Crav 1779	Jacob	Rowa 1768
Isaac	Camd 1782	John	Bute 1766
James	Beau 1779	John	Rowa 1770
James	Curr 1779	Levin	Camd 1782
James	Beau 1786	Samuel	Camd 1782
Jesse	Cart 1779	Thomas	Camd 1782
John	Oran 1779	Wm	Camd 1782
John	Pasq 1779	ROADS, Henry	Bert 1774
John	Beau 1779	John	Bert 1774
John	Crav 1779	Joseph	Cart 1779
Noah	Camd 1782	Wm Jr	Bert 1774
Saml	Surr 1782	Wm Sr	Bert 1774
Timothy	Ruth 1782	ROADSMITH, Paul	Rowa 1768
Wm	Camd 1782	ROAN, Adam	Rowa 1761
Zadock	Surr 1782	Henry	Rowa 1761
RIGHT, Simon	Jone 1779	Henry	Rowa 1770
RIGHTON, Wm	Chow 1785	Henry	Mont 1782
RIGSBY, James	Curr 1779	Henry(Grandson	Rowa 1770
Jesse	Oran 1779	Jesse	Hali 1783
RIKE, Christopher	Oran 1779	John	Hali 1783
RILEY, Daniel	Surr 1782	Lewis	Hali 1783
Edward	Oran 1779	Peter	Rowa 1770
Edward Jr	Oran 1779	Wm Jr	Hali 1783

ROAN, Wm Sr	Hali 1783	ROBERTS, Edward	Rowa 1761
ROARK, Barnabas Jr	Surr 1782	Edward	Rowa 1770
Barnabas Sr	Surr 1782	Edward	Onsl 1771
Bryant	Rowa 1770	Edward Sr	Rowa 1770
David	Rowa 1770	Elizabeth	Chow 1785
Nicholas	Brun 1784	Elizabeth	Wilk 1784
ROBB, Thomas	Curr 1779	Elizabeth	Wilk 1782
ROBBINS, Arthur	Brun 1784	Francis	Hali 1783
Isaac	Rowa 1761	Francis	Wilk 1784
Isaac	Rowa 1768	George	Gran 1785
Jacob	Rowa 1768	George	Wilk 1784
Jacob	Rowa 1770	Ishmael	Dobb 1780
James	Rowa 1768	Jacob	Wilk 1782
James	Rowa 1770	James	Rowa 1770
Jethro	Blad 1784	James	Casw 1784
John	Rowa 1770	James	Chow 1785
John	Mont 1782	James	WilK 1782
John	Gate 1789	James	NorH 1780
Jonathan	Rowa 1770	James	Gate 1789
Joseph	Rowa 1768	James Sr	Dobb 1780
Joseph	Rowa 1770	John	Cart 1779
Martha	Brun 1782	John	Dobb 1780
Mathias	Rowa 1761	John	Rowa 1770
Mathias	Rowa 1770	John	Oran 1779
Michael	Rowa 1761	John	Casw 1786
Michael	Rowa 1768	John	Wayn 1786
Michael	Rowa 1770	John	Casw 1784
Reuben	Wilk 1782	John	Chow 1785
Richard	Rowa 1761	John	Warr 1779
Richard	Rowa 1768	John	Perq 1772
Richard	Rowa 1770	John	Wilk 1784
Wm	Ruth 1782	John	Wilk 1782
Wm	Rowa 1761	John	NorH 1780
Wm	Rowa 1768	John	Surr 1782
Wm	Rowa 1770	John	Perq 1787
Wm & son John	Rowa 1768	Jonathan	Gate 1789
Wm & son John	Rowa 1770	Joseph	Gran 1785
ROBBS, Wm	Oran 1779	Joseph	Gran 1771
ROBBUNS, Isaac	Rowa 1770	Morris	Ruth 1782
ROBER, John	Hali 1783	Nathan	Rowa 1768
ROBERSON, Arthur	Bute 1766	Olive	Surr 1782
Christopher	Bute 1766	Owen	Bert 1774
Cornelius	Mont 1782	Richard	Gran 1771
Edward	Casw 1786	Rosanna	Wilk 1782
Eliz	Perq 1787	Rosannah	Wilk 1784
Ferris	Mont 1782	Samuel	Dobb 1780
George	Warr 1779	Shadrack	Roea 1768
Jacob	Surr 1782	Shadrack	Gran 1785
John	Bute 1766	Solomon	Perq 1787
John	Casw 1786	Stephen	NorH 1780
John	Wilk 1782	Thomas	Dobb 1780
Luke	Mont 1782	Thomas	Gran 1785
Thomas	Casw 1786	Thomas	John 1784
Wm	Surr 1782	Thomas	Perq 1787
ROBERT, James	Surr 1782	Thomas Jr	Chow 1785
ROBERTS, Absalom	Oran 1779	Thomas Sr	Chow 1785
Benj	Perq 1787	Vincent	Casw 1786
Benjamin	Perq 1772	Willis	Chow 1785
Bennett	Wilk 1784	Willis	Gran 1785
Britton	John 1784	Wincher	Curr 1779
Charles	Oran 1779	Wm	Cart 1779
Charles Jr	Oran 1779	Wm	Bute 1766
David	Casw 1784	Wm	Rowa 1770
Edmund	Casw 1784	Wm	Chow 1785
Edward	Rowa 1768	Wm	Gran 1785

Wm	John 1784	ROBESON, John	Surr 1782
Wm	Warr 1784	Peter	Blad 1784
Wm	Wilk 1784	Taddy	Rich 1790
Wm	Mont 1782	Taddy	Rich 1790
Wm	Wilk 1782	Thomas	Blad 1784
Wm	Gran 1771	Wm	Rich 1790
Wm	Perq 1787	Wm	Rich 1790
ROBERTSON, Andrew	Surr 1782	ROBEY, Demsey	Gran 1771
Ann	Hali 1783	Wm	Pasq 1789
Athaniel	Oran 1779	ROBINS, John	Wilk 1782
Benjamin	Rowa 1768	John	Surr 1782
Buckner	Gran 1785	John Jr	Wilk 1782
Burwell	Warr 1784	Thomas	Wilk 1782
Charles	Casw 1784	Wm	Warr 1784
Christopher	Warr 1784	Wm	Perq 1787
David	Oran 1779	ROBINSON, Allen	Cart 1779
David	Casw 1784	Andrew	Oran 1779
Elisha	NorH 1780	Ann	Cart 1779
Elizabeth	Hert 1779	Ann	Bert 1774
Elizabeth	Camd 1782	Chas Jr	Rich 1790
George	Cart 1779	Chas Jr	Rich 1790
George	Curr 1779	Daniel	Oran 1779
Hardy	Wayn 1786	David	Mart 1779
Hardy	Beau 1786	David	Wilk 1784
Henry	Hali 1783	Edward	Oran 1779
Henry	NorH 1780	George	Rowa 1768
Henry	NorH 1780	George	Rowa 1770
Henry	Beau 1786	Henry	Rowa 1768
Isham	Warr 1784	Henry Sr	Mart 1779
Israel	Wayn 1786	Jacob	Beau 1786
James	Pasq 1694	James	Rowa 1768
James	Warr 1784	James	Oran 1779
James	Bert 1781	James	Mart 1779
Jemimah	Warr 1784	James	Casw 1784
John	Rowa 1770	James	Bert 1774
John	Brun 1784	James Jr	Rowa 1768
John	Beau 1779	Joel	Oran 1779
John	Wilk 1782	John	Rowa 1768
John	OnsL 1771	John	Rowa 1770
John	Surr 1782	John	Oran 1779
John	Bert 1781	John	Chow 1785
John	Pasq 1789	John	Perq 1772
John Jr	Curr 1779	John	Wilk 1784
John Sr	Oran 1779	John	Bert 1774
Josiah	Perq 1787	John	Gran 1771
Mary	NorH 1780	John Sr	Mart 1779
Nicholas	Gran 1785	Joseph	Rowa 1770
Peggy	Pasq 1789	Joseph	Casw 1784
Peter	Nash 1782	Luke	Mart 1779
Peter	Warr 1784	Mary	Gran 1785
Thomas	Curr 1779	Mary	Beau 1779
Thomas	Gate 1789	Nathanl	Gran 1771
Thomas	Perq 1787	Nicholas	Gran 1771
Wm	Cart 1779	Reubin	Wilk 1784
Wm	Ruth 1782	Richard	Rowa 1768
Wm	Hert 1784	Robert	Gran 1771
Wm	Warr 1784	Robert Jr	Gran 1785
Wm	Gate 1789	Robert Sr	Gran 1785
Wm	Bert 1781	Samuel	Casw 1784
Zachariah	Rowa 1770	Samuel	Bert 1774
ROBESON, Chas	Rich 1790	Thomas	Casw 1784
Chas	Rich 1790	Thomas	Gran 1785
Chas Sr	Rich 1790	Thomas	Perq 1772
Chas Sr	Rich 1790	Wm	Rowa 1768
Geo	Surr 1782	Wm	Rowa 1770

ROBINSON, Wm	Mart 1779	ROGERS, Sam	NorH 1780
Wm	Samp 1784	Samuel	Mont 1782
Wm	Blad 1784	Sarah	Gate 1789
Wm	Gran 1785	Spencer	Curr 1779
Wm	Perq 1772	Stephen	Gate 1789
Wm	Bert 1774	Thomas	Nash 1782
ROBNINSON, Henry	Tyrr 1784	Thomas	Pasq 1694
ROBSON, Dennis	Dobb 1780	Wm	Dobb 1780
ROCHELLE, John	Gate 1789	Wm	Oran 1779
ROCHESTER, Nathaniel		Wm	Mart 1779
	Oran 1779	Wm	Gran 1785
RODDA, John	Chow 1785	Wm	Jone 1779
Mary	Chow 1785	Wm	Rich 1790
RODEN, Peter	Bert 1781	Wm	Rich 1790
RODET, Francis	Chow 1785	Zelpha	Gate 1789
RODGERS, Aers	Tyrr 1784	ROGERSON, Daniel	Perq 1772
Benjamin	Bert 1774	John	Blad 1784
James	Dupl 1783	John	Perq 1787
John	Brun 1784	Josiah	Perq 1787
John	Tyrr 1784	Mary	Perq 1787
Joseph	Hert 1784	ROLAND, Ajasia	Mont 1782
Major	Curr 1779	Augustine	Mont 1782
Mary	Bert 1774	F.	Casw 1786
Minute	Bert 1774	James	Mont 1782
Thomas	Tyrr 1784	John	Beau 1779
Wm	Bert 1774	John	Beau 1786
RODWELL, John	Warr 1784	Richard	Mont 1782
ROE, Beverly	Crav 1779	Richard Jr	Mont 1782
Cornelius	Rowa 1770	Robert	Beau 1779
James	Beau 1786	Sherwood	Mont 1782
John	Crav 1779	Wm	Rowa 1770
Joshua	Beau 1786	ROLLINGS, Sarah	Beau 1779
Richard	Beau 1786	ROLLINS, Charles	Bute 1766
Robert	Beau 1786	Drury	John 1784
Robt	Perq 1787	Escala	Rowa 1770
Thomas	Crav 1779	Ezekiel	Curr 1779
ROGERS, Daniel	Cart 1779	Saml	Gate 1789
Daniel	Surr 1782	ROLLISON, Francis	Curr 1779
Enos	Gate 1789	Wm Jr	Curr 1779
Hugh	Oran 1779	Wm Sr	Curr 1779
Isham	Surr 1782	ROMBAUGH, Wm	Chow 1785
Isom	Wayn 1786	ROMENGER, Jacob	Surr 1782
James	Hert 1779	Michael	Surr 1782
James	Hert 1784	RONALD, George	Mont 1782
James	Rich 1790	James	Mont 1782
James	Rich 1790	Thomas Jr	Mont 1782
Jethro	Onsl 1771	Thomas Sr	Mont 1782
John	Gran 1785	RONE, Charles	Warr 1779
John	Brun 1782	RONEY, Benjamin	Oran 1779
John	Brun 1782	James	Oran 1779
John	Mont 1782	John	Hali 1783
John	Surr 1782	Wm	Hali 1783
Jonathan	Hert 1779	ROOK, Benj	NorH 1780
Jonathan	Hert 1784	John Jr	NorH 1780
Jonathan	Gate 1789	Joseph	Gate 1789
Joseph	Chow 1785	ROOKER, John	Gran 1785
Joseph	Gran 1785	John	Warr 1784
Joseph	Hert 1784	ROOKS, Charity, widow	
Joseph	Gran 1771		Mart 1779
Mark	Brun 1782	Dempsey	Hert 1784
Milly	Gate 1789	Jacob	Bert 1774
Minute	Bert 1781	Joseph Sr	Gate 1789
Nicholas	John 1784	Wm	Crav 1779
Phillip	Gate 1789	ROPER, Abraham	NorH 1780
Robert	Nash 1782	David	Ruth 1782

ROPER, James	Casw 1784	ROSS, James	Oran 1779
Jesse	NorH 1780	James	Surr 1782
Wm	Casw 1784	James Jr	Bute 1766
ROSBURY, Philip	Onsl 1771	John	Mart 1779
ROSCOE, Arthur	Bert 1781	John	Beau 1779
Thomas	Bert 1781	John	Surr 1782
Wm	Bert 1781	John son of Wm	Mart 1779
ROSE, Alexander	Casw 1784	Levin	Crav 1779
Benj	Wilk 1782	Lewis	Pitt 1786
Benjamin	Casw 1786	Lucy	Nash 1782
Burwell	Nash 1782	Lydia	Camd 1782
Emanuel	Wilk 1782	Mary	Beau 1786
Emmanuel	Rowa 1770	Nathan	Mart 1779
Francis	Nash 1782	Solomon	Gate 1789
Francis	Rowa 1770	Williamson	Nash 1782
Francis Jr	Rowa 1770	Wm	Ruth 1782
Frederick	Gran 1785	Wm & son John	Mart 1779
Howell	Gran 1785	ROSSER, James	John 1784
James	Hert 1779	John King	Warr 1784
James	Hert 1784	Joseph	Perq 1787
John	Bute 1766	Robert	Perq 1787
John	Rowa 1770	ROTH, Elijah	Beau 1779
John	Pasq 1779	Francis	Beau 1779
John	Wilk 1782	John	Gran 1771
John	Onsl 1771	ROTHRACK, Peter	Surr 1782
John	Beau 1786	ROTHRIE, Valentine	Surr 1782
Mary	Chow 1785	ROTTENBURY, John	Warr 1779
Mary	Beau 1779	ROUAN, Edward	Rowa 1770
Mary	Pasq 1789	ROUGHTON, Agnes	Tyrr 1784
Peter	Surr 1782	Daniel	Tyrr 1784
Samuel	Warr 1784	Edward	Tyrr 1784
Samuel	Wilk 1782	Richard	Tyrr 1784
Sarah	Surr 1782	ROUNSEVAL, Benjamin	Rowa 1770
Starling	Wilk 1782	David	Rowa 1770
Thomas	Hali 1783	Josiah	Rowa 1770
Thomas	Gran 1771	ROUNTREE, Eliz	Perq 1787
Wm	Pasq 1694	Francis	Crav 1779
Wm	Bute 1766	Holly	Gate 1789
Wm	Gran 1785	John	Bert 1774
Wm	Hali 1783	John	Crav 1779
Wm	Warr 1784	John	Gate 1789
ROSEBROUGH, James	Rowa 1770	John	Pitt 1786
John	Rowa 1770	Josiah	Gate 1789
Samuel	Rowa 1770	Levina	Gate 1789
Wm	Rowa 1770	Mary	Gate 1789
ROSENBAUM, Alexander		Miles	Gate 1789
	Rowa 1770	Moses	Pitt 1786
ROSHER, John Jr	Blad 1784	Obed	Bert 1774
John Sr	Blad 1784	Penny	Gate 1789
ROSS, Andrew	Oran 1779	Priscilla	Gate 1789
Ann	Warr 1784	Rachel	Crav 1779
Benj	Beau 1786	Rachel	Gate 1789
Charles	Crav 1779	Reuben	PItt 1786
Chas	Pitt 1786	Seth	Gate 1789
David	Jone 1779	Thomas	Oran 1779
David	Surr 1782	Wm	Pitt 1786
Edward	Bert 1774	ROURK, Samuel	Blad 1784
Edward	Crav 1779	ROURKE, Patrick	Beau 1786
Edward	Pitt 1786	ROUSE, Bartlett	Wayn 1786
Elijah	Beau 1786	Jesse	Dobb 1780
Francis	Beau 1786	John	Dobb 1780
Henry	Rowa 1770	Leonard	Rowa 1770
Hugh	Mart 1779	Phillip	Dupl 1783
James	Rowa 1770	Simon	Dobb 1780
James	Bute 1766	Solomon	Wayn 1786

ROUSE, Thomas	Wayn 1786		RUFFEN, Martha	NorH 1780
ROUSHAM, Edward	Tyrr 1784		Nathaniel	NorH 1780
ROVER, James	Casw 1784		RUFFIN, Aves	Wayn 1786
ROW, Christopher	Onsl 1771		Ethelred	Dobb 1780
ROWAN, Adam	Mont 1782		Wm	Bert 1781
Collas	Blad 1784		RUGBY, John	Wilk 1784
Esther	Blad 1784		RULES, Chas	Onsl 1771
Interdim	Surr 1782		RUMBLY, Edward	Cart 1779
John	Brun 1784		RUMMAGE, George	Mont 1782
John	Brun 1782		RUMOOR, Joseph	Jone 1779
Samuel	Blad 1784		RUMSEY, Wm	NBer 1779
ROWE, Ann	Pasq 1779		RUNCHEY, Adam	Dupl 1783
Cornelius	Rowa 1768		Moses	Dupl 1783
James	Beau 1779		RUNDALS, Wm	OnsL 1771
John	Nash 1782		RUNDLES, Jones	Surr 1782
John	Gran 1771		RUNNELS, Amos	Samp 1784
Joshua	Beau 1779		Dred	Samp 1784
Richard	Beau 1779		Ephraim	Cart 1779
Saml	Pasq 1789		Francis	Rowa 1770
Willis	Brun 1782		RUPERT, Onesimus	Rowa 1770
Wm	Nash 1782		RUSCHY, Adam	Dupl 1783
ROWELL, Fredk	NorH 1780		RUSE, John	Brun 1782
Samuel	Dobb 1780		RUSH, Benjamin	Bute 1766
ROWLAND, Elizabeth	Blad 1784		Benjamin	Rowa 1768
Francis	Gran 1771		Crawford	Rowa 1770
George	Curr 1779		Crawford & son	Rowa 1768
James	Blad 1784		Wm	Nash 1782
John	Blad 1784		Wm	Blad 1784
Jordan	Bute 1766		RUSS, David Jr	Blad 1784
Reuben	Wilk 1782		David Sr	Blad 1784
Samuel	Ruth 1782		Edmond	Blad 1784
Thomas	Ruth 1782		Eleazer	Blad 1784
Thomas	Blad 1784		John	Blad 1784
Thomas	Gran 1785		John	Brun 1784
Wm	Warr 1784		Jonathan	Blad 1784
Wm & sons Wm	Bute 1766		Joseph	Blad 1784
ROWLING, Bartholomew			Thomas	Blad 1784
	Bute 1766		Thomas	Brun 1784
Charles	Bute 1766		Wm	Blad 1784
Chas	Wilk 1782		RUSSELL, Benjamin	Cart 1779
Miriam	Bute 1766		Buckner	Surr 1782
Wm	Bute 1766		Charles	Rowa 1770
ROYAL, Daniel	Crav 1779		David	Cart 1779
James	Rowa 1770		Elizabeth	Chow 1785
James	Crav 1779		Geo	Gate 1789
John	Rowa 1761		George	Rowa 1770
John & son Jam	Rowa 1770		Hillyer	Wilk 1782
Joshua	Rowa 1770		James	Bute 1766
Wm	Gran 1785		James	Mont 1782
ROYSTER, Wm Jr	Gran 1785		Jane	Oran 1779
Wm Sr	Gran 1785		Jeremiah	Ruth 1782
ROYSTON, Luke	Brun 1784		John	Cart 1779
ROZAN, Reuben	Blad 1784		John	Ruth 1782
ROZAR, DanieL	Blad 1784		John	Gran 1785
David	Blad 1784		John	Brun 1782
Shadrack	Hali 1783		John	Wilk 1782
ROZELL, John	Camd 1782		John	Gran 1771
RUDD, Thomas	Perq 1787		John & son Jam	Rowa 1768
RUDEN, Henry	Rowa 1770		John Sr	Curr 1779
RUDOLPH, Wm & son Johns			Mary	Ruth 1782
	Rowa 1770		Nicholas	Bute 1766
RUDYNAKER, Wm	Beau 1786		Robert	Rowa 1768
RUFF, Daniel	Dobb 1780		Samuel	Blad 1784
John	Oran 1779		Samuel	Chow 1785
RUFFEN, Dominica	NorH 1780		Thomas	Cart 1779

RUSSELL, Thomas	Blad 1784	RYE, Dun	Rich 1790
Thomas	Pasq 1789	Solomon	Rich 1790
Twitty	Warr 1784	Solomon	Rich 1790
Wm	Bute 1766	RYLAND, Philip	Samp 1784
Wm	Rowa 1770		
Wm	Warr 1784		
Wm	Curr 1779		
Wm	Wilk 1782	SADDLER, Jesse	Gran 1785
RUST, George	Gran 1785	SADE, Samuel	Hali 1783
John	Gran 1785	SAFFRON, Wm	Surr 1782
RUSTULL, John	Cart 1779	SAGE, Wm	John 1784
RUTH, Jacob	Surr 1782	SAIL, Cornelius	Wilk 1784
Jacob	Surr 1782	Dixon	John 1784
Jean	Rowa 1761	John	John 1784
RUTHERFORD, Griffith		John	Wilk 1784
	Rowa 1770	Thomas	Wilk 1784
Patrick	Oran 1779	SAIN, John	Warr 1784
Wm	Casw 1784	SAINSING, Charles	Warr 1784
RUTLAND, Abednego	Hert 1784	James	Warr 1784
Abednego	NorH 1780	Peter	Warr 1784
Chadwick	Hali 1783	SAINT, Daniel	Perq 1787
Charity	NorH 1780	Samuel	Wayn 1786
Jackson	NorH 1780	Samuel	Tyrr 1784
James	Bert 1774	Thomas	Tyrr 1784
James	Bert 1781	Thomas	Perq 1787
John	Bert 1774	SAKEY, John	Surr 1782
John	Bert 1781	SALE, Cornelius	Wilk 1782
Martha	NorH 1780	John	Wilk 1782
Mesic	NorH 1780	Leonard	Wilk 1782
Neilson	NorH 1780	Thomas	Wilk 1782
Roderick	Bert 1781	Wm	Wilk 1784
Sarah	Wilk 1782	Wm	Wilk 1782
Shadrack	Hert 1779	SALKIL, Isaac	Samp 1784
Thomas	NorH 1780	SALL, Stephen	Pasq 1779
Wm	Hert 1784	SALLEY, Peter	Surr 1782
Wm	NorH 1780	SALLINGS, James	John 1784
Wm Jr	Hert 1779	SALLY, Adam	Ruth 1782
RUTLEDGE, James	Oran 1779	George	Ruth 1782
Mary	Surr 1782	SALMON, John	Rowa 1770
Thomas	Dupl 1783	John	Warr 1784
Wm	Rowa 1768	Richard	Samp 1784
Wm	Wilk 1784	SALTER, Henry	Cart 1779
Wm	Wilk 1782	James	Cart 1779
Wm	Surr 1782	James	Blad 1784
Wm Jr	Surr 1782	John	Beau 1786
RUTTER, Michael	Rowa 1770	Peter	Perq 1787
RYALL, Duke	Samp 1784	Wm	Cart 1779
John	Rowa 1761	Wm	Blad 1784
John	Samp 1784	Wm	Tyrr 1784
Joseph	Rowa 1761	SALTS, Anthony	Rowa 1761
Ormand	Samp 1784	Boston	Rowa 1761
Thomas	Samp 1784	SALYER, John	Onsl 1771
Willis	Samp 1784	Samuel Jr	Curr 1779
Wm	Samp 1784	Samuel Sr	Curr 1779
Wright	Samp 1784	SAMBO, Joseph	Brun 1784
Young Owen	Samp 1784	SAMPSON, James	Samp 1784
RYAN, Ann	Bert 1781	James	Crav 1779
Geo	Bert 1781	James	Pasq 1789
George	Bert 1774	John	Samp 1784
James	Bert 1774	John	Casw 1786
James	Curr 1779	Joshua	Pasq 1789
RYBUN, Henry	Jone 1779	Stephen	Hali 1783
RYE, Absalom	Rich 1790	SAMSON, Penelope	Bert 1781
Absalom	Rich 1790	SAMUEL, Ann	Casw 1784
Dun	Rich 1790	Anthony	Casw 1784

SAMUEL, Archibald	Casw 1784	SANDERS, Nahum	Gran 1771
August	Surr 1782	Richard	Dobb 1780
George	Casw 1784	Richard	Casw 1784
George Jr	Casw 1784	Richard	Perq 1772
Mordica	Wilk 1784	Richard	Perq 1787
Reuben	Surr 1782	Richard	Pasq 1789
SANDEFER, John	Hert 1779	Robert	Nash 1782
SANDEFORD, Tomkins	Nash 1782	Samuel	Cart 1779
Wm	Nash 1782	Smith	Casw 1786
SANDEFUR, James	Wayn 1786	Sophia	Cart 1779
John	Wayn 1786	Stephen	Perq 1772
Joseph	Wayn 1786	Stephen	Perq 1787
Robert	Hert 1784	Thomas	Nash 1782
SANDERLIN, Devotion	Camd 1782	Thomas	Cart 1779
Ezekiel	Camd 1782	Thomas	Samp 1784
Jacob	Camd 1782	Thomas	Wayn 1786
James	Camd 1782	Thomas	Surr 1782
John	Camd 1782	Thomas	Perq 1787
John	Beau 1786	Wm	Bute 1766
Joseph	Camd 1782	Wm	Rowa 1770
Levi	Camd 1782	Wm	Wayn 1786
Robert	Camd 1782	Wm	NBer 1779
Robert	Samp 1784	Wm	Bert 1774
Thomas	Camd 1782	Wm	NorH 1780
SANDERLY, John	Beau 1779	Wm	Perq 1787
SANDERS, Adam	Casw 1784	Wm Capt	Casw 1784
Alexander	NBer 1779	Wm Jr	Casw 1784
Archibald	Blad 1784	Wm Jr & bro Jo	Bute 1766
Benj	Perq 1787	SANDERSON, Benjamin	Jone 1779
Benjamin	Wayn 1786	Jesse	Curr 1779
Benjamin	Perq 1772	John	Curr 1779
Charles	Jone 1779	Joseph	Jone 1779
David	Hert 1779	Richard	Curr 1779
Evan	Psaq 1789	Richardson	Perq 1787
Francis	Wilk 1784	SANDERY, Jesse	Surr 1782
Francis	Wilk 1782	Levi	Jone 1779
George	Mont 1782	SANDIFUR, John	Hert 1784
Isaac	Mont 1782	John Jr	Hert 1784
James	Cart 1779	SANDISH, Joseph	Gran 1785
James	Rowa 1770	SANDLEY, Jeremiah	Gran 1785
James	Casw 1784	SANDS, John	Jone 1779
James	NBer 1779	Phillip	Beau 1786
James	Surr 1782	SANDUTEN, Maximillian	
Jesse	Gran 1771		Pasq 1779
John	Nash 1782	SANDY, Jeremiah	Bute 1766
John	Hert 1779	SANFORD, Henry	Gran 1785
John	Cart 1779	Isaiah	Gran 1785
John	Perq 1772	Jesse	Gran 1785
John	Perq 1772	Jesse	Surr 1782
John	Surr 1782	John	Gran 1785
John	Perq 1787	John	Hali 1783
John & son Tom	Bute 1766	John	Surr 1782
Joseph	Onsl 1771	Josiah	Gran 1785
Joseph	Perq 1787	Moses	Gran 1785
Joseph	Pasq 1789	Stephen	Gran 1785
Joshua	Perq 1787	Wm	Surr 1782
Kirby	Bute 1766	Wm H	Surr 1782
Lowry	Pasq 1789	Zechariah	Hali 1783
Mary	Hert 1779	SAPINGFIELD, Mathias	
Mary	Jone 1779		Rowa 1761
Mary	Perq 1772	SAPP, Benj	Surr 1782
Matthew	Surr 1782	Jesse	Surr 1782
Morrison	Perq 1772	SARGENT, David	Casw 1784
Moses	Dobb 1780	Stephen	Casw 1784
Moses	Wilk 1784	Thomas	Casw 1784

SARGENT, Wm	Casw 1784		SAVAGE, Thomas	Mart 1779
SARJENT, John	Surr 1782		Wm	Chow 1785
SARTAIN, Thomas	Gran 1785		Wm	Beau 1779
SARTON, Thomas	Hali 1783		Zack	Bert 1781
SARVER, James	NorH 1780		Zacker	Chow 1785
SASSER, Benjamin	Wayn 1786		SAVAS, Darrel	Curr 1779
Edith	Wayn 1786		SAVERY, Robert	Cart 1779
Joel	Wayn 1786		SAVILLE, James	Camd 1782
SATCHELL, Morris	Wayn 1786		John	Camd 1782
SATERNON, John	Gran 1785		Seth	Camd 1782
SATHREW, Stephen	Beau 1786		SAWKILL, John	Bert 1774
SATTERFIELD, Bidwell			SAWRY, Edward	NorH 1780
	Casw 1784		SAWYER, Alexander	Camd 1782
Geo	Rich 1790		Arthur	Camd 1782
Geo	Rich 1790		Asa	Camd 1782
James	Ruth 1782		Benjamin	Camd 1782
John	Casw 1784		Caleb	Camd 1782
Wm	Rich 1790		Caleb Sr	Camd 1782
Wm	Rich 1790		Charles	Camd 1782
SATTERWHITE, James	Gran 1785		Chas	Wilk 1782
Michael	Gran 1785		Coston	Camd 1782
Michael	Gran 1771		David	Camd 1782
Thomas	Gran 1785		David	Pasq 1779
SAUL, Absalom	Nash 1782		Dempsey	Pasq 1779
SAULS, Abraham	Blad 1784		Demsey	Camd 1782
James	Dobb 1780		Dennis	Tyrr 1784
Mary	Wayn 1786		Ebenezer	Pasq 1779
Ramon	Wayn 1786		Ebenezer	Pasq 1789
Rayman	Dobb 1780		Elisha	Camd 1782
Wm	Warr 1784		Ephraim	Tyrr 1784
SAULSON, John	Warr 1784		Evan	Camd 1782
SAUNDERS, Abram	Gate 1789		Hillary	Camd 1782
Benj	Gate 1789		Isaac	Tyrr 1784
Charity	Gate 1789		Isaac	Pasq 1779
David	Hert 1784		Isaac Jr	Pasq 1789
Elijah	Perq 1772		Isaac Sr	Pasq 1789
Henry	Bert 1774		Jabez	Camd 1782
Henry	Gate 1789		Jacob	Camd 1782
Jesse	Gate 1789		James	Camd 1782
John	Hert 1784		James	Pasq 1779
John	Warr 1784		Jeremiah	Camd 1782
John	Gate 1789		Jesse	Pasq 1779
John T.	Hert 1784		Joab	Tyrr 1784
Joseph	Bert 1774		Job	Camn 1782
Joseph	Gate 1789		Job #2	Camd 1782
Mary	John 1784		Joel	Camd 1782
Nathaniel	Hert 1784		John	Casw 1786
Patrick	Ruth 1782		John	Casw 1784
Poll	Casw 1786		John	Pasq 1779
Richard	Ruth 1782		John	Pasq 1789
Sarah	Gate 1789		Jonathan	Tyrr 1784
Wm	Casw 1786		Joseph	Camd 1782
Wm	John 1784		Lemuel	Camd 1782
Wm	Hert 1784		Levi	Camd 1782
Wm	Warr 1784		Lewis	Camd 1782
SAVAGE, Absalom	Bute 1766		Lot	Pssq 1789
Benjamin	Nash 1782		Margaret	Camd 1782
Britton	Mart 1779		Mary	Rowa 1761
Drury	Nash 1782		Mary	Camd 1782
Kinchen	Nash 1782		Peter	Tyrr 1784
Levin	Surr 1782		Priscilla	Pasq 1789
Loveless	Mart 1779		Richard	Tyrr 1784
Moses	Hert 1779		Robert	Tyrr 1784
Robert	Mart 1779		Shadrack	Camd 1782
Sterling	Mart 1779		Silvanus	Camd 1782

SAWYER, Solomon	Pasq 1779	SCOGGIN, Willis	John 1784
Solomon	Pasq 1789	Wm	Oran 1779
Stephen	Camd 1782	SCONYERS, Wm	Dobb 1780
Stephen	Casw 1786	SCOTCH, George	Perq 1772
Stephen	Casw 1784	SCOTT, Abel	Pasq 1779
Susannah	Camd 1782	Abraham	Hali 1783
Thomas	Camd 1782	Abraham	NorH 1780
Thomas #2	Camd 1782	Abraham	Pasq 1789
Thomas #3	Camd 1782	Andrew	Wayn 1786
Truman	Camd 1782	Arthur	Surr 1782
Tull	Camd 1782	Bellicent	NorH 1780
Willis	Camd 1782	Benj	Surr 1782
Wm	Camd 1782	Clement	Oran 1779
Wm	Casw 1786	Daniel	Surr 1782
Wm	Casw 1784	David	NorH 1780
Wm	Pasq 1779	Drury	Mont 1782
SAXON, John	Oran 1779	Emanuel	Hali 1783
Samuel	Oran 1779	Exum	Hali 1783
Wm	Oran 1779	Jacob	NorH 1780
SAYER, Robert	Onsl 1771	James	Casw 1784
SAYLOR, John	Surr 1782	James	Casw 1786
SCALES, Henry	Rowa 1770	James	Hali 1783
John	Rowa 1770	James	Pasq 1779
Joseph	Rowa 1770	James	Gate 1789
SCARBOROUGH, Austin	Curr 1779	Jeremiah	Surr 1782
Benjamin	Dobb 1780	Jesse	Surr 1782
Benjamin	Samp 1784	John	Nash 1782
Benjamin	Perq 1772	John	Hert 1779
Edward	Curr 1779	John	Ruth 1782
Elizabeth	Curr 1779	John	Oran 1779
Frederick	Dobb 1780	John	Casw 1784
Ignatius	Curr 1779	John	Casw 1786
James	Curr 1779	John	Blad 1784
Jesse	Dobb 1780	John	Gran 1785
John	Camd 1782	John	Hert 1784
John	Samp 1784	John	Warr 1784
John	Curr 1779	John	Crav 1779
John Jr	Curr 1779	John	Surr 1782
John Sr	Camd 1782	John	Beau 1786
Thomas	Curr 1779	John	Pasq 1789
SCARBROUGH, Augustine		Jonathan	Samp 1784
	Pasq 1694	Joseph	Albe 1679
Edward & son S	Bute 1766	Joseph	Rowa 1770
Joseph	Pasq 1789	Joseph	Samp 1784
Luke	Pasq 1789	Joseph	Hali 1783
Stephen	Bute 1766	Joseph	Pasq 1779
SCARBROVGH, Miles	Perq 1787	Joseph	Pasq 1789
SCARFE, James	Camd 1782	Laven	Onsl 1771
John	Pasq 1779	Lemuel	Pasq 1779
SCARLETT, James	Oran 1779	Leven	Chow 1785
James Jr	Oran 1779	Marmaduke	Pasq 1779
John	Oran 1779	Mary	Samp 1784
John Jr	Oran 1779	Nehemiah	Samp 1784
Mary	Oran 1779	Nicholas	Rowa 1770
SCARSDALE, John	Gran 1785	Randall	NorH 1780
SCATTERS, James	Gran 1785	Robert	Pasq 1789
SCHOBER, Gottleib	Surr 1782	Sam	NorH 1780
SCHREYER, Adam	Surr 1782	Saml	Pasq 1789
SCHULTZ, Geo	Surr 1782	Saml Sr	Pasq 1789
SCHUSON, Shadrack	Hert 1779	Severn	Chow 1785
SCOBY, Mathew	Oran 1779	Simpson	Pasq 1789
SCOGGAN, Francis	Casw 1784	Solomon	Pasq 1779
John	Casw 1784	Stephen	Pasq 1789
SCOGGIN, Alexander	Oran 1779	Stephen Sr	Pasq 1779
James	John 1784	Thomas	Wayn 1786

SCOTT, Thomas	Pasq 1789		SELLERS, Benjamin	Blad 1784
Wm	Curr 1779		Christian	Rowa 1761
Wm	Wilk 1782		Duncan	Blad 1784
Wm	Onsl 1771		Elisha	Brun 1784
SCOW, John	Mont 1782		Isaac	Brun 1782
SCREWS, Benj	Onsl 1771		Isham	Samp 1784
Henry	Nash 1782		John	Nash 1782
SCRIVEN, Thomas	Blad 1784		John	Blad 1784
SCRUGGS, Richard	Ruth 1782		Joseph	Samp 1784
SCUDDER, Mathias	Oran 1779		Matthew	Brun 1784
SCULL, Alexander	Hert 1784		Matthew	Brun 1782
Edward	Hert 1784		Samuel	Samp 1784
Elisha	Hert 1784		Simon	Brun 1784
John	Hert 1784		Simon	Brun 1782
SCURLOCK, Joshua	Wilk 1782		Wm	Nash 1782
Thomas	Hali 1783		Wm	Brun 1782
SEA, Isaac	Bert 1774		SELPH, Abraham	Casw 1784
SEABERN, Isaac	Camd 1782		SELS, John	Surr 1782
James	Camd 1782		SELTS, Alan	Warr 1784
SEABROOK, Daniel	Beau 1779		SEMPLE, James	Gran 1785
Daniel	Beau 1786		SENSING, Charles	Bute 1766
John	Beau 1786		James & sons	Bute 1766
SEAGROVE, John	Bute 1766		James (Jr)	Bute 1766
John	Warr 1784		Peter	Bute 1766
SEALEY, Joseph	Nash 1782		SENTER, Samuel	Hali 1783
Thomas	Nash 1782		Wm	Hali 1783
Tobias	Blad 1784		SENTRESS, Wm	Pasq 1779
SEALS, Robert	John 1784		SERATT, John	Casw 1784
Wm	Bert 1781		Joseph	Casw 1784
SEANGARGUS, John	Warr 1784		SERJANT, James	Casw 1786
SEARCY, Aquilla	John 1784		Thomas	Casw 1786
Bartlett	Gran 1771		SERTAIN, Peggy	Warr 1784
Daniel	John 1784		Peggy	Warr 1784
George	John 1784		SERVER, Henry	Oran 1779
Gideon	Gran 1771		SESSAME, John	Hert 1784
James	John 1784		SESSIONS, Benjamin	Hert 1779
John	Gran 1771		Coleman	Blad 1784
John Jr	Gran 1785		Isaac	Perq 1787
John Sr	Gran 1785		John	Hert 1779
Reuben	Gran 1785		Richard	Samp 1784
Reuben	Gran 1771		Samuel	Blad 1784
Richard	Gran 1785		Thomas	Blad 1784
Samuel	Gran 1785		SESSOMS, Isaac	Samp 1784
Wm	John 1784		Nicholas	Samp 1784
SEARLS, Coventon	Crav 1779		Richard	Samp 1784
SEARS, David	Warr 1784		Solomon	Samp 1784
Hebron	Gate 1789		SETTLE, Frank	Wilk 1782
John	Hert 1779		James	NBer 1779
John	Gran 1785		SEVERN, David	Cart 1779
John	Hert 1784		John	Cart 1779
John	Gran 1771		SEVESTON, David	Cart 1779
Rosanna	Oran 1779		SEVILLE, Alexander	Hert 1784
Wm	Gran 1785		SEWARD, Thomas	Bert 1774
SEAVERN, James	Crav 1779		SEWELL, Abraham	Wilk 1782
SEAWALES, Wm	NBer 1779		Chas	Mont 1782
SEBASTIAN, Benj	Wilk 1782		John	Brun 1782
SEDGEX, Ann	Tyrr 1784		John	Mont 1782
SEGRIST, John Jr	Samp 1784		John	Mont 1782
John Sr	Samp 1784		Joseph	Wilk 1782
SELF, Philip	Bute 1766		Thomas	Beau 1779
Willoughby	Bute 1766		Wm	Mont 1782
SELLAR, Benjamin	Brun 1782		SEXTON, Constantine	Pasq 1789
SELLEN, Peter	Surr 1782		Jeremiah	Camd 1782
SELLERS, Archibald	Blad 1784		Jeremiah	Curr 1779
Arthur	Nash 1782		Jonathan	Camd 1782

SEXTON, Josiah	Pasq 1779	SHAW, Daniel	Rich 1790
Lydia	Wilk 1782	Elizabeth	Hali 1783
Malachi	Pasq 1789	Hannah	Hali 1783
Mark	Pasq 1789	Jacob	Surr 1782
Robert	Surr 1782	James	Hali 1783
Saml	NorH 1780	James	Surr 1782
Willis	Pasq 1789	John	Blad 1784
Wm	Pasq 1779	John	Hali 1783
Wm	Beau 1786	Jonathan	Pasq 1779
Zachariah	Pasq 1779	Joseph	Wayn 1786
SEYER, Isham	Hali 1783	Murdock	Rich 1790
SEYMORE, Adam	Camd 1782	Murdock	Rich 1790
Benjamin	Camd 1782	Murdock	Rich 1790
David	Camd 1782	Murdock	Rich 1790
Jarvis	Camd 1782	Murdock	Rich 1790
Robert	Casw 1784	Nathanl	Rich 1790
SHACKELFORD, Francis		Nathanl	Rich 1790
	Casw 1784	Neil	Blad 1784
Francis	Onsl 1771	Neil Jr	Blad 1784
John	Onsl 1771	Norman	Rich 1790
SHACKLEFORD, Willoughby		Norman	Rich 1790
	Dobb 1780	Ralph	Casw 1786
SHADDY, John	Oran 1779	Ralph	Casw 1784
SHADIN, James	Wayn 1786	Robert	Brun 1784
SHADKLEFORD, James	Cart 1779	Saml	Surr 1782
SHAKESPEARE, Saml	Pasq 1789	Samuel	Rowa 1770
SHAKIN, George	Mont 1782	Samuel	Oran 1779
John	Mont 1782	Thomas	Hali 1783
SHAMBLIN, Wm	Surr 1782	Wm	Surr 1782
SHANKLAND, Andrew	Oran 1779	SHEALER, Benjamin	Bert 1774
SHANKS, John	Casw 1786	David	Bert 1774
John	Surr 1782	Ephraim	Bert 1774
John Jr	Surr 1782	John	Bert 1774
SHANNON, Daniel	Curr 1779	Thomas	Bert 1774
Hugh	Oran 1779	Wm	Bert 1774
John	Gran 1771	SHEARER, John	Oran 1779
Wm	Rowa 1770	John	Wilk 1782
SHANNONHOUSE, James	Pasq 1779	SHEARIN, John	Warr 1784
SHARGOT, Thomas	Curr 1779	Joseph	Warr 1784
SHAROCK, Thomas	NorH 1780	Louis	Warr 1784
SHARP, James	NorH 1780	Moses	Warr 1784
SHARPE, Aaron	Oran 1779	Wm	Warr 1784
George	Oran 1779	SHEARING, Isom	Warr 1779
Henry	Oran 1779	John	Albe 1694
Isaac	Oran 1779	John & son Joh	Bute 1766
Jesse	Oran 1779	Joseph	Bute 1766
John	Rowa 1770	Lydis	Albe 1694
John	Oran 1779	Mary	Albe 1694
John	Cart 1779	Wm	Bute 1766
Joseph	Oran 1779	SHEELS, John	Oran 1779
Richard	Rowa 1770	SHEETS, George	Rowa 1770
Starkey	Hert 1779	Joseph	Blad 1784
Thomas	Dobb 1780	Joseph	Beau 1786
Thomas	Oran 1779	Martin	Rowa 1770
Wm	John 1784	SHEFFIELD, Arthur	NorH 1780
SHARPLEY, John	Crav 1779	Robert	Bute 1766
SHARROD, Elizabeth	NorH 1780	SHEHAN, Miles	Bert 1774
Mary	NorH 1780	Thomas	Bert 1774
Wm	NorH 1780	SHEHON, David	Cart 1779
SHARY, Wm	Surr 1782	SHEHORN, Joseph	Wayn 1786
SHAVER, Mason	Hali 1783	SHELL, Stephen	Warr 1784
SHAW, Anguish	Blad 1784	Stephen Jr	Warr 1784
Archibald	Blad 1784	SHELLY, John	Rowa 1770
Daniel	Blad 1784	SHELTON, Burrill	Hali 1783
Daniel	Rich 1790	David	Casw 1784

SHELTON, Edward	Surr 1782		SHERIDAN, George	Oran 1779
Jeremiah	Surr 1782		SHERMAN, Reuben	Warr 1779
Joel	Ruth 1782		Robert	Gran 1785
John	Casw 1784		SHERMOR, Peter	Surr 1782
John	Surr 1782		SHERRARD, Jacob	Pasq 1694
John (parson)	Surr 1782		Thomas	Pasq 1694
Joseph	Surr 1782		Thomas	Bute 1766
Layman	Hali 1783		SHERRILL, Adam	Rowa 1761
Mary	Bert 1781		Aquilla	Rowa 1761
Micajah	Rich 1790		Isaac	Rowa 1761
Micajah	Rich 1790		Jacob	Rowa 1761
Stephen	Ruth 1782		Moses	Rowa 1761
Thomas	Bert 1781		Samuel	Rowa 1761
Wm	Surr 1782		Wm	Rowa 1761
SHEMWELL, Isaac	Gran 1785		SHERROD, Benjamin	Wayn 1786
James	Gran 1785		Henry	Hali 1783
SHEPARD, Absalom	Cart 1779		John	Mart 1779
Elijah	Cart 1779		John Jr	Wayn 1786
Jacob deceased	Cart 1779		John Sr	WAyn 1786
John	Cart 1779		Joseph	Hali 1783
Solomon estate	Cart 1779		Joseph	Hert 1784
SHEPHERD, Boyd	Rich 1790		Robert Jr	Mart 1779
Boyd	Rich 1790		Robert deceasd	Mart 1779
Coleman	Beau 1786		Sarah	Wayn 1786
Hattie	Ruth 1782		Susannah	Mart 1779
Jacob	Surr 1782		SHERRY, Dionecia	Warr 1784
James	Wilk 1782		SHERWOOD, James	Curr 1779
John	Nash 1782		Randolph	Warr 1784
John	Wilk 1782		SHEUTTE, Jacob	Beau 1779
John	Rich 1790		SHEW, Daniel	Blad 1784
John	Rich 1790		SHEWARASH, Abram	Hert 1784
Jordan	Beau 1786		SHIELDS, Jeremiah	Ruth 1782
Laban	Nash 1782		Wm	Mart 1779
Provey	Hali 1783		SHIFFLETT, Wm	Wilk 1782
Providence	Hert 1779		SHILLING, Derrick	Jone 1779
Providence	Hali 1783		SHIN, John	Dobb 1780
Robert	Wilk 1782		SHINE, Daniel	Jone 1779
Solomon	Beau 1786		James	Hali 1783
Thomas	Beau 1786		SHINGLETON, Wm	Beau 1786
Wm	Oran 1779		SHINN, Saml	Surr 1782
Wm	Hali 1783		Samuel	Rowa 1761
SHEPPARD, Abraham Capt.			SHIP, Daniel	Surr 1782
	Dobb 1780		John	Crav 1779
Abraham Col.	Dobb 1780		Josiah	Surr 1782
Absalom	Cart 1779		Mark	Surr 1782
Benjamin	Dobb 1780		Thomas	Surr 1782
Benjamin	Onsl 1771		Willis	Crav 1779
Elijah	Cart 1779		SHIPLAN, Daniel	Blad 1784
George Jr	Onsl 1771		SHIPLEY, Robert	Ruth 1782
Jacob	Cart 1779		SHIPMAN, Daniel	Ruth 1782
Jacob	Surr 1782		Edward	Ruth 1782
James	Surr 1782		SHIPPE, Mary	Pitt 1786
John	Rowa 1770		SHIRLEY, David	Dobb 1780
John	Dobb 1780		Thomas	Mart 1779
John	Cart 1779		SHMIT, Daniel	Surr 1782
John	Onsl 1771		SHOCKER, James	Wilk 1782
John	Surr 1782		SHOCKLEY, Edward	NorH 1780
John	Gran 1771		SHOECRAFT, Wm	Hert 1784
John	Gate 1789		SHOEMAKER, Adam	Surr 1782
John Jr	Rowa 1770		Adam Jr	Surr 1782
Lucy (widow)	Surr 1782		David	Beau 1786
Smith	Onsl 1771		Jesse	Oran 1779
Stephen	Gate 1789		Robert	Surr 1782
Wm	Crav 1779		SHOFTNER, George	Oran 1779
Wm	Surr 1782		Michael	Oran 1779

SHOFTNER, Michael Jr		
	Oran	1779
SHOLAR, Benj	Bert	1781
David	Bert	1781
Ephraim	Bert	1781
John	Bert	1781
Thomas	Bert	1781
SHOLER, Jacob	Hert	1779
SHORES, Frederick	Surr	1782
Henry	Surr	1782
John	Surr	1782
Reuben	Surr	1782
Wm	Warr	1784
Wm	Surr	1782
SHORT, Aaron	Rowa	1761
David	NorH	1780
James	Surr	1782
John	Bute	1766
John	Warr	1784
John	Warr	1784
John	NorH	1780
SHORTRIDGE, George	Bute	1766
SHOUSE, Christian	Surr	1782
Daniel	Surr	1782
Phillip	Surr	1782
SHOWALTER, John	Blad	1784
SHUFFIELD, Arthur	Hali	1783
Robert	Bute	1766
SHULTZ, George	Oran	1779
Mark	Rowa	1770
SHURLEY, John	Wilk	1782
SHUTE, Joseph	Beau	1786
SHY, Jesse	Casw	1786
John	Casw	1786
SIBBETT, Wm	Blad	1784
SIDDALL, John	Casw	1786
SIDDELL, John	Warr	1784
SIDES, Andrew	Rowa	1761
SIERBNA, Dorothy	Gran	1785
SIKES, Benjamin	Curr	1779
Henry	Hali	1783
Henry	Crav	1779
James	NorH	1780
Joel	Hali	1783
John	Nash	1782
John	Camd	1782
John	Casw	1784
John	Tyrr	1784
Joseph	Wayn	1786
Joseph	NorH	1780
Joshua	Samp	1784
Levi	Pasq	1789
Mary	NorH	1780
Millicent	NorH	1780
Nathan	Hali	1783
Philip	Nash	1782
Samuel	Hali	1783
Sarah	Hali	1783
Willoby	Hali	1783
Wm	Nash	1782
Wm	Hali	1783
Zedekiah	Camd	1782
SILBERT, John	Perq	1787
SILER, Benjamin	Brun	1784
Wm	Surr	1782

SILGROVES, Thomas	NBer	1779
SILLS, Benjamin	Hali	1783
Isham	Hali	1783
Joseph	Hali	1783
SILVEY, Edward	Gran	1771
SIMERAL, Edward	Beau	1786
SIMMONDS, Ann	Brun	1784
Thomas	Brun	1784
SIMMONS, Ann	Brun	1782
Anthony	Curr	1779
Argyle	Chow	1785
Asahel	Curr	1779
Benjamin	Brun	1782
Caleb	Curr	1779
David	Jone	1779
Dempsey	Hert	1784
Edward	Onsl	1771
Emanuel	Jone	1779
George	Jone	1779
George	Onsl	1771
Gussett	Jone	1779
Hannah	Beau	1786
Henry	Onsl	1771
Henry Jr	Onsl	1771
Isaac	Brun	1782
Jacob	Chow	1785
Jacob	NorH	1780
James	Tyrr	1784
James	Onsl	1771
Jeremiah	Blad	1784
Jesse	Wayn	1786
Jesse	Curr	1779
John	Cart	1779
John	Samp	1784
John	Casw	1784
John	Chow	1785
John	Gran	1785
John	Bert	1774
John	Brun	1782
John	Curr	1779
John	Gran	1771
John Jr	Bute	1766
Joseph	Bert	1774
Joshua	Hert	1784
Lacy	Hali	1783
Ladock	Hali	1783
Lewis	Oran	1779
Moldon	Onsl	1771
Moses	Brun	1782
Peter Sr	Surr	1782
Robert	Blad	1784
Robert	Curr	1779
Sam	Pitt	1786
Samson	Curr	1779
Samuel	Jone	1779
Samuel	Curr	1779
Ruth	1782	
Thomas	Chow	1785
Thomas	Crav	1779
Thomas	Brun	1782
Thomas	Curr	1779
Thomas	Perq	1787
Willis	Samp	1784
Willis	Curr	1779
Wm	Bute	1766

SIMMONS, Wm	Chow 1785	SIMPSON, John Jr	Pasq 1789
Wm	Curr 1779	John Sr	Chow 1785
Wm	Gran 1771	Joshua	Cart 1779
SIMMS, Benjamin	Blad 1784	Mary	Casw 1786
Britain	Wayn 1786	Mary	Chow 1785
Edward	Warr 1784	Richard	Casw 1786
Elisha	Gran 1785	Richard	Casw 1784
George	Casw 1784	Robert	Cart 1779
George	Casw 1786	Robert	Blad 1784
Isaac	Blad 1784	Robert	Pasq 1779
James	Rowa 1770	Rossiter	Cart 1779
Joseph	John 1784	Sam	Wilk 1782
Joseph	Onsl 1771	Samuel	Chow 1785
Leonard	Gran 1785	Simon	Blad 1784
Leonard	Gran 1771	Thomas	Cart 1779
Mark	John 1784	Thomas	Blad 1784
Matthew	Rowa 1770	Thomas	Mont 1782
Nathl	Gran 1771	Thomas	Onsl 1771
Robert Jr	Wayn 1786	Thomas	Pasq 1789
Robert Sr	Wayn 1786	Thomas Sr	Onsl 1771
Shadrack	Wayn 1786	Wm	Pasq 1694
Sherwood	Gran 1771	Wm	Chow 1785
Sherwood Jr	Gran 1785	Wm	Pasq 1779
Sherwood Sr	Gran 1785	Wm	Curr 1779
Thomas	Gran 1785	Wm	Pasq 1789
Thomas	Gran 1771	Wm Jr	Pasq 1789
Willis	Brun 1782	SIMS, John	Surr 1782
Wm	Blad 1784	SINCLAIR, Robert	Onsl 1771
Wm	Gran 1785	SINGLEMAN, Barnett	Hali 1783
Wm	Beau 1779	SINGLETARY, Benjamin	
Wm	Brun 1782		Blad 1784
SIMON, John	Pasq 1789	Benjamin	Brun 1784
Joseph	Bert 1781	James	Blad 1784
Peter	Rowa 1761	James Jr	Blad 1784
Thomas	Casw 1784	John	Blad 1784
Thomas	Pasq 1779	John	Brun 1784
Thomas	Beau 1786	John	Brun 1782
SIMONS, Absalom	Pasq 1789	Joseph	Blad 1784
Argill	Albe 1694	Richard	Blad 1784
Elisha	Surr 1782	Thomas	Blad 1784
Jeremiah	Pasq 1789	Wm	Blad 1784
Jesse	Pasq 1789	SINGLETON, Brayton	Blad 1784
Joshua	Hert 1779	Daniel	Ruth 1782
Nicholas	Albe 1694	Hannah mother	Dobb 1780
Obediah	Hert 1784	Hannah w of Sa	Dobb 1780
Sarah	Pasq 1789	Peter	Curr 1779
SIMPKINS, Joseph	Crav 1779	Richard	Ruth 1782
SIMPSON, Abraham	Onsl 1771	SINK, Frederick	Gran 1785
Ann	Pasq 1779	Jacob	Rowa 1761
Archibald	Mart 1779	SINKLER, Colden	Rich 1790
Bevard	Onsl 1771	Colden	Rich 1790
Eliz	Pasq 1789	John	Blad 1784
Evan	Chow 1785	SINNELL, Joseph	Warr 1784
Gilbert	Mont 1782	SINVILL, Aaron	Surr 1782
Jacob	Blad 1784	Wm	Surr 1782
Jacob	Tyrr 1784	SIPERY, Barrow	Jone 1779
Jacob	Pasq 1779	SISK, James	Hert 1784
James	Curr 1779	John	Rowa 1770
Joab	Pasq 1789	John	Wilk 1784
John	Rowa 1770	John	Surr 1782
John	Blad 1784	Robert	Wilk 1782
John	Chow 1785	Timothy	Wilk 1782
John	Curr 1779	Timothy	Surr 1782
John	Onsl 1771	Timothy Sr	Wilk 1784
John	Perq 1787	SISSNEY, Stephen	Rowa 1770

SISSON, David	Ruth 1782	SKITTLETHARP, Charles
John	Ruth 1782	Tyrr 1784
Wm	NBer 1779	SKURLOCK, Thomas	Wilk 1782
Wm Jr	Ruth 1782	SKUTT, Edward	Bert 1774
SITZ, Michael	Surr 1782	SKUTT (SCULL?), Elisha
SIVILS, James	Samp 1784	Hert 1779
SIZEMORE, John	Blad 1784	SKYLER, Benjamin	Bert 1774
SKAGGS, James	Albe 1679	SLACK, Josiah	Curr 1779
SKEEN, John	Bert 1781	Nicholas	Curr 1779
Jonathan	Casw 1784	SLADE, Ebenezer Jr	Mart 1779
Joseph	Rowa 1770	Ebenezerr Sr	Mart 1779
Matthew	Rowa 1770	Henry	Mart 1779
Peter	Casw 1784	Henry	Beau 1779
SKELTON, Christopher		Henry Jr	Mart 1779
	Camd 1782	John	NBer 1779
SKIDMORE, Henry & sons		John	Bert 1781
	Rowa 1767	Joshua	Tyrr 1784
John	Rowa 1767	Major	Beau 1786
John	Surr 1782	Samuel	Beau 1779
Thomas	Rowa 1767	Thomas	Hert 1779
SKILES, John	Bert 1781	Thomas	Casw 1786
Wm	Bert 1781	Thomas	Casw 1784
SKINNER, Ann	Perq 1787	Thomas	Hert 1784
Benjamin	Dobb 1780	Wm	Casw 1786
Charles	Hert 1779	Wm	Casw 1784
Charles	Hert 1784	SLATER, Henry	Surr 1782
Emanuel	Nash 1782	SLATTER, Elizabeth	Hali 1783
Evan	Chow 1785	James	Hali 1783
Evan	Tyrr 1784	Solomon	Hali 1783
James	Hert 1779	Wm	Hali 1783
James	Dobb 1780	SLAUGHTER, Geo	Rich 1790
James	Hert 1784	Geo	Rich 1790
James	Perq 1772	Jacob	Gran 1771
Jesse	Dobb 1780	John	Nash 1782
John	Bert 1774	John	Camd 1782
John	Perq 1787	Owen	Rich 1790
Joshua	Perq 1772	Owen	Rich 1790
Kindred	Hert 1779	Solomon	Bert 1781
Mary	Bert 1781	Thomas	Crav 1779
Mills	Gate 1789	Thomas	Bert 1781
Nathl	Perq 1787	Walter	Rich 1790
Nicholas	Nash 1782	Walter	Rich 1790
Richard	Perq 1772	Walter Jr	Rich 1790
Richard	NorH 1780	Walter Jr	Rich 1790
Richard	Perq 1787	SLAVEN, Jethro	Gate 1789
Samuel	Nash 1782	SLAY, Nathan	Rich 1790
Samuel	Perq 1772	Nathan	Rich 1790
Sarah	Perq 1772	Thomas	Rich 1790
Sarah	Perq 1787	Thomas	Rich 1790
Stephen	Perq 1787	SLEDGE, Arthur	Hali 1783
Thomas	Casw 1786	Daniel	Bute 1766
Wm	Nash 1782	Daniel	Warr 1784
Wm	Chow 1785	Isham	Warr 1784
Wm	Perq 1772	James	Warr 1784
Wm	Perq 1787	John	Hali 1783
Wm	Perq 1787	Nathan	Hali 1783
Wm Sr	Dobb 1780	SLOAN, David	Oran 1779
SKIPPER, Bannaster	Rich 1790	David	Wilk 1782
Bannaster	Rich 1790	Fergus	Rowa 1761
Benj	Rich 1790	Samuel	Wilk 1782
Benj	Rich 1790	Thomas	Wilk 1782
Clem	Brun 1784	Wm	Wilk 1782
Grace	Brun 1784	Wm	Onsl 1771
Isaac	Brun 1784	SLOCUM, Ezekiel	Wayn 1786
Jacob	Wayn 1786	Joseph	Wayn 1786

SLOSS, John	Oran 1779		SMITH, Arthur	Hali 1783
Joseph	Oran 1779		Arthur	Jone 1779
SLUDER, Henry & son	Ma		Bazel	Crav 1779
	Rowa 1770		Benj	Wilk 1782
SMALL, Amos	Jone 1779		Benj	Beau 1786
Benjamin	Cart 1779		Benj	Perq 1787
Benjamin	Chow 1785		Benjamin	Samp 1784
David	Gate 1789		Benjamin	Nash 1782
Isham	Perq 1772		Benjamin	Brun 1784
James	Gate 1789		Benjamin	Gran 1785
John	Gate 1789		Benjamin	Hali 1783
John	Pasq 1789		Benjamin	Perq 1772
Jonas	Cart 1779		Benjamin	Brun 1782
Joseph	Chow 1785		Benjamin	Brun 1782
Joshua	Gate 1789		Benjamin Jr	Wayn 1786
Josiah	Chow 1785		Benjamin Sr	Wayn 1786
Obediah	Pasq 1779		Bradley	Rowa 1770
Peter	Albe 1694		Britain	Nash 1782
Rodney	Jone 1779		Bryan	Bert 1781
Saml	Pasq 1789		Burrill	Hali 1783
Thomas	Perq 1772		Cannon	Pitt 1786
Wm	Perq 1772		Charles	Rowa 1770
Wm	Perq 1787		Charles	Brun 1784
SMALLEY, John	NorH 1780		Chas	Surr 1782
SMALLWOOD, Elijah	Surr 1782		Christian	Surr 1782
Elisha	Oran 1779		Conrad	Casw 1784
Wm	Oran 1779		Damon	Beau 1779
SMART, George	Rowa 1770		Daniel	Warr 1784
Henry	Beau 1786		Daniel	Surr 1782
Peter	Bute 1766		Daniel	Rich 1790
Robert & s Geo	Rowa 1770		Daniel	Rich 1790
Wm Jr	Ruth 1782		Daniel	Rich 1790
Wm Sr	Ruth 1782		Daniel	Rich 1790
SMAW, Henry	Beau 1786		David	Rowa 1768
John	Beau 1786		David	Dobb 1780
Wm	Beau 1786		David	Rowa 1761
SMEDLEY, John	Nash 1782		David	Brun 1784
SMILEY, James	Rich 1790		David	Gran 1785
James	Rich 1790		David	John 1784
Thomas	Jone 1779		David	Crav 1779
SMITES, Wm	John 1784		David	Brun 1782
SMITH, Abel	Dobb 1780		David	Wilk 1782
Abner	Samp 1784		David Jr	Brun 1784
Abraham	Hert 1784		Davis	Pasq 1789
Abraham	Tyrr 1784		Dorcas	Camd 1782
Abraham	Warr 1784		Drury	Bute 1766
Abram	Pitt 1786		Easter	Rich 1790
Absalom	NorH 1780		Easter	Rich 1790
Adam	Oran 1779		Edmund	Gran 1785
Adam	Gran 1785		Edward	Mart 1779
Alexander	Rowa 1768		Edward	Wilk 1782
Alexander	Dobb 1780		Edwin	Surr 1782
Alexander	John 1784		Eli	Blad 1784
Ambrose	NorH 1780		Elias	Samp 1784
Amy	Hali 1783		Elias	Bute 1766
Anderson	Gran 1785		Elias	Curr 1779
Andrew	Oran 1779		Elias	Surr 1782
Andrew	Bert 1774		Elijah	Curr 1779
Anguish	Blad 1784		Elizabeth	Hert 1779
Ann	Hert 1779		Emildred	Hert 1779
Ann	Wayn 1786		Erith	John 1784
Anthony	Rowa 1770		Francis	Casw 1786
Archibald	Blad 1784		Francis	Hali 1783
Arthur	Blad 1784		Frederick	Oran 1779
Arthur	Wayn 1786		Frederick	Rowa 1761
			Garrett	Beau 1779

Geo	Surr 1782	John	Camd 1782
George	Samp 1784	John	Samp 1784
George	Bute 1766	John	Bute 1766
George	Rowa 1761	John	Dobb 1780
George	Ruth 1782	John	Rowa 1761
George	Warr 1784	John	Rowa 1770
George	Warr 1784	John	Nash 1782
George	Brun 1782	John	Hert 1779
Grace	Blad 1784	John	Ruth 1782
Guilielumus	Gran 1785	John	Blad 1784
Gulielmus	Gran 1771	John	Wayn 1786
Hardy	Warr 1784	John	Wayn 1786
Hascomb	Gran 1785	John	Brun 1784
Henry	Oran 1779	John	Chow 1785
Henry	Cart 1779	John	John 1784
Henry	Dobb 1780	John	Hert 1784
Henry	Gran 1785	John	John 1784
Henry	Jone 1779	John	Tyrr 1784
Henry	Crav 1779	John	Pasq 1779
Henry	Surr 1782	John	Warr 1784
Henry	Bert 1781	John	Jone 1779
Henry	Pitt 1786	John	Bert 1774
Henry Jr	Cart 1779	John	Crav 1779
Henry Jr	Cart 1779	John	Brun 1782
Henry Sr	Cart 1779	John	Mont 1782
Howell	Samp 1784	John	Curr 1779
Hughes	Chow 1785	John	Wilk 1782
Humphrey	Crav 1779	John	NorH 1780
Isaac	John 1784	John	Surr 1782
Jacob	Tyrr 1784	John	Surr 1782
Jahallet	Beau 1779	John	Gran 1771
James	Camd 1782	John	Beau 1786
James	Samp 1784	John	Beau 1781
James	Blad 1784	John	Pitt 1786
James	Brun 1784	John	Perq 1787
James	Casw 1784	John	Perq 1787
James	Chow 1785	John	Rich 1790
James	Gran 1785	John	Rich 1790
James	Hali 1783	John #2	Oran 1779
James	Hert 1784	John Jr	Gran 1785
James	Warr 1784	John Jr	Bert 1774
James	Jone 1779	John Jr	Bert 1781
James	Crav 1779	John Sr	Camd 1782
James	NorH 1780	John Sr	Gran 1785
James	Beau 1786	John Sr	Tyrr 1784
James	Perq 1787	John Sr	Bert 1781
James	Rich 1790	Jonathan	John 1784
James	Rich 1790	Jonathan	NBer 1779
James Jr	Jone 1779	Jonathan	Gate 1789
James Jr	Rich 1790	Joseph	Oran 1779
James Jr	Rich 1790	Joseph	Dobb 1780
James Sr	Jone 1779	Joseph	Casw 1784
Jannett	Wilk 1782	Joseph	Chow 1785
Jemimah	Oran 1779	Joseph	Perq 1772
Jeremiah	Onsl 1771	Joseph	Crav 1779
Jeremiah	Beau 1786	Joseph	Surr 1782
Jesse	Tyrr 1784	Joseph	Gran 1771
Jesse	Crav 1779	Joshua	Oran 1779
Jim (Littleton	Rich 1790	Josiah	Wayn 1786
Jim (Littleton	Rich 1790	Josiah	Hali 1783
Job	Perq 1772	Josiah	Bert 1774
Job	Perq 1787	Josiah	Bert 1781
John	Rowa 1768	Judith	Hert 1779
John	Oran 1779	Laban	Curr 1779
John	Mart 1779	Laurence	Surr 1782

Lawrence	NorH 1780	Saml	Perq 1787
Leonard	Gran 1785	Samuel	Camd 1782
Lightfoot	Gran 1771	Samuel	Cart 1779
Mark	Dobb 1780	Samuel	Ruth 1782
Mary	Hert 1779	Samuel	Cart 1779
Mary	Blad 1784	Samuel	Blad 1784
Mary	Brun 1782	Samuel	Hali 1783
Mary	NorH 1780	Samuel	John 1784
Mary	Gate 1789	Samuel	Warr 1784
Michael	Rowa 1768	Samuel	Perq 1772
Michael	Tyrr 1784	Samuel	Crav 1779
Michael	Jone 1779	Sarah	Hali 1783
Miles	Hali 1783	Silas	Bert 1781
Mordicai	Pasq 1789	Simon	Blad 1784
Morgan	Crav 1779	Sion	Nash 1782
Moses	Perq 1772	Solomon	NorH 1780
Moses	Wilk 1782	Solomon	Gran 1771
Moses Jr	Hali 1783	Stephen	Warr 1779
Moses Sr	Hali 1783	Stephen	Surr 1782
Nathaniel	Mont 1782	Stewart	Blad 1784
Neal	Rich 1790	Temperence	Onsl 1771
Neal	Rich 1790	Thomas	Oran 1779
Nehemiah	John 1784	Thomas	Mart 1779
Neil	Blad 1784	Thomas	Camd 1782
Nicholas	Dobb 1780	Thomas	Cart 1779
Nicholas	Casw 1784	Thomas	Dobb 1780
Noah	Samp 1784	Thomas	Hert 1779
Perviance	Curr 1779	Thomas	Blad 1784
Peter	Rowa 1768	Thomas	Hali 1783
Peter	Casw 1786	Thomas	Hert 1784
Peter	Rowa 1761	Thomas	Crav 1779
Peter	Rowa 1770	Thomas	Wilk 1782
Peter	Blad 1784	Thomas	Onsl 1771
Peter	Casw 1784	Thomas	Surr 1782
Peter	Hali 1783	Thomas	Gran 1771
Peter	Bert 1774	Thomas	Gate 1789
Peter	Surr 1782	Thomas	Beau 1786
Peter	Bert 1781	Thomas #2	Camd 1782
Philip	Rowa 1768	Thomas & sonWm	Bute 1766
Philip	Wilk 1782	Thomas Jr	Gran 1785
Phillip	NBer 1779	Thomas Sr	Gran 1785
Plath	PItt 1786	Tobias	Oran 1779
Reuben	Oran 1779	Uriah	Hali 1783
Reuben	Warr 1784	Wm	Oran 1779
Reuben	Wilk 1782	Wm	Samp 1784
Richard	Casw 1786	Wm	Cart 1779
Richard	Bute 1766	Wm	Casw 1786
Richard	Dobb 1780	Wm	Dobb 1780
Richard	Rowa 1770	Wm	Rowa 1761
Richard	Blad 1784	Wm	Rowa 1770
Richard	Casw 1784	Wm	Cart 1779
Richard	Hali 1783	Wm	Ruth 1782
Richard	Crav 1779	Wm	Blad 1784
Richard	Wilk 1782	Wm	Brun 1784
Richard & sons	Bute 1766	Wm	Casw 1784
Richard Jr	Bute 1766	Wm	Tyrr 1784
Robert	Oran 1779	Wm	Warr 1784
Robert	Casw 1784	Wm	Wilk 1784
Robert	Gran 1785	Wm	Crav 1779
Robert	Surr 1782	Wm	Mont 1782
Sam	Onsl 1771	Wm	Curr 1779
Sam	Pitt 1786	Wm	Wilk 1782
Sam	Perq 1787	Wm	NorH 1780
Saml	Gran 1771	Wm	Rich 1790
Saml	Gate 1789	Wm	Rich 1790

Wm & son Wm	Bute 1766		SNEED, Wm	Rich 1790
Wm Jr	Rowa 1770		Wm	Rich 1790
Wm Jr	Blad 1784		SNELL, James	Tyrr 1784
Zack	Blad 1784		John	Tyrr 1784
Zechariah	Hali 1783		Roger	Dupl 1779
SMITHER, Gabriel	Wilk 1782		Roger	Samp 1784
SMITHEY, Moses	Brun 1784		Roger	Tyrr 1784
Nancy	Casw 1784		SNELLING, Aaron	Gran 1785
SMITHSON, Isaac	Pasq 1779		Alexr	Gran 1771
Isaac	Pasq 1789		Aquilla	Gran 1771
John	Pasq 1779		Barnett	Gran 1785
John	Pasq 1789		Hugh	Gran 1785
Joseph	Camd 1782		Lettice	Gran 1785
Joseph	Pasq 1779		SNIDER, Cornelius	Surr 1782
Mathias	Pasq 1779		Henry	Surr 1782
Mathias	Pasq 1789		Peter	Surr 1782
Reuben	Pasq 1779		SNIFEL, Nathl	Gran 1771
Reuben	Pasq 1789		SNIPES, John	John 1784
Samuel	Camd 1782		Nathaniel	Gran 1785
Seth	Pasq 1789		SNODEY, Thomas	Pasq 1694
SMITHWICK, Edmund s of Jo			SNOODIE, Thomas	Pasq 1694
	Mart 1779		SNOTTERLY, Phillip	Oran 1779
Edward	Albe 1694		SNOW, Dinah	Camd 1782
Edward & wife	Albe 1694		Frost	Surr 1782
Edward s of Wm	Mart 1779		Henry	Surr 1782
Elizabeth	Albe 1694		Jacob	Surr 1782
John	Mart 1779		James	Casw 1786
Lydia wife ofE	Albe 1694		James	Casw 1784
Ralph	Albe 1694		John	Camd 1782
Samuel	Mart 1779		Spencer	Warr 1784
SMITHY, John	Wilk 1782		Spencer	Warr 1784
SMIYJ, Samuel	Gran 1785		Wm	Surr 1782
SMYTH, James	Pitt 1786		SNOWDEN, Joseph	Camd 1782
Thomas	Beau 1786		Nathan	Camd 1782
SMYTHE, Caleb	Onsl 1771		Zebulon	Perq 1772
Moses	Brun 1782		Zebulon	Perq 1787
SNABERRY, Christr	Surr 1782		SNYDER, John	Surr 1782
SNAP, Lawrence	Rowa 1761		Malachi	Surr 1782
SNEAD, Chas	Surr 1782		Martha	Gran 1785
John	Surr 1782		Nathaniel	Gran 1785
Robert	Onsl 1771		Phillip	Surr 1782
SNEED, Ann	Rich 1790		SOCKLUSE, Thomas	Gran 1785
Ann	Rich 1790		SOISHY, Samuel	NasH 1782
Daniel	Rich 1790		SOLES, McKinney	Samp 1784
Daniel	Rich 1790		SOLOMON, John	Hali 1783
David	Rich 1790		SONELAGE, John	Onsl 1771
David	Rich 1790		SOOK, John	Gran 1785
Dudley	Gran 1785		SORREL, George	Bute 1766
Henry	Wilk 1784		SORRELL, Robert	Gran 1771
Israel	Rich 1790		SORRILL, Wm	Hert 1779
Israel	Rich 1790		SORRILLS, John	Ruth 1782
John	Rich 1790		Wm	Surr 1782
John	Rich 1790		SORRILS, Richard	Surr 1782
John Esq	Rich 1790		SOULE, Joseph	Brun 1782
John Esq	Rich 1790		Sylvanus	Brun 1782
Jonathan	Rich 1790		SOULON, John Baptist	
Jonathan	Rich 1790			Perq 1787
Phillip	Rich 1790		SOUTH, Andrew	Bert 1781
Phillip	Rich 1790		Benjamin	Casw 1784
Saml	Gran 1771		SOUTHALL, Holman	Hali 1783
Samuel	Gran 1785		SOUTHARD, Henry	Surr 1782
Solomon Jr	Rich 1790		Isaac	Surr 1782
Solomon Jr	Rich 1790		Robert	Casw 1784
Stephen	Gran 1785		Wm	Casw 1784
Wilson	Dobb 1780		SOUTHER, Mary	Wilk 1782

SOUTHER, Stephen	Rowa 1767		SPARKS, Wm Jr	Surr 1782
SOUTHERLAND, John	Casw 1786		SPARNON, Joseph	Pasq 1694
John	Hali 1783		SPARROW, John	Oran 1779
Phillip	Dupl 1783		Matthew	Oran 1779
Phillip	Surr 1782		SPAUGH, Adam	Rowa 1761
Reuben	Surr 1782		SPEARMAN, Sam	Onsl 1771
Wm	Hali 1783		SPEARS, Hezekiah	Gran 1771
SOWELL, Aaron	Hert 1779		Joseph	John 1784
Charlie	Bert 1774		Phillip	Gran 1785
Chas	Surr 1782		Wm	Hert 1784
Coreston	Beau 1786		Wm Jr	Gran 1785
Francis	Bert 1774		Wm Jr	Gran 1771
James	Hert 1779		Wm Sr	Gran 1785
James	Bert 1774		Wm Sr	Gran 1771
James	Bert 1781		SPEED, Henry	Bute 1766
John	Bute 1766		Lewis	Oran 1779
Obadiah	Hert 1779		SPEELMAN, Frederick	Casw 1786
Richard	Hert 1779		SPEER, Arthur	Hali 1783
Richard	Bert 1774		Samuel	Hali 1783
Wm	Bert 1774		SPEERS, Andrew	Surr 1782
SOWER, Mary	NorH 1780		Benj	Surr 1782
Phillip	Rowa 1761		Jacob Jr	Surr 1782
SOWLE, Silvanus	Brun 1784		Jacob Sr	Surr 1782
SOZEK, Chatchut	John 1784		John	Surr 1782
SOZELL, Chatchutt	John 1784		Levi	Surr 1782
SPACH, Adam	Surr 1782		Levin	Surr 1782
Adam Jr	Surr 1782		Thomas	Surr 1782
SPAIN, Littlebury	Hali 1783		Wm	Surr 1782
SPALDING, Chas	Gran 1771		SPEIGHT, Ann	Gate 1789
SPANE, Littleberry	NorH 1780		Ann	Bert 1781
SPANN, John	Dobb 1780		Francis	Dobb 1780
Richard	Curr 1779		Francis	Gate 1789
Sarah	Hali 1783		Fullington	Gate 1789
Thompson	Wilk 1784		Henry	Gate 1789
Willis	Hali 1783		Jemimah	Hert 1779
SPARGO, Stephen	Onsl 1771		Jeremiah	Gate 1789
SPARKMAN, Edward	Bert 1774		John	Dobb 1780
Edward	Bert 1781		Joseph	Blad 1784
James	Hert 1779		Joseph	Gate 1789
James	Hert 1788		Moses	Gate 1789
Jesse	Bert 1774		Moses Sr	GatE 1789
John	Dobb 1780		Samuel	Dobb 1780
Levi	Brun 1784		Seth	Dobb 1780
Louis	Gate 1789		Wm	Nash 1782
Rebecca	Bert 1781		Wm	Gate 1789
Reuben	Gate 1789		Wm Capt	Dobb 1780
Richard	Brun 1784		Wm s of CaptWm	Dobb 1780
Thomas	Hert 1784		SPELLER, Henry	Bert 1781
Willis	Gate 1789		Thomas	Mart 1779
Wm	Bert 1774		SPELLING, Frederick	Hali 1783
Wm	Bert 1781		SPELLMAN, John	Pasq 1694
SPARKS, James	Hali 1783		SPENCE, Charles	Dobb 1780
James	Wilk 1782		Chas	Onsl 1771
John	Wilk 1782		David	Camd 1782
John	Surr 1782		David	Pasq 1779
Jonas	Rowa 1761		David	Pasq 1789
Joseph	Surr 1782		Demsey	Camd 1782
Josiah	Hali 1783		Edward	Camd 1782
Matthew	Rowa 1761		Graves	Camd 1782
Matthew	Wilk 1782		Ineel	Dobb 1780
Matthew	Surr 1782		Isaac	Pasq 1779
Reuben	Wilk 1782		James	Camd 1782
Solomon	Rowa 1761		James	Pasq 1789
Wm	NorH 1780		James Jr	Pasq 1779
Wm	Surr 1782		James Sr	Pasq 1779

SPENCE, Jeremiah	Bert 1781	SPIVEY, Moses	Pitt 1786
John	Dobb 1780	Nathl	Gate 1789
Joseph	Tyrr 1784	Seth	Gate 1789
Joseph Jr	Pasq 1779	Wm	Samp 1784
Joseph Sr	Pasq 1779	SPOCK, Jacob	Crav 1779
Lemuel	Camd 1782	John	Crav 1779
Malachi	Camd 1782	Peter	Crav 1779
Mark	Pasq 1789	SPOON, Adam	Surr 1782
Noah	Camd 1782	Christian	Oran 1779
Preacher	Pasq 1779	John	Oran 1779
Reuben	Pasq 1789	SPOONER, John	Tyrr 1784
Saml	Pasq 1789	SPRAY, Arthur	Jone 1779
Solomon	Bert 1781	SPRENLEY, Geo	Surr 1782
Thomas	Camd 1782	SPRING, Ann	Beau 1786
Thomas	Surr 1782	SPRINGER, John	Rowa 1761
Wm	Dobb 1780	Peter	Rowa 1761
Wm	Pasq 1779	Uriah	Oran 1779
Wm	Onsl 1771	SPRINGLE, Chas	Beau 1779
SPENCER, Benjamin	Rowa 1768	Chas	Beau 1786
Benjamin	Casw 1786	Geo	Beau 1786
Benjamin	Casw 1784	George	Beau 1779
Elizabeth	Casw 1786	James	Beau 1786
Elizabeth	Casw 1784	MIchaeL	Surr 1782
Jeremiah	Oran 1779	Peter	Surr 1782
John	Casw 1786	Wm	Beau 1779
John	Casw 1784	Wm	Beau 1786
John	Surr 1782	SPRINGS, Abraham	Beau 1779
Moses	Surr 1782	SPRINKLE, Peter	Surr 1782
Wm	Rowa 1761	SPRINT, Wm	Warr 1784
SPENHAUR, Henry	Surr 1782	SPRUILL, Benjamin Jr	
Jacob	Surr 1782		Tyrr 1784
Michael	Surr 1782	Benjamin Sr	Tyrr 1784
Warner	Surr 1782	Ebenezer	Tyrr 1784
SPERRY, George	Bert 1774	Eliz	Bert 1781
SPICER, John	Onsl 1771	Elizabeth	Bert 1774
Wm	Wilk 1784	Evan	Tyrr 1784
Wm	Wilk 1782	Godfrey	Tyrr 1784
SPIER, Edward	Hali 1783	Hezekiah	Tyrr 1784
Nathan	Hali 1783	James	Tyrr 1784
Wm	Hali 1783	Jeremiah	Tyrr 1784
SPIERS, John Sr	Crav 1779	Jesse	Tyrr 1784
SPIGHT, Henry	Bert 1774	John	Tyrr 1784
Wm	Crav 1779	Joseph Jr	Tyrr 1784
SPILLAR, Henry	Bert 1774	Joseph Sr	Tyrr 1784
SPILLER, James	Samp 1784	Josiah	Tyrr 1784
James	Dupl 1784	Michael	Tyrr 1784
SPILMAN, George	Casw 1786	Nehemiah	Tyrr 1784
SPINK, Henry	Surr 1782	Samuel Jr	Tyrr 1784
SPIRES, Henry	Surr 1782	Samuel Sr	Tyrr 1784
John	Crav 1779	Simon	Tyrr 1784
SPIVEY, Caleb	Dobb 1780	Stephen	Tyrr 1784
Dempsey	Hert 1784	Thomas	Tyrr 1784
Easter	Bert 1781	Wm	Tyrr 1784
Edmond	Samp 1784	SPRY, James	Curr 1779
Elijah	Gate 1789	SPURGEON, Samuel	Rowa 1768
Ephraim	Dobb 1780	Wm	Rowa 1768
Jacob	Wayn 1786	SPURLIN, Zachariah	Surr 1782
Jacob	Gate 1789	SQUIRES, Amos	Crav 1779
Jesse	Gate 1789	Appleton	Beau 1779
Jonathan	Bert 1781	Appleton	Beau 1786
Josephine	Bert 1774	James	Crav 1779
Lydia	Gate 1789	John	Camd 1782
Moses	Bert 1774	Thomas	Camd 1782
Moses	Crav 1779	ST JOHN, Wm	Warr 1784
Moses	Gate 1789	STACEY, Thomas	Perq 1787

STACKS, Abraham	Wilk	1782
STACY, Charles	Albe	1694
Elizabeth	Albe	1694
Francis	Albe	1694
John	Albe	1694
Mary	Albe	1694
Rebecca	Albe	1694
Sarah	Surr	1782
Thomas	Albe	1694
Thomas	Perq	1772
STAFFORD, John	Hali	1783
John	Pasq	1779
John	Wilk	1782
John	Pasq	1789
Joshua	Hali	1783
Josiah	John	1784
Josiah	Pasq	1779
Laban	Casw	1784
Lemuel	Tyrr	1784
Saml	Pasq	1789
Samuel	Perq	1772
Stephen	Pasq	1779
Stephen	Pasq	1789
Thomas	Perq	1772
Thomas	Perq	1787
Wm	Perq	1772
Wm	Crav	1779
Wm	Onsl	1771
Wm	Surr	1782
Wm	Pitt	1786
STAGNER, Barnet	Rowa	1761
George	Rowa	1761
Honeul	Rowa	1761
STAGS, Wm	Surr	1782
STAINBACK, John	Gran	1771
STALKUP, Peter	Oran	1779
Swain	Oran	1779
Tobias	Oran	1779
Wm	Oran	1779
STALLINGS, Daniel	Perq	1787
Easter	Nash	1782
Elias	Perq	1772
Elias & sMesha	Bute	1766
Elizabeth	Nash	1782
Hardy	Mart	1779
Jesse	Bute	1766
Jesse	Perq	1772
Jesse	Perq	1787
Job	Perq	1772
Job	Perq	1787
John	Bute	1766
John	Perq	1772
John	Gate	1789
John	Perq	1787
Josiah	Bute	1766
Josiah	Gate	1789
Kedah	Perq	1787
Luke	Perq	1787
Meshak	Bute	1766
Moses	Nash	1782
Moses	Bute	1766
Moses & sonsRJ	Bute	1766
Nathl	Gate	1789
Reuben	Bute	1766
Reuben	Perq	1772
STALLINGS, Reuben	Perq	1787
Seth	Gate	1789
Simon	Perq	1772
Simon	Gate	1789
Simon	Perq	1787
Solomon	Perq	1787
Zadok	John	1784
STALLSWORTH, Joseph	Oran	1779
STAMP, Richard	Pasq	1779
Richard	Pasq	1789
STAMPS, Timothy	Surr	1782
STANBACK, Thomas	Nash	1782
Thomas	Bert	1774
STANCEL, John	John	1784
STANCELL, John	Dobb	1780
Wm	Dobb	1780
STANDARD, Daniel	Gran	1771
STANDBACK, Thomas	Rich	1790
Thomas	Rich	1790
STANDFIELD, John	Oran	1779
Robert	Casw	1784
Wm	Casw	1786
Wm	Casw	1784
STANDFORD, Anthony	Oran	1779
Charles	Oran	1779
Israel	Oran	1779
James	Oran	1779
STANDIN, Debra	Chow	1785
Elizabeth	Chow	1785
John	Perq	1772
Samuel	Perq	1772
Wm	Perq	1772
STANDLAND, Martin	Jone	1779
STANDLEY, David	Bert	1781
Evan	Camd	1782
Isaac	Dobb	1780
James	Jone	1779
John	Wilk	1782
Loving	Wayn	1786
Moses	Wayn	1786
Sandy Sr	Dobb	1780
Shadrack	Dobb	1780
Wm	Hali	1783
Wm	Wayn	1786
Wm	Surr	1782
STANFIELD, Henry	Rowa	1761
Thomas	Surr	1782
Thomas	Surr	1782
STANFILL, Sam	Wilk	1782
STANFORD, John	Ruth	1782
Sarah	Beau	1779
STANLEY, Christopher		
	Surr	1782
James	Oran	1779
John Jr	Samp	1784
John Sr	Samp	1784
Leven	Samp	1784
Stephen	Samp	1784
STANN, Moses	Gran	1771
STANSBURY, Mary	Casw	1784
STANSLAND, Hugh	Brun	1784
Margaret	Brun	1784
Samuel	Brun	1784
Thomas	Brun	1784
STANTON, Andrew	Pasq	1789

STANTON, Benjamin	Cart	1779	STEPHENS, Charles	John	1784
Christr	Surr	1782	Dinah	Curr	1779
Hope	Cart	1779	Edward	Hali	1783
John	Wayn	1786	Edward	John	1784
John	Brun	1784	John	Nash	1782
John	Crav	1779	John	Oran	1779
John Jr	Perq	1787	John	Hali	1783
John Sr	Perq	1787	Joshua	Nash	1782
Joseph	Cart	1779	Joshua	Samp	1784
Owen	Cart	1779	Matthew	Samp	1784
Thomas	Perq	1787	Matthew	Crav	1779
Wm	Cart	1779	Mildred	Samp	1784
STAPLEFORD, Thomas	Beau	1786	Richard	Hali	1783
STAPLES, Elizabeth	Camd	1782	Richard	Onsl	1771
Thomas	Camd	1782	Susannah	Pasq	1779
STAPLETON, Alexander			Wm	Blad	1784
	Blad	1784	Wm	Warr	1784
STARK, James	Gran	1771	Wm	Gran	1771
STARKEM, James	Gran	1785	STEPHENSON, James	John	1784
STARKES, John	Oran	1779	Louvincia	Pasq	1789
STARKEY, Edward	Onsl	1771	Matthew & sonM	Rowa	1770
John	Onsl	1771	Matthew Jr	Rowa	1770
Jonathan	Casw	1784	Rebeccah	Hert	1784
Peter	Onsl	1771	Solomon	John	1784
Wm	Blad	1784	STEPNEY, Wm	Perq	1772
STARLING, Abraham	Wayn	1786	Wm	Perq	1787
Elisha	Wayn	1786	STEPP, James	NorH	1780
John	Samp	1784	James Jr	Wilk	1782
Powell	Wayn	1786	James Sr	Wilk	1782
Robert	Samp	1784	John	Wilk	1784
Seth	Samp	1784	John	Wilk	1782
Smelly	Samp	1784	John	Gran	1771
STARRETT, Benjamin	Rowa	1761	Joshua	NorH	1780
STATON, Ezekiel	Mart	1779	Thomas	Wilk	1782
Jesse	Mart	1779	STEPTOE, John Jr	Hali	1783
Joseph	Mart	1779	John Sr	Hali	1783
Keziah	Mart	1779	Simon	Hali	1783
STATTEN, John	Surr	1782	STERLING, Adam	NorH	1780
Thomas	Bert	1774	John	Blad	1784
STAUBER, Christian	Surr	1782	John	Ruth	1782
STEALY, Jeremiah	Tyrr	1784	John	Rich	1790
John	Bute	1766	John	Rich	1790
Thomas	Tyrr	1784	Thomas	Blad	1784
Wm	Tyrr	1784	STESICK, Thomas	Surr	1782
STEEL, Alexander	Jone	1779	STEVENS, Absalom	Dobb	1780
John	Oran	1779	Alexander	Brun	1782
John Jr	Oran	1779	Hardy	Samp	1784
Wm	Rowa	1767	Hardy	Rich	1790
Wm	Oran	1779	Hardy	Rich	1790
STEELE, John	Bert	1774	James	Rowa	1767
Joseph	Beau	1786	Moab	Blad	1784
STEELEY, John	RiCH	1790	Ruth	Beau	1779
John	RiCH	1790	Saml	Surr	1782
STEELMAN, Chas	Surr	1782	Wm	Hert	1779
John	Surr	1782	Wm	Casw	1784
Mathias	Surr	1782	Wm	Hert	1784
STEERY, Abram	Gate	1789	STEVENSON, Alexander		
STEP, Joshua	NorH	1750		Brun	1784
Joshua Jr	NorH	1750	Hugh	Perq	1787
Moses	Wilk	1782	John	Pasq	1789
STEPHENS, Abner	Samp	1784	Thomas	Perq	1787
Abraham	Blad	1784	STEWARD, Anguish	Rich	1790
Barnabee	Samp	1784	Anguish	Rich	1790
Benj	Onsl	1771	Thomas	Rich	1790
Charles	Casw	1784	Thomas	Rich	1790

STEWART, Ann	Albe 1694	STOKES, Peter	Surr 1782
Calwell	NorH 1780	Silvanus	Casw 1784
Charles Jr	John 1784	Wm	Dupl 1783
Charles Sr	John 1784	STOLL, Abraham	Rowa 1770
Colfer	NorH 1780	STOLLER, Jacob Jr	Gran 1785
David	Rowa 1761	Jacob Sr	Gran 1785
Dugald	Samp 1784	STONE, Benj	Bert 1781
Elizabeth	Albe 1693	Benjamin	Rowa 1770
Elizabeth	Blad 1784	Benjamin	Bert 1774
Francis	Crav 1779	Benjamin Jr	Bert 1774
Frederick	Hali 1783	Connoway	Surr 1782
Hardy	Rich 1790	Cornelius	Perq 1787
Hardy	Rich 1790	Elisha	Perq 1787
Isaac	Rowa 1761	Enoch	Surr 1782
James	Rowa 1767	Ezekiel	Surr 1782
James	Oran 1779	Isaac	Perq 1787
James	Casw 1784	Jacob	Surr 1782
John	Rowa 1761	James	Rowa 1770
John	Mart 1779	James	Blad 1784
John	Samp 1784	John	Bute 1766
John Jr	Blad 1784	John	Rowa 1761
John Sr	Blad 1784	John	Rowa 1770
Joseph	Rowa 1761	John	NorH 1780
Robert	Beau 1786	John	Gran 1771
Samuel	Oran 1779	John	Perq 1787
Samuel & sons	Rowa 1761	Joseph	Beau 1786
Samuel Jr	Rowa 1761	Lemuel	Pasq 1779
Stephen	Casw 1784	Lemuel	Pasq 1789
Thomas	Tyrr 1784	Masel	Surr 1782
Thomas	Gran 1771	Moses	Perq 1787
Wm	Albe 1694	Nathl	Beau 1786
Wm	Oran 1779	Solomon	Surr 1782
Wm	Blad 1784	Solomon	Bert 1781
Wm	Casw 1784	Thomas	Surr 1782
Wm	Crav 1779	Wm	Casw 1784
Wm	Mont 1782	Wm	Surr 1782
Wm	Surr 1782	Wm	Bert 1781
Wm & wife Eliz	Albe 1693	Wm Sr	Surr 1782
STICE, Charles	Ruth 1782	Zedekiah	Bert 1774
STIGHT, Thomas	Bert 1781	Zedekiah	Bert 1781
STILES, James	Warr 1784	STONER, Conrad	Oran 1779
John	Bert 1774	STOOF, Daniel	Warr 1784
John	Onsl 1771	John	Warr 1784
Joseph	Onsl 1771	STOOS, Daniel	Warr 1784
STILLEY, John	Beau 1786	STOREY, John	Gran 1771
STILLWELL, Isaac	Beau 1786	STORM, John	Blad 1784
John	Rowa 1761	STORY, John	Hali 1783
John	Rowa 1770	Sarah	Hali 1783
STINSON, John	Oran 1779	Wm	Warr 1784
STIVA, Moses	Rich 1790	STOTT, Jacob	Surr 1782
Moses	Rich 1790	John	Pasq 1789
STOCKARD, James	OraN 1779	Wm	Pasq 1789
John	Oran 1779	STOUT, Charles	Oran 1779
STOCKBURGER, Geo	Surr 1782	Chas	Onsl 1771
STOCKER, Hanton	Onsl 1771	Chas Jr	Onsl 1771
STOCKLEY, Joseph	Pasq 1779	Jacob	Onsl 1771
STOCKTON, Samuel	Ruth 1782	Joseph	Oran 1779
Thomas	Ruth 1782	Peter	Oran 1779
STOGDEN, David	Rowa 1767	Peter Jr	Oran 1779
STOKELEY, Joseph	Pasq 1789	Samuel	Oran 1779
STOKELY, John	Warr 1784	STOVAL, Barthold	Gran 1785
STOKES, Arthur	Dupl 1783	Dorcas	Gran 1785
Drury	Tyrr 1784	Drury	Gran 1785
Henry	Mont 1782	John	Gran 1785
Henry	Surr 1782	Wm	Gran 1785

STOVALL, Barth	Gran 1771		STRICKLAND, Wm	Nash 1782
Benj	Gran 1771		Wm	Samp 1784
John Jr	Gran 1771		Wm Sr	Samp 1784
John Sr	Gran 1771		STRICKLIN, Jesse	Rich 1790
Joseph	Gran 1771		Jesse	Rich 1790
STOWE, Abraham	Surr 1782		Lot	Rich 1790
Benjamin	Curr 1779		Lot	Rich 1790
Daniel	Curr 1779		Matthew	Rich 1790
Jeremiah	Curr 1779		Matthew	Rich 1790
Nathl	Beau 1786		STRICKLING, Drury	Hert 1784
Samuel	Curr 1779		Drury	NorH 1780
Susannah	Curr 1779		Joseph	NorH 1780
STRADER, Conrad	Casw 1786		STRINGER, Hester	Dobb 1780
Conrad	Casw 1784		James	Casw 1784
Henry	Casw 1786		Limage	Casw 1786
Henry	Casw 1784		STRINGFELLOW, Henry	Rich 1790
John	Oran 1779		Henry	Rich 1790
STRAHAM, Moses	Blad 1784		Richard	Gran 1785
STRAHORN, Gilbert	Oran 1779		Robert	Rich 1790
John	Oran 1779		Robert	Rich 1790
Wm	Oran 1779		Wm	Rich 1790
STRAIN, John	Oran 1779		Wm	Rich 1790
Thomas	Oran 1779		STROAN, Larkin	Surr 1782
STRANGE, Edmond	Wayn 1786		STRONG, John	Rich 1790
STRATTON, Rachel	Blad 1784		John	Rich 1790
STRAUBS, Solomon	Rich 1790		STROOP, John	Surr 1782
Solomon	Rich 1790		STROOT, Saml	Surr 1782
STRAUGHAN, David	Bert 1774		STROTHER, Francis	Bute 1766
Gilbert	OraN 1779		John	Bute 1766
John	Oran 1779		STROUD, George	Blad 1784
Thomas	Oran 1779		John	Oran 1779
Wm	Oran 1779		Joshua	Oran 1779
STRAWBRIDGE, Wm	Mart 1779		Matthew	Oran 1779
STRECKLE, Reed	Surr 1782		Peter	Oran 1779
STREDWICK, Samuel	Oran 1779		Sion	Dobb 1780
STREET, John	Surr 1782		Wm	Oran 1779
Josiah	Surr 1782		STUART, David	Surr 1782
Moses	Casw 1784		David Jr	Surr 1782
Samuel	Rowa 1770		Elizabeth	Albe 1693
STREETER, John M.	Hali 1783		John	Rowa 1770
STREETMAN, Wm	Surr 1782		John	Surr 1782
STREETY, Wm	Blad 1784		Reuben	Surr 1782
STRICKLAND, Abner	Nash 1782		Saml	Pasq 1789
Abraham	Blad 1784		Wm & wife Eliz	Albe 1693
Benjamin	John 1780		STUBBLEFIELD, Geo	Wilk 1782
Britain	Samp 1784		Thos	Wilk 1782
David	Nash 1782		Wyatt	Casw 1786
Elias	Blad 1784		Wyatt	Casw 1784
Elizabeth	Nash 1782		STUBBS, Edward	Tyrr 1784
Hardy	Nash 1782		Jesse	Tyrr 1784
Henry	Nash 1782		John	Blad 1784
Herman	Nash 1782		John Jr	Tyrr 1784
Herman Jr	Hali 1783		John Sr	Tyrr 1784
Herman Sr	Hali 1783		Levi	Tyrr 1784
Holly	Samp 1784		Micajah	Tyrr 1784
Jacob	Nash 1782		Richard	Tyrr 1784
James	Blad 1784		Richard	Blad 1784
John	Nash 1782		Thomas Jr	Tyrr 1784
Lazarus	Nash 1782		Thomas Sr	Tyrr 1784
Mark	Nash 1782		Wm	Mart 1779
Phillip	Blad 1784		STUCKEY, James	Wayn 1786
Samuel	Samp 1784		John	Dupl 1779
Simon	John 1784		John	Hert 1779
Solomon	Nash 1782		John	Hert 1784
Thomas	Samp 1784		Shemmy	Hali 1783

STUCKEY, Thomas	Gran 1771	SUMMERS, Calip Quaker	
STUDER, Henry	Rowa 1761		Surr 1782
STUDEVANT, Jesse	Hali 1783	George	Casw 1786
Wm	Hali 1783	George	Casw 1784
STUDIARD, Wm	Wilk 1782	James	Casw 1784
STULTZ, Henry	Surr 1782	James	Perq 1787
Jacob	Surr 1782	Jethro	Warr 1784
Jasper	Surr 1782	John	Oran 1779
Phillip	Surr 1782	John	Mart 1779
STURD, Chas	Surr 1782	John	Casw 1786
Nathl	Surr 1782	John	Crav 1779
STURDEVANT, Henry	Warr 1784	John	Surr 1782
Matthew	Warr 1784	Joseph	Oran 1779
STURTHART, Wm	Surr 1782	Joshua	Surr 1782
STUTSMAN, Jacob	Rowa 1768	Joshua (Quaker	Surr 1782
STYRAN, Adonijah	Cart 1779	Mary	Perq 1787
George	Cart 1779	Thomas	Perq 1787
John	Cart 1779	Thomas (Quaker	Surr 1782
John Jr	Cart 1779	Wrightman	Surr 1782
Lemuel	Cart 1779	SUMMERVILE, John	Gran 1785
Richard	Cart 1779	SUMMERVILLE, John	Hali 1783
Samuel	Cart 1779	SUMMETT, Wm	Blad 1784
Wallace	Cart 1779	SUMNER, Benjamin	Mont 1782
Wm	Cart 1779	David	Hali 1783
STYRON, Cason	Crav 1779	Demsey	Gate 1789
STYVESTER, Dorcas	Tyrr 1784	Edwin	Gate 1789
SUBURN, John	Surr 1782	George	Onsl 1771
SUGGS, Absalom	Dobb 1780	James B	Gate 1789
Allgood	Blad 1784	Jesse	Beau 1779
Ezekiel	Blad 1784	Jethro	Gate 1789
Gabriel	Mont 1782	Josiah	Hert 1779
John	Dobb 1780	Josiah	Hert 1784
John	Blad 1784	Luke	Hert 1779
Thomas	Rowa 1768	Luke	Perq 1779
Thomas	Blad 1784	Moses	Hert 1779
Thomas & son T	Rowa 1768	Moses	Hert 1784
SUIT, Wm	Gran 1771	Mourning	Gate 1789
SULBURNT, Clement	Surr 1782	Robert	Hert 1779
SULLIVAN, Edwin	Brun 1784	Robert	Rowa 1768
John	Dupl 1779	Robert	Hert 1784
John	Bert 1781	Seth	Hert 1784
Richard	Beau 1786	SUREGOOD, Angie	Perq 1772
Thomas	Cart 1779	SURET, Simon	Gran 1771
Wm	Dupl 1779	SURLES, Thomas	Oran 1779
Wm	Hali 1783	SURLS, Edward	Dobb 1780
SULLIVANT, Abraham	Bert 1774	Robert	Dobb 1780
Jeremiah	Hali 1783	Wm	Dobb 1780
SUMAN, Thomas	Beau 1779	SURRATT, Thomas	Rowa 1768
SUMERAL, Joseph	Bert 1774	SURRY, Thomas	Gran 1771
Moses	Rich 1790	SUSSMAN, Lazarus	Pasq 1779
Moses	Rich 1790	SUTHER, John	Oran 1779
SUMERAN, Christian	Rowa 1761	Samuel	Oran 1779
SUMMERLIN, Elisha	Bert 1781	SUTHERLAND, Ransom	Gran 1785
Jacob	Bert 1781	SUTTEN, David	Pitt 1786
John	Bert 1774	SUTTON, Ann widow of J	
Jonah	Bert 1774		Dobb 1780
Jonas	Bert 1781	Ashbury	Perq 1787
Joseph	Bert 1781	Beaun.	Blad 1784
Lazarus	Wilk 1784	Benjamin	Dobb 1780
Loganus	Wilk 1782	Benjamin	Perq 1772
SUMMERS, Bastor	Surr 1782	Bomount	Bute 1766
Benjamin	Oran 1779	Charles	Bert 1774
Boster (Quaker	Surr 1782	Chloe	Bert 1781
Caleb	Surr 1782	Christopher	Blad 1784
Caleb (Quaker)	Surr 1782	David	Crav 1772

SUTTON, Dread	Surr 1782	SWANN, Thomas	Pasq 1789
Geo	Perq 1787	SWANNER, Jesse	Beau 1786
George	Nash 1782	Sarah	Mart 1779
Greenbury	Perq 1787	Thomas	Mart 1779
James	Blad 1784	Thomas	Tyrr 1784
James	Perq 1772	SWARTZ, Andrew	Surr 1782
James	Mont 1782	SWAYRIA, John Jr	Casw 1784
James	Wilk 1782	John Sr	Casw 1784
Jeremiah	Perq 1787	SWEARINGEN, George	Mont 1782
John	Dobb 1780	SWEARINGTON, John	Mont 1782
John	Blad 1784	Thomas	Mont 1782
John	Gran 1785	SWEENEY, John Jr	Casw 1784
John	Wilk 1782	John Sr	Casw 1784
John	Surr 1782	SWEES, Adam	Rowa 1770
John	Bert 1781	SWEET, Abraham	Hali 1783
John deceased	Dobb 1780	Benjamin	Blad 1784
Joseph	Albe 1679	Sarah	Hali 1783
Joseph	Perq 1772	Wm	Hali 1783
Joseph	Perq 1772	SWEETING, Dutton	Wilk 1782
Joseph	Perq 1787	SWEM, Michael	Rowa 1768
Nathaniel	Albe 1679	SWIFT, Anthony	Casw 1786
Saml	Perq 1787	Anthony	Casw 1784
Thomas	Dobb 1780	Ephraim	Onsl 1771
Thomas	Oran 1779	John	Casw 1784
Thomas	Bert 1774	Joseph	Tyrr 1784
Thomas	Bert 1781	Thomas	Casw 1786
Thomas	Perq 1787	Thomas	Casw 1784
Wm	Blad 1784	Wm	Casw 1786
Wm	Tyrr 1784	Wm	Casw 1784
Wm	Wilk 1782	SWIM, Adam	Rowa 1768
SWAFFORD, James	Ruth 1782	John	Rowa 1768
SWAIN, Cornelius	Tyrr 1784	SWINDOLL, Parker	Curr 1779
David	Brun 1784	Samuel	Blad 1784
Eleazer	Tyrr 1784	SWINNEY, Daniel	Surr 1782
Eliakim	Tyrr 1784	Edmond	Bute 1766
James	Mart 1779	Jeremiah	Chow 1785
James	Brun 1784	John	Oran 1779
Job	Bert 1774	Joseph	Bute 1766
Job	Bert 1781	Littlebury	Bute 1766
John	Mart 1779	Thomas	Bute 1766
John	Tyrr 1784	Thomas	Gran 1785
John	Bert 1781	Thomas	Warr 1784
John Jr	Tyrr 1784	Wm	Gran 1785
John Sr	Tyrr 1784	SWINSON, John	Tyrr 1784
Joshua	Tyrr 1784	Levy	Mart 1779
Letchworth	Bert 1781	Richard	Tyrr 1784
Levi	Brun 1784	SWISTON, George	Gran 1785
Michael & sonW	Rowa 1768	SWOPE, George	Hert 1779
Richard	Mart 1779	George	Hert 1784
Richard	Bert 1774	SYKES, Isaiah Jr	Blad 1784
Tabitha	Bert 1781	Jacob	Crav 1779
Wm	Mart 1779	Jesse	Blad 1784
Wm	Pasq 1779	Jonathan	Blad 1784
Wm	Bert 1774	Joseph	Blad 1784
Wm son of Mich	Rowa 1768	SYMMONS, Elliott	Perq 1772
SWALLOW, John	Surr 1782	SYMONS, Abraham Jr	Pasq 1779
SWAN, Henry	Beau 1779	Abraham Sr	Pasq 1779
SWANN, Edward	Casw 1784	Abraham Sr	Pasq 1789
Henry	Pasq 1789	Humphrey	Perq 1772
John	Ruth 1782	Jeremiah	Pasq 1694
John	Pasq 1779	Jeremiah	Pasq 1779
John	Pasq 1789	Jesse	Pasq 1779
Peggy	Pasq 1789	John Jr	Pasq 1779
Thomas	Casw 1786	John Jr	Pasq 1789
Thomas	Casw 1784	John Sr	Pasq 1779

SYMONS, John Sr	Pasq	1789	TARKINGTON, Benjamin Jr		
Matthew	Pasq	1789		Tyrr	1784
Thomas	Pasq	1694	Benjamin Sr	Tyrr	1784
Thomas	Pasq	1789	John	Tyrr	1784
SYNNOT, Michael	Oran	1779	Joseph	Tyrr	1784
Sawyer, Wm #2	Camd	1782	Joshua	Tyrr	1784
			Wm	Tyrr	1784
			Zebulon	Tyrr	1784
			TARPLEY, John	Casw	1784
TABB, Thomas	Hali	1783	Thomas	Casw	1784
TABOR, Drury	Gran	1785	TART (?), Nathl	Bert	1781
Ezekiel	Gran	1771	TARVER, Absalom	Dobb	1780
John	Ruth	1782	Jacob	Dobb	1780
John	Bute	1766	John	NorH	1780
Wm	Gran	1785	Mary	NorH	1780
TADLOCK, Absalom	Bert	1781	Millicent	NorH	1780
Edward	Pasq	1779	Saml	NorH	1780
James	Pasq	1779	Samuel	Dobb	1780
John	Pasq	1779	TATE, Andrew	Wilk	1782
Thomas	NorH	1780	Arthur	Surr	1782
TAFF, John	Bute	1766	James	Oran	1779
TAFT, Wm	Casw	1784	John	Oran	1779
TAGART, Abraham	Gran	1785	Joseph	Oran	1779
TALBERT, Joseph	Casw	1784	Nathan	Casw	1784
Thomas	Mont	1782	Travis	John	1784
TALBOT, Isaac	Nash	1782	Waddy	Casw	1784
John	Casw	1786	Waddy	Casw	1786
TALER, Edward	Surr	1782	Wm	Oran	1779
TALLEY, Daniel	Warr	1779	Zacharias	Oran	1779
Frederick	Warr	1784	Zacheus	Oran	1779
Harley	Warr	1784	TATEAN, John	Curr	1779
Henry	Mont	1782	Wm	Curr	1779
Nicholas	Gran	1785	TATLOCK, Edward	Pasq	1789
Reuben	Gran	1785	James	Pasq	1789
Richard	Warr	1784	John	Pasq	1789
Samuel	Oran	1779	TATOM, Barnett	Gran	1771
Wm	Oran	1779	John	Gran	1771
TALMAN, Joseph	Onsl	1771	TATUM, David	Pasq	1789
TALOM, John	Gran	1785	Joseph	Samp	1784
Wm	Gran	1785	Laban	Samp	1784
TALTON, Arthur	John	1784	Richard Jr	Samp	1784
John	John	1784	Richard Sr	Samp	1784
Joshua	Perq	1787	Stephen	Oran	1779
Wm	John	1784	TAUNT, Jesse	Beau	1786
TANDY, Boyd	Pasq	1789	TAYLOE, Abram	Bert	1781
TANKARD, Geo	Beau	1786	David	Bert	1781
TANN, Benjamin	Nash	1782	James	Bert	1781
TANNER, Benj	Onsl	1771	Jonathan	Samp	1784
Benjamin	Dupl	1783	Laban	Samp	1784
Edward	Warr	1784	Richard	Bert	1781
Frederick	Surr	1782	TAYLOR, Abraham	NBer	1779
Jennings	Gran	1785	Abraham	Bert	1774
Jennings	Warr	1779	Absalom	Crav	1779
John	Warr	1784	Armstead	Oran	1779
Joseph	Wilk	1782	Benj	Onsl	1771
Luke	Gate	1789	Benjamin	Nash	1782
Samuel	Dupl	1783	Benjamin	Curr	1779
Wm	Warr	1779	Benjamin	Wilk	1782
TANSIL, John	Bute	1766	Benjamin Jr	Brun	1784
TANT, Wm	Bute	1766	Benjamin Sr	Brun	1784
TARBUTTON, Dwight	Mont	1782	Caleb	Curr	1779
Joseph	Mont	1782	Caleb	NorH	1780
Joseph	Rich	1790	Charles	Casw	1786
Joseph	Rich	1790	Charles	Casw	1784
TARDY, John	Casw	1786	Charles	Pasq	1779

TAYLOR, Charles	Crav 1779	John	Gran 1771
Chas	Wilk 1782	John	Perq 1787
Christopher	Dobb 1780	John	Pasq 1789
Col	Surr 1782	John 2,514 a.	Nash 1782
Daniel	Dobb 1780	John Jr	Blad 1784
Daniel	Nash 1782	Jonas	Hert 1779
Daniel	Pasq 1779	Jonathan	Samp 1784
Daniel	NorH 1780	Jonathan	Wayn 1786
Daniel	Pasq 1789	Jonathan	Curr 1779
Daniel Jr	Blad 1784	Joseph	Dobb 1780
Daniel Sr	Blad 1784	Joseph	Mart 1779
David	Cart 1779	Joseph	Casw 1784
David	Mart 1779	Joseph	Gran 1785
Dicey	Nash 1782	Joseph	Hali 1783
Drury	Nash 1782	Joseph	Crav 1779
Drury	Surr 1782	Joseph	Curr 1779
Ebenezer	Curr 1779	Joseph	NorH 1780
Edmund	Mont 1782	Joseph	Gran 1771
Edmund Jr	Gran 1785	Joshua	Ruth 1782
Edmund Sr	Gran 1785	Joshua	Mart 1779
Edward	Curr 1779	Joshua	Crav 1779
Edward	Surr 1782	Josiah	John 1784
Elizabeth	Pasq 1779	Kitt	Nash 1782
Elkin	Surr 1782	Laban	Samp 1784
Frederick	Blad 1784	Lemuel	Hert 1779
Gabriel	Camd 1782	Leven	Cart 1779
George	GRaN 1785	Louis	Gran 1785
Harbet	Blad 1784	Mary	Camd 1782
Harry 1,094 a.	Nash 1782	Mary	Casw 1786
Henry	Dobb 1780	Mathias	Crav 1779
Henry	Blad 1784	Matthew	Surr 1782
Hillery	Dobb 1780	Michael	Hert 1779
Humphrey	NorH 1780	Michael	Hert 1784
Isaac	Dobb 1780	Mills	Nash 1782
Jacob	Camd 1782	Nathaniel	Chow 1785
Jacob	Blad 1784	Nathl	Gate 1789
James	Oran 1779	Nimrod	Mont 1782
James	Camd 1784	Reuben	Nash 1782
James	Samp 1784	Reuben	Casw 1784
James	Nash 1782	Reuben	Curr 1779
James	Wayn 1786	Richard	Hali 1783
James	Casw 1784	Richard	Surr 1782
James	Gran 1785	Richard Jr	Mart 1779
James	Jone 1779	Richard Sr	Mart 1779
James	Wilk 1784	Robert	Ruth 1782
James	Surr 1782	Robert	Dobb 1780
James	Pasq 1789	Robert	Curr 1779
James Thomas	Curr 1779	Robert	Gate 1789
Jesse	NBer 1779	Sam	Gate 1789
John	Bute 1766	Samson	Mart 1779
John	Dobb 1780	Samuel	Hert 1784
John	Cart 1779	Samuel	Warr 1784
John	Oran 1779	Samuel Jr	Hert 1784
John	Mart 1779	Shadrack	Pasq 1779
John	Camd 1782	Simeon	Oran 1779
John	Chow 1785	Stephen	Dobb 1780
John	Gran 1785	Thomas	Oran 1779
John	Pasq 1779	Thomas	Brun 1784
John	Perq 1772	Thomas	Hali 1783
John	Crav 1779	Thomas	Curr 1779
John	Mont 1782	Thomas	Pasq 1789
John	Curr 1779	Thomas Sr	Curr 1779
John	Onsl 1771	Thornton	Curr 1779
John	NorH 1780	Wilkins	Cart 1779
John	Surr 1782	Winifred	Hert 1784

Wm	Dobb 1780	TERRY, Matthew	Rich 1790
Wm	Camd 1782	Olive	Casw 1786
Wm	Hert 1779	Olive	Casw 1784
Wm	Blad 1784	Rebecca	Casw 1786
Wm	Wayn 1786	Rebecca	Casw 1784
Wm	Gran 1785	Roland	Gran 1785
Wm	John 1784	Roland	Gran 1771
Wm	Pasq 1779	Sarah	Casw 1784
Wm	NBer 1779	Stephen	Gran 1785
Wm	Perq 1772	Wm	Rich 1790
Wm	Mont 1782	Wm	Rich 1790
Wm	Onsl 1771	TETTERTON, Wm	Tyrr 1784
Wm	Gran 1771	TEW, Jeremiah	Samp 1784
Wm	Gate 1789	Philip	Samp 1784
Wm Jr	Camd 1782	THACKER, Elizabeth	Wilk 1782
Wm Jr	Surr 1782	THACKERY, John	Perq 1772
Wm Sr	Surr 1782	Joseph	Perq 1772
TEACHY, Daniel	Dupl 1779	Oliver	Pasq 1789
TEAGUE, Joshua	Rowa 1768	Thomas	Perq 1772
Michael	Surr 1782	THARP, America	Gran 1771
Thomas	Pasq 1779	Charles	Brun 1784
TEARNAGAN, David	Warr 1784	Samuel	Brun 1784
TEASLEY, Abraham	Oran 1779	Thomas	Gran 1771
Abraham	Casw 1784	Tiny	Gran 1785
TEASTER, John	Hert 1784	THAXTON, Thomas	Casw 1786
TEDDER, George	Dobb 1780	THAYER, John	NorH 1780
Thomas	Dobb 1780	THEACH, Joseph	Perq 1787
TEDDYARD, Basel	Surr 1782	Spencer	Perq 1787
John	Surr 1782	Thomas	Perq 1787
TEENIN, Hugh	Oran 1779	THEARIN, Aaron	Warr 1784
James	Oran 1779	THHOMPSON, Richard	Oran 1779
John	Oran 1779	THIGPEN, Cyprian	Dobb 1780
TELFAIR, Peter	Dobb 1780	Job	Dobb 1780
TELLERTON, Wm	John 1784	John	Dobb 1780
TELLERY, John	Hali 1783	Joseph	Dobb 1780
TEMPLE, Aaron & sons		Joshua	Dobb 1780
	Bute 1766	Martin	Dobb 1780
Aaron s of Aar	Bute 1766	THITFORD, George	Oran 1779
Henry mulatto	Bute 1766	Josias	Oran 1779
Jacob	Pasq 1779	Thomas	Oran 1779
James	Pasq 1789	Wm	Oran 1779
Joseph	Pasq 1779	THODAN, Abraham	John 1784
Joseph	Pasq 1789	THOMAS, Abishai	Hali 1783
Moses s of Aar	Bute 1766	Abram	Oran 1779
Thomas	Cart 1779	Absalom	John 1784
Thomas	Pasq 1779	Amos	John 1784
Thomas	Pasq 1789	Amos	Bert 1774
TEMPLEMAN, Mary	Pasq 1789	Amos	Bert 1781
Richard	Pasq 1779	Benjamin	Bute 1766
Samuel	Pasq 1779	Benjamin	Gran 1785
TENNYSON, Abraham	Bert 1774	Benjamin	Hert 1784
TERRELL, Cornelius	Blad 1784	Benjamin	Perq 1772
Jacob	Pitt 1786	Christian	Gran 1785
John	Bute 1766	Daniel	Warr 1784
John	Casw 1784	Daniel	Rich 1790
Philemon	Blad 1784	Daniel	Rich 1790
Wm	Blad 1784	David	Casw 1784
Wm	Pitt 1786	David	Warr 1784
TERRILL, John	Gran 1771	David	Surr 1782
TERRIS, James	Gran 1771	Edmund	Brun 1784
TERRY, Benjamin	Warr 1784	Edward	Oran 1779
James	Gran 1785	Elisha	John 1784
James	Rich 1790	Evan	Curr 1779
James	Rich 1790	Ezekiel	Bert 1774
Matthew	Rich 1790	George	John 1784

THOMAS, George Sr	Jone 1779	Spencer	Bert 1781
Gingo	Blad 1784	Steven	Rich 1790
Griffith	Oran 1779	Steven	Rich 1790
Isaac	Rowa 1768	Thomas	Blad 1784
Isaiah	Bert 1774	Thomas Jr	Wayn 1786
Jacob	Oran 1779	Thomas Sr	Wayn 1786
Jacob	Chow 1785	W.	Cart 1750
James	Oran 1779	Wm	Dobb 1780
James	Bert 1774	Wm	Oran 1779
James	Gate 1789	Wm	Samp 1784
Jesse	Nash 1782	Wm	Blad 1784
Jesse	Cart 1779	Wm	Wayn 1786
Jesse	Oran 1779	Wm	John 1784
Jesse	Blad 1784	Wm	Perq 1772
Jethro	Nash 1782	Wm	Crav 1779
Joel	John 1784	Wm	Curr 1779
John	Nash 1782	Wm	Rich 1790
John	Bute 1766	Wm	Rich 1790
John	Dobb 1780	Wm	Rich 1790
John	Blad 1784	Wm Sr	Rich 1790
John	Brun 1784	Wm Sr	Rich 1790
John	Casw 1784	THOMASSON, Richard	Surr 1782
John	Gran 1785	Thomas	Gran 1785
John	Hall 1783	THOMLINSON, John	Cart 1779
John	John 1784	Wm	Wayn 1786
John	Bert 1774	THOMPSON, Adam	Surr 1782
John	Crav 1779	Alexander	Nash 1782
John	Brun 1782	Alexis	Casw 1786
John	Surr 1782	Alexr	Surr 1782
John	Bert 1781	Andrew	Rowa 1768
Jonathan	Hert 1784	Ann	Wilk 1782
Jonathan	Bert 1774	Anthony	Casw 1786
Joseph	Blad 1784	Arthur	Bert 1781
Joseph	Wilk 1782	Benjamin	Oran 1779
Joseph	Perq 1787	Charles	Blad 1784
Josiah	Bert 1781	Chas	NorH 1780
Lewis	Blad 1784	Close	Wilk 1782
Lewis	Bert 1774	Cuthbert	Casw 1784
Lewis	Rich 1790	Daniel	Blad 1784
Lewis	Rich 1790	Daniel	Hali 1783
Luke	Samp 1784	Daniel	Nash 1782
Martha	Blad 1784	David	Ruth 1782
Martin	John 1784	David	Dobb 1780
Mary	Nash 1782	Edward	Surr 1782
Mary	John 1784	Elizabeth	Chow 1785
Mathew	Gate 1789	Evey	Surr 1782
Matthew	Bute 1766	Geo	Surr 1782
Micajah	Nash 1782	Geo	Gran 1771
Michael	Blad 1784	Harry	Rowa 1768
Morgan	Pasq 1694	Henderson	Surr 1782
Phillip	Casw 1784	Henry	Oran 1779
Richard	Nash 1782	Henry	Nash 1782
Richard	Oran 1779	Henry	Onsl 1771
Richard	Blad 1784	Henry	NorH 1780
Richard	Gran 1785	Hugh	Onsl 1771
Richard	Onsl 1771	Hugh	Rich 1790
Risher	Dobb 1780	Hugh	Rich 1790
Sam	Gate 1789	Hugh Jr	Rich 1790
Samuel	Hert 1779	Hugh Jr	Rich 1790
Samuel	Dobb 1780	James	Oran 1779
Samuel	Hert 1784	James	Samp 1784
Samuel Sr	Hert 1784	James	Wayn 1786
Simon	Rich 1790	James	Bute 1766
Simon	Rich 1790	James	Warr 1784
Solomon	Wayn 1786	James	Surr 1782

THOMPSON, James Jr	Onsl 1771		THORN, Thomas	Hert 1779
James Sr	Onsl 1771		Thomas	Hert 1784
John	Bute 1766		Wm	Hert 1779
John	Rowa 1768		Wm	Hert 1784
John	Oran 1779		Wm	NorH 1780
John	Casw 1786		THORNBURG, Edward	Rowa 1768
John	Wayn 1786		Edward	Rowa 1761
John	Gran 1785		Edward s of Wa	Rowa 1770
John	Ruth 1782		Henry	Rowa 1768
John	Warr 1784		Henry	Rowa 1770
John	Mont 1782		Joseph	Rowa 1768
John	Curr 1779		Thomas	Rowa 1768
John	Onsl 1771		Thomas s of Ed	Rowa 1761
John	Surr 1782		Walter	Rowa 1768
John	Bert 1781		Walter	Rowa 1770
John	Pasq 1789		Wm	Rowa 1769
Joseph	Oran 1779		Wm	Rowa 1761
Joseph	Wilk 1782		THORNTON, Catrain &	s Jo
Judith	NorH 1780			Bute 1766
Mary	Curr 1779		Daniel	Gate 1789
Matthew	Beau 1779		Francis	Warr 1784
Matthew	Beau 1786		Joel	Casw 1786
Michael	Jone 1779		Joel s of Catr	Bute 1766
Neil	Blad 1784		John	Samp 1784
Noah	Bert 1774		John	Rich 1790
Noah	Bert 1781		John	Rich 1790
Rachel	Wayn 1786		Joseph	Perq 1787
Reuben	Bert 1774		Mary	Perq 1772
Richard	Surr 1782		Merryman	Gran 1785
Ruth	Hali 1783		Nathaniel	Samp 1784
Samuel	Bute 1768		Roger	Bute 1766
Samuel	Oran 1779		Roger	Gran 1785
Samuel	Nash 1782		Solomon	Gran 1785
Samuel	Ruth 1782		Thomas	Warr 1784
Theophilis	Oran 1779		Thomas	Jone 1779
Thomas	Oran 1779		Thomas Jr	Samp 1784
Thomas	Wayn 1786		Thomas Sr	Samp 1784
Thomas	Chow 1785		Wm	Gran 1785
Thomas	Gran 1785		Wm	Surr 1782
Thomas	Dobb 1780		THOU, Michael	Tyrr 1784
Thomas	Rich 1790		THRIFT, Isham	Oran 1779
Thomas	Rich 1790		Nathl	NorH 1780
Thomas Jr	Wayn 1786		THROWER, Benjamin	Hali 1783
Trimikin	Nash 1782		Thomas	Hali 1783
Wm	Samp 1784		THURMOND, Thomas	Wilk 1782
Wm	Casw 1786		THURSTON, Elijah	Surr 1782
Wm	Blad 1784		Isham	Surr 1782
Wm	Wayn 1786		Wm	Perq 1772
Wm	Gran 1785		TICE, Jacob	Mart 1779
Wm	Hert 1784		TICKERELL, Sarah	Warr 1784
Wm	Nash 1782		TICKLE, John	Oran 1779
Wm	Cart 1779		Peter	Oran 1779
Wm	Hert 1779		TIFFIN, Thomas	Casw 1786
Wm	NorH 1780		TIGNOR, James	Crav 1779
Wm	Surr 1782		TILGHMAN, Joseph	Dobb 1780
Wm	Bert 1781		Joshua	NBer 1779
Wm Jr	Blad 1784		Moses	Dobb 1780
THOMSON, John	Brun 1782		TILLERY, Joshua	Surr 1782
THORINGTON, Wm	Beau 1786		TILLETT, James	Bute 1766
THORN, Hardy	Hert 1784		TILLEY, Benjamin	Wilk 1782
John	Hert 1779		Bennett	Surr 1782
John	Hert 1784		Edmund	Surr 1782
Merriman	Gran 1785		Henry	Surr 1782
Nicholas	Hert 1784		John	Oran 1779
Pressley	Gran 1785		Jonas	Surr 1782

TILLEY, Lazarus	Surr 1782	TOLAR, Thomas	Wayn 1786
TILLIS, Elizabeth	Mont 1782	Thomas Jr	Wayn 1786
Jesse	Mont 1782	Wm	Wayn 1786
TILLMAN, Geo	Gran 1771	TOLBERT, John	Bute 1766
John	Dupl 1783	Thomas	Rowa 1768
John	Gran 1771	TOLBEY, Wm	Wilk 1782
Tobias	Oran 1779	TOLER, Wm	Samp 1784
TILLOT, Thomas	Curr 1779	Wm	Blad 1784
TILMAN, Richard	Mont 1782	TOLLEY, Sally	Ruth 1782
TILTON, Elizabeth	Wayn 1786	TOLLICOFFER, George	Hali 1783
TILYAM, James T.	Jone 1779	TOLLIVER, Moses	Wilk 1782
TIMMONS, Elisha	Tyrr 1784	TOLSON, Barnett	Gran 1785
TIMS, Arnis	Gran 1785	Benjamin	Crav 1779
Hollis	Gran 1785	Jesse	Cart 1779
TINDALL, John	Dobb 1780	John	Crav 1779
Joshua	Dobb 1780	Wm	Warr 1784
TINER, Benjamin	John 1784	Wm	Rich 1790
Phillip	Blad 1784	Wm	Rich 1790
TINES, Saml	Gran 1771	TOMAS, George	Samp 1784
TINGLE, Clawson	Crav 1779	TOMELSON, Thomas	John 1784
Elizabeth	Crav 1779	TOMES, Caleb	Perq 1772
Gideon	Crav 1779	Christopher	Perq 1772
Solomon	Crav 1779	Foster	Perq 1772
Stephen	Beau 1779	George	Perq 1772
TINKER, Edward	Beau 1786	Joshua	Perq 1772
Peter	Rowa 1761	Morgan	Pasq 1694
TINNISON, Ignatius	Casw 1786	Mr	Albe 1679
TINTON, David	Surr 1782	Zachariah	Perq 1772
TIPP, John	Warr 1784	TOMLIN, Israel	Blad 1784
Nathaniel	Crav 1779	Susannah	Camd 1782
TIPPET, James	Jone 1779	TOMLINSON, John Edge	
John	Jone 1779		NBer 1779
TIPPINS, Samuel	Warr 1779	Moses	Ruth 1782
TIPPITT, Erasmus	Hali 1783	Wm	Bert 1774
John	Gran 1785	TOMPKINS, Moses	Wilk 1782
TISDALE, Henry	Nash 1782	Silas	Wilk 1782
TITTERSON, John	Dobb 1780	TOMS, Cosby	Perq 1787
Wm	Dobb 1780	Foster	Perq 1787
TOALSON, Benjamin	Cart 1779	John	Perq 1787
Jesse	CART 1779	Martha	Perq 1787
John	Cart 1779	TONEY, Arthur mulatto	
Thomas	Cart 1779		Casw 1786
Wm	Cart 1779	John	Hali 1783
TOAMES, Thomas	Pasq 1694	TOOKES, John	Crav 1779
TODD, Daniel	Onsl 1771	TOOLE, Jonathan	Bert 1774
Elizabeth	Pasq 1779	Jonathan	Bert 1781
James	Surr 1782	Mary	Bert 1774
John	Tyrr 1784	TOOLR, Edward	Samp 1784
John	Bert 1774	TOPPIN, Samuel	Chow 1785
John	Bert 1781	TOPPING, Wm	Oran 1779
Moses	Bert 1781	TORBEVILLE, Joseph	Samp 1784
Samuel	Bert 1774	TORKSEY, Caleb	Camd 1782
Thomas	Bert 1774	Jesse	Camd 1782
Wm	Gram 1785	John	Camd 1782
Wm Jr	Bert 1774	Joseph	Camd 1782
Wm Sr	Bert 1774	Phillip	Camd 1782
TOHEL, Michael	Surr 1782	Robert	Camd 1782
TOLAR, Ann	Wayn 1786	Thomas	Camd 1782
James	Curr 1779	Wm	Camd 1782
John	Wayn 1786	TORRANS, Thomas	Dobb 1780
Mathias	Curr 1779	TORRENTINE, Alexander	
Nehemiah	Wayn 1786		Oran 1779
Robert Jr	Wayn 1786	John	Oran 1779
Robert Sr	Wayn 1786	Samuel	Oran 1779
Stephen	Wayn 1786	TORREY, George	Blad 1784

TOTEWINE, Simon	Dobb 1780	
TOUCHSTONE, Jonas	Rowa 1770	
TOUP, John	Surr 1782	
TOW, Joseph	Onsl 1771	
TOWNS, David	Warr 1784	
David & sons	Bute 1766	
David (Jr)	Bute 1766	
Elizabeth	Warr 1784	
James	Warr 1784	
John	Warr 1784	
Richard	Bute 1766	
Richard	Warr 1784	
Thomas	Crav 1779	
TOWNSEND, Eliz	Perq 1787	
Job	Curr 1779	
John	Curr 1779	
John	Wilk 1782	
Joseph	Oran 1779	
Thomas	Blad 1784	
Wm	Blad 1784	
TRACEY, George	Mont 1782	
James	Mont 1782	
Lucy	Mont 1782	
Thomas	Mont 1782	
TRACY, Nathaniel	Ruth 1782	
TRAIN, James	Blad 1784	
TRAMMELL, Peter	Ruth 1782	
Thomas	Ruth 1782	
TRATT, Adam	Onsl 1771	
TRAVIS, Chas	Mont 1782	
James	Mont 1782	
Thomas	Gate 1789	
TREADWAY, Moses	Brun 1784	
TREADWELL, Henry	CRav 1779	
John	Samp 1784	
Mary	Samp 1784	
TREBLE, Christian	Surr 1782	
TREDHAM, Stephen	Mont 1782	
TRENT, Wm	Mont 1782	
TRESWICK, Robert	Onsl 1771	
TREWHITT, Levi	Dobb 1780	
Wm	Dobb 1780	
TRIBBLE, Benj	Wilk 1782	
Elijah	Wilk 1782	
John	Wilk 1782	
Spillsbee	Wilk 1782	
Stephen	Wilk 1782	
TRICKY, Charles	Casw 1784	
TRIGGS, Samuel	Samp 1784	
TRIM, Charles	Casw 1784	
TRIPLETT, Eleanor	Wilk 1782	
George	Brun 1784	
John	Casw 1786	
John	Casw 1784	
Mason	Wilk 1782	
Nimrod	Casw 1786	
Nimrod	Casw 1784	
TRIPP, Henry	Beau 1779	
John	Beau 1779	
John	Beau 1786	
Nicholas	Oran 1779	
Robert	Beau 1779	
Robert	Beau 1786	
Wm	Beau 1779	
TROLLINER, Michael	Surr 1782	

TROLLINGER, Adam	Oran 1779	
Michael	Surr 1782	
TROTMAN, Dempsey	Gate 1789	
Ezekiel	Gate 1789	
Thomas	Gate 1789	
TROUSDALE, James	Oran 1779	
John	Oran 1779	
Wm	Oran 1779	
TROUT, Henry	Ruth 1782	
TROXLER, Barney	Oran 1779	
TROYER, Samuel	NBer 1779	
TRUE, John	Pasq 1789	
TRUEBLOOD, Aaron	Pasq 1789	
Aaron	Pasq 1789	
Abel	Pasq 1779	
Abel	Pasq 1789	
Asa	Tyrr 1784	
Asa	Pasq 1779	
Caleb	Pasq 1779	
Caleb	Pasq 1789	
Caleb Jr	Pasq 1789	
Caleb Sr	Pasq 1789	
Daniel	Pasq 1779	
Daniel	Pasq 1789	
Fisher	Pasq 1779	
Fisher	Pasq 1789	
Jesse	Pasq 1789	
John	Pasq 1779	
John	Pasq 1789	
Joseph	Pasq 1779	
Joseph	Pasq 1789	
Joshua	Pasq 1789	
Josiah	Pasq 1779	
Josiah	Pasq 1789	
Thomas	Pasq 1779	
Thomas	Pasq 1789	
Thomas Jr	Pasq 1789	
Thomas Sr	Pasq 1789	
Timothy	Pasq 1779	
Timothy	Pasq 1789	
TRUELOVE, Wm	Bute 1766	
TRULL, James	Mont 1782	
TRULUCK, George	Crav 1779	
Sutton	Pitt 1786	
TRUMAN, Hardy	Blad 1784	
James	Blad 1784	
Joshua	Bert 1774	
TRUMBLE, Jethro	Bert 1781	
TUBBS, George	Ruth 1782	
James	Ruth 1782	
John	Ruth 1782	
Wm	Ruth 1782	
Wm	Casw 1784	
TUCKER, Abner	Curr 1779	
Benjamin	Nash 1782	
Benjamin s ofJ	Bute 1766	
Curl	NorH 1780	
Drury	NorH 1780	
Enoch	Rowa 1761	
Frederick	Hali 1783	
George	Rowa 1761	
George	Mont 1782	
George & sonWm	Rowa 1768	
Gray	Hali 1783	
Henry	Hali 1783	

TUCKER, Henry	Warr 1784	TURLINGTON, Wm	Mart 1779
James	Surr 1782	TURNAGE, Geo	Pitt 1786
James Jr	Nash 1782	George	Crav 1779
Janes Sr	Nash 1782	Luke	Rich 1790
Joab	Nash 1782	Luke	Rich 1790
John	Dobb 1780	Michael	Oran 1779
John	Warr 1779	Rachel	Rich 1790
John	Beau 1779	Rachel	Rich 1790
John	NorH 1780	TURNBULL, John	Wilk 1784
John	Beau 1786	John	Wilk 1782
John	Perq 1787	TURNER, Abishai	Bert 1781
John & sons Wm	Bute 1766	Abraham	Perq 1772
Joseph	Nash 1782	Amos	Bert 1781
Mary	Rich 1790	Arthur	Tyrr 1784
Mary	Rich 1790	Benj	Onsl 1771
Nathaniel	Rowa 1768	Benjamin	Pasq 1779
Obadiah	Casw 1784	Benjamin	Casw 1784
Obadiah	Casw 1786	Berry	Casw 1786
Reuben	Nash 1782	Charles	Gran 1785
Robert	Rowa 1768	Chas	Pasq 1789
Robert	Wayn 1786	Clear	Hert 1779
Sam	Wilk 1782	Daniel	Blad 1784
Samuel	Rowa 1768	Daniel	Onsl 1771
Samuel	Wilk 1784	David	Bert 1774
Thomas	Nash 1782	David	Bert 1781
Thomas	Hali 1783	Dempsey	Perq 1772
Thomas	Onsl 1771	Dempsey	Pasq 1789
Willis	Hali 1783	Edward	Oran 1779
Willoughby	Nash 1782	Edward	Perq 1772
Wm	Bute 1766	Edward	Wilk 1782
Wm	Dobb 1780	Edward	Bert 1781
Wm	Samp 1784	Edwin	Hali 1783
Wm	Warr 1779	Elias	Rowa 1761
Wm	Surr 1782	Elias	Onsl 1771
TUCKESTON, Caleb	Mont 1782	Elijah	Mart 1779
TUCY, Adam	Blad 1784	Elizabeth	Surr 1782
Edith	Blad 1784	Fielding	Hali 1783
Francis	Blad 1784	George s ofJac	Rowa 1768
Isham	Blad 1784	Healthy	Hali 1783
James Jr	Blad 1784	Henry	Ruth 1782
Joseph	Blad 1784	Henry	NorH 1780
Lewis	Blad 1784	Henry Jr	Casw 1784
Thomas	Blad 1784	Henry Sr	Casw 1784
TUDER, Elizabeth	Gran 1785	Jacob & son Ge	Rowa 1768
Henry	Gran 1785	James	Nash 1782
John	Gran 1785	James	Casw 1786
Owen	Gran 1785	James	Casw 1784
Valentine	Gran 1785	James	Hali 1783
TUESDALE, James	Gran 1785	James	Bert 1781
TUGGLE, Griffin	Gran 1785	Jeremiah	Hali 1783
John	Gran 1785	Jethro	Gate 1789
TUGWELL, James	Gate 1789	John	Bute 1766
TULL, Charles	Dobb 1780	John	Samp 1784
Isaac	Dobb 1780	John	Blad 1784
John	Dobb 1780	John	Hali 1783
Nicholas	Surr 1782	John	Pasq 1779
Wm	Dobb 1780	John	Perq 1772
TULLOCH, Thomas	Oran 1779	John	Bert 1774
Thomas	Hali 1783	John	Onsl 1771
TUNK, Thomas	Casw 1784	John	Beau 1786
TUNNEY, Wm	NBer 1779	John	Perq 1787
TUNNING, Thomas	Casw 1786	Joseph	Bute 1766
TUNSTON, Wm	Wilk 1782	Joseph	Casw 1784
TURLINGTON, John	Nash 1782	Joseph	Perq 1772
Southey	Samp 1784	Joseph Jr	Perq 1787

TURNER, Joseph Sr	Perq	1787
Joshua	Perq	1787
LUVICEY	Hali	1783
Leona	Bute	1766
Lucy	Hali	1783
Martha	Bert	1781
Matthew	Wayn	1786
Matthew	Bert	1774
Matthew	Bert	1781
Moses	Rich	1790
Moses	Rich	1790
Myal	Samp	1784
Peter	Hali	1783
Rhodey(Rhoda?)	Surr	1782
Richard	Pasq	1789
Robert	Cart	1779
Robert	Rowa	1768
Robert	Oran	1779
Robert 100 a.	Nash	1782
Roger	Rowa	1761
Roger	Wilk	1782
Roger Sr	Rowa	1761
Sam	Onsl	1771
Simon	Bert	1774
Simon	Bert	1781
Solomon	Hali	1783
Stephen	Gran	1785
Thomas	Bute	1766
Thomas	Rowa	1761
Thomas	Hali	1783
Thomas	Warr	1784
Thomas	Bert	1774
Thomas	Wilk	1782
Thomas	Onsl	1771
Thomas	Perq	1787
Wm	Nash	1782
Wm	Hert	1779
Wm	Bute	1766
Wm	Samp	1784
Wm	Gran	1785
Wm	Hali	1783
Wm	Hert	1784
Wm	Pasq	1779
Wm	Warr	1784
Wm	Bert	1774
Wm	Bert	1781
TURNEY, Henry	Casw	1786
Wm	Bert	1774
TURON, Thomas	Casw	1784
TUTEN, Sarah	Crav	1779
Shadrack	Crav	1779
Thomas Jr	Crav	1779
Wm	Crav	1779
Zachariah	Crav	1779
TUTER, John	NorH	1780
John	Gran	1771
Owen	NorH	1780
TUTIN, John	Pitt	1786
TUTON, John	Dobb	1780
Wm	Dobb	1780
TUTTLE, Joseph	Pasq	1789
Thomas	Surr	1782
Thomas	Beau	1786
Thomas Sr	Crav	1779
TWEAT, Frederick	Warr	1784

TWEEDY, John	Tyrr	1784
Thomas	Tyrr	1784
TWETTY, Thomas	Warr	1784
TWIFORD, Wm	Tyrr	1784
TWINE, Abraham	Perq	1787
Jesse	Perq	1787
John	Perq	1772
John	Perq	1787
Pleasant	Perq	1787
TWITTY, John	Ruth	1782
Thomas	Hali	1783
TYGER, Wm	Hali	1783
TYLER, Barrymore	Bert	1781
Bartlett	Gran	1771
Ed	Beau	1779
Jacob	Pasq	1779
John	Hert	1779
John	Hert	1784
John	Brun	1782
Lewis	Hali	1783
Moses	Hert	1779
Moses	Hert	1784
Owen	Samp	1784
Perry	Hert	1779
Perry	Hert	1784
TYNER, Arthur	NorH	1780
Benj	NorH	1780
Elizabeth	NorH	1780
James	Wayn	1786
John	NorH	1780
Sarah	Bert	1781
Wm	Wayn	1786
Wm	NorH	1780
TYRE, George	Wilk	1782
John	Wilk	1782
Wm	Crav	1779
Wm	Wilk	1782
UMFLEET, David	Gate	1789
Job	Gate	1789
Wm	Gate	1789
UNDERHILL, Joseph	Chow	1785
Wm	Wayn	1786
UNDERWOOD, Emmanuel	Nash	1782
George	Wilk	1782
Jacob	Nash	1782
James	Casw	1786
Jesse	NorH	1780
John	Bute	1766
John	Wilk	1782
John	NorH	1780
Richard	Gran	1771
Thomas	NorH	1780
UPCHURCH, Benjamin s ofR		
	Bute	1766
Richard & sonB	Bute	1766
Sarah	Wilk	1782
Wm	Gran	1785
Wm	Wilk	1784
Wm	Gran	1771
Wm Jr	Gran	1771
UPTIGROVE, Isaac	Surr	1782
John	Surr	1782

UPTON, Edward	Camd 1782	
Edward	Casw 1784	
John	Perq 1787	
Robert	Blad 1784	
Thomas	Camd 1782	
Willis	Camd 1782	
URGANHART, Alexander		
	Bert 1774	
URQUEERD, Norman	Samp 1784	
USHER, Mary	Bert 1781	
Richard	Rich 1790	
Richard	Rich 1790	
Samuel	Rich 1790	
Samuel	Rich 1790	
Thomas	Rich 1790	
Thomas	Rich 1790	
Wm	Bert 1781	
USSERY, David	Mont 1782	
Elizabeth	Mont 1782	
James	Ruth 1782	
John	Ruth 1782	
John Jr	Mont 1782	
John Sr	Mont 1782	
Joshua	Mont 1782	
Thomas	Mont 1782	
Wm	Ruth 1782	
Wm	Mont 1782	
UTLEY, David	John 1784	
UZZELL, Elisha Jr	Wayn 1786	
Elisha Sr	Wayn 1786	
VAIL, Edward	Chow 1785	
Jeremiah	Beau 1779	
Mary	Beau 1779	
Thomas	Chow 1785	
VALENTINE, Alexander		
	Hert 1779	
Alexander	Hert 1784	
David	Hert 1779	
David	Hert 1784	
Henry	Gran 1771	
Joseph	Gate 1789	
Sarah	Chow 1785	
Thomas	Nash 1782	
VALZ, Johannes	Surr 1782	
VAN DYKE, Thomas	Mont 1782	
VANCE, David	Surr 1782	
John	Mart 1779	
Nathl	Surr 1782	
Saml	Surr 1782	
Wm	Brun 1782	
VANDAMENT, Ed	Beau 1779	
VANDERGRIFF, John	Wilk 1782	
VANDERPOOL, Abraham	Surr 1782	
Winant	Wilk 1782	
VANDYKE, John	Gran 1785	
Joseph	Tyrr 1784	
VANE, Michael	Wilk 1782	
VANHOOK, Aaron	Casw 1784	
David	Casw 1784	
Florence	Casw 1784	
Isaac	Casw 1784	
Lloyd	Casw 1784	

VANHOOK, Thomas	Casw 1784	
VANHOOSER, Jacob	Mont 1782	
Valentine	Rowa 1761	
Wm	Mont 1782	
VANLANDINGHAM, Dawson		
	Warr 1784	
Francis	Nash 1782	
James	Nash 1782	
John	Gran 1771	
Wm	Gran 1785	
VANN, Dempsey	Bert 1774	
Dempsey	Bert 1781	
Eaccas	Gate 1789	
Henry	Samp 1784	
Jesse	Bert 1779	
Jesse	Gate 1789	
John	Bert 1774	
John	Gate 1789	
King	Samp 1784	
Mary	Bert 1774	
Rachel	Gate 1789	
Stephen	Samp 1784	
Thomas	Bert 1774	
Thomas	Gate 1789	
Wm	Samp 1784	
Wm	Bert 1774	
VANNOY, Andrew	Wilk 1782	
Daniel	Wilk 1782	
Francis	Wilk 1782	
John	Surr 1782	
Nathaniel	Wilk 1782	
VANPELT, Anthony	Dobb 1780	
Harmon	Hert 1779	
James	Hert 1779	
James deceased	Hert 1784	
John	Hert 1779	
Orphan	Hert 1784	
Peter	Hert 1784	
Sarah	Hert 1174	
VANTRESS, George	Dobb 1780	
VANWINKLE, James	Wilk 1782	
VARDIN, Ebenezer	Pasq 1789	
VARNEL, John	Gate 1789	
VASS, Phillip	Casw 1784	
Thomas	Casw 1784	
VASSAR, John	Dobb 1780	
VAUGH, Richard	Gran 1771	
VAUGHAN, Fredk	NorH 1780	
James	NorH 1780	
John	NorH 1780	
Wm	NorH 1780	
VAUGHN, Benjamin	Ruth 1782	
Christopher	Nash 1782	
Dempsey	Nash 1782	
Frederick	Nash 1782	
George	Gran 1785	
Gideon	Casw 1786	
Joel	Ruth 1782	
Joel	Rowa 1768	
John	Oran 1779	
John & son Wm	Rowa 1768	
Joseph	Ruth 1782	
Stephen	Nash 1782	
Vinson	Gran 1785	
Vinson	Hali 1783	

VAUGHN, Wm	Hert 1779	VINCENT, John Sr	Bert 1774
Wm	Hert 1784	Peter	Gran 1785
VAULA, Daniel	Warr 1784	Peter	Gran 1771
VAULS, Daniel	Warr 1784	VINES, John	Albe 1694
VAUSE, David	Dobb 1780	John	Brun 1784
Ephraim	Dobb 1780	Joseph	Beau 1779
Wm	Dobb 1780	Mary	Beau 1779
VAUTERS, John	Surr 1782	Samuel	Beau 1779
VEAL, Wm	Rowa 1770	Thompson	Beau 1786
VEASY, Nathl	Bert 1781	Wm	Beau 1779
VEAZEY, Elijah	Gran 1785	VINING, John	Dobb 1780
James	Gran 1771	Kadar	Dobb 1780
Thomas	Gran 1771	Wm	Dobb 1780
Zebulon	Gran 1785	VINN, Wm	Wilk 1782
VEGER, John	Pasq 1694	VINSON, Benjamin	Wayn 1786
VENABLE, John	Surr 1782	Cal	Hali 1783
John Sr	Surr 1782	David	Bute 1766
Wm	Surr 1782	Elisha	Hert 1779
VENTER, Moses	Onsl 1771	James Sr	Hert 1779
VERMILLION, Richard	Beau 1779	Jesse	Bute 1766
Wm	Casw 1784	Jesse	Pitt 1786
VERNON, Isaac	Surr 1782	Levin	Wayn 1786
James	Surr 1782	Peter	Hert 1779
Jonathan	Surr 1782	Phillip	Hali 1783
Jonathan Sr	Surr 1782	Solomon	Wayn 1786
VERNOR, Adam	Rowa 1770	Thomas	Bert 1781
VEST, Bryan	Blad 1784	Wm	Bute 1766
VESTER, Solomon	Nash 1782	VIRGIN, Samuel	Mart 1779
Wm	Nash 1782	Wm	Bert 1774
VICAR, John W	Blad 1784	Wm	Bert 1781
VICK, Benjamin	Nash 1782	VIVRETT, Thomas	Nash 1782
Benjamin	Samp 1784	VOLGER, Phillip	Surr 1782
Cooper	Samp 1784	VOLVEY, Joseph	Tyrr 1784
Henry	Nash 1782	VOSE, Thomas	Beau 1779
Hiseog	Nash 1782	Thomas	Beau 1786
John	Nash 1782	VOSS, Wm	Albe 1679
Jordan	Nash 1782	VULGAR, Geo	Bert 1781
Nathan Sr & so	Samp 1784	Vinner, John	Gran 1771
Richard	Nash 1782		
Richard s of N	Samp 1784		
Robert	Nash 1782		
Wilson	Nash 1782	WACHUP, John	Camd 1782
VICKERS, Elias	Wilk 1782	WADDELL, Chas	Surr 1782
Elijah	Wilk 1782	Gov.	Blad 1784
Samuel	Perq 1772	Hugh	Blad 1784
VICKERY, Christopher		Noel	Surr 1782
	Rowa 1770	WADDINGTON, Abbite & sons
Christopher so	Rowa 1768		Bute 1766
Elias	Wilk 1784	Wm son of Abbi	Bute 1766
John	Rowa 1768	WADDINGTPN, James s of Abb
John	Rowa 1770		Bute 1766
Marmaduke	Rowa 1770	WADDY, Spence	Warr 1784
Marmaduke & so	Rowa 1768	WADE, Abraham	Cart 1779
Wm	Gran 1771	Amey	Gran 1785
VICKORY, Joseph	Mont 1782	Benj	Gran 1771
VINCENT, Aaron	John 1784	Charles	Gran 1785
Alexander	Gran 1785	David	Cart 1779
Alexr	Gran 1771	Isaac	Cart 1779
Drury	John 1784	J.	Cart 1779
Garrett	Ruth 1782	James	Dobb 1780
Jacob	Gran 1785	John	Dobb 1780
Jacob	Ruth 1782	Joseph	Rowa 1768
John	Hali 1783	Joseph	Gran 1771
John	John 1784	Mary	Cart 1779
John	Bert 1774	Richard	Crav 1779

WADE, Robert	Cart 1779	WALKER, Henderson Capt	
Robert	Gran 1785		Albe 1693
Samuel	Dobb 1780	Howard	Wilk 1782
Valentine	Cart 1779	Isaac	Wilk 1782
Valentine Jr	Cart 1779	James	Hert 1779
WADLINGTON, Thomas	Ruth 1782	James	Oran 1779
WAFF, Thomas	Chow 1785	James	Casw 1786
Wm	Chow 1785	James	Casw 1784
WAGGONER, Gabriel	Surr 1782	James	Hert 1784
Henry	Surr 1782	James	Warr 1784
John	Surr 1782	James	Gran 1771
Joseph	Surr 1782	James Jr	Casw 1786
Saml	Surr 1782	Jesse	Casw 1784
Thomas	Surr 1782	Jesse s of Wm	Bute 1766
Wm	Surr 1782	Joel	Nash 1782
WAGMAN, Geo	Surr 1782	Joel	Hali 1783
WAGNER, George	Oran 1779	John	Ruth 1782
Henry	Rowa 1761	John	Oran 1779
Henry	Oran 1779	John	Casw 1786
Jacob	Rowa 1761	John	Blad 1784
James	Oran 1779	John	Casw 1784
John	Oran 1779	John	Gran 1785
WAHAL, James	Curr 1779	John	Tyrr 1784
WAHHOB, Job	Cart 1779	John	Curr 1779
WAINWRIGHT, Milly	Beau 1786	John	Surr 1782
WAIR, Benjamin	Casw 1784	John	Gran 1771
Geo	Bert 1781	Major	John 1784
Wm	Oran 1779	Mary	Gran 1785
WAIT, Josiah	Curr 1779	Moses	Casw 1784
WAITE, Wm	Casw 1784	O'Neal	Curr 1779
WALDEN, Henry	Hali 1783	Peter	Bute 1766
Samuel	Hali 1783	Peter	Oran 1779
Thomas	Pasq 1789	Phillip	Wilk 1782
Wm	Surr 1782	Randolph	Wilk 1782
WALDING, Benjamin	Wayn 1786	Renelder	Wilk 1782
John C.	Warr 1784	Richard	Rowa 1768
Richard	Gran 1785	Robert	Warr 1784
WALDRAVEN, John	Oran 1779	Robert	Surr 1782
WALDREN, Wm	Onsl 1771	Saml	Gran 1771
WALDROP, John	Gran 1771	Samuel	Ruth 1782
Joseph	Gran 1771	Samuel	Casw 1786
WALFORD, Hardy	Bert 1781	Samuel	Casw 1784
John	Bert 1781	Samuel	Gran 1785
Joseph	Bert 1781	Samuel s of Th	Bute 1766
Wm Walker	Bert 1781	Sherrod	Warr 1784
WALKER, Aaron	Beau 1786	Solomon	Gran 1785
Amos	Oran 1779	Solomon	Gran 1771
Amos	Wayn 1786	Stewart	Tyrr 1784
Ann	Surr 1782	Susannah	Cart 1779
Archelaus	Wilk 1782	Thomas	Nash 1782
Baker	Samp 1784	Thomas	Ruth 1782
Caleb	Curr 1779	Thomas	Tyrr 1784
Charles	Blad 1784	Thomas	Beau 1779
Chas	Wilk 1782	Thomas	Curr 1779
Daniel	Casw 1784	Thomas	Beau 1786
Daniel	Beau 1786	Thomas	Rich 1790
David	Bute 1766	Thomas	Rich 1790
David	Surr 1782	Thomas & son S	Bute 1766
Dorothy	Camd 1782	Willis	Curr 1779
Edward	Tyrr 1784	Wm	Ruth 1782
Elisha	Hert 1784	Wm	Bute 1766
Felix	Ruth 1782	Wm	Oran 1779
George s of Wm	Bute 1766	Wm	Gran 1785
Hatton	Hert 1779	Wm	Warr 1784
Hatton	Hert 1784	Wm	Surr 1782

Wm & sons G&J			WALLER, Nathaniel	Gran	1785
	Bute	1766	Nathl	Gran	1771
Wm Jr	Bute	1766	Zephaniah	Gran	1785
Zachariah	Wilk	1782	Zephaniah	Gran	1771
WALL, Abraham	NorH	1780	WALLIS, Andrew	Dupl	1783
Byrd	Casw	1784	Benjamin	Casw	1786
Edward	Blad	1784	Benjamin	Crav	1779
Francis	Nash	1782	Elias	Casw	1786
Francis	Hali	1783	James	Gran	1771
Garrett	Surr	1782	John	Casw	1786
James	Nash	1782	John	Beau	1779
Jesse	John	1784	Joshua	Curr	1779
John	NorH	1780	Rlizabeth	John	1784
John Esq	Rich	1790	Robert	Pasq	1694
John Esq	Rich	1790	Robert	Crav	1779
Joseph	Beau	1786	Stephen	Crav	1779
Joseph Jr	Beau	1786	Thomas	Pasq	1694
Robert	Warr	1784	Thomas	Beau	1779
Robert	NorH	1780	Vallente	Cart	1779
Wm	John	1784	Wm	Gate	1789
Wm	Rich	1790	WALLS, Absalom	Beau	1779
Wm	Rich	1790	Jacob	Wilk	1782
WALLACE, Aaron Sr	Wayn	1786	James	Gate	1789
Adam	Cart	1779	WALLWOOD, Andrew	Albe	1679
David	Cart	1779	WALMSLEY, Thomas	Curr	1779
Elizabeth	Dobb	1780	WALSTON, James	Gran	1785
Gabriel	Onsl	1771	John	Dobb	1780
George	Hali	1783	John	Bert	1774
George	Bert	1774	Jonathan	Curr	1779
Guy	Warr	1784	Mary	Camd	1782
James	Dupl	1783	WALTER, Richard	Ruth	1782
Jane	Wilk	1782	Thomas	Beau	1779
Jaret	Hali	1783	WALTERER, Wm	Wayn	1786
John	Chow	1785	WALTERS, Amos	Beau	1779
John	Hali	1783	Henry	Brun	1784
John	Mont	1782	Henry	Brun	1782
John	Beau	1786	Isaac	Gate	1789
John Jr	Casw	1784	Jacob	Gate	1789
John Sr	Beau	1786	John	Brun	1784
Joseph	Cart	1779	John	Beau	1779
Joseph	Casw	1784	John	Rich	1790
Joseph Jr	Cart	1779	John	Rich	1790
Mark	Cart	1779	John Jr	Beau	1779
Martha	Mart	1779	Lewis	Gate	1789
Mary	Chow	1785	Mary	Beau	1779
Richard estate	Cart	1779	Paul	Casw	1784
Robert	Cart	1779	Rzekiel	Casw	1786
Robert	Gran	1771	Samuel	Brun	1784
Stephen	Cart	1779	Wm	Brun	1784
Thomas	Beau	1786	Wm	Brun	1782
Vallente	Cart	1779	Wm	Gate	1789
Wm	Cart	1779	WALTHER, Henry	Surr	1782
Wm	Rowa	1768	WALTON, Caleb s o Henr		
Wm	Oran	1779		Rowa	1770
Wm	Mart	1779	Clement	Surr	1782
Wm	Chow	1785	George	Perq	1787
Wm	Onsl	1771	Henry	Rowa	1768
Wm	Surr	1782	Henry	Gate	1789
Wm	Gran	1771	Henry & s Cale	Rowa	1770
WALLENTON, Nath	NorH	1780	James	Casw	1784
WALLER, Benjamin	Hali	1783	James	Onsl	1771
Hardridge	Warr	1784	James	Gate	1789
Henry	Surr	1782	Jesse	Wilk	1784
Jacob	Surr	1782	Jesse	Wilk	1782
Michael	Rowa	1761	John B	Gate	1789

WALTON, Joseph	Brun 1784	WARD, John	Surr 1782
Joseph	Gran 1785	John	Beau 1786
Lemuel	Hali 1783	Jonathan	Beau 1779
Peter	Oran 1779	Jonathan	Curr 1779
Richard	Rowa 1761	Joseph	Chow 1785
Timothy	Bert 1781	Joseph	Hali 1783
Wm	Hert 1784	Joseph	Warr 1784
WALTROP, Ezekiel	Ruth 1782	Lewis	Chow 1785
WALWOOD, Jane	Hert 1784	Lodowick	Chow 1785
WANTLAND, Mary	Onsl 1771	Martha	Bert 1781
WARBURTON, James	Bert 1774	Mary	Hert 1784
Jemimah	Bert 1781	Mary	Onsl 1771
Jeremiah	Bert 1774	Mary	Bert 1781
John	Onsl 1771	Moses	Chow 1785
John	Bert 1781	Notty	Bert 1774
Luke	Bert 1781	Phillip	Bert 1774
Winifred	Bert 1781	Phillip Jr	Bert 1774
Wm	Nash 1782	Rice	Albe 1694
Wm	Samp 1784	Richard	Warr 1784
WARD, Anthony	Tyrr 1784	Richard	Onsl 1771
Benj	Gran 1771	Richard	Surr 1782
Benj	Bert 1781	Richard	Gate 1789
Benjamin	Nash 1782	Robert	Hali 1783
Benjamin	Hali 1783	Robert	Curr 1779
Benjamin	Warr 1784	Seth	Onsl 1771
Benjamin Jr	Warr 1784	Simon	Onsl 1771
Bridget	Bert 1781	Solomon	Dobb 1780
Chas	Gran 1771	Solomon	Chow 1785
Daniel	Bert 1781	Solomon	Onsl 1771
David	Dobb 1780	Spellar	Mart 1779
David	Hali 1783	Stephen	Oran 1779
David	Onsl 1771	Thomas	Mart 1779
Dorothy (?)	Beau 1779	Thomas	Brun 1784
Edward	Onsl 1771	Thomas	Chow 1785
Elias	Hali 1783	Thomas	Pasq 1779
Elijah	Hali 1783	Thomas	Bert 1774
Elisha	Hali 1783	Thomas	Brun 1782
Elizabeth	Surr 1782	Thomas	Mont 1782
Enoch	Cart 1779	Thomas	Bert 1781
Ephraim	Chow 1785	Thomas Jr	Chow 1785
Ezekiel	Dobb 1780	Thomas Jr	Bert 1781
Francis	Nash 1782	Willis	Hert 1779
Francis	Pasq 1694	Willis	Pasq 1779
Francis	Mart 1779	Wm	Hert 1779
Freezan	Hert 1784	Wm	Oran 1779
Fruson	Hert 1779	Wm	Chow 1785
Geo	Bert 1781	Wm	John 1784
Henry	Surr 1782	Wm	Tyrr 1784
Hugh	Dobb 1780	Wm	Pasq 1779
Isaac W.	Hert 1784	Wm Sr	Mart 1779
James	Nash 1782	WARDLAW, Joseph	Ruth 1782
James	Oran 1779	WARE, George	Bert 1774
James	Chow 1785	John	Casw 1784
James	Hali 1783	John	Casw 1786
James	Bert 1774	Peter	Mont 1782
Jeremiah	Gran 1771	Roland	Mont 1782
Jesse	Samp 1784	Thomas	Casw 1784
Jesse	Gate 1789	Thomas	CasW 1786
John	Pasq 1694	Thomas	Mont 1782
John	Dobb 1780	Wm Jr	Casw 1784
John	Rowa 1770	Wm Jr	Casw 1786
John	Oran 1779	Wm Sr	Casw 1784
John	Mart 1779	Wm Sr	Casw 1786
John	Samp 1784	WARES, John	Dobb 1780
John	Mont 1782	WARING, Joseph	Samp 1784

WARNER, Frederick	Cart	1779
John	Dobb	1780
Saml	Pasq	1789
Samuel	Pasq	1779
WARNOCK, James	Surr	1782
John	Surr	1782
Matthew	Surr	1782
Saml	Surr	1782
WARPOOL, Robert	Cart	1779
WARREN, Abraham	Crav	1779
Abraham Jr	Crav	1779
Bray	Gate	1789
Edward	Beau	1786
Elijah	John	1784
Elizabeth	Hert	1779
Ethelred	Hert	1779
Goodlaw	Casw	1784
Hedgeman	Casw	1784
Henry	Hert	1779
Henry	Hert	1784
Henry	Perq	1772
Hinchey	Onsl	1771
Jacob	Pitt	1786
James	Mart	1779
James	Casw	1784
Jeremiah	Crav	1779
Jeremiah	Pitt	1786
Jesse	NorH	1780
Job	NorH	1780
John	Nash	1782
John	Casw	1784
John	Chow	1785
John	Gate	1789
John Jr	Casw	1784
Jordan	Hert	1784
Joseph	Bert	1774
Joseph Jr	Mart	1779
Joseph Sr	Mart	1779
Josiah	Bert	1781
Margaret	Hali	1783
Mary	Nash	1782
Nilson	Mart	1779
Richard	John	1784
Robert	Hert	1779
Robert	Mart	1779
Robert Jr	NorH	1780
Samuel	Casw	1786
Thomas	Nash	1782
Wm	Bert	1774
Wm	NorH	1780
Wm	Bert	1781
Wm Jr	Gate	1789
Wm Sr	Gate	1789
WARRICK, Andrew	Casw	1784
John	Beau	1779
Wyatt	Mart	1779
WARRINGTON, John	Tyrr	1784
WARSON, Henry	Casw	1786
WARTER, David	Beau	1786
Jesse	Beau	1786
John	Beau	1786
Zachariah	Beau	1786
WARTERS, Amos	Beau	1786
WARTON, Wm	Casw	1784
WARWICK, Benjamin	Samp	1784

WARWICK, John	Beau	1786
Wm	Hali	1783
WASDEN, Jonathan	Wayn	1786
WASHBURN, Gabriel	Ruth	1782
James	Blad	1784
Reuben	Surr	1782
Richard	Oran	1779
WASHINGTON, John	Gran	1785
Martin	Mart	1779
Richard	John	1784
Wm	Gran	1771
WASSON, Henry	Oran	1779
WAST, Wm	Bert	1781
WATER, Deep	Wilk	1784
WATERFIELD, Abraham	Curr	1779
John	Curr	1779
Michael	Curr	1779
Wm	Curr	1779
WATERS, Armstrong	Dobb	1780
Deep	Wilk	1782
Ezekiel	Casw	1784
Isaac	Tyrr	1784
Jesse	Beau	1779
John	Casw	1786
John	Casw	1784
John	Perq	1787
John Jr	Dobb	1780
John Sr	Dobb	1780
Leven	Onsl	1771
Moses	Wilk	1782
Regimillick	Dobb	1780
Richard	Dobb	1780
Southey	Onsl	1771
Thomas	Casw	1786
Walter	Wilk	1782
Winifred	Dobb	1780
Wm	Dobb	1780
Wm	Mart	1779
WATKINS, Benjamin	Casw	1784
Benjamin	Wayn	1786
Daniel	Samp	1784
David	Samp	1784
Earl	Mont	1782
Henry	Surr	1782
Israel	Rich	1790
Israel	Rich	1790
Jesse	John	1784
John	Bute	1766
John	Samp	1784
John	Blad	1784
John	Wayn	1786
John	Rich	1790
John	Rich	1790
Joseph	Surr	1782
Kesick	Rich	1790
Kesick	Rich	1790
Nancy	Samp	1784
Thomas	Rich	1790
Thomas	Rich	1790
Wilson	Wayn	1786
Wm	Wayn	1786
Wm	Rich	1790
Wm	Rich	1790
WATSON, Alexander	Rich	1790
Alexander	Rich	1790

WATSON, Alexander	Rich	1790	WEATHERFORD, Thomas	Casw	1786
Benj	Surr	1782	Thomas	Casw	1784
Charles	Nash	1782	Thomas Jr	Casw	1786
Daniel	Pasq	1779	Thomas Jr	Casw	1784
Daniel	Oran	1779	WEATHERINGTON, David		
David	Camd	1782		Crav	1779
David	Gate	1789	Robert	Crav	1779
Drury	Surr	1782	Wm	Tyrr	1784
Ezekiel	Samp	1784	WEATHERLY, Thomas	Tyrr	1784
Francis	Mart	1779	WEATHERMAN, Robert	Pitt	1786
Henry D.	Wayn	1786	WEATHERS, James	Gran	1785
Isom	Wayn	1786	WEATHERSBY, John	Mart	1779
James	Blad	1784	Thomas	Mart	1779
James	Oran	1779	Thomas Sr	Mart	1779
James	Jone	1779	Wm	Mart	1779
Jeremiah Jr	Cart	1779	WEAVER, Edward	Gran	1785
Jeremiah Sr	Cart	1779	Edward	Hert	1784
Jesse	Casw	1784	Edward	Gran	1771
John	Ruth	1782	Fredereick	Gran	1771
John	Oran	1779	Frederick	Blad	1784
John	Blad	1784	Jacob	Oran	1779
John	John	1784	James	Gran	1785
John	Hali	1783	Jesse	Hert	1779
John	Wilk	1782	Jesse	Hert	1784
John	Surr	1782	John	Ruth	1782
John Jr	Bert	1774	John	Gran	1785
John Sr	Bert	1774	John	Gran	1771
Luke	Blad	1784	Joshua	Wilk	1782
Mary	Pasq	1779	Maneer	Gran	1785
Matthew	Rich	1790	Mary	Hali	1783
Matthew	Rich	1790	Sarah	Hert	1779
Matthew	Rich	1790	Stephen	Hali	1783
Mosdes	Cart	1779	Thomas	Surr	1784
Moses	Cart	1779	Wm	Hert	1779
Nathl	Surr	1782	Wm	Bute	1766
Needham	Wayn	1786	Wm	Gran	1785
Patrick	Ruth	1782	Wm	Mont	1782
Richard	Hert	1784	Wm	Surr	1782
Sarah	Bert	1781	WEBB, Benjamin	Hert	1779
Solomon	Blad	1784	Benjamin	Hert	1784
Thomas	Mart	1779	David	Casw	1784
Thomass	Surr	1782	David	Gran	1785
Wm	Blad	1784	Elisha	NorH	1780
Wm	Oran	1779	Etheldred	Bert	1774
Wm	Mart	1779	George	Warr	1784
Wm	Blad	1784	George	Onsl	1771
WATT, James	NorH	1780	James	Camd	1782
Peter	Rich	1790	James	Chow	1785
Peter	Rich	1790	James	Wilk	1782
Wm	Wilk	1782	James	Gran	1771
WATTEN, John	Chow	1785	Jeremiah	Ruth	1782
WATTS, Thomas	Casw	1784	Jesse	Onsl	1771
Wm	Casw	1786	Jesse	NorH	1780
WAYMAN, Cosby	Pasq	1789	John	Ruth	1782
Thomas	Pasq	1779	John	Blad	1784
Thomas	Pasq	1789	John	Chow	1785
Wm	Pasq	1779	John	Gran	1785
WAYMIRE, Frederick soRu			John	Hali	1783
	Rowa	1768	John	Wilk	1782
Rudolph & s Fr	Rowa	1768	John	Perq	1787
WEAMS, John	Oran	1779	John	Rich	1790
WEATHERBY, John	Gate	1789	John	Rich	1790
Micajah	Blad	1784	John Sr	Rich	1790
Septernmus	Warr	1784	John Sr	Rich	1790
WEATHERFORD, John	Surr	1782	John Turner	Rich	1790

WEBB, John Turner	Rich	1790
Johnston	Casw	1784
Junior	Brun	1784
Martin	Wilk	1784
Mary	Chow	1785
Mary	Bert	1781
Richard	Hert	1779
Robert	Ruth	1782
Robert	Casw	1784
Robert	Rich	1790
Robert	Rich	1790
Ruth	Surr	1782
Sam	Onsl	1771
Samuel	Brun	1784
Stephen	Nash	1782
Thomas	Ruth	1782
Thomas	Bute	1766
Thomas	Bert	1774
Thomas	NorH	1780
Wm	Dobb	1780
Wm	Blad	1784
Wm	Chow	1785
Wm	Gran	1785
Wm	Perq	1772
Wm	Surr	1782
Wm	Rich	1790
Wm	Rich	1790
Wm Jr	Ruth	1782
Wm Sr	Ruth	1782
Wm Sr	Onsl	1771
Zachariah	Chow	1785
WEBER, Thomas	NBer	1779
WEBSTER, Hosewell	Tyrr	1784
John	Surr	1782
Richard	Surr	1782
WEEKS, Archibald	Onsl	1771
Benj	Onsl	1771
Benj	Perq	1787
Edward	Cart	1779
Isaac	Cart	1779
Jabez	Cart	1779
James	Cart	1779
Joseph	Cart	1779
Joseph	Oran	1779
Juland	Hert	1784
Sam	Perq	1787
Silvanus	Onsl	1771
Stephen	Cart	1779
Theophilus	Onsl	1771
Thomas	Cart	1779
Thomas	Perq	1787
Wilson	Perq	1787
Ziller	Cart	1779
WEIR, George	Blad	1784
Wm	Gran	1771
WEIRDEN, John	Beau	1786
WELBOURN, John	Gran	1785
Zachariah	Gran	1785
WELCH, David	Chow	1785
David	Surr	1782
Edward	Chow	1785
James	Perq	1772
John	Rowa	1768
John	Gran	1785
John	Perq	1772

WELCH, John	Bert	1774
Joseph	Rowa	1761
Louis	Cart	1779
Mary	Beau	1779
Nathaniel	Perq	1772
Richard	Perq	1772
Samuel	Casw	1784
Thomas	Ruth	1782
Wm	Beau	1779
Wm	Beau	1786
WELDON, Penelope	Hali	1783
Randolph	Hali	1783
Samuel	Hali	1783
Wm	Hali	1783
WELKS, Thomas	Bute	1766
WELLS, Absalom	Bute	1766
Charles	Hali	1783
Hardy	Gate	1789
Isaac	Oran	1779
Joel	Brun	1784
John	Ruth	1782
John	Oran	1779
John	Surr	1782
John	Gate	1789
Joseph	Oran	1779
Joseph	Perq	1772
Joseph	Onsl	1771
Joseph	Perq	1787
Joseph Jr	Oran	1779
Joshua	Nash	1782
Micajah	Wayn	1786
Miles	Gran	1785
Miles	Gran	1771
Nathan	Oran	1779
Nathaniel	Onsl	1771
Sam	Bert	1781
Solomon	Nash	1782
Stephen	Nash	1782
Wm	Blad	1784
Zachariah	Wilk	1782
WELSH, Nathl	Perq	1787
Richard	Perq	1787
Walter	Wilk	1782
WELSMEARHOYER, Thomas		
	Gran	1771
WENBERY, Wm	Pasq	1779
WERDEN, John	Beau	1786
WESCOTE, Joshua	Chow	1785
WESHON, Leonard	Surr	1782
WESLEY, Thomas	Beau	1786
WESR, Robert	Brun	1782
WEST, Alexander	Wilk	1782
Andrew	Cart	1779
Ann	Curr	1779
Arthur	Nash	1782
Arthur Jr	Hali	1783
Arthur Sr	Hali	1783
Charles	Wayn	1786
Charles	Pasq	1779
Chas	Pasq	1779
Cyprian	NorH	1780
Edward	Curr	1779
Eli	Cart	1779
Euphamy	Surr	1782
George	Dobb	1780

WEST, George	Hali	1783	WESTRAY, Gulghan	Nash	1782
Isaac	Oran	1779	WETHERINGTON, John	Rowa	1770
Israel	Hali	1783	WETHERS, George	Warr	1784
James	Samp	1784	Reuben	Warr	1784
James	Blad	1784	WHALEBONE, Thomas	Casw	1784
James	Gran	1785	Thomas	Casw	1786
James	Brun	1782	WHALEY, Joseph	Hali	1783
James	Surr	1782	WHARTON, Caleb	Pasq	1779
James	Gran	1771	Ebenezer	Cart	1779
John	Dobb	1780	Edward	Pasq	1779
John	Wayn	1786	Isaac	Pasq	1779
John	Hert	1784	Joseph	Onsl	1771
John	Curr	1779	Robert	Pasq	1779
Jonathan	Oran	1779	Robert	Pasq	1789
Joseph	Bert	1781	Thomas	Onsl	1771
Joseph	Beau	1786	Willis	Pasq	1779
Joshua	Curr	1779	WHATLEY, Michael	Oran	1779
Lemuel	Pasq	1779	WHAYLAND, John	Surr	1782
Levi Jr	Cart	1779	WHEATLEY, Benjamin	Mart	1779
Levi Sr	Cart	1779	Daniel	Wilk	1782
Nathan	Nash	1782	Dinah	Curr	1779
Robert	Bert	1774	Geo	Wilk	1782
Robert	Bert	1781	George	Wilk	1782
SAmpson	Bute	1766	Hardy	Mart	1779
Samuel	Samp	1784	John	Mart	1779
Samuel	Pasq	1779	John	Curr	1779
Simon	NorH	1780	Mary	Mart	1779
Sion	Nash	1782	Robert	Curr	1779
Spencer	Curr	1779	Samuel	Mart	1779
Thomas	Bert	1781	WHEDBEE, Benjamin	Pasq	1779
Willis	Samp	1784	James	Perq	1787
Wm	Nash	1782	Joseph	Chow	1785
Wm	Samp	1784	Mary	Perq	1787
Wm	Hali	1783	Richard	Pasq	1779
Wm	Tyrr	1784	Richard	Perq	1787
Wm	Bert	1774	Saml	Pasq	1789
Wm	Crav	1779	Saml s of John	Perq	1787
Wm	Bert	1781	Thomas	Perq	1787
WESTBROOK, Benjamin	Dobb	1780	Thomas sof Jno	Perq	1787
Henry	Bute	1766	Wm s of John	Perq	1787
James	Wayn	1786	WHEELER, Ambrose	Surr	1782
John	Wayn	1786	Ann	Gran	1785
Moses	Dobb	1780	Benj	Surr	1782
Thomas	NorH	1780	Benjamin	Gran	1785
Wm	Samp	1784	Catherine	NorH	1780
WESTCORD, Simpson	Warr	1779	Henry	Gran	1771
WESTCOT, John	Curr	1779	Isaac	Blad	1784
Stephen	Curr	1779	Jacob	Oran	1779
WESTCOTT, Wm	Hali	1783	Jesse	Surr	1782
WESTER, Arthur	Nash	1782	John	Ruth	1782
John	Samp	1784	John	Oran	1779
Jordan	Samp	1784	John	Crav	1779
Samuel	Nash	1782	John	NorH	1780
WESTMORELAND, Isham	Surr	1782	Samuel	Casw	1784
WESTON, Ephraim	Bert	1774	Wm	Onsl	1771
Ephraim Jr	Bert	1781	Wm	Bert	1781
Ephraim Sr	Bert	1781	WHEELING, Sion	Hali	1783
Jeremiah	Hert	1784	WHEERY, Anthony	Pitt	1786
Jesse	Hert	1779	Wm	Pitt	1786
Jesse	Hert	1784	WHELIS, Mildred	Nash	1782
John	Pasq	1779	Wm	Nash	1782
Nuca	Bert	1781	WHELLUS, Benj	Surr	1782
Simon	Bert	1774	Louis	Surr	1782
Solomon	Bert	1781	Reuben	Surr	1782
Wm	Perq	1772	WHELON, John	Onsl	1771

WHELUS, Hardy	Hali 1783	WHITE, Daniel	Beau 1786
James	Hali 1783	David	Blad 1784
Joseph	Hali 1783	Devotion	Pasq 1789
WHERGIE, Wm	Bert 1781	Edward	Surr 1782
WHERRY, Anthony	Crav 1779	Edward	Perq 1787
Thomas	Ruth 1782	Elizabeth & s	Bute 1766
Wm	Crav 1779	Francis	Beau 1786
WHICKARD, Benj	Gran 1771	Francis	Pasq 1789
John	Gran 1771	George	Casw 1784
WHIDBEE, George	Perq 1772	George	Gran 1785
John	Perq 1772	Griffith	Blad 1784
John	Curr 1779	Henderson	Hert 1779
Joseph	Perq 1772	Henderson	Hert 1784
Michael	Perq 1772	Henry	Cart 1779
Richard	Perq 1772	Henry	Pasq 1694
Thomas	Perq 1772	Henry	Oran 1779
Wm	Curr 1779	Henry	Gran 1785
WHIDDON, John	Nash 1782	Henry	Perq 1772
Lott	Nash 1782	Henry	Curr 1779
Wm	Nash 1782	Henry	Gran 1771
WHITAKER, Abraham	Oran 1779	Henry Jr	Curr 1779
Abram	Beau 1786	Isaac	Gran 1771
Carey	Hali 1783	Isaac	Perq 1787
Edward	Hali 1783	Jacob	Perq 1772
Hudson	Hali 1783	Jacob	Perq 1787
James	Wilk 1782	James	Bute 1766
John	Hali 1783	James	Blad 1784
John	Wilk 1782	James	Camd 1782
Joshua	Rowa 1761	James	BlaD 1784
Mark	Rowa 1761	James	Chow 1785
Mark	Wilk 1782	James	Pasq 1779
Mark	Surr 1782	James	Warr 1784
Mary	Surr 1782	James	Beau 1779
Matthew	Hali 1783	James	Curr 1779
Peter	Oran 1779	James	Surr 1782
Richard	Hali 1783	James	Perq 1787
Robert	Hali 1783	James	Pasq 1789
Thomas	Wilk 1782	James	Pasq 1789
Thomas	Surr 1782	James s of Elz	Bute 1766
Wm	Rowa 1761	Jeremiah	Ruth 1782
Wm	Surr 1782	Jesse	Warr 1784
WHITCHERS, Batson	Beau 1786	Jesse	Perq 1787
Nancy	Beau 1786	John	Nash 1782
WHITE, Abraham	Pasq 1779	John	Camd 1782
Abram	Pasq 1789	John	Casw 1786
Absillia	Hert 1779	John	Blad 1784
Anthony	Pasq 1789	John	Pasq 1779
Armager	Nash 1782	John	Warr 1784
Arnold	Pasq 1694	John	NBer 1779
Arnold	Pasq 1789	John	Perq 1772
Augustine	Ruth 1782	John	Bert 1774
Benj	Gran 1771	John	Gran 1771
Benj	Perq 1787	John	Gate 1789
Benj Jr	Pasq 1789	John	Bert 1781
Benj Sr	Pasq 1789	John	Perq 1787
Benjamin	Hali 1783	John	Pasq 1789
Benjamin	Pasq 1779	John Jr	Bert 1781
Benjamin	NBer 1779	John Sr	Bert 1781
Benjamin	Perq 1772	Jonathan	Gran 1785
Burgess	Gran 1771	Jonathan	Gran 1771
Cadbreath & br	Bute 1766	Jonathan	Perq 1787
Caleb	Perq 1772	Jonathan Jr	Gran 1771
Caleb	Perq 1787	Jordan	Pasq 1789
Charles	Warr 1784	Joseph	Nash 1782
Cornelius	Camd 1782	Joseph	Oran 1779

Joseph	Camd 1782	Thomas	Gran 1785
Joseph	Blad 1784	Thomas	Tyrr 1784
Joseph	Perq 1772	Thomas	Perq 1772
Joseph	Perq 1787	Thomas	Curr 1779
Joseph	Pasq 1789	Thomas	Gate 1789
Joseph Sr	Nash 1782	Thomas	Beau 1786
Joshua	Camd 1782	Thomas	Perq 1787
Joshua	Chow 1785	Thomas	Pasq 1789
Joshua	Perq 1772	Thomsas	NorH 1780
Joshua	Gate 1789	Timothy	Casw 1786
Joshua Sr	Pasq 1789	Timothy	Casw 1784
Josiah	Perq 1772	Valentine	Gran 1771
Josiah	Perq 1787	Vinson	Curr 1779
Lemuel	Pasq 1789	Willis	Camd 1782
Luke	Bert 1774	Willobee	Curr 1779
Luke	Bert 1781	Wm	Bute 1766
Luke	Perq 1787	Wm	Dobb 1780
Luke Jr	Bert 1781	Wm	Blad 1784
Luke Sr	Bert 1781	Wm	Casw 1784
Lydia	Curr 1779	Wm	Gran 1785
Lydia	Perq 1787	Wm	Tyrr 1784
Margaret	Perq 1772	Wm	Pasq 1779
Mark	Gran 1785	Wm	Perq 1772
Mary	Perq 1787	Wm	Crav 1779
Mary Ann	Curr 1779	Wm	Curr 1779
Matthew	Blad 1784	Wm	Surr 1782
Matthew	Perq 1772	Wm	Gran 1771
Matthew	Perq 1787	Wm	Bert 1781
Mead	Chow 1785	Wm	Perq 1787
Media	Hert 1779	Wm & bro Cadbr	Bute 1766
Medice	Bert 1781	Wm Jr	Perq 1787
Micajah	Warr 1784	Wm Sr	Perq 1787
Miles	Perq 1787	Zachariah	Perq 1787
Mordica	Bert 1774	Zephaniah	Pasq 1779
Mordica Jr	Bert 1774	WHITEFIELD, Bryan 25,030lb	
Nathan	Pasq 1789		Dobb 1780
Nathaniel	Gran 1785	Joseph	Wayn 1786
Nathaniel	Pasq 1779	Needham	Wayn 1786
Peter	Rowa 1761	Wm	Hali 1783
Philemon	Gran 1785	Wm Jr	Wayn 1786
Phillip	Gran 1785	Wm Sr	Wayn 1786
Rachel	Perq 1772	WHITEHALL, Hest	Curr 1779
Robert	Dobb 1780	WHITEHEAD, Arthur	Nash 1782
Robert	Casw 1786	Arthur	Hali 1783
Robert	Casw 1784	Benjamin	Nash 1782
Saml	Gran 1771	Benjamin	Hali 1783
Saml	Perq 1787	Bennett	Nash 1782
Saml Jr	Pasq 1789	Cullen	NorH 1780
Samuel	Dobb 1780	David	Perq 1787
Samuel	Pasq 1779	Jacob	Nash 1782
Samuel	NBer 1779	James	Dobb 1780
Samuel	Perq 1772	James	Brun 1784
Seth	Perq 1772	John	Hert 1779
Silas	Chow 1785	John	Crav 1779
Silas	Perq 1772	John	Mont 1782
Solomon	Beau 1779	Lazarus	Nash 1782
Solomon	Beau 1786	Lazarus	Surr 1782
Spencer	Wilk 1782	Mary widow(Wm)	Dobb 1780
Stephen	Ruth 1782	Phereby	Hali 1783
Stephen	Oran 1779	Rahab	Nash 1782
Stephen	Bert 1774	Samuel	Gran 1785
Theophilus	Perq 1772	Simon	Beau 1786
Thomas	Ruth 1782	Simon Sr	Beau 1786
Thomas	Blad 1784	Suzanne	Hali 1783
Thomas	Chow 1785	Thomas	Nash 1782

WHITEHEAD, Thomas	Oran	1779
Thomas	Casw	1786
Willis	Beau	1786
Wm	Nash	1782
Wm	Casw	1786
Wm	Casw	1784
Wm	Hali	1783
WHITEHOUSE, Henry	Beau	1779
John	Nash	1782
John	Cart	1779
Jonathan	Camd	1782
Richard	Onsl	1771
Robert	Cart	1779
Simon	Beau	1779
Wm	Crav	1779
WHITEHURST, Amey	Camd	1782
Gideon	Curr	1779
John	Curr	1779
Sam	Curr	1779
W.	Camd	1782
WHITELEY, George Jr	Mont	1782
WHITELY, Arthur	Hert	1784
George	Mont	1782
James Jr	Hert	1784
Nathaniel	Hert	1784
WHITEMAN, Matthew	Chow	1785
WHITEN, James	Crav	1779
WHITESIDE, Adam	Ruth	1782
Elizabeth	Ruth	1782
James	Ruth	1782
John	Ruth	1782
Samuel	Ruth	1782
Thomas	Ruth	1782
Wm	Ruth	1782
WHITEVED, Robert	Wilk	1782
WHITFIELD, Benj	Bert	1774
Benj	Bert	1781
Benjamin	Nash	1782
Constantine	Dobb	1780
Copeland	Hali	1783
Eliz	Bert	1781
Hardy	Nash	1782
Israel	Nash	1782
John	Nash	1782
John	Gran	1785
Lewis	Wayn	1786
Martha	Mart	1779
Mary	Nash	1782
Mason	Bert	1774
Mason	Bert	1781
Reuben	Nash	1782
Solomon	Nash	1782
Thomas	Nash	1782
Wm	Nash	1782
Wm	Mart	1779
WHITFORD, Martin	Crav	1779
Thomas	Crav	1779
Wm	Crav	1779
WHITLEY, Arthur	Hert	1779
Arthur	Beau	1779
Arthur	Beau	1786
Britain	Nash	1782
Elijah	Samp	1784
Exodus	Mont	1782
George	Nash	1782

WHITLEY, George	Mont	1782
James Sr	Hert	1779
Jonas	Nash	1782
Joseph	Dobb	1780
Joseph	Samp	1784
Nathan	Hert	1779
Needham	John	1784
WHITLOCK, Chas	Surr	1782
Geo	Gran	1771
James	Rowa	1761
Joseph	Rowa	1761
Mark	Rowa	1761
Robert	Casw	1784
Robert	Casw	1786
Silvis	Surr	1782
WHITLOE, Gordon	Gran	1785
John	Gran	1785
WHITLOW, Nathan	Gran	1771
WHITMAN, George	Casw	1784
John	Dupl	1783
Michael	Blad	1784
WHITMEL, Thomas	Bert	1774
WHITMELL, Penelope	Bert	1781
Thomas B.	Hali	1783
Thomas Jr	Bert	1774
WHITMORE, Amos	Camd	1782
WHITNEY, Ebenezer	Wayn	1786
Josiah	Samp	1784
WHITSELL, Adam	Oran	1779
James	Oran	1779
John	Oran	177
Samuel	Oran	1779
WHITSON, Michael	Tyrr	1784
WHITTENTON, Wm	Wilk	1782
WHITTINGTON, Mary	John	1784
Robert	John	1784
WHITTON, George	Casw	1786
WHOOTEN, Patty	Wilk	1782
WHORTON, David	Mart	1779
Elisha	Mart	1779
John	Mart	1779
WHOSTEN, Willis	Pasq	1789
WICKER, Davis	Cart	1779
Thomas	Gran	1785
Wm	Gran	1785
WICKERS, Thomas	Perq	1772
WICKS, James	Surr	1782
WIDEMAN, Henry	Gran	1771
WIER, John	Rowa	1770
WIGGINS, Absalom	Wilk	1782
Baker	Mart	1779
Caleb	Crav	1779
Elihu	Samp	1784
Frederick	Gran	1785
George	Samp	1784
Gershom	Dobb	1780
James	Hert	1779
James	Hert	1784
Joel	Nash	1782
Joel	John	1784
John	Nash	1782
John	Bute	1766
John	Crav	1779
John	Pitt	1786
John Capt.	Mart	1779

WIGGINS, Jonas	Wilk 1782		WILEY, Thomas	Casw 1786
Joseph	Blad 1784		Thomas	Tyrr 1784
Joshua	Hert 1779		Thomas	Pasq 1789
Joshua	Hert 1784		WILHIDE, Mary	Brun 1784
Lemuel	Mart 1779		Phillip	Bute 1766
Mathias	Bert 1774		WILHITE, Jacob	Oran 1779
Matthew	Bert 1781		Mathias	Oran 1779
Sampson	Warr 1784		WILIAMS, Anna	Pitt 1786
Samson	Bute 1766		Jesse	Crav 1779
Samuel	Perq 1772		Joseph	Blad 1784
Samuel	Crav 1779		Richard	Rowa 1768
Thomas	Wayn 1786		Solomon	Gran 1785
Thomas	Gran 1785		Thomas	Rowa 1768
Thomas	Hali 1783		Wn	Rowa 1768
Thomas	Gran 1771		WILIAMSTON, Thomass	Gran 1771
Willis	John 1784		WILIFORD, Samuel	Warr 1784
Willis	Gate 1789		WILIS, Joel	Crav 1779
Willis Sr	Gate 1789		WILKENSON, Judith	Gate 1789
Wm	Hert 1779		WILKERSON, David	Gran 1785
Wm	Samp 1784		David	Gran 1771
Wm	Hali 1783		Hazlewood	Gran 1785
Wm	Hert 1784		James	Bert 1781
WIGGS, Benjamin	Wayn 1786		John	Casw 1784
Henry Sr	Wayn 1786		John	Gran 1785
John	Samp 1784		John	Gran 1771
John	Wayn 1786		Samuel	Rich 1790
John	John 1784		Samuel	Rich 1790
Jordan	Wayn 1786		Wm	Gran 1785
WILBUGS, Thomas	Pitt 1786		Wm	Gran 1785
WILBURN, Daniel	Hali 1783		Wm	Gran 1771
Edward	Surr 1782		WILKES, Isaac	Blad 1784
Edward	Gran 1771		James	Bert 1774
Elias	Wilk 1782		James Jr	Bert 1781
Isaac	Rowa 1761		James Sr	Bert 1781
Wm	Wilk 1784		WILKINS, Elijah	Hali 1783
Wm	Wilk 1782		James	Hert 1779
WILCOX, John	Pasq 1789		James	Samp 1784
Samuel	Ruth 1782		John	Onsl 1771
Stephen	Pasq 1789		John	Surr 1782
Wm	Wilk 1784		Joseph	Chow 1785
Wm	Crav 1779		Michael	Wayn 1786
WILCOXEN, George s of Jo			Richard	Gran 1785
	Rowa 1761		Richard	Gran 1771
Isaac	Rowa 1761		Thomas	Beau 1779
John & son Geo	Rowa 1761		Wm	Blad 1784
Wm	Wilk 1782		Wm	Chow 1785
WILDER, Catherine	Casw 1784		Wm	Gran 1785
Charles	Bert 1774		Wm	Hert 1784
Hopkins	Onsl 1771		Wm	Curr 1779
John	Onsl 1771		Wm	Onsl 1771
Matthew	John 1784		WILKINSON, Anguish	Blad 1784
Michael	Dobb 1780		Archibald	Blad 1784
Michael	Chow 1785		Francis	Oran 1779
Moses	John 1784		John	Casw 1784
Nathaniel	Cart 1779		John	Surr 1782
Robert	Nash 1782		Mary	Blad 1784
Samuel	John 1784		Richard	Blad 1784
Wm	John 1784		Thomas	Casw 1784
Wm	Onsl 1771		Wm	Hert 1779
WILDES, Joshua	Hert 1779		Wm	Blad 1784
WILDMAN, Elias	Rowa 1770		Wm Jr	Blad 1784
WILES, Joshua	Hert 1779		WILL, Henry	Bert 1774
WILEY, Alexander	Casw 1786		WILLARD, Augustine	Gran 1785
James	Tyrr 1784		Benjamin	Mart 1779
Stephen	Tyrr 1784		Curtis	Beau 1779

WILLARD, Frederick	Mart	1779	WILLIAMS, Demsey	Gate	1789
Geo	Surr	1782	Dixon	Mart	1779
James	Gran	1771	Drury	Surr	1782
Jesse	Brun	1782	Edmund	Crav	1779
John	Beau	1779	Edward	Pasq	1779
Martin	Beau	1779	Edward	Dobb	1780
Richard	Mart	1779	Edward	Rowa	1768
Samuel	Crav	1779	Edward	Pasq	1789
WILLEROY, Wm	Camd	1782	Edward	Rich	1790
WILLEY, Alexander	Casw	1784	Edward	Rich	1790
Hillery	Gate	1789	Edward Jr	Rowa	1768
John	Onsl	1771	Eli	Hali	1783
Joseph	Hali	1783	Elias	Curr	1779
Thomas	Casw	1784	Elisha	Hali	1783
Wm	Hali	1783	Elisha	Bert	1774
WILLIAMS, Absalom	Wayn	1786	Eliz	Gran	1771
Alexander	Dobb	1780	Elizabeth	Casw	1786
Amos	Rowa	1768	Elkanah	Pasq	1779
Amos	Onsl	1771	Eschol	Pasq	1694
Ann	Hali	1783	Evan	Dobb	1780
Anne	Chow	1785	Francis	Hert	1779
Arthur	Bute	1766	Francis	Gran	1785
Arthur	Oran	1779	Francis	Hali	1783
Arthur	NorH	1780	Francis	Hert	1784
Arthur	Bert	1781	Francis	Gran	1771
Asa	Camd	1782	Frederick	Oran	1779
Asa	Pasq	1789	Ful	Perq	1772
Ashkenaz	Gran	1785	Geo	Gate	1789
Ashkins	Warr	1784	Geo	Bert	1781
Augustine	Hali	1783	George	Hert	1779
Benj	Bert	1774	George	Ruth	1782
Benj	Onsl	1771	George	Hert	1784
Benj	Bert	1781	Gilstrap	Hert	1779
Benjamin	Dupl	1783	Gilstrap	Hert	1784
Benjamin	Ruth	1782	Godfrey	Beau	1786
Benjamin	Samp	1784	Halon	Gate	1789
Benjamin	Hali	1783	Hardy	Samp	1784
Benjamin	Bute	1766	Hatter	Rowa	1770
Benjamin	Camd	1782	Henry	Casw	1784
Benjamin	Samp	1784	Henry	Gran	1785
Benjamin	Crav	1779	Henry	NorH	1780
Bennett	Casw	1784	Herod	John	1784
Billy	Warr	1784	Hezekiah	Pasq	1779
Brice	Cart	1779	Hollowell	Curr	1779
Buckman	NorH	1780	Howell	Ruth	1782
Caleb	Curr	1779	Humphrey	Oran	1779
Catron	Samp	1784	Isaac	Hert	1779
Charles	Hali	1783	Isaac	Oran	1779
Charles	John	1784	Isaac	Samp	1784
Chas	Curr	1779	Isaac	Perq	1787
Chris	Surr	1782	Isaac (western	Nash	1782
Christopher	Oran	1779	Isaac Sr	Samp	1784
Comfort	Curr	1779	Isaiah	Hert	1784
Cooper	Nash	1782	Isaiah	Bert	1774
Daniel	Casw	1786	Jacob	Casw	1784
Daniel	Gran	1785	Jacob	Bute	1766
Daniel	Pasq	1779	Jacob	Samp	1784
Daniel	Gran	1771	James	Rowa	1761
Davemorgan	Dobb	1780	James	Nash	1782
David	Hali	1783	James	Cart	1779
David	Pasq	1779	James	Hali	1783
David	Wilk	1782	James	Pasq	1779
David Jr	Pasq	1789	James	Rowa	1768
David Sr	Pasq	1789	James	Camd	1782
Dempsey	Gate	1789	James	Bert	1774

James	Curr 1779	Joshua	Dobb 1780
James	Wilk 1782	Josiah	Hert 1784
James	Bert 1781	Josiah	Bert 1774
James Jr	Dupl 1783	Lemuel	John 1784
James Jr	Beau 1786	Leonard	Camd 1782
James Sr	Dupl 1783	Leta	Mont 1782
Jamjes	Wilk 1782	Lewis	Hert 1779
Jean	Rowa 1761	Lewis	Gran 1785
Jesse	Hert 1779	Lewis	Dobb 1780
Jesse	Onsl 1771	Lewis	Curr 1779
Jesse	NorH 1780	Lewis Sr	Onsl 1771
Job	Dobb 1780	Lockhart	Perq 1787
Joel	Nash 1782	Lodowick	Camd 1782
Joel	Samp 1784	Lodowick	Pasq 1789
John	Hert 1779	Louis	Hert 1784
John	Albe 1679	Lucy	Bute 1766
John	Casw 1786	Malachi	Pasq 1789
John	Blad 1784	Mark	NorH 1780
John	Brun 1784	Martin s of Jo	Bute 1766
John	Casw 1784	Mary	Bert 1779
John	Chow 1785	Mary	Bert 1774
John	Gran 1785	Mary	Bert 1781
John	Hali 1783	Miles	Blad 1784
John	Hert 1784	Miles	Gran 1771
John	Warr 1784	Moses	Gate 1789
John	Dobb 1780	Moses	Bert 1781
John	Dobb 1780	Nash	Gran 1785
John	Rowa 1768	Nathan	Samp 1784
John	Oran 1779	Nathaniel	Nash 1782
John	Camd 1782	Nathaniel	Perq 1772
John	Samp 1784	Nathl	Surr 1782
John	Warr 1784	Nathl	Gran 1771
John	Wilk 1784	Nathl Jr	Perq 1787
John	Beau 1779	Nathl Sr	Perq 1787
John	Perq 1772	Nicholas	Curr 1779
John	Bert 1774	Nimrod	Ruth 1782
John	Crav 1779	Nimrod	Warr 1784
John	Crav 1779	Obed	Onsl 1771
John	Curr 1779	Owen	Pasq 1779
John	Wilk 1782	Owen	Wilk 1782
John	Onsl 1771	Owen	Pasq 1789
John	Surr 1782	Perminus	Gran 1785
John	Gran 1771	Peter	Gran 1771
John	Bert 1781	Peter	Perq 1787
John	Beau 1786	Philander	Nash 1782
John & wi Mary	Albe 1693	Phillip	Rowa 1761
John P	Bert 1781	Phillip	Mart 1779
Jonas	Ruth 1782	Phillip	Curr 1779
Jonas	Nash 1782	Price	Dobb 1780
Jonas	Dobb 1780	Rasor	Onsl 1771
Jonathan	Gate 1789	Reuben	Pasq 1779
Jordan	Hert 1779	Reuben	Bert 1781
Joseph	Albe 1694	Richard	Hert 1779
Joseph	Ruth 1782	Richard	Albe 1679
Joseph	Nash 1782	Richard	Hert 1784
Joseph	Hali 1783	Richard	Crav 1779
Joseph	Camd 1782	Richard	Bert 1781
Joseph	Samp 1784	Richard	Perq 1787
Joseph	Perq 1772	Robert	Dupn 1783
Joseph	Curr 1779	Robert	Cart 1779
Joseph	Onsl 1771	Robert	Cart 1779
Joseph	Surr 1782	Robert	Warr 1784
Joseph	Gran 1771	Robert	Dobb 1780
Joseph & s Mar	Bute 1766	Robert	Camd 1782
Joshua	Blad 1784	Robert	Samp 1784

Robert	Warr 1784		Uriah	Camd 178
Robert	Beau 1779		West	Dobb 1780
Robert	NorH 1780		Will	Albe 1693
Robert	Beau 1786		Willis	Pasq 1779
Roger	Mont 1782		Willis	Mart 1779
Roland	NorH 1780		Willis	Pitt 1786
Rowland	Nash 1782		Wm	Hert 1779
Rufus	Pasq 1779		Wm	Ruth 1782
Rufus	Pasq 1789		Wm	Nash 1782
Sam	Perq 1787		Wm	CaRT 1779
Saml	Gate 1789		Wm	Cart 1779
Samuel	Hert 1779		Wm	Wayn 1786
Samuel	Rowa 1761		Wm	Casw 1784
Samuel	Gran 1785		Wm	Gran 1785
Samuel	Hali 1783		Wm	Hert 1784
Samuel	Hert 1784		Wm	Pasq 1779
Samuel	Warr 1784		Wm	Bute 1766
Samuel	Mart 1779		Wm	Dobb 1780
Samuel	Samp 1784		Wm	Rowa 1770
Samuel	Warr 1779		Wm	Mart 1779
Samuel	Perq 1772		Wm	Camd 1782
Samuel	Bert 1774		Wm	Samp 1784
Sarah	Hert 1779		Wm	Warr 1784
Sarah	Nash 1782		Wm	Bert 1774
Sarah	Hali 1783		Wm	Crav 1779
Sarah	Hert 1784		Wm	Mont 1782
Sarah	Warr 1784		Wm	OnsL 1771
Seth	Warr 1784		Wm	Gran 1771
Simon	Hert 1779		Wm	Gate 1789
Simon	Nash 1782		Wm	Bert 1781
Simon	Gran 1785		Wm	Beau 1786
Simon	Bute 1766		Wm	Rich 1790
Simon	Gran 1771		Wm	Rich 1790
Solomon	Warr 1784		Wm Jr	Ruth 1782
Solomon	Mont 1782		Wm Jr	Mart 1779
Spencer	Pasq 1779		Wright	Dupl 1783
Stephen	Mont 1782		Zadock	Hert 1784
Stephen	Onsl 1771		Zebedee	Camd 1782
Stephen	Gran 1771		Zebedee	Pasq 1789
Stephen	Beau 1786		Zebulon	Oran 1779
Stephen s o Ti	Samp 1784		Zebulon	Curr 1779
Talbot	Pitt 1786		WILLIAMSON, Benj	NorH 1780
Thomas	Ruth 1782		Beverly	Hali 1783
Thomas	Bute 1766		David	Cart 1779
Thomas	Gran 1785		George	Hali 1783
Thomas	Hali 1783		Hardy	Samp 1784
Thomas	Hali 1783		Hawley	Casw 1786
Thomas	John 1784		Henry	Wayn 1784
Thomas	Dobb 1780		Henry	NorH 1780
Thomas	Mart 1779		Hugh	Chow 1785
Thomas	Camd 1782		James	Warr 1784
Thomas	Beau 1779		James	NorH 1780
Thomas	Perq 1772		James	Gran 1771
Thomas	Bert 1774		Jeremiah	Casw 1786
Thomas	Curr 1779		John	Hali 1783
Thomas	NorH 1780		John	Jone 1779
Thomas	Surr 1782		John	NorH 1780
Thomas	Gate 1789		John	Perq 1787
Thomas	Beau 1786		John Esq	Casw 1784
Thomas Jr	Beau 1786		John Jr	Casw 1784
Thomas Sr	Curr 1779		Joseph	Pasq 1779
Timothy	Surr 1782		Lewis	Samp 1784
Timothy & s St	Samp 1784		Matthew	Hert 1779
Tobias	Casw 1784		Matthew	Hert 1784
Trimizen	Pasq 1789		Nathan	Casw 1786

WILLIAMSON, Nathan	Casw	1784
Paul	Casw	1784
Priscilla	Hali	1783
Samuel	Blad	1784
Samuel	Tyrr	1784
Shadrack	Rich	1790
Shadrack	Rich	1790
Stephen	Casw	1786
Stephen	Casw	1784
Sterling	Rich	1790
Sterling	Rich	1790
Thomas	Gran	1785
Thomas	NorH	1780
Washen	Pasq	1694
Wm	Chow	1785
Wm	Curr	1779
Wm & son Wm	Bute	1766
Wm Jr	Samp	1784
Wm P.	Wayn	1786
Wm Sr	Samp	1784
Zerubabel	Gran	1785
WILLIAMs, Samuel	Dupl	1783
WILLIFORD, Abner	Bert	1781
Britain	Bute	1766
Britton	Warr	1779
John	Hert	1779
John	Blad	1784
John	Hert	1784
Micajah	Samp	1784
Nathan & s Sam	Bute	1766
Richard	Samp	1784
Richard	Bert	1774
Richard	Bert	1781
Samuel	Warr	1784
Samuel s o Nat	Bute	1766
Stephen	Surr	1782
Wm	Hert	1779
Wm	Samp	1784
Wm	Hert	1784
WILLINGHAM, James	Gran	1771
John	Gran	1785
John	Gran	1771
Thomas	Gran	1771
WILLIS, Agerton	Blad	1784
Anne	Brun	1784
Augustine	Blad	1784
Augustine	Hali	1783
Benjamin	Cart	1779
Benjamin Jr	Blad	1784
Benjamin Sr	Blad	1784
Caleb	Crav	1779
Daniel	Blad	1784
Elizabeth	Blad	1784
Ephraim	Pitt	1786
Francis	Crav	1779
George	Blad	1784
Henry	Casw	1786
Henry	Casw	1784
Henry Jr	Casw	1784
James	Crav	1779
James Jr	Crav	1779
Jeremiah	Blad	1784
Joel	Pitt	1786
John	Blad	1784
John	Warr	1784

WILLIS, John	Crav	1779
John	Pitt	1786
Joseph	Crav	1779
Joseph	Crav	1779
Joshua	Beau	1786
Lewis	Hali	1783
Meshack	Gran	1771
Richard M	Crav	1779
Sam	Beau	1786
Samuel Jr	Crav	1779
Sherrod	Hali	1783
Stephen	Ruth	1782
Thomas	Nash	1782
Thomas	Crav	1779
Wm	Ruth	1782
Wm	Gran	1771
WILLISON, John	Mont	1782
Samuel	Mont	1782
WILLISTON, Andrew	Cart	1779
Daniel	Cart	1779
Ebenezer	Cart	1779
John	Cart	1779
Josiah	Cart	1779
Rabun	Cart	1779
Reuben	Cart	1779
Samuel	Cart	1779
Seth	Cart	1779
Thomas	Cart	1779
WILLOBEE, Edward	Rich	1790
Edward	Rich	1790
Thomas	Camd	1782
WILLOUGHBEE, Caps	Cart	1779
John	Hert	1779
Richard	John	1784
Solomon	John	1784
Wm	Bert	1774
WILLOUGHBY, Anthony	John	1784
WILMER, John	Onsl	1771
WILMOUTH, Thomas	Wilk	1782
Wm	Wilk	1782
WILSON, Abraham	Perq	1772
Abram	Perq	1787
Andrew	Ruth	1782
Ann	Perq	1787
Archelaus	Oran	1779
Benjamin	Camd	1782
Charles	Rowa	1761
Charles	Oran	1779
Christopher	Brun	1784
Daniel	Warr	1784
David	NBer	1779
Edward	Nash	1782
Edward	Oran	1779
Edward	Bert	1774
Edward	Bert	1781
Edward	Bert	1781
Elias & s J&E	Bute	1766
Elias s of Eli	Bute	1766
Elisha Moore	Samp	1784
Geo	Gran	1771
George	Rowa	1768
George	Hert	1784
Henry	Wayn	1786
Henry	Curr	1779
Isaac	Perq	1787

WILSON, Jacob	Perq 1772	Thomas	Beau 1779
Jacob	Perq 1787	Thomas	Perq 1772
James	Ruth 1782	Thomas	Surr 1782
James	Dobb 1780	Thomas Jr	Warr 1784
James	Rowa 1768	Walter	Brun 1784
James	Oran 1779	Willis	Camd 1782
James	Casw 1784	Winifred (?)	Beau 1779
James	Warr 1784	Wm	Ruth 1782
James	Jone 1779	Wm	Oran 1779
James	Beau 1779	Wm	Camd 1782
James	Bert 1774	Wm	Casw 1784
James	Wilk 1782	Wm	Warr 1784
James	Surr 1782	Wm	NBer 1779
James	Bert 1781	Wm	Perq 1772
James s of Eli	Bute 1766	Wm	Surr 1782
John	Nash 1782	Wm	Bert 1781
John	Pasq 1694	Zachariah	Perq 1787
John	Dobb 1780	Zechariah	Perq 1772
John	Rowa 1768	WILSTON, John	Bert 1781
John	Oran 1779	WILTON, Timothy	Bert 1774
John	Camd 1782	WIMBERLY, Abram	Bert 1774
John	Casw 1784	Benj	Bert 1774
John	Gran 1785	Ezekiel	Bert 1774
John	Gran 1771	Ezekiel	Bert 1781
John	Gran 1771	Fred	Bert 1781
John	Pasq 1789	John	Bert 1781
John Sr	Dobb 1780	Levy	Bert 1781
Jonathan	Blad 1784	Malachi	John 1784
Jonathan	Perq 1787	Moses	Mont 1782
Joseph	Blad 1784	WIMMAN, Thomas	Bert 1774
Joseph	Perq 1772	WINANTS, Winant	Bert 1781
Joseph	Pasq 1789	WINBERRY, Winney	Pasq 1789
Lovey	Curr 1779	Wm	Pasq 1694
Luke Sr	Bert 1774	WINBORNE, Bryan	NorH 1780
Mary	Wilk 1782	James	NorH 1780
Mary	Perq 1787	WINBURN, Henry	Hert 1784
Michael	Gran 1771	Josiah	Nash 1782
Moses	Perq 1772	Sarah	Hert 1779
Mumford	Ruth 1782	Thomas	Hert 1784
Penny	NBer 1779	Wm	Hert 1779
Phillip	Surr 1782	WINCHFIELD, Wm	Surr 1782
Rachel	Pasq 1779	WINDFIELD, James	Beau 1786
Rebecca	Pasq 1779	WINDLEY, Aaron	Beau 1786
Reuben	Perq 1772	Israel	Beau 1779
Richard	Warr 1784	Israel	Beau 1786
Robert	Bute 1766	James	Beau 1786
Robert	Oran 1779	Levy	Beau 1786
Robert	Casw 1784	Moses	Beau 1786
Robert	Gran 1785	WINDOM, John	Wilk 1782
Robert	Perq 1772	Thomas	Wilk 1782
Robert	Rich 1790	WINDRON, Thomas	Bert 1781
Robert	Rich 1790	WINDSOR, John	Casw 1784
Sandford	Warr 1784	John	Casw 1786
Sarah	Camd 1782	WINFIELD, John	Hali 1783
Seasbrook	Gate 1789	Sarah	Crav 1779
Seth	Beau 1786	WINFORD, Edmund	NBer 1779
Spencer	Wilk 1782	Edward	NBer 1779
Stephen	Oran 1779	WINFRED, Isaac	Wilk 1784
Stephen	Pasq 1779	James	Wilk 1784
Stephen	Gran 1771	WINFREY, George	Ruth 1782
Tatum	Curr 1779	Isaac	Surr 1782
Thomas	Camd 1782	James	Gran 1785
Thomas	Wayn 1786	WINGATE, Arthur	Brun 1782
Thomas	Casw 1784	Cornelius	Blad 1784
Thomas	Warr 1784	Cornelius	Brun 1782

WINGATE, Edward	Brun	1784
Edward	Perq	1772
Edward	Brun	1782
Edward	Perq	1787
Eliz	Pitt	1786
Elizabeth	Crav	1779
Ephraim	Perq	1787
Isaac	Dobb	1780
Isaac	Pitt	1786
John	Blad	1784
John	Pitt	1786
John	Perq	1787
Michael	Gran	1771
Thomas	NBer	1779
Thomas	NBer	1779
Walter	Blad	1784
Wm	Perq	1772
WINHAM, John	Crav	1779
WINKFIELD, Joseph	Wayn	1786
WINN, Ezekiel	Pasq	1779
Wm	Rowa	1770
Wm	Crav	1779
WINNANT, Peter	Bert	1774
WINNINGHAM, Sherwood		
	Gran	1785
Thomas	Casw	1784
WINNS, Nathan	Bert	1774
WINSCOTT, Abraham	Surr	1782
WINSETT, Francis	Dobb	1780
John	Dobb	1780
Joseph	Dobb	1780
Robert	Dobb	1780
WINSLOW, Benj	Perq	1787
Benjamin	Perq	1772
Caleb	Perq	1772
Caleb	Perq	1787
Jacob	Perq	1772
Jacob	Perq	1787
Jesse	Perq	1787
Job	Chow	1785
John	Perq	1772
John Jr	Perq	1787
John Sr	Perq	1787
Joseph	Perq	1787
Josiah	Pasq	1779
Martha	Perq	1772
Mary	Perq	1772
Obediah	Perq	1772
Pleasant	Perq	1772
Saml	Perq	1787
Thomas	Perq	1772
Wm	Perq	1787
WINSTEAD, Alexander	Casw	1784
Alsey	Casw	1784
Constance	Casw	1784
George	Nash	1782
Joseph	Nash	1782
Peter	Nash	1782
Samuel	Casw	1784
WINSTON, Isaiah	Gran	1771
John	Surr	1782
Joseph	Gran	1771
WINTERS, George	Ruth	1782
James	Hali	1783
Joseph	Hali	1783

WINTERS, Moses	Hali	1783
Thomas	Hali	1783
WISDOM, Joseph	Casw	1784
Joseph	Casw	1786
Larkin	Casw	1786
Martha	Casw	1784
Martha	Casw	1786
WISE, Abel	Wayn	1786
Isaac	Wayn	1786
James	Wayn	1786
Johannas	Beau	1786
John	Blad	1784
John	Wayn	1786
Josiah	Wayn	1786
Thomas	Blad	1784
Thomas	Wayn	1786
WISHEW, John	Curr	1779
Wm	Curr	1779
WITHERINGTON, Charlton		
	Hert	1779
Charlton	Hert	1784
Hardy	Hert	1784
Joseph	Hert	1779
Joseph	Hert	1784
Wm	Hert	1779
Wm	Hert	1784
WITHERMON, Christian		
	Surr	1782
WITHERSPOON, John	Wilk	1778
Martha	Wilk	1782
WITHROW, James	Ruth	1782
John	Ruth	1782
WITTEY, Andrew	Rowa	1768
John	Rowa	1768
Joshua	Oran	1779
Robert	Oran	1779
WODE, David	John	1784
WODERAPPLE, David	Surr	1782
WOLDUN, Joseph	Surr	1782
WOLF, Adam	Surr	1782
Charles	Wayn	1786
Charles Jr	Wayn	1786
Daniel	Surr	1782
George	Ruth	1782
George	Rowa	1770
George	Wayn	1786
Isaac	Blad	1784
Jesse	Wayn	1786
Lewis	Surr	1782
Peter	Oran	1779
WOLLARD, Absalom	Beau	1786
Coleman	Beau	1786
Coverton	Beau	1786
Daniel	Perq	1787
Jeremiah	Beau	1786
John	Beau	1786
John Jr	Beau	1786
Martin	Beau	1786
Martin	Perq	1787
Michael	Beau	1786
Willobee	Beau	1786
WOLLEY, Wm	Mont	1782
WOLSENDER, John	Bert	1781
WOMACK, Abraham	Casw	1784
Abram	Casw	1786

WOMACK, David	Casw 1784	WOODAY, John	NorH 1780
John	Casw 1784	WOODBEE, Matthew	Rich 1790
WOMBLE, Nathan	Jone 1779	Matthew	Rich 1790
WOOD, Aaron	Hali 1783	Wm	Rich 1790
Abraham	Surr 1782	Wm	Rich 1790
Ann & son Wm	Bute 1766	WOODDALE, Joseph	Nash 1782
Benjamin	Beau 1779	WOODEY, James	Oran 1779
Bennett	Warr 1784	Joseph	Oran 1779
Dempsey	Hert 1779	Mary	Oran 1779
Eleanor	Hali 1783	Wm	Oran 1779
Elias	Wilk 1782	WOODHAM, Alice	NBer 1779
Evan	Pasq 1789	Edward	Dobb 1780
Furnival	Samp 1784	Edward Sr	Dobb 1780
George	Ruth 1782	Frederick	Dobb 1780
George	Pasq 1779	WOODHOUSE, Hadley	Curr 1779
Henry	Warr 1784	Henry Jr	Curr 1779
Isaiah	Chow 1785	Henry Sr	Curr 1779
James	Ruth 1782	John	Dobb 1780
James	Dobb 1780	John	Curr 1779
James	Tyrr 1784	John	Onsl 1771
James	Bert 1774	Keziah	Curr 1779
James	NorH 1780	Lemuel	Curr 1779
James	Bert 1781	Markland RevWr	Dobb 1780
Jarrett	Rowa 1770	Wm	Curr 1779
Jesse	Wilk 1782	WOODING, Israel	Beau 1779
Jesse Jr	Onsl 1771	WOODLAND, Isaiah	Beau 1786
Jesse Sr	Onsl 1771	Sarah	Tyrr 1784
John	Ruth 1782	WOODLEY, Hezekiah	Pasq 1779
John	Hali 1783	Hezekiah	Pasq 1789
John	Pasq 1779	John	Perq 1787
John	Warr 1784	Thomas	Bute 1766
John	Beau 1779	Wm	Perq 1787
John	Beau 1786	WOODRIDGE, Simon	NorH 1780
John	Pasq 1789	WOODRUFF, John	Bute 1766
John B	Bert 1781	John	Warr 1779
Jonathan	Onsl 1771	Joseph	Surr 1782
Joseph	Blad 1784	Moses	Surr 1782
Joseph	Perq 1787	Nathl Sr	Surr 1782
Lucy	Blad 1784	Thomas	Surr 1782
Mary	Bert 1781	WOODS, Blaton	Oran 1779
Payton	Gran 1785	Edward	Oran 1779
Philemon	Warr 1784	Harris	Oran 1779
Richard	Pasq 1779	Henry	Oran 1779
Richard	Surr 1782	Hugh	Oran 1779
Richard	Gran 1771	James	Oran 1779
Saml	Surr 1782	John	Oran 1779
Thomas	Pasq 1779	Joseph	Oran 1779
Thomas	Pasq 1789	Richard	Surr 1782
Thomas Sr	Pasq 1789	Samuel	Casw 1784
Wm	Ruth 1782	Sarah	Oran 1779
Wm	Warr 1784	Thomas	Oran 1779
Wm	Bert 1774	Wm	Ruth 1782
Wm	Bert 1781	Wm	Surr 1782
Wm Jr	Bert 1774	WOODWARD, Abraham	Rowa 1770
WOODALL, Christopher		Benjamin	John 1784
	John 1784	Edward	Chow 1785
Jacob	Gran 1785	Elisha	John 1784
John	John 1784	Ethelred	Hert 1779
Joseph	Bute 1766	James	Nash 1782
Wm	Bute 1766	James	Chow 1785
WOODARD, Isaac	Wayn 1786	Jesse	Nash 1782
Joshua	Wayn 1786	Jethro	John 1784
Oliver	NorH 1780	John	Beau 1779
Peter	Ruth 1782	Miles	Chow 1785
Wm	Bute 1766	Richard	Chow 1785

WOODWARD, Thomas	Nash 1782		WORSLEY, Stephen	Crav 1779
WOODY, Henry	Wilk 1782		Thomas	Beau 1779
Talton	Wilk 1782		Thomas	Beau 1786
Wm	Wilk 1782		Wm	Beau 1779
WOOLAID, Martin	Perq 1772		WORTHAM, Edward	Oran 1779
WOOLARD, Absalom	Beau 1779		John	Warr 1784
Jeremiah	Beau 1779		Judson Jr	Warr 1784
Mary	Chow 1785		Wm	Warr 1784
Michael	Beau 1779		WORTHINGTON, Isaac	Hert 1784
WOOLBANKS, John & son Wm			John	Rowa 1768
	Bute 1766		WOTHERINGTON, Nathan	
Richard	Wilk 1782			Dobb 1780
WOOLDRIDGE, Edmund	Surr 1782		Robert	Dobb 1780
Gibson	Surr 1782		Stephen	Dobb 1780
Thomas	Surr 1782		Widow	Dobb 1780
Wm	Surr 1782		WOTHERINGTPON, Cleverly	
WOOLFORTH, Jacob	Surr 1782			Dobb 1780
WOOTEN, Benj	Surr 1782		WRANUM, Sam	NorH 1780
Caleb	Bert 1781		WRAY, Ambrose	Wilk 1782
Chas	Pasq 1789		Baker	Warr 1784
James	Bute 1766		Elizabeth	Wilk 1782
Jeremiah	Bute 1766		George	Warr 1784
Jesse	John 1784		James	Casw 1786
John	Bute 1766		Jesse	Wilk 1782
John	Hali 1783		John	Mont 1782
Richard s o Th	Bute 1766		Lodowick	Ruyh 1782
Robert	Samp 1784		Robert	Casw 1784
Saml	Pasq 1789		Zachariah	Surr 1782
Thomas	Bute 1766		WRENN, John	Warr 1784
Thomas	Pasq 1779		Joseph	Warr 1784
Thomas	Surr 1782		Joseph	Gran 1771
Thomas & s Ric	Bute 1766		WRIGHT, Abraham	Casw 1784
Wm	Hali 1783		Asa	Casw 1784
Wm	Pasq 1779		Augustine & br	Camd 1782
Wm	Curr 1779		Barrabus	Camd 1782
Wm	Surr 1782		Benj	Bert 1781
Wm Jr	Samp 1784		Benjamin	Perq 1787
Wm Sr	Samp 1784		Charles	Camd 1782
WOOTER, Thomas	Surr 1782		Christopher	Pasq 1779
WORD, James	Surr 1782		Clayburn	Casw 1784
WORDAL, Jacob	Gran 1771		Cornelius	Camd 1782
WORDSWORTH, Caleb	Perq 1787		Daniel	Wilk 1782
Thomas	Pasq 1779		Daniel	Surr 1782
Thomas	Perq 1787		Elizabeth	Hert 1784
WORKS, John	Bute 1766		Gamaliel	Camd 1782
WORLEY, Daniel	Bert 1774		Geo	Gran 1771
Daniel	Bert 1781		George	Gran 1785
Henry	Surr 1782		Hannah	Gran 1785
John	Hali 1783		Jacob	Casw 1784
Michael	Rowa 1761		James	Hert 1779
Richard	Rowa 1770		James	Gran 1785
Wm	Wayn 1786		James	Hali 1783
WORNUM, Elizabeth	NorH 1780		James	Hert 1784
WORRELL, Benjamin	Wayn 1786		Jarrett	Gran 1785
Brittain	Hert 1779		Jesse	Warr 1784
David	Wayn 1786		John	Camd 1782
Henry	Wayn 1786		John	Samp 1784
James	Wayn 1786		John	Casw 1784
John	Wayn 1786		John	Chow 1785
Richard	Hert 1779		John	Gran 1785
Richard	Wayn 1786		John	Hali 1783
Richard	Hert 1784		John	Warr 1784
Wm	Bute 1766		John	Crav 1779
Wm	Wayn 1786		John	Mont 1782
Wm	Warr 1784		John	Wilk 1782

WRIGHT, John	Surr 1782	WYNNE, Andrew	Tyrr 1784
John (mulatto)	Casw 1786	Benjamin	Tyrr 1784
John Jr	Bute 1766	George	Tyrr 1784
John Sr & s Mo	Bute 1766	Haskin	Bert 1774
Joseph	Nash 1782	James	Bert 1774
Joseph	Bute 1766	John	Tyrr 1784
Joseph	Oran 1779	Joseph	Tyrr 1784
Joseph	Wilk 1782	Robert	Tyrr 1784
Josiah	Mont 1782	WYNNS, Augustus	Hert 1779
Lemuel	Nash 1782	Benjamin	Hert 1779
Lott & bro Aug	Camd 1782	Benjamin	Hert 1784
Lucy	Onsl 1771	George	Hert 1779
Martha	Hall 1783	George Col.	Hert 1784
Mathias	Camd 1782	John	Hert 1779
Moses	Wilk 1782	John A.	Hert 1784
Moses s o John	Bute 1766	Thomas	Hert 1779
Peter	Camd 1782	Thomas	Hert 1784
Richard	Casw 1784	Wm	Hert 1779
Robert	Samp 1784	Wm	Hert 1784
Sam	Wilk 1782	Wm B. Capt.	Hert 1784
Samuel	Bute 1766	Warwick, Wyatt	Wayn 1786
Samuel	Perq 1772	Whitley, James s of Art	
Thomas	Perq 1772		Hert 1779
Thomas	Crav 1779	Wiggins, Thomas	Mart 1779
Thomas	Surr 1782		
Thomas	Perq 1787		
Winfield	Gran 1771		
Wm	Bute 1766	YANCEY, Ann	Casw 1786
Wm	Camd 1782	Bartlett	Casw 1786
Wm	Casw 1786	Charles	Gran 1785
Wm	Casw 1784	James	Gran 1785
Wm	Gran 1785	James	Gran 1771
Wm	Hali 1783	James Jr	Gran 1771
Wm	Mont 1782	Lewis	Gran 1785
Wm	Perq 1787	Phillip	Gran 1785
Wm	Rich 1790	Richard	Gran 1771
Wm	Rich 1790	Thomas	Gran 1771
Wm Jr	Camd 1782	Thornton	Gran 1785
Wm Sr	Camd 1782	Thornton	Gran 1771
Zebulon	Crav 1779	Willard	Gran 1771
WRIGHTENOUR, John	Oran 1779	Wm	Gran 1785
WRITSMAN, Peter	Oran 1779	YARBROUGH, George	Hall 1783
WYANT, Watkins Wm	Bert 1781	James s o Josh	Bute 1766
WYANTS, Peter	Rowa 1761	John	Bute 1766
WYATT, Christopher	Tyrr 1784	John	Casw 1784
Dempsey	Nash 1782	Joshua & s Jam	Bute 1766
Eliz	Perq 1787	Meno	Bute 1766
Ephraim	Mart 1779	Micajah	Bute 1766
Jacob	Perq 1772	Richard	Bute 1766
James	Nash 1782	Richard	Hali 1783
James	Hali 1783	Samuel	Casw 1784
James Jr	Hali 1783	Wm	Casw 1784
James Sr	Hali 1783	Wm	Warr 1784
Jesse	Hall 1783	Zachariah	Bute 1766
John	Bute 1766	YARNELL, Daniel	Wilk 1782
John	Perq 1772	YARRELL, Peter	Surr 1782
John	Perq 1787	YARRILL, Matthew	Mart 1779
John Jr	Bute 1766	YATES, Abraham	Rich 1790
Joseph	Tyrr 1784	Abraham	Rich 1790
Joshua	Perq 1772	Daniel	Onsl 1771
Nathan	Bute 1766	Isaac	Rich 1790
Nathl	Beau 1786	Isaac	Rich 1790
Solomon	Mart 1779	James	Bert 1774
Wm	Albe 1679	James	Onsl 1771
WYNN, James Boone	Bert 1781	James	Bert 1781

YATES, James	Rich 1790		John	Bute 1766
John	Blad 1784		John	Oran 1779
John	Casw 1784		John	Blad 1784
John	Bert 1774		John	Gran 1785
John	Onsl 1771		John	Hali 1783
John	Bert 1781		John	Crav 1779
Peter	Bert 1774		John	Gran 1771
Peter	Bert 1781		John	Beau 1786
Samuel	Jone 1779		John S.	Samp 1784
Thomas	Casw 1784		Joseph	Oran 1779
Thomas	Onsl 1771		Joseph	Wilk 1782
Thomas	Gran 1771		Joshua	Surr 1782
William	Bute 1766		Luke	Hali 1783
William	Casw 1784		Mary	Blad 1784
William	Bert 1774		Mary	Hali 1783
William	Wilk 1782		Miles	Bert 1781
William	Onsl 1771		Miles	Bert 1774
William	Surr 1782		Norman	Hali 1783
William	Bert 1781		Patterson	Warr 1779
YAVEL, John	Bert 1774		Rachel	Wilk 1782
YEARGEN, John	Warr 1784		Robert	Warr 1784
Samuel	Warr 1784		Robert	Crav 1779
YEARGIN, Andrew	Wilk 1782		Robert Jr.	Ruth 1782
John	Wilk 1782		Robert Sr.	Ruth 1782
YEARLY, John	Hert 1784		Samuel	Surr 1782
YEARNESSEY, Edward	Albe 1694		Sarah	Hali 1783
YEATS, Bazel	Cart 1779		Stephen	Nash 1782
Charles	Cart 1779		Thomas	Bute 1766
Job	Hert 1779		Thomas	Hali 1783
Job	Hert 1784		Thomas	John 1784
Luke	Hert 1784		Whitson	Hali 1783
Priscilla	Hert 1779		William	Nash 1782
Sarah	Hert 1779		William	Ruth 1782
Sarah	Hert 1784		William	Surr 1782
Stephen	Cart 1779		William	Beau 1786
YELVENTON, Hardy	Wayn 1786		YOUNGER, Thomas	Surr 1782
John	Wayn 1786		YOUNT, Andrew s o David	
Noah	Wayn 1786			Rowa 1768
YEOMANS, Eleanor	Grav 1779		David & s AnJo	Rowa 1768
James	Chow 1785		George & s John	Rowa 1768
Joseph	Cart 1779		John s o David	Rowa 1768
Samuel	Cart 1779		John s o Geo	Rowa 1768
YONKER, Michael	Rowa 1761			
YORK, James	Surr 1782			
John	Surr 1782			
Thomas	Surr 1784		ZEAL, Thomas	Bert 1770
YOUNG, Archibald	Hali 1783		Wm	Rowa 1770
Benj	Surr 1782		ZERNELSON, Airs	Tyrr 1784
Daniel	Dobb 1780		Charles Jr.	Tyrr 1784
Dolphin D.	Hali 1783		Charles Sr.	Tyrr 1784
Dorothy	Dobb 1780		ZERNOR, Adam	Rowa 1770
Edward	Bute 1766		ZIGLER, Christopher	Surr 1782
Edward	Mont 1782		ZINSON, Ozias	Bert 1781
Edward	Surr 1782			
Edward Jr.	Bute 1766			
Elizabeth	Bute 1766			
Ezekiel	Surr 1782			
George	Hali 1783			
Isham	Surr 1782			
James	Dobb 1780			
James	Oran 1779			
James	Surr 1782			
Jarrett	NorH 1780			
Jarrard	Hali 1783			
John	Ruth 1782			

LaVergne, TN USA
17 December 2010
209290LV00001B/2/P